# Geological Survey of Illinois

# GEOLOGICAL SURVEY OF ILLINOIS.

A. H. WORTHEN, DIRECTOR

## VOLUME VI.

# GEOLOGY AND PALÆONTOLOGY.

## GEOLOGY,

By A H WORTHEN, and Ass'ts G C. BROADHEAD and E. T COX.

## PALÆONTOLOGY,

By ORESTES St. JOHN, A. H. WORTHEN and F B. MEEK.

ILLUSTRATED
BY JULIUS MAYER & CO, BOSTON, MASS
PUBLISHED
BY AUTHORITY OF THE LEGISLATURE OF ILLINOIS

1875.

JOURNAL CO. BOOK PR
SPRINGFIELD ILL

TO THE

# HON JOHN L BEVERIDGE,

GOVERNOR OF ILLINOIS

SIR

The sixth volume of my report on the Geological Survey of Illinois, the publication of which was provided for by the 28th General Assembly, is herewith submitted Its appearance has been delayed by causes beyond my control, and mainly by the length of time required to engrave the plates and map accompanying this volume, the work in this instance being assigned exclusively to one engraving establishment instead of being divided between two or more, as was done with the preceding volume

Although the Palæontology of the State is by no means completed, and some departments, especially those of the corals and bryozoans, remain almost untouched, while many of our most common fossils have never been fully illustrated, and the descriptions even have not been published in any work now accessible to the general student, yet, in consequence of the manifest desire on the part of the law-making power to cut off all appropriations not deemed by them as absolutely necessary, I have not thought it advisable to make any provision for continuing the work beyond the publication of this volume, which includes the geology of all the counties in the State not heretofore reported on.

Moreover, important facts are constantly being developed in regard to our coal resources, by experiments with the drill, and by shafts sunk in various portions of the Illinois coal field, which should be collated and made available for the information of the public; for it is quite impossible that a State survey covering so large an area as that possessed by the State of Illinois, could be carried on with the detailed accuracy with which such work is prosecuted in the older countries of

Europe, without an expenditure of means far beyond any sum hitherto appropriated for scientific purposes in this State; and, consequently, very much yet remains to be learned in regard to the distribution of our coals and other economical deposits

The large collection of geological specimens accumulated by the Survey remains in the condition it was left by the fire in the Masonic Hall building, where it was formerly kept, no proper place having as yet been provided for its reception, and no provision made for its preservation as a State collection Some disposition should be made of this collection, either to preserve it as the nucleus of a State Cabinet of Natural History, or to dispose of it to some scientific institution where it would be appreciated and properly cared for

In the prosecution of the work I have kept in view two objects that seemed to me of paramount importance, to-wit: First, the development of the material resources of the State, so far as was possible, by making known whatever matters of economical importance the field explorations should bring to light, and secondly, to bring out such scientific results as this rich and comparatively unexplored field made possible, so that the State of Illinois, through its geological survey, might contribute something towards the general stock of scientific knowledge.

Although the scientific results brought out by the survey may not be, and probably are not appreciated by our own people, nevertheless I have the satisfaction of knowing that they are elsewhere, and that the Illinois Reports are esteemed a desirable acquisition to all scientific libraries, both public and private, and the applications for this work since the distribution of the first three volumes, coming mainly from individuals and institutions directly interested in scientific pursuits, would have consumed the entire edition published.

As the alleged reasons for withholding further appropriations to continue the work were based on the necessity of economy, and lest it might therefore be supposed, by those unacquainted with the facts, that there has been an unnecessary expenditure of money in the prosecution of this work, I deem it but just to myself to state in this connection precisely the amount that has been placed at my disposal for carrying on the Geological Survey of the State since it has been under my direction

When the survey came under my control, in March, 1858, the annual appropriation was $5000 per annum, with an additional sum of $500 per annum for topographical work As the latter amount was entirely inadequate to the accomplishment of any practical results in topography, it was expended mainly in the construction of the State map accompanying this volume, and in drawing such county maps as the prosecution of the work rendered necessary, so that the first named sum was all the available means at command to pay the salaries of myself and my assistants in geology and palæontology. for chemical work and chemicals, and the traveling and incidental expenses of the survey. This appropriation continued until the adoption of the new constitution in 1872, when by a provision in that instrument it was abolished In addition to this annual appropriation, the twenty fifth General Assembly made a special appropriation of $10,000 per annum for two years to complete the field work, and five or six additional assistants were employed for that time, and the sum so appropriated was exclusively devoted to this department of the survey

After the expiration of the regular annual appropriation in 1872, by the constitutional provision above referred to, the twenty-seventh General Assembly appropriated the sum of $2000 to defray the entire expense of the Survey for one year, and the succeeding General Assembly appropriated the sum of $3600 per annum for two years to defray the salary of myself and assistant including office and traveling expenses, and $1500 to pay the cost of the drawings required to illustrate this volume. This appropriation expired on the 30th day of June, last The two first volumes of my report were published in 1866, the third in 1868, the fourth in 1870, the fifth in 1872, and the sixth in 1875, this latter volume having been delayed nearly a year by causes already alluded to These six volumes, averaging about 550 pages each and containing 175 full page plates besides numerous wood cuts, were brought out in about nine years on the appropriations above specified From these facts and figures those best qualified to judge can determine, for themselves, whether or not the Geological Survey of Illinois has been conducted with due regard to economy

In taking leave of a work which I have had so long in charge, and to which I have devoted the best years of my life, I can but express my grateful acknowledgments to the many good and true friends of the Survey in various portions of the State, through whose influence and encouragement the work has been brought so near to a final completion, and more especially to those eminent eastern scientists, Prof HENRY, of the Smithsonian Institution, Prof. DANA, of New Haven, and the lamented AGASSIZ, for the loan of rare scientific books from the extensive libraries under their control, and for their personal influence and assistance freely manifested in various ways, by which the best interests of the Survey have been greatly promoted

I have the honor to be

Your obedient servant,

A. H WORTHEN

SPRINGFIELD, ILL., *Sept*, 1875

# TABLE OF CONTENTS.

## PART I.

## CHAPTER XI.

GEOLOGY OF FAYETTE COUNTY



## CHAPTER XII.

GEOLOGY OF MONTGOMERY COUNTY



## CHAPTER XIII

GEOLOGY OF CHRISTIAN COUNTY



## CHAPTER XIV.

GEOLOGY OF SHELBY COUNTY



## CHAPTER XV.

GEOLOGY OF EFFINGHAM COUNTY



## CHAPTER XVI

GEOLOGY OF MOULTRIE MACON AND PIATT COUNTIES



## CHAPTER XVII

GEOLOGY OF GALLATIN COUNTY



## CHAPTER XVIII

GEOLOGY OF SALINE COUNTY



## CHAPTER XIX.

GEOLOGY OF LIVINGSTON COUNTY



# PART II.

## PALÆONTOLOGY OF ILLINOIS

SECTION I.

## DESCRIPTIONS OF VERTEBRATES.



SECTION II

## DESCRIPTIONS OF INVERTEBRATES.

# CHAPTER I.

## COAL MEASURES

The coal area within the boundaries of the State of Illinois may be safely estimated, in round numbers, at about 35,000 square miles, an area nearly three times as great as that of Pennsylvania or Ohio, and equal to one fifth of the productive coal fields of the United States, throwing out of the account the *lignite basins* of the western Territories. A line drawn from Hampton, in Rock Island county, to the junction of the Kankakee and Iroquois rivers, would define approximately the northern line of the Illinois coal field, but from the junction of these streams the boundary line deflects south to the vicinity of Chatsworth, in Livingston county, and thence eastwardly to the Indiana line All the area south of the line above designated, except a narrow belt along the Mississippi to the mouth of the Ohio, and up the latter stream to Battery Rock, is underlaid by the Coal Measures, and nearly all the counties within the above described boundary have afforded some coal, although in several of them the coal lies too deep below the surface to be available without a heavier expenditure of capital than the present demand for fuel would seem to warrant.

The Coal Measures attain an aggregate thickness of about fourteen hundred feet, and may be properly divided into upper and lower measures, taking as a line of demarcation the limestone of Shoal creek and Carlinville, a tough brownish gray rock that is so persistent in its lithological characters and development as to make it a conspicuous horizon in tracing the detailed stratification of the Coal Measures This limestone overlays a thin coal often only three or four inches in thickness, but locally becoming from eighteen inches to two feet or more, as in the vicinity of Highland, in Madison county, where it has been worked in a limited way for many years Above this limestone there is some seven hundred feet of strata belonging to the upper measures, inclosing six or seven seams of coal that range in thickness from six inches to three feet, but none of them attaining to the thickness of those in the lower measures. In Europe a coal seam eleven or twelve inches thick is considered of sufficient value to be worked in the usual way by underground drifting, but in this country seams of less than eighteen inches are generally neglected, except when they can be worked by stripping the coal along the outcrop of the seam.

The following detailed section has been constructed from the most satisfactory outcrops examined in various portions of the State, and is given as an approximately correct description of the most important strata recognized in the progress of the Geological Survey. They are numbered from the bottom upward and may be briefly described in detail as follows, commencing with the highest beds of the upper measures as they were found developed in Effingham and some of the adjacent counties. The best exposures of these upper coals and associated strata were found on the upper course of the Kaskaskia and its tributaries, and to the east and south east including the counties adjacent to the Wabash river, from Clark county on the north to the south line of White county, where the limestone separating the upper and lower measures is found outcropping at New Haven, on the lower Wabash

| | | Ft | In |
|---|---|---|---|
| No 95 | The highest strata recognized in the district above described was found by Mr Broadhead, in Effingham county, and consists of sandstone and sandy shale, upper part gray middle brown, with fragments of fossil plants | 50 | |
| No 94 | Bituminous shales and septaria with *Pleurotomaria sphærulata Spirifer plano convexus, Rhynchonella osagensis, Nautilus occidentalis, N ferratus*, etc | | 6 |
| No 93. | Dark clay shales | 4 | |
| No 92 | Dark ash brown shaly and nodular limestone, containing *Myalina sub quadrata, Aviculopecten occidentalis, Bellerophon Montfortianus, Edmondia, Leda, Macrodon*, etc | 1 | 6 |
| No 91 | Blue and olive shales | 5 | |
| No 90 | Gray sandstones and sandy shales | 26 | |
| No 89 | Thin coal | | 6 |
| No 88 | Fire clay | 5 | |
| No 87 | Buff sandstone | 12 | |
| No 86 | Clay shale with bands of fossiliferous iron ore containing *Leda bella striata, Astartella vera Nucula ventricosa, Spirifer plano convexus, Chonetes Flemingii Myalina sub quadrata, Macrocheilus inhabilis, Pleurotomaria Grayvillensis, Bellerophon Montfortianus, B carbonarius*, and *Orthoceras Rushensis* | 35 | |
| No 85 | Bituminous shales and pyritiferous limestone with argillaceous shales containing silicious wood | 9 | |
| No 84 | Gray pyritiferous sandstone | 30 to 40 | |
| No 83 | Shales with fucoids | 40 | |
| No 82 | Gray limestone with *Fusulina cylindrica? Athyris subtilita, Spirifer cameratus, S plano convexus*, etc | 4 to 8 | |
| No 81 | Calcareous shales with *Orthis carbonaria* and *Productus longispinus* very abundant | 1 | 6 |
| No 80 | Coal No 16, Nelson s coal in Effingham, and the coal on the Embarras in Coles Co | 1 to 3 | |
| No 79 | Fire clay | 1 to 3 | |
| No 78 | Sandstone and shales | 80 to 90 | |
| No 77 | Bituminous shale | 2 | |
| No 76 | Coal No 15, Shelby coal" | 1 to 3 | |
| No 75 | Fire clay | 2 to 5 | |
| No 74 | Buff limestone | | 4 |
| No 73 | Sandstone and shales | 15 to 50 | |
| No 72 | Shales partly calcareous | 10 to 15 | |
| No 71 | Calcareo bituminous shales passing into shelly bituminous limestone, fossils abundant *Euomphalus sub rugosus, Chonetes Flemingii, Productus costatus, P longispinus, Hemipronites crassus, Retzia punctulifera, Lophophyllum proliferum, Orthoceras Rushensis, Erisocrinus typicus, Zeacrinus ? mucrospinus*, and *Periprstis semicircularis* | 2 to 4 | |

| | | Ft | In |
|---|---|---|---|
| No 70 | Coal No 14, "Pana coal" | 1 | 6 |
| No 69 | Fire clay and clay shale | 3 to 5 | |
| No 68 | Calcareous sandstone | 2 to 5 | |
| No 67 | Sandstone and sandy shale | 50 | |
| No 66 | Shaly limestone with fossils similar to those of the bed below | 4 | |
| No 65 | Hard gray limestone containing *Syntrielasma hemiplicata*, *Meekella striato-costata*, *Spirifer cameratus*, *S lineatus*, *Spiriferina Kentuckensis*, *Athyris subtilita*, *Terebratula bovidens*, *Hemipronites crassus*, *Productus longispinus*, *P costatus*, *Stenopora lepidodendroides*, *Lophophyllum proliferum*, *Polypora*, *Synocladia*, etc | 5 to 25 | |
| No 64 | Shales | 6 | |
| No 63 | Coal No 13 | 1 to 1 | 6 |
| No 62 | Bituminous and argillaceous shales locally fossiliferous, containing *Pleurotomaria sphærulata*, *P tabulata*, *P Grayvillensis*, *Macrocheilus inhabilis*, *Goniatites globulosus*, *Orthoceras Rushensis*, *Bellerophon carbonarius*, *Leda bella-striata*, *L Oweni*, *Nucula ventricosa*, *Astartella vera*, *Euomphalus subrugosus*, *Polyphemopsis peracuta* and *Conularia* | 6 to 8 | |
| No 61 | Sandstones and sandy shales | 75 to 85 | |
| No 60 | Dark shaly limestone and calcareous shales with *Hemipronites crassus*, *Athyris subtilita*, *Spirifer cameratus*, *Spiriferina Kentuckensis*, *Synocladia biserialis*, *Productus punctatus*, *P Prattenianus*, *P costatus*, *P longispinus*, etc | 2 to 4 | |
| No 59 | Coal No 12 | 6 inches to 1 | 6 |
| No 58 | Shales | 10 | |
| No 57 | Gray or buff limestone, partly shaly, with *Productus Nebrascensis*, *P longispinus*, *Spirifer cameratus*, *Spiriferina Kentuckensis*, *Synocladia biserialis*, *Polypora*, etc | 5 to 20 | |
| No 56 | Bituminous shale, locally fossiliferous | 2 to 4 | |
| No 55 | Coal No 11 | 1 to 1 | 6 |
| No 54 | Arenaceous and argillaceous shales | 35 to 40 | |
| No 53 | Calcareo bituminous shales containing *Bellerophon carbonarius*, *Pleurotomaria sphærulata*, *Productus longispinus*, *Chonetes Verneuilianus*, and *Lophophyllum proliferum* | 2 to 3 | 6 |
| No 52 | Coal No 10 | 7 inches to 3 | 6 |
| No 51 | Fire clay | 1 to 4 | |
| No 50 | Sandy shales and brown sandstone | 4 to 8 | |
| No 49 | Band of *cone in cone* replaced in White county at Carmi by a band of brown iron ore filled with a minute bivalve shell probably a *Posidonia* | | 2 |
| No 48 | Argillaceous shales with flattened iron stones | 20 | |
| No 47 | Dark ash gray or chocolate colored calcareous sandstones with *Aviculopecten occidentalis*, *Productus Nebrascensis*, *P Prattenianus*, *Myalina subquadrata*, *M Swallovi*, *Euomphalus subrugosus*, *Pinna peracuta*, *Avicula longispina*, *Meekella striato costata*, *Bellerophon crassus* etc | 2 to 5 | |
| | This bed outcrops in the bed of the creek in the south part of the town of Carmi, in White county, and also a mile and a half north of New Haven, at Mr Murphy's place in the south east part of Clark county, at the old John mill site on Crooked creek in Clinton county and was penetrated in the shaft at Centralia, at a depth of about a hundred feet from the surface | | |
| No 46 | Sandy shales and sandstone | 30 to 60 | |
| No 45 | Hard brownish gray limestone of Shoal creek, Carlinville and New Haven and the recognized boundary line between the upper and lower measures Locally the upper layers are shaly and contain numerous fossils, among which are *Productus longispinus*, *Spirifer cameratus*, *Sp lineatus*, *Sp planoconvexus*, *Terebratula bovidens*, *Rhynchonella osagensis*, *Retzia punctulifera*, *Athyris subtilita*, *Chonetes variolata?* *Hemipronites crassus*, *Platyostoma Peoriense*, *Chonophyllum*, etc | 4 to 7 | |
| No 44 | Greenish drab and blue shales | 4 to 6 | |
| No 43 | Bituminous shale | 2 | |
| No 42 | Blue shale, with flattened concretions of iron | 8 to 10 | |
| No 41 | Coal, No 9 | ½ to 2 | |
| No 40 | Fire clay | 1 to 2 | |
| No 39 | Sandy shales and sandstone | 35 to 65 | |

| No. | Strata | Ft In |
|---|---|---|
| No 38 | Calcareo bituminous shale passing locally into an argillaceous limestone abounding in fossils among which the following are the most common *Leda bella striata Nucula ventricosa Astartella vera A varica Bellerophon carbonarius B. Montforti anus B percarinatus Macrocheilus inhabilis M primigenius M ventricosus, Pleurotomaria sphærulata, P Grayvillensis, Productus longispinus, P Nebrascensis, P Prattenianus Phillipsia Sangamonensis, P scitula, Polyphemopsis per acuta, Orthoceras Rushensis, Zeacrinus ? mucrospinus, Erisocrinus typicus, Lophophyllum proliferum*, etc | 2 to 3 |
| No 37 | Coal, No 8 | 1 to 2 |
| No 36 | Dark ash gray fire-clay | 2 to 3 |
| No 35 | Nodular shale passing locally into a hard silicious limestone | 3 to 4 |
| No 34 | Sandy shales and sandstone | 40 to 75 |
| No 33 | Dark ash gray silicious limestone containing *Athyris subtilita Spirifer cameratus, Chonetes mesoloba*, joints of *Crinoidea*, etc | 1 to 7 |
| No 32 | Bituminous shale | 1 to 3 |
| No 31 | Coal, No 7 | 2 to 9 |
| No 30 | Fire clay | 2 to 3 |
| No 29 | Sandstone and sandy shale | 30 to 50 |
| No 28 | Gray argillaceous limestone, with the *Fusulina* figured in vol. 5, pl 26, fig 8 It is associated in Fulton county with *Rhynchonella Osagensis, Spiriferina Kentuckensis* and *Hemipronites crassus* | 3 |
| No 27 | Laminated bituminous shale, with *Lingula umbonata*, and *Cardinia ? fragilis* | 2 to 4 |
| No 26 | Coal, No 6 | 1½ to 5 |
| No 25 | Fire clay | 1 to 3 |
| No 24 | Sandstones and shales | 25 to 75 |
| No 23 | Hard black shale, with concretions of limestone containing numerous fossils among which are *Productus muricatus Clinopistha radiata, Nautilus, Orthoceras*, etc | 1 to 5 |
| No. 22 | Coal No 5 | 4 to 7 |
| No 21 | Fire clay | 1 to 3 |
| No 20 | Sandstone and sandy shale | 30 to 75 |
| No 19 | Bituminous shale and argillaceous limestone | 2 to 4 |
| No 18 | Coal No 4 | 2 to 4 |
| No 17 | Fire clay and clay shale | 2 to 10 |
| No 16 | Sandstone and sandy shale | 50 to 75 |
| No 15 | Bituminous shale passing locally into dark blue limestone and concretions of septaria filled with fossils, *Cardiomorpha Missouriensis, Discina nitida, Productus muricatus P Prattenianus*, with two or three small species of *Goniatites* and *Nautili* | 3 to 6 |
| No 14 | Coal No 3 | 2 to 4 |
| No 13 | Fire clay | 1 to 3 |
| No 12 | Hard, tough steel gray limestone weathering to a rusty brown color, and containing *Spirifer cameratus* joints of *Crinoidea*, etc | 1½ to 3 |
| No 11 | Sandstone and silicious shale | 25 to 30 |
| No 10 | Blue clay shale filled with fossil plants At Murphysboro, Colchester and on Mazon creek in Grundy county, this shale contains concretions of iron ore inclosing fossil plants, insects, crustacea, etc | 2 to 3 |
| No 9 | Coal No 2 | 2 to 5 |
| No 8 | Light gray fire clay | 2 to 3 |
| No 7 | Sandstone and silicious shales about fifty feet in thickness on the northern and western borders of the coal field but in Gallatin county attaining a thickness of about one hundred and forty feet, with some thin seams of coal | 50 to 140 |
| No 6 | Dark argillaceous limestone sometimes highly silicious, and in Rock Island county associated with a band of dark steel gray chert, from six inches to a foot or more in thickness At some localities, as near Seaville, in Fulton county, it contains numerous fossils, among which are *Spirifer cameratus, S lineatus, S opimus, Nautilus occidentalis Productus Prattenianus, P costatus, P nanus, P punctatus, Macrocheilus*, etc This limestone is replaced in Southern Illinois by silicious shales | 3 to 8 |
| No 5 | Bituminous and silicious shales forming the roof of Coal No 1 In Gallatin county this shale is generally silicious, but in the northern portion of the State it is usually bituminous, and contains *Spirifer cameratus, Athyris subtilita, Aviculopecten, Orthoceras*, etc | 3 to 8 |

| | | Ft | In |
|---|---|---|---|
| No 4 | Coal, No 1 | 1½ to 5 | |
| No 3 | Silicious shaly fire clay, containing *Stigmaria ficoides* | 2 to 3 | |
| No 2 | Silicious shales with concretions of carbonate of iron In Gallatin county this bed is from sixty to seventy feet in thickness, but is not found at all in the northern portion of the State | 0 to 70 | |
| No 1 | Coarse sandstone or conglomerate forming the base of the Coal Measures In the southern portion of the State it is largely developed, with an average thickness of more than a hundred feet, but in the northern portion it is seldom found attaining a thickness of more than twenty five to thirty feet, and is often wanting altogether It appears at several localities in Whiteside county, as outliers, of considerable thickness several miles beyond the present boundary of the coal field Its thickness usually ranges from | 20 to 110 | |

Stems of *Sigillaria* and *Lepidodendron* are almost the only fossils it affords, and even these are seldom found in a condition to be specifically determined.

The deepest shaft yet sunk in the State is the one at Centralia, which commences about the horizon of coal No. 11, and has been carried down to the depth of 576 feet. The following is a correct copy of the record kept of the thickness and general character of the beds passed through in this shaft, and is inserted here for comparison with the general section, and with others that may hereafter be sunk through the corresponding strata in other portions of the State.

*Shaft at Centralia*

| | | Ft | In |
|---|---|---|---|
| No 1 | Drift clay and soil | 12 | |
| No 2 | Soapstone (clay shale) | 11 | |
| No 3 | Blue shale | 47 | |
| No 4 | Shale | 0 | 8 |
| No 5 | Limestone | 1 | 6 |
| No 6 | Coal | 0 | 8 |
| No 7 | Blue shale | 24 | 6 |
| No 8. | Soapstone (clay shale) | 2 | |
| No 9 | Limestone | 5 | 6 |
| No 10 | Hard sandstone | 5 | |
| No 11 | Coal | 0 | 2 |
| No 12 | Soft sandstone | 6 | |
| No 13 | Coal | 0 | 6 |
| No 14 | Sandstone | 2 | 6 |
| No 15 | Coal | 0 | 2 |
| No 16 | Soapstone (clay shale) | 4 | |
| No 17 | Limestone | 2 | |
| No 18 | Sandstone | 12 | 2 |
| No 19 | Blue rock | 1 | 6 |
| No 20 | Fire clay | 2 | |
| No 21 | Soapstone (clay shale) | 15 | 6 |
| No 22 | Blue shale | 29 | |
| No 23 | Limestone (Carlinville bed) | 11 | |
| No 24 | Shale | 5 | 6 |
| No 25 | Coal | 0 | 4 |
| No 26 | Clay shale | 4 | |
| No 27 | Sandstone | 10 | |
| No 28 | Shale | 50 | |
| No 29 | Limestone | 1 | |
| No 30 | Shale | 2 | |
| No 31 | Soapstone (clay shale) | 3 | |
| No 32 | Sandstone | 21 | |

| | | Ft | In |
|---|---|---|---|
| No 33 | Blue shale | 70 | |
| No 34 | Coal | 1 | 2 |
| No 35 | Clay shale | 3 | |
| No 36 | Lime conglomerate | 8 | |
| No 37 | Light colored shale | 10 | |
| No 38 | Sandstone | 56 | |
| No 39 | Dark shale | 43 | |
| No 40 | Black slate, with carbonate of iron | 0 | 6 |
| No 41 | Coal | 0 | 1½ |
| No. 42 | Clay shale, with sulphuret of iron | 3 | |
| No 43 | Limestone kidney ore and fire clay mixed | 11 | |
| No 44 | Sandstone with sulphuret of iron | 1 | |
| No 45 | Black slate | 1 | |
| No 46 | Fire clay | 1 | 6 |
| No 47 | Gray limestone | 2 | |
| No 48 | Variegated shale | 8 | |
| No 49 | Coal | 2 | |
| No 50 | Limestone | 8 | |
| No 51 | Blue shale | 2 | |
| No 52 | Gray limestone | 4 | 6 |
| No 53 | Black shale | 3 | 6 |
| No 54 | Gray limestone | 4 | |
| No 55 | Black shale | 12 | |
| No 56 | Blue limestone | 7 | |
| No 57 | Bituminous shale | 2 | 6½ |
| No 58 | Coal | 7 | |
| | Total depth | 576 | |

No 9 of this shaft corresponds with No 47 of the general section, and No. 23 is probably the Carlinville limestone, the equivalent of No 45 of the general section. This shaft is nearer the center of the coal field than any other in the State, and there seems to be a general increase in the thickness of the strata from the borders of the coal field eastwardly, which carries the lower seams to a greater depth from the surface than they were supposed to be, judging only from the examinations made at points remote from the center of the basin. In Sangamon and Macoupin counties the main coal is found generally at a depth of 200 to 240 feet below the Carlinville limestone, while at Centralia the first workable coal reached in their shaft was 373 feet below this limestone, though it is quite possible that the coal found there belongs to a lower horizon than the seams opened in the more northern counties. The borings at Pana, Vandalia and Decatur have not reached any workable coal, so far as reported, though the one made at the two former points was carried far enough to reach the Springfield coal, unless there is a greater increase in the thickness of the overlaying strata than could be reasonably anticipated. The boring with the diamond drill at Decatur was stopped from 80 to 100 feet above the horizon at which the coal should be found, and hence afforded no evidence in regard to the development of the main coals in that county A single boring is, however, in no case a satisfactory test as to the development of coal at a given point, as the drill might strike what the miners term a "horseback," and pass below the coal without showing any indications of the existence of a workable seam.

On the eastern borders of the State, in the counties adjacent to the Wabash river, several borings have been made that failed to find any coal thick enough to be of any value, and it is possible that there are some local areas where there are no heavy beds developed; but this is a point as yet unsettled, and only to be determined by careful experiments at many different localities. It is certainly not a well recognized principle in geology that the central portion of a coal field should be barren, and only the borders productive, and there is no good reason to suppose that the Illinois coal basin will prove an exceptional case in this respect Sir CHARLES LYELL suggests, in his "Principles of Geology," that the facts seem to "imply the existence, during the carboniferous epoch, of islands, instead of an extensive continent, in the area where the coal was found." It we accept this as probably one of the prevailing conditions of the coal-producing epoch, we must expect to find certain areas in the coal fields where the surface was not elevated above the ocean level long enough to yield a forest growth sufficient, when again submerged, to form a coal seam, and consequently local areas of greater or less extent where no workable coal can be found.

It is now a very generally accepted proposition that the vegetable matter necessary to the production of a coal seam grew upon the spot where the coal is found, and was not, as formerly supposed, drifted from an adjacent shore into the ocean's bed, where it was finally covered by sediments and transformed into bituminous coal through the slow chemical processes of succeeding ages Hence coal would only be found where the conditions requisite for a dense growth of tropical plants prevailed, and near the ocean level where the land was liable to submergence. All the remains of animal life found in the limestones and calcareous and bituminous shales that are associated with the coal in this State are of marine origin, showing conclusively that the beds from which they come have been formed beneath the ocean, and not under fresh water, as formerly supposed, and hence our present coal fields must have been low peaty and boggy lands adjacent to the sea shore, and subject to frequent and long continued submergencies, during which the sandstones, shales and limestones separating the various seams of coal were deposited, inclosing the remains of fishes, molluscs and other marine organisms with which the ocean was filled at that period.

In defining the boundaries of the coal field on the State map, we have been compelled to rely mainly on the reports of borings for the counties of Kankakee and Iroquois, as there are few or no natural outcrops of the strata along the borders of the coal area in these counties, and this is also the case with regard to the character of the formations upon which the Coal Measures rest in the counties above named So far as is known at the present time, no Devonian or Lower Carboniferous rocks are known to exist in these counties, and the whole area east of the coal field is supposed to be underlaid by upper and lower Silurian strata; but it is by no means improbable that beds belonging to the Devonian or even the Lower Carboniferous may yet be found in these counties, as these formations are known to underlay the Coal Measures on the Upper Wabash, in the vicinity of Williamsport, in Indiana, in considerable force, and unless they thin out rapidly to the northwest ward, should extend into this State.

# CHAPTER II.

## CLARK COUNTY.

Clark county is situated on the eastern border of the State, and is bounded on the north by Edgar and Coles counties, on the east by the Indiana line and the Wabash river, on the south by Crawford, and on the west by Cumberland and Coles counties. It contains ten full and eight fractional townships, making a total area of about five hundred and thirteen square miles.

The surface of the country in the western portion of the county is generally rolling, though some of the prairies are rather flat. The eastern portion is more broken, especially in the vicinity of the Wabash bluffs, where it becomes quite hilly, and is often broken into steep ridges along the courses of the small streams. The general level of the surface of the highlands above the railroad at Terre Haute, which is a few feet above the level of high water in the Wabash, is from one hundred and twenty-five to one hundred and fifty feet. The principal streams in the western part of the county are North Fork, which traverses the western portion of the county from north to south, and empties into the Embarras river in the eastern part of Jasper county; and Hurricane creek, which rises in the south part of Edgar county, and after a general course of south 20° east, discharges its waters into the Wabash river near the south-east corner of the county. In the eastern part of the county Big creek, and two or three of less note, after a general south-east course in this county, empty into the Wabash river. The North Fork, throughout nearly its whole course, runs through a broad, flat valley, affording no exposures of the underlaying rocks, and the bluffs on either side are composed of drift clays, and rise from thirty to fifty feet or more above the valley, and at several points where wells have been sunk these clays and underlaying quicksands are found to extend to an equal depth beneath the bed of the stream. The creeks in the eastern portion of the county are skirted by bluffs of rock through some portion of their courses, and afford a better opportunity of determining the geological structure of the county.

The Quaternary system is represented in this county by the alluvial deposits of the river and creek valleys, the loess of the Wabash bluffs, the gravelly clays and hard pan of the true drift, and the underlaying stratified sands that are sometimes found immediately above the bed rock.

The drift deposits proper vary in thickness from twenty to seventy-five feet or more, the upper portion being usually a yellow gravelly clay, with local beds or pockets of sand. The lower division is mainly composed of a bluish gray hard pan, exceedingly tough and hard to penetrate, usually impervious to water, and from thirty to fifty feet in thickness This is underlaid by a few feet of sand, from which an abundant supply of water can be had where it cannot be found at a higher level A common method of obtaining water on the highlands in this county, where a sufficient supply is not found in the upper portion of the drift, is to sink a well into the hard pan, and then bore through that deposit to the quicksand below, when an unfailing supply is usually obtained. Bowlders of granite, sienite, trap, porphyry, quartzite, etc, many of them of large size, are abundant in the drift deposits of this county, and nuggets of native copper and galena are occasionally met with, having been transported along with the more massive bowlders, by the floating ice, which seems to have been the transporting agency of our drift deposits.

## *Coal Measures.*

All the rocks found in this county belong to the Coal Measures, and include all the beds from the limestone that lies about 75 feet above coal No 7, to the sandstone above the Quarry creek limestone, and possibly coal No 14 of the general section These beds are all above the main workable coals, and although they include a total thickness of about 400 feet, and the horizon of five or six coal seams, yet none of them have been found in this county more than from 12 to 18 inches in thickness. The following general section will serve to show the relative position and comparative thickness of Coal Measures in this county

| | | | Ft | In |
|---|---|---|---|---|
| No | 1 | Sandstone, nowhere found well exposed | 30 to 40? | |
| No | 2 | Quarry creek and Martinsville limestone | 20 to 30 | |
| No | 3 | Shales lower part bituminous | 10 to 15 | |
| No | 4 | Coal (No 14?) | 1 | |
| No | 5 | Shaly fire clay | 2 to 3 | |
| No | 6 | Sandstone and shale some bands of iron carbonate | 18 to 20 | |
| No | 7 | Bituminous shale | 1 to 2 | |
| No | 8 | Coal (No 14?) | 1 to 1½ | |
| No | 9 | Clay shale and fire clay | 4 to 6 | |
| No | 10 | Cinnamon brown limestone | 3 | |
| No | 11 | Coal (local?) | 0 | 9 |
| No | 12 | Sandy shales passing into massive sandstone below | 40 to 50 | |

| | | Ft | In |
|---|---|---|---|
| No 13 | Dark shales with nodules of arg and fossiliferous limestone | 5 to 8 | |
| No 14 | Hard black shale approaching cannel coal | 1 to 3 | |
| No 15 | Evenly bedded sandstone | 20 to 25 | |
| No 16 | Greenish arg and sandy shales | 30 to 40 | |
| No 17 | Sandstone | 8 to 10 | |
| No 18 | Gray limestone (upper division of Livingston bed) | 5 to 8 | |
| No 19 | Shale enclosing a 6 to 10 inch coal (No 12 ?) | 7 to 8 | |
| No 20 | Limestone, lower bed at Livingston | 7 to 8 | |
| No 21 | Argillaceous and sandy shales | 30 to 35 | |
| No 22 | Coal (No 11 ?) | ½ to 1 | |
| No 23 | Brown and gray sandstones | 24 | |
| No 24 | Shale, lower part bituminous | 25 | |
| No 25 | Coal local | 0 | 7 |
| No 26 | White fire clay | 3 | 6 |
| No 27 | Green clay shale | 3 | 6 |
| No 28 | Shale and sandstone | 36 | |
| No 29 | Chocolate brown impure limestone | 3 to 4 | |
| No 30 | Bituminous shale | 3 to 6 | |
| No 31 | Coal No 10 | 1 to 1 | 6 |
| No 32 | Drab colored shales | 30 to 40 | |
| No 33 | Compact brownish grey limestone | 4 to 5 | |

This limestone is about 75 to 80 feet above the coal in the shaft just across the river from Terre Haute which is No 7 of the Illinois section, and the intervening beds would give the following continuation of the section, if carried down to the horizon of this coal, but they do not come to the surface in Clark county

| | | Ft |
|---|---|---|
| No 34 | Green blue and red clay shales | 10 to 12 |
| No 35 | Sandstone | 12 to 15 |
| No 36 | Argillaceous and sandy shales | 45 to 50 |
| No 37 | Bituminous shale | 1 to 2 |
| No 38 | Coal No 7 | 5 |

The coal afforded by this seam is a rather soft, fat, caking coal, of fair average quality The lower part of the seam contains two or three partings of shale. This seam would be the first workable coal that could be reached anywhere in Clark county, and its approximate depth at any point where it was desirable to bore for it may be determined by reference to the foregoing general section. From the horizon of the Quarry creek limestone to this coal it would be from 350 to 400 feet, and from the horizon of the Livingston limestone from 250 to 300 feet

In the north west part of this county several borings were made for oil during the oil excitement, some of which were reported to be over 900 feet in depth, but as no accurate record seems to have been kept, the expenditure resulted in no general benefit further than to determine that no deposit of oil of any value existed in the vicinity to the depth penetrated The following record of the "Old Well," or "T. R Young well," was furnished to Prof Cox by Mr. LINDSEY

| | Ft |
|---|---|
| Soil and drift clay | 23 |
| Hard pan | 30 |
| Sandstone | 20 |
| Mud stone ? | 20 |
| Coal and bituminous shale | 3 |
| Sandstone | 22 |
| Coal | 1 |
| Sandstone | 5 |

| | Ft |
|---|---|
| Clay shale (soapstone so called) | 23 |
| Black shale | 9 |
| Sandstone | 12 |
| Coal | 1 |
| Sandstone | 90 |
| Mud stone? | 2 |
| Hard rock | 1 |
| Sandstone | 52 |
| | 814 |

The upper part of this boring corresponds very well with our general section, except in the absence of the Quarry creek limestone, which should have been found where they report 20 feet of "mud stone," but whatever that may have been, it seems hardly probable that such a term would be used to designate a hard and tolerably pure limestone

This well was tubed with gas pipe for some 8 or 10 feet above the surface, and water, gas and about a half gallon of oil per day was discharged All the wells, so far as I could learn, discharged water at the surface, showing that artesian water could be readily obtained here, but it was all more or less impregnated with mineral matters and oil, sufficient to render it unfit for common use The 900 foot well must have been carried quite through the Coal Measures, and, if an accurate journal had been kept, the information it would have afforded would have been of great value to the people of this, as well as the adjacent counties It would have gone far towards settling the question as to the number and thickness of the workable coals for all this portion of the State, and the depth at which they could be reached from certain specified horizons, as for instance, from the base of the Quarry creek or Livingston limestones, or from either one of the thin coals of the upper measures that were passed through in this boring As it is, the expenditure was an utter waste of capital, except in so far as it may have taught those directly engaged in the operation the folly of boring for oil where there was no reasonable expectation of finding it in quantities sufficient to justify such an expenditure of time and money

The beds forming the upper part of the general section in this county are exposed on Quarry creek south of Casey and one mile and a half east of Martinsville, on the upper course of Hurricane creek, and the Blackburn branch south east of Parker prairie At the quarry a mile and a half east of Martinsville, the limestone is heavy bedded, and has been extensively quarried for bridge abutments, culverts, etc, on the old National road. The bed is not fully exposed here, and seems to be somewhat thinner than at Quarry creek, where it probably attains its maximum thickness, but thins out both to the north-east and south-west from that point. The upper part of the bed is generally quite massive, affording beds 2 feet or more in thickness, while the lower beds are thinner, and at the base it becomes shaly and locally passes into a green clay shale with thin plates and nodules of limestone. These shaly layers afford many fine fossils in a very perfect state of preservation, though they are neither as numerous or as well preserved here as at the outcrops of this limestone in Edgar county The most characteristic fossils of this formation are *Meekella striato-costata*, *Pleurotomaria turbiniformis*, and *Platyceras Nebrascensis*, associated with *Athyris subtilita*, *Spirifer cameratus*, *S lineatus*, *Spiriferina Kentuckensis*, *Orthis carbonaria*, *Platyostoma Peoriense*, *Terebratula bovidens*, *Chonetes Verneuilianus*, numerous corals like *Heliophyllum*, and large joints of *Crinoidea* Possibly the apparent thinning out of this limestone to the northward in this county may be due to surface erosion, as we nowhere saw the overlaying sandstone *in situ*, and Prof BRADLEY gives the thickness of this bed in Edgar county as about 25 feet, which does not indicate a very decided diminution of its thickness in a north eastwardly direction

Below this limestone, in the vicinity of Martinsville, there are partial outcrops of shale and thin bedded sandstone, with a thin coal, probably No 4 of the preceding section, and south-west of the town, and about three quarters of a mile from it, there is a partial outcrop of the lower portion of the limestone in the bluff on the east side of the North Fork valley, where we obtained numerous fossils belonging to this horizon

West and north west of Martinsville no rocks are exposed in the bluffs of the creek for some distance, but higher up partial outcrops of a sandstone, probably overlaying the Quarry creek limestone, may be found

At Quarry creek, about a mile and a half south of Casey, on sec 28, T 10, R 14, this limestone appears in full force, and has been extensively quarried both for building stone and the manufacture of quicklime It is here a mottled gray, compact limestone, locally brecciated, and partly in regular beds from six inches to two feet or more in thickness At least 25 to 30 feet of limestone is exposed here, and as the overlaying sandstone is not seen, its aggregate thickness may be even more than the above estimate. At its base the limestone becomes thin bedded and shaly, passing into a greenish calcareous shale with thin plates and nodules of limestone, abounding in the characteristic fossils of this horizon At one point on this creek a bed of green shale, about two feet in thickness, was found intercalated in the limestone A large amount of this stone was quarried here for lime, for macadamizing material and for bridge abutments on the old National road, and this locality still furnishes the needed supply of lime and building stone for the surrounding country

At the base of the limestone here there is a partial exposure of bituminous shale and a thin coal, probably representing the horizon of No 4 of the preceding section, below which some ten or twelve feet of sandy shale was seen

At WM HOWE'S place, on sec. 3, T. 9, R 14, we found the following beds exposed below the Quarry creek limestone.

| | Ft |
|---|---|
| Clay shale | 4 to 6 |
| Bituminous shale | 2 |
| Coal | 1 |
| Shaly fire-clay | 2 |
| Sandstone and shale with bands of carb of iron | 20 |
| Coal | 1½ |
| Clay shale | 3 to 6 |
| Compact brownish gray limestone | 3 to 5 |
| Black shale and fire clay partially exposed | 2 to 3 |
| Sandy shale and sandstone | 25 to 30 |

Both the coals in the above section have been worked here, mostly, by stripping in the bed of a small branch. The quality of the coal is good, but, unfortunately the seams are too thin to be successfully worked in a regular way They are the equivalents of the two upper coals in the general section of the rocks of this county.

At Mrs BRANT'S place, on sec 10 of the same township, we found the following section, which varies but little from that above given

| | Ft | In |
|---|---|---|
| Blue shale. | 10 | |
| Bituminous shale | 1 | 3 |
| Coal | 1 | |
| Fire clay | 2 | |
| Shale and sandstone | 20 | |
| Bituminous shale | 1 | |
| Coal | 1 | 3 |
| Clay shale | 6 | |
| Brown limestone | 3 | |
| Shale and sandstone | 25 | |
| Bituminous shale. | 3 to 4 | |
| Coal | 0 | 9 |
| Sandy shale and sandstone | 30 to 40 | |

Tumbling masses of the Quarry creek limestone were found here as well as at Mr HOWE'S place, immediately above the blue shale, at the top of the foregoing sections, and there is probably only a few feet of sandy shale or sandstone intervening between the limestone and the upper shales of these sections Considerable coal has been mined at MRS. BRANT'S place, and these two seams formerly furnished the greater portion of the coal used by the neighboring blacksmiths. It is a true splint coal breaking freely into cuboidal blocks two or three inches in thickness, and free from pyrite. At MR. JOSEPH HOWE'S dwelling house the limestone was found at the bottom of his well, not more than ten to fifteen feet above the upper coal which crops out near by.

On Hurricane branch, commencing on sec. 14, T. 10, R. 13, and extending down the creek for a distance of two miles or more, there are continuous outcrops of sandstone and sandy shales, No 12 of the county section. The upper portion is shaly with some thin bedded sandstone, passing downward into a massive, partly concretionary sandstone that forms bold cliffs along the banks of the stream from 20 to 30 feet in hight At the base of this sandstone there is a band of pebbly conglomerate from one to three feet in thickness, containing fragments of fossil wood in a partially carbonized condition, and mineral charcoal.

The regularly bedded layers of this sandstone have been extensively quarried on this creek for the construction of culverts and bridge abutments in this vicinity, and the rock is found to harden on exposure and proves to be a valuable stone for such uses. Some of the layers are of the proper thickness for flag stones, and from their even bedding can be readily quarried of the required size and thickness.

This sandstone is underlaid by an argillaceous shale, and a black slate which, where first observed, was only two or three inches thick, but gradually increased down stream to a thickness of about fifteen inches. The blue shale above it contains concretions of argillaceous limestone with numerous fossils, among which were *Pleurotomaria sphærulata*, *P Grayvillensis*, *Astartella vera*, *Nucula ventricosa*, *Rhynchonella Eatoniæformis*, *Orthis carbonaria*, and *Lophophyllum proliferum*. These fossils indicate the horizon of No. 13 coal, and in Lawrence, White and Wabash counties we find a well defined coal seam associated with a similar shale containing the same group of fossils, but possibly belonging to a somewhat lower horizon

On Blackburn branch, commencing on sec. 24 in the same township, and following down the stream for a mile and a half, we have a repetition of the same beds of shale and sandstone seen on Hurricane creek, underlaid by the clay shale and black slate, Nos 13 and 14 of the county section.

Near the center of section 4, T. 9, R 12, the following beds were found on Joe's Fork, above the site of the old Anderson mill

| | Ft. |
|---|---|
| Massive sandstone the same seen on Hurricane creek | 25 |
| Dark shales with nodules of arg limestone | 5 to 8 |
| Black shale | 1 to 2 |
| Sandy shale and evenly bedded sandstone | 20 to 25 |
| Greenish colored sandy and arg shales | 35 to 40 |
| Hard concretionary sandstones with softer beds below | 8 to 10 |
| Gray sparry limestone | 5 |
| Shale with 10 inch seam of coal | 8 |
| Brownish gray hard, brittle limestone | 7 to 8 |

The above includes Nos 12 to 20 of the county section. The limestones at the base of the above section are the equivalents of the Livingston limestones hereafter described, and they pass below the bed of the creek here about a mile above the old mill. The sandstone overlaying the upper limestone here, when evenly bedded, is quarried for building stone and affords a very good and durable material of this kind for common use At the mouth of Joe's Fork the lower limestone is partly below the creek bed, the upper four feet only being visible, and above it we find clay shale 2 feet, coal 10 inches, shale 5 to 6 feet, succeeded by the upper limestone which is here only three or four feet thick. The upper limestone at the outcrop here is thinly and unevenly bedded and weathers to a rusty brown color. The lower limestone is more heavily bedded, but splits to fragments on exposure to frost and moisture. It is of a mottled gray color when freshly broken, but weathers to a yellowish brown. Fossils were not abundant in either bed, but the lower afforded a few specimens of *Athyris subtilita*, a coral like *Heliophyllum*, *Productus costatus*, and *Terebratula bovidens*.

At Mr. SPANGLER'S place, on sec. 12, in Melrose township (T. 9, R. 12), a hard, brittle, gray limestone outcrops on a branch of Mill creek. The bed is about eight feet in thickness here, and is underlaid by a few feet of partly bituminous shale and a thin coal from six to eight inches thick. This is probably the same as the upper limestone at the old Anderson mill, or No. 18 of the county section. The rock has been quarried here for lime, and is said to yield a fair article.

On sec. 5, T. 9, R. 10, Prof. COX reports the following section:

| | Ft. | In. |
|---|---|---|
| Covered slop | 20 | |
| Gray shale and shaly sandstone | 10 | |
| Limestone | 4 | |
| Gray fossiliferous shale | 0 | 6 |
| Coal (impure) | 6 in. to 1 | |
| Black fire clay | 0 | 6 |
| Gray shale to the bed of the creek | 2 | |

The fossils observed here in the shale below the limestone were *Productus Prattenianus*, *P. semireticulatus?* *P. punctatus*, *Chonetes mesoloba*, *Spirifer cameratus*, *Athyris subtilita*, *Lophophyllum proliferum*, and *Myalina perattenuata*... *Myalina perniformis*. The limestone and coal of this locality probably belong to Nos. 10 and 11 of the county section.

At the railroad bridge north west of Livingston the following section may be seen:

| | Ft. | In. |
|---|---|---|
| Gray sparry limestone | 7 | |
| Blue shale | 6 | |
| Gray limestone, heavy bedded | 8 | |
| Sandstone and sandy shale | 30 to 40 | |
| Thin coal (reported) | 0 | 6 |

The upper bed of limestone (No. 18 of the county section,) is traversed by veins of calcite and brown ferruginous streaks, that give the rock a mottled appearance when freshly broken. The upper layer of the lower bed is about thirty inches thick, and is a tough, compact, gray rock, that breaks with an even surface and has a slightly granular or semi-oolitic appearance. The lower part of this bed is a mottled gray fine grained limestone, and breaks with a more or less conchoidal fracture. The fossils found in the limestone here were *Athyris subtilita*, *Productus costatus*, *P. Nebrascensis*, *Pinna per-acuta*, *Spirifer cameratus*, *S. plano convexus* and joints of *Crinoidea*. The upper division of this limestone thins out entirely about a mile above the bridge, and passes into a green shale like that by which the limestones are separated. The following section is seen about one mile above the railroad bridge in the creek bluffs and adjacent hill tops:

| | Ft |
|---|---|
| Covered slope, with tumbling masses of Quarry creek limestone | 20 |
| Sandstone, upper part massive, with shaly beds below | 40 to 50 |
| Pebbly sandstone | 8 to 10 |
| Green clay shales with a streak of coaly matter | 21 |
| Limestone, upper division of Livingston bed | 3 to 0 |
| Green shale | 3 to 5 |
| Limestone (partial exposure) | 3 |

The tumbling masses of limestone that are found in the hill tops hereaway, no doubt belong to the Quarry creek bed, which is found in partial outcrops not more than half a mile back from the creek, and from 80 to 90 feet above its level The intervening sandstones and shales which separate these limestones in the north eastern part of Clark county are much thinner than where they outcrop on Hurricane and Mill creeks, in the southern portion, indicating a general thinning out of the strata below the Quarry creek bed to the northward Sometimes I have been inclined to believe that this upper limestone was unconformable to the beds below, and its disappearance beyond Parker prairie to the south-west, where the apparent trend of its outcrop would naturally carry it, seems to strengthen this conclusion, but the outcrops of the underlaying beds are so partial and widely separated that it is difficult to determine this point satisfactorily. At any rate, the thickness of the beds between these limestones north of Livingston does not exceed 75 or 80 feet, while south of Martinsville they are from 125 to 150 feet apart, at least, showing that they thin out rapidly to the northward The upper division of the Livingston limestone can be seen to thin out entirely about a mile north of the railroad bridge north west of Livingston, and the other division must also disappear before reaching Edgar county, as Prof BRADLEY failed to find it there, as will be seen by his report on that county in Vol. IV of these reports The Quarry creek limestone is undoubtedly the same bed described by him as No 3 of his Edgar county section, and if the Livingston beds extended into that county they would be found not more than 60 to 75 feet below his No 3 Possibly this lower limestone may be represented there by his No 11, which is described as a "sandy argillaceous limestone, containing pebbles of black limestone and fragments of fossils," as we have nothing in Clark county that can be correlated with that unless it is one or both divisions of the Livingston limestones. The distance from his No. 3 down to coal No 7 he makes from 185 to 250 feet, while in Clark county the distance from the limestone on Quarry creek to this coal is from 350 to 400 feet

At Mr MURPHY'S place, near the mouth of Ashmore creek, on sec. 29, T 11, R 10, a bed of shelly, chocolate colored, impure limestone, is found outcropping by the roadside at the base of the Wabash river bluffs The section seen here is as follows.

| | Ft | In |
|---|---|---|
| Massive brown sandstone | 30 to 40 | |
| Brown earthy limestone | 3 to 4 | |
| Bituminous shale | 4 to 6 | |
| Coal | 1 | 6 |
| Fire clay and shale | 4 | |

These beds are equivalent to Nos 29 to 31 inclusive of the county section, and the coal at this point is coal No 10 of the Illinois section. The limestone above the coal here contains a fine *Naticopsis* and a *Macrodon* It weathers to a rusty-brown color on exposure, but when first broken the color is a chocolate brown, mottled with dark bluish-gray spots This limestone resembles the brown arenaceous limestone subsequently found two and one-half miles north of New Haven, near the south line of White county, and also in the bed of the creek at Carmi, and I am inclined to believe it belongs to the same horizon, though fossils are by no means as numerous in it in Clark county as at the localities mentioned in White county If this conclusion is correct, it would bring the New Haven limestone on a parallel with that numbered 33 and forming the base of the Clark county section, and they agree very well both in their lithological and paleontological characters.

The coal seam at MURPHY'S averages about 18 inches in thickness, and affords a coal of fair quality.

Tracing the bluff north eastwardly from this point, the beds rise rapidly, and about half a mile from MURPHY'S place there is about 30 feet of drab colored shales exposed beneath the limestone which is here found well up in the hill

At the foot of the bluff on Clear creek, near the State line, a mottled brown and gray limestone 4 to 5 feet in thickness is found, underlaid by 10 or 12 feet of variegated shales, which are the lowest beds seen in Clark county Extensive quarries were opened in this limestone to supply material for building the old National road, and in the debris of these old quarries we obtained numerous fossils from the marly layers thrown off in stripping the solid limestone beds that lay below The fossils found here comprise the following species. *Athyris subtilita, Retzia punctulifera, Spirifer lineatus S plano-convexus, Terebratula bovidens, Platyostoma Peoriense,* and two or three undetermined corals The limestone is a tough, fine grained, mottled, brown and gray rock in tolerably heavy beds, which makes an excellent macadamizing material, and also affords a durable stone for culverts, bridge abutments and foundation walls.

The beds intervening between this limestone and coal No 7 do not make their appearance in this county, but by visiting the shafts now in operation on the west side of the Wabash river, one and a half miles west of Terre Haute, I found a portion of them outcropping at the surface, and the remainder had been penetrated in the shafts and were reported to me by the gentleman in charge of the work. The section from the limestone to the coal would be as follows

| | Ft |
|---|---|
| Brownish gray compact fine grained limestone | 4 |
| Green blue and purple shales | 10 to 15 |
| Sandstone locally in tolerably heavy beds | 12 |
| Argillaceous shales, with bands of iron stone | 40 to 50 |
| Bituminous shale | 1 to 2 |
| Coal No 7 | 5 |

This is undoubtedly the "Danville coal" which has been extensively worked at Danville and at several other points in Vermilion county, where it ranges from 4 to 7 feet in thickness, and is equivalent to No 7 of the Illinois section There it is overlaid by a soft black shale filled with fossil shells in which the calcareous matter is replaced with pyrite, giving to the fossils a beautiful metallic lustre, but unfortunately in many cases the pyrite decomposes if not protected from the atmosphere, and the fossils are soon destroyed Locally No 7 is overlaid by a heavy bed of limestone, as at the Equality and Bowlesville mines, in Gallatin county At the mines opened west of Terre Haute, we found no well preserved marine fossils in the soft shales over this coal, although a careful search was made for them Fragments of fossil wood, either silicious or replaced by pyrite, were abundant in the debris taken from the shafts here, as well as at Bowlesville.

In any attempts that may be made in Clark county to mine coal by shafting to the lower coals, this would be the first seam reached, and its approximate depth at any given locality may be determined by the remarks already made, and especially by reference to the county section In the northern portion of the county the distance from the Livingston or Quarry creek limestones to this coal would be considerably less than in the southern part, for reasons already stated, namely, the thinning out the intervening beds to the northward, and consequently this variation in the relative thickness of the beds in different parts of the county should be duly considered in estimating the probable cost of any extensive operations for coal mining.

## *Economical Geology.*

*Coal*—From what has been already stated in the preceding pages, it will be inferred that there is no great amount of coal accessible in this county except by deep mining In the thin seams outcropping at Mr

MURPHY'S place, near the Wabash river, and at Mr HOWE'S and Mrs. BRANT'S, south east of Casey, the coal varies in thickness from a foot to eighteen inches, and though of fair quality, the beds are too thin to justify working them except by stripping the seams along their outcrop in the creek valleys The coal at Mr. MURPHY'S place has a good roof of bituminous shale and limestone, and could be worked successfully by the ordinary method of tunnelling if it should be found to thicken anywhere to 24 or 30 inches. The higher seams, found at the localities above named, south-east of Casey, are thinner than that at Mr. MURPHY'S, though one or both of the upper ones are said to have a local thickness of 18 inches I see no good reason to believe that the main workable seams that are found outcropping in the adjacent portions of Indiana, should not be found by shafting down to their proper horizon in this county, notwithstanding the reported results of the oil well borings in the north western portion of the county I have observed that in borings made for oil or for artesian water, which are expected to come to the surface whenever they are reached by the drill, it is only in exceptional cases in this State, that any accurate knowledge was obtained even by the persons in charge of the work. of the character of the rocks passed through in the boring; and in many cases the work is placed in the charge of those who are utterly incompetent to determine the proper characteristics of the strata through which the drill was passing Hence, when the enterprise was abandoned, the expenditure proved to be utterly valueless, for the want of a correct and reliable record of the strata penetrated, which, if kept and preserved, might have been of great value to the public at large, as well as to those for whose special benefit the work was prosecuted

*Building Stone*—Clark county is well supplied with both freestone and limestone suitable for all ordinary building purposes. The sandstone bed on Hurricane creek, south east of Martinsville, is partly an even bedded freestone, that works freely and hardens on exposure, and is a reliable stone for all ordinary uses. The abutments of the bridge over the North Fork on the old National road were constructed of this sandstone, which is still sound, although more than thirty years have passed away since they were built. The sandstone bed overlaying the limestone at the old Anderson mill, below the mouth of Joe's fork, also affords a good building stone as well as material for grindstones, and the evenly bedded sandstone higher up on Joe's fork, which overlays the green shales, is of a similar character, and affords an excellent building stone Each of the three limestones in this county furnish an excellent macadamizing material, and the Quarry creek limestone, as well as the beds near Livingston, furnish dimension stone and material for foundation walls of good quality

*Lime*—A fair quality of quick lime is made from both the limestones above named, and on Quarry creek the kilns are kept in constant operation to supply the demand for this article in the adjacent region.

*Potters' Clay*—An excellent article of white clay, suitable for pottery or fire brick, was found in the shaft near Marshall, about 80 to 85 feet below the Livingston limestone, and about fifty feet above the coal in the bottom of the shaft, which was probably the same coal found at Mr. MURPHY'S This bed of clay would probably be found outcropping in the Wabash bluffs, not far below MURPHY'S place.

*Soil and Timber*—The soil is generally a chocolate colored sandy loam, where the surface is rolling, but darker colored on the flat prairies, and more mucky, from the large per cent of humus which it contains. The prairies are generally of small size, and the county is well timbered with the following varieties white oak, red oak, black oak, pin oak, water oak, shell bark and pignut hickory, beech, poplar, black and white walnut, white and sugar maple, slippery and red elm, hackberry, linden, quaking asp, wild cherry, honey locust, red birch, sassafras, pecan, coffee nut, black gum, white and blue ash, dogwood, red-bud, sycamore, cottonwood, buckeye, persimmon, willow, etc. The bottom lands along the small streams, and the broken lands in the vicinity of the Wabash bluffs sustain a very heavy growth of timber, and fine groves are also found skirting all the smaller streams and dotting the uplands in the prairie region As an agricultural region this county ranks among the best on the eastern borders of the State, producing annually fine crops of corn, wheat, oats, grass, and all the fruits and vegetables usually grown in this climate. Market facilities are abundantly supplied by the Wabash river, and the St. Louis, Vandalia and Indianapolis railroad, which passes through the central portion of the county, furnishing an easy communication with St. Louis on the west, or the cities of Terre Haute and Indianapolis on the east.

Before closing my report on this county I desire to acknowledge my obligations to JOHN F. LAFFERTY, ESQ, of Martinsville, for valuable information, and personal attention and assistance rendered me, while prosecuting my examinations in this county.

# CHAPTER III.

## CRAWFORD AND JASPER COUNTIES.

Crawford county contains seven full and several fractional townships, making an aggregate area of about 438 square miles It is bounded on the north by Clark county, on the east by the Wabash river, on the south by Lawrence and Richland counties, and on the west by Jasper. Located on the western side of the Wabash, and traversed by several small streams tributary thereto, the surface is generally rolling, and was originally mostly covered with timber Subsequently a considerable portion of this timbered area has been cleared and brought under cultivation, though there is still remaining an abundance of timber to supply the present, and also the prospective demand for many years The south-west portion of the county from the Shaker mills, on the Embarras, nearly to Robinson, is quite broken, and there are also belts of broken land of greater or less extent on all the small streams The principal water courses in the county tributary to the Wabash river, are the Embarras, which runs diagonally across the south-western corner of the county, the North Fork, traversing its western border from north to south; Crooked creek, also in the southwest part, and Brushy fork, Lamotte creek, Sugar creek, and some other small streams, in the eastern portion of the county.

The prairies are generally small, and are for the most part rolling, and are mainly confined to the northern and western portions of the county, and to the bottom and terrace lands adjacent to the Wabash river One of the earliest settlements made in the State was on one of these bottom prairies in the vicinity of Palestine, in this county.

*Quaternary*—The beds referable to this formation in this county consist of buff or drab marly clays belonging to the loess, which are found capping the bluffs of the Wabash and attaining a thickness of ten to twenty feet or more, and from twenty to forty feet of brown gravelly clays and hard pan, the latter resting upon the bed rock, or separated from it by a thin bed of stratified sand or gravel If these beds were found in a vertical section they would show the following order of succession

| | Ft |
|---|---|
| Buff and drab marly clays or sands | 10 to 20 |
| Brown and yellow gravelly clays | 15 to 20 |
| Bluish gray hard pan | 10 to 25 |
| Sand or gravel | 0 3 |

Generally, these superficial deposits are thin in this county, and at most places the bed rock will be found within fifteen or twenty feet of the surface Small bowlders are frequently met with in the branches, but large ones are quite uncommon, and they are more frequently derived from the limestones and hard sandstones of the adjacent Coal Measure beds, than from the metamorphic rocks beyond the confines of the State, though some of the latter were seen

## *Coal Measures.*

The stratified rocks of this county all belong to the upper Coal Measures, the lowest beds appearing in the bluffs of the Wabash river and the highest along the western borders of the county, and include the horizon of coals Nos 11, 12 and 13, of the Illinois section The only knowledge that we have of the underlaying formations is derived from a shaft and boring made at Palestine landing The shaft passed through the following beds, commencing about six feet above high water level in the Wabash river

| | Ft | In |
|---|---|---|
| Soil gravel and clay | 8 | |
| Loose sand rock | 0 | 4 |
| Shale | 21 | 8 |
| Coal No 10? | 2 to 3 | 6 |
| Fire clay | 3 | |
| Hard limestone | 3 | 6 |
| Sandstone | 21 | |
| Brown shale | 6 | 6 |
| Limestone, with fossils | 0 | 6 |
| Gray sandy shale | 2 | |
| Limestone | 0 | 8 |
| Clay shale | 1 | 4 |
| Limestone | 0 | 6 |
| Sandstone and shale | 38 | 6 |
| Black shale | 2 | |
| Coal No 9? | 0 | 6 |
| Fire clay, not passed through | 123 | 6 |

This shaft was sunk to reach a coal seam reported in a boring previously made to be four feet thick, and at a depth of 123 feet The bore was made about a mile and a half north-west of the shaft, and commenced 15 feet below a thin coal which outcrops in the hill above The bore was made for oil, during the oil fever, and no great reliance can be placed on the reported thickness or character of the strata penetrated The shaft mentioned above was sunk to the horizon of a coal seam reported 4 feet thick in the bore, but on reaching it in the shaft it proved to be 2 feet of bituminous shale and 6 inches of coal

The report of this bore is as follows

| | | Ft | In |
|---|---|---|---|
| 1 | Soil and clay | 4 | |
| 2 | Shale | 15 | |
| 3 | Sandstone | 10 | |
| 4 | Clay shale | 6 | |
| 5 | Coal No 10 | 1 | |
| 6 | Fire clay | 13 | |
| 7 | Limestone | 3 | |
| 8 | Fire clay | 5 | |
| 9 | Limestone | 2 | 6 |
| 10 | Shale | 8 | |
| 11 | Coal No 9 ? | 3 | 6 |
| 12 | Fire clay | 4 | |
| 13 | Sandstone | 43 | |
| 14 | Shale | 5 | |
| 15 | Hard sandstone | 4 | |
| 16 | Shale | 8 | |
| 17 | Gray sandstone | 8 | |
| 18 | Shale | 12 | |
| 19 | Coal reported | 4 | |
| 20 | Fire clay | 5 | |
| 21 | Pebbly shale | 4 | |
| 22 | Dark shale | 15 | |
| 23 | Gray sandstone | 4 | |
| 24 | Dark shale | 39 | |
| 25 | Gray sandstone | 17 | |
| 26 | Black shale | 3 | |
| 27 | Rotten coal, No 8 ? | 3 | |
| 28 | Fire clay | 3 | |
| 29 | Sandstone | 22 | |
| 30 | Shale | 5 | |
| 31 | Sandstone | 4 | |
| 32 | Soft variegated shale | 30 | |
| 33 | Shale, with fatty substance and fetid odor | 7 | |
| 34 | Hard sandstone | 4 | |
| | | 323 | |

If any reliance can be placed on the reported section of this boring, it must have passed through coals Nos 10, 9 and 8, of the general section of the Illinois Coal Measures, and it is noticeable that in the shaft sunk at the landing, they found two thin beds of limestone over the coal at the bottom of the shaft, coal No 9, showing that although this limestone has thinned out very much from what its outcrop shows in Clark county, it has, nevertheless, not quite disappeared. This coal was reported in the boring at 4 feet, without any recognition of the bituminous shale above it, while in the shaft that was sunk down to this horizon in the anticipation of finding a good seam of coal, the bituminous shale proved to be 2 feet thick and the coal only 6 inches

The rotten coal No. 27, of the foregoing section, probably represents coal No 8, which, in Gallatin county, is from 50 to 75 feet above No 7, though no trace of the latter was reported in this bore. The coals intervening between No 8 and 15 are seldom found of sufficient thickness to be worked to advantage except where it can be done by stripping along their outcrops, and hence they are of but little value as a resource for fuel. In the western portion of the county but little coal has been found, and only in a single mine, hereafter to be mentioned, has there been any attempt to mine for coal in a systematic way.

The exposure in the bluffs just below Palestine Landing shows the following beds

| | | Feet |
|---|---|---|
| No 1 | Covered slope of loess and drift | 15 to 20 |
| No 2 | Shelly brown limestone with fossils | 2 |
| No 3 | Bituminous shale and thin coal—No 12 | 1 to 2 |
| No 4 | Sandy shales and sandstone | 15 to 30 |
| No 5 | Bituminous shale, with numerous fossils | 2 to 3 |
| No 6 | Coal—No 11 | 1 |
| No 7 | Hard dark gray bituminous limestone | 2 to 3 |
| No. 8 | Shale | 15 to 20 |

The shelly brown limestone No 2, of the above section, contains numerous fossils, among which I recognized *Spirifer cameratus*, *Productus costatus*, *P punctatus*, *P Prattenianus*, *P longispinus*, *Chonetes Flemingii*, joints and plates of *Crinoidæ*, *Orthis carbonaria*, and some undetermined forms of *bryozoa* Farther west in this county, and in Lawrence also, No 12 coal is overlaid by a buff, calcareous shale, in which *Orthis carbonaria* and *Lophophyllum proliferum* are conspicuous

The bituminous shale, No 5, of the above section I found well exposed at the bridge on Lamotte creek, on the road from Palestine to the landing, and the following group of fossils were obtained from it at this locality: *Pleurotomaria sphærulata*, *P tabulata*, *P Grayvillensis*, *Bellerophon carbonarius*, *B per-carinata*, etc, corresponding with the beds at Lawrenceville and Grayville Numerous bands of carbonate of iron occur in the shales at the base of the above section, both on Lamotte creek and in the river bank at Palestine landing.

Robinson is located on a sandstone deposit overlaying all the rocks found in the bluffs at Palestine landing, indicating a decided dip of the strata to the westward The outcrops of sandstone on the small branch of Sugar creek, which drains the section on which the town is built, show from 15 to 20 feet in thickness of soft brown rock, in which a few small quarries have been opened This portion of the bed affords sandy shales, and thin bedded, rather soft brown sandstone, with some thicker beds towards the base of the outcrop, which are rather inaccessible, from the amount of stripping required to reach them, as well as from the fact that they are partly below the water level in the branch.

At Mr ISAAC C HOLE's place, north of Robinson, on the N. E qr. of sec 16, T. 7, R. 12, more extensive quarries have been opened in this sandstone, and a much greater thickness of strata is exposed The quarries are on a branch in the timber, but there is almost a continuous outcrop along the branch, nearly to the prairie level, showing the following succession of strata

| | Feet |
|---|---|
| Shaly, micaceous sandstone, becoming thicker bedded and harder towards the bottom, and containing broken plants | 30 to 40 |
| Massive bro sandstone (main quarry rock) | 8 to 10 |
| Ferruginous pebbly bed | 3 |

The massive brown sandstone quarried here is locally concretionary, the concretions being much harder than other portions of the bed, and afford a very durable stone. This sandstone, with the shales usually associated with it, probably attains a maximum thickness of 60 to 80 feet, and fills the intervening space between coals Nos 12 and 13 of the general section. It has been penetrated in sinking wells on the prairie at many places north and north-west of Robinson

LAW'S coal bank, formerly known as EATON'S bank, is on the S. W. of the N. E qr of sec 12, T 7, R 13 The coal is a double seam, about three feet thick, with a parting of bituminous shale from two or three inches to two feet in thickness. It is overlaid here by shale and a hard, dark, ash gray limestone, destitute of fossils. One mile up the creek from this mine the coal is said to pass into a bituminous shale. The coal obtained here is rather soft, and subject to a good deal of waste in mining: but as the mine was not in operation when I visited the locality, I had no opportunity of judging of its average quality. A section of the creek bluff at the mine shows the following order

| | Ft | In |
|---|---|---|
| Gravelly clays of the drift | 10 to 15 | |
| Hard, dark ash gray limestone | 1 to 1 | 6 |
| Hard silicious shales, with nodules | 0 | 6 |
| Coal, with shale parting—No 13? | 3 | |

A boring was made here by the proprietor, and a thicker seam was reported to have been found some forty feet below, but if this report is correct, the sandstone usually intervening between coals Nos 12 and 13 is here much below its average thickness, and no such coal is known to outcrop in the county. However, local coals are sometimes developed which only cover very limited areas, and this may be a case of that kind.

Four miles south-west of Robinson a bed of hard, dark gray bituminous limestone outcrops in the bed of Turkey creek, and has been quarried for building stone, for which purpose it is but poorly adapted, as it splits to fragments after a limited exposure to the elements The rock occurs in a single stratum about eighteen inches thick, overlaid by a brown calcareous shale, filled with nodules of argillaceous limestone. The shale contained numerous specimens of *Lophophyllum proliferum*, associated with joints of *Crinoidæ*. The foundation stone for the court house at Robinson was obtained here. This limestone may overlay a thin coal, but I could not learn that any seam had been found in this vicinity, and I could find no outcrop of the beds below the limestone in this neighborhood. In the western portion of the county outcrops are rare, and so widely separated that no continuous section could be made.

On section 4, in Hutsonville township, at Mr. W D LAMB'S place, a bed of limestone is found underlaid by five or six feet of blue shale and a thin coal. In a well sunk here the limestone was found to be five feet in thickness, a tough, fine-grained dark grayish rock, containing no well preserved fossils On Mr EVANS' place, just over the line of Clark county, on sec. 34, T. 8, R. 12, heavy masses of tumbling limestone are to be seen along the creek valley. It is a massive, gray, brittle rock, and contains *Athyris subtilita*, *Spirifer cameratus* and *Productus longispinus*. A mile and a half further up the creek this limestone is found in place, and is burned for lime by Mr DRAKE I believe these limestones belong below the sandstone which is found at Robinson and at HOLE'S quarry

At LINLEY'S mill, on the N. W. qr. of sec. 7, T. 8, R. 13, a hard, dark gray limestone was found in the bed of the creek, only about two feet in thickness of its upper portion being exposed above the creek bed. A quarter of a mile south of the mill, at Mr. REYNOLDS' place, coal is mined by stripping along the bed of a branch. The coal is from 15 to 18 inches thick, overlaid by two or three feet of blue shale, and a gray limestone filled with large *Producti*, *Athyris subtilita*, etc. *Productus costatus*, with its long spines, seemed to be the most abundant species This limestone, and underlaying coal, I am inclined to believe represent the horizon of the upper coal in the bluff at Palestine landing, and No. 12 of the general section

Hutsonville is located upon a bench of sandstone, the lower part of which is concretionary, and the upper part which outcrops in the hills back of the town, is more evenly bedded, and affords some tolerable good building stone. The sandstone extends below the average water level of the river, and is probably altogether not less than 50 to 60 feet in thickness here, and is the equivalent of the sandstone at Robinson and vicinity in the central portion of the county.

At MARTIN'S mill, on Brushy Fork, near the south line of the county, the limestone and shale found at the Lamotte creek bridge, and also at Lawrenceville, representing the horizon of coal No. 11, is well exposed, the creek bluff showing the following section

| | | Feet |
|---|---|---|
| No 1 | Brown sandy conglomerate and concretionary sandstone, found a quarter of a mile east of the mill | 10 to 15 |
| No 2 | Space not seen | 0 |
| No 3 | Micaceous sandstone and shale, top of the bluff | 6 |
| No 4 | Brown and bluish gray micaceous shale | 12 |
| No 5 | Blue shale, partly calcareous, with iron nodules and numerous fossils | 4 |
| No 6 | Hard bituminous limestone | |

The upper bed in the above section was found about a quarter of a mile from the creek, and at a somewhat higher level apparently than the sandstone, No 2, forming the top of the bluff, but the intervening space could not be more than ten or fifteen feet. Pockets of coal were found here in the concretionary sandstone, but although dug into for coal, they proved to be of very limited extent The micaceous sandstone No. 3, of the section, affords some very good building stone, and some of the thin layers are distinctly ripple marked.

The calcareous shale afforded numerous fossils of the same species found at the Lamotte bridge

At Mr. NETTLE'S place, on the N E. qr. of sec. 24, T. 5, R 12, coal has been mined for several years The coal is about 18 inches thick, and has a roof of fine black slate, resembling a cannel coal, nearly as thick as the coal itself. The black slate is overlaid by two or three feet of calcareous shale, containing *Orthis carbonaria*, *Retzia punctulifera*, and joints and plates of *Crinoidæ* This coal I believe to be the same as that near the top of the hill at Palestine landing, and No 12 of the Illinois section

Prof COX reports the following outcrops in this county, at localities which I did not visit "In the hill east of the Shaker mill, sec 32, T 5, R 12, a soft, yellowish, massive sandstone, forming cliffs along the ravines, and in places weathering into 'rock houses,' or oven-like cavities. Section here as follows

| | Ft |
|---|---|
| Soil and covered space | 5 |
| Flaggy sandstone in two to eight inch layers | 8 |
| Solid bedded sandstone | 13 |

Sandy shales, flagstones, and an occasional showing of massive soft sandstone form the prominent geological features of the southern and western portions of the county Around Hebron, four miles south of Robinson, massive sandstone forms cliffs 15 to 20 feet high, probably a continuation of the rock seen at the Shaker mill Two miles and a half south east of Belair, found the following section at Gooden's coal bank

| | Ft |
|---|---|
| Slope of the hill | 20 |
| Hard blue argillaceous shale | 10 |
| Coal (breaks in small fragments) | 1 to 1½ |

This mine is worked by a shaft. A quarter of a mile below, on Willow creek, the same coal is worked on Mr MATHENEY'S place by stripping, where the coal is of the same thickness."

This coal must be as high in the series as No 13 or 14 of the general section, and may be the same as the coal mined near Newton and New Liberty, in Jasper county.

## *Economical Geology.*

*Coal.*—As we have already stated, on a preceding page, all the stratified rocks in this county belong to the upper Coal Measures, extending from coals Nos 11 to 14, inclusive, and as these seams are usually too thin to be worked in a regular way, no valuable deposit of coal is likely to be found outcropping at the surface in the county. The seam at Mr LAW's place, north-west of Robinson, is said to attain a local thickness of three feet, and may be successfully mined where the coal is good. When the demand for coal shall be such as to justify deep mining, the lower coals may be reached at a depth of four to six hundred feet Their nearest approach to the surface is along the valley of the Wabash river, and the depth would be increased to the westward by the dip of the strata and the elevation of the surface.

*Building Stone.*—The best building stone to be found in this county comes from the heavy bed of sandstone above coal No 12, which outcrops at various places in the county, and especially at Mr HOLE's quarries north of Robinson At some localities, a fair article of thin bedded micaceous sandstone is found between coals 11 and 12, as at Martin's mill, on Brushy Fork, near the south line of the county These sandstones afford a cheap and durable material for foundation walls, bridge abutments, etc The limestone four miles west of Robinson, that was used in the foundation walls of the court house, is liable to split when exposed to the action of frost and water, and although seeming hard and solid when freshly quarried, will not withstand exposure as well as the sandstone, if the latter is carefully selected. The limestone at Reynolds' coal bank, near Lanley's mill, stands exposure well, and will afford a durable building stone

*Lime.*—We met with no locality in the county where lime was burned, but just north of the county line of Clark county, at Mr. DRAKE's place, a fair quality of lime is obtained from a limestone apparently the equivalent of that at Reynolds' coal bank

*Iron Ore.*—The shales associated with coal No 11 usually contain more or less carbonate of iron, and at the locality below the bridge on Lamotte creek, near Palestine landing, the quantity seemed to be sufficient to justify an attempt to utilize it. The shale in the bank of the creek shows a perpendicular face of fifteen to twenty feet, and the bands of ore towards the bottom of the bed would afford from twelve to eighteen inches of good ore in a thickness of about six feet of shale. At the river bank, just below the landing, this shale outcrops again, and the iron nodules are abundant along the river bank, where they have been washed out of the easily decomposed shale

*Sand, Gravel and Clay*.—The materials for brick are abundant almost everywhere, and can be had wherever wanted. Good brick clay can be found in the subsoil of the uplands, and sand is found both in the loess deposits of the river bluffs and in the beds of the streams. The second bottom or terrace land along the Wabash river affords an abundance of gravel for road ballast, making cements, etc.

*Soil and Timber*.—From Hutsonville south, there is a belt of alluvial bottom and terrace land, from one to three miles in width, extending to the mouth of Lamotte creek, a distance of about ten miles. This is mostly prairie, and the soil is a deep, sandy loam, and very productive. The upland prairies have a chocolate colored soil not so rich in humus as the black prairie soils of Central Illinois, but yielding fair crops of corn, wheat, oats, clover, etc. On the timbered lands the soil is somewhat variable. Where the surface is broken the soil is thin, but on the more level portions, where the growth is composed in part of black walnut, sugar tree, linden, hackberry and wild cherry, the soil is very productive, and yields annually large crops of all the cereals usually grown in this latitude. The varieties of timber observed in this county were the common species of oak and hickory, black and white walnut, white and sugar maple, slippery and red elm, honey locust, linden, hackberry, ash, red birch, cottonwood, sycamore, coffee nut, black gum, pecan, persimmon, paw-paw, red thorn, crab apple, wild plum, sassafras, red bud, dog-wood, iron wood, etc.

*Indian Mounds*.—One mile south of Hutsonville, on the gravel terrace, and about 200 yards from the river bank, there is a curious group of mounds, 55 in number, and from eight to ten feet in hight. One of the largest mounds is surrounded by a wall of earth raised about three feet above the surface, and from five to six feet in width, inclosing a space of ground about a hundred feet in diameter. This was undoubtedly the site of an ancient village belonging to that mysterious people whom we call the "Mound builders," for the want of some more distinctive appellation, and who once, and probably for a long series of years inhabited the valleys of the Mississippi and its tributaries, as is proven by their earth works scattered over the whole area of the western and southern States. But little is at present known of the character and habits of this ancient people, whence they came or whither they went, and the study of these ancient works, and the ornaments and implements belonging to those who built them, is perhaps the only available clue to their history.

JASPER COUNTY contains an area of 484 square miles, and is bounded on the north by Cumberland, on the east by Crawford, on the south by Richland, and on the west by Clay and Effingham counties The Embarras river traverses the whole extent of the county from north west to south east, and drains nearly the whole of its surface except the south west corner, which is drained by Mud creek, a tributary of the Little Wabash. About one-third of the county was originally timbered land and the remainder prairie, the latter occupying the broad areas of upland between the valleys of the streams, and elevated from sixty to eighty feet above the water courses From Robinson to New Liberty the country is rather low and comparatively level, seldom rising more than twenty or thirty feet above the beds of the small streams The Embarras river runs through a low, flat bottom, from three to five miles in width, with some swampy areas, though generally dry enough to admit of cultivation, but subject to overflow from the high water of the river. Rock exposures are but rarely to be met with in the county, owing, in part, to the soft and yielding character of the sandstones and shales that form the bed rock over the greater portion of the county, and in part to the wide valleys in which the streams have their courses, seldom impinging upon the bluffs sufficiently to expose the stratified rocks

The superficial deposits of this county consist mostly of brown, gravelly clays, and a bluish gray hard pan, the whole aggregating from twenty to forty feet in thickness, and presenting the same character as in Crawford county. These beds thicken to the westward and are considerably heavier in the western part of the county than in the eastern Small bowlders of metamorphic rock are frequently met with in the creek beds or on the hill sides weathered out of these deposits, associated with those derived from the sandstones and limestones of the Coal Measures.

## *Coal Measures.*

From the limited exposures, and the widely separated points where the bed rock can be seen in this county, no general section of the strata was possible, but enough was seen to indicate their general character, and to determine very nearly their relative position in the Coal Measures. The main water courses traverse broad alluvial valleys which gradually slope up to the level of the adjacent highlands, rarely impinging upon the bluffs on either side so as to show the character of the underlaying formations. The lowest beds in the county are probably the shales and shaly sandstones outcropping on the lower courses of the North Fork, and on the Embarras in the vicinity of St. Marie, which probably belong to the heavy shale deposit passed in the boring at Greenup, and belong between coals Nos. 11 and 16 of the general section. The highest outcrops will be found in the north west corner of the county, where the *Fusulina* limestone that outcrops at Churchill's place, near the county line in Cumberland county, may be seen.

At the crossing of North Fork, on the old Palestine and Vandalia road, a blue, sandy shale has been penetrated by a shaft to the depth of about thirty feet in search of coal, but without success. The upper part of this shale bed outcrops in the bank of the stream at an old mill just below the bridge. About a mile further down the creek, a bed of brown, calcareous sandstone is found from 18 to 20 inches thick, which contains *Pinna per acuta*, *Spirifer plano convexus*, *Productus Prattenianus*, *Orthoceras*, *Myalina*, etc.

In the bank of the Embarras, at St. Marie's, a thin bedded micaceous sandstone is quarried at low water, but it splits into thin layers on exposure, and is of but little value as a building stone. A well was sunk here at the steam mill, to the depth of ninety feet, through sandy shales and sandstone, without finding either coal or limstone.

Newton, the county seat of this county, is located on the bluff of the Embarras, and the outcropping beds that form the lower portion of the bluff consist of 25 to 30 feet of soft micaceous shales and sandstones extending below the river bed. About two miles south east of the town, on Brush creek, a sandstone is found that furnishes most of the building stone used in this vicinity. The quarry rock is from eight to ten feet thick, in layers varying from six to twelve inches or more in thickness. The stone is rather soft when first quarried, but becomes harder on exposure and makes a very durable rock for ordinary use. Locally it has a coarsely concretionary structure, the concretions being harder than the surrounding rock, a character frequently observed in the heavy bedded sandstones of the Coal Measures. Below the sandstone there is a variable thickness of shale that becomes bituminous towards the bottom and forms the roof of a coal seam that has been opened and worked to some extent at this locality. The seam was covered up by the falling in of the roof, so that I could not see the quality of the coal or measure its exact thickness, but it is said to be from 2½ to 3 feet thick, and has a shale parting like the seam at the old Eaton mines north west of Robinson. This is probably coal No 14 or 15 of the general section. This coal probably underlays the town of Newton at a depth of eight or ten feet below the bed of the Embarras river, and might be easily mined anywhere along the bluff, by driving an inclined tunnel into the base of the hill above high-water mark down to the level of the coal. A mine could be cheaply opened here in this way, and if the quality of the coal should prove to be good, it would no doubt become a profitable investment in supplying the steam mills and other local demands for coal

Three miles east of Newton, on the road to New Liberty, the same sandstone is met with on the east side of the Embarras valley outcropping in the base of the low hills bordering the valley, and continuing in occasional outcrops to the coal bank one mile west of New Liberty. This coal is probably the same as that on Brush creek a mile and a half south-east of Newton The seam is divided by a bituminous shale varying from six to eighteen inches in thickness, and only the lower division of the seam is mined here, the upper part being too soft and shaly to be of much value A section of the beds above this coal, as seen between Newton and this point, would be as follows .

| | Ft | In |
|---|---|---|
| Micaceous sandstone thin bedded at the top and more massive below | 20 to 30 | |
| Sandy shale with local layers of thin sandstone | 5 to 10 | |
| Bituminous shale | 1 to 3 | |
| Coal, rather soft and poor | 1 to 1 | 6 |
| Shale parting | ½ to 1 | 6 |
| Coal, good | 1 | 6 |

We found no fossils in the shale overlaying this coal on Brush creek, but west of New Liberty we noticed imperfect examples of *Bellerophon carbonarius* and *Spirifer plano-convexus.*

South of Newton a prairie ridge extends for several miles in a southerly direction, along which sandstone is said to be found, and most probably this ridge shows the trend of the sandstone formation in this part of the county.

On Limestone creek, in the south west corner of the county, there is an outcrop of light-gray limestone, that is quarried for building stone and is also burned for lime

The following sections were found by Prof. Cox at localities I did not visit "In the north west corner of the county, on Island creek, an outcrop of heavy bedded sandstone and flagstone commences on sec 16, T. 8, R. 8, and may be traced northward to the county line. The sandstone is brownish colored and makes a fair building stone On Mint creek, sec 1, T. 7, R. 8, the following section was found

| | Ft | In |
|---|---|---|
| Silicious shale | 20 | |
| Gray pyritiferous shale, passing into limestone | 2 | |
| Jet black bituminous shale with fish scales and spines | | 6 |
| Coal, breaking into small cubes | | 6 |
| Fire-clay | | 3 |
| Gray silicious shale and flagstone | 3 | 9 |

This thin coal was sometimes found split by a hard bituminous shale, leaving only about an inch of coal in each division

Section on Slate creek, sec. 9, T 7, R. 8 ·

| | Ft | In |
|---|---|---|
| Grayish buff argillaceous shale | 5 | |
| Calcareo argillaceous shale with fossils | 1 | 6 |

—6

| | | |
|---|---|---|
| Brownish black shales | 2 | 6 |
| Hard black shale | 2 | |
| Gray argillaceous shale | 6 | 6 |

The fossiliferous shale in the above section contained *Euomphalus subrugosus*, *Pleurotomaria Grayvillensis*, *Nucula ventricosa*, *Lophophyllum proliferum*, *Chonetes mesoloba* and a leaf of *Neuropteris*.

Section on the Embarras river, S W qr of sec 31, T 7, R 10

| | | Ft | In |
|---|---|---|---|
| 1 | Covered slope | 10 | |
| 2 | Bluish brown argillaceous shale | 10 | |
| 3 | Brown and black bituminous shale | 3 | |
| 4 | Fire clay | | 3 |
| 5 | Gray fossiliferous limestone | | 10 |
| 6 | Blue argillaceous shale | | 4 |
| 7 | Brownish black impure limestone | 3 | |
| 8 | Blue shale | 2 | |
| 9 | Bluish shaly sandstones | 10 | |

The impure limestone, No 7, contained *Productus longispinus*, *Athyris subtilita*, *Pleurotomaria Grayvillensis*, *Terebratula bovidens*, *Chonetes mesoloba* and *Hemipronites crassus*. The shale under the limestone contained *Myalina sub-quadrata?* *Euomphalus subrugosus*, *Orthoceras Rushensis*, fragments of *Pinna*, etc. Two miles north of St Marie on the west half of sec 7, T 6, R 11, a shaft was sunk twenty feet to the river level and some fragments of impure limestone were thrown out. About a hundred yards up the river this limestone is just at the water's edge. It is 8 or 10 inches thick and contains *Athyris subtilita*, *Spirifer cameratus* and fragments of *Pinna*. It is probably the equivalent of the limestone near Newton.

The second bluff or terrace is about forty feet above low water. About thirty feet above low water in the face of the bluff, there are the remains of an old furnace. It is about three feet in diameter, of a circular form and walled with rock. Around it are pieces of burnt limestone, charcoal and cinders. On the top of the bluff there are a number of Indian mounds arranged in the form of an oblong square inclosing a court. The peculiar arrangement of the mounds, and the presence of mica in the sandstone and also in the drift bowlders found here, led to the belief that silver existed in the rocks and could be extracted from them, and the existence of the mounds and the furnace led to the sinking of the shaft in pursuit of the same precious metal.

On Crooked creek, a half mile west of Brockville, the following section was found

| | Ft | In |
|---|---|---|
| Buff colored limestone without fossils | 4 | |
| Blue argillaceous shale | 3 | |
| Rotten limestone with fossils | | 6 |
| Black bituminous shale | 4 | |
| Blue argillaceous shale | 2 | |

The fossils found in the rotten limestone were: *Athyris subtilita, Chonetes mesoloba?* and *Productus longispinus.* One mile and a half south-west of Harrisburg, on Lick creek, found the following beds

| | Ft | In |
|---|---|---|
| Bluish argillaceous shale | 10 | |
| Black bituminous shale | 4 | |
| Impure limestone with fragmentary fossils | | 6 |
| Bluish argillaceous shale | 2 | |

The water of the creek is slightly saline, and some prospecting for brine has been done in this vicinity."

All the outcrops given on the preceding pages belong to the upper Coal Measures, and range about the horizon of coals No 14 or 15 of the general section From the general trend of the strata it may be inferred that the lowest beds that outcrop in the county are those along its eastern border, and the highest those upon the western.

## *Economical Geology.*

*Coal.*—A limited supply of coal may be obtained from the beds outcropping near Newton and New Liberty, but neither the average thickness of the seams nor the quality of the coal they afford would justify an attempt to work them except in a limited way. The main coals are here from five to six hundred feet or more below the surface, and to reach the bottom of the Coal Measures would require a shaft more than a thousand feet in depth. It will probably be many years before the demand for coal will be such in this county as to warrant the opening of mines at this depth

*Building Stone.*—Building stone of good quality is not abundant, the supply being mainly from the sandstone overlaying the coal at Newton and in that vicinity At some points this bed affords a brown sandstone of fair quality, and at others it passes into silicious shales or shaly sandstones too soft and thin bedded to be used for building purposes. On Limestone creek, in the south western portion of the county, there is a bed of compact gray limestone in layers of a foot to eighteen inches in thickness, that is quarried for foundation walls, etc, for the supply of the adjacent region

*Lime*—The only limestone found in the county that seemed to be at all adapted for use in the lime kiln, was that on Limestone creek in the south-west corner of the county, and a fair quality of lime may be made there for the supply of such portions of the adjacent region as are remote from railroad tranportation

*Sand and Clay*—These common and useful materials are abundant, and good brick may be made at almost any point on the uplands where they may be required Sand for mortar and cement occurs at many places along the bluffs of the Embarras, and may be found in the beds of most of the small streams, and in nearly every portion of the county.

*Soil and Timber.*—The bottom lands of the Embarras have a rich alluvial soil, and when cleared and brought under cultivation, produce large crops of corn, to which they seem best adapted. The soil of the prairie region is a chocolate colored clay loam, similar to that of the adjoining counties, and produces fair crops of corn, wheat, oats and grass. The timbered upland is similar to that described in the report on Crawford county, and the varieties of timber noticed here was nearly the same. Although not possessing so large an area of timbered land as Crawford county, it has nevertheless an abundant supply for a much larger population than it contains at the present time.

# CHAPTER IV

## LAWRENCE AND RICHLAND COUNTIES.

Lawrence county embraces an area of about three hundred and sixty-two square miles, and is bounded on the north by Crawford county, on the east by the Wabash river, on the south by Wabash county and on the west by Richland The principal water courses in the county, besides the Wabash river which forms its eastern boundary, are the Embarras river, which traverses the north east portion of the county, with its affluents Brushy Fork and Indian creek, which drain the northern and central portions of the county, and Raccoon creek and the eastern fork of the Bonpass, which drain the southern part East of Lawrenceville, and lying between the Embarras and Wabash rivers, there is an extensive marsh from two to four miles in width and about ten miles in length, called Purgatory swamp Surrounding this on the east and north, there is a considerable area of bottom prairie, the upper or northern portion being known as Allison's prairie, and the lower portion as the Russelville prairie. In addition to this there are some small prairies in the southern, and also in the north western portion of the county, but the greater portion of its area was originally covered with a heavy growth of timber. The surface is generally rolling, but nowhere so broken that the land cannot be cultivated even along the bluffs of the streams The elevation of the country above the water courses is nowhere very great, and on what may be termed the upland ranges from fifty to about a hundred feet

*Loess and Drift*—In the vicinity of the Wabash river we find beds of brown clay and buff or yellowish marly sands ranging from ten to twenty feet or more in thickness which probably represent the age of the loess These are underlaid by brown or gravelly clays containing small bowlders ranging in size from an inch or two to a foot or more in diameter. On the uplands away from the river bluffs there are usually from fifteen to twenty feet of these gravelly clays above the bed rock, and usually in sinking wells, especially in the northern portion of the county, an adequate supply of water can only be obtained by going from ten to forty feet or more below the drift clays into the underlaying shales or sandstones About Lawrenceville there is usually from five to six feet of brown gravelly clay resting immediately upon the bed rock, and above that from ten to twelve feet of buff or brown clays that are quite free from gravel

*Stratified Rocks* —All the formations that outcrop in this county below the superficial deposits already described, belong to the upper Coal Measures, and include a vertical thickness of not more than one hundred and fifty to two hundred feet On the Wabash river at St Francisville there is an outcrop of massive gray sandstone, which I believe to be the same as that found at Hanging rock Bluff in Wabash county, and the lowest rock seen in this county. The section here is as follows

| | Ft |
|---|---|
| Shale | 8 |
| Impure iron ore | 1 |
| Thin bedded sandstone and sandy shale | 16 |
| Massive gray sandstone | 20 to 25 |
| Unexposed to river level | 10 to 15 |

Just below the dam at Lawrenceville on the Embarras river we find the following section which I believe overlays the beds seen at St Francisville

| | Ft |
|---|---|
| Brown and bluish gray argillaceous shale | 10 to 12 |
| Bituminous and partly calcareous shale with bands of iron ore and numerous fossils | 4 to 5 |
| Black slaty shale | 3 to 5 |
| Dark gray limestone in the river bed | 1 |

The fossiliferous bed at this locality contains *Lophophyllum proliferum*, *Pleurotomaria sphærulata*, *P. tabulata*, *P. Grayvillensis*, *P carbonaria*, *Polyphemopsis per acuta*, *Bellerophon Montfortianus*, *B carbonarius*, *B. per-carinatus*, *Astartella varica*, *Productus longispinus*, *Hemipronites crassus*, *Macrocheilus inhabilis*, and joints and plates of *Crinoidea*.

At the bridge two miles east of Lawrenceville we find a repetition of the foregoing section, but the bluff is much higher and a greater thickness of strata is exposed, giving the following section

| | | Ft |
|---|---|---|
| 1 | Micaceous sandstone and shale passing downward into argillaceous shale | 20 to 25 |
| 2 | Bluish gray calcareous shale, with iron bands and fossils | 4 to 6 |
| 3 | Black laminated shale, with concretions of black limestone | 4 to 5 |
| 4 | Little dark gray limestone, weathering to a brown or buff color | 1½ to 2 |
| 5 | Blue and brown shales partly argillaceous and bituminous | 12 to 14 |

About a hundred yards above the bridge, by an undulation of the strata, the limestone No 4 of the above section is brought down to, and passes under the river bed This would seem to indicate a rapid dip to the northward, but the re appearance of the fossiliferous shale No 2 of this section on Lamotte creek, in Crawford county, some twenty miles north of this, shows that the apparent dip here is only an undulation of the strata, such as may frequently be observed in the Coal Measures of this State Near the upper end of the exposure here a dike of sandstone from six to eighteen inches in width, cuts transversely through the lower bed of shale No. 5 of the above section, having an east and west direction This would seem to indicate that the undulation in the strata here might be due to some disturbing force acting from below The calcareous shale No. 2 of this section contains the same group of fossils found at Lawrenceville The limestone contains *Naticopsis ventricosus, Nautilus sp? Terebratula bovidens, Spirifer planoconvexus, Rhynchonella Osagensis, Athyris subtilita, Clinopistha radiata, Solenomya radiata*, with several undetermined species of small univalve shells This is a very marked horizon in the upper Coal Measures, and the outcrops extend along the valley of the Wabash from below Grayville, in White county, to the central or northern part of Crawford county. The black laminated shale above the limestone contains local concretions of black limestone, with fish scales *Discina nitida*, etc South of the bridge, on the east side of the Embarras, there is an outcrop of micaceous sandstone that affords some building stone of a fair quality, which has been used for bridge abutments, foundation walls, etc., and is probably the equivalent of the upper part of the foregoing section

At Mr F PLUMMER'S place, on the S E qr of sec 25, T 5 N, R 12 west, two wells were sunk, one near his dwelling house, passing through eighteen inches of coal at a depth of eighteen feet, and the other, about a quarter of a mile to the northward, commencing at a level below the bottom of the first, was carried down forty three feet mostly through sandstone and shale, the lower part bituminous, and ending in the calcareous fossiliferous beds of the section at Lawrenceville and the bridge two miles east of that point

At Mr PORTER'S place, adjoining Mr. PLUMMER'S on the south, a well was sunk to the depth of fifty-six feet, through the following beds

| | Ft |
|---|---|
| Drift clay soil etc | 18 |
| Sandstone | 11 |
| Blue shales, bituminous at the bottom | 27 |

The water was obtained in the fossiliferous layers over the black, sheety shale No 3 of the section at the Embarras bridge The coal passed through in the well at Mr. PLUMMER'S house must lay above the sandstone in the Porter well, which had probably been eroded away at that point by water currents during the drift epoch.

At Mr FRITCHEY'S well, a half mile west of Mr. PLUMMER'S, a bed of cellular iron ore occurs in the sandstone near its base, and was passed through in his well about sixteen feet below the surface. The iron ore was reported to be two feet thick in the well, but at the outcrop, a quarter of a mile from the house, its thickness was only about six inches. It appears to be too sandy to be of any value for the production of iron

At Mr. WARRINER's well, a mile and a half northwest of Mr. PLUMMER's, the sandstone was penetrated in a well to the depth of fifty eight feet without reaching the bottom of the bed, and its entire thickness here cannot be less than from sixty to seventy five feet Near its base there is a very hard layer about two feet in thickness, which rings under a blow of the hammer like a compact limestone, probably from a small per cent of calcareous or ferruginous matter in its composition A similar hard layer was observed at the base of the sandstone at Hole's quarry, north of Robinson, in Crawford county, of which this is probably the equivalent. The coal under this sandstone is probably No 12 of the general section, which is somewhat irregular in its development in this county, sometimes affording from eighteen to twenty inches of good coal, while at other places it thins out to a few inches, or is wanting altogether.

At Mr. EMERICH's quarry, two miles and a half north east of Sumner, a heavy bed of sandstone outcrops on a branch of the Embarras, that is probably referable to this same formation The face of the quarry shows from eighteen to twenty feet of massive sandstone, presenting a concretionary structure at the base of the bed, but becoming thinner bedded and somewhat shaly towards the top. This rock has been extensively quarried here for building culverts and bridge abutments on the O and M. railroad. One mile north of the town there has also been a small quarry opened higher up in this formation, where the rock is thin bedded and shaly, but affords some good building stone near the bottom of the quarry, though the overlaying beds are shaly and worthless.

In the Embarras bluffs near Mr. WM. H. MILES' place on the N W. qr of sec 33, T 5, R 12, there is a massive sandstone exposed forming the lower portion of the bluff in connection with a thin seam of coal The section here is as follows

| | Ft | In |
|---|---|---|
| Massive sandstone | 5 to 10 | |
| Ferruginous conglomerate | 2 to 3 | |
| Coal (probably local) | 0 | 8 |
| Slope covered to the river level | 10 to 12 | |

A hundred yards above where this section was seen, the sandstone continues down to the river level with no indications of coal This is probably the same thin coal found on Brushy creek, near Martin's mill, just over the line in Crawford county, and as it is there from forty-five to fifty feet above the creek level, it indicates a westerly dip of the strata equal to about six or seven feet to the mile. No rocks are known to outcrop on the Embarras for some distance above this point, and below there is no considerable exposure between this and the dam at Lawrenceville

Three miles south of Lawrenceville, on Mr. HENDERSON's place, on the south side of Indian creek, and at several other points in the neighborhood a coal seam is found which has been opened and worked in a limited way to supply the local demand for coal. It ranges from twelve to eighteen inches in thickness and is mined only by stripping along its outcrop in the banks of the small streams The seam at Mr HENDERSON'S place is from twenty five to thirty feet above the bed of Indian creek, and partial outcrops of soft shale were seen between the coal seam and the creek level This coal seems to be identical with that at Mr. NETTLE'S, near the south line of Crawford county, and the equivalent of No. 12 of the general section. It outcrops also on Mud creek, three or four miles north-west of Lawrenceville, at several places, and has been worked to a limited extent to supply the neighboring blacksmiths previous to the construction of the O and M. railroad, since which time it has been generally abandoned.

A boring was made some eight or ten years ago at Lawrenceville, to the depth of about four hundred and fifty feet, but no accurate record has been kept of the beds passed through A thin coal was reported at the depth of three hundred and forty feet, and another seam four feet thick near the bottom of the bore, but it seems probable, from all that can be learned at the present time, that the work was not in charge of a competent person, and hence but little reliance can be placed on the reported results. A very good brine was said to have been reached near the bottom of the bore

The following sections and notes are reported by Prof COX, from his examinations at localities not visited by myself "At JOHN LEED'S quarry, on Indian creek, one mile west of the St Francisville road, found the following section

| | Ft | In |
|---|---|---|
| Gray shale | 6 | |
| Carbonaceous shale | 0 | 6 |
| Shale | 0 | 8 |
| Sandstone in even beds from 4 in to 1 foot thick | 3 | |

This sandstone is a durable building stone and was used in the bridge abutments on the Embarras river. On the north bank of the Embarras river, at the Shaker mill, on sec. 32, T. 5, R. 12, the following section was found, the massive sandstone being probably the equivalent of that at St. Francisville :

| | Ft |
|---|---|
| Soil and drift | 5 |
| Thin bedded sandstone, 2 to 8 inches | 8 |
| Massive sandstone | 13 |

Section on Indian creek, three miles south of Lawrenceville :

| | Ft | In |
|---|---|---|
| Soil and drift | 10 | |
| Argillaceous shale, with iron bands | 25 | |
| Impure coal | 0 | 8 |
| Fire clay and gray shale | 5 | |
| Bluish sandstone in the bed of the creek | 1" | |

—7

The eight inch coal in the above section is below that mentioned on a previous page as occurring on Mr HENDERSON'S place in this neighborhood as that is found from 25 to 30 feet or more above the bed of Indian creek, and ranges from twelve to eighteen inches in thickness. The following is an approximate section of the rocks outcropping in this county

| | Feet |
|---|---|
| Brown and gray sandstone the lower part in massive beds | 60 to 75 |
| Coal—No 12 | 1 to 1½ |
| Shale with bands of argillaceous iron ore | 30 to 35 |
| Coal—No 11 | 0 to 1 |
| Sandstone, top thin bedded and shaly bottom massive | 30 to 35 |

The upper sandstone underlays the northern and western portions of the county, and is penetrated in sinking wells nearly everywhere upon the uplands. At its base there is usually a very hard stratum that is sometimes called limestone on account of its hardness, and also a ferruginous bed, that passes locally into a sandy iron ore. The lower sandstone forms the main portion of the Wabash bluff at St. Francisville, and also appears at the Shaker mill on the Embarras, but its outcrop is restricted to the eastern border of the county.

## *Economical Geology.*

*Building stone*—Both the sandstones in the foregoing section afford more or less building stone of fair quality for ordinary use, and extensive quarries have been opened in the upper one in the vicinity of Sumner for the use of the O & M. Railroad Small quarries have been opened in various places in the central and northern portions of the county in this bed to supply the local demand for foundation stone, walling wells, bridge abutments, etc LEEDS' stone quarry on Indian creek, south of Lawrenceville, and one mile west of the St Francisville road, is probably in the lower bed of sandstone, and the rock obtained there is in thin, even beds, ranging from four inches to a foot in thickness.

The limestone associated with coal No. 11 at Lawrenceville, and at the bridge two miles east on the Embarras, is somewhat argillaceous, and consequently cannot be depended on where it is to be subjected to the action of frost and moisture, although it has been used in building the Lawrenceville bridge This is the only limestone that was met with in the county, and being both argillaceous and silicious, it is not adapted either for building purposes or for the lime kiln.

*Coal*—The uppermost of the two coal seams that outcrop in this county has been worked in a small way at several points by stripping, and affords a coal of very good quality; but unfortunately it has been nowhere found thick enough to be profitably mined in any other way.

Just north of the county line in the edge of Crawford county, at Mr. NETTLE's coal mine, the coal is about 18 inches thick, overlaid by about a foot or more of hard bituminous shale resembling a cannel coal. It has been mined here for several years at intervals, by tunneling into the bank along the line of outcrop, but no permanent entry was constructed, and when the work stopped the roof caved in and filled the opening so that a new entry was required as often as the work was resumed

This was the condition of things when I was there, and I was unable to make any satisfactory examination of the quality of the coal. or to determine its exact thickness.

The main coals of the lower measures which are so extensively mined in Gallatin and Saline counties will probably be found here by boring, and if the well bored at Lawrenceville had been in the hands of an expert, and an exact record kept of the thickness and composition of the various beds passed through, the question would have been settled whether there was any thick seam of coal within four hundred feet of the surface in this county. As it is, nothing has been positively determined by this expenditure of money, further than the fact that two coal seams of uncertain thickness were found in the boring, one at a depth of about 340 and the other at 440 feet below the surface. The depth of the seam, when not exceeding four or five hundred feet, is no serious impediment to the working of the coal, if the demand for this kind of fuel is sufficient to justify the investment, and we already have several shafts in successful operation in the State that are over 500 feet in depth Deep mining is the only alternative in this county for obtaining an unfailing supply of this kind of fuel, as the surface seams appear to be too thin at every outcrop at present known in this or the adjoining counties to be successfully worked for the supply of any large demand for coal.

*Iron ore*—The shales intervening between coals 11 and 12 contain numerous bands of argillaceous iron ore, but they are too widely separated at the localities where the shales were met with in this county to be of any practical value for the furnace At the base of the upper sandstone a ferruginous bed is frequently met with, sometimes appearing as a conglomerate of iron nodules in sandstone; but in Mr FRITCHEY'S well, on sec 25, T. 5 N, R 12 W., it was reported to be two feet thick, and consisted partly of a very good quality of brown hematite ore, but other portions were too much mixed with sand to be of any value for the production of metallic iron It was found in the well at a depth of 16 feet, and outcrops about a quarter of a mile to the westward, where its thickness is only about six inches.

*Soil and Timber*—The Wabash and Embarras rivers are skirted with broad alluvial bottoms and level table lands, ranging from two to four miles in width. Some portions of the latter are quite sandy, and constitute the terrace prairies between the Purgatory swamp and the Wabash. The bottoms along the Embarras are heavily timbered with all the common varieties of oak, hickory, ash, elm, maple, black and white walnut, coffeenut, persimmon, cottonwood, sycamore, hackberry, red birch, honey locust, wild cherry, black gum, dogwood, etc. The uplands are generally rolling, and were mostly originally covered with a heavy growth of timber, though much of the surface has been cleared and brought under cultivation since the first settlement of the county. The soil on the rolling uplands is a chocolate colored clay loam, usually very productive, bringing good crops of corn, wheat, oats and grass annually. With a judicious system of cultivation, and a proper rotation of crops, these uplands can be easily kept up to a high standard of fertility. There are some small upland prairies along the western borders of the county, the soil of which does not differ very much from that of the timbered lands adjacent thereto.

RICHLAND COUNTY embraces a superficial area of about three hundred and fifty square miles, and is bounded on the north by Jasper and Crawford counties, on the east by Lawrence, on the south by Wabash, Edwards and Wayne, and on the west by Wayne and Clay counties. There are no large streams in the county, but some of the northern affluents of the Little Wabash drain the western, and the western branch of the Bonpass creek the south eastern portion of the county. The main stream of the Little Wabash also skirts the south western border of the county for the distance of about eight miles. The surface of the county is generally rolling, and its area is nearly equally divided into prairie and timbered land, the latter forming belts along the courses of the streams from one to three miles in width, and the prairies occupying the higher or table lands between the main water courses. The elevation of the prairies above the beds of the principal streams ranges from fifty to about a hundred feet. The south eastern portion of the county on the head waters of the Bonpass is quite broken, and is underlaid by the heavy beds of sandstone and sandy shales intervening between coals 12 and 13, which attain here a thickness of seventy to eighty feet, or more. In the central and western portions the surface is seldom so broken as to render it unfit for cultivation.

The geological formations of this county comprise a moderate thickness of drift clay, sand and gravel, that is everywhere found immediately beneath the soil, except in the creek valleys, where this superficial material has been removed by eroding agencies, and a series of sandstones, shales, etc., embracing an aggregate thickness of 250 to 300 feet, which belongs to the upper Coal Measures, and include the horizon of three or four thin seams of coal.

The drift clays are somewhat thicker in this county than in Lawrence, and the bowlders are more numerous and of larger size Below the brown gravelly clays that usually form the subsoil on the uplands, and range from ten to twenty feet in thickness, there is in many places a bed of hard, bluish gray, gravelly clay, or "hard pan" as it is frequently termed, and below this at some points there is an old soil or muck bed, underlaid by from one to five feet or more of quicksand. Limbs and trunks of trees are frequently found imbedded in this old soil in which they probably grew, or in the bluish gray hard pan immediately above it, but to the present time no authentic specimens of animal remains have been found in them in this State, sufficiently well preserved for identification Some small fresh water and land shells have been found in the quicksands in other portions of the State, but they did not prove to be specifically distinct from those now living.

*Coal Measures*—From the meager outcrops to be seen on the small streams in this county, it would not be possible to construct a continuous section of all the beds that should be found here, but fortunately a boring has recently been made at Olney which will aid us materially in ascertaining the general character of the formations that underlay the southern and eastern portions of the county to the depth penetrated by the drill. This boring for coal was made by Mr. CRANE, to whom I am indebted for the following report of the beds passed through

| | | Ft | In |
|---|---|---|---|
| 1 | Soil and drift clay | 13 | |
| 2 | Yellow sandstone | 28 | |
| 3 | Gray sandstone | 2 | 6 |
| 4 | Black shale (horizon of coal No 13 ?) | 4 | |
| 5 | Clay shale | 29 | |
| 6 | Hard rock (probably sandstone) | 48 | |
| 7 | Clay shale with black slate | 25 | |
| 8 | Hard sand rock | 3 | |
| 9 | Clay shale | 28 | |
| 10 | Hard rock (probably sandstone) | 36 | |
| 11 | Clay shale | 22 | |
| 12. | Black shale and coal (No 12 ?) | 2 | |
| 13 | Clay shale | 31 | |
| 14 | Limestone | 4 | |
| 15 | Shale partly calcareous | 23 | |
| 16 | Limestone | 3 | |
| 17 | Hard rock (probably sandstone) | 36 | |
| | | 337 | 6 |

Two miles and a half south of Olney, in the vicinity of Boden's mill, located on the S E qr of sec 15, T. 3, R. 10 E, there is an outcrop of a thin coal in the creek bed, overlaid by the following strata

| | Ft | In |
|---|---|---|
| Brown sandstone | 10 to 12 | |
| Black shale with concretions of blue septaria | 4 to 6 | |
| Blue clay shale | 5 | |
| Hard silicious limestone with broken plants | 2 | |
| Clay shale with concretions of limestone | 3 | |
| Coal (No 13 of general section) | | 6 |

The black shale in this section is probably identical with No 4 of the Olney boring, and the thin coal below was wanting there or else was passed without observation. Some of the limestone concretions contain fossils, among which I identified *Productus Nebrascensis*, *Bellerophon carbonarius*, *Aviculopecten*, etc. The band of hard silicious limestone found at this locality is a very durable stone and has been quarried for building purposes It is a refractory stone to work, but may be relied on for culverts and bridge abutments where an ordinary sandstone would yield to atmospheric influences

One and a half miles south of Clermont there is an outcrop of the following beds, probably representing the same strata seen at Boden's mill south of Olney

| | | Feet |
|---|---|---|
| 1 | Shale | 1 to 2 |
| 2 | Hard calcareous sandstone | 4 to 6 |
| 3 | Blue shale with calcareous nodules | 3 to 4 |
| 4 | Black laminated shale extending to the creek level | 4 |

The quarry here belongs to the O and M railroad, and an immense amount of stone has been quarried from the calcareous sandstone No 2 of the above section, to be used in the construction of culverts and bridges on that road. This quarry is near the center of sec 16, T 3, R. 14 E

On Mr. P BERRY's place, on the S E qr. of sec 11, T 2, R. 14 E., coal has been mined for several years in a limited way by stripping the seam along its outcrop in the valley of a small stream a tributary of the Bonpass. The coal is about 18 inches thick and of good quality, and is overlaid by a few inches of soft bituminous shale, and an argillaceous shelly limestone which contains *Productus costatus*, *P. punctatus*, *P Prattenianus*, *Spirifer cameratus*, etc The shale contains *Chonetes variolata*, *Orthis carbonaria*, *Lophophyllum proliferum*, *Trematopora*, joints and plates of *Crinoidea*, etc This coal is also mined by Mr STOVER on the N. E. qr. of the same section This is probably coal No. 12 of the general section, and must have been passed through in the boring at Olney, and may be represented by No 12 of the boring at that point.

About five miles north-east of Olney coal has been found on the open prairie at a depth of about 22 feet below the general surface level It was first discovered in digging a stock well, and subsequently an inclined tunnel has been driven down to the coal and preparations made to work it in a systematic way. If the seam retains an average thickness of three feet, it will prove of great value to the county. The roof consists of clay shale with some limestone in bowlder-like masses, though it is possible the limestone masses thrown out in opening the tunnel may belong to the drift clays, and not to the roof shales of the coal This tunnel is on Mr COMBS' place, but the coal has also been found on the adjoining place belonging to Mr. SHOOKS. On another farm a little farther to the west, on sec 18, T. 4 N, R 10 E, a double seam was reported to have been passed through in a bore but a short distance below the surface, the upper one two feet and the lower one three feet in thickness, with a space of about fifteen feet between them These coals, if there are really two distinct seams here, must be about the horizon of No. 15 of the general section, and this is probably about the southern line of outcrop for these coals, as no indications of their presence was found in the boring at Olney or in sinking wells about the city, and from the topography of the surface I am inclined to believe the surface level where these coals have been found is at least forty or fifty feet above the level at Olney.

Prof. COX notes the following sections at points I did not visit: "Section at B. F. HEAP's sandstone quarry on sec. 34, T. 4, R. 10 E.

| | Ft |
|---|---|
| Soil and drift | 8 |
| Soft buff sandstone | 3 |
| Hard gray building stone | 4 |

The gray sandstone is very hard and takes a good finish, stands well but is somewhat marred by carbonaceous spots At Andy Darling's quarry, two miles west of Olney, the quarry rock is overlaid by 8 feet of buff silicious shale, beneath which is a heavy bedded buff sandstone that was quarried for the masonry on the O. and M railroad at the time of its construction

On sec 18, T 3, R 10, on Big creek, found the following section

| | Ft |
|---|---|
| Covered slope | 25 |
| Shaly sandstone | 5 |
| Heavy bedded sandstone | 10 |
| Black bituminous shale | 3 |

A quarter of a mile down the creek a soft buff sandstone in heavy beds from four to ten feet thick alternate with thinner beds of hard bluish sandstone At Higgins' mill, on sec 34, T 3, R 14, in his well located on the slope of a hill rising to the north from Bonpass creek, sixteen feet of sandstone was passed through and a coal seam below it reported to be twenty inches thick. Shaly sandstone and clay shale were seen overlaying the heavy bedded sandstone a few hundred yards above the mill The hills along the Bonpass are from twenty to sixty feet high, composed in part of drift deposits consisting of yellowish clay with gravel and small bowlders, the latter seldom exceeding five or six inches in diameter.

At Wilson Law's coal bank, on sec. 16, T 2, R 14, the section is as follows

| | Ft | In |
|---|---|---|
| Soil and drift | 10 | |
| Buff sandstone and shale | 5 | |
| Bluish gray limestone | 2 | |
| Shale | 0 | 2 |
| Coal | 1 | 8 |

The shale over the coal was filled with fossil shells, corals, etc. The limestone over this coal was also seen three miles north west of LAW'S place, where it was formerly quarried and burned for lime

A quarter of a mile below the Big Creek bridge, south of Olney, found the following section.

| | Ft |
|---|---|
| Soil and drift | 15 |
| Coarse irregularly bedded sandstone | 15 |
| Black marly shale | 13 |

The lower part of the black shale was slaty and contained numerous fossils, *Pleurotomaria tabulata*, *P. Grayvillensis*, *Bellerophon percarinatus*, *B. Montfortianus*, *B. carbonarius*, *Athyris subtilita*, *Productus longispinus*, *Nucula ventricosa*, *Orthoceras Rushensis*, and *Lophophyllum proliferum*. At JAMES C. STEWART'S place, four and a half miles south west of Olney, a black shale outcrops in the banks of Sugar creek about five feet thick, underlaid by a thin coal. A quarter of a mile below at the bridge saw the same conglomerate sandstone that occurs on Big creek, underlaid by the same black shale, which was sometimes marly and contained the fossils mentioned above. It also contains large nodules of impure limestone."

This bituminous shale and thin coal probably represents coal No. 13 of the general section, and this same group of fossils occurs in connection with this coal on the East fork of Shoal creek in Montgomery county.

## *Economical Geology.*

*Building Stone.*—Sandstone of a fair quality for ordinary use is quite abundant, and there is probably not a township in the county where good quarries could not be opened at a moderate expense. Many of these localities have been mentioned in the preceding pages, and but little needs to be said farther in regard to them. The quarries south of Clermont, belonging to the O. and M. railroad, afford a very hard and durable rock, and although the bed is only about six feet in average thickness, it is, fortunately, so situated as to require no great expenditure in stripping, and the rock has already been removed over a surface of several acres in extent. The rock is a very hard, gray, micaceous sandstone and seems to be but little affected by long exposure, and hence affords a desirable material for culverts, bridge abutments, etc. The sandstones in the northern and western portions of the county are for the most part rather soft, but locally they afford some very good building stone, as at Mr. Heap's quarry northeast of Olney, and at Darling's quarry two miles west of that town. The stratum of hard, silicious limestone outcropping on Big creek two miles and a half south of Olney is a durable stone, but is not to be obtained in sufficient quantity to be of much importance as a building stone.

*Coal*.—There are two coal seams cropping out in this county that promise to be of some value in supplying the local demand for fuel, and the upper one, if its thickness at the outcrop should be found persistent over any considerable area, will furnish all needed supplies for the county for many years to come. The lower seam, which outcrops on the head waters of the Bonpass in the south eastern portion of the county, and has been referred to No. 12 of the general section, ranges from sixteen to twenty inches in thickness, and has only been worked by stripping in the creek valleys where it outcrops. It affords a coal of good quality, but unfortunately is generally too thin to be mined profitably in a systematic way. The other seam, five miles north-west of Olney, is about three feet in thickness, and an inclined tunnel has been carried down to it, and preparations made for working it systematically for the supply of the Olney market. This is probably the Shelbyville seam, No. 15 of the general section, which is the thickest seam in the upper Coal Measures, and usually quite persistent in its development. In Shelby county this seam affords a semi block coal of fair quality, hard enough to be handled without much waste, and tolerably free from sulphuret of iron, but showing thin partings of selenite on transverse cleavage. The thickness of the sandstones, shales, etc., intervening between coals 12 and 15 in the valley of the Okaw is about 235 feet, but in this county it is probably somewhat less, though this point could only be determined approximately from the lack of continuous outcrops of the intervening strata. The main coals of the lower Coal Measures are probably from six hundred to a thousand feet below the surface at Olney, and it would require an expenditure of capital to open and work them that the present demand for coal would not justify. If the seam northeast of Olney should be found to retain an average thickness of three feet over any considerable area, it will furnish an abundant supply for all the present demands for coal in this county.

*Lime*.—No limestone was seen in this county that seemed well adapted for use in the lime kiln, though some attempts have been made to use the rock overlying coal No. 12 on the Bonpass for that purpose. It is usually too argillaceous to slack freely when burned, and at best would only produce a very inferior quality of lime.

*Soil and Agriculture*.—The agricultural facilities in this county are similar to those of the counties adjoining, and do not require any extended notice in this place. The surface is generally rolling and pretty equally divided into timber and prairie land. The prairies are usually small, and possess a rich, productive clay-loam soil, that will never require manuring if properly cultivated with a judicious system of rotation of crops. The soil on the timbered lands is less uniform in quality than on the prairies, and its character is generally well indicated by the growth of timber Where this is mainly composed of two or three varieties of oak and hickory, the soil is thin and poor, and will require frequent applications of manure or other fertilizers to keep it up to the ordinary standard of productiveness for western lands. But where the timber growth is largely interspersed with elm, black walnut, linden, wild cherry, persimmon, honey locust, etc., the soil is good, and will rank favorably with the best prairie lands in its productive qualities. A large portion of the timbered land in the county is of this quality, and when cleared and brought under cultivation, it produces nearly or quite as well as the best prairie land.

I am indebted to Mr J B Wolf, of Olney, former county surveyor, for much valuable information, and for personal attention and assistance while at work in the county.

# CHAPTER V.

## WABASH AND EDWARDS COUNTIES.

Wabash and Edwards are two of the smallest counties in the State, and laying contiguous to each other on its south-western borders, they may very properly be described together Their aggregate area is about four hundred and twenty five square miles, and their boundaries are as follows Wabash is bounded on the north by Lawrence and Richland counties, on the east and south by the Wabash river, and on the west by the Bonpass creek Edwards county is bounded on the north by Richland county, on the east by Bonpass creek, on the south by White county, and on the west by Wayne. The only streams of any importance are those forming in part their respective boundaries, the Wabash river, by a south-westerly course, bounding Wabash county on the east and south, and the Bonpass creek, with a course nearly due south, forming the dividing line between them The latter stream winds its sluggish course through a broad alluvial valley showing no outcrops of the underlaying rock formations except at rare intervals. Along the Wabash, exposures of the rocky strata are more numerous, but as the course of the river is nearly on the trend of the underlaying formations, but a limited thickness of strata can be seen along the bluffs of this stream The surface of the uplands is generally quite rolling, but there are some limited areas of rather flat timbered lands above the level of the river bottoms, and forming what may properly be termed terrace lands. Both counties are heavily timbered, though there are some small prairies within their limits A complete list of the trees and shrubs indigenous to Wabash county has been furnished for this report by Dr J Schenck, of Mt Carmel, which will be found further on It is peculiarly interesting because it shows the presence here of some species hitherto supposed to belong exclusively to a more southern latitude.

The geological formations to be seen in this county belong to the Quaternary and the upper Coal Measures The former is more fully developed along the bluffs of the Wabash than elsewhere, and consist of the buff and yellow marly sands and clays of the loess, and a moderate thickness of the gravelly clays of the drift formation.

On the lower course of the Bonpass, in the vicinity of Grayville, and in some of the valleys of the smaller streams, stratified clays are found at the lowest levels seen, which may belong to an older deposit than the drift, and a heavy bed of this kind is reported to have been passed through in the boring south west of Mount Carmel, but as it was overlaid by sandstone, and no rock of this kind is known in this county of more recent age than the Coal Measures, I am inclined to doubt the correctness of the report However it is by no means improbable that there are old valleys along the Wabash, as well as the Mississippi and Ohio, that were filled originally with Tertiary or Cretaceous deposits, some of which still remain, and are now hidden by the subsequent accumulations of loess and drift. Indications of the existence of such beds have been found on the Ohio as far north as Louisville, and on the Mississippi for more than two hundred miles above St. Louis, the evidences being well preserved shark's teeth found at various points within the region specified, some of which are too fragile and delicate to have been transported for long distances by drift agencies without destruction The reported sandstone above the clay in the boring is most probably a Coal Measure bed, and the reported clay beneath it may be a soft clay shale of the same age, such as is frequently met with in the coal bearing formations At Mount Carmel the loess and drift clays are about thirty feet in thickness, which is probably about the average in the vicinity of the river bluffs, while on the uplands, remote from the river, their average thickness is not more than fifteen to twenty feet, and at many points much less.

In Edwards county the Quaternary beds present the same general character, and are considerably thicker in the bluffs on the lower course of the Bonpass than in the central and western portions of the county, where we only find from ten to twenty feet of buff or brownish gravelly clays overlaying the bed rock Near Grayville the creek banks show outcrops of five to ten feet or more of stratified clays, variously colored, and seemingly derived from the decomposition of the clay shales of the Coal Measures, and above these we find from twenty to thirty feet of loess possibly covering a nucleus of gravelly drift clay. To the north and west the loess is not conspicuous, and in digging wells the bed rock is usually reached after passing through ten or fifteen feet of brown drift clays.

## *Coal Measures.*

In the bluffs of the Wabash river, at Mount Carmel, there is an outcrop of sandstone forming the lower portion of the bluff, underlaid by a blue clay shale but partially exposed.

The following is a section of the bluff at this point

| | Ft |
|---|---|
| Loess and drift clays | 30 |
| Soft shaly micaceous sandstone | 13 |
| Massive sandstone, partly concretionary | 20 |
| Blue clay shale—partial exposure of | 3 to 6 |

Springs of water issue from the base of this sandstone, indicating the impervious character of the underlaying beds, even where there is no outcrop of the shales. Locally the concretionary sandstone contains geodes of oxyd of iron, filled with a greenish or buff colored clay The base of the above section is some fifteen or twenty feet above the low water level of the river, and the intervening beds which are probably shales are not exposed. A boring was made here for coal under the direction of Mr J ZIMMERMAN, to whom I am indebted for the following section of the beds passed through, and as the work was done with a hollow drill and prosecuted very carefully, the section is probably a very correct one The bore was commenced just above the low water level of the river, and something like fifteen feet below the base of the foregoing section, and passed through the following beds:

| | | Ft | In |
|---|---|---|---|
| No 1 | Shale | 2 | |
| No 2. | Sandstone | 2 | |
| No 3 | Clay shale | 4 | |
| No 4 | Sandstone | 35 | |
| No 5 | Micaceous sandstone | 0 | 10 |
| No 6 | Hard fine sandstone | 4 | |
| No 7 | Fire clay? | 1 | |
| No 8 | Coal and bituminous shale | 0 | 4 |
| No 9 | Fire clay | 9 | |
| No 10 | Argillaceous sandstone | 2 | |
| No 11 | Blue shale | 1 | 4 |
| No 12 | Fire clay | 3 | 10 |
| No 13 | Calc shale and sandstone | 32 | |
| No 14 | Calc shale, with black streaks | 20 | |
| No 15 | Blue clay shale | 36 | |
| No 16 | Blue fire clay | 4 | 2 |
| No 17 | Coal | 0 | 7 |
| No 18 | Fire clay | 3 | |
| No 19 | Argillaceous limestone | 5 | |
| No 20 | Hard sandstone, parting | 0 | 1 |
| No 21 | Hard gray limestone | 2 | 2 |
| No 22 | Hard gray limestone | 1 | 6 |
| No 23 | Very hard limestone | 2 | |
| No 24 | Calcareous shale | 1 | 3 |
| No 25 | Band of iron stone | 0 | 3 |
| No 26 | Variegated shale | 2 | |
| No 27 | Hard gray limestone | 1 | 3 |
| No 28 | Variegated shale | 0 | 3 |
| No 29 | Hard gray limestone | 2 | 4 |
| No 30 | Variegated shale | 0 | 3 |
| No 31 | Hard gray limestone | 8 | 8 |
| | | 188 | 8 |

This boring was commenced near the horizon of No. 11 coal, and the beds passed through probably extend very nearly to No. 7. The following is the report of a bore made for oil one mile and a half southwest of the court house, commencing in a creek valley:

| | | Ft | In |
|---|---|---|---|
| No 1 | Soil clay etc | 54 | |
| No 2 | Sandstone | 24 | |
| No 3 | Clay ? (probably clay shale) | 45 | |
| No 4 | Sandstone | 2 | |
| No 5 | Bituminous shale (probably blue clay shale) | 32 | |
| No 6 | Sandstone | 1 | 6 |
| No 7 | Bituminous shale | 10 | 6 |
| No 8 | Sandstone | 2 | |
| No 9 | Bituminous shale | 5 | |
| No 10 | Sandstone | 3 | |
| No 11 | Bituminous shale | 4 | |
| No 12 | Sandstone | 1 | 4 |
| No 13 | Bituminous shale showing oily soot | 5 | |
| No 14 | Sandstone | 13 | |
| No 15 | Very hard limestone | 21 | |
| No 16 | Bituminous shale | 8 | |
| No 17 | Sandstone | 2 | |
| No 18 | Coal No 9 | 2 | |
| No 19 | Limestone | 5 | |
| No 20 | Shale | 3 | |
| No 21 | Sandstone | 2 | |
| No 22 | Mixture of sand and limestone | 8 | |
| No 23 | Yellow shale | 4 | |
| No 24 | Sandstone | 12 | |
| No. 25 | Clay shale with pyrites | 12 | |
| No 26 | Sandstone | 15 | |
| No 27 | Bituminous shale | 6 | |
| No 28 | Sandy shale | 70 | |
| No 29 | Sandstone | 60 | |
| No 30 | Micaceous sandstone | 10 | |
| No 31 | Coal No 7 ? | 3 | |
| No 32 | Bituminous shale | 12 | |
| No 33 | Compact limestone | 8 | |
| No 34 | Bituminous shale | 7 | |
| No 35 | Lime and sandstone | 2 | |
| No 36 | Bituminous shale | 5 | |
| | | 482 | 4 |

It is hardly possible that the beds reported as bituminous shale in this bore could be anything more than ordinary blue clay shales, and as a rule I believe that but little dependence can be placed in the reported sections of oil well borings made in this State. By comparing this section with that made for coal it will be seen that there is a wide discrepancy in the descriptions given of the strata passed through in each, and although the oil well boring was carried down to the depth of about seven hundred feet, yet no coal was reported below the three feet seam found at the depth of four hundred and fifty five feet, which probably represents coal No 7 or 8 of the general section. The sandstone No. 2 of the oil well boring may be the same as No 4 in the other, but there is very little correspondence in the lower strata, considering that the distance between the points where the borings were made is scarcely two miles in a direct line.

In the bed of the river at low water there is an outcrop of micaceous sandstone No 2, of the first boring, which contains iron nodules, some of which inclose fossil ferns, and one was found containing *Leaia tricarinata* In the bed of the river, a little further down, an impure argillaceous limestone has been found below the river level.

At Hanging-rock bluff, about three miles north east of Mt. Carmel, there is an outcrop of massive sandstone similar to that at the town, which projects into the bed of the river at low water, and rises above it to the hight of 30 to 35 feet. Three quarters of a mile nearly west of Hanging rock, at Mr REEL'S place, there is an exposure of the beds above the sandstone showing the following section

| | Ft | In |
|---|---|---|
| Soft brown shales | 4 to 6 | |
| Bituminous shale | 1 to 3 | |
| Dark hard bituminous limestone | 3 | |
| Coal—No 10 ? | 1 | 6 |
| Clay shale | 1 to 2 | |
| Massive sandstone | 30 to 35 | |

The limestone here is a steel gray, passing into black, and weathering to an olive brown, and filled with crushed shells of small size, among which *Rhynchonella Osagensis* seemed to be most conspicuous It is possible that the sandstone at Hanging rock belongs below that at Mt Carmel, as the beds seemed to rise to the northward, so far as we could find the rocks exposed, and this sandstone may be the bed No. 4 in the boring made at the river bank. This seems the more probable from the fact that no trace of the limestone or coal has been found above the Mt. Carmel sandstone, where it should appear if these sandstones are identical. Furthermore the outcrop at Hanging rock is about a mile to the eastward of the Mt Carmel bluff, and the general western dip of the strata would naturally bring up the lower beds in this direction Furthermore the rock seemed harder and appeared to be less affected by atmospheric influences at the former locality than at Mount Carmel. If the sandstone is the same at these localities, the limestone and coal at REEL'S place must be a mere local deposit, but I believe this limestone to be identical with that at Rochester mills in the river bank, which represents the horizon of No 10 coal On Coffee creek there is a good exposure of the beds overlaying this limestone, and the following section, commencing in the bed of the river at low-water mark, and extending up the creek for about a mile, shows the general character and relative position of the rocks in this vicinity.

| | | Ft | In |
|---|---|---|---|
| No 1 | Coal, hard and splinty—No 13 ? | 3 | |
| No 2 | Space unexposed | ? | |
| No 3 | Brown shale | 4 to 6 | |
| No 4 | Shaly impure limestone | 1 to 2 | |
| No 5 | Clay shale | 1½ to 2 | |
| No 6 | Black shale | 0 | 6 |
| No 7 | Coal—No 12 | 0 | 4 |

| | | Ft | In |
|---|---|---|---|
| No 8 | Black shale—No 12 | 0 | 6 |
| No 9 | Coal—No 12 | 0 | 6 |
| No 10 | Blue and green clay shale | 2 to 3 | |
| No 11 | Massive gray sandstone | 12 to 20 | |
| No 12 | Clay shale | 15 to 18 | |
| No 13 | Black laminated shale | 2 to 3 | |
| No 14 | Dark shaly limestone | 1 | |
| No 15 | Coal—No 11 | 0 | 10 |
| No 16 | Clay shale | 3 to 4 | |
| No 17 | Hard nodular, dove colored limestone | 2 | |
| No 18 | Soft shales | 15 to 20 | |
| No 19 | Hard bituminous limestone | 1 to 3 | |
| No 20 | Coal No 10 | 1 | |
| No 21 | Sandy shale, and sandstone in the river bed | 8 | |

The limestone No 19 of the above section I believe to be identical with that at REEL'S place, and the sandy shale and sandstone in the river bed at Rochester mills to be the upper part of the Hanging rock sandstone, and the sandstone at Mount Carmel is probably the equivalent of No 11 of the foregoing section The upper coal on Coffee creek, No 1 of the above section, is probably the same formerly worked by Mr SIMONDS and others south west of Mount Carmel, and is either a merely local seam, or a division of No. 12, as there is a heavy bed of sandstone, usually from sixty to eighty feet in thickness, intervening between coals 12 and 13, of which there was no trace here, the covered space represented by No 2 of the section not exceeding 8 to 10 feet in thickness It is possible that the outcrop of No 1, which was only some two or three hundred yards from the outcrop of Nos. 7, 8 and 9, may be only a thickening and reappearing of the same seam at a little higher level. The outcrop at the highest exposure was in the bed of the creek, and no roof but sand and gravel was found above the coal. The shaly brown limestone No 4 of this section contained a few fossils, among which I noticed *Spirifer cameratus*, *Lophophyllum proliferum* and joints of *Crinoidæ* The hard, dove colored limestone contained numerous examples of *Productus Prattenianus*, *Aviculopecten Clevelandicus*, and a small branching coral

The old coal shaft on Mr SIMONDS' place, about three miles southwest of Mount Carmel, has been abandoned for some time, and the sides have fallen in, so that nothing could be learned when I was there in regard to the thickness or quality of the coal, except from those who had worked in the mine when it was in operation The seam is said to average about three feet in thickness, and lays from 30 to 35 feet below the surface

Section of Simonds' coal shaft

| | Ft | In |
|---|---|---|
| Drift clay and soil | 5 | 6 |
| Argillaceous shale | 30 | |
| Limestone | 0 | 6 |
| Coal | 3 | |

This seam has been opened by several parties in this neighborhood, but the shafts have all been abandoned This coal probably corresponds to coal 11 or 12 of the general section

At HERSHEY'S old mill, on Raccoon creek, there is an outcrop of the same fossiliferous shales found at Lawrenceville and Grayville, associated with coal No 11. The section here shows the following beds outcropping in the bluffs of the creek

| | | Feet |
|---|---|---|
| No 1 | Brown sandy shales and sandstone | 8 to 10 |
| No 2 | Blue and gray shales the lower part argillaceous | 20 to 25 |
| No 3 | Blue fossiliferous shale, with iron nodules | 3 |
| No 4 | Black laminated shale | 1 to 2 |
| No 5 | Dark bituminous limestone | 0 to 2 |
| No 6 | Black laminated shale | 1½ to 2 |
| No 7 | Blue clay shale | 6 |

The argillaceous shales No 2 of the above section contain numerous bands of argillaceous iron ore, which are more numerous in No. 3, and contain the same species of fossils that occur in the shale I obtained here the following species: *Pleurotomaria tabulata*, *P sphærulata*, *P. Grayvillensis*, *Bellerophon carbonarius*, *B. percarinatus*, *Polyphemopsis per-acuta*, *Lophophyllum proliferum*, *Dentalium obsoletum*, *Orthoceras Rushensis*, and *Macrodon carbonaria*

At Allendale this fossiliferous shale was found in a well sunk near the railroad, overlaid, as at HERSHEY'S mill, by sandy shales and sandstone, which is found in sinking wells in the higher portions of the town. In one well near the summit level a thin coal 8 inches thick was passed through, with 2 feet of clay shale above it, and about the same thickness of fire clay below. In the vicinity of Oriole the sandstone above this thin coal is found at several places, and quarries have been opened in it for building stone, flag-stones, etc It probably underlays all the highlands in the north west portion of the county.

At JAMES MCNAIR'S well, one mile and a quarter north of Friendsville, the following beds were reported from memoranda furnished by Mr J. ZIMMERMAN

| | Ft | In |
|---|---|---|
| Soil and clay | 18 | |
| Impure coal, (probably bituminous shale) | 2 | |
| Clay shale with iron nodules | 3 | |
| Hard sandstone | 0 | 8 |
| Gray sandstone, in even beds, 4 to 8 inches thick | 15 | |
| Sandy shales | 11 | |
| Hard sandstone in two layers | 2 | 8 |
| Dark bituminous shale | 3 | |
| Coal, said to be good | 2 | |
| | 57 | 4 |

At Mr GILKERSON'S well, in the same neighborhood, after reaching the coal found at the bottom of MCNAIR'S well, a boring was made to the depth of 9 feet below the coal The material obtained from the boring was a milk-white substance resembling fire-clay.

At Hamiker's old mill on the Bonpass, a little north of west from Allendale, a bed of bituminous shale outcrops at the base of the bluff, overlaid by a conglomerate of ferruginous pebbles and a rather soft, thin bedded sandstone The section here is as follows

| | Ft |
|---|---|
| Soft, thin bedded sandstone and shale | 15 |
| Ferruginous conglomerate | 3 to 4 |
| Hard black shale | 2 to 3 |

The black shale extended below the bed of the creek, and I could not learn that any coal had been found underneath it here. These beds resemble the outcrop at the iron bridge on the Little Wabash, between Albion and Fairfield.

Prof Cox reports the following sections at points I did not visit: "On sec 5, T 10, R. 12, there is a bed of light blue clay, very plastic, exposed in the bank of Crawfish creek, as shown in the following section

| | Ft | In |
|---|---|---|
| Soil calcareous shale and limestone | 16 | |
| Coal | 0 | 8 |
| Blue clay | 1 | |
| Sandstone in the bed of the creek | ? | |

The calcareous shale above the coal contains the same species of fossils enumerated from the locality on Raccoon creek at Hamiker's old mill, indicating the horizon of coal No. 11.

"At Emanuel Refl's place, on sec 8, T. 1 S, R 12, blue limestone at the foot of the hill one foot thick, underlaid by a thin coal Bluish shale and sandstone in the hill forty feet above The well at the house went through soil and drift 10 feet, clay shale 1 feet, sandstone 29 feet.

At Little Rock, on the Wabash river, sec. 19, T. 1 N., R. 11 W :

| | Ft |
|---|---|
| Shale and covered slope | 60 |
| Sandstone in solid bed | 30" |

This hill forms a conspicuous land mark on the river, and the sandstone at the base is probably the same as that found at St Francisville, a little higher up the river, in Lawrence county

Edwards County. The outcrops of rock in this county are few and widely separated, and no continuous section of the beds could possibly be made from surface exposures only The sandstones and shales intervening between coals No 11 and 13 are probably the prevailing rocks The following beds may be seen in the vicinity of Albion, in the railroad cut and on the small creek that intersects the town

| | Ft | In |
|---|---|---|
| Shale and shaly sandstone with a pebbly bed at the bottom | 20 to 25 | |
| Sandstone locally hard and concretionary | 8 to 12 | |
| Streak of bituminous shale | 0 | 3 |
| Hard nodular limestone | 2 | |
| Shale with bands of argillaceous iron ore | 4 to 6 | |
| Hard shaly sandstone | 3 to 4 | |

The concretionary sandstone is their main quarry rock here, and it is sometimes quite hard and affords a very durable material for foundation walls Above this there are some layers of even bedded sandstone that, although rather soft when first quarried, become harder after exposure and make a fair building stone

At Dr. SMITH's place, four miles north of Grayville on the west bank of the Bonpass creek, the hill rises to an elevation of about a hundred feet, but the beds forming its upper portion are hidden beneath a covered slope. A thin coal is found in this hill at an elevation of thirty-six feet above the bed of the creek, which is underlaid by sandy shales and sandstones that form a precipitous cliff to the creek bed. The coal is about 8 inches thick and of good quality, and is underlaid by a light-gray fire clay The sandstone and shale below this coal are the equivalents of the beds above the fossiliferous shale in the Grayville section, and the fossil bed of that locality would no doubt be found here a little below the creek bed The thin coal found here has also been met with in sinking wells at Grayville in the upper part of the town About half a mile above this, on the same side of the Bonpass, the same beds outcrop again where an old mill was formerly located At the base of the bluff here there is from ten to twelve feet of blue shales partly argillaceous, and passing upward into a sandy shale and sandstone twenty feet or more in thickness, with a partial outcrop of the thin coal and bituminous shale still higher up This coal probably corresponds to the ten inch seam No. 15 of the Coffee creek section.

At Mr NAILOR's place, six miles north west of Grayville, a coal seam was opened many years since and successfully worked for a time to supply the local demand for coal It is probably the same seam worked by Simonds and others south-west of Mount Carmel The seam is said to be about thirty inches thick and the coal hard and splinty, partaking of the block character.

At the ford on the Little Wabash, eight miles north-west of Albion, on the S. W. qr of sec 7, T 1 S, R 10 E, there is an outcrop of a thin coal associated with the following beds

| | | Ft | In |
|---|---|---|---|
| 1 | Brown ferruginous clay shales | 10 to 12 | |
| 2 | Brash coal | 0 | 10 |
| 3 | Clay shale | 0 | 8 |
| 4 | Brash coal | 0 | 10 |
| 5 | Shale with numerous bands of iron ore | 4 | |
| 6 | Gray sandy shale | 6 | |
| 7 | Iron conglomerate in river bed | 1 | |

The shale No. 5 of the foregoing section contains considerable clay iron ore of a fair quality, amounting to nearly or quite one half of the whole thickness of the bed. If the quantity of iron in this shale should, on drifting into the bluff, prove continuous for some distance, it would eventually justify the erection of an iron furnace in this vicinity. At another old ford about a mile further up the river, the same coals outcrop in connection with a thin bed of nodular argillaceous limestone of a light-gray color, weathering to a yellowish-brown on exposure

Five miles north west of Albion, on the N. W. qr. of sec. 22, T. 1 S., R 10 E, an argillaceous limestone similar to that above mentioned, but rather darker colored, is found underlaying a bed of bituminous shale, as shown in the following section

| | Ft | In |
|---|---|---|
| Sandy shale and thin bedded micaceous standstone | 10 to 12 | |
| Bituminous shale | 1 to 1 | 6 |
| Nodular argillaceous limestone | 2 to 3 | |
| Gray sandy shale with bands of iron stone | 3 to 4 | |

This outcrop seems to be on the same horizon with the beds at the Wabash fords, the coal found there being represented here by the bituminous shale of the above section The thin bedded sandstone has been quarried here for building cellar walls, foundations, etc , and seems to be the best material in the neighborhood for such purposes

At Mr HARTMAN'S mill, on the east side of the town of Albion, there was a boring made for oil some years since, of which the following is a reported section

| | Ft |
|---|---|
| Clay and soil | 7 |
| Shale | 40 |
| Coal | 1 |
| Blue shale | 107 |

The boring was ended in a hard rock, the character of which was not determined. It was made in the creek valley in which the mill is situated, and the first shale struck was probably the upper part of that forming the base of the Albion section given on a preceding page.

Prof COX reports the following section at BEAL'S mill, on Blockhouse creek, a branch of the Bonpass, in the east part of the county

| | Ft | In |
|---|---|---|
| "Drift | 5 | |
| Gray shale with clay iron ore | 12 | |
| Silicious iron ore | 1 | |
| Blue argillaceous shale | 7 | |
| Black bituminous sha'e | 1 | 6 |
| Impure limestone | 0 | 6 |
| Coal in the bed of the creek | 0 | 8" |

All the beds represented by the foregoing sections in these two counties belong between coals No. 10 and 13, and do not attain an aggregate thickness of more than 150 to 200 feet

## *Economical Geology.*

*Building Stone*—A fair quality of building stone may be obtained from the sandstones outcropping in various portions of these two counties as indicated in the sections given on the preceding pages. The best is probably that from the even bedded brown sandstone above No. 11 coal, that is found in the northern and north-western portions of Wabash, and the central and northern portions of Edwards. Quarries have been opened in this sandstone in the vicinity of Oriole, in Wabash county, where a good evenly bedded rock is obtained, the thin layers affording a good flag stone, and the thicker beds material suitable for foundation walls, etc. This sandstone probably underlays all the ridges and highlands in the north west part of the county and will be found accessible at many points as the demand for building stone increases. The sandstone in the river bed at Rochester has also been quarried to a limited extent, and quarries have been opened at WALDEN'S place, between this point and Mt. Carmel, where a fair quality of sandstone has been obtained from a bed that is seemingly the equivalent of the sandstone in the Mt. Carmel bluff.

In the vicinity of Albion sandstone of a fair quality is obtained at several points, some of which is concretionary and very hard, yielding a very durable stone. This concretionary character is not persistent however, but the rock passes locally into a thin bedded sandstone or sandy shale. No limestone was seen in either county that could be recommended as a building stone, although that found at Rochester mills and at Mr. REEL'S place north of Mt. Carmel has been used to some extent in the neighborhood of these outcrops. The rock is argillaceous and locally highly bituminous, and is liable to split into fragments by long exposure.

*Coal*.—The upper coal seam in the Coffee creek section was the only outcrop we were able to find in either of these counties that promised to be of any value for practical coal mining. The coal in this seam ranges from thirty inches to three feet in thickness, and appears to underlay a considerable area in the south part of Wabash and the south western part of Edwards. Several shafts have been sunk to this coal about three miles south-west of Mt. Carmel, where the coal is found from thirty to thirty five feet below the surface. This seam affords a hard splinty or semi-block coal of fair quality, and with judicious management it might be worked to advantage, either by a shaft or perhaps better by an inclined tunnel. The roof seems to be good, and if the thickness of the coal is at all uniform, I see no reason why it may not be made to yield a fair return for the labor and capital required to put a mine in successful operation where the coal lays so near the surface. This is probably the same coal worked at Mr. NAILOR'S place in the south-east part of Edwards several years since, for the supply of Albion and the adjacent region. No attempt has as yet been made to reach the lower seams in either of these counties except at Mt. Carmel, where a boring was made to the depth of 180 feet, but this did not go deep enough to reach No 7, which is the uppermost of the main seams It commenced about the horizon of coal No. 10 or 11, and the depth from this horizon to No 7 is probably from two to three hundred feet

*Iron Ore*—Bands of argillaceous iron ore are found disseminated more or less abundantly through many of the shale beds in these counties, but usually in too limited quantities to be of much value. At the ford eight miles north-west of Albion on the S W quarter of sec 7, T. 1 S, R 10 E, there is a larger quantity of iron ore than was seen elsewhere in this region. The shale bed is four feet thick, and nearly or quite one half of this thickness is a clay iron ore of fair quality Several tons of ore may be collected from the *debris* at the foot of the bluff where it has been washed out of the shale by the river current. Twenty inches of coal of a fair quality immediately overlays the ferruginous shale

*Potters' Clay*—Potters' clay of fair quality is found in the bank of Greathouse creek, near Mt. Carmel, and a bed of fine white clay also occurs on Crawfish creek on sec 5, T 1 S, R 12 E This bed is four feet thick and appears like a good fire clay

*Brick Materials*—Good brick clay is abundant in almost every neighborhood, and sand suitable for mortar and cement may be found in the river bluffs as well as in some of the creek valleys

*Soil and Timber*—The soil on the rolling upland is a chocolate colored clay loam well charged with humus from the decomposition of organic matters, and very productive, especially in wheat, oats and grass In the vicinity of the Wabash bluffs the character of the soil is modified by the sandy marls of the loess upon which they rest, but these soils are very quick and productive, yielding annually large crops of all the cereals usually cultivated in this climate. Along the Wabash and Bonpass there are extensive tracts of heavily timbered bottom lands that have a deep alluvial soil with a sandy subsoil These lands are very productive when cleared and brought under cultivation, and are decidedly the best corn lands in this portion of the State They are subject to annual overflow from the river freshets, but these usually occur in the early spring time and seldom interfere with the production of the usual crops These two counties, though limited in area, have a thrifty and wealthy population devoted mainly to agriculture, the Wabash river and the intersecting railroads furnishing all needed market facilities

I am indebted to Mr. J ZIMMERMAN, of Mt. Carmel, for much valuable information and assistance while engaged in my examinations in this vicinity, and to Dr J SCHENCK for the following complete list of the trees and shrubs indiginous to Wabash county.

*A list of the Forest Trees and Shrubs found in Wabash County.*

Acer rubrum, L., (*Red* or *Swamp Maple*)
" dasycarpum, Ehrhart, (*White* or *Silver Maple*)
" saccharinum, Wang., (*Common Sugar Maple*)
" saccharinum, var. nigrum, (*Black Sugar Maple*)
Æsculus glabra, Willd., (*Smooth* or *Ohio Buckeye*)
Alnus serrulata, Ait., (*Smooth Alder*)
Amorpha fructicosa, L., (*False Indigo*)
Asimina triloba, Dunal, (*Common Papaw*)
Betula lenta, L., (*Cherry* or *Sweet Birch.*)
" nigra, L., (*River* or *Red Birch*)
Carpinus Americana, Michx., (*Iron wood, Hornbeam*)
Catalpa bignonioides, Walt., (*Catalpa; Indian Bean*)
Carya olivæformis, Nutt., (*Pecan nut*)
" alba, Nutt., (*Shell bark* or *Shag bark Hickory*)
" microcarpa, Nutt., (*Small fruited Hickory*)
" tomentosa, Nutt., (*Mocker nut, White-heart Hickory*)
" procina, Nutt., (*Pig nut* or *Broom Hickory*)
" amara, Nutt., (*Bitter nut* or *Swamp Hickory.*)
Celtis occidentalis, L., (*Hackberry, Sugarberry.*)
" Mississippiensis, Bosc, (*Mississippi hackberry*)
Cephalanthus occidentalis, L., (*Button Bush.*)
Cercis Canadensis, L., (*Red bud, Judas tree.*)
Cornus florida, L., (*Flowering Dogwood.*)
" sericea, L., (*Silky Cornel, Kinnikinnik*)
" paniculata, L'Her., (*Panicled Cornel.*)
Corylus Americana, Walt., (*Wild Hazel nut*)
" rostrata, Ait., (*Beaked Hazel nut*)
Cratægus tomentosa, L., (*Black* or *Pear Thorn.*)
" tomentosa var. Mollis
" punctata, Jacq.
" cordata, Ait. (*Washington Thorn.*)
" Crus galli, L., (*Cockspur Thorn*)
" veridis, L.
Diospyros Virginiana, L., (*Common Persimmon*)
Euonymus atropurpureus, Jacq., (*Burning-bush; Waahoo.*)
" Americanus, L., (*Strawberry bush*)
Fagus ferruginea, Ait., (*American Beech*)
Forestiera acuminata, Poir.

Fraxinus Americana, L., (*White Ash.*)
" pubescens, Lam., (*Red Ash.*)
" viridis, Michx., (*Green Ash.*)
" quadrangulata, Michx., (*Blue Ash.*)
Gleditschia triacanthos, L., (*Three thorned Acacia* or *Honey locust.*)
Gymnocladus Canadensis, Lam., (*Coffee Tree.*)
Hydrangea arborescens, L., (*Wild Hydrangea.*)
Hypericum prolificum, L., (*Shrubby St John's Wort.*)
Ilex decidua, Walt.
Juglans cinerea, L., (*Butternut.*)
" nigra, L., (*Black Walnut.*)
Juniperus communis. (*Common Juniper.*)
Lindera Benzoin, Meisner, (*Spice bush; Benjamin bush.*)
Liquidambar Styraciflua, L., (*Sweet Gum Tree.*)
Liriodendron Tulipifera, L., (*Tulip-tree, Poplar.*)
Morus rubra, L., (*Red Mulberry.*)
Negundo aceroides, Mœnch, (*Box elder.*)
Nyssa multiflora, Wang., (*Black Gum, Tupelo.*)
Ostrya Virginica, Willd., (*Hop hornbeam, Lever wood.*)
Platanus occidentalis, L., (*Sycamore, Plane tree.*)
Populus heterophylla, L., (*Cotton Wood, Downy Poplar.*)
" monilifera, Ait., (*Necklace Poplar, Cotton Wood.*)
" tremuloides, Michx., (*American Aspen.*)
Prinos verticillata, Gray. (*Black Alder, Winterberry.*)
Prunus Americana, Marshell, (*Wild Yellow, or Red Plumb.*)
" insititia, L., (*Bullace Plumb.*)
" serotina, Ehrhart, (*Wild Black Cherry.*)
Pyrus coronaria, L., (*Sweet scented Crab Apple.*)
" angustifolia, Ait., (*Narrow leaved Crab Apple.*)
Ptelea trifoliata, L., *Water Ash; Shrubby Trefoil.*)
Quercus alba, L., (*White oak.*)
" obtusiloba, Michx., (*Post oak.*)
" macrocarpa, Michx., (*Bur* or *Over cup Oak.*)
" macrocarpa, var. (?) *Lyrata*, Michx., (*Lyre leaved Oak.*)
" prinus, Willd., (*Swamp Chestnut Oak.*)
" bicolor, Willd., (*Swamp White Oak.*)
" castanea, Muhl., (*Chestnut Oak.*)
" tinctoria, Bartram, (*Black* or *Tanner's Oak.*)
" coccinea, Wang., (*Scarlet Oak.*)
" rubra, L. (*Red Oak.*)
" palustris, Michx., (*Pin* or *Water Oak.*)
" nigra, L., (*Black Jack* or *Barren Oak.*)
" Phellos, L., (*Willow Oak.*)
" imbricaria, Michx., (*Laurel* or *Shingle Oak.*)

Rhus typhina, L., (*Staghorn Sumach.*)
" glabra, L., (*Smooth Sumach.*)
" copallina, L., (*Dwarf Sumach.*)
Salix tristis, Ait., (*Dwarf Gray Willow.*)
" discolor, Muhl., (*Glaucous Willow.*)
" eriocephala, Michx., (*Wooly Headed Willow.*)
" petiolaris, Smith, (*Long stalked Green Osier.*)
" nigra, Marshall, (*Black Willow.*)
" rigida, Muhl., (*Stiff-leaved Willow.*)
Sambucus Canadensis, L., (*Common Elder.*)
Sassafras officinale, Nees, (*Sassafras.*)
Staphylea trifolia, L., (*Bladder-nut.*)
Symphoricarpus occidentalis, R. Brown, (*Wolf* or *Buck Berry.*)
" vulgaris, Michx., (*Indian Currant, Coral-berry.*)
Taxodium distichum, Richard, (*American Bald Cypress.*)
Tilia Americana, L., (*Basswood, Linden.*)
" heterophylla, Vent., (*White Basswood.*)
Ulmus fulva, Michx., (*Slippery Elm.*)
" Americana, L., (*American* or *White Elm.*)
" alata, Michx., (*Winged Elm.*)
Viburnum prunifolium, L., (*Black Haw.*)
" nudum, M., (*White Rod.*)
Zanthoxylum Americanum, Mill., (*Northern Prickly Ash.*)

—10

# CHAPTER VI.

## WHITE AND HAMILTON COUNTIES.

White county has a geographical area of about four hundred and eighty square miles, and is bounded on the north by Wayne and Edwards counties, on the east by the Wabash river, on the south by Gallatin county, and on the west by Hamilton. The Little Wabash traverses the county from north to south through its central portion, and the Skillet Fork enters at the north-west corner, and after a south-east course enters the Little Wabash near the centre of the county. These streams, with their smaller affluents, and the main Wabash river as its eastern boundary, drain nearly the whole area of the county. South of Phillipstown there is a considerable area between the Little and the main Wabash rivers of rather flat land, intersected by a chain of ponds extending nearly due north and south, through townships five and six south, range ten east, which probably marks the course of an old river channel This portion of the county is rather flat and heavily timbered The remainder of the county is quite rolling, and portions of it south and west of Carmi are broken and hilly.

*Superficial Deposits.*—The alluvium, loess and drift, the three principal divisions of the Quaternary, or most recent of the geological systems, are well developed in this county Alluvial bottoms of considerable extent skirt the courses of the main and Little Wabash and Skillet Fork, but being subject to annual overflow, the land is only valued at the present time for the fine body of timber which it sustains The soil, however, is a rich sandy loam, and when cleared and brought under cultivation will prove the most fertile land in the county

The loess is very heavily developed along the bluffs of the Wabash from Phillipstown to Grayville, and ranges from thirty to sixty feet or more in thickness. It comprises a bed of brown clay immediately below the surface, of variable thickness, which is underlaid by the usual ash-gray and buff marly sands, containing the characteristic fresh water and land shells usually found in this deposit

The drift deposits in this county vary from ten to thirty feet or more in thickness, and consist of brown gravelly clays, with some northern bowlders of considerable size. In the vicinity of the Little Wabash, north of Carmi, these seemed to be more abundant than elsewhere, and one was seen near the north line of the county, and about a mile east of the ford on the Little Wabash, that was fully four feet in its longest diameter, by two feet or more in the opposite direction This is the most southerly point in the State where bowlders of this size have been seen

## *Coal Measures.*

The stratified rocks of this county belong to the lower part of the upper Coal Measures, and the lowest beds appearing in the county are to be seen in the bluffs of the Little Wabash, in the vicinity of New Haven and near Carmi these two points being on nearly the same geological level The New Haven limestone appears to be identical with the lowest limestone seen in Clark county, which there lays about seventy five to eighty feet above coal No. 7. Here the space is probably a hundred and fifty to two hundred feet or more, with two thin coals intervening between the limestone and the main coals below. In the solid portions of this limestone fossils are comparatively rare, the only species we were able to find in an hour's search at New Haven being *Spirifer cameratus*, *S plano convexus*, *Productus Prattenianus*, *P. longispinus*, *Terebratula bovidens*, *Rhynchonella Osagensis*, *Platyostoma Peoriense*, joints of *Crinoidea*, etc The rock is hard and brittle, and weathers to a rusty-brown color The section in the vicinity of New Haven, commencing at the base with this limestone and extending north along the small branches putting into the Little Wabash for about two miles and a half to land adjoining Mr. R W Boyd, and belonging to the Jones' heirs, is as follows

| | | | Ft | In |
|---|---|---|---|---|
| No | 1 | Sandstone forming the bed rock on top of the hills. and penetrated by Mr Boyd, in his well . | 13 | |
| No | 2 | Sandstone and sandy shale, passing downward into arg shale (partial exposure) | 40 to 50 | |
| No | 3 | Ferro argillaceous limestone, with fossils | 0 | 3 |
| No | 4 | Ferruginous shale, with fossils . | 0 | 2 |
| No | 5 | Chocolate brown calc sandstone, with fossils . . | 1 | 6 |
| No | 6 | Dark colored shale . . . . . . | 2 to 3 | |
| No | 7 | Coal . . . | 0 | 2 |
| No | 8 | Shaly fire clay . | 2 | 6 |
| No | 9 | Hard sandstone, partly in heavy beds . . | 4 to 6 | |
| No | 10 | Shale and thin bedded sandstone . . | 6 to 8 | |
| No | 11 | Space covered. probably not more than | 15 to 20 | |
| No | 12 | New Haven limestone . | 3 to 4 | |

The three inch band of ferruginous limestone, No. 3 of the above section, contains numerous well preserved fossils, and we obtained from it *Pleurotomaria Grayvillensis*, *Bellerophon carbonarius*, *B Montfortianus*, *Euomphalus sub rugosus*, *Macrocheilus inhabilis*, *Nucula ventricosa*, and

*Polyphemopsis per acuta* The chocolate brown calcareous sandstone below it contains a peculiar group of fossils, among which are *Myalina ampla*, *Aviculopecten occidentalis*, *Avicula longispina*, *Pinna per acuta*, *Schizodus Alpinus ?* *Edmondia Nebrascensis*, *Allorisma sub-cuneata*, *Bellerophon crassus*, *Naticopsis Pricei ?* *Platyceras Nebrascensis*, *Productus Prattenianus*, and some other undetermined forms. This bed is found at Carmi in the bed of a small branch south of the town containing the same group of fossils.

About three-quarters of a mile from New Haven north on Rock creek, the beds numbered from two to ten of the foregoing section are well exposed, and a fair quality of thin bedded micaceous sandstone is quarried for building purposes From this point to Carmi by the road on the west side of the river the country is quite broken, and frequent outcrops of sandstone and shale may be seen in the hill sides and in the banks of the small streams On Grindstone creek, seven miles south of Carmi, a bed of sandstone in rather even beds is exposed on a small branch running into the main creek from the south west. The beds exposed are from twelve to fifteen feet in thickness, and the rock has been quarried for building stone, and some grindstones have also been made from it. Most of the beds are in tolerably even layers, but some portions of the mass show a more or less concretionary structure.

At Carmi we have a repetition of the same beds found in the vicinity of New Haven, with the upper part of the section better exposed, but only extending downwards to No 5 of the section seen near New Haven, the lower part of that section being here below the level of the Little Wabash Commencing with the sandstone to be seen in the north part of town, above the dam, and descending from thence along the river bluffs to the small creek just south of the town, we have the following section:

| | | Ft | In |
|---|---|---|---|
| No 1 | Sandy shales and some sandstone in even beds . . . | 12 | |
| No 2 | Clay shales . . | 16 to 18 | |
| No 3 | Two thin coats parted by a foot or more of clay shale . . | 1 to 1 | 6 |
| No 4 | Brown sandstone quarry rock | 8 to 10 | |
| No 5 | Band of cinnamon brown shale with *Posidonias* . | 0 | 2 |
| No 6 | Dark clay shale . . | 1 | |
| No 7 | Gray sandy shales passing downward into clay shale, with iron stones | 18 to 20 | |
| No 8* | Ferro calcareous chocolate brown sandstone with fossils | 1½ to 2 | |

The lower bed of the above section was only partially exposed in the bed of the creek, where it presents the same general appearance, and contains the same group of fossils as were obtained from No 5 of the section near New Haven I was unable to find more than a partial exposure of it in the vicinity of Carmi. The brown sandstone No 4 of the above section contains numerous specimens of broken plants, is somewhat

* This is equivalent to No 47, of the general section of the Coal Measures, on p 2, *et seq*

ferruginous, and affords a good quality of building stone. The thin band of cinnamon-colored shale seems to have been formed from an impalpable brown mud, and on splitting it in thin layers countless numbers of minute shells like *Posidonia* are found covering the surface of the slabs

In the bank of Skillet Fork, at Mill Shoals, there is an outcrop of thin coal, with a bituminous shale and limestone, as shown in the following section.

| | Ft |
|---|---|
| Hard shelly sandstone | 3 to 4 |
| Hard, black laminated slate, passing locally into clay shale | 6 to 8 |
| Shale, with thin coal | 2 to 3 |
| Hard, fine grained limestone | 2 to 3 |
| Greenish, pebbly shale | 2 |
| Sandy shale, in creek bed | 1 |

These beds afford no distinct fossils, but the limestone and black laminated slate bear a strong resemblance to beds found three miles north east of Fairfield, in Wayne county, and two and a half miles south of Olney, which I have referred to the horizon of coal No. 13 of the general section The cross cleavage planes of the limestone shows *Stigmaria* rootlets, and these were the only indications of organic life we could find in it. The rock is fine grained, of a bluish dove color, the lower portion weathering to a yellowish-buff The beds in the foregoing section are succeeded in the hills north and east of the station by sixty to seventy feet of shale and sandstone, with a thin bed of bituminous shale near the top of the exposure.

At Grayville, on the west bank of the Wabash river, the bluff rises to a hight of more than a hundred feet above low-water level, and affords a fine section of the Coal Measure beds, as follows.

| | | Ft | In |
|---|---|---|---|
| No 1 | Covered slope of loess and drift | 48 | |
| No 2 | Heavy bedded sandstone | 15 | |
| No 3 | Slope with partial outcrops of shale | 25 | |
| No 4 | Silicious shale | 7 to 8 | |
| No 5 | Blue argillaceous shale with bands of fossiliferous iron ore at the bottom | 4 | |
| No 6 | Bituminous shale | 6 in to 0 | 8 |
| No 7 | Calcareous shale, and shaly bituminous limestone | 0 to 3 | |
| No 8 | Black shale | 6 in to 1 | |
| No 9 | Green clay shales, or fire-clay | 1 to 2 | |
| No 10 | Sandy shales and sandstone in river bed | 10 to 12 | |

This section was taken about 300 yards below the ferry landing, and at the lowest stage of water in the river. The beds here lie in wave-like undulations, the black shale in the above section being at one point 15 feet above the river bed, and in a distance of about fifty yards they come down to within about six feet of the river level. In the calcareous shale No 7 of the above section there is a thin band filled with crushed and broken specimens of a small *Myalina*, probably *M perattenuata*. This shale is dark colored and highly bituminous, and contains several species of crushed fossils in addition to that above mentioned, but all identical with those found in the clay iron band at the base of No. 5. Local patches of sandstone and conglomerate in lenticular masses a foot or more in thickness come in at two or three points immediately above the black shales, and where this occurs the shales are compressed into something less than one-half their normal thickness At the upper end of this exposure the calcareo-bituminous shale No 7 is replaced by three or four inches of blue clay shale. The thin bedded sandstones and sandy shales in the river bed contain *Calamites*, and fragments of other coal plants, sometimes inclosed in iron concretions similar to those noticed in the river bed at Mt Carmel. The ferruginous band at the base of the blue shale No 5 of the foregoing section contains many fine fossil shells in a good state of preservation, and the locality has become somewhat noted on this account The species to be found here include the following *Nautilus occidentalis, N globatus ? Cyrtoceras curtum, Dentalium obsoletum, Pleurotomaria tabulata, P sphærulata, P. Grayvillensis, Macrocheilus inhabilis, Ianthinopsis tumida, Euomphalus subrugosus, Nucula ventricosa, Astartella vera, Leda bella rugosa, Lima retifera, Orthis carbonaria*, and *Lophophyllum proliferum.* This is the same group of fossils found on Raccoon creek near the north line of Edward's county, at Lawrenceville in Lawrence county, and on Lamotte creek near Palestine landing, showing that the Wabash river, from the latter point to Grayville, continues on nearly the same geological level

The exposure in the Grayville bluff affords an interesting exhibition of the variable character of the beds occurring at this horizon, and if the upper and lower extremities of this outcrop were only to be seen as separate exposures their identity might not be suspected. At the upper end of the hill a seam of pyritiferous shale from one to three inches thick is all that separates the black laminated shales, while at the lower end they are separated by about three feet of calcareous shale and shaly bituminous limestone Fossils are abundant at the upper end of the exposure in clay iron ore in the lower part of No 5 of the section, while three hundred yards below neither the iron stones nor the fossils they inclose can be found. Hence the difficulty of constructing a connected section in the Upper Coal Measures from the examination of isolated outcrops, which are the only exposures of the strata to be found in this portion of the State

On the Little Wabash at the ford six miles west of Grayville, on sec. 21, T 3 S, R 10 E., the bluff consists of sandstone and sandy shale, inclosing a bituminous shale and thin coal. The section here is as follows

| | Feet | In |
|---|---|---|
| Evenly bedded sandstone and sandy shale . . . .. . . | 30 to 40 | |
| Bituminous shale and thin coal | 1 | 6 |
| Clay shale . . . . . | 5 to 8 | |
| Massive sandstone, partly concretionary .. . . . . . | 10 to 15 | |

A short distance below the ford the bituminous shale and coal appeared to be wanting, wedging out in a distance of about a hundred yards. The upper bed of sandstone is in part a hard micaceous rock, in even layers of moderate thickness, and will afford a good quality of building stone, as will also the concretionary bed below. About half way from Grayville to this ford, in crossing a ridge, there is from 20 to 30 feet of shales exposed, which probably overlay the sandstones at the ford, though the exact connection between them could not be determined

Gossett station, on the Cairo and Vincennes Railroad, is located on a high ridge something more than a hundred feet above the bed of Bear creek At the summit the railroad cut shows about ten feet of coarse, soft, brown sandstone, that decomposes easily on exposure A few feet below this sandstone a thin coal has been found at two or three places in the neighborhood, and some digging has been done here in the expectation of finding it somewhere thick enough to work to advantage, but so far without success A section of the rocks seen in this vicinity show the following order

| | Ft | In |
|---|---|---|
| Brown clay capping the ridge | 10 to 15 | |
| Coarse soft brown sandstone | 10 | |
| Space not seen, probably not more than | 10 to 15 | |
| Sandy shale | 6 | |
| Thin coal | 0 | 4 |
| Sandy shale | 6 | |
| Space not seen | 15 to 20 | |
| Nodular argillaceous limestone, without fossils | 1 to 2 | |
| Sandy shale | 4 to 6 | |
| Even bedded micaceous sandstone | 0 to 8 | |

The lowest bed in this section affords sandstone in smooth even layers from an inch to a foot or more in thickness, which is an excellent and durable stone for flagging, foundation walls, etc, and the thickest beds could be easily cut for caps and sills The rock at this quarry resembles that at McGILLY'S, a mile west of McLeansboro. No outcrop of coal of any value has yet been found in this portion of the county, and the four-inch seam in the above section is not likely to increase in thickness sufficiently to become of any practical value for mining purposes.

The following observations and sections are from Prof COX'S notes in this county "At the Grand Chain, one and a half miles below BLACK'S ferry, the Wabash flows over a hard sandstone, that is here a fine-grained gray rock, excellent for building purposes. It forms a low reef across the stream, creating a strong current, and hence the name, 'Grand Chain' On the Illinois shore the rock is but a few feet above the river bed, and is soon lost under the alluvial bottom. On the Indiana side it forms a ledge in the hills bordering the narrow bottom. At Warrick's riffle, six miles above, this sandstone is again seen at the water's edge, and on the Indiana shore, near the mouth of Rush creek, it is overlaid by a heavy bed of shale, including a soft, calcareous stratum, containing numerous fossils

At WEBB's ferry the equivalent of the Rush creek shale, alternating with shaly sandstone, again makes its appearance, and at Bonpass, a little higher up, we have the following section:

| | Ft | In |
|---|---|---|
| Loess, with characteristic fossils | 30 | |
| Drift clay and gravel | 20 | |
| Buff sandstone | 10 | |
| Shale and covered space | 20 | |
| Thin coal | 0 | 6 |
| Fire clay | 1 | 6 |
| Silicious shale and sandstone | 6 | |
| Argillaceous shale | 25 | |
| | 123 | |

The lower shale in the above section is first seen half a mile below the ferry, and contains fossil plants, *Sphenophyllum*, *Pecopteris* and *Neuropteris*, but too fragile to be preserved

On the western borders of the county, opposite New Harmony in Indiana, there is a large island formed by an arm of the Wabash, called Fox river. This island is low and flat, and subject to overflow Soon after crossing Fox river we ascend the Phillipstown ridge, which bears a little east of north, and strikes the Wabash river at Grayville In this ridge we find the counterpart of the sections at Cut-off, below New Harmony, and at Grayville: but the creeks do not cut quite so deep into the argillaceous shales here, so as to show the lowest beds. Just before reaching Phillipstown, on the New Harmony road, a thin coal is seen in the bank of a branch Below it there is a few inches of fire clay, and then an argillaceous shale, which is seen in the bed of the branch Above the coal, which is mostly decomposed, there is a calcareous band containing fossils similar to those found at Grayville When first quarried this band is firm and hard, but after long exposure it becomes soft. Above the fossil band there is a few feet of argillaceous shale and a bed of sandstone, as seen in the following section

| | Ft | In |
|---|---|---|
| Yellow crumbling clay | 20 to 40 | |
| Loess with fossils | 20 to 30 | |
| Drift with pebbles and small granite bowlders | 35 | |
| Silicious shale | 10 | |
| Sandstone | 2 | |
| Argillaceous shale | 10 | |
| Calcareous fossil band | | 3 |
| Fire-clay | 1 | |
| Thin coal and fire clay | 5 | |
| | 133 | 3 |

About a quarter of a mile south west of this the sandstone of the above section is ten feet thick without seams It is micaceous and soft when first quarried, but hardens on exposure and makes a good durable building stone. Two and a half miles south west of Phillipstown this same ledge of sandstone forms a low cliff along the eastern face of the ridge and in places is weathered into caves, locally called rock houses.

On the road to Carmi the loess is replaced by a loose yellow sand, that forms a bluff on the eastern border of a prairie, which is succeeded by a shallow slough or swamp that was probably once the bed of an arm if not the main stream of the Little Wabash.

Section on Seven mile creek, on the Mt Vernon road and near the ferry on Skillet Fork, sec 30, T 1, R 9 E.

| | Ft | In |
|---|---|---|
| Drift clay | 5 to 6 | |
| Argillaceous shale | 20 | |
| Bituminous shale—black | | 10 |
| Coal | 1 | |
| Fire clay | 3 | |

The black shale contained some poorly preserved specimens of *Polyphemopsis*, *Aviculopecten* and *Nucula ventricosa*. The argillaceous shale twenty feet or more in thickness appears again on the creek a short distance below the opening to the coal.

On Limestone creek north of Enfield, T 4 S, R 8 E, there is an earthy limestone two feet thick passing down into hard silicious fire clay. No fossils in the upper part, but the lower part contains rootlets of *Stigmaria*. This rock has been burned for lime, and hence the name of the creek.

A thin coal is found at the following localities in this county not already mentioned: Sections 16 and 18, T 4, R 8, sec. 8, T. 5, R 10, sec 30, T 4, R 9, sec 21, T. 6, R 8, sec 3, T 6, R 10; and sec 19, T 3, R. 9."

## *Economical Geology.*

*Building Stone*—Sandstone of a fair quality for building purposes is found at a number of localities in this county, as noted in the sections already given in the preceding pages. At Carmi the brown sandstone that forms the bed rock in the south-east part of the town is an even-bedded ferruginous rock, that hardens on exposure and makes a very good building stone. On Grindstone creek, six or seven miles south of Carmi, on the New Haven road, a bed of gray sandstone is quarried for building stone, and affords a durable stone for all ordinary purposes. Near Gossett station an excellent flagstone may be obtained as well as heavier bedded sandstone for other purposes. This rock is micaceous and cuts freely, and could be cheaply wrought into door sills, lintels, window caps and sills, etc.

The sandstone outcropping in the bluffs of the Wabash river from Phillipstown to Grayville affords good building stone at many points, as does that also that outcrops farther south at Grand Chain In the bluffs of the Little Wabash, near the north line of the county, there is from thirty to forty feet of sandstone nearly all of which might be used for building purposes, and the upper beds are in even layers of moderate thickness, that could be cheaply quarried.

*Coal*—No coal seam thick enough to be worked advantageously was found outcropping in the county, and the only resource of this county in that direction is in the main coals of the lower measures These coals may be found here, in my opinion, at a depth of two to four hundred feet in any part of the county At Carmi, and along the Wabash south of Grayville, coal No 7 ought to be found not more than one hundred and fifty feet below the river level, and if that should be found too thin to be worked to advantage, about a hundred feet more would reach No 5, one of the most persistent seams that we have in the Illinois coal basin Situated as Carmi is at the junction of two important railroads, the citizens could well afford to make a test experiment with the drill, in order to determine whether they have coal beneath the surface at a reasonable depth and of sufficient thickness to justify the sinking of a shaft This is a matter of public interest, and so far as the test experiment is concerned, the expense should be shared by the property holders of the town, and when this point is settled private enterprise will do the rest

*Brick materials*—Sand and clay suitable for brick making may be found in every neighborhood, and on the uplands on nearly every farm. Sand for mortar and cement is also abundant at some localities, as between Carmi and Phillipstown, where a bed of clean yellow sand is found replacing the loess

*Soil and Agriculture*—The soil of this county includes three quite distinct varieties, to wit The low alluvial bottoms skirting the main water courses, and subject to annual overflow, the higher alluvial lands south east of Carmi, between the Little Wabash and the chain of ponds already referred to as indicating an ancient river channel, which are mostly above high water, and the rolling uplands forming the northern and western portions of the county There is a small prairie on this second or higher bottom between Carmi and Phillipstown, about five miles in length by two in breadth and also two small prairies on the northern border of the county and partially within its limits, but the remainder of its surface was originally covered with a heavy growth of timber. On the low bottoms between the Fox river and the Wabash, cane brakes are frequently met with, the canes usually ranging from three to six feet in hight. This is the most northerly point that we have observed this shrub growing in Illinois. The soil on the low river bottoms is exceedingly productive, and especially adapted to the growth of corn, and were it not for the annual river floods would be the most valuable land in the county. The higher alluvial land skirting the Little Wabash south of Carmi has a sandy soil, not quite so productive as that on the low river bottoms but yielding fair crops of corn, wheat oats and grass, and easily cultivated. On the uplands the soil is generally a clay loam, similar to that of Wayne and Edwards, but more variable in its productive capacities, in consequence of the inequalities of the surface. On the oak ridges the soil is thin and yields only light crops of corn, but is better adapted to small grains and grass, while the valleys and the level stretches of land between them have a deep loamy soil that is very productive, yielding good crops of all the cereals usually grown in this portion of the State. For a list of the trees of this county the reader is referred to that already given in the report on Wabash county.

HAMILTON COUNTY embraces an area of four hundred and twenty-three square miles, and is bounded on the north by Wayne county, on the east by White, on the south by Saline and on the west by Franklin and Jefferson counties. There are no streams of any considerable size in the county. The northern portion however is drained by the tributaries of Skillet Fork, the main stream intersecting the north east corner of the county, and the southern by the North fork of Saline, several branches of which take their rise near the center of the county and coalesce near the south line to form the main stream. The surface is generally rolling, and was originally mainly covered with timber, though there are two or three small prairies within its borders.

*Superficial Deposits.*—The alluvial deposits in this county are limited to the valleys of the small streams mainly tributary to the North fork of Saline, and are seldom more than a mile in width. They are very heavily timbered with several varieties of oak, hickory, elm, linden, ash hackberry, black and white walnut, poplar, sugar maple, etc. The drift deposits on the uplands range from ten to thirty feet in thickness and consist of yellow and buff gravelly clays, with small bowlders of northern origin varying in size from a few inches to a foot or more in diameter. Branches of trees and sometimes the stems also, of considerable size, are met with in sinking wells through the drift in this county, as well as nearly every other portion of the State, and very frequently the ancient soil in which they grew remains *in situ* beneath the gravelly clays and hard pan of the drift.

*Stratified Rocks.*—The rock formations of this county belong to the upper Coal Measures, ranging from the horizon of coal No. 10 to coal No. 13, and including a total thickness of one hundred and fifty to two hundred feet of rock strata, but affording but little coal thick enough to be worked to advantage.

About a mile a little south of west from McLeansboro, at Mr JAMES McGILLEY'S place, sandstone is quarried to supply the demand for building stone in this vicinity. The stone is of a good quality, very evenly bedded, and can be quarried in slabs of any desirable size, and varying in thickness from two or three inches to two feet. The bed is from five to six feet thick at this quarry, and it affords most of the building stone used in McLeansboro and the adjoining neighborhood The rock dresses easily and hardens on exposure, and can be cheaply cut for window caps and sills, ashlars, etc. The sandstone is underlaid at the quarry by about three feet of shale which farther down the branch thickens to ten or twelve feet, when the banks of the stream become alluvial and no further outcrop is seen for some distance. Above the quarry rock there is a partial outcrop of ten to fifteen feet of sandy shale, with a few thin layers of sandstone intercalated therein, from two to eight inches thick.

At Mr. RICE'S place, about a mile north of McGilley's quarry, there is a band of hard argillaceous limestone from a foot to eighteen inches in thickness, outcropping at a considerable higher level than the sandstone at McGilley's. The limestone is overlaid by fire-clay and a thin seam of coal, which has been worked in a small way by stripping at several places hereabouts The limestone has been burned for lime, but is evidently too impure to slack freely, and moreover, the bed is too thin to be profitably quarried for any purpose It contains no fossils On the north side of the ridge about a quarter of a mile from Rice's, there is another outcrop of the limestone where lime has been burned, and here it is overlaid by a black shale containing concretions of black limestone or septaria

At Mr BARNET'S place, on Hog prairie, the coal overlaying the limestone is from eight to twelve inches thick, with from one to two feet of fire clay between. In the early settlement of the country this coal was worked by stripping to supply the neighboring blacksmiths, but since the opening of the heavy beds in Saline county the work here has been abandoned This limestone is probably somewhere from thirty to forty feet above the highest beds seen at McGilley's quarry, and the following section will show the general relation of the strata seen between Hog prairie and McLeansboro.

| | Ft | In |
|---|---|---|
| Yellow ferruginous shale | 10 | |
| Black, or dark blue bituminous shale | 2 to 3 | |
| Coal | ⅔ to 1 | |
| Fire clay | 1 to 2 | |
| Limestone | 1 to 1 | 6 |
| Space unexposed estimated at | 30 to 40 | |
| Shale and thin bedded sandstone | 10 to 12 | |
| Evenly bedded sandstone at McGilley's | 5 | |
| Sandy shales | 8 to 10 | |

This coal seam is probably nowhere more than twelve to fifteen inches thick in this part of the county, and the coal is rather soft and slaty, but quite free from pyrite, and is a very fair blacksmith's coal. The limestone is a hard fine grained grayish rock, weathering to a yellowish drab, and when thoroughly burned is said to yield a strong dark colored lime.

To the westward of Hog prairie sandstone and sandy shales outcrop at intervals in the small branches and in the hill sides to the Jefferson county line, just beyond which the following beds were seen, and as they probably underlay the north-west part of Hamilton county from the prevailing north easterly dip of the strata, I deem it proper to give a description of them in this place.

At Dr. WILKEY'S place on sec. 36, T. 4 S., R. 4 E., the following section was seen:

| | Ft. |
|---|---|
| Shales, sandy at the top but passing into blue clay shales below | 18 to 20 |
| Calcareo-bituminous shale with fossils, the upper part passing locally into shaly bituminous limestone | 4 to 6 |
| Coal | 1½ to 3 |
| Shaly fire clay | 2 |
| Shaly micaceous sandstone with fragments of plants | 8 to 10 |

Among the fossils found here I recognize the following species: *Orthoceras Rushensis*, *Bellerophon carbonarius*, *B. Montfortianus*, *Euomphalus subrugosus*, *Nucula ventricosa*, *Astartella vera*, *Leda Oweni*, *Macrodon carbonaria*, *Spirifer plano-convexus*, *Chonetes Flemingii*, *Synocladia biserialis*, *Lophophyllum proliferum*, and plates and spines of *Eupachycrinus*.

About a mile north of Dr. WILKEY'S on Mr. JINES' place another coal seam is found where the coal is about eighteen inches thick, and overlaid by a few inches of bituminous shale without fossils, passing upward into a chocolate colored shale, of which about two feet in thickness is exposed on the branch in stripping the coal. This seam is opened on a small branch running north eastward into a tributary of Skillet fork, and the coal dips in the same direction about with the fall of the creek, while the outcrop at Dr. WILKEY'S is on one of the branches of the Middle fork of Big Muddy, which runs to the south and south westward. The coal at Mr. JINES' mine seemed to be harder than that at Dr. WILKEY'S, and while at the latter locality the coal was quite variable in thickness, ranging from eighteen inches to nearly or quite three feet, at the former it varies but little from eighteen inches. I have no doubt but these outcrops are on two distinct seams, probably the equivalents of Nos. 10 and 11 of the general section. In the vicinity of McLeansboro the strata seem to be nearly horizontal, no continuous dip in any direction being perceptible, but to the westward between Hog prairie and the county line there appeared to be a decided dip to the north eastward. These two coals, and possibly a still higher seam, No 12 of the general section, must underlay the north west corner of Hamilton county, and where there is no outcrop they will probably be found at a depth of less than a hundred feet from the surface

Five miles south west of McLeansboro, on the old LOCKWOOD estate, there is a thin coal from six to fifteen inches in thickness, overlaid by bituminous shale, which passes upward into gray silicious shale and sandstone, the latter but partially exposed The coal is rather slaty, and has only been worked to a limited extent by stripping at the outcrop in the banks of a small branch. Neither the quality nor thickness of the coal would justify any attempts at systematic mining here.

On Esq TWIGGS' land, about three miles west of Rectorsville station, a thin coal was found in sinking a shallow well near a sandstone quarry The coal and a few inches of bituminous shale forming its roof lies immediately below the sandstone, but no outcrop of it could be found. It is probably too thin to be of any practical value The sandstone quarry shows a space of about three feet in thickness of soft micaceous evenly bedded rock in layers from one to six inches thick, and contains fragments of plants and numerous casts of *Aviculopecten rectilaterarius* Quarries have been opened at several places in this vicinity in this sandstone, and the coal has been found in several wells, but always too thin to be of any practical value for mining purposes.

At Hood's old mill on the North Fork, about two miles and a half south-east of Rectorsville station, the following beds outcrop in the bluffs of the stream

| | Ft |
|---|---|
| Brown shale | 2 |
| Hard chocolate brown, shaly, micaceous sandstone | 5 |
| Sandy micaceous shale | 14 |

The chocolate colored sandstone at this locality resembles somewhat the brown calcareous sandstone found in the bed of the creek at Carmi, but it is less calcareous here if they are equivalent strata, and contains but few fossils, and none of the species most characteristic of that bed in White county. The fossils observed in it here were *Productus Prattenanus*, *P Nebrascensis*, *Terebratula bovidens*, *Bellerophon*, *Fenestella*, and joints of *Crinoidea* Hand specimens of this sandstone, which is here ferruginous and perhaps slightly calcareous, very closely resemble those from the White county localities, and it is quite possible they may represent equivalent strata, and if so this is probably about the lowest bed outcropping in this county.

The following outcrops are reported by Prof. COX:

"On sec. 23, T 5, R 5, on Knight's prairie, coal is found reported to be eighteen inches thick, overlaid by argillaceous and silicious shale At J. M. McDANIEL'S well on sec 5, T. 5, R 6, passed through eighteen feet of sandstone and two feet of blue shale Mr JOHN HALL, in digging a well on Knight's prairie, struck coal at the depth of seventeen feet Earthy limestone one foot thick exposed at S LANE'S, also at PLATT STEPHENS' on sec 16, T 5, R 7, where it is exposed in the bed of a branch overlaid by ten feet of silicious shale. A thin coal is found on sections 14 and 23, T 5, R. 7."

These isolated sections give the general character of the outcrops to be seen in this county, but they afford no data on which to construct a connected section of the several beds that outcrop within its borders It is probable the total thickness of the strata that appear in natural outcrops within the county do not exceed one hundred and fifty to two hundred feet, and include no important limestones, and no coal seams above fifteen to eighteen inches in thickness except in the north-west corner of the county, where coals Nos 10 or 11 may perhaps be found from two to two and a half feet thick.

## *Economical Geology.*

*Building Stone*—Sandstone of a fair quality for building purposes may be obtained at several places in this county, and the quarry at McGILLEY'S, one mile south west of McLeansboro, furnishes a good material for flagging and for cut stone, as well as foundation walls, etc This quarry furnishes most of the stone used at McLeansboro and in the adjoining neighborhood A similar sandstone is found outcropping on a branch about three miles north west of McLeansboro, a tributary of the Skillet Fork, and several quarries have been opened in the bluffs of the stream In the southern part of the county the supply of good stone is not abundant, but the bed of micaceous sandstone near 'Squire TWIGGS' place, three miles west of Rectorsville station, affords a soft rock in thin beds that is used for walling wells, for foundations, etc The hard chocolate colored micaceous sandstone at Hood's old mill, on the North Fork, near the south line of the county, affords a very durable stone, but is too thin bedded for heavy masonry The only bed of limestone seen in the county is too thin to be of any practical value for building purposes, and is unevenly bedded and nodular in structure

*Coal*—The coal seams appearing above the surface in this county are mostly too thin to be worked systematically, and no coal is mined in the county at the present time except by stripping The coal at Dr. WILKIE'S, just over the line in Jefferson county, attains locally a thickness of about two feet and a half, and if that thickness should prove persistent it might be worked to advantage in the usual way by a tunnel or a shallow shaft This seam probably underlays the north west corner of Hamilton county, and would be found at a depth of fifty to a hundred feet below the surface The seam above it worked by Mr JINKS, north of WILKIE'S, affords a harder coal, but it seldom exceeds a thickness of about eighteen inches, and can only be worked by stripping. The coal on Hog prairie ranges from eight to fifteen inches in thickness, and is not much worked at the present time The main coals lay at a considerable depth in this county, and may be reached by deep shafts whenever the demand for coal shall be such as to justify extensive mining operations The approximate depth to No 7 coal would probably not be more than two hundred to two hundred and fifty feet in the south part of the county, and from three hundred and fifty to four hundred in the northern portion, and No 5 may be found about a hundred feet below No 7 These depths will prove to be no serious obstacle in the way of coal mining whenever the demand for a large amount of coal shall arise

*Lime*—The thin band of limestone below the coal on Hog prairie has been burned for lime, but the bed is too thin to furnish an adequate supply for the wants of the county, and the quality is inferior to that obtained from St Louis.

*Clay and Sand*—Clay suitable for brick making is abundant in every neighborhood, and may be obtained from the subsoil of the upland almost anywhere that it is required, and sand suitable for mortar and cement is also abundant

*Mineral Springs*—There is a Chalybeate spring one and a half mile east of McLeansboro, the water of which is strongly charged with carbonate of iron The water in Dr DEFOE'S well, in McLeansboro, is also highly charged with mineral substances, of which the following qualitative analysis has been furnished by Prof Cox

| | | |
|---|---|---|
| Neutral to test paper | Sulphate of lime | Sulphate of protoxyd of iron |
| Chloride of magnesia | Sulphate of magnesia | Carbonate of lime |
| Chloride of sodium | Sulphate of alumina | Carbonate of magnesia |

Mr J M McDANIEL'S mineral spring north of town, is a strong, saline, sulphureted water, that would probably prove beneficial in cases of general debility The water in Dr DEFOE'S well probably derives its mineral properties from the shale overlaying the thin coal that outcrops on Hog prairie, as that coal and the overlaying shale was passed through in sinking the well, and the two springs above named may derive their mineral ingredients from the same source Possibly this shale may be the same that imparts its mineral properties to the water at several localities in Wayne county, especially west and north of Fairfield

*Soil and Agriculture*—On the main branch of North Fork and on some of the smaller streams in this county there are belts of alluvial bottoms of variable width, that were originally covered with a heavy body of most excellent timber. These lands possess a very rich soil, usually a sandy loam, and when cleared and brought under cultivation they are the most productive lands in the county The prairies are small, and occupy the highlands forming the water shed between the streams The soil is a chocolate colored clay loam of average quality, and produces fair crops of corn, wheat, oats, grass, etc Some of the best timbered uplands are equally as productive as the prairie, especially those on which the timber growth consists in part of black walnut, elm, linden, sugar maple, wild cherry, etc, in addition to the common varieties of oak and hickory The oak ridges along the breaks of some of the streams have a thin soil with a stiff clay subsoil, and need the frequent application of artificial stimulants, in the way of manures, or by fallowing and plowing under green crops, to retain their productive qualities. These lands will produce good crops of wheat and clover, and by judicious management may easily be made to repay the labor of the well skilled husbandman. As an agricultural region this county ranks favorably with those adjacent in Southern Illinois, and the completion of the St. Louis and Southeastern railroad gives to the products of the county an easy access to the St Louis market, or that of the large cities on the Ohio and the Lower Mississippi rivers.

## CHAPTER VII.

### WAYNE AND CLAY COUNTIES

Wayne county embraces an area of seven hundred and twenty square miles, and is bounded on the north by Clay and Richland counties, on the east by Richland and Edwards, on the south by White and Hamilton, and on the west by Jefferson and Marion It is located on the southern border of the prairie region, and at least three quarters of its surface was originally timbered land The prairies are mostly small, the largest being that in the northern portion of the county between Elm creek and Skillet Fork. The principal streams in the county are the Little Wabash, and Elm creek, its principal western affluent, which drains the eastern division, and Skillet Fork, with its numerous small branches which flow through the south-western part of the county

The surface is generally rolling and elevated from fifty to a hundred feet above the beds of the streams. The bottoms on Skillet Fork and Little Wabash are rather low and flat and heavily timbered.

The geological features of this county are very similar to those of Wabash and Edwards, the drift deposits and upper Coal Measures being the only formations exposed In the southern portion of the county the drift clays seldom exceed a thickness of fifteen to twenty feet, and in sinking wells the bed rock is often found at a depth of ten or twelve feet below the surface. Towards the northern boundary of the county they are somewhat heavier, and on Elm creek there are bluffs thirty feet or more in hight that seem to be composed entirely of drift Here the lower portion consists of the bluish-gray hard-pan that has been more particularly described in the report on the more northerly counties, where it is sometimes found from fifty to seventy five feet or more in thickness The upper portion of these superficial deposits may be represented along the bluffs of the Little Wabash by a few feet of loess, but generally it consists of yellowish brown gravelly clays and sand, with numerous rounded pebbles and occasionally bowlders of metamorphic rock of moderate size. Locally the gravelly clays are tinged a reddish-brown color, with the red oxyd of iron, derived probably from the decomposition of a ferruginous sandstone that forms the bed rock in many places in the southern part of the county The undulations of the surface often take the form of long ridges from thirty to forty feet in hight, with a direction nearly parallel with the courses of the streams These ridges usually have a nucleus of sandstone or shale, but their sides are so gently sloping and the drift clays cover them so evenly, that the bed rock is seldom exposed to view. The streams are sluggish and meander through wide, flat valleys, seldom showing any outcrop of the bed rock along their courses. This renders the construction of continuous sections very difficult, and the determination of the true sequence of the strata can only be made in a general way, by the examination of isolated outcrops.

## *Coal Measures.*

At the iron bridge on the Little Wabash, on the stage road from Fairfield to Albion, the following section is to be seen on the east bank of the stream

| | Feet |
|---|---|
| Sandstone partly in regular beds and partly massive | 25 |
| Pebbly conglomerate, with fragments of coal and mineral charcoal | 2 to 4 |
| Black laminated shale with concretions of bituminous limestone | 3 |
| Dove colored clay shale with fossil ferns | 2 to 3 |
| Shaly sandstone appearing some distance below | 3 to 4 |

No fossils were found here that would enable me to fix the horizon of these beds, but they presented nearly the same lithological characters as the outcrop at Hamicker's old mill on the Bonpass, in Edwards county. At Beech Bluff, three or four miles above the bridge, the sandstone is more massive, and extends to the river level, showing no outcrop of the underlaying beds

At Massillon, on the west bank of the Little Wabash, on the N. W. qr of sec 15, T 1 S, R. 9 E, the bluff is composed mainly of sandstone and sandy shale, with a few feet of argillaceous shales near the river level containing several bands of clay iron ore. This outcrop seems to be identical with that at the old ford three miles above in Edwards county, and it is quite probable the thin coal found there is here a little below the river bed. A thin coal is found here in the sandstone some twenty feet or more above the river level, but it is probably only a local deposit or "pocket," such as may be frequently met with in the sandstones of the Coal Measures

Mill Shoals is situated on the Skillet Fork, just over the line in White county, but the section made in this vicinity is partly in Wayne, and is as follows

| | Feet |
|---|---|
| Sandstone in thin beds—partial exposure of about | 6 |
| Bituminous shale with streak of impure coal near the top | 2½ to 3 |
| Sandstone and sandy shale | 40 to 50 |

| | Feet |
|---|---|
| Space unexposed | 15 to 20 |
| Hard shaly sandstone in the bank of Skillet Fork | 3 to 4 |
| Hard, black laminated slate, passing locally into clay shale | 6 to 8 |
| Shale, with a thin coal | 2 to 3 |
| Hard, fine grained limestone without fossils | 2 to 3 |
| Greenish, pebbly shale | 2 |
| Sandy shale | 1 |

The three upper beds in the foregoing section are found in Wayne county about three quarters of a mile north east of the village. Prof. COX reports a section six miles south east of Fairfield, which seems to be nearly a repetition of that at Mill Shoals, as follows

| | Ft |
|---|---|
| "Yellow clay and drift | 15 |
| Sandstone and locally some shale | 45 |
| Gray silicious shale | 10 |
| Thin coal | — |
| Limestone without fossils | 2" |

These two sections will give a general idea of the prevailing character of the rocks in the south part of Wayne county The following is a section of a well bored for oil by Major COLLINS on sec. 25, T 2, R 7

| | Ft | In |
|---|---|---|
| Soil and subsoil | 3 | |
| Sandstone | 50 | |
| Slate—(shale ?) | 27 | |
| Coal | 3 | 6 |
| Clay and blue shale | 2 | |
| Hard gritty rock | 4 | |
| Hard yellow rock | 1 | |
| Hard sandstone | 8 to 10 | |
| Dark slate—(shale?) | 28 | |
| White sandstone | 66 | |
| Black shale | 4 | 6 |
| | 207 | |

It is proper to state here again what we have already said on more than one occasion, that reports of oil wells are to be taken with due allowance, in consideration of the fact that the persons having the work in charge were seldom qualified to determine the true character of the beds through which their drill was passing, and we see in the above section that no attempt was made to define the character of two beds of hard rock, while the beds denominated slate were probably shale, with possibly a thin bed of slate intercalated therein In this way bituminous slate is often mistaken for coal, and where the substance is reduced to an impalpable powder by the drill no one but an expert can fully determine the one from the other by the material brought up in the sand pump

At Mr BLACK's place, about two miles north west of Fairfield, there is an outcrop of hard, dark, bluish gray limestone, weathering to a buff color, which is overlaid by clay shale, with a thin coal or bituminous shale intercalated therein, as indicated by a streak of smutty material to be seen a few feet above the limestone. A thin coal, sometimes as much as eighteen inches in thickness, occurs at another locality under a limestone similar to this, and the same may possibly be found here by digging a few feet below the rock. The limestone has been quarried here as well as on the adjoining farm for building stone and for lime, and ranges from two to three feet in thickness.

On Mr. J. H. THOMAS' place, on sec. 17, T. 1 S., R. 8 E., a thin coal has been found below a limestone similar to that above mentioned. The coal was opened a few years since by sinking a shaft some 15 or 20 feet in depth, and the coal is reported to have been 18 inches thick, and the limestone two feet. The shaly portion of the limestone contained a few fossils, among which we identified *Orthis carbonaria*, *Spirifer cameratus*, *Chonetes Verneuiliana*s and *Lophophyllum proliferum*.

On Mr. E. PILCHER's land, on sec. 20 of the same township, a bed of black shale crops out on a hill side at an elevation considerably above the coal shaft above mentioned, and was penetrated to the depth of fifteen feet in search of coal, but without finding it. On the opposite side of the hill, and below the level of the black shale, a calcareo-silicious rock has been quarried for building stone. It has a slaty structure, and is filled with fragments of broken plants, and appears to be the exact equivalent of the arenaceous limestone found at Mr. BODEN's place two miles and a half south of Flora. The bituminous shale at Mr. PILCHER's place contains rounded bowlders of black limestone that weather to a bluish dove color, and similar concretions were seen at the exposure south of Flora, which leaves no reasonable doubt of the identity of the beds at these points. A short distance south of Mr. PILCHER's land limestone was formerly quarried for lime burning, but the outcrop is now covered up. The relative position of the beds above described is indicated in the following section:

| | Ft. | In. |
|---|---|---|
| Bituminous shale, with concretions of black limestone | 15 to 20 | |
| Slaty arenaceous limestone, with broken plants | 2 to 4 | |
| Shale partially exposed | 10 to 15 | |
| Dark limestone | 2 | |
| Shale (thickness not determined) | | |
| Coal | 1 | 6 |

This is probably coal No. 13 of the general section.

On Mrs. WILLIAMS' place on the N. W. qr. of sec. 29, T. 1 S., R. 7 E., about seven miles north-west of Fairfield, there is an outcrop of 15 to 20 feet of sandy and argillaceous shale, containing numerous bands of kidney iron ore of good quality. A thin coal has been passed through in digging wells in this neighborhood, and either underlays these shales entirely or is intercalated in them. This outcrop closely resembles that at McDANIELS' place near the north line of the county, hereafter to be mentioned, and the well water in this vicinity is impregnated with epsom salts, like wells and springs at the locality above mentioned. Between this locality and Fairfield, and about three miles a little south of west from the town, an even bedded sandstone is quarried for building purposes similar to that at Hoag's quarry north of Xenia This sandstone probably underlays the shales outcropping at the Williams place three or four miles to the westward, and the coal there is either a local deposit or else represents coal No 14 of the general section.

On sec. 21, T 2 N. R. 6 E, in the bluffs of Bear creek, near the north line of the county, a massive sandstone outcrops for some distance along the bluffs of the stream in perpendicular cliffs from twenty to thirty feet in hight. This sandstone was struck in the boring at Flora at the depth of about sixty feet, and was penetrated to the depth of eighty four feet The outcrops on Bear creek probably represent only the lower portion of the bed.

On sec 27 T 2 N, R 6 E, argillaceous and sandy shales with bands of kidney iron ore crop out in the slopes of the hills at various points, showing an aggregate thickness of twenty feet or more, with a bituminous shale or impure coal near the top of the exposure A well sunk here struck a vein of water at the depth of twenty one feet so strong that it soon rose to the surface and has been flowing freely to the present time It has a strong taste of epsom salts, and produces an effect similar to that drug upon those who use it At Mr Eli McDaniel's place, adjoining the above, a spring of the same kind of water is found, somewhat stronger in mineral properties than that in the well The water here seems to derive its mineral properties from the bed of argillaceous shale which forms the bed rock in this vicinity, as wells sunk in the overlaying sandstone afford pure water

The following additional notes and sections are reported by Prof Cox in this county "At Liberty they pass through sandstone in digging wells from ten to forty feet, and obtain good water On sec 30, T 2, R. 7, limestone is obtained for building and for lime Bed three feet thick, upper part shaly, contains *Productus longispinus, Macrocheilus inhabilis, Athyris subtilita, Productus costatus* and joints of *Crinoidea.* The same limestone is exposed at Whitaker's, on sec 25, T 2, R 7. A thin coal is usually found beneath the limestone, and a thin, impure coal or bituminous shale is frequently seen in the shales above it Clay iron ore occurs in a grayish shale seven miles north of Fairfield, exposed by a wash on a hill side On sec 34, T 1 S, R 9 E, the following beds are seen

| | Ft | In |
|---|---|---|
| Heavy bedded sandstone | 25 | |
| Arenaceous shale | 10 | |
| Black slaty shale | 2 | |
| Pyritiferous shale with fragments of shells | 0 | 3 |
| Fire clay (good quality) | 1 | |
| Clay shale | 0 | 6 |
| Shaly sandstone in river bed | 2" | |

From the foregoing sections and remarks it will be seen that there is but little diversity in the character of the rocks exposed in this county. They probably represent a total thickness of one hundred and seventy-five to two hundred feet or more, comprising mainly sandstones and shales, most of which decompose readily on exposure, and are therefore seldom found in bold outcrops

## *Economical Geology.*

*Building Stone*—Sandstone of a fair quality for building purposes is tolerably abundant, and quarries have been opened in nearly every township in the county. Three miles a little south of west from Fairfield, an excellent sandstone is quarried on a small branch tributary to Skillet Fork. The rock is in smooth even layers, and resembles the sandstone of Hoag's quarry, near Xenia Along the Little Wabash a heavy bedded sandstone is found throughout its course in the south-eastern part of this county, which, from the bold cliffs it forms at many points along the bluffs of the stream will no doubt afford a large amount of durable building material Six miles south-east of Fairfield a good flag sandstone is quarried in large slabs six inches thick Three and a half miles north of Jefferson, on sec 30, T 1 N., R 6 E, a grayish sandstone of good quality is quarried in large slabs from a foot to eighteen inches in thickness A similar stone is also quarried by Mr PHILLIPS, on sec. 16, T 1 N, R. 7. E. These are some of the most valuable quarries opened at the present time, but others equally good may be opened at various places in the county as the wants of the people may require. The limestone over the eighteen inch coal seam has been quarried at almost every point where it outcrops, but the bed is thin, and the supply to be obtained from it, without too great expense in stripping, is rather limited

*Coal*—The only coal in the county that promises to be of any value for practical mining, is the eighteen inch seam north and north east of Fairfield This might be worked in a limited way, either by stripping or by an inclined tunnel near its outcrop, but the seam is too thin to furnish an adequate supply for the general market. The main coals of the lower measures may be reached in the southern portion of the county at depths varying from three to five hundred feet, and in the northern portion from five to eight hundred.

*Iron ore*—Bands of iron ore of good quality occur at several places in the shales of this county, and have been noted in the sections already given They seem to be in sufficient quantity at several localities to eventually become of some economical value In Great Britain, bands of six to eight inches in thickness are said to be worked successfully, and we find many localities in our Coal Measures where from twelve to eighteen inches of good ore can be obtained from a vertical thickness of five or six feet of shale. The shale containing the iron ore observed in this county underlays a considerable area in the central and western portions, mainly in ranges 6 and 7 east At Mrs. WILLIAMS' place, on the N W. qr. of sec 29, T 1 S, R 7 E, iron ore of good quality seemed to be quite abundant, and also at several places on the ravines near Mr McDANIEL's place, not far from the north line of the county. Prof Cox also notes an outcrop of clay iron ore in a grayish shale seven miles north of Fairfield, and also on sec. 15, T 1 N, R. 8 E

*Potters' Clay*—A good clay suitable for pottery or fire brick was found on sec 34, T 1 S, R 9 E, but at the outcrop it was only one foot thick Possibly it may be found at some other locality near by, where it is thick enough to be utilized for the manufacture of pottery or fire brick.

*Clay and Sand*—Materials for brick can be obtained from the subsoil of the uplands almost anywhere in the county, and from the abundant supply of wood for fuel, brick can be cheaply made in sufficient quantity to supply all future demands for this indispensable building material

*Soil and Agriculture*—The soil in this county is mainly a dark ash-gray or chocolate colored clay loam, less highly charged with organic matters or humus than the black prairie soils of Central Illinois, but yielding fair crops of corn, wheat, oats and grass, both clover and timothy, and with judicious treatment will retain its fertility without any expense for artificial fertilizers. The ridges afford excellent fruit farms, and apples, peaches, pears, cherries and the small fruits may be grown here in the greatest abundance The cultivation of the grape has only been attempted in a limited way, but the broken timbered lands could be profitably cultivated in vineyards. As an agricultural region this county ranks favorably with the adjoining portions of Southern Illinois

CLAY COUNTY embraces a surface area of about four hundred and sixty six square miles, and is bounded on the north by Effingham and Jasper counties, on the east by Jasper and Richland, on the south by Wayne, and on the west by Marion and Fayette The Little Wabash river runs diagonally across the county from north west to southeast, and with its affluents, Elm creek on the south, and Muddy creek on the north east, drain nearly the whole of its area The surface of the county is nearly equally divided into prairie and timbered land, the latter forming wide belts along the streams, and the former occupying the highest areas between them The difference of level between the creek bottoms and the adjacent highlands is not very great, probably nowhere exceeding fifty to seventy five feet Locally the streams are bordered with precipitous bluffs from forty to fifty feet in hight, and at other points there is a gradually sloping surface from the bottoms up to the level of the adjacent prairie The bottoms along the Little Wabash vary in width from one to three miles, and are subject to overflow during the annual spring freshets, and hence have not been brought under cultivation, but are still covered with primeval forests of excellent timber. The alluvial soil of these bottoms is exceedingly rich, and if subdued and brought under cultivation would produce abundant crops of corn, and all the cereals usually cultivated in this latitude.

*Drift Deposits*—The uplands are covered with blue and yellow drift clays ranging from ten to forty feet in thickness, and possibly along the bluffs of some of the streams they may attain even a greater thickness than that above indicated The surface of the bed rock was often eroded into valleys of considerable extent before the drift was deposited, and being subsequently filled with these gravelly clays, the deposit is not uniform, but is much thicker in some places than in others

In the borings at Xenia and Flora, the bed rock was struck at the depth of thirteen or fourteen feet, and generally upon the prairie in sinking wells, the drift clays and gravel beds are found to range from ten to twenty feet. In the bluffs at Elm creek south of Flora and at some other points in the county, they attain a thickness of thirty to forty feet The upper part is generally a brown or buff gravelly clay with occasional bowlders of a foot or two in diameter, and the lower part where the deposit attains its greatest thickness consists of bluish or ash-gray clay or hard pan as it is usually denominated, from its being more compact and harder to penetrate than the brown clay above it. Bowlders of granite, sienite, greenstone and quartzite are not uncommon, and occasionally nuggets of native copper and small specimens of galena are to be met with in these gravelly clays in this county.

*Stratified Rocks*—The rock formations proper in this county all belong to the upper Coal Measures, and the only seam in the county that has been worked to any extent is No 16 of the general section, and the highest seam but one known in the State There have been three borings made in the county, one at Xenia and two in the vicinity of Flora, but none of them were carried down far enough to reach the main workable coals of the lower measures The Flax mill boring on the eastern edge of Flora, is reported as follows

| | | Ft | In. |
|---|---|---|---|
| 1 | Soil and drift clay | 13 | |
| 2 | Sandy shale and gray sandstone | 47 | |
| 3 | Black shale and coal, No 14? | 3 | |
| 4 | Hard sandstone | 84 | |
| 5 | Clay shale (soapstone) | 33 | |
| 6 | Black shale | 3 | |
| 7 | Shaly limestone | 2 | 6 |
| 8 | Coal? No 13? | 7 | 3 |
| | | 192 | 9 |

A shaft was commenced near where this boring was made, and carried down to the depth of one hundred and fifteen feet, mainly through sandstone and sandy shale The flow of water in the shaft was so strong as to seriously interfere with the prosecution of the work, and finally filled it to within about five feet of the surface of the ground, where it still remains. The shaft terminated in the heavy bed of sandstone No 4 of the preceding section Another boring two miles to the westward of this, near the Fair Grounds, was reported as follows

| | | Ft | In |
|---|---|---|---|
| 1 | Soil and drift clay | 13 | |
| 2 | Sandstone | 40 | |
| 3 | Clay shale (soapstone) | 7 | |
| 4 | Hard gray sandstone | 35 | |
| 5 | Hard rock (probably sandstone) | 3 | |
| 6 | Sandstone | 47 | |
| 7 | Impure limestone | 4 | |
| 8 | Black shale | 8 | |
| 9 | Limestone | 8 | 6 |
| 10 | Clay shale (soapstone) | 37 | |
| | | 205 | 6 |

These borings commence at least forty or fifty feet below the coal and limestone north west of Louisville, and were discontinued before reaching the horizon of any workable coal The boring at Xenia was carried to the depth of 450 feet passing through three thin coals, one of which was reported to be four feet thick. The following is the section of this boring as furnished by Captain DYER

| | | Ft | In |
|---|---|---|---|
| 1 | Soil and drift | 14 | |
| 2 | Clay shale (soapstone) | 92 | |
| 3 | Bluish gray sandstone | 31 | |
| 4 | Coal No 13? | | 9 |
| 5 | Crevice? (probably soft fire clay) | 1 | 6 |
| 6 | Clay shale (soapstone) | 3 | |
| 7 | Limestone | 1 | 6 |
| 8 | Conglomerate | 3 | |
| 9 | Bluish gray sandstone | 4 | |
| 10 | Blue shale | 64 | |
| 11 | Hard rock | 1 | |
| 12 | Black shale, No 12? | 9 | |
| 13 | Sandstone | 12 | |
| 14 | Blue shale | 14 | 6 |
| 15 | Coal No 11? | 4 | |
| 16 | Fire clay | | 6 |
| 17 | Sandstone | 15 | |
| 18 | Pebbly rock | 2 | |
| 19 | Shale | 2 | 6 |
| 20 | Blue shale | 29 | |
| 21 | Micaceous sandstone | 4 | |
| 22 | White sandstone | 4 | |
| 23 | Rock with a few fossils | 1 | |
| 24 | Coal, No 10? | 1 | 6 |
| 25 | Fire clay | 2 | 6 |
| 26 | Sandstone | 11 | 6 |
| 27 | Blue shale | 4 | |
| 28 | Sandstone | 2 | |

| No. | Stratum | Ft | In |
|---|---|---|---|
| 29 | Black shale | 15 | |
| 30 | Flint rock? | 10 | |
| 31 | Shale | 23 | |
| 32 | Hard rock | 4 | |
| 33 | Shale | 11 | |
| 34 | Sandstone | 7 | |
| 35 | Clay shale | 6 | |
| 36 | Sandstone | 14 | |
| 37 | Blue shale | 6 | |
| 38 | Gray sandstone | 14 | |
| | | 444 | 9 |

So far as it is possible to correlate this section with what is known of the upper Coal Measure strata of Central Illinois, I am inclined to believe that the 10 foot bed of hard rock described in the boring as *flint* is the limestone of Shoal creek and Carlinville, which is usually a very hard rock, and that the succeeding coals are 10, 11, 12, and 13 of the general section The small coal outcropping north of Hoag's quarries about two miles, at JACOB SPIKER'S place, is probably No 15, and the next succeeding seam would be the Nelson coal of Effingham county, which outcrops in this county about two miles north-west of Louisville, and at several points north-west of there in the bluffs of the Little Wabash and its tributaries, and will be more particularly described further on in this chapter

One mile north of Xenia a fine evenly bedded freestone is extensively quarried by Mr HOAG The rock is a rather fine-grained sandstone in even layers from two inches to two feet in thickness, and can be easily quarried in large slabs. It is partly brown and partly of a bluish gray color, dresses freely and hardens after being taken from the quarry, and is the best building stone known in this portion of the State The rock is as evenly bedded as the magnesian limestone of Joliet, and the thin layers make good flagstones, while the heavier beds afford a fine quality of cut stone for ashlars, window caps and sills, lintels, etc. A large quantity of this stone is furnished to the city of St Louis, where it bears an excellent reputation as a superior building stone About eight feet in thickness of this freestone is worked in this quarry, the heaviest beds ranging from one foot to thirty inches in thickness This sandstone is overlaid in the vicinity of this quarry with twenty to twenty five feet of soft brown shale with numerous bands of iron ore, closely resembling the shales on the waters of Raccoon creek south west of Flora and described in the report on Wayne county The water of a well sunk in this shale, about half a mile north of Hoag's quarry, has the same taste as that at McGannon's spring near the north line of Wayne county, and I have no doubt the shales are identical. The shale here contains numerous bands of iron ore of good quality, and several points were observed on the small branches north east of the quarry, and not more than a mile distant, where from twelve to sixteen inches of good ore could be obtained from a vertical thickness of four or five feet of shale. The thin coal at Spiker's place overlays this shale, and the beds exposed there gave the following section:

| | | Ft | In |
|---|---|---|---|
| Bituminous shale | | 4 | |
| Hard blue limestone (septaria) | 6 inches to 1 | | 6 |
| Blue shale | 1 ft to 1 | | 6 |
| Coal | | | 6 |
| Fire clay and clay shale | | | ? |

A few well preserved fossils were found in the septaria over the coal, among which were *Nautilus occidentalis*, *Macrocheilus inhabilis*, *Productus pertenuis*, *Spirifer cameratus*, *Myalina sub quadrata*, *Chonetes*, joints of *Crinoidea*, etc. All the beds exposed from Hoag's quarry to this point are probably above those passed through at the Xenia bore.

At Mr. JOHN LAMKINS' place about two miles north-west of Louisville, on the N W qr of sec 20, T 4, R. 6, there is an outcrop of gray limestone underlaid by a coal seam which ranges from twelve to eighteen inches in thickness, and is worked by Mr LAMKINS in a limited way, affording a coal of fair quality. The limestone over the coal is a compact, hard, gray rock, ranging from three to four feet in thickness, containing numerous fossils that may be obtained from the calcareous shaly layers associated with the limestone, in a fair state of preservation, The section here is as follows

| | Ft | In |
|---|---|---|
| Buff shale with iron bands | 5 to 8 | |
| Compact gray limestone | 3 to 4 | |
| Calcareous shale | 2 to 3 | |
| Coal | 1 to 1 | 6 |
| Clay shale or fire clay | 1 to 2 | |
| Sandy shales | | ? |

The fossils observed here include the following species *Orthis carbonaria*, *Fusulina cylindrica*, *Spirifer cameratus*, *Spiriferina Kentuckensis*, *Lophophyllum proliferum*, *Productus longispinus*, *P. costatus*, and *P punctatus*.

On sec 10, T 4, R 5, this limestone is found on Crooked creek but little above the creek bed, and the coal if found here at all would be below the water level.

On the S. W. qr. of sec. 25, T 5, R 5, about two miles east of Larkinsville, the coal and the overlaying limestone outcrop in the bluffs of Dismal creek. The limestone is here from four to five feet in thickness, and the coal is reported to be about the same as at Lamkins' place There is here from ten to twelve feet of sandy shale exposed in the bluffs of the creek below the coal.

On sec 16, T 4, R 5, near the north-west corner of the section, a bed of hard shaly sandstone outcrops in the banks of a small branch, overlaid by a slaty bituminous shale a foot or more in thickness, containing lenticular masses of black limestone or septaria. The shaly sandstone was about three feet in thickness, and it probably overlays the limestone and coal at Lamkins' place, though the exact connection between them was not determined.

On the S. E. qr. of sec 21, T. 4, R 6, a sandstone quarry has been opened where the rock shows a perpendicular face from four to six feet in thickness The sandstone is overlaid by a buff colored shale succeeded by a black laminated shale containing concretions of black or dark-blue limestone or septaria, containing a few fossils.

On section 16, in the same township, a hard sandstone is found in the bluffs of Crooked creek which resembles the rock at the quarry on section 21, and it is here underlaid by shaly sandstone and shale to the water level If these sandstones are identical the section here would show the following order of succession

| | Feet. |
|---|---|
| Black laminated shale with septaria | 5 to 6 |
| Buff or drab shale | 6 to 8 |
| Sandstone (quarry rock) | 4 to 6 |
| Sandy shale partial exposure | 12 to 15 |

Just below the mouth of Crooked creek, in the bluffs of the Little Wabash, we find the following section

| | Feet |
|---|---|
| Soil and drift clay | 12 to 15 |
| Soft shales partly argillaceous | 15 |
| Irregularly bedded sandstone | 3 to 4 |
| Sandy shales | 12 to 15 |

These beds outcrop at intervals along the bluffs of the stream from the mouth of Crooked creek to Louisville, and at the old mill dam we find nearly a repetition of the above section, as follows:

| | Ft | In |
|---|---|---|
| Black laminated shale | 2 to 3 | |
| Coal | | 6 |
| Buff and blue shales—partial exposure | 6 to 12 | |
| Irregularly bedded hard sandstone | 1 to 6 | |
| Sandy shales extending below the river bed | 10 to 12 | |

The thin coal in the above section is locally overlaid by a few inches of chocolate colored shale, passing into a hard blue limestone containing a few fossils, among which we were able to identify the following *Productus Prattenianus*, *Chonetes granulifera*, *Lingula umbonata?* *Pleurotomaria carbonaria*, *Macrocheilus*, etc This thin coal is probably identical with that at Mr SPIKER's three miles north of Xenia, and is either a local seam or else represents coal No 15 of the general section The beds on the Little Wabash at Louisville underlay the limestone and coal at Lamkins' place and on Dismal creek, but the exposures were too isolated to obtain a complete section of the strata.

Four miles south west of Flora, on a branch of Raccoon creek, sandstone and sandy shale outcrops along the bluffs of the stream for some distance. The bed is altogether some ten or twelve feet in thickness, the upper part a sandy micaceous shale passing downward into micaceous sandstone interstratified with the shales. The sandstone strata vary in thickness from six to fourteen inches, and when freshly quarried the rock is rather soft, but hardens on exposure and becomes a durable building stone The quarry opened here belongs to Mr. JOHN McGANNON, and is located on sec 3, T 2, R 6 E. On section 4, in the same township, a massive sandstone outcrops in the bluffs of Raccoon, in an apparently solid bed, projecting in some places several feet over the bed of the stream by the wearing away of the lower strata

On Bear creek, another tributary of Elm creek, just over the line in Wayne county, on sec 21, T 2 S, R 6 E, this massive sandstone is found in perpendicular cliffs of 20 to 30 feet in hight above the bed of the stream. This is probably a part of the sandstone passed through in the shaft and borings at Flora, and it forms the bed rock over a considerable area in the south part of Clay and the northern part of Wayne counties

On Willow branch, about six miles south west of Flora, a blue argillaceous shale is found containing several bands of argillaceous iron ore of good quality. The exposure of shale is twenty feet or more in thickness, with a streak of smutty coal or bituminous shale near the top of the exposure The water that percolates through the shale becomes highly impregnated with salts, and acts as an effective cathartic on those using it freely This shale probably overlays the massive sandstone on Raccoon creek, but we found no continuous outcrop that would enable any one to determine, definitely, their true relations

The following notes of localities I did not visit are reported from the notes of Prof Cox "On a branch of Skillet Fork on sec 32, T. 4, R 5, found the following beds

| | Ft |
|---|---|
| Drift clay | 4 to 5 |
| Blue argillaceous shale | 8 |
| Bituminous shale and limestone in the bed of the creek | 1 |

Crystals of selenite (sulphate of lime) of small size were found disseminated through the shale, and are reported to be abundant at many points on this branch and also on the main creek

On Mr. R. T ROBERTS' place, two miles and a half south of Clay City, a thin coal is found underlaid by fire clay and argillaceous shale. The section of the exposure here is as follows.

| | Ft | In |
|---|---|---|
| Soil and drift | 10 | |
| Shale | 0 | 6 |
| Coal | 0 | 6 |
| Fire clay | 0 | 4 |
| Argillaceous shale | 1 | |
| Silicious shale | 2 | |

In digging a well on the the top of the hill about a quarter of a mile from this outcrop, Mr ROBERTS went through from four to six inches of fossiliferous limestone which probably belongs above the coal

Three quarters of a mile south of Maysville is a sandstone quarry owned by HUGH MILLER The rock is of a yellowish gray color, and the exposure from seven to eight feet thick The so called "salt pond" is on the south half of sec 4, T 3, R 8, and is a bog surrounded by high ground Sticks may be thrust into it through the spongy mass to the depth of ten or fifteen feet, and cattle, and formerly wild animals also, resorted here for water.

At Moore's quarry, on sec 14, T 4, R. 6, there is a fine grained buff sandstone that was used in the foundation, and also for caps and sills for the Masonic Hall building in Louisville There are three layers of the rock exposed from 8 to 10 inches thick, over laid by two feet of siliceous shale

At J ELKINS' place, on sec 36, T 5, R 5, the following section was found.

| | Ft |
|---|---|
| Soil and drift | 2 |
| Gray argillaceous shale | 8 |
| Limestone in the bed of the creek | ? |

Down the creek the limestone is two feet thick, the upper part full of encrinite stems and *Fusulina cylindrica* The limestone is quite compact and will take a good polish Still lower down on the creek there is a thin coal below the limestone This limestone is again seen on Limestone creek, on sec. 34, T 6, R 4" near the north line of the county."

The limestone above mentioned is undoubtedly the same as that found over the coal at Lamkins' mine near Louisville, and on Dismal creek east of Larkinsburg, and a limestone very similar in appearance is found on Muddy creek near the north-east corner of the county, where it is quarried both for lime and for building stone.

## *Economical Geology.*

*Coal*—The only coal seam in the county that promises to be of any value for mining operations is that at Mr. LAMKIN'S place northwest of Louisville, and this is so unevenly developed that there are probably but few localities in the county where it will prove to be of any practical value At some points it affords from 18 to 20 inches of good coal and possibly may thicken at some localities to a little more than that, while at others it thins out to a few inches or is wanting altogether, and its place is only indicated by a thin streak of bituminous shale. Where well developed it affords a very good quality of coal, and may be worked to advantage in a limited way to supply the local demand. I believe it to be the same as the Nelson coal found in the south west corner of Effingham county, which is No 16 of the general section and the highest workable coal in the State.

The main coals of the lower Coal Measures are probably from eight hundred to a thousand feet below the surface in any part of this county, and borings or shafts should not be encouraged unless parties are prepared to go to that depth The coal seam reported to have been found four feet in thickness in the boring at Xenia, could not have been lower in the series than No 11 or 12, and if its thickness was correctly ascertained it is probably only a local thickening of one of these upper coals Having been present at the time the drill passed through this coal in the Xenia boring, I can certify to the excellent quality of the samples brought up in the sand pump, but I could not testify as to the thickness of the seam The distance to the lower coals is, of course, no serious impediment to their being mined successfully whenever the demand for coal shall be such as to justify such an expenditure of capital as will be required to open up a mine at this depth.

*Building Stone*—Sandstone of fair quality for building purposes is found at several localities in the county, and the quarries near Xenia, described on a preceding page, afford a freestone of superior quality, that is extensively quarried for exportation to St. Louis and other points where a stone suitable for architectural display may be required. This rock has a very even texture, dresses freely, and can be easily cut into elaborate designs for ornamental work. A rock similar to this in appearance outcrops on Raccoon creek south of Flora, which probably belongs to the same bed, as the general trend of the strata appears to be from north-west to south east Other sandstones that afford a fair quality of building stone outcrop in various parts of the county as has already been noted in the preceding pages The limestone over the eighteen inch coal seam in the northern part of the county will afford a very hard and durable stone, but requires a greater amount of labor to quarry it and prepare it for use than the sandstone found in the same neighborhood, and hence has been but little used.

*Lime*—The only rock in the county that seems at all adapted to the manufacture of lime is the limestone above mentioned as overlaying the eighteen inch coal at Lamkins' mine, and outcropping at several other points in the north part of the county This rock varies in thickness from two to four feet, and seems usually pure enough to afford a fair quality of lime, and has been burned for that purpose in a limited way at two or three points in the county.

*Iron Ore*—Bands of iron ore of good quality intercalated in a bed of shale was observed in two or three places in the county, especially on the upper course of Elm creek, and on some small tributaries of the same stream south west of Flora and near the Wayne county line.

*Clays*—Clay suitable for pottery occurs on Mr BOTHWELL's place, one mile south of Clay City, and good brick clays may be found in almost every neighborhood in the subsoil of the uplands.

*Mineral Springs.*—At Mr SAILOR's place, about eight miles east of Louisville, on the N. E. qr. of sec 25, T. 4, R. 7, there are several springs, the waters of which have some reputation for their medicinal qualities The springs apparently have their origin in the quick-sands below the drift clays, and the water comes bubbling up very freely at numerous points along the valley of a small branch Gas escapes quite freely from these springs at intervals, giving the water the appearance of boiling under a strong heat After a short time the boiling motion ceases, and the water remains quiet until the escaping gas again sets it in motion. An analysis of this water has been made, and I was promised a copy of the result for publication in this report, but it has not come to hand.

*Soil, Timber, etc*—The soil in this county presents no marked variation from that in the adjoining counties, and need not be discussed farther in this place. Although much of the timbered land has been subdued and brought under cultivation since the first settlement of the county, the rapid growth of the remaining portion, with the addition of the brushy lands, which, since the annual fires have been kept down, have been covered with a fine growth of young timber, has nearly or quite kept up the original supply, and there is probably about as much timber in the county at the present time as there was in its early settlement.

We are indebted to Mr. H. S. WATSON and Mr S JOHNSON, of Louisville, for important information and personal assistance while prosecuting our work in this county.

# CHAPTER VIII.

## CUMBERLAND, COLES AND DOUGLAS COUNTIES

Cumberland county contains eight full and four fractional townships, making a total area of 336 square miles, and is bounded on the north by Coles county, on the east by Clark, on the south by Jasper and Effingham, and on the west by Effingham and Shelby. The Embarras river traverses the county from north to south, and this river and its tributaries are the only streams of any note within its borders The central portion of the county along the river and its affluents is well timbered, while the eastern and western portions are mainly prairie. The bottom lands along the river are usually from a half mile to a mile or more in breadth, and heavily timbered with the usual varieties of timber found growing upon the bottom lands in Central Illinois The prairie lands are from seventy five to one hundred feet above the level of the river, and are generally rolling, though occasionally tracts of level prairie are to be found

The superficial deposits of this county comprise the alluvial bottoms of the Embarras and its tributaries, and a considerable thickness of gravelly clays and hard pan which increases in depth to the northward. In the southern portion of the county the drift deposits range from twenty to forty feet in thickness, consisting mainly of brown or buff gravelly clays with numerous bowlders; but to the northward this thickness is increased to fifty or seventy five feet, the lower portion being a bluish-gray hard pan similar to that seen in Clark, and described in the report on that county Bowlders of considerable size are not uncommon, and native copper and also specimens of the sulphuret of that metal are said to have been found in the drift gravel in this county A bed of potters' clay of fair quality is found in the drift clays in the vicinity of Greenup from four to six feet in thickness, from which a fair article of stoneware is made

*Coal Measures*.—All the rock formations of this county below the drift belong to the upper Coal Measures, and include the beds intervening between the Quarry creek limestone of Clark county and the

Shelbyville coal of Shelby county, making an aggregate thickness of 200 to 250 feet. Not more than one half of these beds are exposed in the county, and we have to rely on the borings made at Greenup, and a general acquaintance with the outcrops in adjoining counties, for a full description of the strata

The following is a record of the bore made just north of the town of Greenup, by Messrs. DUNLAP & Co , in 1866, for oil

| | | Ft |
|---|---|---|
| 1 | Shale | 51 |
| 2 | Sandstone | 11 |
| 3 | Shale | 102 |
| 4 | Black bituminous and gray shale | 17 |
| 5 | Very hard rock (limestone ?) | 5 |
| 6 | Gray shale and sandstone | 69 |
| 7 | White sandstone and shale | 45 |
| 8 | Sandstone | 35 |
| | | 335 |

The very hard rock No. 5 which was found here at the depth of 181 feet is probably the Quarry creek limestone Another boring was subsequently made by Mr. TALBOT near his mill at the railroad depot, for coal, and the following is his report, given from memory:

| | | Ft | In |
|---|---|---|---|
| 1 | Soft sandstone | 15 | |
| 2 | Gray shale | 65 | |
| 3 | Black shale | 2 | |
| 4 | Hard sandstone | 8 | |
| 5 | Shale, dark colored towards the bottom | 20 | |
| 6 | Hard sandstone | 5 | |
| 7 | Shale | 8 | |
| 8 | Dark hard rock | 4 | |
| 9 | Shale | 13 | |
| 10 | Hard rock, probably limestone | 3 | |
| 11 | Shale | 17 | |
| 12 | Black shale | 5 | |
| 13 | Coal | 0 | 3 |
| 14 | Clay shale | 20 | |
| 15 | Black rock | 1 | 8 |
| 16 | Dark shale | 8 | |
| 17 | Black slate | 8 | |
| 18 | Coal | 0 | 3 |
| 19 | Fire clay | 4 | |
| 20 | Shale with pebbles | 16 | |
| | | 223 | 2 |

As this boring was made especially in search of coal, it is probable that closer attention was given to the character of the beds passed through than at the other, and the section reported corresponds much better with the outcrops in Clark county. The hard rock, which I presume represents the Quarry creek limestone, was found in the Talbot boring at a depth of 140, while at the Dunlap well it was reported at 181 feet, although the latter well was commenced at a level at least ten to fifteen feet below the former, hence we may infer that the reported depth of the boring was no more reliable than the character of the strata that were penetrated Both these borings commence below the Fusulina limestone which outcrops in the bluffs of the Embarras from the bridge west of Greenup to the north line of the county

In the bluffs of the Embarras, one mile west of Greenup, we find the following section at the bridge on the old National road

| | Ft | In |
|---|---|---|
| Gravelly drift clay buff yellow and ash gray | 32 | |
| Thin bedded micaceous sandstone | 6 | |
| Argillaceous shales with a streak of coaly matter | 16 | |
| Impure ferruginous limestone (*Fusulina* bed) | 1 | 6 |
| Thin bedded sandstone and sandy shales | 15 | |
| Slope covering shales to river bed | 12 | |

A mile north of the bridge the limestone thickens to three feet or more, and is a nodular gray argillaceous rock, rather more calcareous than at the bridge below, nodular and thin bedded, but containing a few of the fossils that are more abundant in it near the north line of the county This is the only limestone found in the county, and varies in thickness from 18 inches to 8 or 10 feet, or more, at the different outcrops examined. It is usually too argillaceous to slack freely when burned, and too nodular and irregularly bedded along the Embarras to furnish a good quality of building stone

The sandstone underlaying the limestone in the above section affords layers from 6 to 18 inches in thickness, and was used in the abutments for the bridge at this point, but not being carefully selected, the shaly layers soon gave way, endangering the whole structure so that it had to be abandoned

On the branch north of the town of Greenup, where the oil well was located, the following beds outcrop in the bluff on the south side of the stream

| | Feet |
|---|---|
| Yellow drift clays | 10 to 12 |
| Nodular brown impure limestone | 1½ to 2 |
| Sandy and argillaceous shales, with thin layers of sandstone to the creek bed | 35 to 40 |

A short distance above Ryan's ford, and about two miles below the north line of the county, this limestone is well exposed, showing a bench of rough, irregularly bedded, brownish gray, nodular, argillaceous limestone, from 8 to 10 feet in thickness, outcropping just above the bed of the river The upper part of the bed is of a brownish-gray, and the lower part a greenish gray color Numerous small fossils were found in the limestone at this locality, among which were the following well known species *Athyris subtilita*, *Terebratula bovidens*, *Retzia punctulifera*, *Rhynchonella Osagensis*, *Spirifer cameratus*, *S lineatus*, *S. planoconvexus*, *Fusulina cylindrica*, some undetermined corals, etc The limestone is underlaid here by a greenish clay shale, of which not more than two feet in thickness was visible above the bed of the river. Descending the river from the ford towards Greenup the limestone gradually rises in the river bluff, and four miles below Ryan's it is found about twenty feet above the river level, associated with sandstone and shale, forming the following section

| | Ft |
|---|---|
| Thin bedded nodular argillaceous limestone . | 5 |
| Evenly bedded sandstone . | 6 |
| Sandy shale with thin layers of sandstone | 15 |

The *Fusulina cylindrica* and several other species of the fossils enumerated as occurring at Ryan's ford were found here, but they were less numerous than at the other locality.

On Mr CULLUM's land south-west of Jewett, the S. E. qr. of the S W. qr of sec 26, T 9, R 8, a quarry has been opened in a hard bluish-gray micaceous sandstone, of which some 8 to 10 feet is exposed The rock is very hard and affords a durable building stone. A quarter of a mile below this quarry, on the main creek, sandy shales form the main portion of the bluff, overlaid by a hard, brittle argillaceous limestone, which was seen only in tumbling blocks, indicating a thickness of about 18 inches The beds were nowhere well exposed, but seemed to hold the following relative position .

| | Ft | In |
|---|---|---|
| Hard gray micaceous sandstone . | 8 to 10 | |
| Impure limestone . . . | 1 | 6 |
| Blue and brown sandy shales . | 25 to 30 | |

Following down the creek these lower shales appear at intervals in the bluffs of the stream nearly to the bridge south of Jewett North of the bridge towards the town several quarries have been opened in the same bed of sandstone that appears on Mr CULLUM's place.

On Long Point, a tributary of the Embarras, which enters the main river from the eastward six miles south of Greenup, we were unable to find any outcrops of rock, the bluffs of the stream being composed, so far as could be seen, of drift clays from 30 to 10 feet or more in thickness

On Webster creek, sec. 33, T. 9, R. 8, a thin coal is found from 4 to 6 inches thick, associated with the following beds

| | | Ft | In |
|---|---|---|---|
| No 1 | Blue and brown argillaceous shales . | 3 | |
| No. 2 | Band of brown argillaceous iron ore with fossils | 6 in to 0 | 8 |
| No 3 | Shale clay | 0 | 4 |
| No 4 | Coal | 0 | 6 |
| No 5 | Bituminous shale | 2 | |
| No 6 | Clay shale partially exposed . | 10 to 15 | |
| No 7 | Concretionary sandstone and sandy shale | 12 to 15 | |
| No 8 | Gray and brown impure limestone | 2 | |
| No 9 | Dark gray sandy shales . . . | 20 to 25 | |

The band of argillaceous iron stone, or more properly speaking an argillo ferruginous limestone, contains numerous fossil shells in a fine state of preservation, among which the *Euomphalus subrugosus* was most abundant, associated with *Aviculopecten carboniferus*, *Yoldia sub-*

*scitula* ? *Phillipsia scitula*, *Pleurotomaria sphærulata*, *P Grayvillensis*, *Rhynchonella Osagensis*, *Productus longispinus*, *P Lasallensis* ? *Entolium aviculatum*, *Bellerophon percarinatus*, *Polyphemopsis peracuta*, *Macrocheilus inhabilis*, *Nucula*, *Orthoceras*, *Nautilus*, *Lophophyllum proliferum*, etc

The impure limestone, No 8 of the foregoing section, I am inclined to regard as identical with the *Fusulina* bed, although I could not find the characteristic fossils in it at this locality. This limestone thins out in the south part of the county, and the most southerly outcrops observed contain few or no fossils, but the outcrops are so continuous on the Embarras and its western affluents that there seems to be no doubt that they all belong to the same formation

In Coles county this limestone continues along the valley of the Embarras at least as far north as the mouth of Brush creek, where it overlays a seam of coal, No 16 of the Illinois section, while the 6 inch coal in the foregoing section most probably represents the thin coal, or highest seam of the general section

Prof COX reports a coal seam about a quarter of a mile west of the county line in Shelby county, which from its thickness and general character agrees very well with the Shelbyville coal, or No 15 of the general section "This is on Mr HANCOCK's place on sec. 12, T 10, R. 6, where the following beds were seen

| | Ft | In |
|---|---|---|
| Blue argillaceous shale | 3 | |
| Fire clay | 0 | 3 |
| Coal | 1 | 6 |
| Slate parting | 0 | 1 |
| Coal, hard and impure | 1 | |

About 200 yards west of the point where the coal was opened, on a branch of the Little Wabash river, there was ten feet of blue argillaceous shale above the coal, which further down the stream gives place to a thick bedded sandstone"

He also reports the *Fusulina* limestone on Bear creek, sec. 22, T. 10, R 8, near Mr JOHN PRATHER'S, where the bed is 4 feet thick, overlaid by 20 feet of sandstone. At Prairie City the limestone was passed through in sinking the well at the mill, and found to be 4 feet thick, with shales above and below it.

The trend of the strata in this county is evidently very nearly north and south, as the course of the Embarras is on nearly the same geological level through this county and Coles for a distance of 25 to 30 miles or more, and the dip, if any, is apparently to the westward There are no streams in either county that intersect the general outcrop in an east and west direction, and no connected section of the outcropping formations could therefore be made The small streams do not cut through the heavy drift deposits, and hence exposures of the Coal Measures are only to be met with on the Embarras and the lower courses of its main affluents.

## *Economical Geology.*

*Coal*—No workable coal outcrops in this county, unless the seam mentioned above as occurring on the waters of the Little Wabash just over the line in Shelby county may be found in the north-west corner of Cumberland The coal below the *Fusulina* limestone in Coles county seems not to have been developed in Cumberland, and the seam above the limestone is too thin to be of any practical value. For deep mining in this county a shaft would have to be carried down from six hundred to a thousand feet to reach the main coals of the lower measures This would require an expenditure of capital that the present demand for coal in this county would scarcely justify, and hence it will probably be some years before any serious effort to reach the lower coals will be made In the counties laying west of this, including Bond, Fayette, Montgomery and Shelby, according to the report of Mr BROADHEAD, it is about six hundred feet from the Shelbyville coal (No 15) down to the Danville seam (No. 7 ?), which would be the first one of the main coals that would be reached here, and if that failed to be well developed, about a hundred feet more would have to be penetrated to reach the next workable seam below.

*Building Stone.*—The best building stone met with in this county is the sandstone south and southwest of Jewett station, and that quarried in the vicinity of Greenup, in the bluffs of the Embarras The former is a hard, gray, micaceous sandstone, that stands exposure well, and may be relied upon for bridge abutments and culverts, as it will probably resist successfully the influence of frost and moisture The other is a rather soft, brown sandstone, that will answer well for dry walls, but liable to crumble on long exposure to the elements The *Fusulina* limestone, where sufficiently thick bedded, will also furnish a fair quality of stone for rough walls, and several quarries have been opened in it in the northern and western portions of the county

*Lime*—The limestone just mentioned, which is the only rock of the kind found in the county, is too impure to make a good lime, though we saw one or two points where an attempt had been made to burn it, but evidently with indifferent success. At some points it looked as though it might possess hydraulic properties, and it is quite probable that by burning and grinding a very good water lime might be made from it

*Iron Ore*—Bands of kidney ore or carbonate of iron of a fair quality were found at several points in the shales over the *Fusulina* limestone, but in too limited quantities to be of any practical value for smelting purposes.

*Sand and Clay*—Clays suitable for making brick may be found almost anywhere in the sub-soil of the uplands, and sand for mortar or cement occurs abundantly in the valleys of the streams

*Soil and Timber*—In the southern part of the county the soil is rather thin, with a subsoil of light drab colored clay, but in the northern portion it is darker colored and more productive, and has a subsoil of yellow clay Much of the prairie and a portion of the timbered land is rather flat and requires thorough draining to make it productive The bottom lands on the Embarras are from a half mile to a mile or more in breadth, and were originally covered with a heavy growth of timber, but portions of it have been cleared and brought under cultivation, and are very productive, though subject to occasional overflow The varieties of timber in this county appeared to be about the same as in Clark, and need not be enumerated again here A supply of water may usually be obtained in the gravelly drift clays above the hard pan, but at some localities it can only be had by boring or digging through the hard pan to the quick sands below.

COLES COUNTY embraces an area of over five hundred square miles, and is bounded on the north by Douglas county, on the east by Edgar and Clark, on the south by Clark and Cumberland, and on the west by Moultrie and Shelby The principal water courses in the county are the Embarras river, which traverses its eastern portion from north to south, and the Okaw or Kaskaskia, which runs diagonally across the north-western corner of the county. The greater portion of its surface is prairie, though there are belts of excellent timber skirting all the water courses, and the southeastern part of the county along the Embarras and its tributaries is heavily timbered

This county lays in that portion of the State where the drift deposits attain nearly to their maximum thickness, and bowlders of considerable size are quite commonly to be seen on the surface of the prairies but partially imbedded in the soil The total thickness of the drift in this county ranges from fifty to one hundred and fifty feet or more, the upper part consisting of a variable thickness of brown or buff gravelly clays, and the lower of blue clays or hard pan, the latter sometimes underlaid by gravel and quicksand.

In the boring for oil at Charleston, fifty five feet of drift was reported as follows

| | Ft |
|---|---|
| Soil and yellow clay | 18 |
| Sand and gravel | 8 |
| Blue clay (hard pan) | 16 |
| Bowlder clay | 13 |

At Mattoon, wells have been sunk from seventy five to one hundred and fifty feet without reaching bed rock, and all the way through drift clays and gravel, and sometimes without obtaining even then an adequate supply of water

At Mr. THEOPHILUS VAN DOREN'S, on Kickapoo creek, there is a deposit of chocolate colored sandy loam two and a half to three feet thick filled with fragments of partially decomposed or carbonized vegetable matter which was once without doubt a surface deposit. It is associated with a bed of brownish gray pipe clay, and is overlaid by gravelly drift clays This old soil has been passed through at other localities in digging wells in this county, at a depth of thirty to fifty feet from the surface, and its position appears to be below the drift clays, and above the quicksands that usually form the lowest part of this formation. The gray pipe clay at VAN DOREN'S is apparently a good potters' clay. In digging and boring through the drift deposits in this county, veins of inflammable gas are sometimes struck about the horizon of this old soil, derived probably from the partially decomposed vegetable matters with which it is filled. Trunks of trees and smaller fragments of wood are frequently found in sinking wells through the drift deposits in this portion of the State, and these constitute the only fossils hitherto obtained from it in this county. Probably if the quick sands below the hard pan were accessible, some remains of fresh water or land shells might be obtained from them, but no traces of either fresh water or marine animals have as yet, so far as I know, been found either in the brown clays or the blue hard pan of the drift

## *Coal Measures.*

The stratified rocks of this county all belong to the upper Coal Measures, and correspond very nearly to those already described in Cumberland, except that the *Fusulina* limestone is rather thicker and more evenly bedded in this county than it is further south The course of the Embarras river still follows the trend of the strata, and the limestone alternately appears above and then sinks below the level of the river bed.

At Hanging Rock, just above the Cumberland county line, a bed of soft concretionary sandstone may be seen at the base of the bluffs, extending from thirty to forty feet above, and also projecting below the level of the river bottoms It shows no regular lines of bedding in the lower part of its outcrop, and the rock is so soft and crumbles so easily under a blow from the hammer that at some localities it is difficult to obtain a good hand specimen A little further up the river there is about fifteen feet of dark-bluish shale cropping out beneath the sandstone

At McCann's ford the same limestone apparently that was left at Ryan's ford just below the north line of Cumberland county, appears in a bench on the west side of the river, where it is underlaid by ten or twelve feet of sandy, micaceous shale The full thickness of the limestone was not seen here, the upper part having been cut away in the erosion of the river valley The limestone is said to outcrop again a mile above McCann's, but I did not find the exposure No rocks are seen on the east side of the river above the ford for two or three miles, and the hills, which are from a hundred to a hundred and twenty five feet in hight, were mainly composed of drift material The following section shows the relative position of the rocks found in the south part of this county:

| | Ft |
|---|---|
| Soft, brown, micaceous, shaly sandstone, passing down into an unstratified concretionary mass | 30 to 40 |
| Sandy and argillaceous shales | 15 to 20 |
| Rough, gray, unevenly bedded limestone | 8 to 10 |
| Dark gray micaceous shale | 10 to 12 |

The coal which is found beneath the limestone higher up the river seems to be undeveloped here, as it is also in Cumberland, and no indications of it were seen south of the road running east from Charleston.

Three miles a little south of east from Charleston, near the bridge on the road to Westfield, the sandstone which forms the upper division of the foregoing section crops out at the foot of the bluff on the west side, where quarries have been opened in it for building stone This sandstone is considerably harder here than at Hanging Rock, and affords a very good material for bridge abutments, foundation walls, etc The lower twenty feet of the bed here is but partially stratified, but the upper portion is evenly bedded, and as it hardens on exposure it affords a very good building material Near the bridge there is an exposure of about fifteen feet of argillaceous shales with bands of carbonate of iron, and just at the water's edge below the bridge there is a partial outcrop of the upper part of the limestone. The outcrop of sandstone at the quarry measures thirty-three feet in thickness including some shaly layers at the top of the exposure.

A half mile below the Westfield road on the river, Prof. Cox reports the following detailed section, but whether above or below the main sandstone is not stated, though they are probably above that rock.

| | Ft | In |
|---|---|---|
| "Gray friable shale, with several bands of iron stone | 20 | |
| Fossiliferous iron stone | 0 | 6 |
| Friable shale | 1 | |
| Black shale | 0 | 8 |
| Gray clay shale | 5 | |
| Impure coal | 0 | 2 |
| Sandstone | " | " |

He also reports the following beds as occurring above the sandstone on the river three miles east of Charleston.

| | Ft | In |
|---|---|---|
| "Drift | 15 | |
| Buff argillaceous shale | 4 | |
| Calcareous shale, with fossils | 0 | 1 |
| Gray iron stone with fossils | 0 | 6 |
| Brownish black shale with fossils | 0 | 1 |
| Black hard shale | 0 | 8 |
| Blue shale | 5 | |
| Brash coal | 0 | 3 |
| Sandstone, showing on the opposite side of a hill a vertical face of | 35 " | |

Above Baker's mill, which is located on sec 25, T. 12, R. 10, he reports a similar section, that shows a thickening of some of the beds:

| | Ft | In |
|---|---|---|
| "Covered slope | 40 | |
| Limestone with fossils | 1 | |
| Gray shale | 0 | 6 |
| Black shale | 8 to 10 | |
| Calcareous pyrite band | 0 | 3 |
| Blue shale | ? | |
| Sandstone, thin bedded at the top and heavy bedded below | 20 to 30 " | |

On another ravine leading to the river he reports the following section, showing still further changes in the lithological character of the beds above the sandstone.

| | Ft | In |
|---|---|---|
| "Limestone | 0 | 6 |
| Bituminous shale | 0 | 8 |
| Gray shale | 2 | |
| Decomposing gray shale | ? | |
| Sandstone | 3 | |
| Coal | 0 | 3 |
| Blue clay | 0 | 3 |
| Coal | 0 | ½ |
| Blue shale, with fossil plants | 2 | |
| Brash coal | 0 | 1 |
| Blue argillaceous shale | 3 to 5 | |
| Solid sandstone, not measured" | | |

At the old mill on the Pole cat creek, known as the Whorl mill, the following beds are to be seen

| | Ft | In |
|---|---|---|
| Sandstone, in thin beds, with pebbles in lower layers | 10 to 12 | |
| Hard black shale | 0 | 10 |
| Clay shale | 6 to 8 | |
| Coal | 0 | 3 |
| Sandy shale | 2 to 3 | |

About two hundred yards to the westward of the mill the sandstone extended below the bed of the creek, showing a decided dip of the strata in that direction. This locality was visited especially on account of the reported occurrence of silver or some other valuable mineral at this point, but the reputed silver proved to be nothing more than the glittering scales of mica which was very abundant in the sandstone.

On the Embarras, about a mile and a half or two miles below the mouth of Brush creek, a hard brown argillaceous limestone from eight to ten feet in thickness outcrops above the bed of the stream and overlays a seam of coal that has been worked to a limited extent in this vicinity. This limestone is rather darker colored and more heavily bedded than the *Fusulina* limestone of Cumberland county, and might be supposed to belong to a higher level, but on comparing hand specimens I found it resembled its equivalent, the limestone over the Nelson coal in Effingham county, rather more than it did the specimens from Cumberland. However, these upper Coal Measure limestones are somewhat variable in their lithological characters, and though I did not find the *Fusulina cylindrica* in it in Coles county, I am still inclined to believe that it is a representative of that limestone. The fossils found here were *Spirifer cameratus*, *S lineatus*, *Productus longispinus*, *Spiriferina Kentuckensis*, *Athyris subtilita*, *Platyostoma Peoriense*, a delicate coral allied to *Cyathoxonia*, and joints of *Crinoidea* The section seen here was as follows

| | Ft | In |
|---|---|---|
| Brownish gray unevenly bedded limestone | 8 to 10 | |
| Dark shale | 1 | |
| Coal | 1 to 1 | 3 |
| Clay shale | 1 | |

Higher up stream towards the mouth of Brush creek, some ten or twelve feet of sandy shale with bands of carbonate of iron are seen under the beds in the foregoing section

A shaft was sunk for coal in this vicinity on the S W. qr of sec. 21, T 13, R 10, near the bank of the Embarras, the following report of which was furnished to Prof. Cox

| | Ft | In |
|---|---|---|
| Drift clay | 20 | |
| Limestone | 2 | |
| Coal | 1 | |
| Clay shale (soapstone) | 3 | |
| Soft blue sandstone | 5 | |
| Clay shale | 1 | |
| Coal | | 8 |
| Clay shale | 5 | |
| Sandstone | 5 | 6 |
| Coal | | 7 |
| Clay shale | 2 | |
| Hard bluish sandstone | 3 | |
| Dark clay shale (soapstone) | 20 | 6 |

The foregoing sections on the Embarras river and the boring at Charleston by the Charleston Petroleum and Mining Company, affords the only data for determining the geological features of this county.

The following is a correct copy of the record of this boring

| | | Ft | In |
|---|---|---|---|
| 1 | Soil and drift clays | 55 | |
| 2 | Yellow sandstone | 21 | |
| 3 | Hard limestone | 11 | |
| 4 | Shell rock (shale?) | 2 | |
| 5 | Coal, No 16 | 1 | 4 |
| 6 | Hard slate (shale?) | 8 | 9 |
| 7 | Clay shale (soapstone) | 13 | |

| | | Ft | In |
|---|---|---|---|
| 8 | Hard flint? | 3 | |
| 9 | White sandstone | 12 | |
| 10 | Shale and shaly slate | 26 | |
| 11 | Coal No 15 | 2 | |
| 12 | Hard shale | 15 | |
| 13 | Clay shale | 10 | |
| 14 | Blue limestone | 8 | |
| 15 | Shale and sandstone | 14 | |
| 16 | Soft white rock | 13 | |
| 17 | Shale and slate | 27 | |
| 18 | Sandstone | 31 | |

The limestone No 14 of the above section, I believe to be the Quarry creek bed of Clark county, and the distance between that bed and the limestone of the Embarras, (No. 3 of the section,) which is here only about 93 feet, while at Greenup it is 130 feet or more, shows the same thinning out to the northward of the beds above the Quarry creek limestone, that was observed in Clark county in the strata below that rock Hence, the main coals, if found fully developed here, would be reached at a depth somewhat less than in Cumberland. The total thickness of the outcrops to be seen along the Embarras river, in this county, does not exceed a hundred feet of Coal Measures, and includes the horizon of coal No 16 of the general section and the thin coal above it. Coal No 15 should be found underlaying nearly the whole of this county, if it has not been cut out by denuding agencies It is the thickest of the upper seams, sometimes attaining a thickness of 2½ to 3 feet. It has been worked for many years in the vicinity of Shelbyville in shafts and inclined tunnels, and affords a semi block coal of good quality

## *Economical Geology.*

*Coal*—No outcrop of a coal bed thick enough to be worked to advantage was found in the county, and unless No. 15 may be found beneath the heavy drift deposits in the western part of the county, there is no hope of obtaining an adequate supply of this indispensable article of fuel without sinking to the main seams in the lower part of the Coal Measures A shaft from six to eight hundred feet in depth might reach No 7 or the Danville seam, but it would require one more than a thousand feet deep to reach the bottom of the Coal Measures in any part of this county.

*Building Stone*—Sandstone of a fair quality for building purposes may be obtained at various points along the bluffs of the Embarras river, and the rock obtained from the quarries near the Westfield road appears to be a durable stone, can be easily quarried, and has been very generally used for the supply of the adjacent region In the southern portion of the county the rock is comparatively soft, and at the few outcrops examined did not promise well as a building stone. The limestone which outcrops along the river is thicker bedded than in Cumberland, and between the railroad bridge and the mouth of Brush creek quarries have been opened in it at several points, where a hard brownish gray limestone in beds from four to eighteen inches thick has been obtained for building purposes. The western portion of the county is quite destitute of rock of any kind except the drift bowlders found upon the surface or in the valleys of the small streams

*Lime*—The limestone on the Embarras is too argillaceous to be successfully used for making quick lime, and as this is the only limestone of any considerable thickness found in the county, some other region must be depended on for a supply of this article

*Clay and Sand*—Brick clays are easily obtained from the subsoil in almost any portion of the upland, and a potters' clay of fair quality is found in the drift deposits on the Kickapoo Sand can be readily obtained either from the beds of the streams, or may be found in many places interstratified with the drift clays

*Iron ore*—Bands of carbonate of iron in small quantities were found interstratified in the shales above and below the heavy bed of sandstone that forms the lower portion of the bluffs on either side of the Embarras river

*Soil and Timber*—The prairies in this county, which constitute by far the greater portion of its surface, have a deep, black, loamy soil, highly fertile, and ranking among the best prairie lands in the State On the timbered ridges adjacent to the streams the soil is thinner, but nevertheless productive, and especially adapted to the cultivation of wheat and other small grains, clover and fruit On these ridges oak and hickory is the prevailing timber, but as the surface becomes more level toward the prairie region, we also find elm, linden, hackberry, wild cherry and honey locust, and on the bottom lands along the streams cottonwood, sycamore, ash, red birch, willow, coffeenut, black walnut, white and sugar maple, etc, etc

DOUGLAS COUNTY is bounded on the north by Champaign, on the east by Edgar, on the south by Coles, and on the west by Moultrie and Piatt It embraces eight full and seven fractional townships, which give it an area of about four hundred and ten square miles The Okaw or Kaskaskia river drains the western portion, and the Embarras the central and eastern portion of the county. These streams are skirted with timber, but the greater portion of its surface is prairie

The whole area of the county is covered so deeply with drift clays that there is no outcrop of the underlaying Coal Measure strata in the county. From the exposures in the adjoining counties it is known that the underlaying beds belong to the upper Coal Measures, and probably include two or three of the upper coals, but the extent to which they are developed here can only be determined with the drill. It is not probable that any heavy bed of coal will be found short of six to eight hundred feet from the surface, though one of the upper seams. two or three feet thick, might be found at a moderate depth.

The drift clays are similar to those described in the counties of Edgar, Coles and Moultrie, but only the upper part of this deposit is to be seen in the natural outcrops in the bluffs of the streams The soil is mainly a deep, black, vegetable mould, characteristic of the prairie lands throughout the central portions of the State, and is very productive. yielding annually heavy crops of all the cereals grown in this latitude.

# CHAPTER IX.

## WILLIAMSON AND FRANKLIN COUNTIES.*

Williamson county embraces a superficial area of twelve full townships, or four hundred and thirty two square miles, and is bounded as follows: on the north by Franklin county, on the east by Saline, on the south by Johnson and Union, and on the west by Jackson.

The western portion of the county is drained by the Big Muddy and its tributaries, the main stream intersecting the north western corner of the county, while Crab Orchard creek, its main southern affluent, traverses the central portion from east to west, passing out of the county near the center of its west line. The eastern and south eastern portions are drained by the main branches of the middle and south forks of Saline, which have their rise in this county, and with a westerly course discharge their waters into the Ohio, the highlands in the eastern portion of this and Franklin forming the water shed that separates the waters of the Ohio from those flowing west into the Mississippi.

In the northern part of the county the surface is quite rolling, and in some portions broken and hilly, while the central part is generally level, and the southern part quite broken, especially near the south line of the county, where the conglomerate and heavy bedded sandstones of the lower Coal Measures are the prevailing formations. There is, however, but little land in the county that is too much broken for cultivation, and as an agricultural region this county ranks among the best in Southern Illinois. Originally the surface was mostly covered with a heavy growth of timber, the prairie lands covering but a small fraction of its area. Some of the broken lands were originally but thinly timbered, forming what is known in the Western States as "oak openings," through which one could travel with but little more difficulty than on the open prairie; but now where these lands have not been brought under cultivation, they are densely covered with a heavy growth of

---

* These two counties and the county of Livingston were assigned to Mr. H. C. Freeman in the spring of 1866, and he was paid in full for surveying and reporting on them, but failing to obtain any report from him, though repeatedly promised, and after a delay of eight years waiting for him to fulfil his obligations, I was compelled, when all the rest of the counties had been reported on and this volume was otherwise ready for the press, to go into these counties myself and make such examinations as the limited time and unfavorable season would permit. A. H. WORTHEN.

young timber, which was previously kept down by the annual fires that swept over the county previous to its settlement by the dominant race

The principal varieties of timber noticed on the ridges were black, white and black-jack oak and hickory, and on the more level portions of the uplands in additions to these we find elm, linden, black and white walnut, sugar maple, black gum, wild cherry, honey locust, bur and post oak, pa paw, persimmon, sassafras and poplar, and on the creek bottoms the prevailing varieties are cottonwood, sycamore, red birch, coffeenut, pecan, ash, soft maple, redbud, dogwood, elm and hackberry

The geological formations to be found in this county belong to the Quaternary and lower Coal Measures The Quaternary is represented by a series of brown and yellow clays, sometimes mixed with gravel and small bowlders, and ranging from twenty to forty feet or more in thickness These beds are generally pretty uniform both in their depth and general character, and seem to partake largely of the character of the sandstones and sandy shales that form the underlaying bed rock Locally they become quite gravelly, and contain small bowlders of granite, hornblende, quartzite and trap rock, seldom exceeding six inches to a foot in diameter, though a few were seen in the county of more than twice the size just indicated. Nothing resembling the bluish-gray hard pan that constitutes the lower portion of the drift deposits in the more northerly counties was seen here, but the yellowish sandy and gravelly clays that form the main portion of the deposit here rest directly upon the stratified rocks of the Coal Measures.

## *Coal Measures.*

All the lower coals are found in this county, the outcrops embracing a part of the conglomerate sandstone that underlays the hilly region along the southern line of the county, and all the succeeding beds up to the horizon of coal No. 10 of the general section At Bainbridge, three miles south west of Bolton, in the north-east corner of Johnson county, a seam of coal has been opened about three feet to three and a half in thickness, which is probably coal No 1 of the general section, and from the trend of the strata, which is to the north of west, this coal must be found in the south-west portion of Williamson county In the bluff north of Bolton there are two seams that probably represent coals 2 and 3 of the general section. The lower one has been opened at two or three points in the vicinity of the village by tunneling into the hill on the outcrop of the coal, which averages about three feet in thickness, with a roof of bituminous shale The coal has a parting of clay shale about a foot above the bottom of the seam from three to four inches in thickness The upper seam is from 15 to 18 inches thick, and is underlaid by a sandy fire clay with *Stigmaria*, passing into a hard nodular sandstone, below which there is a bed of dark steel gray, tough limestone, weathering to a rusty brown color, and closely resembling that underlaying the upper seam at Murphysboro. It is from eighteen inches to two feet in thickness here, and contains joints of *Crinoidea* and *Spirifer cameratus* The coal is overlaid by a massive sandstone, partly concretionary and partly in regular layers, that is quarried for building stone, for which it seems well adapted. The following is a section of the bluff at this point

| | Ft | In |
|---|---|---|
| Quartzose sandstone | 20 to 25 | |
| Coal | 1 | 3 |
| Silicious fire clay | 2 | |
| Hard steel gray limestone | 1 | 6 |
| Slope with partial outcrops of shale | 40 | |
| Bituminous shale | 2 | |
| Coal | 3 | |
| Covered slope to the railroad level | 20 to 25 | |

The coal obtained from the lower seam here contains a good deal of iron pyrites, and in quality is rather below the average of our Illinois coals, but it answers tolerably well for steam purposes

At the crossing of Sugar creek, about three miles north of Bolton, on the Marion road, a massive sandstone outcrops in the banks of the stream extending to the hight of fifteen to twenty feet above the creek level, overlaid by a thin bedded sandstone, of which about the same thickness could be seen. A coal seam has been opened here beneath the sandstone and some coal taken out for blacksmiths' use, but it was hidden by the high water when I was there, and hence I could neither determine its thickness nor ascertain the quality of the coal it afforded. This is probably coal No 4 of the general section

At the water mill on the south fork of Saline river, about two miles below the bridge on the road from Bolton to Marion, another seam of coal is found associated with the following beds

| | Ft | In |
|---|---|---|
| Brown sandy shale | 4 to 6 | |
| Band of hard bluish gray limestone | 0 | 6 |
| Bituminous shale | 5 | |
| Coal No 5 | 2 | |
| Nodular clay shale | 2 | |

The brown shale at the top of the foregoing section may be seen in a hill side near the mill where it is about twenty feet thick, and its full thickness is probably as much as forty to fifty feet. The coal at the mill is rather hard and splinty, but is said to work well in the forge. The upper four inches is a cannel coal. This mill is located on the S. E. qr. of the N. W qr of sec 4, T 10 S, R 4 E

At the bridge over the South Fork, two miles above the mill near the old town of Sarahsville, a thin coal outcrops by the side of the road, associated with shale and thin bedded sandstone. This is above the section seen at the mill The following is the section here:

| | Ft |
|---|---|
| Thin bedded sandstone | 8 to 10 |
| Sandy shale | 4 to 6 |
| Coal No 6 | 1 |
| Sandy shales to the water level | 12 to 15 |

Davidson's mine, one mile and a quarter south of Crab Orchard, belongs to a still higher level, and the coal is there five and a half feet in thickness overlaid by bituminous shale and a dark bluish gray impure limestone A little to the eastward of the coal mine the overlaying sandstone is well exposed in the bed and banks of a shallow ravine, showing a thickness of twenty to twenty-five feet This sandstone stands exposure well, and when found in beds of sufficient thickness for heavy work furnishes a durable building stone. About three quarters of a mile east of Davidson's mine the thin coal that outcrops at Sarahsville was found in the bed of a small branch, and apparently from forty to fifty feet below Davidson's coal A section of the beds seen here show the following order of succession

| | Ft |
|---|---|
| Brown and buff sandy shale and sandstone | 20 to 25 |
| Dark ash gray limestone | 2 to 3 |
| Bituminous shale | 1 to 1 |
| Coal No 7 (Davidson's) | 5 to 6 |
| Fire clay | 2 |
| Unexposed | 30 to 40 |
| Brown and buff sandy shale | 10 |
| Coal No 6 | 1 to 1½ |
| Blue sandy shale exposed | 1 |

On Mr WILEY'S land, two miles and a half southwest of Marion, a thin coal has been found on Crab Orchard creek, which is probably identical with the thin seam in the foregoing section

At Mr MOTSINGER'S mine, one mile and a half west of Crab Orchard village, the coal is about five feet thick with a roof of bituminous clay shale The coal is of fair quality, tolerably free from pyrite, and the upper eighteen inches is a good smith's coal. About a hundred yards to the south of the coal opening the hard, dark, ash gray limestone usually found above No 7 coal has been quarried and burned for lime, though but poorly adapted to that purpose The coal here and at Davidson's is mined by tunneling into the hill side on the outcrop of the seam.

On Mr FRANK ENSMINGER'S place, one mile east of Crab Orchard, the following beds overlaying coal No 7 were seen.

| | Ft |
|---|---|
| Hard sandstone in thin beds | 8 |
| Blue sandy shale | 4 to 6 |
| Brown shale and sandstone | 10 to 12 |
| Blue shale | 8 to 10 |
| Cinnamon colored limestone | 1 |
| Bituminous shale | ½ to 1 |
| Coal, said to be six inches thick | ½ |

About a mile and a half north-east of Mr. ENSMINGER'S, on the S. E. qr of the N E qr of sec 16, there is an outcrop of the same cinnamon-brown limestone mentioned in the foregoing section, and the coal below it is said to be from two to three feet thick, and has been mined in a limited way for blacksmiths' use. This is probably coal No. 8 of the general section, and has been mined by stripping in the valley of a small creek. Owing to recent heavy rains the holes from which the coal had been taken were full of water, and the thickness of the seam could not be measured

South of Mr ENSMINGER'S on sec 32, T 9, R 4, coals No 5, 6 and 7 may all be seen within a short distance. No 5 is here from two to six feet thick, while No 7 is pinched out to about three feet The following section was seen here:

| | Ft. | In |
|---|---|---|
| Dark gray massive limestone | 4 to 6 | |
| Bituminous shale | 3 to 5 | |
| Coal No 7 | 0 to 5 | |
| Fire clay and clay shale | 2 to 3 | |
| Massive sandstone | 15 to 18 | |
| Sandy shale | 10 to 12 | |
| Blue and brown clay shale | 15 to 20 | |
| Coal No 6 | 1' to 1 | 10 |
| Brown and blue shales | 20 to 30 | |
| Dark steel gray limestone | 1 | |
| Bituminous shale with concretions of limestone | 4 | |
| Blue shale | 8 to 10 | |
| Coal No 5 (Ensminger's coal) | 1½ to 6 | |

One locality was noticed on the creek where the above section was made, where the massive sandstone beneath coal No 7 seems to have pinched the coal entirely out, but a half mile to the eastward it comes in again and ranges from two to five feet in thickness The bituminous shale over Ensminger's coal contains numerous large concretions of black limestone which weathers blue on exposure, but contain no fossils at this locality. This seam I believe to be the same as that at the water mill on the south fork of the Saline, though it is much thicker here than there, and varies from one and a half to six feet in a distance of less than half a mile Owing to the limited demand for coal, no systematic mining has yet been attempted here, but an extensive coal mining business could be easily and cheaply carried on whenever this portion of the county is provided with railroad facilities, or manufacturing enterprises shall be established to create a market for the almost inexhaustible supply of coal now hidden beneath the soil

At Dr SMITH'S old place, south of Corinth, where a shaft was sunk several years since in search of silver, the following section was found.

| | Ft |
|---|---|
| Brown shale | 10 to 15 |
| Blue shale partly bituminous | 8 to 10 |
| Coal No 10 | ? |

| | Ft |
|---|---|
| Fire clay, good | 2 to 3 |
| Sandstone | 10 to 15 |
| Blue clay shale | 4 to 6 |
| Hard brownish gray limestone | 6 to 9 |
| Bituminous shale | 2 to 4 |
| Coal No 9 | 2 |

The limestone exposed here I believe to be the same as that at New Haven, on the Wabash, and the equivalent of the Carlinville and Shoal creek bed. The fire clay above the limestone was only partially exposed, and may be somewhat thicker than above indicated and appeared to be of a suitable quality for pottery or fire brick

About a mile and a quarter north of Corinth, a shaft was sunk some years ago in search of silver ore, which passed through this limestone at the depth of about forty two feet. I am indebted to Mr. SHAW, who sunk this shaft, for the following data, given from memory, of the beds passed through in this shaft

| | Ft | In |
|---|---|---|
| Surface soil and clay | 9 | |
| Sandstone | 22 | |
| Clay shale | 2 | 6 |
| Limestone | 9 | |
| Bituminous shale | 1 | 6 |
| Rotten coal. | 2 | |
| Fire clay | 2 | |
| Hard rock probably sandstone | ? | |

A few fossils were observed in the fragments of limestone thrown out of this shaft, but belonging to species common throughout the Coal Measures An outcrop of the upper sandstone near by showed a bed of ferruginous conglomerate about two feet thick, composed in part of almond shaped nodules of brown oxyd of iron

At Dr MITCHELL'S place, on sec 22, T 8, R. 4, a bed of hard, brittle limestone occurs in a single layer about a foot in thickness. It contained *Naticopsis ventricosus*, *Productus longispinus*, and joints of *Crinoidea* I am inclined to regard this limestone and the shales associated with it as the highest beds to be seen in this county, and probably the equivalent of the ferruginous beds usually found associated with coal No. 11 in the Wabash valley At Mr ROBERTS place, on the north side of the village of Corinth, coal was found in his well about fourteen feet from the surface. It was penetrated, according to the report, about two feet without passing through it. On ELIJAH MUSE'S place, near the north-east corner of the county, an inferior quality of coal said to be two feet thick outcrops in the bed of a small creek These thin coals probably belong above the limestone at Dr. SMITH'S place, and may represent the horizon of coals 10 or 11 of the general section, which are seldom found of sufficient thickness to be of any economical value. The foregoing sketch comprises all the coal seams probably occurring in this county, and it only remains now to note some of the most important outcrops of coals Nos 5 and 7 not heretofore mentioned, as these are the only seams that are of sufficient thickness to justify mining operations on an extended scale at the present time

Spiller's mine, two miles north of Marion was the first one opened in this county, and has now been worked for about twenty-five years. The coal is obtained by stripping along its outcrop on a small creek, and the coal ranges from six to ten feet in thickness The upper four feet is a good smith's coal and presents the irridescent appearance characteristic of the variety known as "peacock coal" The roof is sometimes composed of hard, black shale, but locally this is replaced with a dark blue clay shale, succeeded by a dark, ash-gray limestone which in this vicinity ranges from four to six feet in thickness, and weathers to a bluish drab color on exposure. The following beds may be seen in the vicinity of Spiller's mine.

| | Ft |
|---|---|
| Shaly buff limestone | 2 to 3 |
| Hard dark ash gray limestone | 4 to 5 |
| Blue argillaceous shale | 4 to 6 |
| Bituminous shale | 0 to 2 |
| Coal No 7 | 6 to 10 |
| Fire clay and clay shale | 2 to 4 |

The argillaceous shale over the coal contains numerous small, irregular shaped nodules of pyritiferous clay, but no fossil plants were found here, though they occur in the roof shales of this coal at Carterville The limestone contains but few fossils and these belong to species common everywhere in the Coal Measures, such as *Spirifer cameratus*, *Athyris subtilita*, and *Productus longispinus* Neither the limestone nor bituminous shale are very regular in their development, and at some localities both are wanting, and the roof of the coal consists of clay shale overlaid by sandstone The coal has a parting of hard black shale about an inch thick some two feet from the bottom of the seam, and there are also several other leaf like partings of shale separating the coal into distinct layers or strata.

A shaft sunk some years ago on the western borders of the town of Marion, is said to have penetrated a coal seam six feet in thickness at the depth of about fifty feet below the surface This was probably coal No. 5, as the outcrop of Spiller's coal is two miles north of the town, and at about the same level as the surface on which the town is built, and the general dip of the beds being to the north eastward, that seam would outcrop above the level of the town A thin coal has also been found in sinking wells in the town, probably No. 6, which belongs some forty to fifty feet below the Spiller coal.

The Carbondale Coal and Coke Company have opened a mine near Carterville station and are working No 7 with a sloping tunnel carried down to the level of the coal, which lays about forty feet below the surface The seam is here from eight to nine and a half feet thick of clean, bright, glistening coal, presenting the finest appearance to the casual visitor of any mine we have visited in the State The roof consists of about fifteen feet of blue shale slightly bituminous at the bottom, and showing the remains of numerous fossil plants where the coal has been removed This coal is quite free from pyrite, cokes well, and the product finds a ready market at the Iron Furnaces at Grand Tower The same parting of bituminous shale noticed at Spiller's may be seen here It is about an inch in thickness and some two feet above the bottom of the coal, and there are some other leaf like partings that divide the seam into regular layers The dip at this mine is said to be about two inches to the yard in a north-westerly direction, but this is probably local About half a mile north east of the opening this seam crops out in the bottom of a ravine, where the coal is much less than its average thickness and is underlaid by two feet of fire clay and a nodular gray limestone which weathers to a yellowish buff color, and is from eighteen inches to two feet thick. The seam was first opened in this ravine, and considerable coal taken out by tunnelling into the side of the hill

At Crane station, a half mile east of Carterville, a shaft was sunk to the depth of about forty feet to a seam of coal three feet eight inches thick, overlaid by a heavy bed of bituminous shale Operations had been suspended here when I visited this locality, and the shaft was partially filled with water, so that no satisfactory examination could be made except from the material thrown out The coal is said to be quite different from that obtained at Carterville, being harder and containing more pyrite. The coal is overlaid by a heavy bed of bituminous shale, with concretions of dark pyritiferous limestone, and nodular masses of bluish gray limestone resembling those occurring over Ensminger's coal south east of Crab Orchard If the dip determined in the mine at Carterville is continuous over any considerable area, that seam would be thrown out here, and I am of the opinion that this is the case, and that the coal at this station is No 5, though it is somewhat thinner here than at Ensminger's, and from some local cause contains a greater amount of pyrite In the roof shales thrown out at the air shaft we found several species of fossils, among which we recognized *Chonetes mesoloba*, *Productus longispinus*, *P. Prattenianus*, *Athyris subtilita*, *Spirifer cameratus*, *S. lineatus* and joints of *Crinoidea*

From what has already been said in regard to the development of the lower coals in this county, and from the sections given on the preceding pages, it will be seen that the main coals from No 2 to No 7 inclusive are found on the eastern borders of the county, and all but No 4 distinctly recognized and examined. It is probable however that there is a gradual thinning out of these lower measures to the westward, and it is quite likely that some of these coals may not be found at all in the western part of the county, or if found, will prove to be too thin to be of any practical value; but the outcrops are too meagre in that portion of the county to enable any one to trace out the exact sequence of the strata successfully Borings have been made along the line of the railroad west of Carterville, and are said to have found no workable coal, but my efforts to obtain a record of the strata passed through in these borings for publication in this report were unsuccessful.

## *Economical Geology.*

*Coal*—The great mineral resource of this county will be found in its coal deposits, which are surpassed by but few portions of the State of equal extent Nearly one-half of the county, comprising its northern portion, is underlaid by coal No 7, the thickest seam to be found in the State, and it is probably nowhere more than from 75 to 200 feet below the surface It outcrops at many points in township 9 south, and ranges 2, 3 and 4 east, and will be found underlaying nearly all the area north of these outcrops No 5 lays from 100 to 150 feet below No 7, but its development in the western portion of the county is at present an unsettled problem. It is however developed over a large area in the north western part of the county. These two seams will yield from ten to twelve million tons of coal to the square mile, and they probably underlay nearly one half of the entire area of the county All that is required to make this one of the most prosperous coal mining regions in the State, is a ready market for the vast stores of mineral fuel that are now hidden beneath the surface, awaiting the capital and skilled labor necessary for their full development This market could be obtained by direct railroad communication with some large coal consuming city like St. Louis, Chicago or Cincinnati where the coal products of the county could be sent at a minimum cost for transportation, instead of passing over two or three different lines of road as is now necessary in order to reach a reliable market, thus increasing the cost of transportation until it equals or exceeds the full value of the coal on its delivery in market

*Building Stone*—Sandstone of fair quality for ordinary use may be found in abundance in nearly every township in the county, and the brown sandstone overlaying coal No. 7, north east of Marion and in the vicinity of Crab Orchard, dresses well and hardens on exposure and forms an excellent material for caps and sills, and for all the ordinary uses for which a dressed stone is required In the vicinity of Bolton, and through the southern portion of the county, the sandstones associated with the lower coals are abundant, and that overlaying coal No 3 affords an excellent material for dressed work as well as for heavy masonry

*Lime*—Lime has been burned at several places in the county from the dark-gray limestone overlaying No 7 coal, but it affords only a poor quality of dark colored lime that is mostly used as a top dressing for the poorer qualities of soil The limestone which is sometimes found beneath this coal would probably afford a better quality of lime, if it should be found outcropping where it could be obtained at a moderate cost of labor With proper railroad facilities, however, lime could be obtained from Union county at a less cost than it could be manufactured from any of the limestones met with in this county

*Iron Ore*—There is a notable quantity of *limonite* or the brown oxyd of iron, occurring in the shales and sandstones of the lower Coal Measures but often too much mixed with sand or other silicious matters to be of any economical importance Bands of carbonate of iron or "kidney ore also abound in the shales of the lower measures, but from the limited time devoted to the examination of the county I was unable to give as much attention to this subject as was desirable Bands of good ore of this kind aggregating a thickness of sixteen to twenty inches in a depth of six feet of shale, would be worthy of the attention of the iron manufacturer, in view of the unlimited supply of coal to be found here suitable for the use of the smelting furnace

*Brick materials*—Good brick clays may be found in every neighborhood and on nearly every farm, the ordinary subsoil clays affording a suitable material for this purpose, and clean white sand of an excellent quality for mortar and cements is found in abundance about two miles north of Marion. It is composed entirely of rather coarse angular grains of white quartz Sand suitable for brick and for ordinary purposes may be found in the creek beds, and also in the hillsides in almost every neighborhood

*Soil and Agriculture*—There is considerable variety in the quality of the soils in this county, and their relative value for agricultural purposes may generally be determined by the growth of timber they sustain Perhaps the poorest quality of soil may be found on the post oak flats of which the area in this county is small, and next in order would be the oak ridges where the timber growth consists mainly of black, white and black-jack oak These lands possess a thin soil, and if constantly cultivated require to be well manured, or frequently sown to clover and the green crop turned under with the plow They produce fair crops of wheat, oats and grass if judiciously managed, and are excellent fruit lands Next in value we would place the small prairies and the adjacent uplands, where the timber growth consists of the usual varieties of oak and hickory interspersed with black walnut, elm, linden, wild cherry, sassafras and honey locust. The soil on these lands is a dark chocolate colored clay loam with a yellowish clay subsoil, and they produce good crops of corn, wheat, tobacco, castor beans and cotton and excellent crops of timothy and clover.

Tobacco is one of the staple products of the county, and during the rebellion cotton was planted extensively in this portion of the State, and was found to succeed so well that it has continued to be one of the staples of this county, most of the farmers raising all that is required for home consumption, besides exporting annually from eight hundred to fifteen hundred bales. The rolling lands are well adapted to the growth of fruit, especially peaches, which seldom fail on the high sandstone ridges in the southern part of this county. Apples, pears and small fruits flourish well and produce abundant crops, and some varieties of grapes would doubtless succeed well, though the Catawba has not succeeded well here, the fruit being subject to rot badly after a few years cultivation.

There are but few counties in Southern Illinois that possess a finer soil, or that present greater inducements for the investment of capital in agricultural pursuits than Williamson. The extension of the railroad, now terminating at Marion, through the county, giving increased facilities for the transportation of its agricultural products to market, would undoubtedly bring large accessions to the population and wealth of the county, and add largely to the present value of all the improved lands within its limits.

I take pleasure in acknowledging my obligations to Dr. LODGE of Marion, and Dr. MITCHELL of Corinth, for important information and for personal attention and assistance while engaged in the survey of this county.

FRANKLIN COUNTY contains nearly twelve townships or about 420 square miles, and is bounded on the north by Jefferson, on the east by Hamilton and Saline, on the south by Williamson, and on the west by Jackson county and the Little Muddy river. This county lies on the southern border of the prairie region, and about one quarter of its area was originally prairie and the remainder heavily timbered, but much of this timber has been cleared off in the agricultural improvement of the county. The prairies are small, seldom exceeding a breadth of two or three miles, and are mostly rather flat, and there are also wide belts of low flat bottoms on all the main water courses in the county. The rolling and hilly uplands are heavily timbered with the common varieties of oak and hickory, and the best soils also sustain a heavy growth of elm, linden, wild cherry, black walnut, honey locust, etc.

That portion of the county lying between the Big and Little Muddy's is generally quite rolling, and the above named varieties of timber indicate a very productive soil, and this land is undoubtedly equal to any in the county for farming purposes. Big Muddy river and its affluents drain nearly the whole area of the county, the main stream running a little to the west of south through its central portion, while the Middle and South Forks drain the south eastern, and the Little Muddy the north-western, forming its western boundary for about ten miles from the north line. These streams furnish an abundant supply of water for stock, but are too sluggish to furnish any valuable water power for manufacturing purposes.

The geological formations in this county, like those in Williamson, consist altogether of Drift and Coal Measures, the latter belonging mainly, however, to the upper instead of the lower division of that formation.

*Drift*—The drift deposits of this county differ but little from those observed in Williamson, and are found to consist mainly of brown and yellow sandy clays, with gravel and small bowlders. Occasionally those of a larger size were met with, the largest ranging from two to three feet in diameter. It is a notable fact that bowlders of metamorphic rocks similar to those found in Northern Illinois, as well as specimens of native copper, are found in Southern Illinois beyond the southern limit of the bluish gray "till" or hard pan that usually constitutes the lowest division of the drift deposits in the central and northern portions of the State. Frankfort, near the southern border of the county, is located on a hill from eighty to one hundred feet above the level of the surrounding country. No outcrop of stratified rocks was found in any of the deep gulleys that furrowed its sides, though it probably has a nucleus of Coal Measure shales or sandstone. Otherwise the drift clays are much thicker here than they have been found in any other portion of the county. Their average thickness may be stated at about thirty feet, though in many places the bed rock has been struck in sinking wells at the depth of ten to fifteen feet from the surface.

## *Coal Measures.*

Wherever the streams cut through the drift clays they expose a series of sandy and argillaceous shales and sandstones with an occasional outcrop of bituminous shale or thin seam of coal, all of which belong to the Coal Measures and mainly to the upper division of that formation. The lowest beds to be found in the county outcrop in the south west portion and comprise the sandstone shales and thin coal that intervenes between the Spiller coal two miles north of Marion and the limestone that usually overlays coal No. 9. This limestone was met with on the S E (?) qr of sec 22, T. 7 S R 4 E, about two miles a little south of east of Frankfort, and from its nearest outcrop in Williamson county, which was at Dr SMITH's old place about two miles and a half south east of Corinth, its trend seems to be nearly north west, though it probably bends to the northward before reaching the west line of the county. It should be found on the Big or Little Muddy's, but owing to the excessive rains of the past season no examinations could be made on these streams while I was at work in this county.

At Mrs EWING's place, on the S W qr of sec 23, T 7 S, R 4 E, the following beds were found, that must overlay the limestone above named

| | Ft | In |
|---|---|---|
| Sandy micaceous shale | 10 to 15 | |
| Band of ferruginous conglomerate | 1 | |
| Bituminous shale | 3 to 4 | |
| Thin coal | 0 | 6 |
| Brown sandy shale with fossil plants | 3 to 4 | |
| Dark blue micaceous shale | 5 | |
| Brown shale | 10 to 15 | |

The coal noted in the above section varies in thickness in this vicinity from two to eighteen inches, and is probably a local seam overlaying the limestone which outcrops about half a mile to the west of this point. This limestone is here a hard even bedded rock of a steel-gray or brownish gray color, weathering to a yellowish drab. It dips gently to the north eastward with the fall of the small branch on which it is found, and only about three feet in thickness of its upper layers could be seen. The only fossils we noticed in it were *Athyris subtilita*, *Spirifer lineatus*, *Rhynchonella Osagensis*, and *Productus longispinus*. Coal No. 9 will probably be found a few feet below the limestone; but as it is usually too thin to be of any economical value, there is no inducement to expend either capital or labor in its development. Coal No 7 (Spiller's coal) should be found here at a depth of 125 to 150 feet below this limestone, and will be the first one of the main coals to be reached by a shaft in this county.

About two miles and a half west of Benton, and a mile south of the DuQuoin road, there is an outcrop of soft ferruginous sandstone overlaid by sandy shale. The beds exposed were about fifteen feet in thickness, and at one point a thin coal was found below the sandstone. The rocks here have a strong resemblance to those seen in the vicinity of Shaw's shaft north of Corinth in Williamson county, and if the equivalents of them, the Carlinville limestone will be found not very far below the level of the Big Muddy river. A similar bed of sandstone outcrops on Dr HICKMAN's place a mile and a half south west of Benton, and the thin coal associated with it outcrops on a small branch where coal has been dug by stripping off the overlaying clay. The coal dips to the westward a little more than the fall of the small branch that runs in the same direction. The coal on the outcrop of the seam is not more than six inches thick, but near by it was said to have been found from a foot to eighteen inches thick It is overlaid by a ferruginous sandstone, one layer of which is a conglomerate of iron pebbles.

Two miles north of Benton on a small branch emptying into Big Muddy there is an outcrop of sandstone interstratified with shale presenting an exposure of fifty to sixty feet of strata Following down the branch for about three quarters of a mile we found the following succession of beds

| | Ft |
|---|---|
| Micaceous sandstone interstratified with shale | 10 to 15 |
| Micaceous shale | 20 to 25 |
| Sandstone | 12 to 15 |
| Micaceous shale | 6 to 8 |
| Sandstone in creek bed | |

This locality furnishes all the building stone used in Benton and the surrounding neighborhood, and the quarries here furnish an excellent freestone for foundation walls and for dressed stone, as it cuts freely and has proved to be a reliable building stone. The beds appear to dip gently to the north eastward, and probably overlay the thin coal and sandstone seen at Dr. HICKMAN'S place, south-west of the town

At the ford on the Big Muddy, at the crossing of the road from Benton to Mulkeytown, there is an outcrop of about six to eight feet of brown sandy shale overlaid by about twenty feet of brown and yellow gravelly drift clay, containing numerous small bowlders from an inch to a foot in diameter. South of this for about three miles no outcrop was found on the east side of the Big Muddy, the bluffs forming low sloping hills that appeared to be composed entirely of drift material. Further to the southward, where the Frankfort and DuQuoin road crosses, a thin coal is said to outcrop, but I did not visit the locality This may be coal No 8 of the general section.

A boring was made just on the western borders of the town of Benton which was suspended on reaching a hard gray limestone at the depth of one hundred and sixty two feet. The record was carried away by the person in charge of the work, and so no details could be obtained of the several beds passed through The limestone found at the bottom of this bore was probably the same as that met with two miles east of Frankfort. This rock was mistaken for the Lower Carboniferous formation and the work consequently abandoned, when in fact it was really the bed which separates the upper and lower Coal Measures, and is at least six hundred feet above the base of the lower measures Two or three thin seams of coal were reported in this bore, but none thick enough to be of any value

Three miles and a half west of the Big Muddy bridge, on the road from Benton to DuQuoin, a coal about one foot in thickness has been opened at the outcrop and some coal taken out for the use of the neighboring blacksmiths Still further west, in the barrens of Little Muddy, another outcrop of coal has been found about two miles south of the DuQuoin road None of the seams outcropping in this county are thick enough to be successfully worked in a regular way

All through the north eastern portion of the county sandstones and sandy shales are the prevailing rocks, and these outcrop at numerous points on the East Fork and its tributaries, from the Shawneetown road east of Benton to the north east corner of the county, and numerous quarries have been opened for building stone, in this portion of the county. Sandstone has been found at the following points in the county in addition to those already mentioned

On sec 14, T 6, R 1, on sec 19, T 5, R 2; on secs 1, 2 and 26, T 6, R 2, on sec 20, T 7, R 2, on secs. 27, 33 and 34, T. 5, R 3, on secs. 4 8, 9 and 17, T. 6, R 3, on secs 12, 13 and 14, T. 6, R. 3, on secs 20, 30 and 36, T 6, R 3, on secs 1, 2, 3 and 5, T 5, R 4, on secs 8, 10, 15 and 21, T. 5, R 4, on secs. 1, 5 and 12, T 6, R 4, on secs 24 and 30, T. 6, R. 4, on secs 1, 2, 8 and 11, T. 7, R. 4, on secs 12 and 30, T. 7, R. 4; on sec. 2, T. 7, R 3.

Limestone is also reported in the north-east corner of the county, on sec 11, T 5, R 4 This may be the same bed that was found underlaying the thin coal on Hog prairie, in Hamilton county.

## *Economical Geology.*

*Coal* —No coal seams thick enough to be worked in a regular way are known to outcrop in this county, yet its entire area is underlaid by the main coals of the lower measures which outcrop in the adjoining counties on the west and south In the southern and western portions of this county the Spiller coal (No 7 of the general section) may be reached at a depth of one to two hundred feet, while in the central and north-eastern portions it is probably from three to five hundred feet to this seam, and as much as eight hundred to a thousand to the base of the Coal Measures At the present time there is but little inducement for the investment of capital in coal mining operations in this county, nor will there be until some foreign demand shall be created by the construction of railroads through this portion of the State giving this county direct and cheap transportation to some of the large coal consuming centers of the West

*Building Stone* —Sandstone of fair quality is abundant in the central and eastern portions of the county, and some of the quarries like that two miles north of Benton afford an excellent quality of freestone, that hardens by exposure, dresses easily, and becomes a durable and handsome building stone. Sandstones of fair quality for common use may be found on nearly all the streams and more especially on the East Fork and its tributaries.

*Lime.*—The only outcrop of limestone suitable for the lime kiln that we saw in this county was found about two miles a little south of west from Frankfort. Only about three feet in thickness of the upper part of the bed was uncovered, but it is probably from six to ten feet thick when fully exposed. The rock is a hard gray, rather evenly bedded limestone, and has been quarried in a small way for building stone, but I saw no evidence that any attempt had been made to manufacture lime from it here. It seems to be somewhat argillaceous, and might not slack freely when burned.

*Soil and Agriculture.*—There is considerable variety in the character of the soils of this county, though there is probably not a section of land within its limits that would not yield a fair return to the husbandman for the labor necessary to bring it into cultivation. The botom lands are rather low and subject to overflow, and are therefore somewhat neglected. The prairies are generally small and rather level, and are often surrounded by a limited area of post oak plats, which have a thin soil and are generally regarded as the poorest lands in the county. The prairies have a more productive soil, but are inferior to the best timbered lands. For all farming purposes the rolling timbered lands that were originally covered with a growth of oak and hickory interspersed with black walnut, elm, linden, wild cherry, honey locust, sassafras, etc., are more productive, and will bear continued cultivation without artificial stimulants longer than any other uplands in this portion of the State.

The soil and agricultural products of this county are very similar to those of Williamson, though somewhat less attention is given here to the cultivation of tobacco, and cotton is only grown for home consumption. Stock raising, in the absence of railroad facilities for the transportation of flour and grain to market, is perhaps the most profitable branch of farming now, and beef and pork constitute a large part of the farm products of the county at the present time. Well improved farms can be purchased here at prices ranging from ten to twenty-five dollars per acre, and at these figures should command the attention of those who are seeking to invest in lands already under cultivation.

To Major WM. MOONEYHAM, of Benton, I am under obligations for much valuable information in regard to points of especial interest in this county.

# CHAPTER X.

## BOND COUNTY.

*Section of the rocks belonging to the upper Coal Measures in Bond, Fayette, Shelby, Montgomery and Christian counties.* By G. C. BROADHEAD.

| No. | | | Ft. | In. |
|---|---|---|---|---|
| 1 | Shales and sandstone | | 45 | |
| 2 | Limestone | | 1 | |
| 3 | Fire clay | | 2 | |
| 4 | Shales passing into sandstone | | 30 | |
| 5 | Limestone, with *Allorisma*, etc. | | | 4 |
| 6 | Shales at top, sometimes changing to argillaceous limestone | | 55 | |
| 7 | Sandstone, points at bottom | 4 to | 40 | |
| 8 | Shaly bituminous limestone and bituminous shales | 4 in. to | 4 | |
| 9 | Coal No. 15, 18 in. to 3 ft., generally | | 1 | 10 |
| 10 | Fire clay | 15 in. to | 5 | |
| 11 | Limestone, buff color | 0 to | 4 | |
| 12, 13 | Shales and sandstone, 15 to 30 in Shelby, in Fayette 75 (?) | | 50 | |
| 14 | Calcareous shales, fossiliferous | | 4 | |
| 15 | Shales | | 7 | |
| 16 | Calcareous and bituminous shales | | 2 | |
| 17 | Coal, No. 14, near Pana, on Beck's creek | 16 in. to | | 22 |
| 18 | Fire clay | | 5 | |
| 19 | Sandy limestone | | 5 | |
| 20 | Sandstone and shales | | 50 | |
| 21 | Shaly limestone | | 4 | |
| 22 | Limestone | | 4 | |
| 23 | Shales | | 6 | |
| 24 | Bituminous coal, No. 13 | 12 in. to | | 16 |
| 25 | Fossiliferous shales | | 8 | |
| 26 | Sandstone and shales | 75 to | 85 | |
| 27 | Limestone, hard blue | | 2 | |
| 28 | Coal, No. 12 | 2 to 10 in. | | 2 |
| 29 | Shales | | 10 | |
| 30 | Shales and limestone, fossils numerous | | 4 | |
| 31 | Limestone | 13 to | 16 | |
| 32 | Bituminous | | 4 | |
| 33 | Coal, No. 11 | | | 17 |
| 34 | Mostly shales | | 30 | |
| 35 | Blue and bituminous shales | | 1 | 6 |
| 36 | Calcareo bituminous shales—fossils | | 2 | |
| 37 | Coal, No. 10 | | | 7 |
| 38 | Fire clay | | 4 | |
| 39 | Sandy shales | | 3 | |
| 40 | Cone in cone (*Tutenmergel*) | | | 2 |
| 41 | Ironstone | | 1 | |
| 42 | Argillaceous shales and flattened ironstone nodules | | 20 | |

| | | Ft | In |
|---|---|---|---|
| 43 | Sandy limestone, numerous fossils | 2 | |
| 44 | Sandstone fossils | 2 | 6 |
| 45 | Sandy shales | 30 | |
| 46 | Sandstone—fossils | | 8 |
| 47 | Gray shales and sandstone | 30 | |
| 48, 49 | Shoal creek limestone | 4 | |
| 50, 51, 52 | Clay and bituminous shales | 16 | 6 |
| 53 | Coal No 9 | | 10 |
| 54 | Fire clay | 2 | |
| 55 | Sandy shales | 4 | |

Connected section from highest rocks of Effingham to lowest in the above named counties, condensed

| | | Ft | In |
|---|---|---|---|
| Sandstones and shales | | 108 | |
| Coal No 17 | | | 6 |
| Sandstone limestone and shales | | 145 | |
| Coal No 16—Nelson's coal | | | 16 |
| Sandstones and shales | | 90 | |
| Coal No 15—Shelby coal | | 1 | 10 |
| Shales and sandstone | | 65 | |
| Beck's creek coal No 14 | | 1 | 8 |
| Shales and sandstone some limestone | | 74 | |
| Coal No 13 Lower Hickory creek | 12 in to | | 16 |
| Sandstone and shales | | 95 | |
| Coal No 12 | 2 to 10 in | | 3 |
| Mostly limestone some shales | | 34 | |
| Coal No 11—Litchfield and Lake fork | | | 17 |
| Shales | | 42 | |
| Coal No 10 | | | 7 |
| Shales sandstone limestone, ironstone etc., including Shoal creek limestone | | 112 | |
| Coal No 9 | | | 10 |
| Shales and fire clay | | 6 | |
| Total upper Coal Measures | | 780 | |

Bond county is bounded on the north by Montgomery, on the east by Fayette, on the south by Clinton, and on the west by Madison county Its area is about 380 square miles Its surface originally consisted of about half prairie and half timber, but at present all the prairie and some of the timbered land is in cultivation or under fence.

*Topography, Timber and Soil*—The surface is diversified by mounds, hills, valleys and plains. It is mostly drained by Shoal creek and its tributaries; their general course is southward, with the Kaskaskia river and Hurricane creek on the east The most broken part of the country is probably near Bethel bridge on Shoal creek, where the hills are about 100 feet high In the southern part of the county the hills are low. The country is generally somewhat broken for about a mile on each side of Shoal creek. The ravines are deep and somewhat abrupt, with hillsides covered with a growth of white oak, black oak and hickory, sloping back to poor flats, with a growth of post oak, black oak, black jack and black hickory At the edge of the prairie on the west side o

Shoal creek the soil is rather thin, with a growth of black-jack and post oak; but further out on the prairie it becomes better. On the east side of Shoal creek, between the forks, near the edge of the prairie, there are some wet pin-oak flats blending into flat prairies.

Near East Fork the hills are lower than those of Shoal creek. Near the stream there is generally a good growth of white oak, black oak, hazel, hickory and sassafras. This is good wheat land. Eastwardly the country changes, and occasionally there are high sandy mounds, often a hundred feet above the creek bottoms, which, when not too sandy, are quite productive, supporting a natural growth of dog wood, sassafras, white oak, white walnut, hickory, black oak and ash, and on the shaded hillsides there are many ferns. Near the east county line a series of these mounds extend from the southern to the northern part, generally rising to about 50 feet above the surrounding plains, with which they almost imperceptibly connect by exceedingly gentle slopes. Sometimes these mounds extend into connected ridges, where we may find a luxuriant growth of vines, red and white elm, cherry, hickory, sassafras, ash, hazel, mulberry, black oak, red oak and local groves of sugar trees. Occasionally they present a beautiful and picturesque view, gently rising and falling in the distance, resembling a low range of mountains. The plains are often four or five miles wide, generally with a very sandy soil, inferior to that of the mounds.

The banks of Beaver creek are low, not often more than 10 to 15 feet high, and the adjacent country is generally flat. Along its margin may be found pin oak, laurel oak, persimmon, crab apple, hazel, plum and elm.

The smaller creeks generally go dry during the summer. The beds of all the streams are very sandy, their bottoms are wide, rich and heavily timbered, among which may be found, bur oak, red oak, sugar tree, black walnut, white walnut, hackberry, elm, honey locust, hickory, sycamore, birch and mulberry. On the hills there is an abundant supply of white and black oak timber.

*Drift.*—The bowlders seen in this county were all small, but among them were granite, quartzite, greenstone sienite, fragments of coal and fossils from the Devonian. In the western part of the county the drift is not well developed, but is best seen near Greenville. At the bridge on East Fork, three miles north east of Greenville, fragments of coal were found, which was a sufficient bait to the inexperienced to induce searching for more coal in the drift deposits. A shaft was sunk 87 feet to rock, when the water broke in and checked any further work. The upper ten feet passed through was yellow clay, below it blue clay extending to the bottom, becoming darker as they descended; at 25 feet a large lump of coal was found, and wood at 20 feet from the surface. The creek bank here shows.

| | | Ft |
|---|---|---|
| 1 | Red clay with some sand | 10 |
| 2 | Beds of clay with some reddish sand, somewhat stratified, with blue sandy clay at bottom | 30 |

At Greenville the drift extends from the creek to the summit of the hill, a distance of about 100 feet vertically, on top there is a deep red clay. The road washings disclose beds of coarse sand, pebbles and bowlders. The washings on the hillside filter the sand very much, and towards the bottom there are deposits of very fine clean sand.

At JOHN HALL'S, three miles east of Greenville, there was found in his well conglomerate masses of rounded drift pebbles, evidently cemented together by the silicious matter in solution in the infiltrating water. I noticed a fragment of magnesian limestone with many small pebbles and some sand closely adhering to it

It is evident that over the whole of this part of the State, including all of the counties I have examined, the surface was formerly 50 to 100 feet higher than at present, the missing portion having been composed of sands, clays, pebbles and bowlders, that this continued until near the close of the drift period, that the Pleistocene sea still spread over the country, with the exception of a few of the highest mounds, that the sea subsided at a rate sufficiently rapid to wear away most of the upper clays and bear them away, leaving finer sands strewn along the surface just as we see exemplified at present at the Greenville hill.

## *Coal Measures.*

Outcrops are seen on Shoal creek, Locust Fork, Dry Fork and Lake Fork. The total thickness in this county is about 220 feet, all belonging to the upper series, from No 26 to No 53, and include about three coal beds The following is a general section of the Coal Measure rock in Bond county. [Note—the numbers used correspond to those used in my general section in this and adjoining counties, see page 128, *et seq* ]

| | | Ft | In |
|---|---|---|---|
| No 26 | Clay shale | 0 | 8 |
| No 27 | Dark shaly limestone | | 10 |
| No 28 | Coal, No 12 | | 3 |
| No 29 | Shale | 13 | |
| No 30 | Shale and limestone | 8 | |
| No 31 | Limestone | 13 | |
| No 32 | Blue and bituminous shale | 4 | |
| No 33 | Coal, No 11 | 0 | 17 |
| No 34 | Mostly shale | 39 | |
| No 35 | Blue and bituminous shale | 1½ | |
| No 36 | Calcareo bituminous shale, fossils | 2 | |
| No 37 | Coal No 10 | 0 | 7 |
| No 38 | Fire clay | 4 | |
| No 39 | Sandy shale | 3 | |
| No 40 | Tutenmergel | 0 | 2 |
| No 41 | Iron stone | 1 | |
| No 42 | Argillaceous shale and flattened ironstone nodules | 20 | |

| | | Ft | In |
|---|---|---|---|
| No 43 / No 44 | Sandy limestone and sandstone, fossils | 4½ | |
| No 45 | Sandy shale | 30 | |
| No 46 | Sandstone fossils | 0 | 8 |
| No 47 | Gray shale and sandstone | 30 | |
| No 48 / No 49 | Shoal creek limestone | 4 | |
| No 50 / No 51 / No 52 | Clay and bituminous shale | 10½ | |
| No 53 | Coal No 9 | | 10 |
| No 54 | Fire clay | 2 | |
| No 55 | Sandy shale | 4 | |

The rocks occupying the highest geological position are those seen on Dry Fork and Lake Fork. On a branch of Lake Fork, near McCracken's, I observed the following beds

| | | Ft | In |
|---|---|---|---|
| No 26 | Brown and drab clay shales | 8 | |
| No 27 | Band shaly limestone, with *Bryozoa* | | 10 |
| No 28 | Coal No 12 | | 3 |
| No 29 | Clay shales the lower part a nodular limestone bed | 7 | |

On the head of Dry Fork the same beds occur, thus

| | | Ft |
|---|---|---|
| 1 | Limestone with fossils *Hemipronites crassus*, *Athyris subtilita* and *Synocladia biserialis* | 2 |
| 2 | Shales with brown iron stone nodules | 5 |
| 3 | Shale | 8 |
| 4 | Limestone No 31 | 10 |

Part of the same section, one mile down stream, appears as follows

| | | Ft | In |
|---|---|---|---|
| 1 | Dark coarse shaly limestone abounding in *Polypora*, *Synocladia biserialis* contains also *Productus Nebrascensis*, *Aviculopecten* and *Spiriferina Kentuckensis* | | 4 |
| 2 | Drab clay shale | 8 | |
| 3 | Buff Limestone, referred to No 31 with many remains of *Crinoids* contains also *Productus longispinus* | 5 | |

On Lake Fork, near McCracken's coal bank, limestone (No 31) is thirteen feet thick and has many minute particles of calcareous spar disseminated; the bottom bed of one foot consists of dark ash colored limestone, beneath this is four feet of bituminous and blue shale resting on seventeen inches of coal This coal I have marked as No 11, counting upward, and its place in the section is No 33

From this downward, according to the record of the Litchfield boring, there is thirty-nine feet vertical thickness to the next rocks coming under my observation In a descending series we next observe on the tributaries of Dry Fork, in sec. 19, T. 6 N., R. 4 W.,

| | | Ft | In |
|---|---|---|---|
| No 34 | Clay shale | 12 | |
| No 34½ | Rough calcareo ferruginous bed with *Bellerophon carbonarius*, *Pleurotomaria sphaerulata*, and *Macrocheilus* | | 3 |
| No 35 | Lead blue calcareous shale | | 8 |
| No 35½ | Bituminous shale | | 8 |
| No 36 | Lead blue calcareous shale fossiliferous it is sometimes a limestone contains *Productus longispinus*, *Chonetes variolata*? *Ch. Verneuiliana* and *Lophophyllum proliferum* | 2 | |
| No 37 | Bituminous coal | 0 | 7 |
| No 38 | Dark olive fire clay | 4 | |
| No 39 | Green sandy shales, containing rough brown nodules | 3 | |

| | | Ft | In |
|---|---|---|---|
| No 40 | Cone in cone, good specimens | 0 | 2 |
| No 41 | Four inches ironstone at top and bottom, separated by four inches of dark shales, contains *Hemipronites crassus*, and *Productus Prattenianus* . . | 1 | |
| No 42 | Argillaceous shale with flattened ironstone concretions | 20 | |
| No 43 | Ash gray silicious limestone, upper surface sandy and shelly, made up almost entirely of fossils, including *Aviculopecten occidentalis*, *Hemipronites crassus*, *Productus Nebrascensis*, *Athyris subtilita*, together with *Myalina Swallovi*, *Euomphalus subrugosus*, *[illegible]*, *Pinna per-acuta*, *Chonetes granulifera*, and *[illegible]* . | 2 | |
| No 44 | Brown sandstone, fracture sometimes shows a greenish shade, contains *Pinna per-acuta* and *P. [illegible]*. This is sometimes merged into that above and they then both present the characteristics of a ferruginous sandstone | 2½ | |
| No 45 | Drab clay shale with flattened concretions of ironstone | 30 | |
| No 46 | Dark drab indurated sandstone with some remains of a few fossils, could scarcely distinguish species. *Aviculopecten occidentalis* | | 8 |

Two miles above Bethel bridge, on Shoal creek, there are thin layers of No 46 containing *Myalina Swallovi*, *Aviculopecten occidentalis*, with fragments of plants (*Calamites*). Just below, on the creek, No 47 appears thus:

| | | Ft |
|---|---|---|
| 1 | Shaly ferruginous sandstone with ironstone concretions . . | 6 |
| 2 | Blue sandy shale | 2 |
| 3 | Sandstone, upper part sometimes gray, indurated below, and bright brown, lower part dark gray, with carbonaceous bands | 4 |
| 4 | Gray micaceous sandy shale and shaly sandstone . . | 3 |

Half a mile east of Bethel bridge the following beds are exposed:

| | | Ft |
|---|---|---|
| No 42 | Drab argillaceous shale with concretions of ironstone . | 12 |
| No 43 / No 44 | Sandy limestone and sandstone .. . | 3 |
| No 45 | Argillaceous shale . | 17 |

East of Fairview, near the east county line, on a branch of Hurricane creek, there is exposed about six feet of chocolate colored sandstone (part referred to No 46), containing *Productus Prattenianus*, *Aviculopecten occidentalis*, and remains of plants (*Calamites*). The position of this rock would indicate that the easterly dip of the rocks in this county does not exceed thirty feet across its whole breadth. Below No 46 are seen on Shoal creek occasional outcrops of thin bedded gray sandstone amounting to about thirty feet in total thickness.

| | *Shoal Creek Limestone* | Ft | In |
|---|---|---|---|
| No 49 | At many places on Locust Fork there crops out about four feet of an ash blue limestone with a somewhat splintery fracture, jointed vertically, the upper part shelly on exposure; contains *Productus longispinus*, *Spirifer lineatus*, *Sp. cameratus*, *Productus Nebrascensis*, *Rhynchonella Osagensis*, *Retzia punctulifera*, *Athyris subtilita*, *Chonetes granulifera* and *Hemipronites crassus* . . | 4 | |

Below this are seen on Locust Fork:

| | | Ft | In |
|---|---|---|---|
| No 50 | Greenish drab clay shale . . . | 2½ | |
| No 5[illegible] | Blue shale, somewhat bituminous . . . | 2 | |
| No 51 | Bituminous shale | 2 | |
| No 52 | Blue clay shale, with occasional flattened concretions of pyritiferous ironstone and septaria | 10 | |
| No 53 | Coal No 9, good except lower 2 in | | 10 |
| No 54 | Light blue fire clay, from a few inches thick to two feet. Next below is three feet of yellow and brown sandstone in one inch layers, then argillaceous shale. Passing eastwardly down the creek the rocks dip about twenty feet per mile. One mile south west at the county line, there is a local dip north of four feet in a hundred | | |

## *Economical Geology.*

*Coal*—McCracken's, on Lake Fork, is the only place where coal in any quantity has been taken out, and it is only when the creek is dry that this can be advantageously worked. The coal is seventeen inches thick and of good quality, it is dug out at several other places on Lake Fork, and has also been found on the head of Dry Fork. The other coal beds seen in this county are too thin to be worth working Shafts have been sunk in the drift clays for coal east of Greenville, but in order to reach any valuable coal bed they will have to go about 225 to to 300 feet or more below the general surface of the county

*Building Material*—The only really good building rock is the Shoal creek limestone, of which TOBIAS FILES and Mr. REAMS have good quarries The sandy limestone No 43 is also good for building purposes, and it may be procured one mile south-west of JAMES VALLENTINE'S, on a branch of Dry Fork Plenty of good limestone for lime can be procured on Lake Fork, on the head of Dry Fork and on Shoal creek near the north county line

*Fire-clay.*—No 38 may prove to be a good material for fire brick, and good clay for common bricks can be everywhere procured

*Water*—Springs are scarce Good water can generally be procured at twenty to thirty feet beneath the surface.

*Soil and Agriculture.*—On the mounds and white oak ridges the soil generally inclines to a red color, on the flats it is of a whitish or gray color and often quite sandy. The richest soil is that of the bottoms, next the high mounds, then the prairie in the south west part of the county, and next succeed the white oak lands and the flats. There is a small area of very good limestone soil near Locust Fork, with a growth of red oak, white oak, shell bark hickory, elm, hackberry, laurel oak, black oak, black walnut, mulberry, red bud, sassafras, and honey locust. The average yield of wheat is good, occasionally varying from fifteen to thirty bushels per acre, of corn, thirty to forty, very rarely on the best mound slopes reaching seventy five bushels per acre.

# CHAPTER XI.

## FAYETTE COUNTY.

This county is bounded on the north by Montgomery and Shelby, on the east by Effingham and Clay, on the south by Marion and Clinton, and on the west by Bond and Montgomery. It embraces an area of 720 square miles It is intersected by the Kaskaskia river from the north-east to the southwest, nearly equally dividing it Dismal creek flows south eastwardly through T 5 N, R 4 E All the other streams are tributaries of the Kaskaskia river, including East Fork, Flat, Carson, Richland, Hickory, (three forks,) Sand, Camp, Linn, Sugar, Rock, Big, Moccasin, Wolf and Waller's creeks on the east, with Hurricane, Buck, Bear, Buckmaster, Ramsey, Asher's, Beck's and Mitchel's creeks on the west

*Topography and Timber* —In passing from the streams to higher land we generally ascend by white oak slopes to post oak flats, thence to flat prairies, around which there is generally a margin of pin oak and sometimes black jack and post oak Between the various streams there are flats and mounds, the latter rising from fifty to seventy five feet above the flats There is a low mound in T 4 N, R 1 W, another in T 7 N, R 1 E. The mound just west of Vandalia is about ninety feet above the plains Occasionally they occur along the prairie between Hurricane creek and Kaskaskia river, and there is one large mound north west of Bowling Green East of Beck's creek the rise is gentle from the post oak flats to the white oak mounds about sixty feet above On the post oak flats and flat prairie we often find swampy places and sometimes ponds In the north part of T. 5 N., R. 1 W., there is a remarkable chain of ponds several miles long trending east and west, and mostly connected Their margins are marshy, with a growth of *Cephalanthus occidentalis* or button bush, pin oak, rose, maple *iris* and rushes Some are said to contain fish Northwardly towards Vandalia there are several other ponds Township 5 N, R 4 E, is generally very gently undulating Dismal creek rises from very gentle depressions in the flat prairies, no bluffs appear for several miles, but near the Chicago railroad they are sixty to seventy feet high and rise by long gentle slopes.

T. 4 N., R. 1 W., east of the river, is mostly flat with a gradually rising low mound in the south part. Near Carson, Flat and Richland creeks the country is gently undulating, with low hills near the streams, passing from rich land with pin oak, laurel oak, *cornus* and willow near the prairie, to land with elm, ash, pig nut and common hickory, hazel and plum, thence to open post oak flats. Near Hickory creek the country is somewhat broken into short white oak ridges blending into post oak and white oak flats. Near the creek the hills are not over fifty feet high. East of Vandalia to the prairie the country undulates very gently, having mostly a gray soil with sometimes an abundant growth of hickory, varied by richer land with black oak, white oak, shell bark hickory, laurel oak and flats with post oak and black oak. Passing thence along an undulating prairie down the gentle slopes of Sugar creek to Big creek and London City, there are broken white oak hills spreading out into flats with post oak, black oak, black jack and black hickory. On Rock and Wolf creeks the hills are sometimes sixty feet high, and on the bottoms as well as those of Sugar creek sugar trees are very abundant. The bottoms of Big and Wolf creeks are tolerably wide and flat and sustain a growth of red birch, sycamore, bur oak, coffee tree, ash, red mulberry, hickory, *cornus* coral berry and *amorpha fruticosa*. Beck's creek is rather a sluggish stream with wide and often wet pin oak bottoms; thence to the higher lands there are long slopes reaching to the flat post oak ridges. The neighboring prairies have a margin of pin oak, laurel oak and swamp white oak. Ramsey is a clear stream with a sandy bed, its bottoms are wide and high enough for good farming lands. On its bottoms may be found linden, buckeye, white walnut, bladder nut, hornbeam, hackberry, sugar tree, with iron wood, service berry and Spanish oak (?) on the hill sides. Lower down the stream the hills are low, but above the railroad they are more abrupt. From Vandalia westwardly to the county line the country is mostly flat with occasionally small prairies, a few low drift mounds, some ponds and some good timbered land with white oak, black oak and hickory, and occasionally poorer land with post oak, and richer land with sassafras, elm and ash. Hurricane creek is rather a sluggish stream, its bottoms are rich and often wet, varying in width, sometimes being a half mile wide and increasing near the Kaskaskia river. On its bottoms I observed sassafras trees one and a half feet in diameter and rose bushes twenty feet high, and the trees generally are very tall. Other trees observed on its bottoms were bur oak, hackberry, red bud, ash, elm, shell bark and pig nut hickory, hazel, wild allspice and grape vines. East of Fairview the growth on Hurricane bottoms consist mostly of pin oak and swamp white oak. The trees are larger and taller near the Kaskaskia river, one hickory growing on a hill side was noticed, four inches in diameter and sixty feet high. The Kaskaskia river (or Okaw, as it is commonly called,) has a deep channel and often sandy banks. Its bottoms below Vandalia are generally two miles wide, diminishing to one mile at the north county line. On the bottoms there is a heavy growth of timber, including pin oak, walnut, red oak, bur oak and cotton wood; and in wet places opposite Vandalia I noticed *Catalpa bignonioides*. The hills south of Vandalia are from fifty to seventy-five feet high. Towards the northern part of the county they are generally higher, being about 80 feet near the north county line, and 150 feet near the mouth of Beck's creek. On the other streams the hills are lower. On Buck creek are found *cornus florida*, white walnut, hornbeam, sugar tree, black gum, red oak, ash, linden, cotton wood, sycamore and white oak.

## *Stratigraphical Geology.*

In this county the formations consist of the Quaternary and the Coal Measures.

*Alluvium.*—The wide flat bottoms of the Kaskaskia embrace an extensive area of alluvium.

*Prairie Formation.*—The prairie near Dismal creek has a grayish soil containing a few small concretions of oxide of iron. Nine miles east of Vandalia on the national road the prairie soil contains a good deal of iron ore.

On Flat prairie, ten miles south west from Vandalia, the roadside washings expose:

| | | Ft. |
|---|---|---|
| 1 | Dark soil | 1 |
| 2 | Dark brown clay with darker stains exposed | 2 |

This I consider older than the alluvium, and may be equivalent to the Bottom prairie of the Mo. Geol. Report.

On the north side of Big creek there is exposed six feet of dark and buff clays, containing small nodules, probably loess.

*Drift.*—This formation is well developed in this county. A well near Ramsey was dug 100 feet deep through clay and gravel to solid rock. The mound west of Vandalia is about 100 feet above the general surface of the surrounding country, and 55 feet of drift is exposed on the bank of the river at the National road bridge. This would make the total thickness of the drift in this county not less than 150 feet; probably a little more, but not over 200 feet.

On the bank of the Kaskaskia river, at the National Road bridge, the upper 15 to 20 feet consists of red clay with coarse sand and gravel below, with 30 to 35 feet of blue clay at the bottom. The blue clay is very hard and compact, and contains numerous small rounded pebbles. One mile south-west the railroad cut exhibits red clay, sand and pebbles at the top, below, gray and brown beds, with alternations of beds of sand and pebbles, the latter sometimes partially cemented together.

The mound west of Vandalia has ash colored clay at the top, and darker colored clay and pebbles below, then brown sand, pebbles and bowlders, two-thirds up the hill side there is a fine spring of pure water issuing out of the brown sand. One and a half miles south-west of Vandalia the river bluffs are formed of steep, broken drift hills, with blue clay and bowlders at the bottom, overlaid by brown sand, towards the upper part there is a two foot stratum of ferruginous sandstone passing into a hard iron ore. Its firm hard appearance might induce one to think it belonged to an older age than the drift, but it lies at about the same horizontal level along the hillside, and is also found cropping out in other ravines at the same elevation, with drift sands below. Furthermore, its frequent occurrence in this county, and also in others, associated with the same drift beds, shows that it must belong to this formation The blue clay at this place is quite hard, and the water passing over it forms a tufaceous deposit on the surface In the ravines there are many fine springs of water issuing from the base of the sand beds

On Buck creek, near the Kaskaskia bottoms, there is a dark gray clay and sand conglomerate, which when struck emits a dull hollow sound. A good spring of water flows from just over it, and a tufaceous deposit is there formed.

Twelve miles south-east of Vandalia masses of ferruginous conglomerate were observed similar to that found near Vandalia. A well here shows 8 feet of sand at the top, and 18 feet of sand and pebbles below. In the road north of Greenland I observed—

| | | Ft |
|---|---|---|
| 1 | Buff clay and gray sandstone | 5 |
| 2 | Ferruginous sandstone | 4 |
| 3 | Buff clay and pebbles | 4 |
| 4 | Blue clay and pebbles in sight | 6 |

In sec 31, T. 6 N., R. 2 E, on the land of GEORGE PHIFER, a broken stratum of coal 1½ inches thick occurs in the drift, with blue clay and pebbles both above and below One unacquainted with geology might imagine a permanent coal bed to be here.

A similar place was examined on Bear creek, five miles from Vandalia The hill is here 27 feet high, and near the middle there is a thin stratum of black sand, beneath this are streaks and fragments of coal enveloped by red sand and small bowlders, and near the base of the hill there is a mass of Coal Measure fire clay. There are also masses of sandstone and limestone not much worn, all evidently drifted but a short distance. Other bowlders found here are of granite, sienite and quartzite.

At the mill on Beck's creek, in sec 10, T 8 N, R 2 E, Coal Measure limestone is seen apparently resting on a bed of drift; some of the sand and pebbles are even cemented to the limestone, which must have been overhanging when the drift was deposited, and the latter washed beneath.

*Mounds*—In the western part of the county there are many mounds rising above the general surface of the country 50 to 90 feet, and occasionally there are a few east of the river The various clays, sands and pebbles found on these mounds, and entering into their composition, present the same character peculiar to mounds found in other counties.

Among the drift bowlders found in this county are sienite, granite, hornblende rock, greenstone, quartzite, sandstone, limestone and clays from the Coal Measures No very large bowlders were found.

## *Coal Measures*

On account of the non-appearance of certain intermediate beds necessary in the connection, we can only approximate the thickness of the Coal Measures in this county; but there is sufficient data to assume that the total thickness may reach 350 feet, ranging from No. 1 to No. 46, of the section of upper Coal Measure strata, and include the horizon of four coals, viz 13, 14, 15 and 16, although the latter has not yet been found in the county.

The rocks occupying the highest geological horizon in this county are probably those on Dismal creek, of which the following is a section:

| | | Ft |
|---|---|---|
| No 1 | Sandy shale | 10 |
| No 2 | Dull limestone, upper part nodular, middle in even layers, no fossils seen | 5 |
| No 3 | Clay shales with nodules, middle red, remainder olive colored | 12 |
| No 4 | Sandy shales and thin beds of hard, gray sandstone | 21 |

The next highest beds are found on Hickory and Rock creeks

*On Hickory Creek*

| | | Ft |
|---|---|---|
| No 1 | Sandy shales in the middle are dark micaceous and carbonaceous partings, below there are occasional thin beds of sandstone, color yellow, drab and gray | 20 |
| No 2 | Sandstone, hard, gray and brown, ferruginous and yellow, part of it for 100 feet horizontally is a vermilion red, containing *Lepidodendron* and *Sigillariæ* | 5 |
| No 3 | Slaty coal and bituminous shale, passing into a cannel coal, at Odell's contains *Solenomya radiata* and *Aviculopecten Whitei*, equivalent to No 15 Shelby coal | 3 |
| No 4 | Dark blue clay shales stained brown | 1 |
| No 5 | Yellow clay | 2 |
| No 6 | Soft yellow sandstone and shales | 3 |
| No 7 | Greenish blue clay shales | 2 |

In passing down stream a quarter of a mile the rocks rise 1 foot in 60

| | | Ft | In |
|---|---|---|---|
| No 8 | One and a half miles down stream there is exposed 25 feet of clay shales, they may be as much as 50 or 75 feet in thickness. Men boring at Odell's report 80 feet below No 3 (coal No 15) without reaching any coal. In the road near the creek at Shibtown the following beds were seen | | |
| No 9 | Dark grayish blue shaly limestone sometimes in solid layers suitable for building purposes, contains remains of fossils | | 8 |
| No 10 | A few inches of shale | | [illegible] |
| No 11 | Coal—smut in the road—in a well | 1 | |
| No 11½ | Fire clay covered by *debris* at this place | 4 | |
| No 12 | Ochrey brown sandy shales with nodules of ironstone and some hard rough masses of sandstone | 25 | |

Below this there may be 25 to 50 feet more of sandy shales, to the next lowest rock seen at Richardson's coal bank, in sec 27, T. 6 N., R. 2 E.

| | | Ft | In |
|---|---|---|---|
| No 14 | Yellow clay shales | 6 | |
| No 15 | Dark gray shelly limestone passing into a calcareous shale, very fossiliferous, contains *Hemipronites crassus*, *Chonetes Flemingii*, *Spirifer cameratus*, *Productus Nebrascensis*, *Aviculopecten occidentalis*, *Myalina ampla*, *Myalina Swallovi*, *Leda arata*, *Monopteria gibbosa*, *Schizodus*, *Macrodon*, *Edmondia*, *Phillipsia Sangamonensis*, *Poteriocrinus* ? near *P. hemisphericus*, stems of Crinoids, *Synocladia biserialis* and *Fistulipora* | 4 | |
| No 16 | A few feet of clay shale and a few inches of dark shale | | |
| No 17 | Covered by *debris*—Bituminous coal (13) said to be | | 16 |

Below the forks of Hickory creek there is exposed 8 feet of thin bedded sandstone. On the South fork of Hickory, part of the above section appears thus.

| | | Ft | In |
|---|---|---|---|
| 1 | Bituminous shale | | [illegible] |
| 2 | Dark blue shaly limestone | | 6 |
| 3 | Bituminous coal (coal No 14) | | 10 |
| 4 | Olive clay shale | 2 | |
| 5 | Nodular arenaceous limestone, contains *Productus Prattenianus*, *Allorisma* and a large *Pleurotomaria* | 2 | |
| 6 | Dark red and olive clay shales with nodules and concretions of ironstone | 4 | |

A quarter of a mile down the creek there is about 40 feet of hard sandstone and sandy shales.

On Rock creek and Wolf creek coal No. 15 (Shelby coal) with the adjacent rocks is found. At Pfiffer's and at Joel Blakely's the section is as follows

| | | Ft | In |
|---|---|---|---|
| 1 | Yellow and brown sandstone, containing remains of plants, with a few red ochrey bands at the lower part | 35 | |
| 2 | Soft black shales | 1 | |
| 3 | Coal (15) | | 18 |
| 4 | Clay with some nodules of limestone | 4 | |
| 5 | Rough looking fine grained buff limestone, no fossils except a few Crinoid stems | 4 | |
| 6 | Sandy shale | 8 | |

Below the forks of Moccasin there is exposed 25 feet of shales, the upper 5 feet sandy, below dark bluish olive clay shale. At 12 feet from the bottom there is a 5 inch calcareous stratum, abounding in *Myalina subquadrata*, also contains *Leda arata*, *Schizodus*, *Lingula*, *Macrodon* (large Sp.), and fragments of crinoids. This bed is probably 30 or 40 feet below coal No 15

Near Howard's Point the following beds are below coal No 15 In sec 36, T 7 N, R 2 E, there is an outcrop on the head of Camp creek of about 2 feet of hard grayish-blue fucoidal sandstone, which turns dark brown on exposure

At Howard's Point part of the same sandstone appears thus:

| | | Ft |
|---|---|---|
| 1 | Yellow shaly sandstone | 1 |
| 2 | Hard bluish gray sandstone | 1 |
| 3 | Sandy shales and thin beds of chocolate colored sandstone | 10 |

A quarter of a mile down the creek, there is 15 feet of dove colored clay shale In the lower part are concretions of sulphuret of iron and carbonate of iron and lime

| | | Ft | In |
|---|---|---|---|
| No 2 | Dark shales lower part bituminous, sometimes there is a bed of dark shaly limestone | 1 | 6 |
| No 3 | Bituminous coal (No 14) | | 10 |
| No 4 | Dove colored fire clay | 4 | |
| No 5 | Thickly laminated soft chocolate colored and red sandy shales | 4 | |

On Kaskaskia river, in sec 28, T 9 N, R 3 E

| | | Ft | In |
|---|---|---|---|
| 1 | Slope from hill top about | 60 | |
| 2 | Olive clay shales with some ferruginous concretions | 7 | |
| 3 | Dark blue shaly limestone | | 4 |
| 4 | Brownish ash calcareous shales contains *Athyris subtilita*, *Chonetes Flemingii*, crinoid arms and columns | 2 | |
| 5 | Bituminous coal (No 14) | | 14 |
| 6 | Fire clay | 4 | |
| 7 | Coarse rough nodular sandy shales some hard nodular, sandy and calcareous beds containing *Productus Prattenanus* *Aviculopecten*, etc | 6 | |

Down the river 300 yards the same sandstone appears at the water's edge

At Brown's coal bank on the west fork of Beck's creek, at the county line, in the south part of sec 22, T 9 N, R. 1 E., the coal is said to be 16 inches thick, capped by dark slate. The section is

| | | Ft | In |
|---|---|---|---|
| 1 | Dark lead blue limestone dull appearance, weathers ash blue | 1 | |
| 2 | Lead blue calcareous shales abounds in *Productus Nebrascensis*, *Orthis carbonaria* *Retzia punctulifera* *Athyris subtilita* also contains *Spirifer plano convexus*, *Spiriferina Kentuckensis* | 2 | |
| 3 | Coal (14) | 16 to 22 inches | |

A half mile down the creek there is found.

| | | Ft | In |
|---|---|---|---|
| 1 | Ferruginous limestone rather shaly, contains remains of crinoids and *Lophophyllum proliferum* | | 6 |
| 2 | Light greenish clay shales | 2 | |
| 3 | Thinly laminated sandy shales | 2 | |
| 4 | Hard bluish gray or drab calcareous sandstones | 1 | |
| 5 | Drab and blue clay shales | 8 | |

In sec. 30, T. 9 N., R 2 E, (known as the Gooden coal bank) we have

| | | Ft | In |
|---|---|---|---|
| 1 | Drift slope | | 7 |
| 2 | Dull ash blue shaly limestone weathers to a dirty drab, fossils are *Productus Nebrascensis*, *P Prattenanus*, and *Chonetes* | 1 | 6 |

| | | Ft | In |
|---|---|---|---|
| 3 | Clay shales | 8 | |
| 4 | Thinly laminated clay shales with plants | 1 | |
| 5 | Clay shales in thin layers in the creek, beneath there is said to be a thin seam of coal | | 1 |

An interesting group of rocks occurs on Ramsey creek, comparatively isolated from any other group in this county, no other outcrop being observed within six miles, but from the topography of the country it is apparent that their position is below that of the rocks previously mentioned. Their position is near No. 22 of section on page 128.

Section at the railroad on Ramsey creek and just below:

| | | Ft | In |
|---|---|---|---|
| 1 | Sandstone and sandy shale | 21 | |
| 2 | Clay shales with compact nodules of iron ore | 7 | |
| 3 | Semi bituminous dark slate | | 2 |
| 4 | Indurated clay shale a few inches | | 1 |
| 5 | Even bed of iron stone, outside brown, fracture purplish drab, abounds in *Estheria*, also contains *Aviculopecten* | | 2 |
| 6 | Light-blue argillaceous shale | 4 | |
| 7 | Drab colored clay shales or fire clay | 4 | |
| 8 | Drab clay shales nodules in the upper part, lower part talus of above, about | 15 | |
| 9 | An ½ to ¾ mile down the creek we have an ash blue limestone, upper part turns brown and shells off on exposure | 3 | |

The lower part is sometimes shelly; abounds in *Syntrilasma hemiplicata*, also contains *Meekella striato-costata*, *Chonetes*, *Spirifer cameratus*, *Sp. lineatus*, *Spiriferina Kentuckensis*, *Athyris subtilita*, *Terebratula bovidens*, *Hemipronites crassus*, *Productus longispinus*, *P. costatus*, *Nautilus*, *Stenopora lepidodendroides*, *Polypora Synocladia*, and *Lophophyllum proliferum*; it has also dark fucoidal veins passing irregularly through it.

| | | Ft | In |
|---|---|---|---|
| 10 | Clay | 1 | |
| 11 | Coarse gray limestone, contains only a few crinoid stems and a few remains of fish teeth | 2 | 6 |
| 12 | Yellow clay and nodules of limestone | | 7 |

About two miles down the creek there is an outcrop on the hillside of about two feet of even bedded chocolate colored and yellowish sandstone, with twenty five feet of sandy shale beneath, and towards the foot of the bluff, two inches of blue, compact limestone with a pot metal ring; this is probably near No. 4 of above section. One and a half miles further down the creek, at a ford, the following appears:

| | | Ft |
|---|---|---|
| 1 | Drift of sand and clay | 7 |
| 2 | Sandy shales | 4 |
| 3 | Yellow, ochre colored sandstone | 2 |
| 4 | Gray shales with ironstone concretions abounding in some very nice fossils, including *Leda arata*, *Solenomya radiata*, *Myalina*, resembling *M. meliniformis*, *Schizodus* near *S. Rossicus*, *Allorisma*, *Aviculopecten* and *Edmondia* | 5 |

No. 4 of this section is near No. 5 of the section at the railroad bridge. The course of Ramsey creek is generally south east. From the above it will be seen that the rocks have a slight dip down stream.

On Beck's creek at the mill, in sec 10, T. 8 N., R. 2 E., there appears 6 feet of buff limestone abounding in *Syntrilasma hemiplicata*, and *Lophophyllum proliferum*, also contains *Athyris subtilita*, *Productus costatus* and *P. punctatus* This bed of limestone is seen extending along the creek for 100 feet, and has a regular local dip of 17° On Hurricane creek, near the line of Bond county, east of Fairfield, beds of sandstone occur containing fossils resembling those of No. 46.

## *Economical Geology.*

*Coal*—Much anxiety was manifested by the citizens of Vandalia on the subject of coal. At present their supplies are brought by rail from Perry county.

Coal 15 or Sheby coal is only found near the head of Hickory creek 2½ miles from the east county line, and northwardly near the county line on Rock creek and Wolf creek.

At Jas P. Odell's, in sec 34, T 6 N, R. 3 E., a slaty coal has been taken out, but as yet is not much used. A shaft was in process of being sunk, and had reached 80 feet, without coming to any other coal

On the land of Joel Blakeley, near Rock creek, an 18 inch seam has been worked, the upper and lower two inches pyritiferous and 14 inches of good coal. At Blakeley's bank part of the coal bifurcates, and insinuates thin veins into the overlaying sandstone.

The neighboring hills are low and the coal can be easily reached Mrs Mary Grant and Mrs Phifer also have coal banks in the same vicinity This coal crops out one foot thick at the edge of the water of Wolf creek, in sec. 12, T. 8 N, R. 3 E

Coal No 14 crops out on the Kaskaskia river at Wm Thomas' in sec. 2, T. 9 N., R. 3 E, 14 inches thick, at Jas Brown's near the north county line on the waters of Beck's creek, in sec 21, T. 9 N, R. 1 E, 16 to 22 inches thick, a half mile north of Howard's Point 10 inches. On the south fork of the Hickory, in sec. 10, T. 5 N., R. 2 E, it is 10 inches; at Col Forman's 18 to 20 inches

Only at Brown's and Col Forman's has there been much mining.

At Brown's a drift 2½ feet high has been run into the hill, but recently nothing has been done At Forman's, in sec 1, T. 5 N, R 2 E, a good many pits have been dug at various places on the bottom and a good deal of coal taken therefrom at different times. On the bank of a branch the coal appears very well, extending nearly horizontally along the stream for about 50 feet, and 20 inches thick, with 4 feet of fire clay beneath; at one place the coal measures 2 feet in thickness. A trace of this coal appears in the road at "Slabtown"

Coal No 13—Banks have been opened at two places on Little Hickory creek, viz at Wm. Hamilton's, in the S. W. qr. of the N. W. qr. of sec. 26, T. 6 N., R. 2 E, and at Wm. Richardson's, in sec 27, T 6 N, R. 2 E. At Hamilton's several pits have been dug on low ground near the creek, but they are now filled with *debris*. At Richardson's the coal was taken from the side of the bluff, but is now hidden from view by the talus from above; the thickness of the seam is reported to be from 16 inches to 2 feet, and the coal of good quality. These places can be worked without much cost

On Beck's creek, about a mile above the Shelbyville road, a good deal of coal has been taken from the creek, but the water is generally in the way This is known as the Goodeen coal bank A bed of coal is reported to be at the bottom of the Kaskaskia river, in the S E corner of T. 9 N., R 2 E, but the water is generally at least 6 feet over it

The western boundary of coal No 15 is a north and south line two miles from the east county line The western boundary of coal No 14 is nearly parallel to the last and three miles west of it, with an outlier of a few miles square near the north county line, east of the railroad.

The western boundary of coal No 13 passes northwardly near the middle of R 2 E, crossing Kaskaskia river near the mouth of Beck's creek, and thence north westwardly. West of this line no coal beds have appeared in the county.

The coal under the Shoal creek limestone is about 230 to 240 feet below the lower Hickory creek coal Coal No. 7 is 375 to 500 feet below coal No 13. From this I would suppose that in order to reach a good workable coal, a shaft would have to be sunk 300 to 500 feet at Vandalia, at that depth coal No 7 (6 to 8 feet thick) might be reached *

*Iron Ore*—Thin beds and concretions of carbonate of iron ore are common in the Coal Measure shales, but were not found sufficiently abundant to work in this county. On the National road, nine miles east of Vandalia, I noticed a deposit of very dark colored oxide of iron in prairie clay or soil, it crops out about 4 inches thick, in a rough massive stratum around the margin of a washed place of 50 feet square, on one side it is 6 inches beneath the surface and on the other 2 to 3 feet. The clay at this place is probably of older age than the soil or alluvium, probably nearly, if not quite as old as the loess Small concretionary nodules of a similar variety of iron ore are often found washed out of the prairie clays

The ferruginous sandstone, previously spoken of under the head of "Drift," may sometimes be considered an iron ore, it is abundant near Vandalia, and is also found near Greenland and at William Porter's on Little Hickory

*Building Rock*—There is a good sandstone quarry near Ramsey creek, two miles below the railroad. the rock is generally about 2 feet thick and of good quality, part of the stone arch culvert on the I C R. R. at Vandalia, was procured here.

* See section of shaft and boring at Vandalia, at the close of this chapter

The *Syntrilasma* limestone on Ramsey creek has been very extensively used on the railroad, and also in bridge abutments on the National road. Part of it seems to stand the weather well, but a good deal has been cracked by frost. The lower bed under that containing *Syntrilasma*, has the appearance of being a very durable stone, but I am not aware that it has been used.

The buff limestone, on Beck's creek near its mouth, would probably make a very good lime.

In sec. 10, T. 5 N., R. 2 E., there is a quarry of hard brownish-gray sandstone, rather irregular in its character, changing color on exposure. It has been used in some bridge abutments on the National road, but has not proved durable.

At Wm. Yokes', north of the National road, nine miles east of Vandalia, there is a good sandstone quarry. The rock is thin bedded, tolerably hard, but works freely and is of even thickness. On Dismal creek, near Laclede, there is a five foot bed of buff limestone, which makes a tolerably good building rock and good lime.

*Road Material*.—At Vandalia there are very extensive beds of sand and rounded gravel, very suitable for road beds and much used for ballasting on the railroad. Several lumps of native copper have been found in this county; one a half pound and another 10 ounces in weight.

*Soil and Agriculture*.—The Kaskaskia bottoms embrace a large area of, as yet, untilled lands, being subject to annual overflows, which has heretofore been a drawback to their cultivation, but there certainly will be a time when these lands will be sources of great wealth. The prairies in the southern and south-east parts of the county probably contain the best upland; the other prairies have generally a thin soil, similar to that on the post oak flats but probably richer. Much of the timbered land is poor, but there are occasionally very rich spots of elm and cherry land, for example, on the Vandalia and Carlyle road.

The best uplands will produce 40 to 50 bushels of corn per acre; other lands 25 to 30.

A good average of wheat is 20 bushels per acre, the timbered land producing the best crops.

Recently the bugs have been quite destructive to the potato crop; but generally, with proper culture, very fine crops can be raised. I would suppose that on the broken ridges fine vineyards could be made, but none have yet been started.

*Wells and Springs*.—There are some very good springs in this county, generally originating in the drift sands, and are sometimes a pleasant chalybeate.

On the land of Geo Phifer, in sec 31, T. 6 N, R 2 E, there are several chalybeate springs issuing from the sands of the drift, and Mr P. says that they always have the same flow of water In the hills south of Vandalia there are a good many fine springs of mostly very pure and clear water.

In the north part of the county, the wells are 12 to 18 feet deep, with weak veins of water. A well on Rock creek prairie was dug 39 feet and plenty of water obtained

One mile south of Vandalia a well was dug 30 feet, mostly through sand with some clay at the top, and plenty of water procured. On a hill, at an elevation of about forty feet above, another well was dug 60 feet deep, through similar material, with no water, near the latter, another was dug 65 feet deep, mostly passing through sand, to water. A half mile north is another well, 30 feet deep, through clay and sand, with plenty of water

*Antiquities*—There are a good many ancient mounds of human construction in this county; a few near Vandalia, some on Hurricane creek, and some near Ramsey But few of them have been opened I obtained only a few flint arrowheads and a stone hatchet made of sienite, and picked up a few broken fragments of pottery near the site of a mound that had been opened.

A particular examination of these mounds might develop some interesting relics

In conclusion I would state that I am under many obligations to Mr. TEVIS GREATHOUSE, of Vandalia for assistance in furnishing maps, and am also particularly indebted to Dr G W. BASSETT, of the same place, for assistance in making collections, in getting information, and for spending several days in assisting me.

NOTE—Since the foregoing report was made by Mr. BROADHEAD, a shaft was sunk at Vandalia to the depth of 377 feet 3 inches, and a boring from the bottom of the shaft to a total depth of about 574 feet

The following section of this shaft and boring was furnished by Dr. G W BASSETT, of Vandalia

| | | | Ft | In | Total | |
|---|---|---|---|---|---|---|
| No | 1 | Soil and yellow clay, sand, gravel, bowlder clays and quicksand (drift) | 94 | 6 | | |
| No | 2 | Hard sandstone | 1 | 2 | 95 | 8 |
| No | 3 | Dark sandy, clay shale | 6 | 3 | 101 | 11 |
| No | 4 | Clay shale | 4 | 3 | 106 | 2 |
| No | 5 | Black shale | 10 | 2 | 116 | 4 |
| No | 6 | Dark gray shale | 7 | 4 | 123 | 8 |
| No | 7 | Coal, No 10 | | 10 | 124 | 6 |
| No | 8 | Fire clay | 8 | 9 | 133 | 3 |
| No | 9 | Hard gray shale, with iron nodules | 17 | | 150 | 3 |

| | | Ft | In | Total | |
|---|---|---|---|---|---|
| No 10 | Hard gray sandstone | 7 | 11 | 158 | 2 |
| No 11 | Bituminous shale | 7 | 10 | 166 | |
| No 12 | Clay shale | 5 | 6 | 171 | 6 |
| No 13 | Dark gray, sandy shale | 16 | 2 | 187 | 8 |
| No 14 | Fire clay | | 4 | 188 | |
| No 15 | Hard gray sandy shale | 9 | 5 | 197 | 5 |
| No 16 | Dark gray shale | 11 | 2 | 208 | 7 |
| No 17 | Lime conglomerate | 3 | | 211 | |
| No 18 | Clay shale | 2 | 8 | 213 | 8 |
| No 19 | Shale | 3 | | 216 | 8 |
| No 20 | Bituminous limestone with *Pinna per acuta*, etc | 2 | | 218 | 8 |
| No 21 | Fire clay | 5 | | 223 | 8 |
| No 22 | Clay shale | 4 | | 227 | 8 |
| No 23 | Dark clay shale with *Arca rectilaterarius* | 38 | 2 | 265 | 10 |
| No 24 | Bituminous shale | 1 | 5 | 267 | 5 |
| No 25 | Limestone, Carlinville and Shoal creek bed | 4 | 3 | 271 | 8 |
| No 26 | Gray shale | 27 | 6 | 299 | 2 |
| No 27 | Bituminous shale | 1 | 2 | 300 | 4 |
| No 28 | Coal No 9 | | 6 | 300 | 10 |
| No 29 | Bituminous shale | | 3 | 301 | 1 |
| No 30 | Gray shale | 1 | 8 | 302 | 9 |
| No 31 | Gray sandstone | 1 | | 303 | 9 |
| No 32 | Gray shale | 21 | 7 | 325 | 4 |
| No 33 | Coal No 8 | | 9 | 326 | 1 |
| No 34 | Fire clay | 1 | | 327 | 1 |
| No 35 | Bituminous shale | 1 | 6 | 328 | 7 |
| No 36 | Sandstone | 3 | 7 | 332 | 2 |
| No 37 | Sandy shale | 13 | | 345 | 2 |
| No 38 | Dark gray shale with bands of iron ore | 7 | 3 | 352 | 5 |
| No 39 | Bituminous shale with fossil shells and ferns | 2 | 6 | 355 | 11 |
| No 40 | Coal | | 1 | 356 | |
| No 41 | Clay with iron stone concretions | 9 | 3 | 365 | 3 |
| No 42 | Sandstone with fossil ferns | 9 | 2 | 374 | 5 |
| No 43 | Sandy shale with clay parting | 2 | 10 | 377 | 3 |

*Bottom of shaft*—boring as follows

| | | Ft | In | Total | |
|---|---|---|---|---|---|
| No 44 | Sandstone | 111 | | 488 | 3 |
| No 45 | Limestone | 2 | | 490 | 3 |
| No 46 | Clay shale | 9 | 10 | 500 | 1 |
| No 47 | Gray sandstone | 5 | 7 | 505 | 8 |
| No 48 | Shale | 8 | 10 | 514 | 6 |
| No 49 | Clay shale | 6 | | 520 | 6 |
| No 50 | Bituminous shale | 5 | 6 | 526 | |
| No 51 | Dark gray shale | 5 | 2 | 531 | 2 |
| No 52 | Clay shale, with lime nodules | 12 | | 543 | 2 |
| No 53 | Bituminous shale | 1 | | 544 | 2 |
| No 54 | Gray shale | 5 | 11 | 550 | 1 |
| No 55 | Blue clay shale | 4 | | 554 | 1 |
| No 56 | Gray clay shale | 12 | 3 | 566 | 4 |
| No 57 | Limestone | | 10 | 567 | 2 |
| No 58 | Bituminous slate and coal | | 6 | 567 | 8 |
| No 59 | Fire clay | 6 | | 573 | 8 |
| No 60 | Limestone | | 8 | 574 | 4 |

This shaft and boring reaches a depth of 574 feet without finding a workable coal The shaft at Centralia was sunk to the depth of 576 feet, at which depth a seam of coal 7 feet in thickness was found. This coal is 373 feet below the Carlinville limestone in that shaft, and if the strata retain the same thickness at Vandalia, their boring terminated 80 feet above the Centralia coal seam. It seems from these shafts and borings that there is a very decided increase in the thickness of the strata associated with the lower coals in the central portion of the State, and that they will be found at a greater depth here than at points nearer the borders of the coal field. The parties interested in the matter at Vandalia should prosecute their boring at least to the horizon of the coal seam at Centralia, to determine, if possible, whether that coal extends into Fayette county.

A. H. W.

# CHAPTER XII.

## MONTGOMERY COUNTY.

This county is bounded on the north by Christian, on the east by Christian, Shelby and Fayette, on the south by Fayette, Bond and Madison, and on the west by Macoupin. Its superficial area is 19½ townships or 702 square miles

*Topography.*—On Ramsey creek the hills are low and the country gently undulating; near Nokomis there are several mounds, with long, gentle depressions between, stretching off into rich plains. Westwardly, across the country, through townships 10, 11 and 12 N., the country is for the most part rather flat. Near the East Fork of Shoal creek the hills are generally low, becoming higher as we descend the stream; in the south part of T. 8 N., they are 40 to 50 feet high. On Shoal creek and Middle Fork the hills are 40 to 50 feet high, and rise by long, gentle ascents.

On the West Fork of Shoal creek the country is generally broken for a few miles from the stream, and the hills are 60 to 70 feet high. Near Lake Fork the hills are not very high. In the south half of the county between the main streams there are occasional mounds, often a mile or more across their base and about 50 feet above the adjacent plain, with which they are connected by a long descent.

*Timber and Prairie*—Probably a little less than two-thirds of the area of this county is prairie. The northern part is mostly prairie; the southern has a large proportion of timber. Near Hurricane creek there are post oak flats, changing to low white oak hills near the creek. At the edge of the prairie the growth is mostly laurel oak, sumach, hazel, plum, etc Near Ramsey creek the upland growth consists of white oak, black oak, post oak, laurel oak, hazel and sassafras The East Fork hills have mostly pin oak, black oak and post oak, changing near the prairies to laurel oak, black oak and hazel. Shoal creek hills have mostly white oak, black oak, sassafras and hickory, changing to poorer flats, with post oak, black jack and black hickory, often extending to the prairie Near Hillsboro the growth is principally black oak with some white oak, hickory, sassafras and hazel

Near Walshville and Lake Fork the country is gently undulating, with a growth principally of plum, black walnut, honey locust, wild cherry and grape vines Wild vines loaded with grapes were observed nearly everywhere in the woods, proving the soil to be naturally well adapted to the grape.

Post oak flats occur near West Fork as far up as T 10 N.

Sugar trees are occasionally found along the Middle and West Forks, and some extensive groves are found on the bottoms of main Shoal creek.

The following comprises a list of such trees and shrubs as were observed occurring in this county crab apple, ash, prickly ash, red birch, bladder nut, buckeye, box elder, button bush, bitter sweet, blackberry, coralberry, choke cherry, common cherry, coffee tree, *cornus*, (2 species), cottonwood, *Clematis Virginiana*, elder, grape, (4 or 5 species,) gooseberry, black haw, hackberry, honey locust, *hop tree*, hazel, shellbark and thick shellbark hickory, pig nut hickory, black hickory and common hickory, iron wood, linden, white maple, sugar tree, red mulberry, pa-paw, persimmon, plum, black, red, white, post, laurel, pin, chestnut, blackjack, bur and swamp white oak, red and American elm, red bud, raspberry, rose, red root, poison oak, sassafras, service berry, sarsaparilla, sumach, trumpet creeper, Virginia creeper, willow, (several species,) and black and white walnut.

## *Geological Formations.*

Washings in the road at Walshville show 8 feet of brownish buff clay with but few pebbles Along the various streams are occasional exposures of sand and pebbles with some beds of brownish yellow clay. Five miles north east of Litchfield, 45 feet of drift is exposed, the lower part a compact bed of dark clay, with some sand and pebbles. In sec. 8, T 8 N, R 3 W, the following description was given me of the various clays passed through in well digging

1.—Soil. 2—Yellow clay or hardpan, at 24 feet reached a 3 foot bed of sand, then soft moist clay

Seventy-five yards from this another well was dug, showing in the upper part brownish yellow clay at 20 feet, and at 38 feet was a 2 foot bed of sand, and at 42 feet, specimens of wood.

On the head waters of Ramsey there are many springs slightly chalbyeate, and some containing sulphate of iron, issuing from beds of drift sand and pebbles.

There is certainly evidence that at some former period of time the whole surface of the county was 50 to 75 feet higher than at present; that since the original drift deposition (it may have been just at the close of the Drift period) large masses of these deposits were washed off, leaving occasional mound like elevations, several of which may be seen near Nokomis, a few between the East and West forks, and the hills between Hillsboro and Butler.

## *Coal Measures.*

The upper Coal Measures appear in part in this county, and underlay all the superficial deposits, and include coal beds No 11 and No. 13, with a trace of No 12, and embrace about 150 feet of rocks, reaching from the base of No 33 to No. 20 of upper Coal Measure section.

Nos 20 and 21.—In sec 12, T. 10 N., R 1 W., there crops out along the creek 8 feet of sandy shale and blue limestone, close by is an outcrop of brown shaly soft limestone, containing *Hemipronites crassus* and Crinoid stems, a *Machrocheilus* and *Spirifer cameratus* were also found. The exact thickness between 21 and 22 is unknown, the outcrops are ten miles apart with no evidence of a continuous easterly dip, but it is probable that 25 or even 50 feet may intervene.

*Rocks on the East Fork of Shoal creek.*—In sec. 24, T. 8 N, R 3 W, we have

| | | Ft |
|---|---|---|
| 1 | Mostly dark lead blue shales, upper part sandy with brown nodules of iron stone, the lower two thirds calcareous with many fossils *Productus Nebrascensis, Spirifer cameratus Pleurotomaria hemisphericus*, *Bellerophon montfortianus, B Carbonarius, Orthoceras cribrosum, Leda bellistriata* a fossil near *Solenscus typicus Bryozoa* and a few branching corals | 10 |
| 2 | Ash blue limestone, jointed and shelly on top contains *Productus Prattenianus, Chonetes, Aviculopecten, Pecten ? Aviculatus* and *Prod Boonensis* .. . | 1 |

The last named limestone I regard as No 22 of my upper Coal Measure section. North east of Irving on East Fork, and down stream for a mile, there are occasional outcrops of an ash blue hard shelly limestone, abounding in a large variety of *Productus Prattenianus;* it also contains *P. costatus, P punctatus, P. Nebrascensis, Spirifer cameratus, Aviculopecten carboniferus, Chonetes Verneuiliana, Ch. Flemingii*, and a branching coral.

In sec 7, T 8 N, R 2 W, obtained the following section

| | | Ft |
|---|---|---|
| 1 | Masses of tumbled limestone with *Hemipronites crassus, Productus Nebrascensis, Edmondia* and *Bryozoa* . . . | [illegible] |
| 2 | Dove and brown clay shales . . . . | 4 |
| 3 | Coal . | 1 |
| 4 | Greenish blue fire clay | 2 |
| 5 | Olive shales changing to darker colored below, contains a few brown ironstone concretions, the middle part abounding in a large *Pleurotomaria* similar to one found by Mr Meek at Rulo in Nebraska, the fossils are very fragile a species of *Machrocheilus* is also found, thickness exposed about . . . . | 8 |

A quarter of a mile up stream the limestone appears in a regular layer, stretching across the bed of a small branch.

Three miles up stream many fossils were collected, weathered out of the shale beds in a fine state of preservation, including beautiful specimens of *Pleurotomaria sphærulata*, *P. tabulata*, *Orthoceras*, *Macrocheilus paludinaformis* and one like the *M. primigenius*, but with body whorl and spire more elongated, *Goniatites globulosus*, *Bellerophon carbonarius*, *Leda bella striata*, *Nucula Ventricosa*, *Astartella vera*, *Conularia*, *Leda Oweni*, *Euomphalus sub rugosus*, and *Polyphemopsis per acuta* These shales contain round and oblong clay and ironstone concretions.

In sec 28, T. 10 N, R. 3 W., a few fossils were obtained indicating the presence of the same beds as those last named.

The upper blue limestone, named above, undulates along East Fork for about eight miles, and I regard it as equivalent to No 22 of my general section. Near sec 36, T 8 N, R 3 W., on the east fork of Shoal creek, there crops out eight feet of sandy shale and sandstone. On West Fork, at the bridge on the Hillsboro and Walshville road, there is a bluff of 35 feet of bluish gray sandy shales, with a thin bed showing markings resembling those of *Fucoides cauda galli*, and containing one *Bellerophon*. East of Litchfield, at the creek bluffs, is seen 30 feet of sandy shale, and below that 10 feet of thick bedded sandstone resting on limestone Four miles up stream this sandstone is quite ferruginous at the base and contains many remains of plants, *calamites*, *sigillariæ*, etc One mile further up stream there was observed 45 feet of dark-ash micaceous sandy shale. On Five mile creek, in sec. 26, T 10 N, R. 5 W., there is 12 feet of sandy shales with a thin bed of partially carbonized wood containing a fossil fern. A quarter of a mile up the creek there is an exposure of 16 feet of olive drab clay shales with ironstone nodules. These shales are evidently continuations of the same beds and make the total thickness of No 26 not less than 85 feet.

No 27 to 33 inclusive —The best exposures of these beds are on Lake Fork and at Litchfield The section on Lake Fork at the Bond county line, near McCracken's coal, is as follows.

| | | Ft | In |
|---|---|---|---|
| 1 | Drift slope | 20 | |
| 2 | No 27—Lead blue limestone, with crinoid stems and *Athyris subtilita* | 2 | |
| 3 | No 28—Coal | | 2 |
| 4 | No 29—Blue clay shales | 10 | |
| 5 | No 30—Shales and shaly limestone abounding in fossils, but many are much crushed, including *Spirifer cameratus* *Productus punctatus* *P Nebrascensis* *Spiriferina Kentuckensis* *Hemipronites crassus* *Productus Prattenianus* *Athyris subtilita*, *Terebratula bovidens*, *Myalina sub quadrata*, a *Macrocheilus*, a *Pleurotomaria*, and one fish tooth | 4 | |
| 6 | No 31—Ash gray limestone, in the lower part there is from one to one and a half feet of dark ash colored limestone often traversed by fine lines of calc-spar, fossils not abundant contains *Productus longispinus* | 13 | |
| 7 | Bituminous shale | 4 | |
| 8 | No 33—Coal No 11 | | 17 |

Part of No 27 appears two and one half miles north west in the bed of the creek, containing *Spirifer cameratus*, *Fistulipora*, *Productus costatus*, *P. Nebrascensis*, *P Prattenianus*, and *Myalina subquadrata*. The fossils here have a well preserved and nacreous appearance On Rocky branch, east of Litchfield, No 31 appears thus

| | | Ft | In |
|---|---|---|---|
| 1 | Ferruginous limestone containing *Pinna peracuta* Bryozoa *Prod Nebrascensis*, and *Synocladia biserialis* | 0 | 2 |
| 2 | Nodular drab shale soon becoming a firm bed of rock . . . . . | 2 | |
| 3 | Rough and irregularly bedded limestone lower part a pretty bluish gray has a few small drusy cavities with crystals of calc spar fossils are *Athyris subtilita*, crinoid stems *Prod longispinus* *Aviculopecten carboniferus*, *Terebratula bovidens*, and *Spirifer cameratus* . .. .. . . . . | 16 | |

One and a half miles south-west of Bethel part of No 31 crops out along the creek, the upper portion an even bedded bluish gray sub-crystaline limestone. but below it is more irregularly bedded *Productus longispinus* abounds, associated with *Aviculopecten carboniferus*. Four miles N E of Litchfield the upper part of No 31 is a thick bedded brownish gray limestone abounding in *Rhynchonella osagensis*.

## *Economical Geology.*

*Coal.*—On J. Wilson's land, sec 7, T 8 N, R. 2 W, coal No 13, (No. 24 of upper Coal Measure section) has been mined, that used was from near the out crop and does not appear very favorably. the quality and thickness might improve by thorough opening The same coal has also been taken out on the land of Jno L Newsman, in sec 28, T. 10 N, R 3 W. I was informed that it was 18 inches thick, but I could not thoroughly examine it on account of the overlaying *debris* On the land of Mr McCracken near the south county line (probably in Bond county), coal 13 is 17 inches thick. Occurring as it does below the bed of the creek, it can only be reached at low water, and even then the labor of one man is required most of the time to keep the pit sufficiently dry for two others to work, but with this trouble it will repay very well to work for neighborhood purposes. The same bed has also been worked at Ross' old mill, on Shoal creek, at the south county line, and may also be reached just below the surface of the water on Shoal creek above Long bridge. At the limestone quarries on the creek near Butler it may be reached at about 10 to 14 feet beneath the bed of the creek, also about 4 feet beneath the darker colored limestone at the base of Michael Cleary's quarry east of Litchfield

Section of the Litchfield shaft, conducted by ANDREW HOWARD

| | Ft | In |
|---|---|---|
| Clay and hard pan . . | 35 | |
| Soft blue sandstone in thin layers . | 18 | |
| Blue shale | 16 | |
| Black calcareous shale | 1 | |

| | Ft | In |
|---|---|---|
| Light blue limestone | 4 | 6 |
| Gray limestone | 4 | |
| Black shale (probably coal) | 1 | |
| Limestone with fossils | 22 | 6 |
| Black slate and coal | 3 | |
| Fire clay | 3 | |
| Clay shale | 1 | |
| Limestone | 4 | |
| Soft slaty sandstone | 30 | |
| Blue shale | 12 | |
| Black and white sandstone | 4 | |
| Black slate and bituminous limestone | 2 | |
| Coal (No 10) | 0 | 6 |
| Fire-clay | 6 | |
| Hard and soft limestone—dark ash color | 12 | |
| Soft sandstone | 8 | |
| Slate | 5 | |
| Hard black and white sandstone | 7 | |
| Black slate and coal | 1 | |
| Blue and red sandstone | 2 | |
| Shaly sandstone | 38 | |
| Blue slate | 10 | |
| Black slate and coal | 1 | |
| Fire clay | 6 | |
| Soft limestone (Carlinville bed ?) | 5 | |
| Sandstone | 18 | |
| Coal impure—No 9 | 0 | 4 |
| Sandstone | 23 | |
| Bituminous shale | 1 | |
| Coal—No 8 ? | 0 | 4 |
| Blue shale | 3 | |
| Limestone | 0 | 6 |
| Shale | 24 | |
| Shale with numerous iron bands | 42 | 8 |
| Black slate | 4 | 6 |
| Shale | 1 | |
| Limestone—hard | 3 | |
| Shale and iron bands | 8 | 6 |
| Limestone—solid | 4 | 6 |
| Shale | 2 | |
| Nodular limestone | 1 | 6 |
| Shale with nodules of black limestone | 4 | |
| Black shale with fossil shells | 12 | |
| Fire clay | 3 | |
| Gray shale | 19 | |
| Coal | 3 | |
| Fire clay | 1 | 6 |
| Nodular limestone | 4 | |
| Shale and sandstone, about | 40 | |
| Coal | 1 | 6 |
| Sandstone and some shale | 45 | |
| Coal, with shaly parting No ? | 5 | |

*Building Rock.*—On East Fork, about sec. 26, T. 8 N., R. 3 W., there is a tolerably good bed of hard bluish limestone On Rocky Branch, east of Litchfield, there are extensive quarries of pretty good limestone, the beds are rather irregular, but the rock is very extensively used for ordinary stone work and makes very good lime. North of the railroad, on the West Fork, there are several outcrops of a brown and gray limestone in three feet beds. The same rock is also found four miles further up stream At the latter place part of it presents a beautiful bluish-gray variegated appearance. I regard this limestone as possessing much durability, and, being in a thick even bed, may become in time very useful for large columns. I believe it to be equivalent to that used in the construction of the old State House at Springfield.

West of Butler there are good quarries of limestone for lime, and it is also much used in the neighborhood for ordinary building purposes.

*Soil and Agriculture*—The richest land lies in the northern part of the county mostly north of the line between Tps 9 and 10 N. East of Nokomis there are a few high mounds quite rich on top and along their sides, and especially so in the valleys between. The northwest townships have a rich soil and are capable of producing heavy crops of corn and wheat. Southwardly, on the prairie, good wheat crops and occasionally good corn crops are produced In many places fresh plowing will disclose rich spots alternating with poorer land. This is due to the existence of what are commonly called "scalds" These "scalds" are spots of very thin, poor soil, with naturally a very scanty vegetation, mostly *Ambrosia bidentata.* Good manuring and deep plowing might make these barren spots more productive With careful tillage, deep plowing and thoroughly rolling or harrowing, so as to render the soil quite loose, good crops of wheat can be raised on most of the whitish soils. On ordinary land, by good preparation and sowing with a drill the farmer may feel sure of twenty-five to thirty bushels of wheat per acre.

# CHAPTER XIII.

## CHRISTIAN COUNTY.

This county is located near the center of the State, is regular in outline excepting the northern boundary, is twenty one miles in width from east to west, and thirty two in greatest length from north to south, and is bounded on the north by Macon and Sangamon, on the east by Macon and Shelby, on the south by Shelby and Montgomery, and on the west by Montgomery and Sangamon counties Its superficial area is about nineteen and a half townships or seven hundred and two square miles.

### *General Features, Soil, Timber, etc.*

On the north it is drained by the Sangamon river, and the central, southern and western parts of the county are watered by the South Fork of Sangamon and its tributaries, Bear, Locust Fork, Prairie Fork and Flat creeks The smaller streams sometimes are nearly dry, but the two main forks of Sangamon generally flow the year round. The South Fork is rather a sluggish stream, with muddy banks, but occasionally, as at Taylorville, the water is clear and fresh, indicative of latent springs

The topographical features of this county do not vary much in different localities The prairies in the southeast are rolling, often rising into mounds In every other part of the county they are flat or very gently undulating. Near the streams the slopes are often very gentle In the southern half of the county we very rarely find a bluff twenty-five feet high, and in passing down the South Fork no broken nor hilly land is seen until we get below Taylorville Four miles north west of Taylorville the country is rather hilly, the hills about sixty feet high, but not often too steep to admit of cultivation A few miles further down, there is a gradual descent from the prairie to the river, the bluffs of which are about twenty feet high. In the northeast the slopes are often so gentle as to render it impossible to trace a line between the upland and lowland

On the North Fork of the Sangamon there are occasional-drift bluffs thirty to fifty feet high, capped with a heavy growth of white oak, but the white oak lands do not often extend more than a quarter of a mile from the river, giving place to a more undulating surface, with a growth of elm, hickory, oak, sassafras, cherry, hazel, etc

This county consists mostly of prairie, the timbered land being confined to a narrow belt along the streams On the South Fork of the Sangamon the timber belt is generally about three miles wide, and along the other streams from one to two miles The prairies are generally flat, with a luxuriant growth of resin weed, two species, viz *Silphium laciniatum* and *S.* ***terebinthinaceum*, golden rod, *solidago*, several species, *Liatris* or blazing star, two species, and the beautiful and delicately colored *Physostegia Virginiana* and *Gerardia tenuifolia* Occasionally, on the basin-like depressions or flat marshy spots on the prairies, I found *Iris versicolor* and *Vernonia fasciculata*.

There is not much difference in the quality of the prairie soil, it being all a rich black loam of from one to two and a half feet in depth, and in the northern part of the county slightly sandy The soil along the edge of the prairie near Taylorville is quite sandy; eastwardly for six miles there are occasional spots of poor sandy soil, with post oak and black jack, but this often gives place to better land with white oak, black oak, hazel and sassafras or cherry, laurel oak, hazel, pin oak, hickory, plum and crab apple Along Locust Fork its whole length, and on South Fork above the mouth of Locust Fork, both on the bottoms and hill sides the soil is deep and rich, with principally a growth of American elm and *cornus*. On Bear creek the soil and growth is similar On and near Musquito creek the soil is rich and black, with a growth of elm, linden, coffee tree, cherry, red oak, hickory, red bud, spice bush, hackberry, black walnut, honey locust, ash, mulberry, etc West of Musquito creek, on the slopes leading to the North Fork, the timbered land is quite sandy and the growth variable; on some soil black oak predominates, where there is much clay mingled with sand there is a growth of red elm, sassafras, etc, when there is still more clay, laurel oak, American elm, white oak, black hickory, shell bark hickory, red bud, black oak and sassafras

On the south side of South Fork, below the mouth of Bear creek, the prairie land often approaches the stream, and the adjoining woodland growth reaching to the river bank consists of laurel oak, elm, hickory, linden and sassafras

North of the South Fork there are white oak hills occasionally spreading out into flats.

---

NOTE.—*The *S. terebinthinaceum* abounds on the rich prairies of Illinois, whereas in Missouri I have only found it on the post oak and black jack barrens in the southern portions of the State

Along the Sangamon river and adjacent hills there is a good supply of very good timber, consisting of white oak, bur oak, black walnut, red oak, elm and linden

Out on the prairies the farmers have planted many hedges of Osage orange, and they seem to thrive very well Near Rosemond I noticed a thrifty berberry hedge

*Crops*—This is an excellent corn producing county, generally averaging forty to fifty bushels per acre, and often sixty to seventy five can be raised Fall wheat gives a fine return to the farmer, but requires the ground to be well broken and grain put in with a drill It will average fifteen bushels and often reach twenty-eight to thirty-two per acre As yet there have not been many orchards planted, but the apple crop is generally sure and the peach trees often bear two years in succession Where the prairies are grazed down blue grass naturally springs up and soon affords excellent grazing

The Geological Formations of this county include the Quaternary and the Coal Measures.

## *Quaternary*

Under this head were recognized the alluvium, loess and drift The alluvium includes the soil and recent deposits from the streams, and the black clays of the wide rich Sangamon bottoms are good examples of alluvium. On Musquito creek the exposures along the banks show as much as six feet of dark rich loam. On the south fork of the Sangamon the black loam is often ten feet or more in depth

The loess is but partially developed, and is scarcely recognized as separate from the drift.

East of Taylorville the washings in ravines exhibit about ten feet of buff and brown clays and sand which may be referred to the loess; and in digging wells, about ten to fifteen feet of similar clay is passed through, reaching beds of sand and gravel, in which good streams of water are generally found. Sand beds are often reached within eight feet of the surface. The well at the hotel in Taylorville is thirty-eight feet deep, passing through eight feet of dark and light clay; then sand, gravel and clay to the bottom Good streams of pure and pleasant tasting water are generally reached at a depth of from twelve to sixteen feet on the prairies, sometimes as much as twenty feet, and very rarely they have to dig deeper; but in the timber wells have to be dug deeper, often twenty to thirty five feet

Bluffs of well marked drift deposits are often seen along the streams, and consist of brown sand with rounded pebbles and bowlders, and brownish-yellow and blue clay

On Prairie Fork of Bear creek, ten miles south of Taylorville, the washings on the hillsides exhibit at the top soft brown clay, and below clay with many small rounded pebbles On the North Fork of the Sangamon, one mile west of the east county line, the river bluff is fifty feet high, the upper portion of blue and dark brown clay with sand and pebbles; below there is a loose mass of sand and pebbles, sometimes cemented into a rough sandy conglomerate, at times sufficiently firm and regular to make rough walls Below this there is a dark colored bed of finely comminuted sand and clay Two miles further down stream there is a low bluff of dark drift clay with pebbles and small bowlders at the bottom and brown clay at the top At this place I observed a quantity of bituminous shale, a little coal and some fragments of limestone, all associated with the drift.

The drift bowlders in this county are generally small, and their character and composition various Among them may be found greenstone, quartzite, granite, sienite, epidote rock, corals from the Devonian and limestone from the Silurian, but no peculiar drift fossils.

At Pana, the I. C. R R, passing through a mound, exhibits the following section

| | | Ft | In |
|---|---|---|---|
| 1 | Soil and subsoil | | 18 |
| 2 | Ash brown clay | 8 | |
| 3 | Brown clay and small rounded pebbles | 15 | |

This section is similar to what may be found in all the mounds of this part of the State.

## *Coal Measures.*

This formation as seen in this county embraces a thickness of about 230 feet, in which are visible two coal seams, only one of which is of workable thickness These measures underlay the whole of the county, although there are no outcrops in the south west, nor do we find any in the north east quarter of the county, they being restricted to a small district south of Pana, to Locust Fork, to South Fork for ten miles up the stream from the west county line, on North Fork for three miles from the west line of the county, and one other outcrop between the forks The deep drift deposits cover the rocks in other places These rocks belong to the upper Coal Measures and their position in my upper Coal Measure section is from No 12 to No 32 inclusive.

The highest rocks (geologically speaking) are the beds south of Pana at or near White's coal bank, of which the following is a section

| | | Ft | In |
|---|---|---|---|
| 1 | Drift of clay pebbles, etc | 23 | |
| 2 | Clay shale | 10 | |
| 3 | Blue and bituminous shale part quite calcareous, passing into a dark colored lime stone | 4 | |

| | | Ft | In |
|---|---|---|---|
| 4 | Bituminous coal (No 14) | | 16 to 22 |
| 5 | Fire clay | 5 | |
| 6 | Rough looking hard gray sandstone, sometimes in thin even beds (No 2) of the section | 4 | |
| 7 | Sandy shales, with iron stone concretions | 15 | |

There is here a regular southerly dip at the rate of thirty feet to the mile, extending from Pana for four miles south It is probable that near or north of Pana the rocks are horizontal and soon dip north-westwardly, which they evidently do ten miles north-west of Pana, although the dip is slight.

The next rocks in descending order crop out on Locust Fork on sec. 2, T 11 N, R 1 W, and just north They belong near No 21 of the section, and appear thus.

| | | Ft |
|---|---|---|
| 1 | Dark blue clay shales, with some regular layers of lenticular concretions of iron stone and occasional strata of brown ferruginous shales, containing remains of fossils, including *Prod longispinus*, *Bellerophon*, *Crinoidal* stems, etc., part exposed, remainder in shaft—total | 31 |
| 2 | Ash gray limestone, weathers drab, has thin shaly partings, abounds in *Prod costatus*, *P longispinus*, *Athyris subtilita*, also contains *Prod Nebrascensis*, *Sp cameratus*, *Prod Prattenianus*; a fish tooth and one specimen each of *Syntrilasma hemiplicata* and *Allorisma subcuneata* were obtained from it | |

I regard the rocks of the above section equivalent to the Ramsey creek Fayette county beds The limestone (No 2) contains the fossils of the *Syntrilasma* limestone of Ramsey creek, although but one specimen of that fossil was found The lithological character, thickness and fossils are the same as beds found on Beck's creek, Fayette county, and the overlaying shales (No 1) are similar to corresponding beds at the railroad bridge on Ramsey creek Down the creek three miles there appears in the creek four feet of lead blue argillaceous limestone, equivalent to No 22 of the section The upper beds are shaly, the lower part a firm, even thick bed of subcrystalline fine grained deep blue limestone, having a conchoidal fracture The upper shaly part is traversed by fucoidal markings and contains many fossils, mostly *Prod. Prattenianus*, *P Nebrascensis* and *Sp cameratus*, but fragments of a *Nautilus* and *Bryozoa* were also found here.

A mile further down stream rocks near No 25 crop out in the bank of the creek, of which the following is a section

| | | Feet |
|---|---|---|
| 1 | Soft yellow, ochrey calcareous shales | 5 |
| 2 | Dark olive clay shales | 2 |
| 3 | Deep blue fucoidal sandstone and sandy shale | 1½ |
| 4 | Bituminous shales | ? |

Fossils found in Nos 1 and 2 were *Pleurotomaria sphærulata*, *Spirifer cameratus*, *Sp plano-convexus*, *Productus longispinus*, *P Prattenianus*, *Orthis carbonaria*, *Retzia punctulifera*, *Lophophyllum proliferum*, *Macrocheilus*, (small sp ), *Bellerophon*, crinoid stems, and one fine specimen of *Pleurotomaria tabulata*

The next in descending order is 12 feet of sandstone (No 26), seen on South Fork, five miles below Taylorville The upper part is shaly, the lower beds thick, hard and gray, and a softer brown with dark specks, contains remains of *Calamites*, *Sigillaria*, and other coal plants.

*Nos* 27, 28 *and* 29 —In sec 29, T 14 N, R 3 W, a quarter of a mile above Greenwood's mill, I observed at the top—

| | Ft | In |
|---|---|---|
| Red shales | 1 | |
| Dark olive calcareous shales containing *Athyris subtilita* a small *Macrocheilus Nucula ventricosa* and crinoid stems | 2½ | |
| Coal No 12 | | 10 |
| Slope to limestone No 30 of general section | 3 | |

Three miles above Ralston's bridge, on the South Fork of the Sangamon, observed Nos 30 and 31, as follows:

| | | Ft | In |
|---|---|---|---|
| 1 | Ash gray compact limestone showing facets of calc spar, very few fossils | | 8 |
| 2 | Shales with nodules of buff limestone abounding in fossils *Productus costatus Productus longispinus, Spirifer cameratus Spiriferina Kentuckensis Athyris subtilita Chonetes variolata?* Crinoid stems *Fistulipora* and *Synocladia biserialis* | 3 | |

At Ralston's quarry, in sec. 3, T. 13 N, R 3 W., we have—

| | | Feet |
|---|---|---|
| 1 | Slope from top of hill | 20 |
| 2 | Gray limestone, fossils are *Productus costatus, P punctatus Spirifer cameratus, Spiriferina Kentuckensis, Hemipronites crassus* | 1 |
| 3 | Like the last but more shelly fossils about the same | 1 |
| 4 | Green shales | 1 |
| 5 | Brown shales with nodules of limestone, abounds in *Athyris subtilita* Crinoid stems and plates *Lophophyllum proliferum Sp cameratus* | 1 |
| 6 | Gray or drab limestone but few fossils those seen were *Athyris subtilita Productus longispinus, P Prattenanus* and *Lophophyllum proliferum* | 9 |

Part of the same at Greenwood's mills, as follows

| | | Ft |
|---|---|---|
| 1 | Clay and sandy alluvium | 1 |
| 2 | Clay with nodules of brown limestone containing *Chætetes, Fistulipora, Athyris subtilita, Productus Nebrascensis, P costatus, P Prattenanus P punctatus* | 2 |
| 3 | Gray or brown and buff limestone, contains *Productus longispinus, P Prattenianus, P punctatus P costatus P Nebrascensis, Sp cameratus, Hemipronites crassus Athyris subtilita* and *Lophophyllum proliferum* | 12 |
| 4 | Bituminous shale (No 32) in sight | 2 |

At North Fork mills, on the North Sangamon river, in sec 13, T. 15 N, R 3 W, we have—

| | | Ft |
|---|---|---|
| 1 | Slope clay and sand—drift | 50 |
| 2 | Limestone upper part gray and nodular, lower part more firmly bedded, soon weathers brown fossils *Productus longispinus P costatus P Prattenanus, P Nebrascensis, Athyris subtilita Spirifer cameratus, Hemipronites crassus* | 8 |
| 3 | Clay shales, contains a *Crinoid* allied to *Poteriocrinus hemisphericus* | 2½ |
| 4 | Limestone weathering brown | 4 |

Three miles down stream, near the west county line, the lower part of the last section appears 7 feet thick, with brown shaly partings between the beds, which abound in *Athyris subtilita*, the other fossils are *P costatus, P Nebrascensis, P. Prattenianus* and *Lophophyllum proliferum*

The limestones above described (Nos 30 and 31) correspond to similar beds at Litchfield and on *Lake Fork in Montgomery county.

## *Economical Geology.*

*Coal*—South of Pana coal has been taken out at several places along the head waters of Coal creek; but at the time of my visit the only place worked was White's bank, on sec. 34, T 11 N., R. 1 E. The seam here is about 22 inches thick, of good quality, and obtained by drifting into the hill side at an elevation of about 30 feet above the level of the creek. The position of this coal in the geological series is about 420 feet above coal No. 7, and corresponds to No. 14, counting from lowest coal upwards, and is numbered 17 in my general section of this and adjoining counties A ten-inch seam crops out a quarter of a mile up stream from Greenwood's mill, but the coal is of poor quality. Beneath the limestone at Greenwood's mill, and a little below low water, a 17 inch seam ought to be found, the same bed also probably exists beneath the limestone at North Fork mills, probably six feet below low water This coal is probably about 365 feet above coal No. 7.

*Building material.*—South of Pana Mr Burke has a quarry of hard gray sandstone, which appears to be very durable At Mr Walcher's, six miles north west of Pana, on Locust Fork, there is four feet of ash gray limestone, weathering bluish drab The beds are rather thin, but the rock is of good quality On Jas. P. Durban's land, two miles north west of Walcher's, there is a very good quarry of deep blue limestone; the lower bed, if properly quarried, would make a pretty and durable building stone.

Ralston's and Greenwood's quarries, on the South Fork of Sangamon, each contain several good beds of building stone, and make excellent lime. There are similar quarries at the North Fork mills, and three miles west

The lower two feet at Stokes' quarry, in sec. 16, T. 14 N., R. 3 W., would probably make a pretty marble; it is a fine grained, even-textured, dove colored limestone, with many lines and specs of calc spar.

---

*Note —I also believe them equivalent to Nos 162 to 166 of my Missouri river section, published in Vol 2, No 2 Trans St Louis Acad Sci., St Louis, 1866 The limestones of the North and South Fork of Sangamon closely resemble both in lithological appearance and fossils, beds in the northern part of Cass county, and those near Randolph, in Clay county Missouri

# CHAPTER XIV.

## SHELBY COUNTY.

Shelby county is bounded on the north by Christian, Macon and Moultrie, on the east by Moultrie, Coles and Cumberland, on the south by Effingham and Fayette, and on the west by Montgomery and Christian. It embraces an area of about 755 square miles, about two-thirds of which is prairie land. Its surface is agreeably diversified by mounds, hills, valleys and plains.

*Streams.*—The principal streams are the Little Wabash river in the south east, and the Kaskaskia and its tributaries in the central and western portions of the county.

*Topography*—The hills skirting the "Okaw" or Kaskaskia river are generally 60 to 70 feet high, but 4 miles north east of Shelbyville they attain a hight of 130 feet. For the distance of a half mile to a mile from the river the country is somewhat broken. The growth on these hills consists for the most part of white oak with some black oak and hickory. The bottoms vary in width from a quarter of a mile in the northern to three quarters in the southern part, and are generally from 14 to 16 feet above the ordinary stage of water in the rivers, with sometimes a second bottom a few feet higher. During wet seasons the river often extends over the first bottom several feet in depth. Near the margin of the stream are found birch and willows, on the lower bottoms elm, maple and sycamore, and on the higher bottoms sometimes sugar tree and bur oak Other trees occurring here are ash, pin oak, coffee tree and honey locust Where the bottoms are low and the soil very sandy mixed with river drift, *Vernonia fasciculata* is the most abundant plant.

The south-east portion of the county is flat, between the streams. The timbered part of townships 9 and 10 consists mostly of flat post oak ridges, with thin light ash soil changing locally to better land with an abundant growth of hickory; and at the edge of the prairie pin oak and laurel oak, with hazel undergrowth Along the hillsides white oak predominates. The hills near Green creek attain a hight of about 40 feet; on Little Wabash generally 25 to 30 feet. Passing northwardly along the west fork of Little Wabash, the change from low to high ground is very gradual, the country at the same time increasing in fertility. The growth in the south part of township 11, R. 6 E., consists of elm, grape vines, wahoo, laurel oak, black haw, arrow wood, hazel, and honey locust Farther north the land continues rich, with a growth principally of bur oak, shell bark hickory, black walnut, chest nut oak, pignut hickory, sassafras, red bud, ash and mulberry, and a carpet of pennyroyal and goosegrass Near Windsor the surface is either flat or gently undulating, with a deep rich black soil. From the high ground at Windsor there is an exceedingly easy descent towards Sand creek. At the edge of the timber north west I noticed four species of *Cratægus*, also laurel oak, elm, pin oak and hickory, and the surface of the ground was covered with pennyroyal On Richland and Brush creeks the hills are not generally very high—about 50 feet near the mouth of Richland, becoming lower further up stream. its bottoms are one-eighth to one quarter of a mile wide and not too low to be cultivated, and have a growth of white walnut, elm, black walnut, sycamore, coffee tree, bur oak, sassafras, red bud, coral berry, and raspberry. From the bluffs the ascent is gentle to white oak and post oak flats and small prairies In the southern part of the county on the west side of the Kaskaskia river, broken and flat ridges extend to the flat prairies; towards the centre of the county these gradually rise to the mounds.

Between Mitchel's and Beck's creeks there are a series of mounds extending from the southern part of the county as far north as Mud creek Northwardly near Prairie Bird there are several low mounds. The soil on the highest is of a reddish color, sometimes containing a good deal of gravel and sand The high timbered mounds near Williamsburg have on them a good growth of white oak, black oak, shell bark and common hickory, red bud, sassafras and hazel. The mound slopes are very rich, and sustain a growth of elm, cherry, walnut, hickory, mulberry, hackberry, red bud and hazel

The bottoms of Beck's creek are one quarter of a mile wide, low and flat, with mostly pin oak, laurel oak, elm, ash, hackberry, buckeye, maple and sugar trees; the hills are low, sloping at 15° to 20°, and sustain a growth of white oak. black oak, shell bark hickory, plum, hazel, etc. Near the edge of the neighboring prairie the surface is flat and sometimes swampy, with pin oak and button bush (*Cephalanthus occidentalis*)

Robinson's and Mud creeks are sluggish streams with muddy banks and wide bottoms and generally low hills, the highest not above 50 feet in hight. On the hills the timber for the most part consists of white oak, black oak and occasionally post oak and black jack, sometimes there are low ridges where black oak and black hickory prevails, with shell bark hickory, white oak, sassafras and hazel, and locally elm land. Skirting the prairie are found elm, hackberry, honey locust, laurel oak, black haw, arrow wood, *cornus* and hazel.

From Prairie Bird northwardly there is gently undulating rich land, and occasionally there are small thickets with elm, plum, honey locust and hazel

Near Flat branch there is some gently sloping and very fertile land with a growth mostly of red and American elm, black walnut, shell bark and pignut hickory. mulberry, bur oak, red bud, *cornus*, hazel, buckeye, red oak, prickly ash and grape vines There are occasional spots with a luxuriant growth of *Impatiens fulva* and *I. pallida*, indicating a rich moist soil

The prairie in the northern part of the county is either flat or very gently undulating, with some wet or swampy depressions, and possesses a rich soil

The river bottoms and neighboring hills afford an abundant supply of good timber.

## *Geological Formations.*

The formations in this county include the Quaternary and upper Coal Measures

*Quaternary*—A well on Kaskaskia bottoms, 2 miles below the mouth of Jordan's creek, presents · 1st, soil and dark clay—5 feet; 2d, sandy material with some pebbles—11 feet

The hills at Shelbyville exhibit about 50 feet of sand and clay, with many rounded pebbles of various sizes, including mica slate, sienite of various colors, granite several kinds, including graphic granite, quartzite, greenstone, chert. etc At an old well 3 miles above Shelbyville, a drift bluff is well exposed At this place the sand and pebbles have partially united, forming disconnected layers of rather firmly cemented conglomerate. At Lilly's mill there is a brown conglomerate in the drift similar to that above named.

On the Wabash river the drift is only partially developed Below the forks I observed 12 feet of chocolate and buff colored clays, the lower part sandy, with a few small pebbles. Near Williamsburg the washings expose a reddish brown clay, with rounded pebbles on the north side of the ridge. A well was dug by Mr. Draper on J Gallagher's farm 72 feet deep. He states that the first 38 feet was through clay to sand, then a muddy sand, with occasional leaves and sticks and one log; from 52 to 72 feet he bored to stiff clay.

## *Coal Measures.*

In this county there are exposures of about 175 feet of upper Coal Measures, from No 1 to No 20, in which are included about two workable coals, Nos 14 and 15 The following is a condensed section of the various beds

| | | Ft | In |
|---|---|---|---|
| 1 | Shales and sandstone not recognized | | |
| 2 | Limestone, dove colored | 4 | |
| 3 | Fire clay | 2 | |
| 4 | Shales passing into sandstone | 30 | |
| 5 | Limestone | 0 | 4 |
| 6 | Shales at top changing to argillaceous limestone | 55 | |
| 7 | Sandstone | 4 to 40 | |
| 8 | Shaly bituminous limestone and bituminous shales | 4 in to 4 | |
| 9 | Coal No 15 | 18 in to 3 | |
| 10 | Fire clay | 15 in to 5 | |
| 11 | Limestone | 0 to 1 | |
| 12 | Shales and sandstone | 15 to 30 | |
| 13 | Shales | | |
| 14 | Calcareous shales | 4 | |
| 15 | Shales | | |
| 16 | Calcareous and bituminous shales | 2 | |
| 17 | Coal near Pana | 16 to | 22 |
| 18 | Fire clay | 5 | |
| 19 | Sandy limestone | 5 | |
| 20 | Sandstone | | |

No 1 of the above section was not recognized in this county, but occurs in Moultrie No 2, five miles from Windsor, at a mill on Sand creek, extends quite across and down stream for 200 feet. Four miles north-east of Shelbyville, on and near the river, there is seen 4 to 4½ feet of limestone, the upper one foot sometimes shaly and fossiliferous, containing *Spirifer cameratus*, *Sp lineatus*, *Spiriferina Kentuckensis*, *Productus punctatus*, *Athyris subtilita*, *Hemipronites crassus*, and crinoid stems The lower part is of a gray or dove color, and contains few fossils In the same neighborhood we find just beneath the fire clay (No 3) 20 feet of sandy shales At various places on the river there are beds of buff sandstone, making the entire thickness of sandstone and shales (No. 4) amount to 30 feet. No. 5 is 4 inches of tough and very coarse dark gray limestone, mottled with dove colored spots, abounding in fossils, including *Myalina subquadrata*, *Pinna per acuta*, *Allorisma subcuneata*, *Prod Prattenianus*, *Nautilus occidentalis* and *Aviculopecten occidentalis* At an old mill on the Kaskaskia river, four miles above Shelbyville, it is found about three feet above low water; one mile up stream it is seen sticking out of the bank at about the same distance above the water; at the latter place it is easily recognized, and very good fossils can be procured; but at the former it is not so firm, and the fossils are almost blended with the rock itself.

Below the last, and included in Nos. 6, 7 and 8 of my section, there is about 96 feet of sandy and argillaceous shale, sandstone and argillaceous limestone, with calcareous and bituminous shale. The upper part consists principally of argillaceous shale; below, the beds are not all persistent, and are interchangeable. The argillaceous shale sometimes assumes the form of a deep blue argillaceous limestone It crops out near Kaskaskia river, one mile above the mouth of Long branch, 25 feet in thickness, with 15 feet of thin-bedded sandstone separating it from coal No. 15 Near the railroad one mile west of Robinson's creek it is 30 feet in thickness. Its beds are very irregular, with buff shaly partings Its fracture is smooth, conchoidal, the thinner beds shaly, and the only fossils found were two specimens of *Chonetes variolata* ? .

The sandstone (No 6) is also changeable, both gradually and abruptly. Sometimes it is entirely absent, its place being occupied by sandy shales, as on Little Wabash river; at other places it is a thin bedded sandstone. Two miles south east of Shelbyville it changes rapidly to a shale, again to a sandstone, and again to a shale. Sometimes it rests on the coal as at Smith's, then it is separated from the coal by bituminous shales. which I have seen beginning at 0, and in a short distance increasing to 1½ feet in thickness.

At Lilly's mill a calcareous shale overlays the coal, which, in 200 feet distance, thickens from 0 to 3 feet; it is divided, after a short distance, by 2 feet of clay shales, and the upper part becomes a firm bed of limestone.

There are but few fossils in these several beds, in the sandstone, *Sigillaria* and *Calamites*, and probably *Cordaites* in the shales In the calcareous shales the fossils are very much crushed, but I could distinguish *Athyris subtilita, Sp. Kentuckensis, Prod Prattenianus* and *Bryozoa.*

The following sections were obtained at the various outcrops of coal, from which the changeable character of the adjacent rocks will be seen. On Copperas creek, west of Nioga, at J. Young's coal bank—

| | | Ft | In |
|---|---|---|---|
| 1 | Drab and blue shale | 3 | |
| 2 | Bituminous coal | 0 to | 20 |
| 3 | Fire clay | 1 | |
| 4 | Slope | 10 to 15 | |
| 5 | Chocolate and drab colored arenaceous limestone | 2 | 6 |
| 6 | Slope | 5 | |
| 7 | Sandstone, hard and rough | 5 | |

On Little Wabash, one mile above the mouth of Copperas creek—

| | | Ft | In |
|---|---|---|---|
| 1 | Clay and drift | 25 | |
| 2 | Clay shale | 14 | |
| 3 | A little black slate | | |
| 4 | Bituminous coal | 0 to | 22 |
| 5 | Fire-clay at top for a few feet, then clay shales, with nodules of ironstone, one nodule with zinc-blende etc | 18 | |

A mile up stream the coal is four feet above the water, and a quarter of a mile further it is two feet above, and capped by 12 feet of gray shale, passing into thin beds of sandstone.

J. Gallagher's coal on Richland creek, in sec. 33, T. 10 N., R. 4 E., is capped by about 30 feet of sandy and argillaceous shales. South of this on Brush creek we have shales above, with dark lead-blue shaly limestone, containing remains of fossils, just over the coal

At Wm A. Rudy's, in the north half of the south east quarter of sec. 14, T. 9 N., R. 3 E., the coal is 18 inches thick, with clay shales above, and blue fire clay beneath The hills here are about 50 feet high

At Mrs. Matthews', a quarter of a mile east, the coal is capped by 2 inches of dark lead blue calcareous shale Half a mile down Richland creek it is 20 feet above the water, with 5 feet of yellow clay beneath, resting on 16 feet of thin bedded, dark gray and brown sandstone.

In sec 6, T. 9 N., R. 4 E., the section is—

| | | Ft | In |
|---|---|---|---|
| 1 | Olive clay shales | 4 | |
| 2 | Bituminous coal | 1 | 6 |
| 3 | Fire clay | 2 | |
| 4 | Buff limestone, fracture gray | 4 | |

The coal at this place is seen occupying the bed of a small dry branch, and is easily taken out On land of S Syfert's, near by, the coal is a little thicker On Mrs Fancher's land, in the S. E. qr sec 32, T 10 N., R. 4 E., we have—

| | | Ft | In |
|---|---|---|---|
| 1 | Argillaceous shales | | |
| 2 | Coal | | 22 |
| 3 | Fire clay | 5 | |
| 4 | Sandstone in thin beds alternating rough, hard, with gray ripple marked, and thicker brown beds | 15 | |

I saw a very good grindstone that had been made from the last named sandstone

The following is a section at Lilly's mill, in sec 1, T 9 N., R. 3 E

| | | Ft | In |
|---|---|---|---|
| 1 | Slope gentle | 60 | |
| 2 | Drift clay, sand and pebbles | 10 | |
| 3 | Ash blue clay shale | 4 | |
| 4 | Calcareous shale changing to shaly limestone | 0 to 3 | |
| 5 | Coal | | 22 |
| 6 | Fire clay | 3 | |
| 7 | Hard and soft shales, shaly and thickly bedded gray and grayish blue, very changeable within a short distance | 20 | |

No. 4 at one place is separated by a two foot bed of clay shale from No 5, and becomes a firm but thinly laminated limestone At the mouth of Long Branch in sec. 10, T. 10 N., R. 3 E., we have:

| | | Ft |
|---|---|---|
| 1 | Brown ash clay a few pebbles in the lower part | 20 |
| 2 | Bituminous coal the upper one foot has thin bands of clay shale—the lower is good coal | 3 |
| 3 | Upper part fire clay, in middle are buff nodules of arenaceous limestone | 16 |

A mile up stream the coal is twelve feet above the water in the river. One mile south of Shelbyville the coal is at the water's edge, and we have

| | | Ft | In |
|---|---|---|---|
| 1 | Sandy shales | 55 | |
| 2 | Coal thin seam | 0 | 2 |
| 3 | Calcareous shales fossiliferous | 1 to 2 | |
| 4 | Bituminous coal | 2 | |

Two hundred yards down stream a sandstone begins in the lower part of No. 1 and gradually thickens to four feet.

The following are the results of observations on Robinson's creek. At a coal bank on the S hf. of the S W. qr. of sec 21, T 11 N, R 3 E, the section is:

| | | Ft | In |
|---|---|---|---|
| 1 | Gray sandstone | 25 | |
| 2 | Ferruginous bed | 0 | 5 |
| 3 | Black shale | 0 | 10 |
| 4 | Coal | 2 | 8 |

One hundred yards south of the last locality.

| | | Ft | In |
|---|---|---|---|
| 1 | Limestone with thin laminæ of coal traversing the lower part | 5 | |
| 2 | Ochrey ferruginous stratum | 0 | 5 |
| 3 | Blue and dove colored clay shales | 0 | 4 |
| 4 | Coal | 2½ | |

The hills at this place are about fifty feet high. Near the railroad in the south part of the S. W. qr. of sec. 17, T. 11 N., R. 3 E, at William Howard's

| | | Ft | In |
|---|---|---|---|
| 1 | Sandstone | | |
| 2 | Dark gray calcareous shale thinning out at the old opening it appears forty feet from the entrance | 2 | |
| 3 | Coal | | 18 |

At Minto's, a short distance north:

| | | Ft | In |
|---|---|---|---|
| 1 | Sandstone | | |
| 2 | Ferruginous conglomerate | 1 to 4 | |
| 3 | Dove colored clay shales | | 16 |
| 4 | Coal | | 18 |
| 5 | Fire clay | | 15 |
| 6 | Hard limestone | 2 | |

One hundred and fifty yards further up

| | | Ft | In |
|---|---|---|---|
| 1 | Sandstone | | |
| 2 | Calcareo bituminous shale | 4 | |
| 3 | Coal | 0 | 20 |
| 4 | Fire clay | | |

One mile west the sandstone appears in a branch on the north side of the railroad, and further up the branch there is thirty feet of deep blue argillaceous limestone.

At Smith's coal bank on sec. 5, T. 11 N, R. 3 E., the coal is capped by about forty feet of thick bedded soft gray and brown sandstone. Occasionally there rests upon the coal about four inches of bituminous or blue shale. At one place the shale commenced at 0 and thickened to 1½ feet within 100 feet distance Below the coal there is not over one and a half feet of fire clay, and then a hard nodular limestone.

A half mile west of Prairie Bird on sec. 30, T. 12 N , R 3 E , on Brush creek

| | | Ft | In |
|---|---|---|---|
| 1 | Soil and buff clay | | |
| 2 | Soft buff sandstone | 8 | |
| 3 | Thinly laminated light blue shales | 4 | |
| 4 | Bituminous coal | | 18 |
| 5 | Fire clay | 2 | |
| 6 | Coarse rough nodular calcareous sandstone | | |

The hills near this place are about thirty feet high and of easy slope. Down the creek a half mile the coal is seventeen inches thick and capped by ten feet of chocolate-colored sandy shales.

On the land of J Armstrong, on sec 35, T 12 N , R 2 E , there is over the coal four or five feet of firm gray or brown sandstone containing plants

Below the hard sandstone on Copperas creek, previously mentioned, there is two feet of bituminous shales resting on two feet of dark-blue clay shales. These beds are probably near the horizon of coal No 14.

Between coal Nos 14 and 15 there is about forty feet of sandstone and shale Coal No. 14 was only found on the waters of Beck's creek.

On Mrs. Sides' land, one and a half miles south of the railroad, we have

| | | Ft | In |
|---|---|---|---|
| 1 | Sandstone, at one place very hard, at another soft | 5 | |
| 2 | Ferruginous shales passing into a conglomerate | | 4 to 12 |
| 3 | Lead blue calcareous shales | 2 | |
| 4 | Coal | | 14 to 15 |
| 5 | Fire clay | | |

At one place the sandstone is scarcely separated from the coal. In the south part of sec 2, T 10 N , R 1 E , I observed as follows:

| | | Ft | In |
|---|---|---|---|
| 1 | Mostly chocolate colored argillaceous shales | 10 | |
| 2 | (= No 14 of upper Coal Meas Sec ) Calcareous shales containing *Hemipronites crassus Spiriferina Kentuckensis, Lophophyllum proliferum, Zeacrinus*, and a crinoid resembling *Erisocrinus* | 1 | |
| 3 | Blue and bituminous shales | 3 | |
| 4 | (= No 16 of upper Coal Meas Sec ) Dark lead blue calcareous shales, passing into a shaly limestone, abounds in *Spirifer plano convexus* and *Hemipronites crassus* also contains *Orthis carbonaria Orthoceras cribrosum, Pleurotomaria Sphærulata, Chonetes Flemingii Productus costatus Sp cameratus, Euomphalus sub rugosus, Lophophyllum proliferum* | | |

Besides the above named fossils there is found on the Fayette county line *Prod. Nebrascensis, Prod longispinus, Retzia punctulifera, Spiriferina Kentuckensis*, and *Orthis carbonaria*

| | | Ft | In |
|---|---|---|---|
| 5 | Bituminous coal | | 20 to 22 |
| 6 | Fire clay, calcareous nodules in the lower part | 5 | |
| 7 | Hard rough calcareous sandstone containing *Productus Prattenianus* | | |

No. 3 of the above section sometimes reposes on the coal These rocks preserve a slight southerly dip for ten miles, and are found on Beck's creek at the south county line about the same distance above the creek, but northwardly for four or five miles they rise more rapidly.

## *Economical Geology.*

On a small branch of the Kaskaskia river, four miles north east of Shelbyville, I was informed that there was a six-inch seam of coal A small pit has been dug here and some coal taken out, but the place was filled up with *debris* at the time of my visit. The limestone No. 2 of upper Coal Measure section crops out very near, so that it is probable that this coal is the equivalent of that found on Limestone creek and at Nelson's in Effingham county.

Two coal beds are worked in this county, the upper, sometimes spoken of as the "Shelby coal," I refer to No. 15 coal, it varies in thickness from eighteen inches to three feet, but is generally about twenty-two inches thick It crops out on Copperas creek and at several places above its mouth near Little Wabash river, at the water's edge, near Shelbyville, and occasionally for ten miles south, on Richland creek and its tributaries, on Robinson's creek near the railroad, above on Mud creek and Brush creek below Prairie Bird, and on Beck's creek at the railroad. It is generally a firm, good coal, tolerably free from impurities. A good deal of labor and money has been spent at various places in mining for it. The following are the principal places that have been worked

At J. Young's, in sec. 24, T. 10 N, R. 6 E., several pits have been dug, but at present the place is abandoned On the west side of Little Wabash river, in the north half of township 10 north, there have been several workings for coal, but at present all are abandoned. In sec. 10, T. 10 N., R. 6 E., Cornelius Barrett reports having passed through three feet of coal in the bottom of a well thirty feet from the surface Coal has been taken out from several of the neighboring ravines. Wm Rudy's, J Gallagher's, Henry Allen's on Richland creek, and the railroad bank on Brush creek, have been worked at various times The coal at these places is above the ordinary stage of water in the creek At Mrs. Matthews', the coal was taken out of pits sunk in the bed of a branch of Richland creek. Coal crops out at many places within three miles of Lilly's mill, and is generally of easy access. A good deal has been taken out on land of the heirs of Middlesworth, in and near sec. 6, T. 9 N., R. 4 E. At these places it is easily mined. On sec 32, T 10 N, R 4 E, they have drifted a short distance in the hill side and got very good coal; a spring of water issues from beneath. At Lilly's mill it occurs very favorably for side drifting, but no work has yet been undertaken there. Formerly a very good quality of coal was dug a quarter of a mile below the mill. A good deal of side drifting has been done on the land of Nichols and Whitfield, on Long branch. A few years ago quantities of coal were taken out at low water, one mile south of Shelbyville, but at present the miners have retreated to a short distance back on the bluffs and sunk shafts. Sam Kelly's, on Jefferson Brewster's land, is fourteen feet deep to coal, the coal is twenty four to twenty eight inches thick and of good quality, with three feet of underclay. Near this there are two other shafts.

J. J. Cline has run in two drifts, one for one hundred and fifty feet, with six rooms at the side from sixteen to twenty one feet wide, one of them fifty feet long; it was opened in October, 1866. Since then he has taken out one hundred and fifty thousand bushels of coal. He has to haul it one mile to the railroad, or about four miles to Shelbyville.

Near Robinson's creek station and one mile from Cline's coal banks, a good deal of coal has been taken out, mostly by drifting into the hill-side.

Litton Smith's coal lies mostly beneath the creek bed; a great many pits have been dug and about forty three thousand bushels taken away. The creek only runs a few months in the year, so that water is no serious drawback to the miner. At the other openings up the creek, near Prairie Bird, but little mining has been done. At Elliott's, on the Terre Haute railroad, they have drifted and also sunk pits, where the coal is only sixteen inches thick.

I now come to speak of the Beck's creek or Pana coal, No. 14. On a small branch leading into the West fork of Beck's creek, in the south part of section 15, township 9 north, range 1 east, on land of the heirs of Samuel Roberts, some mining has been done. I observed several old pits, now filled with water and rubbish; the coal was said to be sixteen inches thick. On Beck's creek, in sec. 31, T. 10 N., R. 2 E., twenty one feet of shales and thin bedded sandstone were observed resting on two feet of bituminous shale at the water's edge. I was informed that coal had been taken out of the creek at this place. Six miles north the coal appears a few feet above the water in Coal Bank creek. None of these places are now worked.

*Building Stone.*—The silicious limestone on Copperas creek appears to be excellent and durable for heavy work. For the construction of culverts on the Illinois Central railroad a good deal of sandstone was quarried on the west side of the East fork of Little Wabash river; the rock appears to be durable, but is hard and irregularly bedded. Two miles south east of Shelbyville good gray sandstone has been quarried.

The limestone occurring on Sand creek and west of Kaskaskia river, four and five miles north-east of Shelbyville, affords a superior building rock; it was used in the construction of the Shelbyville railroad bridge. The deep-blue argillaceous limestone west of Robinson's creek has been used for common culverts and rip raps on the Terre Haute Railroad. It seems durable, but is very irregularly bedded, and often has too much clay in its composition Some of the sandstones of this county will make very good coarse grindstones

*Sand and Material for Roads.*—Good sand for plastering can be procured on Little Wabash and Kaskaskia rivers, on Sand creek and from some of the drift exposures. The sands and numerous rounded pebbles of the drift are destined to be of great utility in the construction of roads, especially at Shelbyville, where there is an almost inexhaustible supply of it. Good clay for bricks occurs everywhere. Limestone good for lime can only be procured four and five miles above Shelbyville and on Sand creek

*Soil and Agriculture.*—A pretty good idea of the soil of this county may be gathered from the first part of this report. The soil of most of the northern half of the county is a dark rich loam, the broken land near the streams being not so rich South of the Terre Haute railroad and in the southwestern part of the county, the soil of the flat prairie and timbered lands is thin, on mound slopes it is rich and very productive. Near Windsor, and south and west for six miles, both prairie and timbered land is rich. The woodland near Flat branch is all very good and capable of producing all crops raised in this latitude. Most of the northern part of the county and the timbered land and mound slopes in the south are good wheat lands.

The general average of fall wheat is 20 to 25 bushels.

The finest crops of corn are raised in the northern part of the county, generally averaging 45 to 50 bushels per acre, and according to Mr. L Smith he has raised on rolling upland 80 bushels per acre. The flat prairies and post oak and white oak flats in the south produce indifferent crops of corn.

*Water*—For supplies of water, the people chiefly depend on wells Their depth is variable, from 20 to 50 feet, on the flat prairies not so deep as on the hilly lands.

One and a half miles north of the south county line, on the west side of Beck's creek, I observed a number of chalybeate springs, some impregnated with sulphur, others quite sweet. Tere is a fine spring of excellent water at Mr. Johnson's a half mile north of Williamsburg

In sections 5 and 6, T 10 N, R 3 E, a lake possessing the euphonious name of *Muntonomah* extends over an area of several hundred acres. Around its margin are many broad leaf water plants, and *Cepha-*

*lanthus occidentalis* is also abundant. It is a clear fresh water lake and is nearly level with the upland flat prairie. Lake Emtah, in sec. 5, T. 9 N., R. 5 E., is another quite large body of water.

Before closing I will mention a natural curiosity in sec. 32, T. 10 N., R. 7 E., on the west side of Little Wabash river, a quarter of a mile above a saw mill. Two elm trees grow close to each other, relatively 3 and 2½ feet in diameter; from the latter a large limb branches off about 4 feet above the ground, crossing to the other tree, to which it soon unites, then separating again, but solidly uniting at 10 feet from the ground, forming one trunk of three feet in diameter.

# CHAPTER XV.

## EFFINGHAM COUNTY.

This county is bounded on the north by Shelby and Cumberland, on the east by Cumberland and Jasper, on the south by Clay and Fayette, and on the west by Fayette It has an area of 486 square miles, probably more than one-half of which consists of timbered land.

*Streams*—The Little Wabash river passing southwardly nearly equally bisects the county. Its tributaries are: on the east, Lucas, Big Bishop with its forks, Little Bishop and Ramsey creeks, Big and Little Salt creeks and Brush creek, Green creek and Sugar Fork; on the west are Fulfers and Limestone, Big and Brocket's creeks, Second creek, Funkhouser, Blue Point and Shoal creeks.

*Topography*—The higher surface land is either flat prairie or flat wood land, some post oak, some white oak, some hickory and oak, and some pin oak flats, changing mostly to white oak on the breaks and slopes Above the flats there are a few low mounds, not so abundant nor so elevated as in the counties west; one or two in the eastern part, Blue Mound in the north west, and the low ridge at Mason The mound or ridge at Mason is probably two miles across its base and but little over fifty feet high, descending very gently for over a mile to prairie flats which are soon merged into post oak flats.

Near the south county line the Wabash bluffs are sometimes 80 feet high, near the railroad bridge they are 30 to 40 feet, near Ewington about the same, and 50 to 80 feet near the north county line

The bottoms of Little Wabash are an eighth to a quarter of a mile wide

The hills near Salt creek are often quite abrupt, sometimes 75 feet high; its bottoms are low and narrow, and its channel full of quicksands Near Sugar creek, Shoal creek, and Green creek, the hills are somewhat steep, bottoms very narrow and beds of the streams very sandy. Near the other streams the hills are generally low and of easy ascent and the bottoms rather wide.

*Timber and Prairie*—The prairie in the western part of the county is very flat with occasional ponds, on the margin of which may be found

*Cephalanthus occidentalis* and *Iris versicolor;* at the border of the prairie we found red oak and some laurel oak, on the flats west of the prairie post oak and shell bark hickory; in the woods between the prairies and Ewington hazel, laurel oak, hickory, sassafras, ash, etc.; and near the river white oak is more abundant

On the prairie north of Ewington there are occasionally small willows and a low species of *cornus*

On the bluffs of Sugar Fork we found white oak, Spanish oak, iron wood, sugar tree, and on the bottoms buckeye, sycamore, ash, bur oak, red oak, red bud, elm, hornbeam, and linden.

On the flats near Shoal creek we found white oak, shell bark hickory, post oak, and black oak; and on the hills and flats near Funkhouser's and Big creeks white oak, shell bark hickory and black oak.

The streams west of the Little Wabash river take their rise in very gentle depressions in the prairies

The banks of Fulter creek, on the prairie, are muddy and fringed with *cornus*, plum, cherry, grape vines and willow.

Lower down stream we found on the bottoms, white walnut, sugar tree, elm, grape vines, *clematis*, trumpet creeper, red birch, ash and sycamore

## *Geological Formations.*

*Quaternary.*—At the top of the drift there are beds of brown clay, which may probably be referred to the Loess West of Little Wabash there is exposed in the National road 4 to 6 feet of brown clay resting on blue clay with bowlders.

*Drift*—On the bank of Green creek near the north county line a deposit of altered drift is exposed thus

| | | Ft |
|---|---|---|
| 1 | Brown soil | 1 |
| 2 | Brown sandy clay | 6 |
| 3 | Brown sandstone | 4 in to 1 |
| 4 | Sand and pebbles | ? |

Other drift sections were observed, as follows.

In the railroad cut south of Watson:

| | | Ft |
|---|---|---|
| 1 | Brown clay (Loess?) | 8 |
| 2 | Clay and sand with some pebbles | 20 |

On Bishop's creek.

| | | Ft |
|---|---|---|
| 1 | Brown and buff clay (Loess?) | 12 |
| 2 | Blue clay and bowlders | 15 |

On Salt creek

| | | Ft | In |
|---|---|---|---|
| 1 | Brown and buff clays and sands, a few small springs at the bottom | | ? |
| 2 | Sandy conglomerate | | 6 |
| 3 | Blue clay and bowlders | 8 | |

On National road, 3 miles west of Ewington:

| | | Ft. |
|---|---|---|
| 1 | Brown clay | 6 |
| 2 | Brown clay and gravel | 6 |
| 3 | Sand and gravel, blue and brown clay and gravel in a tolerably even bed, partly formed into a conglomerate | 6 |
| 4 | Drift of sand and bowlders some of the latter very large | 25 |

In sections 17 and 30, T 8 N, R 5 E, there are regular beds of ferruginous drift conglomerate 2 to 3 feet in thickness. In the first named locality a coral was found of Lower Silurian age.

Six miles north-west of Effingham a pocket of black clay was observed, resembling the black humus deposits of the drift mentioned in my report of Moultrie and Macon counties.

A citizen of Effingham engaged in well digging gave me the following general section of wells:

| | | Ft |
|---|---|---|
| 1 | Soil and subsoil | 1 |
| 2 | White buff and blue clay (loess?) | 10 |
| 3 | Red clay and gravel—hard pan | 3 to 4 |
| 4 | Hard pan, blue or gray clay and gravel, as much as 24 feet, general average | 12 |
| 5 | Sometimes black clay | |

He generally found good streams of water in the sand and gravel beneath the hard-pan, lumps of coal and pieces of wood were found at twenty feet from the surface. One well at Effingham, forty four feet deep, had brown and black clay at the bottom and afforded plenty of water.

The surface of this county, like that of others which I visited, gave evidence of having once been much higher than at present, and the few low mounds scattered over the county are not connected, as we found them in other counties, but are isolated, often many miles apart.

## *Coal Measures.*

There are 285 to 300 feet of upper Coal Measure rocks in this county, the highest beds about 190 feet above the highest rocks of Shelby county. They include the horizon of three coal beds, viz: 15, 16 and 17. The following is an approximate section of the beds in this county:

| | | Ft | In |
|---|---|---|---|
| 1 | Sandstone and sandy shale, upper part gray, middle brown with plants | 60 | |
| 2 | Bituminous shale and septaria | 6 | |
| 3 | Dark clay shale | 4 | |
| 4 | Shales and nodular limestone, fossils | 1½ | |
| 5 | Blue and olive shales | 5 | |
| 6 | Gray sandstone and sandy shale | 26 | |
| 7 | Dark shale and thin beds of gray limestone | 5 | |
| 8 | Coal No 17 | 0 | 6 |
| 9 | Fire clay | 5 | |
| 10 | Mostly buff sandstone | 12 | |
| 11 | Clay and calcareous shales, fossils | 20 | |

| | | Ft | In |
|---|---|---|---|
| 12 | Similar to No 11, with fossils | 13 | |
| 13 | Bituminous shale and pyritiferous limestone | 9 | |
| 14 | Gray pyritiferous sandstone | 30 to 40 | |
| 15 | Shale with fucoids | 40 | |
| 16 | Cherty beds | 4 | |
| 17 | Limestone | 4 | |
| 18 | Calcareous and bituminous shale | | 16 |
| 19 | Nelson's coal, No 16 | | 16 |
| 20 | Fire clay | } 40 | |
| 21 | Shale ? | | |
| 22 | Sandstone | 30 | |
| 23 | Coal No 15, or Shelby coal | 1 | |
| 24 | Fire clay | 3 | |
| 25 | Nodular limestone | 2 | |

The rocks on Salt creek include the upper part of the section Nos 1 to 11, inclusive, and are more particularly described as follows.

| | | Ft |
|---|---|---|
| 1 | Just south of Effingham, the road passes over irregular beds of mostly hard gray sandstone with some shaly beds | 15 to 20 |
| 2 | In a ravine lower down the branch sandy shale, with coal smut | 6 |
| 3 | At the quarry below, yellow and brown sandstone with many plants near the upper part including *Calamites* etc | 30 |
| 4 | Dark gray pyritiferous sandy shale and sandstone, probably 12 or 15 feet in sight | 8 |
| 5 | Up a branch to the west, bituminous shale with thin coal laminæ, contains a calcareo pyritiferous bed of septaria, changing to a broad flat, 5 inch bed of rock, perpendicularly jointed forming rhomboidal blocks it contains a few very pretty fossils *Pleurotomaria sphærulata Spirifer plano convexus, Rhynchonella Osagensis, Nautilus occidentalis* and *Nautilus ferrata* ? | 6 |
| 6 | Dark olive shale and clay | 4 |
| 7 | Dark ash brown shaly and nodular limestone, abounding in a *Myalina* like *M sub quadrata*, narrow and regularly rounded at the anterior margin also contains *Aviculopecten occidentalis, Bellerophon Montfortianus, Edmondia* a small *Pleurotomaria, Leda* (coarsely striated), *Macrodon* (like *M carbonaria*), and a small univalve | $1\frac{1}{2}$ |
| 8 | Black and olive shale | 1 |
| 9 | Olive clay shale | 4 |
| 10 | Rough thinly bedded gray sandstone and sandy shale | 3 |

At a quarry half a mile further down the creek, Nos 4 and 5 crop out with the rocks below to No. 11.

| | | Ft |
|---|---|---|
| 11 | Hard blue and gray even bedded sandstone | 6 |

Two miles southwest, on a western branch of Salt creek.

| | | |
|---|---|---|
| 12 | Mostly dark olive or chocolate colored sandy and clay shale | 17 |
| 13 | Dark shale, with two 1 inch even beds of gray limestone, abounding in remains of fossils, including *Hemipronites crassus, Spirifer plano convexus, Chonetes Flemingii*, an *Edmondia*, a Trilobite, crinoid stems and plates, *Stenopora lepidodendroides*, etc | 1 |
| 14 | Dark olive and slate colored shales | 4 |
| 15 | Bituminous coal (No 17) | $0\frac{1}{2}$ |
| 16 | Light dove colored fire clay, nodules in the middle | 5 |
| 17 | Sandy shale with brown nodules | 2 |
| 18 | Down the same branch, and on Salt creek, are occasional outcrops of thick and thin bedded gray buff and drab sandstone and shale, No 10 of the county section, in all about | 20 |
| 19 | On Big Salt creek, half a mile above its junction with Little Salt, are twenty feet of clay shale, near the middle are two fossiliferous beds of carbonate of iron, with calcareo argillaceous shales between, and abounding in very pretty fossils, viz *Leda bella striata Astartella vera, Nucula ventricosa Spirifer plano convexus Chonetes Flemingii, Myalina sub quadrata, Macrocheilus inhabilis, Pleurotomaria Grayvillensis, Bellerophon Montfortianus, Bellerophon carbonarius, Bellerophon Sp ?* and *Orthoceras cribrosum* | ? |

In sec 27, T. 6 N., R. 6 E, on a small branch tributary to Ramsey, we get

| | | Ft |
|---|---|---|
| 1 | (10 of county section) Brown soft sandstone, towards the bottom hard and gray, plants in the upper part at the bottom there is a calcareous bed containing *Nautilus occidentalis*, *Macrocheilus* (small sp), *Diplodus*, etc | 8 |
| 2 | Fine grained, dark dove-colored limestone containing some very nice fossils, *Rhynchonella Osagensis* *Productus costatus* *P longispinus*, *P Prattenianus*, *Euomphalus subrugosus*, *Schizodus*, *Orthoceras cribrosum* *Goniatites* | 1 |

This limestone is also found on P H Hume's land, in sec. 35, T 7 N, R. 6 E, containing only *Productus longispinus* On Shoal creek there is a limestone which may also be its equivalent

| | | Ft. |
|---|---|---|
| 3 | (Last section continued) Bituminous shale containing a bed of carbonized and silicified wood also a 1½ inch bed of pyritiferous limestone | 4½ |
| 4 | Clay shale | 4 |
| 5 | (14 of county section) Hard sandstone and shale | 10 |

On the Wabash river, near the south county line, the last named sandy shales are thirty feet thick, containing, in the upper part, lenticular and regular beds of ironstone, with ferns and *Calamites* It is often very pyritiferous, as seen at the old mill on Fulfer creek, one mile from Little Wabash river, also in the Wabash bluffs at the railroad, where it contains some finely striated stems of plants On Big creek we find the sandstone containing similar stems and some ferns There is also on Big creek twenty to forty feet of drab, dove and dark-colored sandy shales containing ironstone concretions, some of the latter with spherical shaped small brown balls embedded in the side of the concretion

On Little Wabash river, in sec. 35, T 7 N., R 5 E, there is an outcrop of rocks as follows (Nos 11 and 12 of county section):

| | | Ft |
|---|---|---|
| 1 | Rough dark calcareous shale or shaly limestone and shales abounds in *Spirifer plano convexus*, *Nucula ventricosa*, *Productus longispinus* also contains *Athyris subtilita* *Productus costatus*, *Bellerophon*, etc | 2 |
| 2 | Blue and bituminous shales | 3 |
| 3 | Dark bluish olive argillaceous shale | 7 |

A quarter of a mile below, thirty feet of hard, gray and yellow sandstone forms the river bluff, in it are found plants, *Calamites* and fruit On a small branch of Fulfer creek, in sec 2, T. 6 N., R 5 E., there are thick beds of brown and buff sandstone (No. 10), tracing it around the bluff to the creek it is high up in the hill, a little further, on a lower horizon, there are outcrops of bituminous shale and limestone, evidently belonging to No. 13 of county section. One mile up the creek, at an old mill site, a fine section, including parts of 12, 13 and 14, was obtained, as follows

| | | Ft. | In |
|---|---|---|---|
| 1 | Various colored shales with lenticular beds of carbonate of iron In a gray shale at the base are found casts of *Lophophyllum proliferum* and *Spirifer plano convexus* | 25 | |
| 2 | Blue shales and calcareous iron stone, fossils very abundant in both, including *Prod costatus* *Sp plano convexus* *Orthis carbonaria*, *Leda arata*, *Athyris subtilita*, *Orthoceras* *Pleurotomaria Grayvillensis*, *Diplodus* | | 2 |
| 3 | Blue clay shales | | 3 |

| | | Ft | In |
|---|---|---|---|
| 4 | Compact dull-ash pyritiferous limestone with fossils *Productus* (small sp) *Sp plano convexus, Leda arata, Hemipronites crassus, Bellerophon Montfortianus, Euomphalus sub rugosus* | 1 | |
| 5 | Blue shales, fossils as above | 5 | |
| 6 | Ash brown shales | 1 | |
| 7 | Coarse ash blue pyritiferous limestone, contains *Prod. Prattenianus* | 0 | 4 |
| 8 | Shales | 4 | |
| 9 | Bituminous shales | 6 | |
| 10 | Ash blue pyritiferous limestone | 1 | |
| 11 | Shales, thin seams of coal and some bituminous shale | 2 | |
| 12 | Gray pyritiferous sandstone | 15 | |

A specimen collected from a portion of the last is of very even thickness and marked with fine ripple like striæ The rocks here have a local dip of 5° to 10° south, 25° west.

One mile west we have

| | | Ft |
|---|---|---|
| 1 | Bituminous shale with black concretionary limestone in the upper part | 3 |
| 2 | Dark blue limestone mottled with black fucoidal markings contains some beautiful fossils, including *Productus Boonensis P Prattenianus, P longispinus, P costatus Rhynchonella osagensis, Retzia punctulifera, Hemipronites crassus, Schizodus,* (like *S Rossicus*) *Edmondia, Orthoceras cribrosum, Bellerophon per carinata, Nautilus,* (like *N elliptica,*) *Euomphalus sub rugosus, Macrocheilus,* (like *M Newberryi,*) and one like *M ventricosus* | |
| 3 | Blue and bituminous shales | 10 |

The following is the section on Shoal creek·

| | | Ft | In |
|---|---|---|---|
| 1 | Ash blue clay shale | 15 | |
| 2 | Dark gray shaly limestone | 2 | |
| 3 | Bluish drab limestone with the following fossils *Nautilus occidentalis Nautilus, Prod semi reticulatus, P longispinus P scabriculus ? P costatus, Chonetes Flemingii, Athyris subtilita, Spirifer plano convexus, Hemipronites crassus, Rhynchonella osagensis Terebratula bovidens,* and *Orthoceras cribrosum* | 1 | 3 |
| 4 | Dark ash blue clay shales | | 10 |
| 5 | Bituminous shales | 4½ | |
| 6 | Blue limestone, lower part shelly and contains some fossils *Prod Prattenianus, P semi reticulatus, Spirifer cameratus,* and *Myalina sub quadrata* | 2 | |
| 7 | Bituminous coal | | 6 |
| 8 | Fire clay | 3 | |
| 9 | Sandstone | 25 | |
| 10 | Red shale | 4 | |
| 11 | Hard gray sandstone | 6 | |
| 12 | Sandy and clay shales with some nodules | 18 | |

On the head of east fork of Shoal creek, one mile north east of last section:

| | | Ft | In |
|---|---|---|---|
| 1 | Dark ash clay shales | 2 | |
| 2 | Brown calcareo arenaceous bed | 1 | |
| 3 | Semi bituminous shale, contains *Bellerophon* | | 2 |
| 4 | Dark blackish bituminous limestone | | 6 |
| 5 | Dark ash fire clay | 2 | |
| 6 | Hard drab sandstone | | |

The following on Limestone creek.

| | | Ft | In |
|---|---|---|---|
| 1 | Sandy shale | 2½ | |
| 2 | Hard drab sandstone | 2½ | |
| 3 | Buff drab and olive clay shales | 4 | |
| 4 | Red clay shales | 1½ | |

| | | Ft | In |
|---|---|---|---|
| 5 | Olive clay shales | 3 | |
| 6 | Hard sandstone | 3 | |
| 7 | Mostly clay shales | 5 | |
| 8 | Limestone | 3 | 2 |
| 9 | Coal No 16 | | 16 |
| 10 | Drab sandy shales | 8 | |

The last named limestone (No 8) is No. 17 of the general section in this county and regarded as the equivalent of No. 2 of the section in Shelby county, the shales and sandstone above it are similarly developed on the south fork of the Kaskaskia, in Moultrie. The limestone occupies the bed of Fulfer creek, two miles above the mouth of Limestone creek, extending quite across, and is beautifully jointed by perpendicular cracks meeting at oblique angles, thereby forming rhomboidal blocks This limestone dips down stream and is soon out of sight beneath the water It is not found below the mouth of Limestone creek, and the overlaying sandstones and shales appear in its stead. Its fossils mostly occur near the middle and are *Spirifer cameratus*, *Productus punctatus*, and *P longispinus*. On Limestone creek the limestone rests directly on the coal. At Mahon's quarry it is separated by eight inches of clay, and the coal rests on five feet of thinly laminated buff and gray sandy shales.

At G W. Nelson's, in sec. 20, T. 6 N., R. 4 E, a section of his well shows

| | | Ft |
|---|---|---|
| 1 | Chocolate colored shales | 14 |
| 2 | Blue shales | 6 |
| 3 | Clay and nodules of limestone and some peculiar looking fucoids, flat, with round edges and a spiney hirsute appearance | 18 |

A half mile west at the coal bank the section continues thus:

| | | Ft | In |
|---|---|---|---|
| 1 | Loose cherty rock with casts of fossils, *Hemipronites crassus*, *Productus punctatus*, *Spirifer cameratus*, *Prod costatus*, *Chonetes* | 2 | |
| 2 | Bluish drab limestone under ground it has a white surface Its fossils are *Athyris subtilita* and *Leptodomus* | 4 | |
| 3 | Dark blue and buff shales | | 8 |
| 4 | Calcareo bituminous shales | 2 | |
| 5 | Coal (No 16) said to be | 3 | |
| 6 | White clay | | |

I regard the limestone and coal at Nelson's equivalent to that of Limestone creek—it agrees with the dip

The lowest rocks occur on Beech creek, and consist of:

| | | Ft |
|---|---|---|
| 1 | Sandstone the lower three or four feet streaked with thin seams of red oxyd of iron | 30 |
| 2 | Coal (No 15, or Shelby coal) | 1 |
| 3 | Ash blue clay | 3 |
| 4 | Earthy limestone mostly nodular | 2 |
| 5 | Coarse drab shaly sandstone | |

## *Economical Geology.*

*Coal.*—There are no thick beds of coal in this county, and excepting "Nelson's," no workable beds.

Mr. G. W. Nelson's coal bank is on a high prairie in sec. 20, T. 6 N., R. 4 E. A pit has been opened, and good coal procured, but when I was there it was full of water, so that the thickness could not be correctly ascertained; but I was informed that it was 3 feet. Six miles down the creek, at Mahon's, it is 10 inches; and on Limestone creek, in sec. 18, T. 6 N., R. 5 E., it is 16 inches thick. These several outcrops—the one at the head of the creek, the other six miles below in the bed of the same creek—indicate a decided easterly dip. The same coal is also found on Big creek, in sec. 25, T. 7 N., R. 4 E. At these several places it is of variable thickness, and only separated from the overlaying limestone by a few inches of clay. I have catalogued this coal as No. 16, counting from the lowest. Except at Nelson's, neither black slate nor shale was observed overlaying it. At Nelson's the black shale is calcareo-bituminous and fossiliferous.

On Salt and Brush creeks there is a 6-inch seam of bituminous coal, which I have marked as No. 17; its sure guide is two thin, even layers of gray limestone, occurring about 4 feet above, and abounding in *Spirifer plano-convexus*. This coal was reported to me to be 16 inches and 2 feet in thickness, but I observed it nowhere so thick. On Salt creek, near the mouth of Brush creek, several pits have been dug at different times, but are now all full of earth and rubbish.

A thin coal seam observed in sec. 26, T. 9 N., R. 5 E., may be referred to either No. 16 coal, or else locally between 16 and 17, but I am in doubt regarding its exact horizon.

Coal No. 15 is only found on Beech creek, a branch of Rock creek, in sec. 30, T. 8 N., R. 4 E., one foot in thickness, with thick-bedded sandstone overlaying it. A shaft at Effingham, in order to reach coal No. 5, would have to be sunk about 900 to 950 feet.

*Iron ore.*—The drift conglomerate occurring in sec. 17, T. 8 N., R. 5 E., is 3 feet thick, and contains a good deal of iron ore. It crops out on a point of the hillside, extending for 30 feet across. A similar deposit occurs near the mouth of Big creek, in sec. 30, T. 8 N., R. 5 E. Coal Measure shales on Big creek abound in many concretions of oxyd and carbonate of iron; there are also some in other localities, but the quantity is insufficient.

The sandstone below Effingham, in the fossiliferous portion, is very ferruginous. Red oxyd of iron occurs on Beech creek in sandstone over coal No. 15.

*Building rock.*—On Sugar fork, near its mouth, there is a good quarry of hard sandstone, and one of silicious limestone on Green creek above the mouth of Sugar fork.

A very good quarry is that of Eversman's on Salt creek bluffs, two miles south of Effingham. The rock is a firm, gray sandstone, in even beds. Very good sandstone, in thick beds, occurs in the bluffs of Shoal creek near its mouth, on Fulfer creek, in sec 2, T 6 N., R. 5 E.; near Ramsey creek, half a mile from its mouth, in sec 27, T. 6 N., R 6 E, and on Big creek, in sec 29, T 9 N, R 5 E

On Limestone creek, and on Fulfer creek for two or three miles above the mouth of Limestone, there are good limestone quarries. A good deal of rock used on the National road was obtained at Mahon's quarry on Fulfer creek, also north-west on Big creek. I do not consider this rock of superior quality; that on the National road has undergone the test of twenty five years, and is very much cracked by frost The lime stone at Nelson's coal bank is apparently of better quality. All these limestones will make tolerably good lime.

The various streams nearly all abound in a good quality of clean sand, useful for plastering, etc

*Potters' clay.*—The buff and darker clays from just beneath the soil of the white oak lands is very much used at Effingham to make common pottery

*Supply of water.*—Good water can be procured anywhere by digging. On the prairies in the south-east it is obtained at from 12 to 20 feet; at Effingham, 30 to 44; at Watson, 16, in South west, 20; at Mason, 18 to 30 The deepest wells I heard of were G. W. Nelson's of 50 feet, through clay and Coal Measure rocks to good limestone water, and Jesse Newman's, at Mason, 145 feet, with scant supply of water. On the prairie, between Big creek and Fulfer, I detected a strong taste of sulphate of iron in water from a well 25 feet deep Near the mouth of Fulfer, in sec 2, T 6 N., R. 5 E, there is a chalybeate spring of very excellent water; it issues from beneath thick bedded Coal Measure sandstone.

On Brush creek, one mile from its mouth, there is a never failing spring of very good water. It is called by some a sulphur spring, but I could detect no taste of sulphur.

*Soil.*—There is more or less sand mingled with the soil of this county. The yield of corn is generally about 40 bushels per acre. Some persons think the country is too flat to be good wheat land; the general average is 20 bushels per acre—sometimes, but rarely, 30. When the seasons are not too dry good vegetable crops can be raised. The soil is well adapted to raising most kinds of fruit, but as yet orchards are not numerous The peach crop sometimes fails

At Mason I saw some very thrifty young pines growing in a yard, indicating their adaptation to this soil.

*Scalds*.—On the prairies in this county there are often found "scalds," or spots of barren and almost entirely unproductive land; fresh plowings often disclose spots of light and dark soil. The few plants found growing on these barren spots are of the same genera and species of those growing on poor land by the roadsides, or on and near an abandoned road, especially on a post oak flat, and consists mostly of *Erigeron divaricatum* and *Ambrosia bidentata*. If the character of these scalds results from the same causes producing the wastes on and near roads, it must have been produced by the tramping or wallowing of buffaloes.

In Missouri I have often seen places known as deer licks or buffalo wallows, and the growth on them is also the same as on the prairie scalds

So far, they may be buffalo wallows; but if they are wallows or licks, we would expect them to be basin-shaped, but they are generally about level with the surrounding plain.

In concluding I must tender my sincere thanks to Mr W. B. COOPER, of Effingham, for the presentation of specimens of silver ore from Nevada, and I am also under many obligations to Mr GEO W. WRIGHT, of Effingham, for valuable assistance in giving me lists of many important localities in the county, by which my labor was much reduced. To Dr. CORNWELL, of Mason, I also am obliged for assistance

# CHAPTER XVI.

## MOULTRIE, MACON AND PIATT COUNTIES.

Moultrie is bounded on the north by Piatt and Macon, on the east by Douglas and Coles, on the south by Shelby, and on the west by Shelby and Macon counties. It comprises an area of about 339 square miles, a little more than one fourth of which is timbered land It is drained by the South and West forks of Kaskaskia river and their tributaries. The timbered belt along the main streams varies from two to four miles in width The West fork of Kaskaskia is a sluggish stream with low muddy banks and does not run in dry seasons The South Fork is the only stream with any lasting quantity of water, it runs during ordinary seasons, and below Sullivan has low sandy banks, but eastwardly they are muddy. On the bars we found many pretty mollusks, including *Unio zigzag*, *U dilatata*, *Alasmodonta truncata*, *Melania*, *Paludina*, *cyclas*, etc

*Topography*—The prairies are either nearly flat or very gently undulating The timbered land, gradually sloping near the heads of creeks, becomes more uneven near the main streams, but there is no extensive tract of broken land The bluffs on the South fork of Kaskaskia, near the east county line, are sometimes forty feet high, but for four or five miles down stream are not often over twenty feet in hight, and spread out into white oak flats. Southwest of Sullivan the hills are sometimes sixty or eighty feet high, but not very abrupt.

*Prairies*—There is an extensive tract of nearly flat prairie west of the West fork of Kaskaskia, the north east quarter of the county is nearly all a very gently undulating or flat prairie, still, in great part, preserving its native state, and we here find tall grasses *Liatris* (two species), *Solidago*, *coreopsis*, *Monarda* (horsemint), resin weed (two species), *Veronica Virginica*, several species of aster, *Vernonia Noveboracensis*, *Dipteracanthus ciliosus* and *Eryngium yuccæfolium*.

The above imperfect list of species evidently indicates a transition from a wild state Occasionally swampy depressions are found, or marshy ponds with *Physa*, etc, and such plants as *Vernonia fasciculata*, *Lythrum alatum*, etc On the dry, low elevations are occasional clumps of hazel and low willow

## *Stratigraphical Geology.*

The formations in this county consist of the Quaternary and limited Coal Measure outcrops

*Alluvium*—This includes the soil, the loose material and more recent formations along the streams.

Below Sullivan, the soil of the South fork of Kaskaskia bottoms is very sandy, and along the stream there are many sandbars The sandy bottoms are often entirely covered with a growth of *Vernonia fasciculata.* The principal trees and shrubs are spice bush, sassafras, white and red elm, mulberry, red bud, grape vines, Virginia creeper, trumpet creeper, cottonwood, sycamore, white maple, hickory, coral berry, ash, black walnut, hazel and *cornus.*

Three miles south east of Sullivan, on land of George Purvis, on the west bank of Kaskaskia, I discovered the head of a bison. It measured across the forehead above the eyes twelve inches, the same between the roots of the horns; the latter were short, thick and slightly curved. The hill above the bank is probably twenty-five feet high, the bank about eight feet high, forming a narrow bench with the hill, of about ten feet in width, in this bench or terrace, a few feet from the top, the skull and part of the cervical bones were found, the surrounding clay was black rich loam There were several trees two feet in diameter growing on this terrace

*Drift*—The drift is of great depth in this county At Sullivan, which is about as high ground as any other part of the county, a well was dug 210 feet deep without reaching any older formation Mr PATTERSON, who had charge of the digging, informed me that he passed through

| | | Ft |
|---|---|---|
| 1 | Yellowish clay | 15 |
| 2 | Green clay | 10 |
| 3 | Whitish clay and some gravel | 6 |
| 4 | At 60 feet from top struck a soft white sandstone (probably a bowlder), then 21 feet alternations of sand gravel red clay blue clay, etc at 81 feet struck a big bowlder at 110 feet blue clay, continuing to 210 feet next 5 feet of quicksand—he could go no further A strong vein of water came in at 15 feet from the surface, also at 105 feet, another at 180 feet the last rising to within 5 feet of the top, but subsided to 15 feet It has a strong sulphate of iron taste | |

On Whitley's creek, on land of Daniel Brown, the following section of drift was exposed

| | | Ft |
|---|---|---|
| 1 | Soil at top with a growth of white oak and black hickory below brown clay, with a few small pebbles | 8 |
| 2 | Mostly blue and brown clay, with pebbles | 10 |
| 3 | Black spongy stratum, apparently vegetable mold, with no pebbles, when struck gives a hollow sound | 4 |
| 4 | Buff clay and brown sands, with talus from above | 11 |

Up a ravine a hundred yards distant is a fine spring of exceedingly clear pleasant tasted water four feet in depth, bubbles of sulphuretted hydrogen occasionally rise to the surface; no taste of sulphur was perceptible, but there was a slight odor of it The spring is on the land of Daniel Brown, and there are several similar springs near by

On the edge of the prairie near the east county line, a half mile south of the river, a well was dug twenty-two feet, through first, yellow clay, lower six or eight feet blue clay, then bored twelve feet through blue clay to a bed of black sand and vegetable mold, in which plenty of water was obtained. The latter dark material is probably the equivalent of No 3 of section at Brown's, and is also equivalent to a similar bed seen on Big creek, in Macon county.

On the South fork of Kaskaskia, below the mouth of Whitley's creek, observed as follows:

| | | Ft |
|---|---|---|
| 1 | Soil, local drift, etc | ? |
| 2 | Blue clay with a few pebbles at the lower part a very dark stratum of clay | 8 |
| 3 | Brown sand and small bowlders | 5 |
| 4 | Blue and brown sand and clay with some pebbles and bowlders | 8 |
| 5 | Very comminuted fine sand bed, some of it concretionary | 3 |
| 6 | Dark purplish blue sands | 4 |
| 7 | Talus of above, with fragments of coal etc | ? |

From the appearance of the dark stratum in Nos. 2 and 7, James W. Loomis & Co have run in a drift for seventy feet in search of a coal bed. of course they were unsuccessful The dark stratum at Daniel Brown's also induced certain parties to dig in search of coal A little knowledge of geology would have taught them the futility of searching for coal at these places

Drift bowlders of various kinds of metamorphic rocks are often found alone on the prairies, especially in the northern part of the county. Four miles north east of Sullivan there is a bowlder of granite 10+5+8 feet, surrounded only by the black prairie soil; how deep it lies beneath is not known.

## *Coal Measures.*

I was informed that near Sullivan Mr. John Patterson had dug a well 200 feet deep, through drift clays, and struck a soft sandstone, into which he bored 43 feet This is probably equivalent to No. 1 of my general section of the Coal Measure rocks observed in Shelby and adjoining counties. The top of this rock is probably about 140 feet above the Shelby coal (No 15) On the South Fork of Kaskaskia, two miles above the junction, I obtained the following section.

| | | Ft | In |
|---|---|---|---|
| 1 | Long slope of drift, along which are strewn many bowlders of various kinds | 50 | |
| 2 | Drab sandy shale | 5 | |
| 3 | Rough chocolate colored limestone | | 4 |
| 4 | Olive clay | 2 | 6 |
| 5 | Red clay | 2 | |
| 6 | Dark olive clay | 2 | |
| | To low water in the river | | |

North west of the above, on West Fork above the ford, I found many tumbled blocks of limestone sticking out of the bank, at a regular elevation above the water in the creek. They are somewhat surrounded by a local drift, but apparently about their proper place. Down the river a few miles, in Shelby county, this limestone (No 2 of general section) crops out in regular layers 4 feet thick I regard the above named Coal Measure rocks as equivalent to those seen on Limestone creek in Effingham county I would therefore say that a shaft would have to be sunk about 330 feet at Sullivan in order to reach coal No 15 or probably 850 feet to reach coal No 7

*Springs and wells*—There are but few springs in this county On the south-east and north east portions of the county water is generally obtained at a depth of from 15 to 22 feet Some wells on the prairies north of Bethany are but 13 feet deep. In digging, blue clay is generally passed through, and water found in the beds of sand. A well at the mill near Sullivan was dug 80 feet deep, with no water; six rods from it one was dug 30 feet deep, and water procured

*Soil*—We have here the prairie soil and the soil of the timbered land, each differing from the other, both in appearance and in relative fertility The prairie soil is very nearly of the same character every where, is very black, and generally 1½ feet or more in depth Around Sullivan, although it has been cultivated for many years, it does not seem to be impoverished, but still retains great fertility, producing annually 40 to 50 bushels of corn per acre, and often reaching 75—never less than 20; wheat 15 to 30, often 30 to 35; and barley 46 bushels per acre.

Near Whitley's creek there is a very narrow strip of probably less than a quarter of a mile in width extending along the stream for four miles from its mouth, with a growth mainly of white oak, black oak, and hickory, and sometimes sugar tree. Near the prairie this gives place to a richer land, with crab apple, thorn, plum, etc, further up stream the soil becomes still richer, with backberry, elm, walnut, honey locust, laurel oak, ash, bur oak, and sometimes chestnut oak. This soil is very productive, yielding, according to Mr Smizer, a general average of 50 bushels of corn per acre, and as high as 83, with 33 of wheat.

Around Bethany the growth is very similar, but the soil is generally of a lighter color, containing a few pebbles, the growth is honey locust, elm, backberry, hazel, laurel oak, hickory, linden, grape vines, *cornus*, cherry, coral berry, mulberry, and a surface covered with grass and pennyroyal

Between this and Sullivan the growth is somewhat different, consisting of black oak, hazel, hickory, sassafras, and occasionally bur-oak, walnut and *cornus*. This land is very well adapted to the growth of fruit, and yields excellent crops of wheat, averaging 20 to 25 and sometimes as much as 35 bushels per acre.

There is generally a belt a mile in width of poorer land with a yellowish soil extending along the South Fork, often spreading out into white oak flats, with a growth principally of white oak, black oak, post oak and low willow. Indifferent corn and tolerably good wheat can be raised on this soil.

Good Osage orange hedges have been planted, and succeed very well in this county, and there are also some willow hedges.

MACON COUNTY is bounded on the north by DeWitt, on the east by Piatt and Moultrie, on the south by Moultrie, Shelby and Christian, and on the west by Christian, Sangamon and Logan counties.

It embraces an area of about 555 square miles, the greater part of which is prairie, the timber being restricted to a three mile belt along Sangamon river, becoming narrower towards the eastern part of the county, a similar belt near Big creek, and a two mile strip along Friends' creek. There is a quantity of good timber both on the hills and bottoms, including white oak, black oak, bur-oak, red oak, laurel oak, pin oak, swamp white oak, chestnut oak, hackberry, hickory, elm, honey locust, sassafras and ash. White walnut and blue ash are found on the bottoms of Big creek, but are not common.

The general surface of the country is flat or gently undulating on the prairies, becoming more hilly as we approach the streams. From the northern part of the county the surface declines with gentle undulations southwardly to the timber, and from the high prairie in the north there is a fine southward view to the Sangamon timber ten miles distant. West of Harristown the slopes are extremely gentle from the high prairie to the Sangamon bottoms. Eastwardly the timbered land is more hilly, becoming quite broken near Decatur, with lower hills near the east county line. Near Decatur the hills rise by long slopes to a hight of about 90 feet above the bottoms, and are higher than the general surface of the country a little south. On Sangamon river near the east county line, and on Big creek north of Mt Zion, the hills are not often over 30 or 40 feet high.

Near the edge of the prairie south of Niantic there is a low sandy ridge with a growth of bur oak, black walnut, red oak, hackberry and hickory, changing to black oak, elm and hickory, then to black oak, hickory, elm and laurel oak. Where clay predominates pin oak and elm constitute the principal growth; the richest spots abound in cherry, laurel oak, hazel, elm, mulberry, redbud and black walnut. A well dug at this place gives the following section:

| | | Ft |
|---|---|---|
| 1 | Clay | 24 |
| 2 | Dry sand | 10 |
| 3 | Yellow and mottled clay | 3 |
| 4 | Quicksand with water | |

Two hundred yards distant another well was dug with somewhat different results, passing through 27 feet of clay to clay and gravel, with a fine stream of water at the bottom

Near Decatur, and for three miles west and eastwardly on Sangamon hills, the soil is of a light mulatto color, reddish-brown clay with a few pebbles appearing near the surface Near Decatur the growth is black oak, white oak, hickory, hazel and some walnut Near the edge of the prairie the growth is principally bur oak, laurel oak, hickory, hazel, plum and cherry, passing from the timber to the prairie the change is rapid from the light colored and yellowish soil of the timber to the deep rich black prairie soil.

Two miles south of Decatur the soil and growth changes from that of the black oak land to richer, with groves of elm, white oak, walnut, hickory, sassafras, vines, chestnut oak, laurel oak and mulberry

Near Mt Zion are tracts of good land, with white oak, walnut, chestnut oak, hazel, sugar tree and buckeye; the washings disclose some gravel. On the hillsides are goose grass and pennyroyal On the bottoms of Big creek blue ash, white walnut, sugar tree, elm, linden, with large buckeye and bur oak trees are found.

Pin oak and laurel oak are generally found at the edge of the prairies

On Sangamon bottoms there is plenty of good timber, including bur oak, red oak, black walnut, elm, linden, hackberry, buckeye, hickory, etc.

*Prairies.*—In many places the prairies still preserve their native beauty, covered with tall grass and adorned with Flora's bright gifts, among which are found the delicately beautiful *Physostegia Virginiana*, *Gerardia tenuifolia*, *Gentiana puberula*, with the coarser plants *Silphium laciniatum* and *S terebinthinaceum*, *Liatris* (2 or 3 species) *Helianthus*, *Solidago*, etc

## *Stratigraphical Geology.*

The geology of this county is only "surface." Except in one well, no older formations than the Drift have been discovered; at about 100 feet in a well at Macon it is said solid rock was struck, which may be doubted, inasmuch as large bowlders are often found in the clays of that vicinity

*Alluvium*—This includes the soils and recent formations along the streams. The Sangamon banks are 8 or 9 feet high and composed of dark clay, vegetable mould and a little sand. On the gravelly shoals many small shells are often found, belonging to the genera *Paludina*, *Melania*, *Cyclas* and *Unio*, where the water is more sluggish *Anodontas* are common.

On the flat prairies there are many small marshy tracts, fresh plowing of one of them disclosed to view remains of old shells of the genus *Planorbis* and *Lymnea*. It is not improbable that in a few years most of these ponds or marshes will be drained and cultivated, and the calcareous material of the shell remains will be found a useful addition to the productiveness of the soil.

*Drift.*—At Decatur there appears 6 to 10 feet of mostly yellowish-brown clay, then similar clay with bowlders and pebbles extending downwards several feet, then blue and brown clay and pebbles.

On Big creek, in sec. 4, T. 15 N., R. 3 E., the drift appears thus:

1. Thirty feet of drift clays with loose pebbles, sand and clay; at lower part comminuted sand and clay. On the lower slope of this is an abundant growth of *Equisetum* or scouring rush, associated with *Gentiana alba* and *Pedicularis lanceolata*.
2. Eight feet. The upper part dark brownish black, lower part black and apparently of vegetable origin; no pebbles seen; when struck a hollow sound is produced. *Debris* from above falling over unites with this, forms a marshy talus, on which were growing *Lobelia syphilitica*, *Sagittaria variabilis* and several other marsh plants.

The above drift section is very similar to an outcrop on Whitley's creek in Moultrie county.

Bowlders and pebbles of granite, quartzite, altered sandstone, porphyry, limestone, chert, etc., are found along the streams and irregularly scattered on the prairies, and sometimes very large ones are found alone on the flat prairie. Three miles south of Oakley observed a bowlder of gray granite of an irregular shape, measuring 8 feet across in two directions, and sticking up 4 feet above the ground. The surrounding soil is rich and black and no other bowlders were seen near by.

*Wells.*—At the railroad depot, Decatur, Mr. Isaac C. Pugh informed me that a well had been dug 90 feet deep through sand and gravel, but no permanent stream of water was reached. Mr. Pugh's well is 35 feet deep and affords plenty of water.

On the flat prairie south of Decatur water is found at a depth 13 feet.

Near the east county line, south of the railroad, it is reached at from 12 to 57 feet, but the supply fails in dry seasons; but at 27 to 40 feet fine streams are generally obtained, occurring in beds of sand beneath the blue clay. In the north-east part of the county water is obtained at from 10 to 20 feet from the surface, and near Forsyth from 16 to 30. On the rolling prairies in the western part of the county, water occurs at very irregular depths.

Harristown is located on what seems to be an elevated prolongation of a low drift ridge. At this place a well was dug through 10 feet of yellow clay, then 70 feet of blue clay with no sand, and only surface water obtained Two miles north-west, also on high prairie, another well was dug 30 feet deep, and has generally contained about 25 feet in depth of water.

*Springs*.—In sec 4, T. 17 N., R. 2 E., there is a large spring, the water of which is reported to contain sulphur, but I could not detect its presence.

On the land of John Good, near Bethel church, 4 miles north west of Decatur, is a boiling spring Carburetted hydrogen gas accompanied with small white flakes frequently escapes to the surface. The surface of the water presents a slightly iridescent appearance, it is very cold and pleasant to drink, with a faint taste of sulphur Along its margin a small species of *Physa* is found. The flat ground is marshy for as much as an acre in extent

In the Decatur fair grounds are several large and fine springs *

*Agriculture*.—It is apparent from what I have heretofore said, that all the prairie land is very rich, most of the timbered land either rich or of fair quality, and all capable of producing fine crops On the prairies, especially in the northern part of the county, fine corn crops are annually produced, in ordinary seasons yielding 65 bushels per acre and often more. Although the soil is very rich, good wheat crops are rare, fall wheat extremely uncertain, except near the south county line. The farmers generally sow spring wheat and raise from 15 to 20 bushels per acre They consider the ground too loose for fall wheat, but sometimes raise good crops of it on new land Other grains, oats, barley and rye yield well. The potato grows finely when not injured by the bug, but late vines during the last few years have suffered very much from their depredations

*Fruit*.—As yet, there are very few bearing orchards, but the county bids fair to become a good apple growing district. There are only one or two small vineyards near Decatur, and they promise well, this soil I believe to be admirably adapted to the vine Other small fruits when planted do well The peach crop of 1868 was very good, but such crops may not be expected every year.

A few good hedges were observed on the prairies The Osage orange does very well. I observed, growing, some good walnut groves on the prairies

---

* NOTE.—Mr WM A WILSON of this county, living ten miles south of Decatur, struck gas on his farm in the autumn of 1871, at a depth of 45 feet It came from immediately beneath the hard pan and was found at seven different localities on the place and the flow appearing to be constant he utilized it in furnishing his dwelling house with both light and fuel It comes from a bed of quick sand beneath the hard pan which has been penetrated to the depth of fifteen feet without reaching the bottom When last heard from some eighteen months after its discovery, the gas still continued to flow without any apparent decrease in the quantity

A quarter of a mile east of this gas well another boring was made which at a depth of about fifty feet passed through a bed of black peaty soil some four or five feet in thickness but no gas was found

A H W

In conclusion, I would say that for richness of soil Macon county will favorably compare with any other county in this portion of the State

NOTE —Since the foregoing report was written a boring was made at Decatur with a diamond drill, by the Western Coal Mining Company; and I am indebted to Mr BEAN, their agent here, for the following record of the work The boring stopped at the depth of 507 feet, 1 inch, and in my opinion from 85 to 100 feet above the horizon of the Springfield and Howlett coal. The following is the record of this bore

| | Ft | In |
|---|---|---|
| Surface soil clay gravel etc (drift) | 113 | |
| Coarse micaceous sandstone | 4 | |
| Arenaceous clay shale | 34 | |
| Grayish limestone | 4 | |
| Dark clay shale | 6 | 6 |
| Light clay shale | 12 | |
| Micaceous sandstone | 18 | |
| Clay shale | 24 | |
| Dark slaty clay with fossils | 2 | |
| Light slaty clay | 3 | |
| Red shale | 10 | |
| Brown and red shale with shells | 11 | 2 |
| Hard conglomerate | 3 | |
| Coal with red clay and gravel | 1 | 4 |
| Fire clay | 3 | 6 |
| Arenaceous clay shale | 7 | 1 |
| Hard lime conglomerate | 3 | |
| Bluish clay shale | 4 | |
| Soft micaceous sandstone | 21 | |
| Dark gray shale with ironstone | 9 | |
| Clay and quicksand ? | 3 | |
| Blue limestone | 1 | 6 |
| Gray sandy shale with fossils | 22 | 1 |
| Gray limestone | 11 | 6 |
| Black and gray shale | 7 | |
| Mud vein (fire clay ?) | 2 | |
| Blue limestone | 11 | 9 |
| Hard conglomerate | 2 | 1 |
| Blue shale and some rock | 13 | 8 |
| Hard gray, sandy and micaceous shale | 44 | 6 |
| Black shale | 2 | |
| Coal hard and bright | 1 | 2 |
| Fire clay | 9 | 9 |
| Bluish sandy clay shale | 8 | 4 |
| Mud vein (fire clay) | 2 | 1 |
| Dark, slaty clay with fossils | 17 | 4 |
| Hard conglomerate rock | 1 | 4 |
| Dark shale with fossils | 4 | 8 |
| Sulphur balls | | 6 |
| Lime conglomerate | 5 | |
| Red sandy clay shale | 20 | |
| Bluish clay shale with shells | 8 | 3 |
| | 507 | 1 |

The 11 feet 9 inch blue limestone found in this bore at the depth of

345 feet is probably the same as the Carlinville and Shoal creek bed, which is usually from 210 to 210 feet above the Springfield coal.

A. H. W.

PIATT COUNTY is bounded on the north by DeWitt and McLean, on the east by Champaign and Douglas, on the south by Moultrie, and on west by Macon and DeWitt counties It embraces an area of about 436 square miles, most of which consists of prairie,

The prairies of this county are very rich and in a great measure still preserve their native wildness, are beautiful in the summer season, covered with tall grass adorned with many beautiful flowers, among which are the rose, *Liatris*, (2 sp.) *Physostegia Virginiana*, *Phlox pilosa*, *Gerardia tenuifolia*, *Lobelia spicata*, *Lythrum alatum*, *Echinacea*, *Gentiana puberula*, *Veronica Virginica*, *Aster sericeus*, and several other species of aster; together with coarser plants, including *Monarda* (horsemint), *Solidago* (several species), *Silphium* or rosin weed (3 species), *Pedicularis lanceolata*, *Eryngium yuccæfolium*, *Nabalus asper*, *Helianthus* (several sp ), *Ceanothus*, etc Marshy spots and ponds are often seen, even on the highest prairies, some of them containing living shells of the genus *Physa Lymnea* and *Planorbis*, and having on their margin a growth of *Lobelia cardinalis*, *Vernonia fasciculata* and *Aster carneus*

*Streams*.—Willow Branch heads in several large springs N W of Bement, one of these on Thomas Davis' land is said to contain sulphur, but if so, the quantity must be very minute, for I could not detect its presence This spring spreads out into a large grassy marsh.

The South Fork of Kaskaskia river rises in the south east part of the county, a little east of Bement, runs southwardly for 12 miles and enters Moultrie county, along it there is a strip of timber varying from one to two miles in width The West Fork takes its rise in the south west and runs southwardly, soon entering Moultrie: there is but little timber near it, only first a fringe of willows with a few crab apple bushes beyond, lower down, the thorn (*Cratægus*) appears, then plum and cherry, next cherry, plum, pin oak, laurel oak, elm, still further down, elm, red and white oak, hickory and bur oak

The largest stream in this county is the North Fork of the Sangamon river, which traverses the county from north east to south west, and along its margin are many springs which afford a constant supply of pure water. In the river we found many very pretty mollusks similar to those already enumerated in the adjoining counties

*Timber and Topography*.—Near the Sangamon the hills are low and of easy ascent, the highest not over 15 feet, the neighboring country is not broken, but somewhat hilly for a half mile from the stream. Along the river and Goose creek there are timber belts of about two miles in width The total area of timbered land in the county probably does not exceed 50 square miles.

The prairies are bordered with a growth of laurel oak, pin oak, hickory, cherry, plum and crab apple, with sometimes bur oak and black walnut. Between the prairies and the Sangamon bluffs we found white oak, sassafras, shellbark hickory, black oak and hazel, on the sloping bluffs, white oak, black oak, service berry, iron wood, black haw, red tree, sugar tree, linden, ash, red oak, walnut, red elm and poison oak. Good timber abounds on the bottoms, including black walnut, bur oak, ash, maple, hickory, honey locust, hackberry, mulberry, red oak, linden, sycamore, and a few blue ash trees were observed.

Away from the streams the country is either flat or very gently undulating, rising by easy ascent to the upland prairie and gradually blending into the higher mound like elevations

## *Stratigraphical Geology.*

No formations, older than the Drift, appear in this county

The character of the *alluvium* is similar to that of the adjoining counties and it includes the soil and recent deposits along the streams.

*Drift* —At the bridge on Sangamon river, near Monticello, it is thus exposed

| | | Ft |
|---|---|---|
| 1 | Yellowish brown clay | 5 |
| 2 | Clay, sand and bowlders | 5 |
| 3 | Dark ash brown clay fine sand and a few pebbles | 4 |
| 4 | Black clay | 1 |
| 5 | Clay streaked, black and dark brown with ochrey red | 8 |

On Sangamon bluffs, four miles below Monticello, there is exposed

| | | Ft |
|---|---|---|
| 1 | Brown clay | 6 |
| 2 | Pebbles and clay | 10 |
| 3 | At top dark brown clay, below reddish brown finely communuted sand and clay | 14 |

Between Monticello and Centreville the road washings disclose three to four feet of bright brown clay, sometimes brown sand, pebbles and bowlders.

On the prairies there are bowlders of granite of various colors, generally gray, red and grey sienite and sienitic granite, quartzite and altered sandstone, gneiss and greenstone; and in the altered drift we found Devonian fossils and fragments of Coal Measure rocks.

Springs highly colored with oxyd of iron are often found issuing from the drift sands On Willow Branch, in sec 29, T 19 N., R 5 E, there are many such springs, some of them strongly chalybeate In one of them gas arises and a quantity of brown sediment is deposited on its sides; the ground in front is very marshy for the space of two acres

The bluff at this place is about thirty feet high and composed of brown sand and small rounded pebbles. Three quarters of a mile up the Sangamon river there is a similar marsh.

*Wells*.—In the timbered land wells have to be dug deeper than on the prairies and on the higher rolling prairie deeper than on the flat prairie. In the northern part of the county plenty of water is reached at twelve to twenty feet; on high prairie north east of Bement, fifteen to thirty feet, on high prairie, near Monticello, twenty to thirty feet; in the south-west, eighteen to thirty feet.

In sec. 26, T. 16 N., R. 5 E., Mr. LOVE has a well ten feet deep, passing through clay to sand, but the water sunk in the sand, a half mile west, plenty of water is obtained at five feet depth. At the Monticello hotel the well is fifty-five feet deep, the water generally standing at twelve feet from the surface, but in the summer of 1867 it sunk to forty seven feet from the top. At Centreville a well was dug on the hillside thirty-six feet deep, passing through six feet of yellow clay and sand at the top, then blue clay with occasional streaks of sand and some pebbles, a little quicksand near the bottom, and at the bottom a stratum of dark clay and sand, with a weak stream of water. The bottom of this well is near the horizon of the bottom of Sangamon river. One hundred feet distant, and at an elevation of twenty feet higher, a well was dug twenty-six feet deep and a good stream of water procured.

*Soil and Agriculture*.—The soil may be divided into two classes, the prairie and the timber. The timber is a loose, mulatto soil, producing good vegetables, and for fruit and vines is said to be quicker and better than the prairie, and is evidently dryer.

The prairie consists of dark, rich, loose loam, sometimes containing a little gravel; after the first sod plowing, if left thus for one season, a species of *Helianthus* grows up very thick over it to the almost entire exclusion of all other plants.

The southern prairies, I was informed, could be plowed within two days after very heavy rains.

The prairie soil seems admirably adapted to the growth of corn, the yield averaging fifty bushels and often more per acre. This is not a good wheat growing county; crops of spring wheat have been generally good, but this year (1868) the yield was not a half crop. Fall wheat is uncertain, but sometimes yields well, better than the spring wheat.

# CHAPTER XVII.

## GALLATIN COUNTY.

Gallatin county is one of the most interesting counties in the State, not merely geologically, but also in an economical point of view.

A marked feature in the topography of this county is an axis of disturbance or upheaval that crosses it, in an east and west direction, along the southern tier of sections on the parallel of township 9. The ridge, which is formed by this line of uplift, attains an elevation of three hundred and forty two feet above the high water of the Ohio river, and has received the name of "Gold Hill"

Its summit is capped with the conglomerate or millstone grit, a massive sandstone that usually contains small quartz pebbles, and lies at the base of the Coal Measures in this part of the State, whilst along the northern face of the ridge the Chester sandstone and limestone, which comprises the upper group of the Lower Carboniferous, are brought to the surface, and show, as well as the superimposed conglomerate, a strong dip to the south, varying in places from ten to forty degrees Especial attention was directed to discover a reversal of dip or anticlinal axis, but at every locality visited on the north side of the ridge, the strata from top to bottom were basseting at a high angle to the north On the east end, approaching the Ohio river, Gold Hill descends with a very gradual slope, and is lost in the alluvial of the overflowed bottom back of Shawneetown. In front of this town, on the Illinois shore, the rocky axis here crossed by the Ohio river is exposed to view at low water, where the conglomerate and superimposed strata lie in great confusion, but generally show an unmistakable dip of from ten to twenty five degrees to the south, as shown in the diagram, which represents a horizontal section of the rocks running north and south. The basseting conglomerate seen on the north end of this section appears to jut against a reddish, coarse-grained micaceous sandstone, that lies apparently horizontal, and may be traced along the water's edge for several hundred yards up the river, without presenting any appearance of an anticlinal axis. It weathers roughly and is coated in spots with a saline efflorescence, and is charged in

*Section at Shawneetown, Gallatin county, Ill., of Millstone-grit and overlying shales exposed at low water of the Ohio river.*

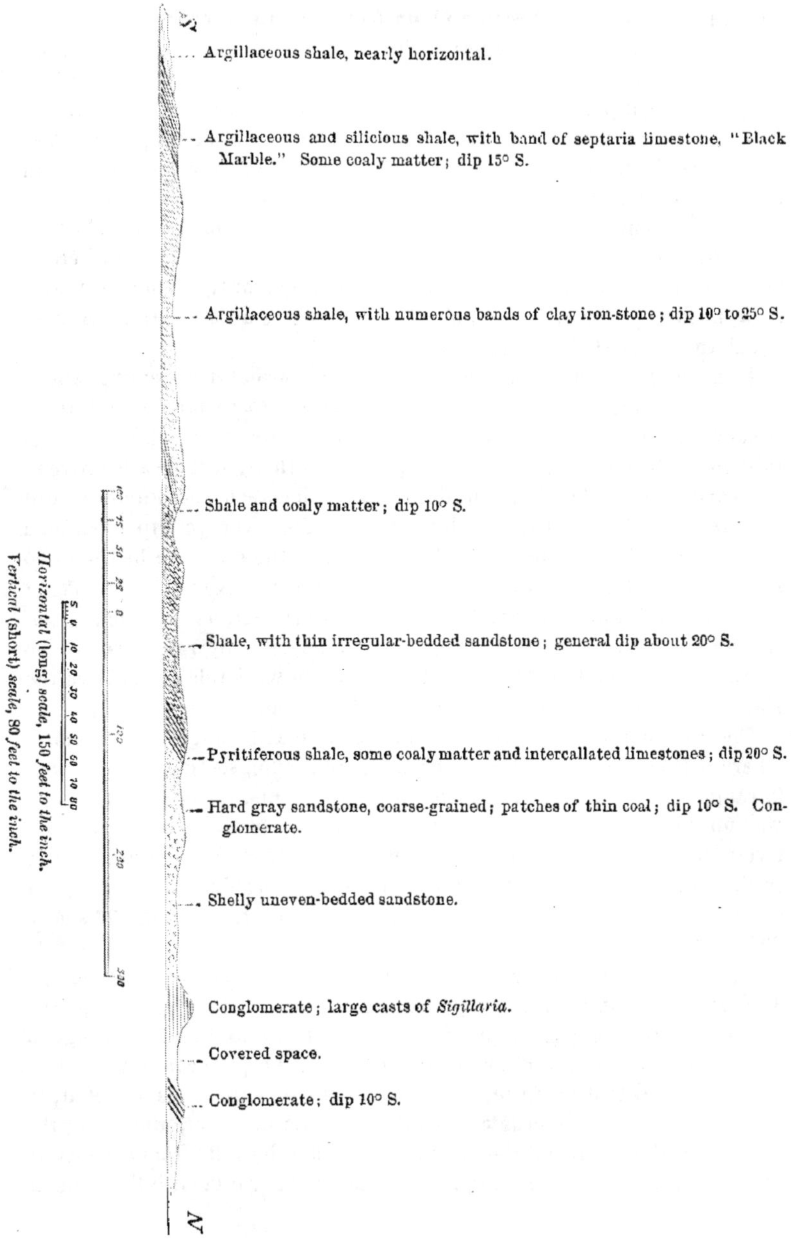

places, also, with iron ore, that forms a kind of ferruginous conglomerate or pudding stone, and here and there small patches of coal, but no regular seam. Large stems of *Sigillaria* are imbedded in it, one of which is twelve inches broad and six feet or more in length.

On the south end of the section the argillaceous shales lie also, apparently horizontal, after passing a short distance below the point where they show a dip of fifteen degrees Several thin seams of coal are seen, as shown in the section, but so crushed and broken up that it is difficult to determine with certainty their position in the vertical section of the Coal Measures hereafter to be described. The coaly matter in the shale dipping ten degrees, may occupy the position of the Battery rock coal, or No 1 of the section above referred to. Several intercallated bands of limestone occur in the section; one, a black septaria rock, is susceptible of a fine polish, and presents an appearance almost equal to the Irish black marble.

A casual observer of the tilted rocks at Shawneetown landing would be likely to exaggerate the thickness of the strata to far beyond what is shown in the above diagram, the measurements for which were carefully made by stepping the distance, and it is thought they will prove to be nearly exact The horizontal length is between nine hundred and fifty and one thousand feet, which, taking the average dip at fifteen degrees, would make the vertical thickness of the strata to be from two hundred and thirty to two hundred and fifty feet Now, if we make a reasonable allowance of one hundred and sixty feet, as the thickness of the millstone grit at this locality, it will be seen by reference to the vertical section of the Coal Measures that no workable coal, above the Battery rock coal No 1, has been brought to the surface here.

There is another low depression in the Gold Hill range in this county where it is crossed by Saline river, at Island riffle, section 36, township 9, range 8. At this locality a Coal Measure sandstone is exposed, but I was unable to determine its position in the measures, or to decide positively upon the direction of its dip. which is but slight, and apparently to the north-east, while at Dorsey's riffle, a short distance above, the shales and thin bedded sandstone in the river are dipping 35° south, 30° west

"Coal Hill" is the name of a short range of hills commencing on sec. 4, T 10, R 9, and terminating on sec 8 of the same township and range. With the exception of Coal Hill ridge and another range of hills that skirt along the north side of Saline river, the country south of Gold Hill and east of Saline has but a slight elevation, much of it, in fact, is subject to overflow. South of the Saline river, and along the waters of Eagle creek, the country is broken by hills from seventy to one hundred and fifty feet high. Another short range of hills, lying to the north of the Gold Hill axis and running nearly parallel thereto, terminate at or near Equality, on the west side of the north fork of the Saline The remainder of the county north of the Gold Hill axis is destitute of prominent hills, with the exception of an elevated narrow ridge running nearly north and south along the road from New Haven to Shawneetown, and terminating within three miles of the latter place

Gallatin county is well supplied with water courses Besides the Ohio and main Wabash rivers on its eastern boundary, the Little Wabash river enters the county at the village of New Haven, and flows through the north eastern corner to form its junction with the main Wabash twenty miles above the confluence of the latter stream with the Ohio The north fork runs through the north western portion and joins the Saline river at the town of Equality, on the eastern border of the county, while the latter river in its course cuts through the Gold Hill axis about three miles below Equality and flows out at the south-eastern corner of the county to form its junction with the Ohio river just above the Battery Rock coal mines, in Hardin county Eagle creek, a large tributary of the Saline river on the south, and its numerous affluents, ramify through the south-western portion of the county. Besides these streams, it may be mentioned that there are a few ponds or small lakes seen in the low lands of the Ohio and Wabash rivers, which are supposed by many, with seeming plausibility, to be the remains of old river channels

## *Stratigraphical Geology.*

The geology of this county will be best understood by an examination of the section on page 202, in which is shown the chronological order of all the strata visible in this county.

*Lower Carboniferous* —Along the northern face of the Gold Hill ridge, in two or three places the upper part of the lower carboniferous rocks has been brought to the surface by the axis of disturbance which produced this noted ridge These rocks belong to what is designated in the first volume of the report on the geology of Illinois as the "*Chester group*"

The most easterly exposure is on the S. hf. of sec. 33, T 9, R 9, about three miles east of Shawneetown, where the following section was obtained

| | Ft |
|---|---|
| Covered slope to top of ridge | 50 |
| Conglomerate with pebbles | 50 |
| Irregular bedded sandstone | 20 |
| Covered, sandstone and shale | 90 |
| Limestone with Archimedes | 55 |
| Covered to high water of Ohio | 40 |
| | 305 |

The rocks in this section basset to the north at an angle of 20°. The Chester limestone exposed near the base is, for the most part, a coarse crystalline, grayish rock filled with small entrochites, the organic structure of which is almost obliterated by crystallization, which gives a glimmering lustre to the freshly broken fragments. It is remarkably poor in other fossils, for after a long and diligent search, I was finally able to obtain only a very badly preserved specimen of *Archimedes* and a few fragments of a small *Spirifer*, too imperfect for determination. There is a thin stratum of fine grained bluish limestone, in which no trace of organisms could be found, lying between strata of the gray rock and near the lower part of the exposure.

The large amount of talus strewed along the base on the north side of Gold Hill, covers up the lower strata so completely that I was compelled to make two separate trips, having a guide each time, and to spend two days in searching before being able to find the limestone at this locality. It is true lime had been burned here, but so long ago that people generally knew nothing about it. Though, for the causes herein stated, this limestone could be traced for only a few hundred feet along its outcrop, it is thought that it may extend half a mile or more along the ridge until it disappears through an east and west depression beneath the drainage of the county. To the west of sec 33 the ridge gradually sinks and is crossed by the Saline river in sec 31, T. 9, R. 9, and in sec 36, T. 9, R. 8, at what is known as Island Riffle, where rapids are formed by the stream flowing over a coarse grained, yellowish sandstone which weathers roughly, and the position of which, in the series, is above the Conglomerate, but I was unable to determine its exact place in the vertical section. After crossing to the west side of the Saline river, and following up the stream to sec 27, T. 9, R. 8, the Chester limestone makes its appearance again high up in the ridge, and forms with its associate strata an abrupt escarpment. They basset to the north at an angle of about 10°.

The following section was taken at low-water of the Saline :

| | Ft |
|---|---|
| Soil, drift and covered | 60 |
| Quartzose sandstone mostly covered up, probable equivalent of the Chester sandstone | 50 |
| Chester limestone gray, with thin seams of calc spar, has a paucity of fossils, yielded a fragment of *Productus elegans* | 23 |
| Covered to low water of Saline | 70 |
| | 201 |

Besides dipping to the south, which is the regular pitch of the strata in the ridge, there is here also an east and west wave of elevation and depression, which carries the limestone down from forty to fifty feet, a few hundred yards to the east, where the old salt springs—formerly known as the "Nigger Works"—break out in the bank of the Saline river, apparently at the junction of the limestone with the sandstone which lies above it Consequently, we may consider this as the geological horizon of the main salt brine of this portion of the State

With the exception of a small outlier of Chester limestone in the south western part of the county, near the corner of Pope and Hardin counties, no other localities are known in Gallatin where the sub carboniferous rocks can be found outcropping; and wherever examined these rocks, quite contrary to what is usual, show a remarkable paucity of organic remains, and the few that were observed it was found impossible to preserve

## *Coal Measures.*

The section which accompanies this report represents the entire thickness of coal strata in Gallatin county, and contains, it is believed, all the workable beds of coal, together with some of the most important thin seams that are to be found in the county.

Section of the rocks in Gallatin county

| | | | | Ft | In |
|---|---|---|---|---|---|
| No | 1 | Silicious shale | | 10 | |
| No | 2 | Heavy bedded sandstone | 5 to | 40 | |
| No | 3 | Siliceous and argillaceous shale | | 25 | |
| No | 4 | Limestone (Carthage rock ?) | | 8 | |
| No | 5 | Shale and thin Coal No 9 | | 3 | |
| No | 6 | Shales partly bituminous and calcareous | | 30 | |
| No | 7 | Bituminous shale | | 2 | |
| No | 8 | Coal No 8 | | 2 | |
| No | 9 | Siliceous shale and sandstone | | 40 | |
| No | 10 | Limestone | | 4 | |
| No | 11 | Bituminous shale | 0 to | 3 | |
| No | 12 | Coal No 7 | 4 to | 7 | |
| No | 13 | Sandstone and shale | | 41 | |
| No | 14 | Coal No 6 | | 2 | 6 |
| No | 15 | Shales and thin bedded sandstone | | 65 | |
| No | 16 | Bituminous shale | 2 to | 5 | |
| No | 17 | Coal No 5 | | 5 | |
| No | 18 | Fire clay | | 3 | |
| No | 19 | Clay shale with iron stone | | 3 | |
| No | 20 | Sandstone and shale | | 78 | |
| No | 21 | Shale partly bituminous | | 2 | |
| No | 22 | Coal No 4 | | 2 | 6 |
| No | 23 | Shale and thin bedded sandstone | | 42 | |
| No | 24 | Thin coal (local) | | 0 | 4 |
| No | 25 | Fire clay | | 5 | |
| No | 26 | Shale with iron stones in upper part | | 43 | |
| No | 27 | Coal No 3 | | 3 | |
| No | 28 | Sandstone and shale | | 19 | |
| No | 29 | Bituminous shale | | 5 | |
| No | 30 | Coal No 2 | | 4 | |
| No | 31 | Argillaceous shale | | 20 | |
| No | 32 | Thin bedded sandstone and siliceous shale with thin coal | | 60 | |
| No | 33 | Hearth sandstone | | 20 | |
| No | 34 | Argillaceous shale | | 40 | |

| | | Ft | In |
|---|---|---|---|
| No 35 | Coal No 1 . . . . . . . . . . . 1 ft 8 in to | 1 | |
| No 36 | Argillaceous and siliceous shale | 70 | |
| No 37 | Conglomerate sandstone | 110 | |
| No 38 | Bluish argillaceous shale (Lower Carboniferous) | 15 | |
| No 39 | Thin coal (Lower Carboniferous) | 0 | 4 |
| No 40 | Argillaceous shales (Lower Carboniferous) | 10 | |
| No 41 | Covered space with sandstone (Lower Carboniferous) | 60 | |
| No 42 | Chester limestone (Lower Carboniferous) | 55 | |
| No 43 | Covered space | 40 | |

No. 1 or "Battery-rock coal" is not worked in Gallatin county, and no exposure of the seam could be recognized with any degree of certainty It is thought probable that the thin seam of coal rash shown in the horizontal section of the disturbed strata in front of Shawneetown, and a thin seam, opened some years ago by Mr Baker, on sec 36, T. 9, R. 9, west of Shawneetown, and near the eastern terminus of Gold Hill, may be that seam, but no reliable evidence was found to establish this conclusion In the decomposing shales above the rash coal in the river bank at Shawneetown, a few fossils were seen, that are thought to be characteristic of much higher strata, as *Bellerophon carbonaris*, *B per-carinatus*, *Productus longispinus* and *Spirifer cameratus*, but they crumbled to pieces on being removed from their matrix. If the actual horizon of this coal is above No. 1 in the vertical section, and near the horizon of No 7, as its fossils and the associated limestone seem to indicate, it shows a remarkable thinning out of the intermediate strata, and a total absence of workable coal, for the Conglomerate can not be more than one hundred and ten or one hundred and thirty feet below it, provided that the latter rock is referable to the Battery-rock Conglomerate. I am aware that the coal seams thin out to the northward of "Gold Hill," but at the same time I believe that the associated strata increase, instead of diminish in thickness in that direction.

The opening to the thin coal west of Shawneetown (section 36) in "Gold Hill' was entirely filled with rubbish, and no good view could be had of it. The strata are all basseting to the north at an angle of 20° to 40°, which renders it almost impossible to work a coal from such an outcrop Mr BECK, who had been, I believe, interested in the mine, accompanied me to the locality, and he expressed the opinion that the seam was found to be two feet thick in the opening. Judging from what I could see, the coal is of an inferior quality, and resembles very much the coal in front of Shawneetown. The following section will show its position in the ridge, commencing from the high water of the Ohio river, which point was determined by the drift wood along the foot of the ridge

| | Ft |
|---|---|
| Covered slope and soil | 10 |
| Buff sandstone | 10 |
| Sandy shale and flagstone | 100 |
| Blue soft shale | 2 |

| | Ft |
|---|---|
| Flag sandstone | 10 |
| Gray and blue shale with ironstone | 40 |
| Coal mostly *rash* | 2? |
| Covered | 30 |
| High water of the Ohio river | ? |
| | 204 |

The buff colored massive sandstone, near the top of this section, forms a vertical wall in many places along the ridge, and, from this point, gradually descends to the east, so that where last seen in that direction, about a quarter of a mile distant, it is found to be only sixty feet above highwater; a rate of dip that would carry it to the water's edge in front of Shawneetown.

In Hardin county, below the mouth of the Saline river, and opposite the town of Caseyville, in Kentucky, the Conglomerate rises into a vertical wall known as the "Battery-rock," and forms here the western bank of the Ohio river. It is divided into two beds, by a very thin parting of shale and coal. The latter is very irregularly bedded and is not anywhere more than a few inches in thickness, and, though not considered persistent, it is seen at the mouth of Tradewater river, on the opposite side of the Ohio. My measurement of that portion of this rock seen above low water, taken with an Aneroid barometer, made the lower bed fifty and the upper sixty feet thick, and the space between low water and the coal, which is here referred to No 1, one hundred and eighty feet

The "Battery rock coal," as it is called, is the equivalent of the seam worked by Bell, Cook and Casey, on Tradewater river, in Kentucky; and also the equivalent of the Ice-house seam, or No 3 of Owen's section, and likewise it is believed to be synchronous with the Cannelton seam, in Indiana, and the Hawesville seam in Kentucky, on the eastern margin of the basin

On Tradewater river this coal ranges from two and a half to five feet in thickness, but back of Caseyville, and on Shotwell's property, in Union county, Kentucky, it averages only from eighteen to twenty-two inches At Battery rock also it is a thin seam, rarely reaching twenty-two inches At every locality where this coal was seen it has from one to four inches of coal-rash at the bottom, above which the coal is highly bituminous, and is held in excellent repute by steamboat men on the Ohio river.

Battery rock coal has been opened in three or four places along the river front, but it is too thin and too subject to horse backs to admit of extensive mining operations The gray colored roof shales contain a few fossil plants belonging to the genera *Lepidodendron* and *Stigmaria*, *Pecopteris lonchitica* and *Neuropteris hirsuta*, but they are too friable to be preserved. No fossil shells were found, though *Lingula umbonata* is common in the roof shales of this coal on the opposite side of the Ohio, and on Tradewater river

The following section obtained along the river, commencing at Battery-rock ferry and extending up stream nearly to the mouth of Saline river, will serve to show the position of No 1 coal and the conglomerate, together with the change of level at the various places given.

Section at Battery-rock ferry

| | Ft | In |
|---|---|---|
| Soil, clay drift, and covered space | 50 | |
| Massive gray sandstone, (hearth stone) | 20 | |
| Shale, mostly silicious | 40 | |
| Coal, No 1 .. 1 ft 4 in | to 1 | 10 |
| Silicious shales passing down into flagstone | 70 | |
| Conglomerate, upper member | 60 | |
| Thin coal, wedged in | 0 | 4 |
| Conglomerate, lower member | 50 | 0 |
| Low water of the Ohio | 0 | 0 |
| | 292 | 2 |

Three quarters of a mile above the ferry, in a north-west direction, N. 40° W, the top of the Conglomerate is just at the water's edge, while three quarters of a mile again above this, and half a mile below Sellers' paper mill, the base is eighty feet above the river, where the following section was taken

| | Ft | In |
|---|---|---|
| Conglomerate sandstone forming a cliff (Shows 70 feet thick at Sellers paper mill, where large masses have broken off and tumbled to the plain below, one block larger and more conspicuous than the others, has received the name of "Stack Rock.") | 35 | |
| Blue argillaceous shales, with numerous bands of carbonate of iron comprising altogether from one to one and a half feet of good iron ore, one band four to six inches thick, contains a number of imperfect casts of fossil shells *Athyris subtilita*, *Macrocheilus inhabilis*? *Spirifer cameratus*? small *Bellerophon*, *Nucula* and a fragment of a *Cyathophylloid* coral | 14 | |
| Coal reported from a bore | 0 | 8 |
| Sandy and argillaceous shale | 7 | |
| Covered to low water | 58 | |
| | 114 | 8 |

Half a mile above Sellers' paper mill, in a direction N. 47° W., coal No 1 is ninety five feet above low-water, and may be seen above and below the mouth of coal creek ; and one half mile above the last locality, in a direction N 61° W, it is one hundred and twenty-two feet above low water, at T. Rees & Co's mines The general dip of the strata is north, about 20° east, and the irregularity in the elevation of the Conglomerate and coal along the river bluff is mainly due to the position of the exposure being on one or the other side of the strike line, and furnishes no evidence of more than one seam of coal above the conglomerate at the localities here cited *

* Since this report was written I visited this locality in company with G E SELLERS, Esq, of Bowlesville and traced the bluffs carefully from Battery rock to the mouth of the Saline From this examination I am confident there are two seams of coal above the Battery rock coal outcropping between these points, which either represent coals Nos 2 and 3 of the general section given on page 2 *et seq* of this volume, or else they are local seams that have not been seen elsewhere

A H W

*Coal No* 2, or "four-foot seam," as it is generally called here, is the next workable coal in the ascending order, it has been reached by a shaft on the Saline river, in Gallatin county, at the Independent Coal Company's mines, where, as well as in Union county, Kentucky it is uniformly four feet thick, and of fine quality for steam and manufacturing purposes, the color brownish black, it has a laminated or splinty structure, with carbonaceous partings, and appears to be remarkably free from sulphur The space between Nos 1 and 2 is about one hundred and forty (140) feet, and contains, on the Kentucky side of the Ohio, two or more thin seams of coal, but no bed that is thick enough to be worked.

The Independent Coal Company work both No. 2 and No. 3 from the one shaft, which commences just below No. 4, or "Well coal," and is one hundred and fourteen feet deep The following section, made from this shaft, will exhibit the character of the strata passed through.

Section of the Independent Coal Company's shaft, sec 35, T 10, R 9, coal dips N 10°, E. about 3°

| | Ft | In |
|---|---|---|
| Soil and clay | 10 | |
| Sandstone | 6 | |
| Blue argillaceous shale | 8 | |
| Silicious shale, with iron stone | 18 | |
| Coal, thin | 0 | 4 |
| Fire clay | 5 | |
| Silicious shale, with iron stone | 40 | |
| Gray, sheety sandstone, with bitumen | 3 | |
| Coal No 3 | 3 | |
| Fire clay | 0 | 6 |
| Sandstone | 8 | |
| Silicious shale with iron stone | 10 | 6 |
| Black bituminous, hard slate | 5 | |
| Coal, No 2 | 4 | |
| | 121 | 4 |

The space between No 2 and 3 coal is only twenty-four feet in this shaft, but it is nearly double this depth at Shotwell's mines in Kentucky.

*Coal No* 3—Is of fair quality, but it contains some sulphur, and its reputation in the market is not quite so good as that of the seam below it

In drifting or running an entry to the west in this shaft after coal No. 3, a serious fault was encountered; the coal was abruptly terminated by a solid wall of sandstone, and was not recovered up to the time of my visit. No. 2 was being worked in the same direction, with a view to learn if it also is affected by the fault, and to endeavor to discover its nature My opinion is that the coal will be found above the level of the entry, as the sandstone which occupies its place appears to be the same as the rock which underlies this seam

A few hundred yards above the Independent Company's shaft, No. 3 outcrops in the bank of Saline river, and No 2 was reached there by a shaft thirteen feet below the bed of the stream. The old works at this locality have long since been abandoned, and the openings are filled up with rubbish, brought by the overflows of the Saline river

Near the foot of the hills, a few hundred yards north of the above mines, and on land belonging to the same company, No. 4 coal was struck by sinking a well, and was subsequently bored through at the company's office. It is two and a half feet thick and lies between ninety and one hundred feet above No 3, as proved by the bore at the office and by the section of the shaft above given

Nos 5, 6 and 7 are seen in their regular sequence outcropping in the hill on the Independent Company's property north of the shaft, and on the above section No 5 is from eighty eight to one hundred feet above No 4 This space is filled with thin bedded sandstone and shales, with more or less iron ore It is generally a little less than five feet thick, though usually called in this county and Union county, Kentucky, the "five-foot coal" The color is a dull black, and on the Saline river it is often marked by a beautiful play of colors, giving rise to the appellation of "peacock coal" It contains a large percentage of fixed carbon, and but for the sulphur bands which are mixed with it, would prove the very best coal for steam and manufacturing purposes in the basin It has been extensively mined for the supply of steamboats, both along the Ohio river in Kentucky, and on the Saline river in this county, but from injudicious mining or other causes, it has fallen into bad repute, and Nos. 2 and 3 have for the time being supplanted it in public favor. The poor reputation which has befallen this seam I have no doubt may be traced to the coal not having been properly screened and not separating it from the sulphur bands with which it is contaminated

No 5 has been opened and worked at many places on sections 27, 35, 21 and 9, township 10, range 9, and was reached in a bore on Eagle creek, on section 13, township 10, range 8, on the south side of the Saline It has been worked by a shallow shaft to furnish fuel for Ross' mill at Equality, and can be seen in the bed of the Saline river at the latter place when the river is extremely low About two miles southwest of Equality, on the eastern edge of Saline county, it is worked by drifting into the hill, and furnishes the fuel to evaporate the brine of the salt works owned by Messrs Temple & Castle

The black bituminous roof shales of No 5 coal contain, usually, an abundance of beautiful, compressed shells, completely gilt with brilliant yellow pyrites of iron This shale, with its fossil treasures, rapidly decomposes when exposed to the weather, and can be preserved only when obtained fresh from the mines, and properly cared for. When I visited the mines on the Saline river for the purpose of making this report, no fresh shale was being brought from the mines, and the old would not bear handling, especially when it contained pyritiferous fossils, but would crumble into fragments The most abundant shells are *Aviculopecten rectilaterarius, Productus longispinus, Nautilus decoratus, Solenomya soleniformis, Nucula ventricosa, Orthoceras Rushensis, Pleurotomaria Grayvillensis, Bellerophon carbonarius*, and *Chonetes mesoloba.*

*Coal No. 6*.—Lies from sixty to seventy feet above No 5, is from two to three feet thick, and was formerly worked on the Saline river at Tolbert's mines, and on the Curlew mines' property, near Caseyville, in Kentucky; the quality is said to be very good, but the old openings have long since been filled up, and there was no chance of collecting specimens or of seeing the solid coal The outcrop of this seam was seen at the localities above cited for No 5. In the hill at Equality it is of very poor quality, and is not over fifteen to twenty inches thick. At this latter locality it is underlaid by a massive sandstone, and the latter is underlaid by gray and buff silicious shales, with ironstones down to the black shales overlying No 5 coal.

*No 7 Coal*.—This seam lies from one hundred to one hundred and twenty feet above No 5, and is at some localities from eight to nine feet thick Its color is a jet black, it breaks into cubes and has numerous cross fractures lined with salts of calcium The bed is divided into two seams by a parting of fire clay from half an inch to four inches or more in thickness, and near the top of the seam there is a very thin sulphur band (bi sulphide of iron), which seldom exceeds one eighth of an inch in thickness That portion of the bed above the fire clay parting is generally considered the best, and in Union county, Kentucky, at the Curlew mines, this part of the seam is assimilated to a cannel coal. No. 7 has been opened and mined on the Independent Coal Company's land in connection with No 5, also, at Tolbert's, in section 21 township 10, range 9, and at Boswell's a half mile north of the former mines. At these localities the bed is from three to four feet thick, the clay parting is two inches thick, and is eight inches from the bottom of the bed The following section was taken at Boswell's mine, section 26, township 10, range 9

| | | | Ft | In |
|---|---|---|---|---|
| Covered slope | | | 0 | |
| Thick bedded sandstone | | | 9 | |
| Flagstones | | | 6 | |
| Silicious shale | | | 4 | |
| Gray limestone | | | 3 | |
| Black shale | | | 2 | |
| Coal | 2 4 | Coal No 7 | 3 | 2 |
| Fire clay | 0 2 | | | |
| Coal | 0 8 | | | |
| Covered | | | 0 | |
| | | | 27 | 2 |

The direction of the dip is north 10° east, at the rate of about three inches to the yard. In the decomposing roof shale, at the mouth of this mine, *Aviculopecten rectilateraius* and *Cardinia? fragilis* were seen, but they were too friable to bear handling. As the strata rise, from Boswell's, in the direction of the Saline river, No 7 is found high up in the ridge on the Independent Coal Company's property, and No 5 outcrops near the base. On the property of Mr. Hines, section 13, township 10, range 8, on Eagle creek, No 7 is seen outcropping in the bed of the creek, but following to the south some two hundred yards, on the rise of the strata, it is found thirty-three feet above the creek, where it has been mined to a limited extent by Mr. Hines, for fuel to run his saw mill. At these outcrops the overlying limestone could not be seen; however, Mr Hines informed me that it made its appearance at the end of his drift, where I was unable to see it for want of lights, but I fully satisfied myself of the identity of the bed by the clay parting and sulphur band, the former ten inches from the bottom, and the latter a few inches below the top. Mr. Hines informed me that at the creek he bored forty feet below this seam, and passed through a lower coal that was two and a half feet thick, this latter is in the position of No. 6. Along Eagle creek, westward to the county line, No. 7 has been reached in wells, and can be traced in a north-east direction to Bowlsville. At Bowlsville, on sections 8 and 9, township 10, range 9, in the range called Coal Hill, Nos. 7, 6 and 5 outcrop. Coal No 7 outcrops on both sides of Coal Hill, and has been opened in a number of places at various elevations above high water of the Ohio river of 1848, as determined by E. F. LEE, Civil Engineer.

The following descriptions of these openings are given to show that no reliance can be placed on the local dip of a coal seam as a means of identifying the beds over any great extent of country:

At the Mason entry into No. 7 coal, on the north part of section 9, the seam is ninety eight feet above high water of the Ohio, is three feet ten inches thick, has a clay parting of two inches, about one foot from the bottom, and a thin band of sulphur near the top. Above the seam is:

| | Ft | In |
|---|---|---|
| Shale | 1 | 6 |
| Dark limestone | 4 | |
| Black bituminous shale | | 8 |
| Coal No 7 | 3 | 10 |
| Fire clay | | ? |

One hundred yards to the north east, near the line between sections 9 and 4, seventy-eight feet above high water, there is another opening showing a dip of the strata, on this part of Coal hill, to the north east at the rate of twenty feet in four hundred of horizontal distance.

Section at the Vaughan entry

| | Ft | In |
|---|---|---|
| Shale | | 4 |
| Limestone | 5 | |
| Shale | | 6 |
| Coal No 7 | 4 | |
| Fire clay | | |

The coal at this entry is one hundred and forty six feet above high water, showing a rise to the south west of forty-eight feet in nineteen hundred and fifty.

Section at Forrester entry

| | Ft | In |
|---|---|---|
| Limestone | 2 | |
| Shale | | 6 |
| Coal No 7 | 4 | |
| Fire clay | | ? |

At the Forrester entry, near the middle of section 8, the elevation is one hundred and thirty nine feet above high water, showing a difference of only seven feet in half a mile, which apparently indicates that it is nearly on the strike of the formations on this part of the hill. The limestone here has diminished to two feet.

At the Barlow entry, near the middle of the south east quarter of section 8, the coal is eighty four feet above high water, which shows a dip S 10° E, of fifty-five feet in a horizontal distance of fourteen hundred and fifty feet

Section at A Barlow entry

| | Ft | In |
|---|---|---|
| Shale | | 6 |
| Coal No 7 | 4 | |
| Fire clay | | ? |

At this entry, on the north side of section 8, the coal is one hundred and twenty eight feet above high water, and the limestone is absent, being replaced by shales The coal is four feet thick and has the sulphur band and clay parting

On the north-west quarter of the same section, the limestone is in place again, and the coal is one hundred and two feet above high water, showing a south west dip of twenty six feet in one thousand one hundred On the north-east quarter of section 7, at the Jones entry on Coal creek, No 7 coal is at high water mark, showing a dip of 6° or 7° to the west, and a fall of one hundred and two feet from the last entry, in rather less than half a mile.

At the town of Equality on the western boundary of the county, Nos 5, 6 and 7 occur in their regular sequence, as seen at Bowlsville, the Independent Company's mines, and other places. At these localities all three beds have been opened, and more or less mined, to supply the home market.

No 7 is usually four feet thick in the many openings where it is mined in the streets, and around the town The miners report the dip here to be in every direction; that is, that no two openings show the same pitch, and that they can hardly pronounce upon any decided dip. The identity of the bed is proved by the presence of the limestone roof, sulphur band, and clay parting. The following section shows the strata in the hill at Equality

| | Ft | In |
|---|---|---|
| Soil and drift | 25 | |
| Sandstone | 15 | |
| Silicious shale | 5 | |
| Limestone | 4 | 6 |
| Shale | | 6 |
| Coal No 7 (with clay parting) | 4 | |
| Fire-clay | | 6 |
| Shale and massive sandstone | 45 | |
| Coal No 6 | 1 | 6 |
| Sandy flag stones, and light blue shale with iron stones | 68 | |
| Black shale | 2 | |
| Coal No 5 in shaft at Ross's mill | 5 | |
| | 176 | 0 |

About two miles, a little west of north, from Equality, No 7 coal was seen at low water of the North Fork of the Saline river, making a descent in that direction of nearly one hundred feet, it was traced along the bank of the river for more than half a mile before it disappeared under the low lands to the northward Coal was first mined in this county at the above locality, and was hauled at an early day to Equality over bad roads, before the fact was known that every family in the town could, if they so desired it, have a coal mine in their own yard North of this locality no workable coal has been found in the county.

At Christmasville, eight or nine miles north of Equality, in the northwestern part of the county, and where the bridge crosses the North Fork of the Saline river on the road from Equality to Carmi, there is exposed in the bank of the river a few feet of argillaceous and siliceous shales, containing a thin fossiliferous band of calcareous sandstone, as shown in this section

| | Ft. | In |
|---|---|---|
| Soil to the street of the village | 10 | |
| Yellow argillaceous shale with iron stones | 5 | |
| Ferruginous calcareous sandstone, with casts of fossil shells | | 3 |
| Schistose gray sandstone | | 6 |
| Hard sandstone | | 8 |
| Schistose sandstone | 1 | |
| Bluish argillaceous shale, some coaly matter | 3 | |
| Low water North Fork of the Saline | | |
| | 20 | 5 |

The fossils found in the three-inch band of the above section are *Aviculopecten occidentalis*, *Edmondia reniformis*, *Athyris subtilita*, *Pternea gibbosa*, *Myalina Swallovi*, *M. meliniformis*, *Eumicrotis Hawni*, *Macrocheilus primigenius*, *Schizodus Sp ?* *Turritella ? Stephensana*, *Bellerophon nodocarinatus*, *Allorisma Sp ?* *Pleurophorus sub costatus*, etc.

About three and a half miles north of Shawneetown the following section was obtained at "Roundpond hill," which forms a part of the ridge or range of hills reaching northward to New Haven on the Little Wabash river:

| | Ft | In |
|---|---|---|
| Soil and drift | 10 | |
| Shale | 5 | |
| Limestone ("Carthage rock") | 6 | 8 |
| Black bituminous shale | 1 | |
| Coal No 9 | | 6 |
| Shale, in covered space | 20 | |
| Reddish schistose sandstone weathers rough | 15 | |
| Argillaceous and siliceous shale | 30 | |
| Black sheety shale | 2 | |
| Calcareous shales, with nearly the same species of fossils as are found at Grayville, Ill and Rush creek Posey county Indiana *Leda bella striata Nucula ventricosa Bellerophon carbonarius, B. Montfortianus B. percarinatus, Macrocheilus primigenius, Myalina sub quadrata, Pleurotomaria sphærulata P Grayvillensis, and Schizodus Sp ?* | | 6 |
| Coal No 8 | | 3 |
| Fire clay | | 6 |
| Siliceous shale | 6 | |
| Covered to low water of the pond | 10 | |
| | 108 | 9 |

The limestone at the top of this section is generally poor in fossils, but it contains at this place large crinoid stems and a few shells; among which were recognized *Productus longispinus* and *Athyris subtilita.* The rock is a hard gray limestone which weathers roughly and readily splits up into irregular slabs, with reddish brown stains of oxyd of iron on the weathered surface It occupies in the geological horizon the position of a similar limestone which is seen opposite Wabash island. on the east side of the Ohio river, in Union county, Kentucky, and at Carthage, one mile below Uniontown, it has been designated by OWEN, in the Kentucky report, as the "Carthage Limestone"

At New Haven, on the Little Wabash river, this limestone is seen in the bank of the river, where the following section was obtained:

| | Ft | In |
|---|---|---|
| Covered slope to street in New Haven | 10 | |
| Limestone Carthage | 4 to 5 | |
| Black sheety shale | 1 | 6 |
| Thin coal | | 3 |
| Fire clay and shale | 3 | |
| Reddish gray sandstone | 4 | |
| Gray micaceous sandstone | 4 | |
| Siliceous shale | 5 | |
| Low water | | 9 |
| | 32 | 6 |

The limestone has here, also, a paucity of fossils, *Productus longispinus* and large stems of encrinites only were seen The thin bedded sandstone of this section extends across the river, and though forming a serious barrier to navigation, furnishes a good foundation for a mill dam, which supplies a valuable and never failing power for manufacturing flour and for other mechanical uses.

## *Quaternary Formation.*

*Drift and Loess*.—The drift deposit occupies the hills and ridges all over the county, resting uncomformably on the Carboniferous rocks, and is from ten to twenty feet thick, composed chiefly of yellow, more or less plastic, clay, containing small rounded gravel with occasionally a granite or trappean bowlder. The largest erratic rock seen in the county is a granite bowlder, about one foot broad and one and a half feet long, lying by the side of the road from Shawneetown to Equality. No fossils, scratches or groove marks were observed in this transported material.

*Loess*.—The loess is from ten to forty feet thick, and occupies the top of the ridges along the road from Shawneetown to New Haven. This deposit is usually characterized by a whitish gray calcareous clay or marl, that contains an abundance of land and fresh water shells, belonging to species now living in this State, with the single exception of *Helicina occulta, Say*, which has not, I believe, been found living north of Arkansas.

## *Economical Geology.*

Besides the many beds of mineral fuel so extensively spread over this county, and already discussed in a general way, there is an inexhaustible reservoir of salt brine underlaying its surface.

The brine springs of Gallatin county were worked at an early date under the management of army officers, at a time when the General Governmennt reserved from sale all lands containing salt springs. Though there are outbreaks of saline springs at various places in this county, and though the water courses, creeks and their branches, and the river, all contain more or less salt, from which circumstance arose the name of Saline river for the principal water course which runs through the southern part of the county, yet, though thousands of dollars have been spent and fortunes lost in the search, there has never been any profitable brine found in the county, except on the north side of Saline river, about one mile south of the town of Equality, on section 19, township 9, range 8, and near what is known as the "Half moon," a semi circular excavation as its name implies, that was made by the buffalo and other wild animals that congregated in vast herds to lick the muriatiferous earth. The diameter of this remarkable excavation is about one hundred yards, and the depth varies from six to eight feet.

The surface level is from ten to twelve feet below high water mark and the soil is a river or lacustrine deposit, of fine, whitish, clay loam, containing in spots many fresh water shells belonging to species now living. Beneath this alluvial soil, the excavation at the "Half moon" shows a yellowish clay, mixed with gravel and sand, which belongs to the age of the Drift This locality must have been, likewise, a favorite resort for the *Mammoth* and *Mastodon*, huge monsters that roamed in immense numbers over the country when the present site of the salt works was an alluring swamp, for there has been found, from time to time, resting on this drift in the Half-moon, a great many bones belonging to these extinct animals While examining this locality several small fragments of the enameled crowns of Mammoths' teeth were picked up, the less enduring parts of the structure having mouldered into dust The liability of fossil bones to crumble and fall to pieces immediately after their exposure to the air, has been a serious drawback to their collection, and many valuable specimens have, in consequence, been lost to science for want of knowing how to secure their preservation

It may not, therefore, be out of place here to state to the citizens who may be interested in the promotion of geological science that bits of paper should be glued over the specimen as fast as the parts are exposed by the removal of the earth, as in this manner highly interesting bones may be removed with safety from their matrix of earth, which without this precaution would drop into useless fragments A further preservation may be secured by subsequently boiling the bones or teeth in a weak solution of glue, which will supply the lost animal matter and cement the earthy particles firmly together.

Teeth of the Mastodon were found last summer close to the water's edge in front of Shawneetown. I subsequently visited the locality and saw that the bones were imbedded in a shallow deposit of bluish clay, resting upon yellow clay and gravel, which corresponds in geological time with the bone beds at the Half Moon

While the Saline salt works were under the control of the General Government, the strong brine on the Kanawha had not been discovered, consequently an immense district of country had to receive its supply of salt from these works The brine then used required from one hundred and twenty five to two hundred and eighty gallons to make one bushel (fifty pounds) of salt Between one and two thousand hands were employed, and the yield of the works has been estimated at eighty to one hundred bushels of salt *per diem* So greatly was the demand beyond the power of the works to supply, that, as I am informed, applicants for salt coming from Tennessee, Kentucky, Indiana, and other parts of the country were regularly ticketed, and could be supplied only by awaiting their proper turn. No one thought of stopping for the drainage of the salt crystals, but all were glad to receive it as soon as it was cool enough to handle, and to start off with their pack horses loaded with sacks of salt from which the water trickled as they journeyed home. The fuel required to evaporate such an immense amount of water, stripped the country of timber for miles around, and the expedient was resorted to of conveying the brine for miles in wooden pipes, to the rapidly receding forest. The idea never once occurred to these early salt makers that the five-foot bed of coal through which their wells generally were dug, could furnish, ready at hand, a never-failing supply of the best and cheapest fuel.

After the establishment of salt works on the Kanawha river, in Virginia, and at Pomeroy, in Ohio, the Saline mines could no longer profitably compete in the market; therefore, the works were finally abandoned and every vestige of former prosperity was effaced by the ravaging hand of time, and all efforts to revive the manufacture of salt on the Saline river, until recently, proved a ruinous loss to the parties engaged in it.

About the year 1850 the Saline property was purchased by Messrs. Temple & Castles, the present proprietors, who soon thereafter commenced to bore a new and deeper well. The first brine was struck in this well at 108 feet, at 600 feet a cavity with some gravel was passed, and at 1,100 feet the bore stopped in brine which marks 7.2° of Baume's saltometer, and requires only seventy-five gallons to make a bushel (fifty pounds) of salt, which is fully as strong as the brine of the Kanawha. The well is not artesian, but the brine comes within a few feet of the surface and is pumped. Messrs. Temple & Castles were not present when this well was bored, and no further record was made of the rocks passed through, except noting a five foot bed of coal at forty feet below the surface. This coal outcrops in the river at Equality, also in the hills one mile to the west, and being referable to coal No. 5 of the general section, it serves to establish a starting point, by means of which the horizon of the saline reservoir in the rocks below may be determined with a tolerable degree of accuracy. The first brine at 108 feet is probably in the shales overlaying the sandstone above coal No. 4, the cavity with gravel at 600 feet is about the place of the shale dividing the Conglomerate in two members, as seen at the Battery Rock and elsewhere, while the 1,100 feet may stop in the Chester limestone, which therefore, forms the base of the muriatiferous rocks in this part of the State. It is my opinion, also, that the strong brine has its main lodgment in this limestone—finding its way upward by hydrostatic pressure through permeable strata—and that it is more or less reduced in strength by the fresh water which it encounters on the way.

At the old "Nigger Works," on sec. 27, T. 9, R. 8, the saline spring, as before mentioned, issues out from near the junction of the Chester sandstone and limestone, marking only 4° of Baume—a diminution in strength that may be accounted for on the hypothesis above stated, from the fact that several springs still less brackish break out a few feet higher up the bank, the latter tending to show the liability of the brine to mix with fresh water as it approaches nearer to the surface. The main spring emits a distinct odor of sulphuretted hydrogen, and it may possess important therapeutic properties.

Around these brine springs fragments of Indian pottery are found in great plenty, some of which are ornamented with bands of vertical lines arranged with considerable taste. To judge by the curvature of some of these fragments, the vessels to which they belonged were not less than four or five feet in diameter, a size truly astonishing, made, as they appear to have been, of common clay and fragments of fresh-water shells. From the large size of these pots it is natural to infer that they were used as evaporating pans by a pre-historic race of salt manufacturers. The rapid destruction of iron evaporating pans, together with their cost, is a heavy tax to the modern salt-maker; therefore, if a more durable and less expensive pan could be formed of some kind of clay, it would prove a large saving in the cost of production of salt; and it would be strange indeed should we be able to hit upon a valuable idea from the lost arts of the Mound builders.

Messrs Temple & Castles re-commenced the manufacture of salt at the "Saline" about the year 1856, from the brine of their new well, which was analyzed for them by Prof. GEO. COOK, of New York.

I was kindly permitted to take a copy of this analysis for publication:

"Specific gravity, 1.047. 100 parts of brine contains 7.2 per cent. of dry matter.

| The brine contains in 100 parts | | | The resulting salt contains in 100 parts |
|---|---|---|---|
| Chloride of sodium (common salt) | 6.2431 | —— | 86.77 |
| Chloride of calcium | .3996 | —— | 5.55 |
| Chloride of magnesium | .2124 | —— | 2.95 |
| Sulphate of lime | .3448 | —— | 4.79 |
| | 7.1999 | —— | 97.06 |
| Water | 92.8000 | | |
| | 99.9999 | | |

Traces of bromide of sodium, chloride of potassium, iodide of sodium and chloride of iron."

The "Saline" brine is of the same strength as the Kanawha, and requires seventy-five gallons to make a bushel (fifty pounds) of salt. I have no analysis of the latter brine for comparison, but I have been informed that it contains more chloride of calcium and less sulphate of lime. The sulphate of lime in the "Saline" brine is a source of much annoyance, and large sums of money were expended by Messrs Temple & Castles before their efforts to get rid of it were crowned with success. They are now, however, manufacturing an article of salt that ranks equal to the Kanawha in purity and antiseptic properties.

When I first visited the "Saline" in the summer of 1867, the average product of the works was from thirty to forty barrels of salt *per diem*; since then it has been increased to double that quantity. There is a system of manipulations connected with the operation of making good salt from this brine that belongs exclusively to the company. It has been established by an outlay of large sums of money spent in experimenting, by much anxiety, and with failure after failure. Taking this property, with the previous disastrous failures staring them in the face, Messrs. Temple & Castles have built up a successful manufacture which is creditable to themselves as enterprising gentlemen and of incalculable importance to the county. It is therefore hoped that they will reap, as they deserve, a rich reward for their meritorious labor.

They have adopted the plan of graduation houses, as in parts of Germany and France, for concentrating the natural brine before it goes into the evaporating pans. These houses consist here of two frames from two hundred to two hundred and fifty feet long, and forty to forty-five feet high; the longest of the two is divided into two parts, so that the brine may be divided into three grades. Thorn bushes are spread on parallel horizontal frames, arranged from top to bottom of the houses, so that the brine, which is pumped and forced to the top of the frames, may descend in a shower through the whole series. After passing the brine, successively, in this manner, over the three houses, the graduation in favorable weather carries it from 7° 2 to 9° 5. From the third house, or after the third graduation, the brine is conveyed to the pans, where the evaporation is completed over the fire. The fuel used for this purpose is stone coal, mined on the company's land one mile west of the works, from No. 5 coal, which is here of excellent quality and almost entirely free from sulphur. It is brought to the works on a tram road, and about three hundred bushels are consumed in the manufacture of thirty five barrels of salt.

*Iron ore.*—More or less clay iron-stone is found with the shales of the coal throughout the county, but at no one locality in quantity sufficient to make it of commercial value.

*Building stone.*—There is an abundance of good freestone, suitable for building purposes, all along the Gold hill axis, along Eagle creek and its tributaries in the south, at Equality, and in the river bank at New Haven. Some members of the Chester limestone might answer for building stone, but as a general rule it will not endure where unprotected from rain and frost. A black septaria limestone, belonging to the Coal Measures, which is exposed at low water in the river bank at Shawneetown, is susceptible of a remarkably fine polish, and being chequered with veins of white calc spar, it presents a beautiful appearance, but can only be obtained in small pieces, owing to its almost inaccessible position and extreme brittleness

*Quick lime*.—The Chester limestone, in the Gold hill ridge, is a rich source of excellent lime The limestone over No. 7 coal, and the Carthage limestone in Round Pond hill, and at New Haven, will make good lime also, though not generally so pure as the former

*Potters clay*.—The fire clays forming the bottom of the coal beds in this county that have been tried do not, I am told, make a good potter's clay, but there is reason to believe that the search has not been thorough, and that some of the clays on the Saline river will be found suited for manufacturing the ordinary stoneware of commerce Plastic clay for bricks can be had in most places over the county

*Soil and Agriculture*.—The soil in the eastern part of the county is principally derived from sediments deposited by the inundations of the Ohio river, and by washings from the Quaternary and Carboniferous strata of the high ground It is in most places a sandy loam, rich in elements of fertility, and is especially adapted to growing Indian corn.

The bottom lands along the main Saline river and its main tributary, the North Fork, though partaking, in part, of the character of the Ohio river bottom land, contains a large proportion of a light colored, fine sedimentary clay loam, which is compact, and tenacious of water, and therefore difficult to bring into good cultivation If properly worked, it would bring good crops of grain, provided the season is favorable; but a very dry or a very wet season is peculiarly injurious to crops on this soil This latter variety of soil has been derived principally from the argillaceous shales of the Coal Measures, and its general want of fertility is owing to its physical condition, and not to any deficiency in the proximate constituents of plant food Underdrainage would prove an efficient means of bringing land of this description into a high state of cultivation The soil of the yellowish, gravelly, clay land in the north west part of the county, is derived from the drift, and is formed of the *debris* of the rocks rasped and ground to fragments by ancient rivers of ice, which moved over the northern part of this continent with snail like pace, during that period of the earth's history known as the *Glacial epoch* This third variety of land will grow all the cereals, grasses and clover well, but it is better adapted for small grain than for corn, and it is particularly good for clover

On the ridges between Shawneetown and the Little Wabash river there is a calcareous clay soil, derived from the loess, which, in an agricultural point of view ranks next to the sandy loam of the river bottom lands

Tobacco, sorghum, and some cotton are cultivated in this county; but the principal crops are the cereals and clover Apples, peaches and pears grow remarkably well, and the taste for orchard-culture is reported to be constantly on the increase. As yet but little attention has been paid to the cultivation of the grape. Messrs Temple & Castles, at the salt works, are cultivating a young vineyard containing about eight hundred vines, of which the greater number are Concord, with some Catawba and Delaware, together with a few of the more recent varieties, such as Norton's Virginia, Iona, Israella, Ives' seedling, and Diana. The Concord and Catawba succeed remarkably well, the other varieties have not yet been sufficiently tested to be pronounced upon with certainty. While enjoying the kind hospitality of these gentlemen I had an opportunity to make a substantial test of the wine which they made from their vineyard, and feel satisfied that it will compare favorably with the native wines of the professional wine maker.

*Timber.*—This county is abundantly supplied with all the usual varieties of trees found in this latitude. On the river bottoms, particularly in the eastern and northern part of the county, large black walnut, white, red and black oaks, hickory, and poplar predominate. On the high lands, in other parts of the county, oak and hickory are the principal timber, on the flat, wet land, post-oak prevails; and along some of the sloughs and ponds there is a fine growth of large cypress

# CHAPTER XVIII.

## SALINE COUNTY.

Saline county is bounded on the north by Hamilton county, on the east by Gallatin, on the south by Pope, and on the west by Williamson.

In shape it is a parallelogram and embraces about eleven townships; therefore it has an area of about three hundred and ninety-six square miles

Its topography is marked by the Gold Hill axis, which, beyond the boundary of Gallatin county forms a conspicuous elevation in the south-eastern part of this county, where it is known as "Prospect Hill" The hight of this hill, as determined by barometrical measurement, is five hundred and ninety feet above the low water of the Saline river. Though the Gold Hill axis disappears beneath the lowlands to the west of this hill, it is again seen as a conspicuous ridge of massive conglomerate sandstone in the south-western corner of the county, near the village of Stone Fort.

Viewed from the summit of Prospect Hill, the northern, middle and western part of this county appears to be perfectly level, but it is nevertheless much broken by hills and ridges, that range in elevation from ten to eighty feet above the high water mark of the streams. However, a large portion of the county is level, and much of the land may be termed "wet," with here and there a not inconsiderable swamp Harrisburg, the county town, is situated nearly in the geographical center of the county, and is built on a hill fifty to sixty feet high, formerly known as "Crusoe's Island," from the fact that it is entirely surrounded by bottom land which is subject to inundation during periods of great freshets The approaches to the town are consequently made by levees. Notwithstanding the apparently unfavorable situation, Harrisburg is a thriving town, and is looked upon as one of the healthiest localities in Southern Illinois The Vincennes and Cairo railway runs through this place, and makes it a point of considerable commercial importance The principal water-course is the Saline river, which, with its tributaries, the South Fork and Little Saline, drain the southern, while the other two main tributaries, the North Fork and Middle Fork, drain the remainder of the county These streams, as well as the smaller tributaries, have generally low banks, which are occasionally overflowed, at which times the water spreads over an extensive area of what is termed "bottom land."

## *Geological Formations.*

The geological formations of this county are the Chester limestone and sandstones forming the upper part of the Lower Carboniferous series, the Millstone-grit and lower Coal Measures, and the drift or glacial deposits of the Quaternary or Post Tertiary epoch

*Chester Group*—The rocks belonging to this group are seen on the north side of a ridge, in the south eastern part of the county, where they have been brought to the surface by the Gold Hill axis, and basset at a high angle to the north The following section was taken at Prospect Hill, which is supposed to be the highest point on this ridge, and it will serve to show the relative position of the Millstone grit with reference to the Chester group

Section taken at Prospect Hill, on section 10? township 10, range 7; average dip of strata 10° south

| | | Ft |
|---|---|---|
| Millstone grit a pebbly sandstone | | 160 |
| Covered space, sandstone ? belonging to the Chester group | 120 | |
| Archimedes limestone | 2 | |
| Green marly shale and covered space | 20 | |
| Gray limestone "cave rock" | 25 | |
| Covered space | 120 | |
| Quartzose sandstone | 20 | |
| Cherty limestone | 30 | |
| Covered sandstone ? | 20 | |
| Chester group | | 357 ? |
| | | 517 |

It was found impossible to determine with accuracy the thickness of the members under the Millstone grit at the place where the above section was obtained, or in fact at any other locality along the line of disturbance in this county, on account of the tumbled masses of rock which lie strewed over the side of the mountain in such a manner as to admit of only an occasional glimpse of what exists beneath them; however, I believe that this section will convey a pretty accurate idea of the sequence of the strata, and gives the total thickness of the exposed rocks of the Chester group, which cannot fall far short of three hundred and fifty seven feet Neither in the lower member of the group, nor in the gray limestone containing the "Cave," could any trace of fossils be found, but in the band of limestone exposed above the green marly shales, a fragment of *Archimedes* was found associated with eutrochites.

There is at Prospect Hill, in the limestone marked "Cave rock" in the above section, a subterranean cavern, which has acquired considerable local notoriety. Accompanied by Mr. TEMPLE, one of the proprietors of the salt works (to whom I am under many obligations for acts of kindness), I undertook to explore this cave, but we forgot to supply ourselves with candles before leaving the salt works, therefore we had to undertake the task with a glass coal oil lamp, which was procured from a farm house close by, but with a light so liable to accident a partial examination was all that it was deemed prudent to make. The entrance is through a hole not more than two feet high, by three feet broad, down which the descent is rather abrupt to the bottom of the cave, where we found ourselves in a narrow, tortuous gallery, averaging from three to five feet in width and twenty feet in hight. We went along the main gallery and a number of its branches and cut-offs, until it was supposed that we had penetrated at least a quarter of a mile beyond the entrance. still we saw no end nor any appearance that seemed to indicate that the exploration might not be continued much farther, yet it was thought advisable to return on account of the danger to be encountered, should we have the misfortune to break the lamp, for notwithstanding every branch or turn that was passed has been marked by some thoughtful explorer with the figure of an arrow scratched on the limestone wall to indicate the direction to be taken in returning, nevertheless this unfailing guide would be of no avail amidst the intense darkness of subterranean passages. The walls and roof were covered with moisture, but the floor was quite dry. It is said that the cave usually contains a spring of cool sulphur water, and we hoped to obtain from it a refreshing drink, but no water was seen along our route; the bed of the sulphur spring pointed out by Mr. TEMPLE, was now dry, probably from the effects of the severe drouth which had prevailed in this county for several months. A great many bats were observed clinging to the roof, with their heads hanging down, some of which were alarmed by the proximity of our lamp, and taking wing, whizzed about our faces, as if to scrutinize closely the enemies who dared to penetrate into their dark abode. The occasional widening of the galleries formed small, irregularly shaped rooms, some of which gave evidence of having been at one time very beautiful, but the stallactites with which they were once adorned, have nearly all been broken off by thoughtless visitors, who thus wantonly destroyed the sublime architectural works of quaint and inimitable patterns that were brought into existence during long periods of chemical action, in Nature's great workshop. One cannot help expressing deep mortification on contemplating the ruthless and blind destruction of that which makes these subterraneous grottoes beautiful as Aladdin's garden, and the defacers merit universal condemnation.

No thorough exploration has yet been made of this cave. therefore, as it appears to be quite extensive, it is possible to discover chambers or rooms surpassing both in size and decorations those at present known.

While in the cave diligent search was made, but no trace of organic remains could be found in its walls, which are formed of decomposing limestone

Much still remains to be learned regarding the effect of the disturbance which has brought the Gold Hill strata to the surface, as to the influence which it may have had in modifying the shape of the coal-basin for here as at other places before mentioned, on the north side of the ridge the coal bearing strata are seen apparently undisturbed

A very good mineral spring issues from about the junction of the limestone and sandstone, on Mrs Ross' place at the foot of Prospect Hill It furnishes a bountiful flow of clear, cool water, that possesses a faint odor of sulphuretted hydrogen gas, and leaves a white sediment on the "gum," and on the sides of the little branch to which it gives rise The reputation which it has acquired is no doubt well deserved, and if suitable buildings were erected to accommodate the public there is reason to believe that it would become a place of considerable resort during the summer months, especially for invalids suffering from general debility Its medicinal effects are most likely to be alterative and aperitive.

The Lower Carboniferous limestone appears above the surface also. on secs 36 and 35, T 9, R. 7. near the line of Gallatin county. The hill above it at this locality is eighty feet high, and exhibits the following succession of strata

| | Ft |
|---|---|
| Slope covered with chert | 55 |
| Red clay mixed with chert | 20 |
| Blackish gray limestone veined with calc spar | 5 |
| | 80 |

The limestone in the above section dips to the south at an angle of 40° It is a hard close textured rock, traversed by veins of white calc-spar that would make it a beautiful marble, if polished

## *Coal Measures.*

The Millstone grit, or Conglomerate, as it is indiscriminately called by geologists—lies in this county conformable to the Chester group, and is at the base of the productive Coal Measures Its position has already been indicated in the section given of the strata at Prospect Hill, where it is principally represented by a massive redish brown sandstone that contains. at many places along its exposure, small rounded pebbles of quartz It is sometimes divided into two members by a few feet of shale; but I was unable to detect this parting at Prospect Hill, probably on account of the tumbled masses of rock and *debris* which may have covered it up.

The Conglomerate is also seen in the south eastern and south western part of the county On sec 34, T 10, R 6, at what is known as the "Stone Fort," it is a massive pebbly sandstone sixty to seventy feet thick, where it forms an abrupt escarpment on the south face of the ridge, 150 to 160 feet above the Little Saline river which flows along the foot of the ridge This ridge appears to be a continuation of the Gold Hill axis, and so far as I have been able to discover in traversing its course, the strata present here the appearance of an anticlinal axis, as they dip about 10° to the northward

The name of the latter locality is derived from an old fort like inclosure built upon the highest part of the Conglomerate. It contains an area of three or four acres, which is surrounded by a semi-circular wall of sandstone three or four feet high The rocks of which this wall was built furnish no evidence of having been quarried, but on the contrary, present the appearance of having been loose stones picked from the surface and thrown into the wall-heap without any attempt at order in their arrangement This ancient fort was well protected on the south side by a bastion or perpendicular wall of Conglomerate sixty to seventy feet thick on its exposed vertical face. In this "fort" we have undoubtedly another monument of a pre historic race of men who inhabited this Continent at so remote a period that no clue to their history can be obtained from the existing races of Indians—the tradition of whose forefathers give no account of the Mound and Fort builders

While standing on the parapet of this ancient strong-hold, the mind naturally wandered back over the immense lapse of time since this fortress or citadel was thronged with beings who were filled with hopefulness, or oppressed with all the cares and anxieties of life peculiar to man, and who, no doubt, felt proud of the supposed security against their foes obtained by the selection of so strong a position. Here probably they placed their sentinels to give the alarm on the first approach of an enemy; here likewise, the *elite* of the community may have assembled to contemplate the grand and beautiful scenery around their strong hold, for, then as now, the Little Saline river had cut its passage through the Conglomerate ridge, and its banks were strewed with cyclopean blocks fallen from the parent mass above.

*Coal No.* 5—This bed of coal is the fifth in the ascending order on Saline river in Gallatin county, but in Saline county it is the lowest workable seam that I have been able to identify It is opened and worked by Messrs Temple & Castles, on sec 21, T 9, R 7, one mile west of the salt works, where it outcrops on the east side of a short ridge bearing a little east of south from Equality. The mouth of the mining entry is twenty feet above high water of the Saline river; and as the same bed was passed through at forty feet below the surface in the salt well one mile directly east of this entry, it shows the dip to be to the east at the rate of seventy feet per mile, if an allowance of ten feet is made for the place of high water mark above the salt well The following section was made at this mine, starting from high-water of the Saline river.

Section at Messrs. Temple & Castles' coal mine on sec. 24, T 9, R. 7 Coal dips east at the rate of seventy feet per mile:

| | Ft | In |
|---|---|---|
| Slope covered with drift | 60 | |
| Grayish white micaceous sandstone | 30 | |
| Gray siliceous shale | 25 to 35 | |
| Black slate | 2 | |
| Coal No 5 ("five foot coal,") | 4 | 8 |
| Fire clay | 2? | |
| Covered slope | 18 | |
| High water of the Saline river | 0 | |
| | 151 | 8 |

About 300 bushels of this coal are consumed daily at the salt works, under the evaporating pans and boilers. It appears here to be free from the sulphur bands so common in coal No. 5 at Equality and other localities, consequently it has acquired a high reputation for smithing purposes. There is in the roof shales an abundance of compressed marine shells coated with yellow pyrites of iron, which gives them the appearance of having been gilded. They are, however, for the most part in a bad state of preservation, and rapidly decompose after exposure to the atmosphere. The shells most common in this shale are. *Aviculopecten rectilaterarius, Productus longispinus, Nautilus decoratus, Nucula ventricosa ?* and *Orthoceras Rushensis*

There is an outcrop of coal dirt on the side of the ridge opposite to the above mine on sec 25, T. 9, R. 7, that is referable, also, to coal No. 5. No opening has been made to test the thickness and quality of the coal at this outcrop, but it is my opinion that No 5 coal will be found thinning out to the south-west and west, and will in the latter direction almost, if not entirely, give out after passing west of the third tier of sections in range seven, and in the former direction it is represented in the vicinity of Whitesville by only an eighteen-inch seam.

At the outcrop on sec 25 it is underlaid by several feet of fire-clay, which contains bands of gray ironstone of a character similar to that which is seen under the coal at the salt works, only it appears to be in much larger quantity at the former place

At the crossing of Saline river, on sec. 26, T. 9, R. 7, the gray silicious shales, commonly over No 5 coal in this part of the coal field, outcrop in the bank of the river, and may be traced for half a mile or more along the stream

West of the mines, at the salt works, and on the extreme western side of the ridge in which those mines are situated, at Mr. Whissen's, on sec. 23, T 9, R 7, a coal that is reported to be four feet thick was struck in digging a well On account of the mineral character of the water no use was made of this well, and it is now filled up, but pieces of coal can still be found mixed with the *debris* of gray and black shale that was thrown out at the time of digging. The agreement of the shale and superimposed sandstone with the rocks seen at Equality, and on the east side of the same ridge above No 5 coal, can leave no doubt as to its synchronism with that bed. The following section gives the succession of rocks in the hill that lie above the coal in Whisson's well:

| | Ft |
|---|---|
| Reddish coarse grained sandstone | 60 |
| Silicious shale | 20 |
| Gray, argillo silicious shale | 15 |
| Black slate, (reported in well) | 2 |
| Coal No 5, " " | 4 |
| | 101 |

About one mile south of the above locality a four foot bed of coal is reported in a well at Mr. Taylor's place, which I refer also to No. 5.

*Coal No 7*—This is the next coal in the ascending order that was seen in Saline county

At Equality, on the eastern edge of Saline county, Nos. 5, 6 and 7 coals are seen in regular sequence, but westward the two lower beds are replaced by shales, and No. 7 increases in thickness.

Three and a half miles west of Equality, on sec. 15, T 9, R 7, at Mr Grear's, coal No. 7 was passed through in sinking a well It is said to be four feet thick, and is overlaid by a limestone as at Equality. In some fragments of the limestone lying around the well a few fossils were detected *Athyris subtilita, A Roysii? Spirifer cameratus*, and *Lophophyllum proliferum.* In a ravine about fifty feet east of the well the limestone outcropped, and is overlaid by shales and shaly sandstone, as follows

| | Ft | In |
|---|---|---|
| Drift and soil | 25 | |
| Hard gray limestone | 2 | 6 |
| Shale | ? | |
| Coal, No 7 | 4 | |

Between Mr Grear's place and Harrisburg No 7 is found on some of the low ridges, but the greatest part has been removed by denudation, though there may be outcrops of it before reaching the Horse swamp and the broad bottom land along the middle fork of the Saline river.

The thin bedded rock in the mound-like hill upon which Harrisburg is built is in part the representative of the sandstone over No 7 coal, and in confirmation of this Dr Pearce informed me that he had a well dug some years ago in the bottoms on the west side of the town, which struck a bed of coal at the depth of eighteen feet Plenty of water was obtained, but it was so contaminated with sulphurous salts from the coal that it was considered unhealthy, and the well was filled up, without previously testing the thickness of the coal.

One mile west of Harrisburg, on Mr. Dove's farm, a coal was drilled into at the depth of twenty one feet; but here again nothing was ascertained in regard to its thickness. It is possible that immediately around Harrisburg, to the north and west, coal No 7 will prove to be only a thin seam. However, at Mr. Warfield's, six miles north-west of the town, on sec. 10 or 11, T 9, R 5, there is an outcrop of coal in the bank of Bankston creek, which is reported to be four to five feet thick. This must be No 7, for though I was unable to see the coal, on account of high water, the sandstone, which lies above it, was traced from Harrisburg to the north western corner of the county.

The thick beds of coal, in this county, are found in the south western part, chiefly between the South fork of Saline river and the parallel of township 8 One and a half miles south east of Harrisburg, on sec 26, T 9, R 6, the first place at which coal No 7 is seen west of the middle fork of Saline river, is at Mr Ingram's mine, being readily recognized by all the peculiar features characterizing that bed at Equality, and at the other localities referred to in the report on Gallatin county, namely a limestone above the shale roof, a thin band of bisulphide of iron nearest to the top of the coal, and a parting of clay nearest to the bottom of it

At Ingram's mine No. 7 is five to six feet thick The entry from which the coal is mined runs with the dip of the strata, which prevents the outward drain of the percolating water, and the mine is consequently wet and disagreeable to the workmen This inconvenience can readily be avoided by a small expenditure in opening another entry on the north side of the hill, where the drift may be carried along the rise of the strata, and thus secure a natural drainage.

Section taken at Ingram's mine—dip 3° east of north

| | Ft |
|---|---|
| Soil and drift | 10 |
| Thin bedded, soft sandstone | 20 |
| Gray limestone | 8 to 10 |
| Coal, No 7 | 5 to 6 |
| Covered slope | 5 |
| High water, middle fork of Saline river | |
| | 51 |

One mile west of Ingram's mine, on sec. 27, T. 9, R 6, Mr Norman is mining No 7 coal, both by stripping and drifting, on opposite sides of the hill. The coal here has about the same thickness as at the former mine, with a similar succession of strata in the hill above the drift, but the limestone is reduced to four feet, and contains a few fossil shells badly preserved, of which *Spirifer cameratus*, *Athyris subtilita*, and *A. Royssii ?* only could be determined. The quality of the coal at these two mines is not of the best, as it is more or less contaminated with sulphur, which renders it unsuitable for blacksmithing It has, however, a good reputation as a grate coal for household uses

From Norman's No. 7 can be traced, on the parallel of township 9, west to the county line. Within this district it has been worked by stripping at a great many places, where it lies exposed in the creek bottoms At these exposures the limestone is not always visible, but it may be seen all along the ridges.

Only a few of the mines west of Norman's, where the coal is worked by stripping, have gone to the bottom of the bed, this is owing in a great measure to the interference of water, when the excavation is carried below the level of the creek bed, and partly to the fact that the upper part of the coal bed contains less sulphur It was found impossible, therefore, under such circumstances, at most of the mines, to get the exact thickness of the coal, but the general impression is that it will average about six feet

At Miller's mine, on sec. 3, T. 9, R. 5, and at Russel's mine, on sec 29, of the same township and range, the limestone overlaying the coal forms in places a conspicuous wall five to six feet thick, along the valley of Coal creek; it is a hard gray rock containing a few fossils, including *Productus longispinus*, *Spirifer cameratus*, *Athyris subtilita*, *Productus semi reticulatus*, and *Chonetes mesoloba*

The Miller coal has a jet black color, is very free from sulphur and has a good reputation in the neighborhood for smithing purposes.

At Holeman's mine also, on section 29, of the above township and range, coal dirt is seen above the main coal, in the position occupied by No 8

In the bank of the Little Saline river, on sec 23, T 10, R 5, at Hay's mill site, there is an exposure of the coal with a thick parting of clay, which on my first visit to the locality I was disposed to refer to one of the lower coal beds of the general section, and I then held the same opinion with regard to the coal bed in the south-western corner of the county, at the village of Stone Fort But subsequent investigations have proved to my satisfaction that there is but little probability that any bed of coal of workable thickness can be found below No. 7, west of the line of range 7 in Saline county. I now, therefore, with still some doubt on the subject, refer the former coal to No. 7, and the latter to No 8.*

* NOTE.—From an examination of the Coal Measures in Williamson county, which joins Saline on the west, I found all the lower coals from No 2 to No 7 well developed, from which it would seem that the conclusion above expressed is not well authenticated for the coal beds in the vicinity of Stone Fort cannot possibly belong higher in the series than coals No 2 or 3 of the general section A H W

The section obtained on the Little Saline river is here given

| | Ft. | In |
|---|---|---|
| Soil | 2 | |
| Drift yellowish clay with gravel | 10 | |
| Ferruginous schistose sandstone | 8 | |
| Coal | 1 | 6 |
| Fire clay | 2 | |
| Coal | 1 | 2 |
| Low water of the river | 0 | |
| | 24 | 8 |

The Little Saline river, after cutting its way through the Conglomerate ridge at the old fort, as before mentioned, runs through a low bottom until it reaches the above mill site, and forms its junction with the South Fork of the Saline river a quarter of a mile beyond.

In the south east part of Saline county and on the south side of Prospect Hill, No. 7 coal outcrops at several places and has also been struck in digging wells. As yet no effort has been made to open mines in this part of the county, consequently it is difficult to determine definitely in all cases the synchronism of the seams At Mr Nicomb's pottery, on sec. 14, T. 10, R. 7, there are two seams of coal partially exposed in the face of a bluff bank of a creek, one of the head waters of Eagle creek. The lower of these lies in the bed of the creek, separated from the upper seam by eleven and one half feet of argillaceous shale and three and one half feet of good fire clay An opening which had been made to test the thickness and quality of the lower bed is now filled up by the caving in of the bank and washings of the creek; therefore no opportunity was afforded of seeing or measuring it myself. Mr Nicomb, however, who made the opening and mined the coal for burning at the pottery, informed me that it was two and a half feet thick From the marked appearance of there having been a slide in the bluff I was, at first, rather disposed to believe that the lower coal was in fact only a portion of the seam above, broken off and brought down by the sliding of the shale, but Mr. Nicomb is confident that this cannot be so, as they neither agree in thickness or quality, the lower seam being as he says a good burning coal, and has beneath it a very dark colored fire clay that cannot be used at the pottery, whereas the fire clay beneath the upper seam is light colored, works well and not only makes good stone ware, but is, likewise, excellent for fire-brick, in fact he considers it the best potters' clay in this part of the coal basin The coal is only about one foot thick, of inferior quality and resembles the coal at the village of Stone Fort, being composed principally of carbonaceous shale, alternating with thin bands of bituminous coal. Without being fully satisfied, from the want of further evidence, as to the truth of the conclusion arrived at, I am nevertheless inclined to believe that the upper seam of coal at the above locality is No. 8, and the lower one No 7.*

Section of the bluff at Nicomb's Dip of strata, 5° N., 20° E

| | Ft | In |
|---|---|---|
| Schistose sandstone | 5 | |
| Coal rash, No 8? | 1 | |
| Fire clay, good for stone ware and fire brick | 3 | 6 |
| Argillaceous shale | 11 | 6 |
| Coal No 7? reported to be | 2 | 6 |
| | 23 | 6 |

About three quarters of a mile south-west of Nicomb's the following section was obtained, the dip of the strata being the same as at the above locality:

| | Ft |
|---|---|
| Strewed with chert, top of hill | 20 |
| Thick bedded sandstone, with some pebbles | 60 |
| Covered slope, strewed with sand rock | 80 |
| Bed of creek | 0 |
| | 160 |

The sandstone in this section, which is inferred to be the Conglomerate, on account of finding a few pebbles in it, was followed along the dip until it disappeared beneath the strata at Nicomb's

*Coal No. 8?* The coal at the village of Stone Fort, in the south western corner of the county, is referred to this number and horizon, but not without some doubt on the subject, for it is just on the margin of the basin, where the seams are subject to much variation, both as regards the quality of the coal and the thickness of the strata Therefore, unless it is seen in connection with No. 7, especially where so little has been done to develop the coals, it is not always possible to distinguish the former from the latter bed. At the village of Stone Fort the strata dip a little east of north at an angle of 20°, which, taken in connection with the dip of the rocks at the old fort, about two miles to the east, appears to indicate that this village also is on the prolongation of the Gold Hill axis of Gallatin county. The following section was taken at the village of Stone Fort †

| | Ft | In |
|---|---|---|
| Sandstone | 15 | |
| Bluish silicious shale | 2 | |
| Yellowish argillaceous shale and yellow clay | 1 | 6 |
| Coal rash No 8? | 3 | 6 |
| Friable silicious shale | 10 | |
| Soft fluggy stone in cube like blocks | 2 | |
| | 34 | |

* These are probably divisions of coal No 1 or 2, both of which are occasionally divided, forming two distinct seams A H W

† This section may be compared with that given in the report on Williamson county, on page 114, the section being in the bluff back of the village of Stone Fort now called Bolton, where coals 2 and 3 have been opened in the face of the bluff A H W

The sandstone at the top of this section forms a cliff that skirts the eastern edge of the village and bassets to the southward at an angle of 20°. It is a whitish brown micaceous rock, easily quarried in large blocks that can be split with wedges, in pieces of any required size. The facility with which this stone can be worked, its beauty and durability have brought it into great requisition for building chimneys, foundations to houses and various other kinds of masonry, for all of which it is well adapted.

The coal which is marked No. 8? has been imperfectly opened on the basseting face of the cliff, and some coal taken out. The quality is not good for fuel, and consists of alternate layers of bituminous coal and carbonaceous, soft, fissile shale, largely composed of fragments of obscure plant stems, and belongs to a class known as coal rash. Though it is not good for burning it may prove to be a valuable fuel for smelting and foundry use, as it appears to be remarkably free from sulphur. To properly test and work this coal a shaft should be sunk on the north eastern edge of the village, where it can be mined on the rise of the strata, not on the pitch, as has been attempted. By this means there would be a natural drainage for the water usually met with in coal mines, and admit of operations being carried on with ease and comfort to the miners.

In the north part of Saline county there are two or more thin seams of coal of indifferent quality, and of but little, if any, commercial value, consequently there has been scarcely any steps taken by the citizens towards their development. In the neighborhood of Gallatin, near the north western corner of the county, on section 9, township 8, range 6, Mr. L. Karns has opened a thin seam of coal, and was endeavoring to work it by drifting into the hill.

This coal may be traced all through the northern part of the county, and is not found at any locality to exceed one foot in thickness.

The section at Karns' mine is as follows, dip of strata 5° W. of S.:

| | | Ft | In |
|---|---|---|---|
| Covered space drift and soil | | 22 | |
| Yellow ferruginous, brecciated limestone very silicious | | 8 | |
| Soft blue clay shale | | 0 | 6 |
| Coal | 8 in | 1 | |
| Bluish shale, with stems of plants | | 5 | |

The limestone is very impure; it has a reddish-brown color derived from the large amount of oxyd of iron with which it is contaminated. It has a brecciated appearance, and seems to be destitute of fossils, in the former respect it resembles very much the brecciated limestone under the sandstone, at Merom, on the Wabash river, above Vincennes.

A limestone that is more or less impure, but not nearly so thick as the limestone in the above section, can be traced through the northern part of the county, usually in connection with a thin seam of coal, the latter is referred to the same horizon as the coal at Karns' mine. The intercalated limestones, in the space between the sandstone and the limestone above No. 7 coal, in the northern part of Saline county, possess a variable character, and seldom exhibit the same features at any two localities.

*Drift.*—The drift in this county is characterized by a yellow plastic clay mixed with small gravel, with occasionally a granite bowlder as large as a goose egg, more rarely as large as a man's head. In some places the clay is replaced by sand, which forms the only source of supply in this county for the sand which is used in mortar for plastering houses and for masonry The drift is from ten to twenty feet thick, and extends all over the county, except where it has been removed by denudation or other causes.

## *Minerals.*

*Copper.*—I was informed by Dr. SMITH, a very intelligent and observant gentleman, who lives near Gallatin, in the northern part of the county, that he had at different times found small pieces of native copper both in this county and the southern part of Hamilton, in ravines or washed places, and in the beds of branches The doctor spoke of a gentleman who had picked up in the bed of a branch, near Gallatin, a lump of native copper larger than a hen's egg. The latter specimen is still owned in the town, and Dr. SMITH tried to procure it for my inspection, but the parties to whom it belonged were away on a visit, and it was locked up in their residence From the malleability and other characteristic tests to which the specimens were subjected by Dr. SMITH, they are proved beyond a doubt to be native copper

The circumstances connected with the finding of small quantities of native copper in Hamilton and Saline counties, clearly indicate that it came from the drift deposit. Therefore, it will be useless to expend time and money in searching for valuable mines of copper in this county, The drift, as before stated, covers a large portion of Saline county, and is composed of material transported by glacial agency from and beyond the copper regions to the northward.

*Salt.*—At an early period, when the agents of the General Government were manufacturing salt at the Saline works, in Gallatin county, some speculative adventurers dug a well on the Middle Fork of the Saline river, about two miles east of Harrisburg, it is reported, that at the depth of eighty feet they found a brine from which a considerable quantity of salt was made. At this late day, it is impossible to obtain any information respecting the quality or number of gallons which it required of this brine to make a bushel of salt, but there is reason to believe, from the geology of the district, that brine, just as pure and strong as that now worked at the "Saline," can be found by boring in the vicinity of Harrisburg In order to test the matter, the bore should penetrate the muriatiferous shales which lie below the Conglomerate On the Middle Fork of the Saline river, or on the bottom land at Harrisburg, a bore would start from a geological horizon fifty to sixty feet above the wells at the "Saline," yet, it is believed that the great salt repository will be reached at a much less depth than at the "Saline," from the thinning out of the subordinate coal strata

*Building Stone.*—There is an abundance of good limestone for building purposes in the south eastern part of the county, where the Lower Carboniferous rocks have been brought to the surface by the Gold Hill axis. In the south-western part there is a durable and handsome sandstone, which is very extensively used for building foundations to houses and for chimneys It can be obtained in large blocks and is easily worked. The sandstone in the northern part of the county answers very well for ordinary building purposes, but is not so good as that found in the south western part

*Quicklime*—The Coal Measure limestone, which overlies No 7 coal, makes a very fair article of dark lime at some localities, but generally contains too large a quantity of impurities, and owing to the extra cost of quarrying, it will never be extensively used for that purpose The Lower Carboniferous limestone, at Prospect Hill, in the south eastern part of the county, can furnish a bountiful supply and of excellent quality.

*Plastic Clay*—Good clay, suitable for fire-brick and stone ware, is found in the south-eastern part of the county, and Mr NICOMB has established a pottery there and is making out of this clay, both fire brick and stone ware.

Good clay, for making the ordinary brick used for building purposes, may be found in the drift deposits throughout the county

*Timber*—For the most part Saline county is well timbered and can furnish a large quantity of black walnut, white oak, cypress and poplar lumber. Besides the trees suitable for lumber, there is the usual variety for this latitude of forest growth.

*Agriculture*—The soils of this county are very similar in their physical features to those of Gallatin county.

Along the water courses there is, in places, a black sandy loam, very rich in organic matter, which supports a fine growth of black walnut, poplar, large oaks, hickory, dog wood and spice bushes. Then, there are extensive tracts, known as post oak flats, which have an ashen colored, close, compact clay soil that holds water like a jug. When properly ditched and drained, the latter soil is highly productive, being rich in all the elements of fertility Without under drains, however, it will require much labor to bring it into a productive condition, and will need to be subsoiled to as great a depth as it is possible to attain with the plow Though not naturally as productive as the first mentioned soil, which ranks equal to any in the State, it will, nevertheless, prove fully equal to it for growing small grain, provided it is under drained An intermediate soil, which ranks between that of the post oak flats and the sandy loam, is known as the "gum land," which, like the former, requires ditching and draining to bring it into good condition

The foregoing soils have all been derived from the disintegration and wearing away of the sandstones, argillaceous shales and calcareous rocks of the Coal Measures, but there is still another characteristic soil, which occupies the greater portion of the county, that is composed of yellowish tenacious clay and sand, with more or less rounded gravel and small bowlders. On the highest points and on the low rolling land, the drift soil has a depth varying from ten to twenty feet or more This is a good, strong soil; but, owing to the tenacious nature of the clay which forms its principal part, it, also, requires more or less draining. It is particularly good for small grain and clover, and grows fine crops of tobacco Considerable attention is paid to the cultivation of the latter article in Saline county, and there are large warehouses at Gallatin and Raleigh for the purpose of preparing the tobacco for shipment

Conclusion —Saline county is rapidly filling up with immigrants from other parts of the country and bids fair to be a populous and wealthy county. The Vincennes and Cairo railroad runs nearly diagonally through the center of the county, and will materially aid its commercial prosperity by opening a market for its vast stores of fossil fuel.

To Dr Mitchel, of Harrisburg, and to the citizens of the county generally, I here tender my sincere thanks for their kind assistance in promoting the interest of the Survey.

# CHAPTER XIX.

## LIVINGSTON COUNTY

This county comprises the congressional townships Nos. 27, 28, 29, and 30 north, and ranges east of the third principal meridian Nos. 3 to 8 both inclusive, making 24 townships, with 3 townships and 3 half townships additional on the south comprised in township 26 north, and ranges 6, 7, and 8 east, and township 25 north, and the north half of ranges 6, 7, and 8 east, equal altogether to 28½ townships or 1,026 square miles This is increased, however, about 18 square miles owing to the north tier of sections in the three half townships being two miles long from north to south, making the aggregate of the county 1,044 square miles.

The Big Vermilion river, running from south east to north west through the county, divides it into nearly equal parts, and this stream affords the only means within the county of determining its geology below the surface, excepting the coal shafts and a few borings.

These data would be meagre without the aid of the exposures of LaSalle county north of it, which furnish the key to the geology of Livingston

The great anticlinal axis which crosses the Illinois river near Utica, in LaSalle county, and which is very clearly defined in the north bluff of the Illinois valley, having its central line two miles west of Utica and a direction of south 33° east, extends through Livingston county, its central line lying a little east of the Vermilion river—the course of this stream evidently having been determined by the influence of this axis, with which it is, in its general direction, nearly or quite parallel

After a full investigation of LaSalle county, Livingston county in its general features is easily determined; yet there are details with respect to the Coal Measures—particularly in that portion of the county lying east of the Vermilion—that can only be ascertained as time develops them through the aid of coal shafts and borings.

Along the Vermilion and west of it the Coal Measures appear to be as complete, generally, as found in the corresponding part of LaSalle county. Soon after passing to the east of it the disturbance of the axis referred to, appears

Almost the entire area of the county belongs in the Coal Measures, the exception being a small strip in the south east part, equivalent to about one and a half townships in area The eastern boundary of the Coal Measures within the county has been determined approximately. Prof F. H. BRADLEY traced the line in Will and Kankakee counties, in the latter running south through the centre of the second tier of sections east of the west line of that county to the south line of sec. 32, T. 31 N . R 9 E, thence bearing a little west to the centre of sec. 32, T. 30 N, R 9 E No further evidence of it could be obtained without boring, and it was considered that a straight line from this latter point to the rim of the basin—as determined at Chatsworth—would be a close approximation to correctness. This would make the county line cross the outcrop at the south east corner of T 29 N, R 8 E, and thence a straight line to Chatsworth in the south west half of sec 4, T. 26 N., R. 8 E From thence, whether this line continues in the same direction to the south line of the county, or whether it bears eastward, is yet unknown. Some indications of the northern boundary of the Coal Measures in Iroquois county favors the latter supposition.

The general character of the surface of the county is rolling prairie and very little broken along the Vermilion river, which, with its branches, is fringed with timber. The south-east part of the county is quite high land From four to six miles south of the county line, in Ford county, about the centre of T 24 N., R. 7 E., is the highest land of this region, and the Illinois Vermilion the Wabash Vermilion, the Mackinaw and Sangamon rivers all have their sources here near together

East of and parallel with the Vermilion is a ridge which may be traced from a point west of Chatsworth, north westerly into LaSalle county, into T 32 N, R. 3 E. This is gravelly and sandy, giving it a distinctive character, as compared with the adjacent prairie.

*Drift*—The drift of this county is very variable and thinnest in the north west part of the county—in the vicinity of the Vermilion, and throughout the course of this stream it is much thinner than away from it on either side. At Pontiac, in the north part of the town, it is eighteen feet at Fairbury and vicinity it is from a few feet to ninety feet, at Odell, Matson's boring reported it two hundred feet to sand and water, and three hundred and fifty feet to rock, showing a great depth of drift. Wells there have a very unequal supply of water. Some in town get abundance at five to ten feet, others fail to get water at one hundred feet. In two borings water was obtained at about ninety-five feet in gravel, while others got none, showing that the two gravel beds so general in LaSalle county furnishing water, have run out. and that here the gravel and sand are in veins rather than stratified over extensive areas This, however, may apply only to the eastern side of the Vermilion. The well at the station at Odell was down one hundred and thirty feet Record as follows

| | Ft | In | Ft | In |
|---|---|---|---|---|
| Soil | | | 4 | |
| Yellowish blue clay | 5 | | 9 | |
| Blue clay | 66 | | 75 | |
| Gravel with some sand | 5 | | 80 | |
| Blue clay | 15 | | 95 | |
| Gravel with sand | 2 | | 97 | |
| Blue clay | 8 | | 105 | |
| Gravel | 0 | 4 | 105 | 4 |
| Blue clay | 22 | 8 | 128 | |
| Gravel | 0 | 4 | 128 | 1 |
| Blue clay | 2 | | 130 | |

At Dwight, on the N E qr of sec. 12, T. 30, R 6 E, a boring of twenty five feet was reported all drift, and the well was abandoned at that depth from tools getting fast Water at fifteen to twenty feet

A boring was reported in the S. W qr. of sec 21, T. 28 N., R. 9 E, of one hundred and five feet in drift, but no statement whether this reached the bottom of it This is over the line two miles. in Ford county

At Chenoa, at the railroad crossing, a well bored one hundred and thirty feet struck water at ninety feet, and at one hundred and thirty feet, both rising to within thirty feet of the surface, or so reported This is probably from gravel in drift

At Avoca and west of it water is found from six to eighteen feet from the surface East of this, thirty to forty feet, and not so reliable as west of the Vermilion

Sand is found on sec 27, T. 27 N, R 6 E, between Fairbury and Avoca, with three feet of soil above it, and also found on sec. 1, T. 27 N., R. 5 E, on the west side of the ridge half a mile west of the Vermilion—reported sixteen feet deep and resting on coarse gravel Pontiac is supplied with sand from this point

The country between Fairbury and Chatsworth is a succession of ridges rising gradually towards Chatsworth, the highest point being one or two miles west of Chatsworth, and this is probably one hundred feet or more higher than the ridge at Fairbury.

The upper limestone of the shafts at Fairbury is traced in the wells, and along low ground outcrops in a north westerly direction, showing the drift at less depth. It appears on Indian creek, two miles south-west of town, and also outcrops three and a half miles north-west of town This limestone underlies a low ridge which is observable running in a north westerly direction in the prairie Two miles east of Fairbury is a ridge higher than the one on the west. The railroad cuts through it to a depth of five or six feet, showing a considerable amount of drift, mainly derived from the Niagara limestone A limestone reported six miles south and one mile west of Forest, is probably the continuation of the low ridge near Fairbury above referred to.

At Chatsworth two borings three quarters of a mile apart show much difference in thickness of drift. In the S E. qr. of sec. 4 it is eighty-four or eighty-eight feet, which includes an old vegetable dirt bed In the S. E. qr. of sec 3 the drift is two hundred and twenty one feet according to the record of the boring at the sugar works, and in this, water was struck at a depth of fifty two feet in gravel, again, at seventy-five feet in quick-sand, a third vein at one hundred and nine feet in sand and gravel The water of these three veins rose to within twenty-seven feet of the surface A fourth vein in gravel at two hundred and ten feet rose to within twenty five feet of the surface

## *Coal Measures.*

The Big Vermilion river, from the north line of the county to Pontiac, affords many exposures that help to determine the changes in the Coal Measures.

A coal bank on the S. W. qr. of the S E qr of sec 1, T. 30 N, R 3 E, shows the Streator coal, which is here divided by a clay seam fifteen inches thick, leaving thirty-three inches of coal above and twelve inches of coal below it The coal here is a little below the bed of the river, and a quarter of a mile below, it is at the river level A quarter of a mile above the mine the coal at Newtown mill is in the bed of the river below the dam A half mile below the mine the clay parting is only one eighth of an inch thick

Glenwood mill is on the N. E qr of sec. 12, about the middle of the quarter section The river runs north 35° west, and the sandstone above the shale that overlies the coal at Streator, shows here with a dip south 35° east, one foot in ten. At the mill the dam rests upon the coal.

One mile above the dam the coal appears again It was worked in 1860 and 1861, and said to be three and a half feet thick.

One hundred and twenty rods north of the south line of sec 18, T 30 N, R 4 E, the coal is four and a half feet thick on the east side of the river At the south line of sec. 18 the coal is under the river not more than eight feet. Farther down the river a short distance, on the west side, the coal is three feet thick

At the north west corner of the S E. qr. of the N. W. qr. of sec 19, T 30, R 4 E, a limestone nearly six feet thick appears where the river makes a bend west This rests on a blue clay, and appears to be No

12 of the general section of LaSalle county Fossils found in it were *Productus longispinus, Spirifer cameratus, Sp lineatus, Athyris subtilita,* and *Cyathoxonia.*

The same limestone appears again in the elbow of the river on the right bank, on the south part of section 19, near the middle line, also in a detached mass slipped down in the east part of the S E qr. of sec 19, with the underlying greenish clay and shale forming the bank

Sandstone appears on the north line of sec 30, T 30, R 4 E, near the middle corner This seems to be No 49 of the general section of LaSalle county. The base is shaly, discolored by water bands of coal and coal-plant fragments This sandstone continues in sight to the mouth of Long Point creek, on the left bank of the river, in the south-east corner of sec 29; then reappears on the right bank just above the mouth of Long Point creek The dip shows well here to the north east one foot in twenty In the N. E qr of the N W. qr. of sec 32, in the bend of the river, the direction of the dip is a little more east, and the massive sandstone is overlaid by a bed of silicious and micaceous shale, on which rests a clay shale of light blue color, the silicious shale being a grayish light blue In the clay shale are two bands of limestone some what like ironstone, irregular, separated by clay shale, and each about one foot thick The main sandstone appears again one quarter of a mile below the mouth of Mud creek, on the left bank of the river, and at the mouth of Mud creek is the underlying shaly sandstone This is near the middle of sec 32.

Continuing up the river this sandstone appears in the south part of sec. 5, T 29, R 4, with five or six feet of the underlying shales. One-quarter of a mile further up, and probably in the north part of sec 8, coal comes in suddenly, with section as follows

| | Ft | In. |
|---|---|---|
| Sandstone | ? | |
| Coal . . . | 1 | 6 |
| Fire clay | 1 | |
| Shale . . . | ? | |

This 18 inches of coal is generally represented elsewhere, and in LaSalle county, by fragments and wafer seams of coal. The fire clay is absent A thin shaly sandstone of 18 inches is here found two feet below the coal

South east three quarters of a mile or less, in a straight line from this point, a coal seam appears in the bed of the river Its thickness could not be determined, but is at least one and a half feet. The right bank shows argillaceous shales, with bands of nodules, and thin shales indicating the Streator coal The dip is between south-east and east This point is a little below the mouth of Scattering Point creek, and is probably in the north part of the south east quarter of sec 8. The shales in the right bank of the river in the north west quarter of sec. 9 in that part of the river which runs near the west line of the section appear to be the same just referred to. In the bend of the river at the middle of the north west quarter of sec 9 the strata of sandstone and shale dip about west one foot in twenty. Ten rods further up the river the dip is a little south of east at the same rate.

Near the south line of sec 9 the same sandstone shows again, and dips south-easterly. In the bank of the river in the S E qr. of sec. 16, the S W qr of sec. 15, and the N W. qr of sec. 22, the limestone before referred to appears in loose masses, the banks formed of the underlying blue clay. A slippery bank, and the limestone slipped down, is, everywhere it appears, characteristic of this portion of the vertical section, often obscuring the details. Near the north line of sec 22, and a quarter of a mile east of the north-west corner, the limestone in place is down to the river level. The character of this rock to disintegrate into irregular fragments is exhibited here in abundant loose, coarse limestone gravel, two to four inches in diameter.

From this point to Allen's mill, in the south-west quarter of sec 23, nothing noticeable is to be seen. This limestone appears again at the mill dam, and also at the ford, two miles and a half below Pontiac, and at Pontiac. The fossils are *Spirifer cameratus*, *S lineatus*, *S plano convexus*, *Productus longispinus*, and *Bellerophon*.

The branches of the river in this county afford no aid in determining the rock strata, excepting at a very few points, the drift concealing everything below. Above Pontiac but little rock exposure is found.

The details given of the tracing of the river up to Pontiac show the upheaval of the Coal Measures continued as in LaSalle county, and also seem to indicate some slight local disturbances or parallel axial lines with the main axis.

On Rook's creek, in the N W qr of the N E qr. of sec. 23, T 28, R. 4 E, a sandstone is quarried. The section is as follows

| | Ft |
|---|---|
| Sandstone in thin laminæ | 5 |
| Sandstone in thick beds, slightly micaceous, bluish color, fine building stone | 2 |
| Shaly sandstone to water level | 1 |
| Dip S 80° W | 1 in 10 |

One hundred yards west, down the creek, it shows again. Two hundred yards west, on the left bank of the creek a limestone comes in, stratified in masses, brecciated, about five feet altogether—no fossils. The sandstone shows again in the bed of the creek about 80 to 100 rods in a south east course.

Section of coal shaft at Pontiac, as furnished from the record of the company

| | | Ft | In | Ft | In |
|---|---|---|---|---|---|
| 1 | Drift clay | | | 18 | 9 |
| 2 | Limestone | 1 | 5 | 20 | 2 |
| 3 | Blue shale | 5 | | 25 | 2 |

| | | Ft | In | Ft | In |
|---|---|---|---|---|---|
| 4 | Limestone | 4 | | 29 | 2 |
| 5 | Brown shale | 4 | | 33 | 2 |
| 6 | Red shale | 2 | | 35 | 2 |
| 7 | Blue shale | 1 | | 36 | 2 |
| 8 | Limestone | 17 | 6 | 53 | 8 |
| 9 | Black slate | 1 | | 54 | 8 |
| 10 | Brown shale | 8 | 2 | 62 | 10 |
| 11 | Limestone | 6 | | 68 | 10 |
| 12 | Dark shale | 2 | | 70 | 10 |
| 13 | Limestone | 5 | | 75 | 10 |
| 14 | Red shale | 16 | | 91 | 10 |
| 15 | Blue shale | 40 | | 131 | 10 |
| 16 | Black slate | 14 | | 145 | 10 |
| 17 | Black slate | 19 | | 164 | 10 |
| 18 | Black slate | 12 | | 176 | 10 |
| 19 | Rock—limestone? | 4 | 6 | 181 | 4 |
| 20 | Soapstone | 1 | | 182 | 4 |
| 21 | Coal | 4 | 6 | 186 | 10 |
| 22 | Dark slate—2 in clay on top | 12 | | 198 | 10 |
| 23 | Brown shale | 7 | | 205 | 10 |
| 24 | Dark slate | 6 | 6 | 212 | 4 |
| 25 | Brown shale | 12 | | 224 | 4 |
| 26 | Very dark clay | 7 | | 231 | 4 |
| 27 | Black slate | 50 | | 281 | 4 |
| 28 | Rock—limestone | 7 | 6 | 288 | 10 |
| 29 | Soapstone | 18 | | 306 | 10 |
| 30 | Limestone | 6 | | 312 | 10 |
| 31 | Soapstone—hard | 20 | | 332 | 10 |
| 32 | Black slate—hard | 30 | | 362 | 10 |
| 33 | Septaria, containing bitumen | 2 | | 364 | 10 |
| 34 | Fire clay? | 3 | | 367 | 10 |
| 35 | Coal | 2 | 6 | 370 | 4 |
| 36 | Fire-clay | 3 | 6 | 373 | 10 |

I do not regard the section as a reliable one. Some specimens of *Aviculopecten rectilaterarius*, found in the waste pile, were reported as from No 27 of the section, and *Productus longispinus*, said to be from No 34.

The following is a copy of A. Matson's boring at Pontiac, one-quarter of a mile north-east of the coal shaft, made in 1863:

| | | Ft | Ft |
|---|---|---|---|
| 1 | Drift | | 18 |
| 2 | Limestone | 1 | 19 |
| 3 | Blue slate | 9 | 28 |
| 4 | Hard rock | 4 | 32 |
| 5 | Red shale | 13 | 45 |
| 6 | Blue shale | 20 | 65 |
| 7 | Hard rock | 10 | 75 |
| 8 | Light colored shale | 20 | 95 |
| | Hard rock | 4 | 99 |
| 10 | Red shale | 18 | 117 |
| 11 | Blue shale | 30 | 147 |
| 12 | Black shale | 9 | 156 |
| 13 | Blue shale | 44 | 200 |
| 14 | Coal shale | 3 | 203 |
| 15 | Coal | 1 | 204 |
| 16 | Blue shale | 23 | 227 |
| 17 | Black shale | 5 | 232 |

Shaft of H L. Marsh, Fairbury, on south-west qr. sec 4, T. 26, R. 6 E.:

*Section*

| | | | | Ft | In | Ft | In |
|---|---|---|---|---|---|---|---|
| 1 | Black soil | | | 2 | | 2 | |
| 2 | Yellow clay | | | 14 | | 16 | |
| 3 | Blue clay | | | 8 | | 28 | |
| | Soft blue clay | | | 4 | | | |
| 4 | Quicksand | | | 5 | | 33 | |
| 5 | Limestone | | | 3 | 6 | 36 | 6 |
| 6 | Blue clay | 5 | 10 | 10 | 10 | 47 | 4 |
| | Red and brown clay | 5 | | | | | |
| 7 | Limestone | | | 10 | 2 | 57 | 6 |
| | Limestone, shale and clay | | | 7 | | 64 | 6 |
| 8 | Blue clay | 5 | 5 | 10 | 11 | 75 | 5 |
| | Red clay | 5 | 6 | | | | |
| 9 | Limestone | | | | 4 | 75 | 9 |
| 10 | Coal 0 3, slate, 2 ft | | | 2 | 3 | 78 | |
| 11 | Blue clay | | | 5 | 1 | 83 | 1 |
| | Red clay | | | 5 | | 88 | 1 |
| | Red clay, very dark | | | 7 | 3 | 95 | 4 |
| 12 | Blue limestone, very hard | | | 1 | 2 | 96 | 6 |
| 13 | Red clay | | | 8 | 10 | 105 | 4 |
| 14 | Sandstone, fine and light colored at top, coarser descending | | | 70 | 0 | 175 | 4 |
| | Sandstone in thin bands, interstratified with thin bands of clay | | | 9 | | 184 | 4 |
| 15 | Soapstone | | | 31 | 8 | 216 | |
| 16 | Coal | | | 4 | 10 | 220 | 10 |
| 17 | Fire clay | | | 26 | 8 | 247 | 6 |
| 18 | Limestone, hard | | | 1 | 2 | 248 | 8 |
| 19 | Slate, dark | 2 | | 31 | 8 | 280 | 4 |
| | Slate, light | 15 | 6 | | | | |
| | Slate, dark | 10 | 8 | | | | |
| | Slate, black | 1 | 5 | | | | |
| | Slate band of nodules | 0 | 2 | | | | |
| | Slate, black with some coal | 1 | 11 | | | | |
| 20 | Clay light colored soft | | | 1 | 11 | 282 | 3 |
| 21 | Limestone | | | 6 | | 288 | 3 |
| 22 | Soapstone, light, sandy | | | 3 | 2 | 291 | 5 |
| 23 | Slate, dark soft | | | | 7 | 292 | 0 |
| 24 | Sandy shale | | | 1 | 5 | 293 | 5 |
| | Sandy shale, changing to clay shale at bottom | | | 38 | 7 | 332 | |
| 25 | Sandstone micaceous and shaly at top, harder at bottom | | | 40 | 7 | 372 | 7 |
| 26 | Shale soft at top and hard at bottom | | | 8 | 11 | 381 | 6 |
| 27 | Coal | | | 2 | 5 | 383 | 11 |
| 28 | Fire clay | | | 20 | 6 | 404 | 5 |
| 29 | Sandstone sandy shales, with thin clay bands, to | | | | | 571 | |

From the coal No 27 the section was ascertained by boring in bottom of shaft. Water was noticed at 427 feet The upper sixteen feet of No 25, reported to contain *calamites* and large wood like fossils, body being of sandstone, probably *Sigillaria* incrusted with coal Limestone No 5 of the section outcrops near town.

The shaft and boring of Amsbury & Jones, on south-west qr. of sec. 2, at Fairbury, exhibits the following section, as reported by them

*Section*

| | | Ft | In | Ft | In |
|---|---|---|---|---|---|
| 1 | Soil | | | 2 | 6 |
| 2 | Yellow clay | 8 | 8 | 11 | 2 |
| 3 | Blue clay and mixed with sand | 9 | 7 | 20 | 9 |
| 4 | Gravel, with little water | 1 | 1 | 21 | 10 |
| 5 | Hard pan, sand and gravel, with little clay, cemented and very hard | 39 | 2 | 61 | |

| | | Ft. | In | Ft | In |
|---|---|---|---|---|---|
| 6 | Blue clay | 29 | 4 | 90 | 1 |
| 7 | Black and brown shale mixed, changing into sandstone, and bottom 6 or 8 feet contains fossil plants covered with coal crust making gray colored debris, water abundant at bottom of this | 43 | | 133 | 4 |
| 8 | Sandstone | 14 | | 147 | 4 |
| 9 | Clay, light colored | 4 | | 151 | 4 |
| 10 | Coal (working this bed) | 4 | 2 | 155 | 6 |
| 11 | Fire-clay, with pyrite balls | 8 | | 163 | 6 |
| 12 | Red shale | 7 | | 170 | 6 |
| 13 | Sandstone | 4 | | 174 | 6 |
| 14 | Limestone | 0 | 7 | 175 | 1 |
| 15 | Shale | 6 | | 181 | 1 |
| 16 | Limestone | 1 | 6 | 182 | 7 |
| 17 | Blue shale or clay | 21 | | 203 | 7 |
| 18 | Coal | 0 | 2 | 203 | 9 |
| 19 | Sandstone | 3 | | 206 | 9 |
| 20 | Blue shale or clay | 2 | | 208 | 9 |
| 21 | Coal | 0 | 2 | 208 | 11 |
| 22 | { Shale 7 } { Shale or dark clay 10 } | 17 | | 225 | 11 |
| 23 | Black slate and little coal | 2 | | 227 | 11 |
| 24 | Fire clay | 1 | 6 | 229 | 5 |
| 25 | Sandstone | 5 | | 234 | 5 |
| 26 | Fire clay | 7 | | 241 | 5 |
| 27 | Limestone, hard | 1 | 8 | 243 | 1 |
| 28 | Fire clay | 3 | 6 | 246 | 7 |
| 29 | Sandstone | 11 | | 257 | 7 |
| 30 | Blue clay or shale | 45 | | 302 | 7 |
| 31 | Coal | 3 | 6 | 306 | 1 |
| 32 | Fire clay | 1 | 0 | 307 | 1 |
| 33 | Sandstone | 2 | 0 | 309 | 1 |

The mine is wet, water dripping from the sandstone, No. 8 of the section, the clay next above the coal giving way, and varying from two to eight feet in thickness. H. L. Marsh's mine is dry.

Chatsworth boring, west of town, for coal, south east qr. sec 4, T 26, R 8 E

*Section*

| | | Ft | In | Ft | In |
|---|---|---|---|---|---|
| 1 | Soil, blue clay and sand | | | 65 | |
| 2 | Soft sandstone (sand?) | 15 | | 80 | |
| 3 | Vegetable dirt bed, grains of wood discernable like old rotten logs and portions of leaves | 4 | | 84 | |
| 4 | Fire clay (so called) | 4 | | 88 | |
| 5 | Sandstone | 35 | | 123 | |
| 6 | Shale | 13 | | 136 | |
| 7 | Coal or black slate | 0 | 2 | 136 | 2 |
| 8 | Fire clay | 1 | | 137 | 2 |
| 9 | Soapstone or shale | 11 | | 148 | 2 |
| 10 | Coal | 1 | 3 | 149 | 5 |
| 11 | Fire clay | 3 | | 152 | 5 |
| 12 | Soapstone | 15 | | 167 | 5 |
| 13 | Black slate | 1 | 6 | 168 | 11 |
| 14 | Soapstone or shale | 31 | 1 | 200 | |

To coal or slate, a thin bed, with iron pyrite

This boring is fifty feet from the railroad, near east line of section 4.

Artesian well, at Chatsworth, south-east qr sec. 3, T. 26, R. 8 E.:

*Section*

| | | | Ft |
|---|---|---|---|
| 1 | Soil and clay | | 4 |
| 2 | Yellow clay | 4 | 8 |
| 3 | Blue clay | 44 | 52 |
| 4 | Sand and gravel | 8 | 60 |
| 5 | Blue clay | 10 | 70 |
| 6 | Sand | 5 | 75 |
| 7 | Hard pan (clay and gravel) | 53 | 128 |
| 8 | Sand | 7 | 135 |
| 9 | Hard pan and clay | 52 | 187 |
| 10 | Soft clay and gravel | 13 | 200 |
| 11 | Soapstone | 21 | 221 |
| 12 | Limestone | 69 | 290 |
| 13 | Limestone | 94 | 384 |
| 14 | Limestone | 70 | 454 |
| 15 | Limestone | 115 | 569 |
| 16 | Black slate | 40 | 609 |
| 17 | Gritstone | 80 | 689 |
| 18 | Limestone | 65 | 754 |
| 19 | Limestone | 70 | 824 |
| 20 | Dark shale | 36 | 860 |
| 21 | Limestone | 147 | 1,007 |
| 22 | Flint? | 109 | 1,116 |
| 23 | Dark gray shale, with streaks of flint | 84 | 1,200 |

A comparison of the two borings above shows an abrupt change from the Coal Measures to the older rocks and a great difference in the depth of the drift.

PART II

# PALÆONTOLOGY OF ILLINOIS.

## SECTION I.

## DESCRIPTIONS OF FOSSIL FISHES.

By ORESTES ST JOHN and A. H. WORTHEN.

# PREFATORY NOTE.

It was our intention, originally, to preface the work on Fossil Fishes with an introductory chapter on the stratigraphic or time history of these interesting remains But as our inquiries progressed it became apparent, not only that the means at the disposal of the Survey were wholly inadequate to allow the completion of the investigation of the materials already in hand, but that our information bearing on their distribution in certain horizons was insufficient for conclusive results We have, therefore, limited our observations to such facts as are actually accessible, believing that, so far as they go, they contribute something to our knowledge of these important data to the palæontologist. These, so far as it was possible to do, have been explicitly stated in connection with the descriptions in the following pages.

It was our fortune at an early day, and during the progress of our investigations, to interest and receive the earnest coöperation of a few gentlemen, whose opportunities enabled them to furnish most important data and material, all of which was generously placed in our hands Messrs FRANK SPRINGER and CHARLES WACHSMUTH, of Burlington, Iowa, have not only contributed large accessions in material, but it is to Mr. SPRINGER, and subsequently to Mr. WACHSMUTH, that we owe the discovery of the ichthyic horizon in the upper part of the Kinderhook at that place, as well as some excellent explorations in the superincumbent Burlington formations, and Keokuk limestone, in south eastern Iowa. The interest which these gentlemen have evinced in the work, and we may include as well that of others, and material aids which we owe to them, render anything like an adequate acknowledgment of their share of this important part of these investigations impossible in so brief an account as the present. While these explorations in the lower formations were progressing, Mr. W. C. VAN HORNE was prosecuting similar and most exhaustive researches in the St. Louis formation; besides it is largely due to him that opportunity was afforded one of the writers to make a thorough examination of this formation in the environs of St. Louis, where it presents its most typical development An interesting result of these explorations was the ascertaining that the fishes range through a considerable thickness of limestone strata, at least forty feet, instead of occurring in "fish-beds" of a few inches, or feet at most, in thickness, as obtained in the Kinderhook, Burlington, Keokuk, and probably the Warsaw formations, as well as the superincumbent Chester beds. The interest and variety of the remains from the St Louis beds is not excelled, while at the same time they are as markedly characteristic in faunal facies as are the fishes whose remains occur in horizons of more limited vertical extent As an illustration of the latter horizons, no finer example occurs to us than that discovered by Mr. SPRINGER and Mr WACHSMUTH in the Kinderhook at Burlington, where two distinct "fish beds," separated by only a few feet of intervening strata, exhibit in the main quite peculiar faunal characteristics, though there are many found common to both horizons During his residence at Boonville, Dr. G. A. WILLIAMS has prosecuted a careful examination of the stratigraphy of the Keokuk and Warsaw divisions in Central Missouri, with especial reference to the distribution of their contained fish remains. The results of his explorations show a remarkable conformity to the stratigraphic phases of these formations as they appear in Iowa and Illinois, and which information should be embodied in an exhaustive treatise on the stratigraphy of the Lower Carboniferous deposits. We are also indebted to Mr L. A. FULLER, Professors B. F. MUDGE and JAMES TODD, Mr. ALEX BUTTERS, Prof. J J. STEVENSON, and Dr A. LIPTON, for important information and material derived from the Coal Measure formations, and extending from West Virginia in the Appalachian region to the plains of Kansas west of the Missouri.

Of the magnificent collections brought together by these explorations, and those previously made by one of the authors during the many years occupied in the geological examination of the country bordering upon the Upper Mississippi, which latter formed the basis of the work on the Fishes in the preceding second volume of this report, by Messrs. Newberry and Worthen, we have been able to make only partial use for the present work. Indeed the *Cochliodonts* and *Mylodonts* alone would require space equal to that here devoted to the *Hybodonts* and *Petalodonts.* It is a matter of time, and ample at that, for the entire work to reach completion, and in the respite which necessity compels, it is to be hoped that no opportunity will be allowed to escape whereby additional data and collections may add to and perfect our knowledge of the history of these fragmentary and for the most part scattered remains of the earliest vertebrates in our earth's history.

We have also received many courtesies from other sources, which have enabled us to avoid the perpetration of errors in nomenclature, besides adding much information which will be of value in monographing the carboniferous fishes Dr JOSEPH LEIDY has not only furnished us, at our solicitation, with important references to his own labors in this field, but he kindly secured for us the loan of the original specimens described by him, from the Museum of the Academy of Natural Sciences of Philadelphia. Mr. F. B. MEEK also forwarded us for examination such specimens as have found their way to the great collections of the Smithsonian Institution, from the surveys of Dr HAYDEN, Lieut. WHEELER, and others. And Prof. SAFFORD placed in our hands such fish remains as he has come upon in his geological investigations in Tennessee In connection with this work we have also had occasion to acquaint ourselves with facts occurring abroad and which it was not possible to obtain from our own resources We would here acknowledge the highly interesting communication with which Lord ENNISKILLEN has favored us, especially with reference to the *Cochliodonts*, which it was our intention at one time to include in the present work. We would also refer to the very favorable opportunities which one of the writers owes to Dr. CHAS. A. WHITE, for prosecuting examinations intimately connected with the study of the Fossil Fishes as they occur throughout the Carboniferous deposits in the State of Iowa, and which have enabled us the more successfully to compare the stratigraphy of the two regions on either side of the Mississippi.

In the execution of the lithographing of the plates illustrative of the subjoined text, Mr. MAYER has exercised a degree of patience with our wishes, and skill, for which the plates themselves are sufficient witness.

In conclusion, it is but justice to ourselves to state, that, however excellent our material has been, the present work has been prosecuted principally during leisure between hours which duty devoted to other palæontological labors little akin to these more special investigations. Yet we would gratefully acknowledge the favorable facilities these same opportunities have placed in our reach, and to which we are more indebted than it were possible to express It is due to the authorities of the Museum of Comparative Zoology at Cambridge, where we were allowed every privilege it was in our power to take advantage of, to express our deep obligations for opportunities which perhaps are to be found to the same extent in no other quarter for these special purposes.

# VERTEBRATES.

## GENUS PHŒBODUS, St. J. and W.

### PHŒBODUS SOPHIÆ, St. J. and W.

Pl I, Fig 14

The magnesian beds overlying the coraline limestone of the middle Devonian, in the Cedar valley of Iowa, have afforded, amongst other interesting ichthyic remains more particularly characteristic of the Devonian age, a couple of peculiar forms of minute teeth which unquestionably belong to that section of the *Hybodonts* represented by the *Cladodi*, and of which they are the earliest representatives thus far detected in America To one of these forms we have given the above generic and specific designations. The other has received the name *Bathycheilodus McIsaacsii.*

The former of the above mentioned forms is represented by very small teeth, the largest of which do not exceed 0.2 inch in lateral diameter and about one third less in greatest hight, general proportions strong, symmetrical. Base irregularly elliptical in outline, strongly produced in front and faintly excavated at the median line, the antero-interior angles approximate, and laterally curved to the rounded extremities, broadly though irregularly rounded behind; the angles in front are occupied by a strong, lateral, pad-like prominence, which is more or less distinctly bilobed and beveled to the deeply excavated inferior surface; posterior margin slightly burled, postero superior surface moderately convex and surmounted by a laterally elongated, well defined prominence, which is situated nearly midway between the base of the crown and the posterior border to which the surface abruptly slopes, and extending laterally nearly half the diameter of the base The coronal region consists of three strong cusps, of which the exterior pair are largest, strongly diverging and moderately recurved or nearly vertical, antero posteriorly compressed or suboval in section, apparently without distinct cutting edges, the median cone similar in shape, erect, more or less produced in front and continued to the shallow median depression in the basal border, from the lateral portion of which the coronal region is sharply defined by a delicate sulcation in the angle extending laterally from the median notch; in the angles between the median and the strong lateral cusps arise a delicate rudimentary denticle on either side, but which are generally obsolete, possibly in consequence of abrasion The coronal cusps are apparently smooth; however, in some examples a few faint vertical striæ or thread like lines are discernible, the surface in all cases highly polished; the basal region is more or less roughened, with here and there large punctæ or foramena

The teeth here mentioned bear intimate relations to the form from the Kinderhook beds of the Lower Carboniferous, which we have referred to the genus *Pristicladodus* of McCoy. This resemblance is strongly marked in the general outline of the base and position of the coronal cusps. But the absence of the deep median slit in the posterior margin of the base, the confluent antero inferior basal prominence, and the sharp definition therefrom in the lateral portions of the coronal region, constitute an assemblage of features which seem to preclude their reference to that group

Dedicated in grateful and filial remembrance.

*Position and locality*. Magnesian beds of the middle Devonian; Waterloo, Iowa.

## GENUS BATHYCHEILODUS, St. J. and W.

### BATHYCHEILODUS McISAACSII, St J and W.

Pl I, Figs 12 13

Teeth minute, robust, symmetrical Base laterally elongated, subelliptical in outline, gently sinuose in front, and margined by a relatively deep ridge which extends two thirds the distance across the base, produced downward and outward, defining the moderately excavated inferior surface, which is posteriorly beveled, posterior margin broadly arched, lateral extremities sharply rounded and more or less produced, postero superior surface moderately convex and traversed by a narrow central ridge nearly as extensive as the lateral diameter and direct, sharply bevelled to the margin behind, surfaces more or less roughened. Crown well-defined from the base, gently constricted in front and laterally, posteriorly sloping into the basal surface, and consisting of a prominent ridge which is produced into a strong, rapidly tapering, anteriorly compressed and posteriorly rounded median cone, with well-defined cutting edges, flanked by a pair of nearly equally strong, slightly diverging and recurved lateral denticles of similar shape, with a minute intermediate denticle in the angles between the lateral cones and the erect median cusp; the outer coronal face is ornamented with a few relatively strong, sharp crested, vertical ridges, which descend to the basal line, though generally obsolete in the lower half of the face, with similar, though perhaps less strongly marked costæ in the posterior face, when the surfaces are not abraded a dense enamel like layer occurs, which in the posterior face distinctly defines the basal limit of the crown. Lateral diameter of base one to two-tenths inch, or about twice the hight of the teeth.

The affinities of the teeth described above are so intimate with *Cladodus* as strongly to suggest their identity with that genus. Yet we cannot mistake the characteristics which pertain to the form in question and by which it is distinguished from the typical forms of the latter genus The coronal region even more strongly suggests relationship with *Phœbodus* and *Pristicladodus*, as remarked in its entire definition from the basal region, forming indeed an elevated ridge from which arise the *Cladodus* like cusps, in a manner very similar to that observed in the above mentioned genera But in the basal characters we find a marked divergence from the latter genera, and an equally striking likeness to that of *Cladodus*, with, however, this distinction, in the present teeth the anterior basal border is uniform, without a break such as produced by median excavation or prominence.

Their occurrence with the previously described form, *Phœbodus Sophiæ*, with which they bear intimate resemblance in size, has raised the question as to their relations with these teeth. Of course, it is possible they represent the dentition of opposite jaws, in which case there would be even a less marked dissimilarity than obtains respectively in the teeth of the upper and lower jaws of some of the modern sharks, as instanced in *Scymnus* But, while we have no further evidence of such being the fact, the unmistakable characters upon which their distinctive features are based can scarcely be reconciled with a diversity of which we have no analogy in the allied genus *Cladodus*.

These, with the preceding described teeth, are among the earliest palæontological acquisitions of one of the writers, and it is with no inadequate sense of his deep obligations for the early training and subsequent friendship, that the present form is respectfully dedicated to Mr. PATRICK MCISAAC, of Iowa.

*Position and locality* · Magnesian limestone of the middle Devonian, Waterloo, Iowa.

## GENUS PRISTICLADODUS, McCoy, (amended.)

The genus *Carcharopsis* of Agassiz, (Poiss. Foss III, p. 313, *C. prototypus*, carb limest, Yorkshire and Armagh,) was founded upon imperfectly preserved teeth, which probably are more intimately allied to the form described by McCOY under the name *Pristicladodus dentatus* than with that described as *P. Goughi*, (McCoy, Brit Palæ Foss, p 642, 643) Thus associated, we have two generic groups which appear to be respectively defined by the following characters:

CARCHAROPSIS.—Principal cusps very strong, erect, compressed in front, rounded behind or sublenticular in transverse section; broadly expanded at base so as to occupy nearly the entire lateral diameter of the base, lateral angles sharp and deeply and regularly crenulated, extremities occupied by one or two more or less slender, conical lateral denticles, which are as isolated as is the case in typical *Cladodus*, coronal faces smooth or faintly striated vertically Base in outline like *Cladodus*, moderately produced and broadly rounded posteriorly; extremities more or less sharply rounded, anterior face sinuose, terminating below in a well defined continuous basal ridge, which occupies the greater extent of the anterior border, inferior surface excavated, postero superior surface moderately convex, roughened possibly into pad-like prominences

PRISTICLADODUS—Principal cusp very strong, erect, sigmoidally recurved, lenticular in section, more compressed in front than behind, rapidly converging to the apex, lateral edges sharp and more or less distinctly undulated or simple, lateral cusps relatively very strong, sometimes even more massive than the median cusps, divergent, similar in shape to the median prominence with which they are connected by a prominent sharp curved intervening ridge, anterior coronal surface marked with sharp more or less irregular costæ, which converge in the intermediate crest, producing a faint denticulation, sometimes forming quite strong spinose processes The costæ in the lateral cusps ascending from the basal line diagonally to the inner margin of the cusps, where they often form a spinose edge or become obsolete, the posterior face is generally less strongly costate, perhaps, in some forms or individuals, smooth The base generally like *Cladodus*, posterior expansion occupied above by a more or less distinct convexity, broadly rounded behind, extremities rounded or truncated, anterior margin sinuose, laterally more or less broadly rounded into the extremities with distinct protuberances occupying the anterior angle either side of the mesial depression and connected by a low ridge; inferior surface moderately excavated, and in some forms at least the posterior border is deeply notched near the median line.

Perhaps the base is generally narrower antero posteriorly in the former genus than it is in *Pristicladodus*, the anterior marginal border forms an uninterrupted ridge, while in the latter group it is sinuate at the median line, with well-defined protuberances in the anterior basal angles The coronal region is still more diverse in the two groups, the present one being distinguished by the strong cuspidate lateral cusps, whereas in *Carcharopsis* the lateral cones are more numerous, smaller and isolated, and the lateral margins of the median cusp are deeply crenulated in the same manner as in some of the earlier and modern Squaloids. The form described by Dr NEWBERRY under the name *Carcharopsis Wortheni*, from the Chester limestone of Alabama, (Geol. Ill II, p. 69, Pl. 4, fig. 14,) is a typical representative of the genus first recognized by Prof. Agassiz and intimately allied to, though probably specifically distinct from, *Pristicladodus dentatus* of McCoy. Whether or no the latter form is identical with the original species noticed by Agassiz, *Carcharopsis prototypus* of the same horizon, we have not been able to ascertain; but from the comparative reference made by Prof. Agassiz, there can be little doubt as to the generic identity of the two above mentioned forms.

It will be observed from the preceding diagnosis that the teeth mentioned herein, and in the following description, are separable into two well defined groups by not inconspicuous characteristics peculiar to their respective representatives; and in assigning to each of these groups appellations which we believe to have been originally applied to quite different forms, in part at least, by Profs AGASSIZ and McCOY, we have been guided by such facts as are accessible to us, only desiring to render due justice to our own authorities.

## PRISTICLADODUS SPRINGERI, St. J. and W.

Pl I, Fig 7 11

Under the above designation we refer to a peculiar form of teeth from the Kinderhook formation, which is represented by a unique example in the collection of Mr SPRINGER, and, although the specimen is in a very satisfactory state of preservation, we have referred it with some doubt to *Pristicladodus*, together with other specimens which are referred to further on

Teeth under medium size, in general outline like *Cladodus* and in the particulars of form intimately related to *Pristicladodus*, according to the definition of that genus previously given Base moderately thick, in outline elliptical, beveled on both surfaces along the broadly rounded posterior margin, outer margin slightly inverted and defined below by a faint marginal ridge, with strong basal protuberances in the angles upon either side of the mesial depression, which latter extends upwards forming a deep triangular area in the base of the median cusp, extremities more or less produced beyond the coronal portion, lateral angles truncated. rounded behind, inferior surface gently excavated and occupied transversely to the long diameter by a low median fold, which, however, may not be of permanent occurrence, and faintly grooved or roughened in the same direction; the upper surface of the posteriorly produced base is not fully exposed, but appears to be gently convex with obscurely defined median prominence. Crown very prominent, compressed, abruptly constricted basally in front, and consisting of three stout, acutely pointed, trenchant cusps, strongly compressed in front, broadly rounded behind, of which the median one is the largest, regularly and gradually tapering, gently deflected laterally and more strongly recurved, sublenticular in transverse section; lateral cusps comparatively very strong, compressed with sharp lateral angles rapidly tapering, strongly divergent or laterally deflected and recurved at a considerably greater angle than the median cone, with which they are intimately connected by the elevated intervening crest; the coronal surface in front is delicately marked with numerous sharp, more or less irregularly disposed costæ, whose extremities along the basal margin are thickened with obscure indications of spinose processes, and which, ascending the coronal prominence, are deflected or converge in the cusps, where they are bifurcated, and towards the apices replaced by implanted costæ, which become obsolete before reaching the lateral edges, which latter are smooth and sharp above, but faintly denticular in the sharp intermediate coronal crest; both surfaces appear to be similarly ornamented, but in the inner face of the principal cusp the costæ are more numerous and abruptly terminated in the smooth area bordering the margins. Lateral diameter of base .50 inch, antero posterior diameter .18, greatest hight of tooth .32, elevation of the intermediate coronal crests 13 inch.

Associated with the above Mr. WACHSMUTH has found several specimens of a minute form of teeth, which offer at first glance a wide contrast to the tooth described, but which, on more familiar acquaintance, seem to present closer affinities with that specimen than at first suspected. The latter form, which we have designated under the provisional term *P. armatus*, although variable individually, is chiefly distinguishable from the above by its smaller size, proportionately stronger lateral cones which exceed the dimension of principal cusp, and the presence of intermediate processes, which latter often spring from the inner margins of the lateral cusps. The outer aspect of the coronal cusps are strongly ridged with flexuose costæ, which become obsolete in the cones and especially in their inner margins, where they give rise to the delicate processes which correspond to the intermediate denticulation of the crest in the first mentioned specimen; the inner face of the crown is more strongly arched, and apparently quite free from vertical costæ, although there are faint indications of striæ. The character of the basal region is very similar to the tooth previously mentioned, although relatively of less lateral extent, the antero inferior protuberances more strongly developed and generally, though not always, more closely approximated, a deep narrow notch interrupting the posterior border, and the postero superior surface broadly convex, with indications of a broad, low mesial pad. The latter teeth range from .11 to .30 inch in lateral diameter

Without authentic specimens exhibiting all the intermediate phases, it is not possible positively to assert the specific identity of the forms above described But, considering the intimate characteristics which they in common possess, it seems highly probable that their individual peculiarities may be attributable to the variable expression of the dentition of different parts of the jaws.

The elegant unique fossil first noticed above is distinguished by superficial characters which widely remove it from any form with which we have had opportunity to make comparison. In the continuity of the coronal prominence, and in the form of the basal portion, it bears much resemblance to the form described by Prof. McCoy under the name *Pristicladodus Goughi*, from the lower Carboniferous schists of Ireland. It is distinguished from that species, however, not only by its small size, but more especially by the even lateral angles of the cusps, the denticulations being restricted to the coronal crest intervening between the principal and lateral cusps, (although in the instance of the variety *P. armatus* these denticulations encroach far up the lateral border of the lateral cones, retaining their distinct spinose character,) and which bear a closer relation to the peculiar indentations observed in the above named species than they do to the crenulated edges of *Carcharopsis dentatus* (McCoy sp ) from the Carboniferous limestone of Derbyshire. Indeed, as previously expressed, there seems to be sufficient reasons for doubting the generic identity of the two species described by McCoy, and however disinclined we might be to refer the present form to an intimate relationship with *C. dentatus*, the same objections would not obtain in the case of *P Goughi*, with which latter form there exist more prominent features in common, and which seem to constitute sufficiently distinctive peculiarities to justify the recognition of their distinct generic character.

*Position and locality*—Not common in the lower fish bed of the Kinderhook, also in the upper fish-bed of the same formation; Burlington, Iowa

## GENUS CLADODUS, Agassiz

### CLADODUS EXILIS, St J and W.

Pl I Figs 1 6

Teeth very small and symmetrically formed Base elliptical in outline, inferior surface moderately excavated with a relatively broad beveled belt along the posterior margin, anterior surface constricted along the basal line of the crown and considerably depressed in the middle or just beneath the principal cone, terminating below in a rather prominent mesial ridge, which is sometimes faintly sinuous in front, and extending one third to one half the lateral diameter of the base, with well defined lateral angles; the upper surface of the posterior portion of the base presents a well marked pad or ridge, in lateral extent corresponding nearly with the antero-inferior mesial ridge, gradually sloping to the posterior edge, and separated from the crown by a narrow distinct intervening channel, or, in worn specimens, the surface presents a more or less regular convexity in the region of the pad. The crown consists of a strong, erect or slightly deflected, gradually tapering and slightly sigmoidally curved median cusp, more compressed in front than behind, slightly compressed laterally with sharp cutting edges, lateral denticles normally two on either extremity, slender and tapering to a sharp point with distinct cutting edges, the inner pair about half the size of the exterior pair, and ornamented with numerous exceedingly delicate, closely arranged parallel striæ, the same as appear in the median cone, the striæ of the inner face being appreciably finer than those in the opposite face, in both faces becoming obsolete just before reaching the lateral edges, and ordinarily extending nearly to the apices in front In rare instances three pairs of lateral denticles have been observed in teeth which otherwise differ in no particular from the normal condition described above The largest specimens observed attain a lateral diameter of base of .35 inch and from that size down to .15 inch, with a hight of .18

Although not numerously represented, we have had opportunity, through the zealous interest of Messrs SPRINGER and WACHSMUTH, to examine a fine series of this elegant little form, of which there are several nearly perfect individuals. The form differs so markedly from any of its associates in the same beds, as scarcely to require the mention of its distinctive peculiarities But compared with later succeeding forms, this closely resembles in form, and in many, if not most, of its external details the teeth known under the name *C. micropus*, N. and W, of the Burlington and Keokuk division The chief distinction consists in the diminutive proportions of the Kinderhook teeth as contrasted with the large dimensions attained by the Burlington and Keokuk form, while in some minor respects the present form bears even closer resemblance to the forms of the same group occurring in the St Louis and Chester divisions, and which is especially noticeable in the exceeding delicacy of the coronal striation and the nearly perfect symmetry in the proportions

It is worthy of remark that the largest individuals of the form under consideration occur in the second or upper fish-bed of the Kinderhook division, but these scarcely exceed the smallest examples of *C. micropus*, while they present readily appreciable characters by which they may be recognized from that form in all its stages The striæ are uniformly more numerous and crowded than in *C micropus*, being also less divergent laterally in the median cone in front, similar differences are observed in the inner face of the coronal cusps, where the striation is conspicuously coarser and more sparce than in the present form Compared with *C. politus*, N and W, of the Chester division, the same differences are observed; while the more frequent occurrence of a third small accessory denticle *exterior* to the larger pair of lateral cones (though this feature also obtains in *C micropus*,) exhibit additional distinctive characters in *C exilis*, whenever a third denticle makes its appearance, it is apparently always developed in the angle at the base of the median cone and first lateral denticle. There is, however, considerable diversity in the teeth referred to *C. micropus*, and until it is well understood, in connection with those forms which appear in later deposits of the same period, we may not be able to determine the exact relationship of these various forms

*Geological position and locality* Not uncommon in both ichthyic horizons in the Kinderhook division, Burlington, Iowa

## CLADODUS SPRINGERI, St. J and W

Pl 2, Fig 1-13

Teeth attain medium size, base strong, subelliptical in outline, broadly and more or less regularly rounded behind; anterior border gently arched, rarely even faintly sinuose, rounded at the obtuse lateral extremities, gently inbeveled and produced below in a strong median prominence of somewhat variable extent, but usually about one-third the lateral diameter of the base, laterally defined, and sloping to the moderately concave inferior surface, which is bordered by a more or less distinct beveled area along the obtuse posterior margin, postero-superior surface gently convex, and surmounted by a strong, roughened prominence, which closely borders and conforms to the posterior margin, widely spaced from the base of the crown, and of variable lateral extent, in this respect apparently conforming to the distance between the obscure marginal angles, hence in laterally elongated bases it is of proportionately greater lateral extent than in more abbreviated individuals, as represented by the small teeth, in which it is reduced to a strong pad like prominence scarcely one fourth the greatest diameter of the base To some extent the same is true of the anterior basal ridges, though in some examples it assumes the condition, but without the distinct definition, of the median ridge in the larger teeth, or those which present the normal aspect of the form. In well preserved specimens there is less variability in the coronal region than remarked in the basal portion, the crown nominally presenting a strong median cone flanked on either hand by four pairs of lateral denticles alternating in size, the exterior pair stout, moderately deflected laterally, and recurved at an angle greater than the median cone, which they resemble in shape, perhaps less symmetrical; the median cone gradually tapers to the acute apex, sublenticular in transverse section, gently convex in front, strongly arched posteriorly, with sharp lateral edges, compressed or faintly depressed at the base in front, and marked with more or less closely and somewhat irregularly arranged angular costæ, which bifurcate descending, with intercalated costæ above, and which ascend half or two thirds the distance to the apex in front, in the posterior face they are more delicate and more closely crowded or numerous; in front the costæ terminate in slight basal knobs, probably the worn bases of accessory processes, and which appear in the lateral extremities, often forming a dense border of spinose processes encircling the anterior border of the crown, and flanking the base of the exterior denticles; the lateral denticles are similarly striated in the anterior face, a few strong, sharp ridges terminating in the apex, the posterior face occupied by delicate thread like ridges

The form under consideration is the most numerously represented of the Kinderhook *Cladodi*, the original collection of Mr SPRINGER offering the means of a comprehensive study of the form under the varied aspects which it displays, and which, but for this extensive material, would lead to serious misconception of the character presented by the widely diverse individuals of which it is composed. In selecting material for illustration, we have aimed not so much at giving a graduated series, as to illustrate by a few well chosen examples the variable character of individuals of various sizes, positions, and conditions of preservation Perhaps the most marked variableness is directly attributable to abrasion, by which, especially in the smaller teeth, the spinose processes at the base of the crown have suffered most, in the majority of the teeth there remaining scarcely a vestige of these processes, while, at the same time, even the lateral denticles themselves have been subjected to partial, and sometimes in the case of the more delicate ones, total obliteration Denuded of their distinctive characteristics, these teeth scarcely present a suggestion of their real specific identity, while amongst themselves they are even more diverse than the greatest extremes exhibited by well expressed examples Yet we have observed in these smaller teeth variations in the number of true lateral denticles, which indicate that in this respect there was not absolute uniformity In some of the normal examples one extremity may bear an extra denticle, in others there may be one or two denticles wanting And in abnormally (?) developed teeth, as also in specimens which have suffered most from abrading agencies, there may occur but two and three denticles on either extremity, or but a single one on one and a pair or three denticles upon the opposite extremity Amongst the more minute examples teeth less than .15 of an inch in lateral diameter, and larger, the median cone often presents a coarse costation quite in contrast to that ordinarily presented, and which has led to the conclusion that the forms exhibiting this feature never belonged to the rows constituted by the larger teeth, but pertain either to the anterior or posterior portions of the jaws

The teeth referable to the form above described have some general resemblance to *C. succinctus*, of the fish-bed next above the horizon whence these were derived, but even a cursory comparison will at once reveal the wide distinctions between them, as exhibited in the basal region, and the fine costation of the median cone. The worn examples also resemble *C. alternatus* of the same horizon—a smaller and more symmetrical form, destitute of accessory processes, and otherwise well marked specifically, as shown in the illustrations of Pl II, in which both forms are represented

It affords us pleasure to associate the name of our friend Mr. SPRINGER with this fine form, as a slight token of our appreciation of the valuable aids he has contributed to this work

*Position and locality* Lower fish-bed of the Kinderhook formation, Burlington, Iowa.

## CLADODUS EXIGUUS, St J. and W.

Pl 3, Fig 13-15

Teeth of small size, though rather stoutly fashioned. Base long, or subelliptical in general outline, extremities obtusely rounded, slightly sinuous in front, and arched, moderately excavated below, and gently beveled along the posterior margin, the exterior mesial ridge occupying two thirds or more of the lateral diameter of the base, and forming a continuous, strongly marked ridge projecting downward and slightly outward, or sometimes more or less distinctly divided into two lobes by a faint median constriction in the inner side, along which it is always sharply beveled toward the concavity of the root, from the body of which it is more or less distinctly defined laterally, posteriorly the base is gently rounded, and surmounted by a well marked ridge, which makes an abrupt descent to the posterior margin, with which it is parallel, and separated from the crown by a shallow channel, surfaces irregularly roughened and pitted Crown slightly constricted along the basal line in front, the sinuosity of the usually deep basal region extending up into the median cone as a faint depression, while the enamel of the inner face terminates in a faint line, median cone strong, laterally deflected and generally strongly recurved, rapidly tapering to an obtusely rounded point, compressed in front and broadly rounded behind, with sharp lateral edges, lateral denticles four on either extremity, alternating more or less irregularly in size, in shape resembling the median cone; the exterior pair relatively strong and outwardly and posteriorly curved, the outer basal line is marked by irregularly disposed tubercles or processes, which are more markedly developed in the lateral regions, and sometimes flank the exterior denticles, besides the latter, the lateral denticles are ornamented with one or two, perhaps rarely more, sharp costæ, while the median cusp in some individuals bears five or six similar costæ, irregularly spaced, implanted or rarely bifurcated descending, and seldom reaching two thirds the distance towards the apex; the costa of the inner face are apparently equally irregularly developed and more delicate, and usually obsolete in the lateral denticles A well proportioned specimen of medium size measures in greatest lateral diameter of base .38 inch, greatest hight of tooth .32.

Although the general features presented by the teeth here recognized are quite persistent, a considerable range of variation occurs in individuals, rendering it difficult in many instances to determine their identity, especially in worn and otherwise mutilated or abnormally developed specimens. In some respects the form bears intimate comparison with *C. Wachsmuthi*, as especially noticeable in the base, which is almost the exact likeness of the latter form, the coronal region, on the other hand, presents an equally striking resemblance to *C Springeri*, with which it is associated, and from which it is recognized chiefly by the fewer accessory processes and costæ in the outer aspect, and its dwarfish and less symmetrical proportions. It is possible that it may prove to belong to the former of the above named forms, but no exactly similar individuals are as yet known from the horizon in which *C. Wachsmuthi* occurs, while the characters which serve to distinguish the individuals from either of the forms mentioned, would also seem to indicate their distinct specific character.

In this connection, it is interesting to note the absence of *C. Springeri* in the ichthyic bed which affords the form described under the name *C Wachsmuthi;* or, in other words, the stratigraphic limitation of each respective form with which that under consideration in one or other way is intimately allied, while the normal examples of each form present at a glance appreciable peculiarities

*Geological position and locality* Not uncommon in fish-bed No 1 of the Kinderhook division of the Lower Carboniferous, Burlington, Iowa

## CLADODUS WACHSMUTHI, St J and W

Pl 3, Fig 1-7

This species presents considerable variation, not only in the teeth from different parts of the jaws, but also in the various sizes, with, however, a well-defined normal standard, which may be defined as follows Base thick, moderately expanded behind and broadly arched, with a more or less strong sinuous curvature along the outer margin, and nicely rounded at the lateral angles, in front the base is distinctly constricted along the line of union with the crown, expanding outward in its descent, and terminating in a rather strong marginal belt, which generally stretches across two-thirds or more of the median region, and more or less abruptly terminated laterally, the inferior surface of this belt or ridge is, when well preserved, flattened and beveled inward and in rare instances it is observed to be more or less distinctly bilobed, in which cases the belt is relatively of narrower lateral extent, but never cut down so as to break the continuity of the ridge viewed from the outer side, the interior surface has its greatest depression immediately below the anterior border, and is usually distinctly beveled along the inner margin. superior surface distinctly defined from the coronal region, moderately convex, and surmounted by a continuous, narrow, pad like prominence, which occupies half or two-thirds the lateral diameter of the base, and abruptly sloping to the posterior margin; sometimes the surface immediately above the pad is deeply excavated, and the posterior margin somewhat distinctly channeled, but in the majority of teeth, perhaps, the pad presents a gently rounded prominence, and in worn specimens it may be obsolete; both basal surfaces are irregularly corrugated antero posteriorly and pitted by irregularly disposed foramina Crown sharply defined in front and laterally from the base, and a faint line sweeping around the median cone and contracting in the lateral portions, indicating the basal termination of the enamel behind The central and external cusps are connected by a sharp, compressed and deeply denticulate crest, the intermediate denticles irregularly alternating in size; the exterior pair in the normal state are remarkably large, more strongly compressed in front than behind, with sharp cutting edges, the apices almost always directed toward the median cone, in many instances, the larger exterior pair are flanked by a second pair of denticles with a minute intervening cusp, and all are ornamented in the outer face by more or less strongly marked carinæ, which are either simple or give off spinose processes towards their bases, which latter are more strongly developed in the lateral than in the median portions of the crown, the median cusp is strong, trenchant, sigmoidally curved and laterally deflected, compressed in front and broadly rounded behind, with a slight depression occupying the basal portion in front, the carinæ are more strongly developed in front than in the opposite face, though their development is very irregular, as shown in a large suite of specimens—in some individuals there being very few and these scarcely reaching one third the distance towards the apex, while in others they show several sharp, close set costæ implanted and bifurcated in their descent, the carinæ are relatively coarser and far less numerous in the lateral denticles, though always irregularly disposed, the inner face of the crown exhibits similar variableness in the development of the costæ, though relatively corresponding to their development in the opposite face, in some examples the inner face of the principal cone is quite smooth, with only faint costæ visible in the lateral portions, in others, again, the costæ are quite numerous, but in all cases they are less strong than in the outer face, the carinæ are sharp, the intervening space presenting a slight and regularly concave channel when they are crowded, in the principal cone they are terminated before reaching the lateral edges in front, and the same is true of the posterior face—the lateral costæ being shortest and soonest becoming obsolete Large individuals exceed an inch in greatest lateral diameter of base and one fourth to one third greater than the entire hight of the tooth

The score and a half or more of individuals to which I have had access, through the kindness of Mr WACHSMUTH, in drawing up the foregoing description of this interesting and beautiful species, present a range in size from teeth of .2 inch in lateral diameter to those measuring nearly one inch in the same direction; and otherwise exhibiting considerable diversity in the details, especially the superficial ornamentation. These latter may be best represented in the illustrations which have been introduced.

*Position and locality*. Authentic examples of the species have thus far been observed only in the upper fish bed of the Kinderhook, at Burlington, Iowa, where Mr WACHSMUTH, to whom we have dedicated the species, has obtained a beautiful series of specimens.

## CLADODUS SUCCINCTUS, St. J and W

Pl 3, Fig 8-12

Associated with the last described teeth, *C Wachsmuthi*, is a form almost as numerously represented, which seems to offer persistent peculiarities sufficient for its recognition under almost all circumstances. Very similar in form and size to *C. Wachsmuthi*, they may be chiefly distinguished from that form by the squat outline of the crown viewed in front, stouter median cone, which is marked by strong downward bifurcating costæ which extend nearly, sometimes quite, to the apex, and which are generally nearly equally strongly marked, though more numerous, in the posterior face, where they are rarely bifurcated, the outer basal line of the crown is generally occupied by strongly developed accessory processes, especially in the lateral portions, with, however, exceptions in the case of occasional small teeth in which they are absent, and here are found certain features which go far towards indicating the possible specific indentity of these teeth with the form last described, since the present examples present precisely the same basal characters as observed in *C. Wachsmuthi*, while the coronal costæ, excepting the accessory processes, may be found to differ only in the degree of their development In the normal examples, the outer face of the base is slightly inflected, instead of projecting outward, as is conspicuously the case almost always in the above mentioned form.

It is not improbable the form here noticed may prove to be merely a variety of *C Wachsmuthi*, but with the present material this is not clearly demonstrable, while on the contrary, its distinguishing peculiarities are readily recognizable on careful examination.

*Geological position and locality* Not uncommon in the upper fish bed of the Kinderhook division; Burlington, Iowa.

## CLADODUS ALTERNATUS, St J and W.

Pl 2, Fig 14-18

Teeth below medium size, symmetrical and very graceful in form. Base semi elliptical or trapezoidal in outline, thick, posterior margin broadly rounded in the median region, rapidly so or obliquely truncated laterally to the obtusely rounded lateral extremities, anterior border of moderate depth and slightly produced outward, nearly straight or gently depressed in the middle and rounded at the lateral extremities, and produced downward into a rather strong median ridge, which occupies half to two thirds of the lateral diameter of the base, well defined laterally and beveled to the inferior surface, inferior surface nearly plain or gently excavated, with a narrow beveled belt along the greater portion of the posterior margin; postero superior surface moderately convex, occupied nearly centrally by a sharply defined, linear prominence, in lateral extent nearly equal to half the diameter of the base. Coronal portion slightly constricted along the basal line in front, gently depressed at the base of the principal cone which latter is very strong, vertical to the horizontal plane of the base or slightly recurved sigmoidally, more or less laterally deflected, or erect, gently convex in front, strongly arched behind, lateral margin compressed, sharp and gradually converging to the acute apex; lateral denticles normally four on either extremity, alternately arranged in pairs, sometimes with delicate rudimentary denticles appearing in the angles of the persistent ones, exterior pair more or less divergent and recurved, similar in shape to the median cone, though less compressed in front; coronal surface ornamented with sharp, thread like, regularly arranged costæ, which, in the median cone seldom reach more than half the distance to the apex in front, with rather a wide plain space bordering the margin in which the lateral costæ become obsolete; in the lateral denticles the costæ are very similar but less numerous, and extend nearly to the apices, in the posterior face they are equally regular in disposition, but more numerous and delicate A specimen of ordinary size measures in greatest diameter of base .28 inch, antero posterior diameter .13, greatest hight of tooth .32, a smaller tooth of greater lateral diameter is .18 inch in lateral diameter, lesser diameter .08, hight about .15 inch

This beautiful little form is represented by a fine series of specimens in the collections of Messrs WACHSMUTH and SPRINGER, which exhibit remarkable persistency in the distinctive characteristics, and which, in well preserved specimens, readily enable their determination. The form is most intimately allied to *C Springeri*, with which it is associated; but, as has been shown in connection with the observation on that form, the present are not to be confounded with the minute and worn examples of the above form which they most resemble in outline, but from which they are distinguished by the greater lateral extent of the anterior basal ridge, the shallow mesial depression, the finer and more regular costation, and absence of accessory spinose processes along the anterior basal border of the crown

*Position and locality* The earlier and most numerous acquisitions of Mr SPRINGER are from the lower fish bed of the Kinderhook, but Mr. WACHSMUTH has obtained a few specimens from the upper fish bed of the same formation, which are undistinguishable from the earlier teeth; Burlington, Iowa.

CLADODUS INTERCOSTATUS, St J. and W.

Pl I, Fig 11

Teeth of small or medium size Base subelliptical in outline, moderately thick, posterior margin broadly rounded, with obtuse angles, extremities more or less sharply rounded, anterior margin sinuose, with a broad mesial depression, slightly produced, anterior angles occupied by well defined protuberances, which are connected by a well marked basal ridge; inferior surface moderately excavated, beveled along the posterior margin, postero-superior surface moderately convex, surmounted near the posterior margin by a laterally elongated, narrow, roughened prominence equal to about half the lateral diameter of the base, both superior and inferior surfaces irregularly pitted Crown gently constricted in front, obscurely defined behind, median cone symmetrical rapidly tapering to an acute point, gently recurved, sublenticular in transverse section with trenchant edges, broadly arched behind, in front compressed and towards the base slightly excavated, both faces occupied by strong, sharp costæ, those in the posterior face perceptibly finer and terminating in the lateral margins, in front a strong ridge extends from base to apex parallel with and separated from either border by a rather wide slight depression, the intermediate space being occupied by equally strong bifurcated and implanted costæ; lateral denticles two on either extremity, the exterior pair as strong again as the intermediate denticles, strongly deflected laterally or divergent, and recurved at an angle greater than the median cone, subcircular in section with sharp cutting edges, inner pair slightly produced in front, similar in section and ornamentation to the larger denticles, a few strong vertical costæ occurring in either face and occupying the low intermediate coronal ridge A specimen of medium size measures in greatest lateral diameter of base 36 inch, antero posterior diameter 12, greatest hight of teeth 29 inch.

The above description applies to a form not numerously represented in our collections, and with regard to the affinities of which with other teeth associated with them, there is matter of some doubt. All the individuals which have been identified with the above form are small, and some of these show indications of a third rudimentary lateral denticle, while there are others which possess a fourth pair, but with precisely the same, or even relatively coarser coronal costæ With these also occur in considerable abundance a larger form, which is characterized by several lateral denticles, and along the outer coronal margin a greater or less development of spinose processes, while the costæ are relatively finer, though similarly disposed, and the base offers no essen tial feature different from that of the teeth described above. These large teeth are almost always much abraded, so that even so fine a series as that obtained by Mr. SPRINGER fails to afford a satisfactory solution of their specific relations Until recently they were regarded as probably referable to *C. deflexus*, N. and W ; but the explorations of Mr WACHSMUTH have brought to light in the lower Burlington fish-beds a form which is unquestionably identical with the latter form—the exact stratigraphic position of the originals of which was not known. However, a comparison of them with the specimens discovered by Mr. WACHSMUTH affords almost conclusive proof that they were derived from the same horizon Their distinguishing characteristics, as compared with the teeth above referred to from the upper Burlington horizon, consists in the relatively stronger lateral denticles, the laterally deflected principal cone, and the exceedingly delicate and crowded striation, possibly, also, the narrower postero anterior diameter of the base and the less prominent anterior basal angles and protuberances.

In the absence of material in a perfect state of preservation, it is impossible to determine the nature of the variations noticed above; and however impressed we are with their probable specific identity, the material does not, as is the case with some of the Kinderhook forms, exhibit all the phases of gradation which alone can furnish indubitable evidence of such identity Considering only the first described individuals, one cannot fail to appreciate certain intimate resemblances to *C zygopus*, N. and W. of the Chester; but taking into account the *ensemble* presented by the teeth noticed above, there is little difficulty in drawing the distinctive features of the species We regret that our means have not made it possible to present as fair a representation of these teeth as of some of the other forms of this remarkable group.

The Keokuk limestone has furnished a few fragmentory specimens representative of a closely allied form, if not specifically identical with that first described above; but of the latter we have only a few individuals, and these are not sufficient for a critical comparison necessary to establish their relationship with the upper Burlington form. Closely agreeing in shape and size, they are distinguishable by the much coarser striation of the coronal cusps, there being not more than half the number of striæ usually observed in the present form. It is not improbable these teeth constitute the remains of a form distinct from the above, in which event we would suggest for them the specific designation *C Keokuk.*

*Position and locality* Not uncommon in the upper Burlington fish bed, Louisa and Des Moines counties, Iowa , Henderson, Warren and Adams counties. Illinois The Keokuk specimens are known to occur at Hamilton, Illinois, Keokuk and Bentonsport, Iowa.

### CLADODUS GOMPHOIDES, St. J. and W.

Pl 4, Fig 12-16

Teeth robust, low in stature, of medium or large size Base slightly sinuate in front, antero inferior angles moderately prominent, and thence broadly rounded to the lateral extremities, which are also rounded or obtusely angular, and broadly rounded behind, basal ridge well defined at the antero inferior angles, depressed in the middle and merging into the margin laterally; inferior surface moderately excavated, defined behind by a rather broad beveled belt parallel with the posterior margin, postero superior surface slightly convex, with a more or less distinct continuous or sometimes interrupted and roughened basal ridge occupying the posterior half of the surface and extending about three-fourths the lateral diameter, and rather abruptly beveled to the posterior margin Coronal cusps very strong, proportionately low, thick, rapidly tapering to the obtusely pointed apices, sublenticular in transverse section, both faces presenting rather strong, sharp costæ which increase mainly by implantation or rarely bifurcating, and slightly more numerous and crowded behind, median cone very strong, turgid, rarely faintly depressed at base in front, and generally flanked by two pairs of lateral denticles, of which the inner pair is sometimes rudimentary or obsolete, in other examples they are strongly developed, the exterior pair slightly deflected laterally and recurved: constricted along basal line in front, also well defined from base behind

The form here noticed is represented by a few specimens, among which there are only three or four perfect teeth Although individually varying to some extent, their specific identity is quite apparent, and at the same time they seem to be readily distinguishable from other forms associated in the same deposits. However, in the case of *C. bellifer*, a form which we have indicated from a few large teeth derived from the same locality, the chief distinctive features in contrast with the present form consists in the more flattened anterior coronal faces and the more strongly anteriorly produced position of the smaller or intermediate pair of lateral denticles. A large suite of specimens might indeed present a series of individuals which would connect the extremes here indicated by supplying the intermediate and at present missing gradations, without which opinion one way or other is mere conjecture.

*Geological position and locality* · In the fish-bed of the upper Burlington limestone, Buffington creek, Louisa county, Iowa.

### CLADODUS BELLIFER, St J and W.

Pl 4, Fig 10

The teeth attain large size. Outline of base subelliptical, extremities rounded, posterior margin broadly rounded, anterior border of moderate depth, slightly inbeveled, gently concave in the middle, rather abruptly rounded laterally, median ridge occupying half or more of the lateral diameter, moderately prominent as are also the anterior basal angles, inferior surface gently concave, with broad beveled belts along the posterior margin, postero superior surface occupied by a prominent, narrow ridge which extends over two-thirds the lateral diameter, abruptly defined behind and parallel with the posterior border Crown slightly constricted basally in front, median cone strong, gradually tapering, moderately recurved or nearly vertical to the horizontal plane of base, sublenticular in transverse section with sharp lateral edges, much compressed below in front, gently convex above, strongly so behind, apex sharp or obtusely truncated from wear, lateral denticles two on either extremity, moderately strong, exterior pair slightly divergent, recurved in the same plane as the median cone and similar in shape, inner pair prominently produced in front and generally much abraded, coronal surfaces without trace of ornamentation, presenting a smooth appearance, as from wear. A remarkably fine large specimen in the collection of Mr SPRINGER measures in greatest diameter of base 1 4 inches, antero posterior diameter 62, greatest hight of tooth 1 20 inches

The collection of Mr. SPRINGER contains a few examples of the form above described, which show considerable variation in size, and always the appearance of wear, but well characterized by the advanced position of the inner pair of lateral denticles. In the latter respect it resembles *C. occidentalis*, Leidy, of the Coal Measures, although otherwise not intimately related to that form, as indicated by the continuity of the anterior basal ridge and the prominence in the postero-superior surface. The worn condition of the specimens renders it doubtful whether the coronal surfaces were plain or their costæ obliterated by abrasion

*Position and locality* Upper Burlington fish bed, Louisa county, and Burlington, Iowa

### CLADODUS PRÆNUNTIUS, St J. and W

Pl 4, Fig 17

We have provisionally recognized, in a unique example in the collection of Mr SPRINGER, the representation of a distinct form The tooth is of medium size, strong, symmetrical proportions. The base is very similar in general outline to that of *C. intercostatus* and *C. gomphoides* from the same horizon, agreeing with the latter in the vertically arched outline and produced lateral extremities, while the prominence of the protuberances in the anterior basal angles resemble the former form, but it differs from both of these forms in the central position of the ridge in the postero superior surface The crown consists of a strong, erect slightly recurved median cone, and a single pair of strong lateral denticles; median cone compressed in front, strongly arched behind, with sharp lateral angles, and gently excavated in the outer basal region; lateral cones less compressed or more regularly lenticular in transverse section, produced in front slightly in advance of the median cone, and slightly deflected laterally, in the intermediate angle a faint trace of a rudimentary denticle is observed; the coronal surfaces are smooth, polished, presenting evidences of wear, which may have obliterated all traces of costation except the most obscure vestiges of striæ in the anterior basal region of the principal cone Lateral diameter of base about .84 inch, antero posterior diameter .33, hight of tooth .72.

The tooth above noticed bears a strong resemblance to *C Van Hornei* of the St. Louis limestone, although it is distinguishable by its more delicate proportions, greater breadth between the anterior basal angles, and more erect lateral cones The contour of the base will readily serve to distinguish it from individuals of the *C. micropus* group, which possess but a single pair of lateral denticles; while the absence of the strong costation so characteristic of *C. intercostatus*, as also almost equally of *C. gomphoides*, render its identity with either of the latter forms questionable Yet we cannot overlook the fact, in view of the superb collections from this horizon, of the singular isolation of the individual here referred to, and which would lead us to seek specific identity with one or other of the above mentioned forms, rather than for evidence corroborating the interpretations based upon a unique and evidently imperfect specimen.

*Position and locality*. Upper Burlington fish bed; Louisa county, Iowa

### CLADODUS RARICOSTATUS, St. J. and W.

Pl 4, Fig 18

Tooth small Crown well defined from the base in front, and consisting of a strong, rapidly tapering, laterally deflected, recurved median cone, which is much compressed, sublenticular in transverse section, trenchant, with a triangular depression occupying the base in front, and form lateral denticles on either side, alternating in size, divergent and recurved in nearly the same plane as the median cone, which they resemble in form, though perhaps less compressed, the external pair about one fifth the hight of the median cone; the outer face of the principal cone is faintly ornamented by a few diverging thread like striæ which rise in the triangular depression, dispersed and becoming obsolete in the middle region of the cone—the lateral portions and denticles apparently quite smooth and polished The basal portion is not well exhibited, as also the posterior aspect of the crown, gently arched vertically, anterior border gently sinuose, apparently uninterrupted, slightly produced, anterior basal angles inconspicuous, and gently rounded into the slightly produced lateral extremities Greatest hight of tooth .36 inch, lateral diameter of base .45 inch

The unique example before us differs from its associates in the same horizon in the sparseness of the coronal striæ and the compressed condition of the principal cusp. In general outline it agrees intimately with the teeth which we have provisionally recognized under the name *C Keokuk* from the same horizon, of which rare form it may possibly prove to be a much abraded example. But the imperfect condition of the lateral portions of the original specimens of the latter form prevents a critical comparison, and in view of the very strong vertical ridges with which the principal cusp of that form is ornamented, the tangible differences seem sufficient to raise a doubt as to its specific identity with the present form

*Position and locality:* Upper fish-bed of the Keokuk limestone; Keokuk, Iowa

## CLADODUS ECCENTRICUS, ST J. and W.

Pl 4 Fig 4

There occurs in the St Louis limestone a form of which comparatively few representatives have been found up to the present time, and these, with one exception, are not in a sufficiently perfect state of preservation to answer the purpose of an exhaustive comparison with allied forms Of the latter Messrs NEWBERRY and WORTHEN have described a form from the Chester limestone, *C politus*, with which the present teeth bear the most intimate resemblance, if indeed they prove not to be specifically distinct. Perfect examples of *C. politus* are beautifully striated with thread like striæ, precisely in the same manner as in the present teeth, and which also recalls *C. Fulleri* of the Coal Measures But among the teeth under consideration, a single and elegantly preserved specimen, which was obtained by Prof WORTHEN at St. Louis, exhibits characters which, if they prove not to be abnormal, render its reference to the Chester form exceedingly improbable The tooth in question is distinguished by the somewhat eccentric proportions of the base, which is very produced laterally, deeply excavated interiorly, deeply arched inward between the quite prominent antero inferior angles, and broadly rounded into the more or less sharply rounded lateral extremities, the antero median ridge moderately prominent The median cone does not differ essentially from that of *C. politus*, being erect, gradually tapering, compressed in front and strongly rounded posteriorly, and ornamented with numerous closely arranged striæ, the lateral denticles, however, present the somewhat anomalous feature of possessing in one extremity a third relatively strong cone exterior to the larger lateral denticle, and which in lateral divergence and recurvation corresponds to the exterior denticle in the opposite extremity; the lateral cones are nearly circular in section, but ornamented in the same manner as observed in the great cone The hight of the specimen particularly described above, and which represents about the largest size attained by the other teeth, is about 40 inch, lateral diameter of base 42 inch

It is possible that the tooth noticed above may prove to be distinct from those with which it is associated, but we are inclined to regard it as an abnormally developed tooth, or perhaps it represents a peculiarity in the teeth from a particular part of the jaws.

Mr. VAN HORNE has also obtained from the Warsaw beds a very similar form of teeth, but in the imperfect state of preservation which without exception prevails in the few specimens thus far known from that horizon, it is quite impossible to more than recognize their general resemblance to the section of the genus represented by the above mentioned forms

*Position and locality* Upper beds of the St Louis limestone, Alton, Illinois, St. Louis, Missouri.

### CLADODUS VAN HORNEI, St. J. and W.

Pl 4, Fig 5

Teeth of large size, robust Base irregularly elliptical, massive, moderately arched, inferior surface deeply excavated, beveled belt narrow, posterior margin thick, angularly rounded, extremities strongly produced and sharply rounded, anterior border deep, produced, sinuose, anterior basal angles prominent, and occupied by obtuse protuberances, gently rounded into the extremities, and separated by a rather wide depression, which extends up into the median cone, postero superior surface occupied by a strong lateral prominence in extent equal to half the diameter of the base, and abruptly defined behind, surface coarsely roughened Crown distinctly constricted at base in front, obscurely defined behind, median cone very robust, rapidly tapering to an acute apex, laterally deflected, rather strongly recurved, gently arched in front, strongly convex posteriorly, with compressed, sharp cutting edges; lateral denticles one on either side, relatively strong, divergent, similar in form and recurvation to the principal cone, with which they are connected by a low, sharp coronal crest; the anterior face is marked with a few short, sharp-crested, widely spaced costæ, which are apparently confined to the basal region, the greater extent of the cusps being smooth, and beautifully polished, as also the posterior face, with the exception of a faint carina in the angle between the cones, and which may terminate in a delicate rudimentary denticle A medium sized specimen measures 1.25 inches in lateral diameter of base, and about equal to the greatest hight of the tooth, antero-posterior diameter .45 to .50, hight of median cone 1 inch, hight of lateral denticles about .55 inch

The recognition of the present form is based upon a few specimens discovered by Mr. VAN HORNE, one of which presents a nearly perfect tooth of medium size. Another consists of the base of a remarkably large individual, measuring in greatest diameter 1.80 inches, postero anterior diameter .75, and agreeing intimately with the lesser specimen in form and contour. Others exhibit worn and fragmentary examples of smaller teeth The peculiarities possessed by these teeth readily distinguish them from other forms of the genus, and, with the exception of a single specimen in the collection of Mr. SPRINGER from the upper Burlington limestone, which has been provisionally referred to a distinct species, under the name of *C prænuntius*, it has no intimate ally. It is one of the largest and most interesting species as yet made known, and must have belonged to fishes of truly formidable size, and we have a commensurate pleasure in dedicating the species to its discoverer

*Position and locality* Rare in the upper beds of the St. Louis limestone; Alton, Illinois.

## CLADODUS EUGLYPHEUS, St. J. and W.

Pl IV, Fig 1 3

Teeth minute, or attaining a size below the medium Base defined in front by a broad, moderately deep sinuation, extending between the angles produced by the antero inferior bosses, thence retreating to the lateral extremities, which are produced and sharply rounded to the broadly curved posterior margin, moderately excavated below, a faint marginal rim between the antero inferior bosses, and faintly beveled behind, postero superior surface gently arched and occupied by a pair of rather prominent protuberances or bosses, which are separated by a narrow intervening channel, and defined from the crown by a broader, shallow depression; surface roughened by irregular sulci and minute pits Crown defined from base in front by a distinct channel, median cone more or less deeply excavated at base in front. more or less irregularly tapering to the apex, more compressed in front than behind, with sharp cutting edges, lateral costæ ascending to the apex in front, limiting a rather broad furrow extending along the lateral margin, intermediate space occupied by a few strong, sharp costæ, which coalesce with the lateral ridges at more or less irregular intervals, posterior face marked by a few simple costæ somewhat more slender than those in front, and successively disappearing in the lateral margins ascending, lateral denticles normally four on either extremity, the exterior pair long, but proportionately more slender than the median cone, more or less divergent and recurved, with sharp cutting edges, and bearing in front two to four costæ, which are sometimes bifurcated descending, intermediate denticles alternating in size, the middle pair about half the size of the exterior pair, their bases being continued in a marked prominence into the antero inferior bosses of the base, ornamented with one or two sharp costæ, and flanked on either side by a smaller delicate denticle, which usually bears a single sharp ridge in front

The description is based upon minute teeth not uncommon in the St. Louis limestone at Alton and St. Louis, and which present considerable individual variation from the normal condition noticed above In some specimens there are only three lateral denticles on one side, and the disposition of the coronal costæ also presents less or more slight divergence from that stated above, as shown in the figures of the two minute teeth from the above mentioned localities. From the same formation at Pella, Iowa, we have examples of apparently the same form, but which attain nearly twice the size of the largest specimens yet observed at the more southern localities, and which are otherwise distinguishable by the absence, or rudimentary condition, of the smaller pairs of lateral denticles, possibly the result of attrition or wear, and the apparent though not relatively more numerous coronal costæ in front.

This form, at first glance, appears to be closely allied to *C. zygopus*, N. and W, of the Chester formation, it is, however, readily distinguishable from that form by the greater number of lateral denticles and sparser coronal costæ, as well as its generally smaller size In the number and irregular development of the lateral denticles only does it bear intimate comparison with *C intercostatus*, of the Upper Burlington limestone.

*Geological position and localities*: Not uncommon in the upper beds of the St Louis limestone, Alton, Illinois, and St. Louis, Missouri, a few specimens have been obtained from the calcareous shales in the same formation near Pella, Iowa.

### CLADODUS FULLERI, St. J. and W.

Pl. IV, Fig. 9.

Mr. L. A. FULLER has discovered in the shale in connection with coal No. 3? at Bloomington, Illinois, a remarkable specimen which exhibits no less than the entire jaws of a fish whose dentition proclaims its affinities with the genus *Cladodus*. The cartilages of the jaws, though somewhat crushed and flattened, are quite distinct in their general outline, and would at first glance be pronounced as those belonging to a *Plagiostome*, in general shape bearing a striking resemblance to the jaws of the *Squali*, as illustrated in the genus *Odontaspis* of the existing seas. The rami of the lower jaw are characterized by their great depth in the region posterior to the middle, and apparently broadly rounded to the articular extremity; the rami of the upper jaws are somewhat crowded forward, vertically narrower and more produced in front. The rami of both the upper and lower jaws appear to have been somewhat thickened in the dentigerous region, and very thin in the opposite borders, with indications of the longitudinal folds, the anterior protuberances and the posterior shallow excavations, while the structure is unmistakably that of semiosseous cartilage, in all which particulars it closely agrees with the jaw cartilages of the more modern order of *Selachians*. The greatest length of the jaw is about 11 inches, greatest vertical depth of the rami of the lower jaw 2.5 inches, that of the upper rami probably less than 2 inches.

The teeth are evidently displaced, as appears from the very irregular arrangement, or, indeed, apparent want of order in their present disposition, being collected in a disordered group between the anterior extremities and extending backward three fourths the distance to the articular extremities. So far as it is possible to determine, there would seem to be less diversity in form than occurs in *Odontaspis*, the arrangement being the same, or apparently in serial rows from within outward. The largest individuals exposed are considerably less than half an inch in hight, and about the same in lateral extent of base. Individually, the teeth are symmetrical in shape, base strong, gently sinuous in front, broadly rounded posteriorly, the inferior surface moderately excavated; the anterior marginal border relatively narrow, broadly arched inward between the antero lateral shoulders, which are moderately produced and between which the border is very gently arched downward; the postero superior surface of the base is unknown. The crown consists of a strong, moderately tapering, trenchant median cusp, which is compressed or gently arched in front and slightly excavated towards the base, broadly rounded behind, with a slight sigmoidal curvature from base to apex, and ornamented in either face with exceedingly delicate thread-like striæ, which are more numerous and crowded in the basal region in front, but sparser and somewhat irregularly implanted above, and extending two-thirds or three-fourths the distance to the acute apex, with a rather wide plain space parallel with either edge and reaching half way towards the base, upon either extremity there are apparently but two lateral denticles, of which the exterior pair are relatively strong, subcircular in section, or less compressed than the median cone, very slightly deflected laterally, more strongly recurved than the median cusp, and similarly finely striated, the inner pair of denticles are less than half the size of the outer ones, similar in shape and slightly advanced in the basal border above the antero inferior angles A large-sized tooth measures in hight .30 inch, hight of outer denticles .12, lateral diameter of base .34, antero posterior diameter about .12. The smaller teeth distinguishable are, perhaps, half the dimensions of that above measured

The preservation of the specimen under consideration is such as not to afford a distinct knowledge of all the details—the shale in which the specimen is imbedded so closely adhering as to necessitate the most careful and laborious manipulation in developing the specimen, which, we regret, we have not had the opportunity to perform. But the general features as exhibited by the teeth, may be satisfactorily ascertained and these would appear to indicate less individual variableness than obtains in some species which have been determined from isolated teeth Minute speck-like bodies are associated with the mass, which possibly represent portions of the shagreen, since they present a much more uneven or papilious surface than observed in the surface of the cartilage itself

We have long had in our possession a little tooth from the Middle Coal Measures of Iowa, which we have come to regard after careful comparison as identical with the above described teeth, with the smallest of which it agrees in size. The basal region in front, however, is more strongly arched downward in the middle and relatively deeper; but the coronal cusps in number and ornamentation apparently present no marked feature by which it is distinguishable from the typical examples associated upon the jaws described above

It is our intention eventually to give this interesting specimen a more careful study than it is possible at the present time to bestow upon it And, in connection with some fragmentary jaws discovered by Prof. WORTHEN in the St. Louis formation, which we believe to be the first veritable examples of their kind found in American Carboniferous deposits, if not indeed elsewhere, we hope to obtain more definite knowledge of their systematic relations in the great class of which they are among the earliest representatives

It gives us much pleasure to associate the name of Mr. FULLER with the above described species

The full complement of plates having been made up prior to the reception of the remarkable specimen discovered by Mr FULLER, its full illustration has unavoidably been deferred. That of the Iowa specimen, however, with the description, will enable the recognition of other individuals that may hereafter be found

*Position and locality* Carbonaceous shale overlying coal No 3 ? at Bloomington, Illinois, and in the lower portion of the middle Coal Measure, Dallas county, Iowa

## CLADODUS PANDATUS, St J and W.

Pl IV. Fig 9

We here refer to a unique example of a minute form in the Coal Measures, which in general outline and size closely resembles *C Fulleri* of the same horizon, from which, however, it is readily distinguishable by the presence of more numerous lateral denticles The base is markedly sinuous in front, relatively deep, moderately arched downward and inbeveled, produced downward into a strong continuous marginal border between the quite prominent antero inferior angles, broadly rounded at the extremities and posteriorly, inferior surface rather deeply excavated, postero superior surface moderately convex, with an ill-defined basal pad, which apparently stretches across the greater diameter and about midway between the base of the crown and the posterior margin The median cone is proportionately strong, gradually tapering, very slightly curved sigmoidally, and produced obliquely outward beyond the line vertical to the horizontal plane of the base, compressed in front, broadly rounded behind, with delicate cutting edges, the lateral wings are occupied by an irregularly alternating series of three or four pairs of relatively small denticles, with indications of accessory denticles in front and flanking the large exterior cones, which latter are moderately deflected laterally and recurved, the inner ones more erect, and similarly ornamented as the median cone, which latter is marked by numerous closely arranged thread like striæ. Greatest hight of tooth about .19 inch, lateral diameter of base 21

The form described is further distinguishable from *C carinatus* by the less regular disposition of lateral denticles and the more numerous and delicate striation The specimen is somewhat worn, but the general characters are well exhibited, and in the light thrown upon the extent of variableness of individual teeth by the remarkable jaw discovered by Mr FULLER, there would appear to be no doubt as to its specific distinctness from *C Fulleri* The form apparently belongs to the section represented by *C. Springeri*, of the earliest member of the Lower Carboniferous

*Position and locality* Limestone above coal No 9, at Carlinville, Illinois.

### Cladodus carinatus, St. J. and W.

Pl IV, Fig 6 7

Teeth very small, lateral diameter about equal to the greatest hight, generally robust. Base relatively massive, sub elliptical in outline, gently arched vertically, broadly and regularly rounded behind, rather deeply sinuate in front and abruptly rounded into the more or less acutely rounded extremities, anterior basal angles occupied by prominent anteriorly produced protuberances which are connected by a low marginal ridge, inferior surface moderately excavated, pitted, postero superior surface unknown. Crown more or less produced and constricted basally in front, and deeply excavated in the median region median cone strong, sub circular or sub lenticular in transverse section with delicate cutting edges, rapidly tapering to an acute point, erect or laterally deflected and nearly vertical to the horizontal plane of the base, lateral denticles normally four on either side, alternating in size, the exterior pair relatively very large, more or less strongly divergent and recurved, in form similar to the principal cusp; the anterior face of the median cone is marked with sharp crested, more or less regular and crowded costæ, which appear stronger in the lateral denticles and less crowded, and obsolete in the swollen basal region, ornamentation of posterior face not known. A medium sized tooth measures 17 inch in lateral diameter of base, hight .15 inch.

Only two authentic examples of the present form have come to our notice—one obtained by Mr FULLER, from the horizon of coal No 5, and the other from bed No 30 of the general section of the Middle Coal Measures of Iowa. Both specimens being derived from nearly the same stratigraphic position at localities distant from each other, much interest attaches to their discovery on account of the evidence they furnish relative to the value of these remains in the identification of strata associated with particular coal horizons at remote localities.

The Iowa specimen is still smaller than that measured, and presents an interesting feature of individual variation. The median cone is eccentric, or to one side of the median line, and the short extremity exhibits only two long, slender denticles, while the opposite end possesses the full complement in its armature Otherwise, in the form, disposition and ornamentation of the coronal cusps, as also the basal region, the characters possessed in common indicate the most intimate relationship between the two specimens Compared with other forms, perhaps this bears the strongest resemblance to *C euglypheus* of the St. Louis Limestone, it is, however, distinguished from that form by the finer striation and greater depth of the anterior basal region.

*Position and locality* · Carbonaceous shale accompanying coal No 5, at Girard, Ill., and bed No 30 of the middle Coal Measures, Guthrie Co , Iowa.

## GENUS LAMBDODUS, St J. and W.

Teeth small, base posteriorly produced, more or less laterally expanded, long elliptical or sub circular in outline, broadest behind the cornua, slightly produced in front, gently concave, or sometimes convex below, superior surface convex A single strong, slightly sigmoidally curved, recurved, eccentric cornua arises from the anterior angle of the base, terminating in a sharp apex, compressed in front, broadly rounded behind, with more or less distinct cutting edges and irregular vertical costæ.

The teeth recognized under the above generic term were at first supposed to pertain to some part of the dental economy of *Cladodus* The accession of material, mainly through the efforts of Mr. SPRINGER, affording a more complete knowledge of the individual characteristics of the teeth of the two most abundantly represented forms, has resulted in the development of no further intimacy with the above genus, while it has conclusively proved the persistency of the characteristics which distinguish them from *Cladodus*, and lead to the recognition of their generic distinctness It is distinguished from *Cladodus* by the single coronal cornua, the absence of lateral denticles The basal portion bears some resemblance to *Thrinacodus*, but the coronal features are entirely dissimilar The genus is, so far as at present known, restricted to the Lower Carboniferous formations, occurring in considerable abundance in the upper Burlington and Keokuk limestones, and extending upwards in the St Louis and Chester formation.

### LAMBDODUS COSTATUS, St J and W.

Pl V, Fig 3

Teeth of small size. Base laterally oval or sub-circular in outline comparatively thin, inferior surface slightly concave, anterior border moderately produced and slightly thickened Coronal cusp strong, gradually tapering to the acute apex, slightly deflected laterally and sigmoidally curved backward, slightly compressed laterally, ovate section, with sharp cutting edges well defined towards the apex, but generally obsolete below; anterior face occupied by six to ten strong sharp crested costæ, which increase by implantation, becoming obsolete towards the apex where the exterior pair merge into the lateral margins, producing the sharp cutting angles, strongest in the middle, and towards the base of the cone often swelling into strong plicæ, which give off subordinate carinæ by bifurcation, posterior face apparently destitute of striæ or costation A perfect, medium sized tooth will measure in greatest antero posterior diameter of base .26 inch, lateral diameter .31, thickness 10, hight of cone 32, greatest diameter at base about .12 inch.

The form here described was first brought to our notice by Mr. SPRINGER, and subsequently fine suites of specimens have been obtained at the localities in the environs of Burlington They usually occur as strong cusps without the base, which has been worn or broken away. But even in this condition they may be readily identified, the strong costation of the outer face serving to distinguish them from similarly preserved specimens of the forms with which they are associated, *L. calceolus*. As in the case of the latter form, there occurs in the Keokuk limestone a very similar form of teeth, but our material from that horizon is insufficient more than to establish the fact of the close relationship existing between them and the Upper Burlington teeth A large suite of specimens may disclose differences by which they may be distinguished from each other, such as we have pointed out in connection with the above mentioned form.

*Position and locality* In the fish bed horizon of the Upper Burlington limestone, Louisa and DesMoines counties, Iowa, and localities in Henderson and Warren counties, Illinois. The localities in the Keokuk limestone are in the vicinity of Warsaw, Ill, Boonville. Mo, where Dr WILLIAMS has obtained specimens of the Keokuk teeth; Bentonsport, Iowa

## LAMBDODUS CALCEOLUS, ST. J. and W

Pl V, Fig 5

Teeth small Base moderately thick, elliptical in outline, narrow, greatest expansion posterior to the coronal cusp, in front slightly produced, narrower than behind and rounded, posterior extremity usually obliquely rounded or truncated The coronal cusp rises from the anterior extremity of the base, in a strong, rapidly tapering, conical, slightly twisted cone, which bulges outward, recurved and more or less deflected from a vertical line, in hight probably two thirds the antero posterior diameter of the base; the transverse section of the cone is elliptical or sub oval, the long axis being in the same direction as that of the base, lateral angles sharp, though generally obsolete from wear, outer face marked by rather fine, irregularly disposed sharp crested carinæ, inner face apparently smooth, the enamel like layer terminating inferiorly in a faintly defined border A specimen of ordinary size measures in greatest diameter of base 45 inch, lateral diameter 24, depth 15, hight of cone about 30, greatest diameter at base 14, lateral diameter 11 inch.

The teeth of this form present considerable individual variation, which appears to be mainly attributable to wear We have a few specimens from the Keokuk limestone, which are very intimately allied to the form especially referred to above, to which we have provisionally referred them, as a variety, under the designation *L robustus* The latter teeth are uniformly more robust, and, although the base has the same outline viewed from above, it is deeper and sometimes strongly angular or heeled in the inferior surface, instead of being plane, as almost always occurs in the Upper Burlington teeth, the anterior extremity of the base is also more prominently produced, while the form of the cone, which in the few examples examined is worn smooth, is in no marked degree unlike that of the form described. The differences between these forms are strikingly similar, in degree, to those which distinguish the teeth of *Cladodus micropus*, N. and W, in the same horizons; and it is not, perhaps, unreasonable to look for a greater intimacy in the relationship of these two groups, than the data possessed at this moment would seem to justify

*Position and locality*—Not uncommon in the fish-bed of the Upper Burlington, Louisa and DesMoines counties, Iowa, and localities in the same horizon in Illinois The Keokuk form occurs at Warsaw, Illinois, Keokuk and Bentonsport, Iowa, and Lagrange, Missouri.

### LAMBDODUS TRANSVERSUS, ST J and W

Pl V, Fig 4

A single specimen of a minute tooth from the St. Louis limestone, apparently referable to the above genus, is distinguished by its relatively great lateral diameter of base, which is two and a half times greater than its antero posterior diameter, comparatively thick, laterally oval in outline, anterior border nearly equally produced with the posterior margin, and beveled to a thin edge, coarsely roughened The coronal cusp is very strong, rapidly tapered, moderately recurved, antero posteriorly compressed, lenticular in transverse section, lateral angles acutely rounded, surface smooth. Hight of tooth 07 inch, cone nearly central lateral diameter of base .15, antero-posterior diameter .06 inch

The present form appears to be most nearly allied to *L. costatus* of the Upper Burlington limestone, from which it is distinguishable by its greater lateral diameter of base and more compressed and centrally situated coronal cusp. The unique example described belongs to Mr. VAN HORNE'S collection.

*Position and locality*: Upper beds of the St. Louis limestone, Alton, Illinois.

### LAMBDODUS HAMULUS, St. J. and W.

Pl V, Fig 26

Teeth small. Base strong, thick, laterally compressed, posteriorly produced and truncated or rounded, inferior surface nearly plane or slightly arched laterally and nearly straight from front backwards, contracted anteriorly where it terminates in an obtuse marginal prominence or border, which distinctly defines the base from the crown, postero superior surface moderately convex laterally, with a more or less well defined mesial ridge extending from the base of the cone to the posterior border, both surfaces more or less roughened and longitudinally striated. Coronal cusp strong, gradually tapering, prominently produced in front, recurved, laterally compressed, thickest in front, presenting an ovate transverse section, apparently smooth. Hight of tooth about .18 inch, antero posterior diameter of base .25, lateral diameter .16, vertical depth of base in middle .09, greatest diameter of cone at base .10, lateral diameter .08, hight of cone .15 inch.

The above form is clearly related to *L. calceolus* var. *robustus*, of the Keokuk limestone; indeed so intimate is the resemblance, that, were the present tooth obtained from the same horizon, one would scarcely hesitate, in the absence of means for more critical comparison, to refer it to that form. But, occurring in a position several hundred feet above that in which the above mentioned form is found, in a division which is otherwise quite distinct from the Keokuk beds, there are also certain peculiarities presented by the form here described, which, should they be found to be persistent, must establish its distinct specific character. The most striking of these apparently distinctive characteristics are, the more prominent forward projection of the cone, and the reversed position of the ovate transverse section, which in the Keokuk form is narrowest in front, and its base less symmetrical.

*Position and locality*: Rare in the lower fish bed of the Chester limestone, Chester, Illinois.

### LAMBDODUS REFLEXUS, St J and W.

Pl V, Fig 25

Teeth of small size. Base broad, apparently rectangular, laterally and posteriorly expanded, considerably produced in front beyond the base of the corona and broadly rounded, margin thin, interior surface slightly concave, both surfaces irregularly striated or roughened Coronal cusps strongly recurved, slightly twisted, gradually tapering to an acute point, laterally compressed, ovate in transverse section with the broad margin anterior, apparently smooth and polished Elevation of tooth about .27 inch, lateral diameter of base about .30

The single example of the above form at present known, unfortunately, does not preserve the entire outline of the base, especially the posterior border, although in other respects it is quite perfect, permitting satisfactory comparison with other allied forms Of the latter *L costatus*, from the Upper Burlington limestone, bears the most intimate resemblance to the form under consideration, which, however, is distinguished from that species by its thinner base, which is more prominently produced along the front border, and the more strongly recurved cone. With *L transversus*, from the St. Louis limestone, it agrees in the central position of the coronal cusp, but differs in a marked degree in other particulars, as its more slender or much higher cusp, which latter is laterally instead of antero posteriorly flattened, as in that form. The apparent smooth surface of the cone may be due to attrition. but there is no evidence of costation or other superficial ornamentation

*Position and locality* Upper fish bed of the Chester limestone ; Chester, Illinois.

## GENUS HYBOCLADODUS, St J. and W.

The collection from the Upper Burlington and Keokuk formations afford a few examples of a group of teeth, which presents certain peculiar combinations of external features not hitherto observed in the dental remains of the *Hybodonts* of the Lower Carboniferous epochs. They consist of strongly cuspidate teeth, with a broad, posteriorly expanded base, in which last respect they exhibit an unmistakable affinity to *Cladodus*, but differing so widely in other and no less important particulars, as to leave little doubt as to their distinct generic character

Teeth attain medium size. Base elliptical in outline, vertically arched between the extremities, which are more or less sharply rounded, anterior face nearly straight, curved laterally, terminating below in a well defined marginal border or ridge, posterior margin broadly rounded, inferior surface excavated immediately behind the marginal border, with a beveled space extending along the posterior margin, superior surface more or less convex and beveled to the posterior edge. Crown well defined from the base, constricted in front and laterally, forming a sub acute crest, gradually increasing in prominence from the extremities towards the middle, culminating in a more or less prominent antero-posteriorly compressed median cone; both coronal surfaces are marked with more or less regular, vertically or radiatingly disposed plicæ or ridges, the apical terminations of which produce a delicate, sometimes strong, denticulation in the crest, crown enameled

In the group of teeth here designated, the crown bears a strong resemblance to that of *Hybodus* (especially *H plicatilis*, Agassiz, of the European *Muschelkalk*), and also *Mascalodus*, while its affinities with *Orodus* are, perhaps, less striking. Indeed this peculiar group apparently presents a *Hybodus* like crown planted upon a *Cladodus* base, or, in other words, a combination of characters which, separately considered, find their peculiar development in groups or genera pertaining to remotely separated geological epochs That it constitutes a type holding a position intermediate between *Hybodus* and *Cladodus*, combining in its external features characters which are peculiar to one or other of those genera, and thence forming, as it were, a connecting link between these geologically widely separated groups, seems to be most apparent.

In his great work on the Fossil Fishes of the Old Red Sandstone,* Professor AGASSIZ has described a form of teeth under the name *Cladodus simplex*, from the Devonian in the environs of St. Petersburg, which seems to exhibit precisely the same coronal features pertaining to the teeth under consideration. But, since its base is imperfect, important characters are wanting, without which its identity with the present genus cannot be determined I have also recently examined a specimen obtained by ROBERT DRINKWATER, from the Coal Measure shales near Manchester, England, which appears to be generically identical with the teeth designated above, though it differs in having the lateral portions of the crown occupied by a few very strong, conical tuberculations, the median cone relatively low, and ornamented by a few strong, sharp, bifurcated vertical costæ I have not been able to ascertain whether the form here indicated has been described

* Pois Foss du Vieux Grès rouge, p 124 Tab 33. figs 29, 30, 31

### HYBOCLADODUS PLICATILIS, St J and W

Pl V, Fig 9

Teeth of medium or small size, symmetrical in form Base elliptical in outline, gently arched vertically, lateral extremities neatly and regularly rounded, the postero superior surface beveled to the broadly expanded and rounded posterior margin, anterior face gently arched, or nearly straight, slightly recurved at the extremities, forming a well-defined marginal ridge projecting downward and slightly outward, moderately excavated below, and bordered posteriorly by a rather wide beveled belt, sometimes coarsely striated or punctate Crown occupying nearly the entire lateral diameter of the base, strongly constricted basally in front, moderately so behind, lateral extremities obtuse, crest sub acute, regularly rising into the prominent median cone, which is lenticular in transverse section with delicate cutting edges, more or less nearly vertical and slightly recurved; the anterior face is marked by rather strong vertical plicæ which originate in slight protuberances, sending off bifurcations above and below, those above producing a delicate denticulation in the lateral portions of the crest, but which are generally obsolete from abrasion, the plicæ in the median cone perceptibly finer than those in the lateral extremities, the vertical plications in the posterior face are very like those described, except that they may be less strong. A medium sized tooth is .36 inch in lateral diameter, hight .21, antero posterior diameter of base .12 inch.

The individuals of this beautiful form vary considerably in size, attaining twice the size of the specimen indicated in the above measurements. However rare perfect teeth are, fragments of the crown are not infrequent, and when these show any portion of the lateral extremities, or the anterior median region of the base, they are not likely to be confounded with *Cladodus*, which they somewhat resemble, as also *Orodus*, especially worn specimens

*Position and locality* Fish bed of the Upper Burlington limestone; Louisa county, Iowa.

### HYBOCLADODUS TENUICOSTATUS, St J and W.

Pl V, Fig 10

The collections from the Keokuk limestone afford a few imperfect specimens of strongly cuspidate teeth, which are apparently referable to the above genus, though specifically distinct from the last described form from the Upper Burlington None of the examples before us preserve the base entire, but the symmetrical, gracefully tapering median cone is well shown in all, and a specimen from Warsaw exhibits one extremity of the coronal portion nearly entire, also enough of the base remains to render its generic identity with the last noticed form almost certain

In general form the present form bears a close resemblance to *H. plicatilis*, being symmetrically proportioned and apparently of nearly the same dimensions The base appears to be somewhat narrower, its inner margin more attenuated and rather more strongly arched laterally than in the case of the former species The coronal crest is sharp along the lateral portions, and produced into a strong, regularly tapering median cusp, which is slightly compressed, with sharp lateral edges extending half way to the apex The basal portion of the crown is slightly excavated in front, and the lateral and median portions are ornamented with fine, angular, thread like vertical costæ, which become coarser near the extremities, obsolete in the upper half the median cone and more numerous and crowded in front than behind Lateral diameter of medium sized specimen about .15 inch, hight .38

Associated with the above teeth, there occurs a form which possesses peculiarities which seem to indicate a distinct species, which we have provisionally designated by the name *Hybocladodus intermedius*, on account of its relationship to *H. plicatilis* of the Upper Burlington Particularly is this relationship displayed in the wide base, the posterior expansion of which is even greater than in the latter form. The median cone approaches near that of *H tenuicostatus*, and, while the ornamentation of the crown is coarser than observed in the latter, the costæ are more regular and widely spaced than in the former species The two imperfect specimens representing the form here alluded to, show only enough to render doubtful their identity with either of the forms above mentioned, though not sufficient to enable a satisfactory elimination of their specific characters

*Position and locality* Fish bed horizon of the Keokuk limestone; vicinity of Warsaw, Illinois, Keokuk and Bentonsport, Iowa

## HYBOCLADODUS COMPRESSUS.

Pl V, Fig 8

*Helodus compressus* NEWBERRY and WORTHEN, 1866, Geol Ill II, p 78, Pl V, Fig 1, not *Helodus compressus* N and W, vol iv, p 360, Pl III, Fig 15

Teeth small Crown antero posteriorly compressed, and remarkable for the laterally deflected, stout, low, obtuse median cone; besides the crest is suddenly compressed to a thin edge, interrupted by faint serrations, and laterally produced at an acute angle beyond the base; the body of the outer face is occupied by short, nearly vertical plicæ, while that of the inner face is smooth in all our specimens, though in well-preserved individuals it will probably be found to be similarly ornamented The base presents all the characteristics of the above group of teeth, the anterior marginal ridge is well defined, nearly straight, and but slightly arched vertically, inferior surface moderately excavated, the posteriorly expanded portion projects sharply downward at a slight angle to the posterior crown face, broadly rounded along the inner margin. Lateral diameter of crown about .35 inch, or slightly exceeding that of the base, elevation of outer face of tooth .16, greatest thickness of crown at base .07, antero posterior diameter of base .10 inch

The original of the present form, although somewhat abraded in the coronal portion, and so imbedded as to expose only the outer aspect of the tooth, is readily identified with more perfect specimens since obtained from the same horizon at other localities, which latter teeth exhibit, apparently, unquestionable generic relationship with *Hybocladodus*, and dissimilar in all essential characters from *Helodus*, as evidenced by the peculiar form of the base and acuminate crest The compressed crown and laterally deflected median cone afford the widest contrast with the typical species *Hybo. plicatilis*, with which it is associated, but which more intimately ally it with *Hybo nitidus*, described from the Chester limestone, from which latter, however, it is distinguished by its more compressed crown, and, perhaps, greater regularity of the crest line, etc.

*Position and locality* Fish bed of the Upper Burlington limestone, Louisa county, and Augusta, Iowa

## HYBOCLADODUS NITIDUS, St. J. and W

Pl V. Fig 7

Teeth very small Outline of base elliptical, considerably expanded posteriorly in the same horizontal plane as the crown, and gently arched vertically, moderately excavated below, anterior marginal ridge strong and well defined from the crown, slightly produced outward. Crown strong, prominently distended in front, defined from the base behind by a slight angle, constricted at the extremities, crust obtusely angular, median prominence eccentric, strong, and laterally deflected, with a small obtuse secondary cone at either extremity, surfaces apparently destitute of ornamentation

This species is founded upon a single specimen, a nearly perfect tooth, which measures scarcely one tenth of an inch in lateral diameter, and is the sole representative of the genus thus far brought to our knowledge in the upper division of the Lower Carboniferous deposits Closely allied to *Hybo compressus* of the upper Burlington limestone, it is readily distinguished from that form by its more robust proportions, less compressed crown, and less obliquely produced posterior expansion of the base. The median cone presents the same lateral deflection, although it is relatively less prominent, and it is possible the present form may possess similar vertical rugæ as appear in the crown of the above form

*Position and locality* Chester limestone, Chester, Illinois.

## GENUS THRINACODUS, St. J and W.

Teeth of small size. Base posteriorly produced in a long, sometimes twisted, vertically flattened, or laterally compressed, clavate plate, longer than wide, anterior face narrow, and abruptly beveled from the basal line of the crown, posterior extremity more or less obtusely rounded, inferior surface narrow, plane or faintly excavated, superior surface gently convex, concave antero posteriorly, or corresponding to the curvature of the inferior surface From the antero superior extremity of the base spring three more or less relatively stout, nearly equal, trenchant, acutely pointed, recurved cusps, the exterior pair divergent, the central one more or less vertical, slightly sigmoidally curved, transverse section sublenticular, compressed in front, rounded behind, with simple cutting edges, and more or less strongly costate in either face

The generic peculiarities of the teeth here referred to, as contrasted with *Diplodus*, Agass, with which they are most intimately allied, consists in the relative more slender base, which lacks both the antero inferior protuberance and the postero superior pad like prominence characteristic of the above genus The coronal cusps are also nearly equal in size, the cutting edges are destitute of crenulations, and their anterior and posterior faces more or less strongly ridged vertically. The form of the trident-like cusps are very like that of *Cladodus*, being slightly constricted basally in front and faintly defined from the base behind

As here defined, the genus includes the forms originally described by Messrs NEWBERRY and WORTHEN, under the name *Diplodus incurvus* and *D duplicatus*, of the Keokuk limestone, which seem to be undistinguishable from a form not uncommon in the upper Burlington limestone.

### THRINACODUS NANUS, St. J and W.

Pl V, Fig 1 2

Teeth minute. Base thick, moderately produced posteriorly, or apparently sub elliptical in outline, constricted or rounded below, and faintly excavated; coronal cusps nearly equal in size, terminating in a sharp point, with sharp lateral edges, lenticular in transverse section, more compressed in front than behind, the exterior pair diverging and recurved, central cone erect or laterally deflected, and ornamented with a very few sharp, irregularly disposed costæ in the outer faces Hight of medium size tooth 0.5 inch, and .07 inch between the tips of the exterior denticles.

The few individuals showing the crown entire present the appearances described above But the collections afford several imperfect teeth, apparently referable to the same species, which show the base considerably produced posteriorly, flattened and slightly twisted, precisely in the same manner as in the allied forms occurring in the succeeding Burlington and Keokuk divisions. In case of this identity, the laterally elliptical outline of the base, as described above, is probably due to mechanical abrasion.

These teeth are most intimately allied to the form which occurs in the Burlington limestone, *Thrinacodus incurvus*, (N and W sp) from which, indeed, they are chiefly distinguishable by their exceedingly minute size The costæ seldom exceed three in the outer face of the coronal cusps, the inner face showing obscure traces of fine and more numerous striæ.

*Geol position and locality:* Not uncommon in the upper fish-bed of the Kinderhook division, Burlington, Iowa.

## GENUS MESODMODUS, St J. and W.

Teeth laterally elongated Base consisting of one inferiorly flattened, posteriorly obliquely produced, massive plate, of which the posterior face slopes downward and slightly backward at an obtuse angle to the posterior crown face, anterior face slightly produced along the shoulder which extends parallel with the base of the crown, vertical or beveled, and occupied by a more or less prominent median protuberance which extends to the edge of the inferior surface, both faces more or less roughened or pitted, lateral angles truncated or rounded and more or less constricted above, equaling the lateral diameter of the crown Crown rising along the anterior border, sharply constricted in front and laterally, and well defined, sometimes constricted, from the posterior basal face, nearly equaling the base in antero posterior diameter, but more or less compressed along the crest, which rises into a more or less prominent median or submedian cusp, vertical or laterally deflected and recurved, usually compressed, with distinct, sometimes sharp cutting edges; the lateral portions of the crown are more or less strongly denticulated, the extremities bearing slightly more prominent cusps than the intermediate spaces, both faces more or less strongly ridged vertically, the outer face of the median cone often strongly buttressed and descending to the basal protuberance, coronal surfaces covered with a polished enamel like layer.

The teeth of the several forms of the present genus at present known, are small, or attain medium size. The individuals of certain forms are very variable, and yet, when perfect, their minor or specific characteristics are readily determinable The affinities of the genus are clearly intermediate between *Orodus* and *Hybocladodus* of the Carboniferous genera, and its relation to the Jurassic *Hybodus reticulatus* of Agassiz, would appear to be most intimate, but for the presence of the median protuberance in the anterior face of the base. The general and somewhat marked resemblance to *Cladodus*, as especially displayed in the denticulation of the lateral extremities, recurvation of the median cusps, and the posterior expansion of the base of certain forms, suggest a much more intimate relationship of the latter genus with *Orodus* than has before been pointed out. The genus thus far is known only in the lower members of the Lower Carboniferous, extending from the Kinderhook upwards to the Keokuk formation.

### MESODMODUS EXSCULPTUS, St J and W.

Pl V, Fig 18-22

Teeth attain medium size, though very variable, according to the position they occupied upon the jaws. Perhaps three varieties may be recognized, at least for the purpose of their specific definition, and which are supposed to represent the dentition of the median, anterior and posterior portions of the jaws, although these merge into one another so that there is practically a regular gradation from one extreme to the other Of these the median teeth are the largest and most symmetrical, attaining nearly an inch in lateral diameter. They are gently and regularly arched between the extremities, which are sometimes curved forward, though generally directed backward, or nearly linear. The base nearly or quite equals the crown in hight and lateral diameter, exceeding the antero-posterior diameter of the crown, massive, obliquely and moderately produced posteriorly, or nearly vertical to the crown, posterior face gently convex vertically, anterior face beveled from the narrow shoulder to the broad inferior surface, which latter occupies nearly the same horizonal plane as the crown, both basal faces are more or less coarsely roughened, the anterior face more so than the posterior, inferior surface smooth, or pitted with minute foramena Crown moderately convex and slightly compressed immediately beneath the crest in either face, the posterior slightly exceeding the anterior face in elevation, gently constricted inferiorly, extremities slightly produced laterally, crest acute, minutely denticulated, and gradually ascending to the more or less eccentric median prominence, which forms the apex of an obtuse angle, slightly deflected laterally toward the shorter extremity, gently convex or distended in the middle before and behind, supported in front by the moderately prominent basal protuberance, the coronal faces are uniformly sculptured in strong, sharp, closely arranged, sometimes bifurcated vertical ridges, one, two or more of which culminate in the minute denticulations along the crest, which latter are more or less irregularly developed, or variable in prominence, the extreme lateral ones sometimes quite prominent, the interspaces are occupied by short thread-like lines descending from exceedingly delicate denticulations in the crest and rising from the base, producing in the highly polished enameled surfaces the most exquisite coronal ornamentation.

The anterior teeth are smaller, typical examples averaging .4 inch in length. The base is relatively more massive, less beveled or slightly produced in front, inferior surface very gently arched upward, sometimes straight, plane, converging to the posterior margin, forming one side of an equilateral triangle, of which the other two sides constitute respectively the posterior and anterior corono basal faces in the lateral wings of the tooth. The average hight of the crown about equals the depth of the base, it is slightly constricted inferiorly, rapidly converging to the crest, which is flanked laterally by somewhat stout, laterally deflected, recurved denticulations, and thence, with intermediate lesser and variable denticulations, approaches the abruptly produced, eccentric median prominence, which is situated about one third the distance from one or other extremity, the sharp rounded apex directed towards the short extremity and recurved, in elevation as great again as the lateral wings, lenticular in transverse section with sharp cutting edges, the base in front somewhat more prolonged into the basal protuberance and posteriorly notched than occurs in the median teeth, the coronal sculpturing is the same as described in the former variety, the chief differences distinguishing the present one consisting in the relatively more massive, inferiorly expanded base, the stouter denticles at the lateral extremities, and more prominent, compressed median cone.

Associated with the above varieties, a third occurs, which, more intimately like the median teeth in form and general proportions, is distinguishable by its linear outline, the median prominence being scarcely distinguishable, the body of the teeth being quite regularly and very gradually attenuated from the short to the long extremity, the crest interrupted by more or less widely spaced denticulations, the intervals between which are most delicately wrought into short vertical ridges The anterior basal area presents a series of small protuberances corresponding to the denticulations in the crest, as shown in fig 20 b—a feature not observed in the other varieties. These teeth are also of smaller size than the median teeth, from which fact, and their linear outline, they may be regarded as having constituted the posterior rows upon the jaws

For the means of studying this interesting form in all its phases, we are indebted to the careful investigations of the local fauna of the Kinderhook at Burlington first begun by Mr FRANK SPRINGER, and subsequently in connection with Mr. WACHSMUTH, which have been prosecuted with most valuable results in the acquisition of abundant and authentic materials The teeth under consideration differ in so marked a degree from the upper Burlington form of the genus, as scarcely to require detailed comparison Among themselves, the varieties described above exhibit every degree of gradation, by which they are shown to be merely the varied dentition of one and the same form While in the ornamentation of the coronal region, as also the form of the base, there is marked persistence in all the teeth, the coronal contour presents a range of variableness which, in extreme examples, hardly affords a clue to their specific identity, as is shown in what we have termed the anterior and posterior teeth

*Position and locality* Common in the lower fish bed of the Kinderhook, a solitary specimen said to have been derived from the upper fish bed of the same formation, occurs in the collection of Mr. GILES, now in the Museum of Comparative Zoology at Cambridge, Burlington, Iowa

## MESODMODUS EXPLANATUS, St J and W

Pl V, Fig 15-17

Teeth minute. Base irregularly long elliptical, or elliptical, in outline, moderately arched upward, beveled in front from the narrow, generally obscure shoulder, protuberance proportionately large, globular, median, inferior surface plane or faintly excavated, posterior face produced downward and backward at a slight angle, or sometimes nearly at right angles to the vertical plane of the crown, broadly rounded along the posterior margin, extremities rounded, anterior face coarsely roughened, posterior face more finely pitted. Crown prominent, compressed, slightly constricted basally, lateral angles divergent, anterior face moderately convex, posterior face less so, median prominence more or less produced, median and obtusely rounded, or eccentric, the acute apex laterally deflected towards the short extremity, recurved, lateral wings occupied by one to three relatively prominent secondary cusps, which are connected with each other and the median prominence by the sharp coronal crest, very variable in occurrence, sometimes a pair on either extremity, of which the exterior are smallest, sometimes one strong cusp on the short extremity, and three in the long opposite wing, again, the one extremity being formed by the even prolongation of the sharp lateral edge of the median cusp, with only a single denticle upon the opposite extremity, surfaces enveloped in a polished enamel like coating, and marked, especially in the basal half, by a few short, sharp, thread like vertical lines, which become obsolete in the upper portions of the crown Lateral diameter of a symmetrical medium sized specimen .19 inch, antero posterior diameter about .07, greatest elevation of tooth .09 inch, some specimens are proportionately shorter and more considerably produced posteriorly, others are narrower, but the specimen measured probably represents the normal proportions of the teeth

We have examined but few examples of the form described above, which, however variable among themselves, exhibit a persistence in coronal markings which readily confirms their specific identity. They bear, at least in some examples, even closer resemblance to *M ornatus* of the Upper Burlington, than they do to *M exsculptus*, with which latter they are associated It seems barely possible, indeed, that they may pertain to the latter form, but their distinctive features, as exhibited by the comparatively smooth coronal surfaces and sparsely denticulate crest, and the broader basal support, do not harmonize with the variable characters of the latter form, while their individual variation is quite as marked, though apparently never approaching that of *M. exsculptus* sufficiently to furnish satisfactory evidence of their specific identity.

*Position and locality* Rare, in the lower fish-bed of the Kinderhook; Burlington, Iowa

## MESODMODUS ORNATUS, St J. and W.

Pl V, Fig 12-14

Teeth very small, lateral diameter about equal to twice the hight. Base subcrescentiform in outline, broadly produced posteriorly and rounded, gently concave in front, anterior face low, beveled, roughened, protuberance median or submedian, moderately prominent, posterior face gently convex laterally, forming an obtuse angle with the posterior crown face, finely punctate, inferior surface slightly oblique to the horizontal plane of the crown, relatively broad, plane or faintly concave, gently arched upward, lateral extremities sharply rounded in front. Crown relatively strong, prominent, more or less strongly produced in front and constricted inferiorly and laterally, well defined from the base behind, principal prominence median and vertical, or eccentric and laterally deflected, the apex directed towards the short extremity, recurved, strongly buttressed in front, the vertical ridge terminating in the basal protuberance below, lateral wings sharp crested, and bearing a strong secondary cusp at the extremities, which is sometimes flanked exteriorly by a smaller denticle, one or more similar denticles between the lateral cusps and the median prominence; in the perfect condition, these denticulations are observed to be produced by the convergence in the crest of one or two relatively strong, vertical ridges, which appear in both faces, though more conspicuous in front, the median buttress forming a prominent, angular ridge, which is perhaps ornamented with delicate thread-like lines. A specimen of medium size measures .10 inch in lateral diameter, greatest hight .06, antero-posterior breadth of base .04 inch.

The present form also presents considerable variability, though perhaps to a less extent than noticed in the preceding forms, and which would appear to be largely due to the state of preservation of the individual teeth. Our material contains several examples some of which are larger than the typical individuals, but which are perfectly smooth, simply exhibiting the general coronal contour, the crest, median and lateral prominences obtusely rounded—features doubtless attributable to abrasion, as they otherwise differ in no respect from the typical examples. The form recalls that previously mentioned under the name *M. explanatus*, with which, indeed, it bears resemblances in general outline and proportions; but the coronal ridges are stronger, and the anterior face of the median cusp is much more prominently buttressed. A specimen obtained by one of the writers from the Keokuk limestone, though not perfect, exhibits no appreciable differences by which it can be distinguished from the present form.

*Position and locality*. Not rare in the fish-bed of the Upper Burlington limestone, Buffington creek, Louisa county, and at other localities in the same horizon, in Illinois and Iowa.

## Genus ORODUS, Agassiz

### Orodus? parallelus, St. J. and W.

Pl. V, Fig. 23

Teeth very small, occurring in serial rows, apparently soldered at their bases, which thus form a common support, probably also occurring isolated, stoutly built, and symmetrical. Individually, the base is very strong, very obliquely produced backward, anterior face deeply channeled and defined from the crown by a narrow, sharply projecting hori zontal shoulder posterior face nearly plane or slightly beveled below, laterally abruptly truncated and angular, inferior surface broad and flattened in nearly the same plane as the crown, both sides coarsely roughened. Crown equaling the greater diameter of the base, strong, linear, slightly constricted interiorly, extremities very gently curved forward and abruptly truncated vertically, crest nearly central, sharp, even, or in some examples produced into a slight submedian prominence, outer and inner faces nearly equal in hight and gently arched vertically, in the outer face bounded by delicate coronal plicæ forming a belt ascending obliquely from the basal border to the upper coronal angles, constituting the only semblance of basal folds, both faces are similarly ornamented with numerous angular, slightly deflected or divergent vertical ridges, irregularly bifurcated below, with short implanted ridges extending downward from the crest, sometimes more or less interrupted in their direct course, producing a delicate and singularly beautiful sculpturing, and covered by a dense enamel like layer. Length of medium sized specimen 19 inch, hight 08, elevation of crown 03, greatest antero posterior diameter of crown .04 inch

Of the present form we have examined only two examples, and the identity of one of these (an imperfect tooth which exhibits certain peculiarities in common with the type), is not well established The form of the individual teeth readily distinguishes them from other species of *Orodus* but this very peculiarity, and the manner in which the specimen occurs, has led us to question its generic identity. The type consists of two teeth, in every respect perfect individually, but which are firmly united at their bases, the inferior surface of this basal plate is evidently no part of the ossified mandibular support, on the contrary, it always constituted the inferior surface of the bases of the teeth, as shown by the presence of a faint suture indicating the margins of independent teeth It is hardly probable that the two teeth in the example described constituted the complete row, which was doubtless made up of several additional individuals, yet there is not the slightest evidence of other teeth having been as intimately connected with them as they are with themselves—there being no fracture or other sign suggesting such intimate association. Hence, it would appear that, under certain conditions, the consolidation of two or more contiguous teeth by the impingement of their bases, which are soldered into a common basal support, may be effected, and the occurrence of specimens in this condition, therefore, may not indicate a departure from the normal condition of more than abnormal importance

The peculiar evenness of the coronal crest, which, in the type, is destitute of median prominence, though such a character is more distinctly exhibited in the doubtfully referred specimen previously mentioned above, and its regular parallelism, seem to point to a more intimate relationship with a group of closely allied but generically distinct teeth, which were first made known by Messrs NEWBERRY and WORTHEN under the name *Lophodus* (Ill Rep, vol. IV, p. 360), a designation which, unfortunately, is preoccupied, and for which we have substituted *Agassizodus* But the teeth under consideration lack the very essential characters by which the teeth of *Agassizodus* are distinguished, that is, the strongly buttressed anterior coronal face, in the present teeth both faces presenting the same degree of vertical corrugation The appearance of the vertical ridges also recall that in *Mesodmodus exsculptus*, but they are much more delicate in the present form, while there exists not the faintest trace of the sub coronal protuberance in the anterior border such as characterizes the above genus

*Position and locality* Rare in the areno magnesian beds in the upper part of the Kinderhook formation, near Richmond, Washington county, Iowa.

## ORODUS WHITEI, St J and W.

Pl VI, Fig 23

A unique specimen, discovered by Dr. WHITE, presents a series of eight teeth apparently firmly soldered at their bases into a common basal support, which is remarkable for the slightly spirally inrolled outline and contour, recalling the shape of the dental plates of some of the *Cochliodonts*. Together the teeth occupy a deltoidal figure, of which the diameter in the direction of inrollment nearly corresponds to that of the inner margin, which is broadly rounded and from which the teeth successively and regularly diminish in size, the exterior or oldest tooth of the series being about one third the greatest diameter of the inner or newest tooth, the anterior margin is gently arched, while the opposite margin, corresponding to the "oblique" margin of *Cochliodonts*, is slightly concave or sigmoidally curved from the subacute postero-inner angle to the outer inrolled extremity, the median cones of the individual teeth form a prominent coronal ridge, slightly posterior to the median line, which traverses the series from the inner to the exterior extremity. The inferior surface is smooth or faintly striated in the direction of inrollment, transversely marked by obscure sulci, which apparently indicate the former presence of sutures, and though exceedingly faintly marked, they correspond in position to the interspaces separating the individual teeth composing the series, and which, as seen from the side, are too apparent to be mistaken Individually, the teeth comprising the series are quite uniform in appearance, the extreme outer individuals showing unmistakable evidence of attrition from wear while fulfilling their functions during the life of their possessor, but which becomes less and less noticable towards the inner or newer teeth of the row, or those which have not been brought into position for use, and the innermost one is nearly perfect. Wherever the crowns have suffered abrasion, the surface presents a coarse punctate structure, otherwise it appears to be enveloped in the usual polished enamel like layer. In outline as seen from above, the crown is moderately arched backward, the lateral extremities more or less constricted at the base of the great cone, thence very gradually diminishing towards the extremities where they are abruptly truncated, viewed from the side, the general outline is slightly arched, the median cone forming a conspicuous conical, slightly eccentric prominence, with indications of irregularly disposed subordinate tuberculations in the lateral wings, which appear more strongly defined in the larger inner teeth, apparently indicating the gradual introduction of modifications in the coronal contour of teeth found at different stages in the growth of the animal to which they belonged; the crown is sharply constricted along the basal line in both faces, the smooth inbeveled portion bearing faint traces of a delicate reticulated ornamentation, above which the coronal surfaces are occupied by numerous rather strong more or less regular vertical folds, with short plicæ occupying the interspaces immediately beneath the crest, and more slender ridges encircle the median cone, which latter is produced into a small callosity near the base in front at the point of impingement with the preceding tooth; the crest forms an obtusely angular or obscurely defined submedian line in the lateral wings, apparently obsolete in the median cone, and in the majority of the teeth of the series it is entirely obliterated by wear Base equaling or slightly exceeding in its greater diameter that of the crown, forming an oblique plate which is flattened in the same plane as the crown below and smooth, produced along the inner margin and roughened by irregular coarse vertical folds and pits, deeply channeled in front, with a narrow shoulder extending just beneath the base of the crown. The following measurements present the comparative dimensions of the second and eighth tooth of the series Greatest length .68 inch, and .25 inch, breadth across median cone 15 inch, and .04 inch, hight at median cone 13 inch, and .03 inch.

The specimen herein described presents the anomalous feature of several teeth of the same row so firmly united at their bases as to form a continuous and solid basal plate, with, however, faint traces of sutures indicating the individuality of the several component teeth, which, taken separately, present no features by which they may be distinguished from typical forms of *Orodus*. Whether this condition is due to chemical action subsequent to their deposition, and by means of which changes in the mineral constituents have taken place whereby their substance seems to merge into uninterrupted continuity along the lines of impingement, or whether it is the result of the co ossification of these parts in the course of the life of the animal of whose dental armature they formed a part, is not so apparent from the examination of this example. It is well known that in some of the existing *Mylio donts*, especially *Aetobatis* of Muller, the anterior teeth become so solidly impacted in their basal portions as to present virtually the condition of a solid scute capable of great resistance. And in the various other genera, representatives of which occur in the Tertiary deposits, the series are as often firmly cemented, the posterior or newer teeth being perhaps most generally found isolated, the same as would be the result in macerating an existing jaw. In other extinct families, however, we meet with identical instances where two or more teeth of the same row have become firmly welded together, *e g*, a specimen of *Chomatodus elytra* (N. and W. sp.) showing five or six teeth intimately united at their bases, and one other marked instance represented by a beautiful little form discovered by Mr. VAN HORNE in the St Louis limestone, *Desmiodus tumidus*, amongst the many specimens of which we have examined, it is no uncommon occurrence to find series of two to six or eight teeth, exhibiting different stages of solidification, from those in which the suture is unmistakable to those where the inferior surface is nearly smooth with scarcely a vestige of division, as in the present form In none of the latter have several contiguous rows of teeth been found, and their association upon the jaw can only be inferred from the outline presented by the examples of isolated rows. Hence, it is extremely hazardous attempting to ascertain the character of the jaws upon which these teeth were planted—whether they were of the transverse type so characteristic of the typical *Rays*, or, on the other hand, approached the anteriorly pointed type common to the *Cestracionts*, as also the *Cochliodonts*. The extremely rapid diminution in size of the teeth from behind outward, and the consequent deltoidal figure which they collectively present, strikingly bring to mind the *Cochliodonts*, and especially that group to which Prof AGASSIZ applied the name *Psephodus*, forms in which the mandibles were produced forward much after the fashion of *Cestracion*. Presuming, on the other hand, that these teeth rested upon a transverse jaw similar to that of the great Carboniferous type *Agassizodus*, it is necessary to assume there were very few rows, probably not more than three or five, in evidence of which, however, the facts are as yet meagre and unsatisfactory.

The individual teeth present characters in their ornamentation and contour which readily distinguish them from other forms of *Orodus* from the same deposits, examples of which are noticed in this report. The ornamentation of the coronal region bears somewhat close resemblance to *O major* of the Lower Burlington limestone but in the latter form the base is relatively narrower and of greater depth They may also be compared with the Keokuk form *O carinatus*, from which it differs in the relatively broad crown and obtusely angular crest.

*Geological position and locality* The specific designation is given in honor of Dr C. A WHITE, by whom the unique specimen described was found in the upper beds of the Kinderhook formation, Legrand, Marshall county, Iowa

## ORODUS DECUSSATUS, St J and W

Pl VI, Fig 10-15

Teeth of small and medium size, attaining .75 inch in length, symmetrical though somewhat variable in form, laterally elongated, vertically arched, extremities slightly curved forward. Base comparatively shallow, especially in the large median teeth, oblique to the crown, beyond the inner margin of which it is more or less strongly produced forming a wide, linear area, with angular lateral extremities, inferior surface smooth, beveled to the thin posterior edge, deeply channeled in front with a more or less well defined angulation or shoulder parallel with the coronal margin The crown is moderately arched vertically, and presents a large median cone, more or less eccentric to the middle, flanked by two to four smaller though well marked denticulations in either wing, which regularly and rapidly diminish in size toward the extremities, and which are ornamented, in the same manner as the principal cone, by a few very strong, rather widely spaced ridges converging towards the apices of the prominences, which latter are connected by a more or less obscure coronal crest, the vertical ridges are quite regular in the posterior face, but in the anterior, or more abrupt face, they irregularly bifurcate descending, each bifurcation bearing the delicate lateral decussations which constitute the peculiarly ornate characteristics of the form The anterior teeth are much smaller, base proportionately deeper and narrower, generally more considerably arched, median prominence strongly produced inferiorly behind, lateral extremities rapidly attenuated, contour and ornamentation similar to the median teeth, with indications of basal plicæ, and varying in length from .15 to .5 inch Posterior teeth long, nearly linear, depressed, crown slightly arched, principal cone submedian, obtusely conical or scarcely distinguishable from the contiguous denticles, of which latter three or four occur in one wing and probably one or two less in the opposite extremity, relatively large and radiatingly sculptured, as described above. The median prominence is often truncated from wear, but in the perfect condition it is obtusely conical, as are also the lateral denticles; the entire surface of the crown may present a fine granulose punctation, generally, however, this structure is visible only in worn surfaces, the lateral extremities of the crown being enveloped in a polished enamel-like layer.

The present form was first brought to our notice by Mr SPRINGER, and subsequently Mr WACHSMUTH made interesting accessions to the material illustrating the species, from the same locality. It is distinguishable from *Orodus mammillaris*, N and W, with which it is somewhat closely allied, by the less regular and stronger radiating ridges in the coronal prominences, and which are more delicately decussated instead of being strongly beaded or nodose, as in that form. In their perfect condition the teeth of this species are amongst the most beautiful and highly wrought of the numerous species of the genus; and even when imperfect from long use or abrasion, they may be in most cases recognized from the above named species, and readily so from other species in the same and succeeding formations.

*Position and locality* Not uncommon in the lower fish bed of the Kinderhook formation; Burlington, Iowa.

## ORODUS DÆDALEUS, St. J. and W.

Pl VI, Fig 7 8

Teeth somewhat variable in form, of medium or small size, attaining 7 inch in length. Large median teeth laterally elongated, nearly straight, and moderately arched vertically Base relatively shallow, obliquely expanded and rapidly beveled to a thin edge behind, the opposite side presenting a broad channel, which separates the plane inferior surface from the crown; the crown exceeds the root in breadth and hight, forming in the middle a strong symmetrical conical prominence, which is strongly distended toward the base behind and in front, where it terminates in a slight node, and is abruptly defined from the lateral wings, which extend on either side in nearly linear direction, or very gradually converging to the rounded extremities, which are slightly deflected posteriorly, the crest and apical point are submedian, or situated nearer the outer margin of the crown, more regularly and broadly convex posteriorly than in front, in the lateral portions of the crown produced into a series of well defined tuberculations, which are ornamented with delicately decussated radiating ridges, two or three of which are continued downward from each cone and merged into the irregularly plicated or reticulated basal border which is more coarsely developed in the outer margin and somewhat closely resembling the plicated basal margins in *O. plicatus*, the large central cone is beauti fully marked with delicate ridges radiating from the apex to about the middle, where they are interrupted and deflected, or replaced by intercalated ridges, which are gathered in an elegant reticulated border at the base of the inner face, a slight mesial ridge ascending the outer face of the great cone, giving off at intervals a few lateral secondary ridges. A somewhat smaller variety, in position probably anterior to the teeth just described, varying from .15 to .5 inch in length, are recognized by their more strongly arched outline, the lateral wings often anteriorly deflected, root narrower and less obliquely produced along the inner margin, central cone relatively larger, and the denticulations of the lateral crests decreasing in number with the abbreviation of the lateral wings—otherwise presenting no marked contrast with the large median teeth. In the perfect condition the crown is enveloped in a firm, polished enamel like layer, a fine punctation appearing in worn surfaces

In general outline the present form is somewhat like *O. elegantulus*, N. and W, of the Upper Burlington limestone, although a direct comparison of the two forms discovers differences which widely distinguish them specifically, as remarked in the details of coronal sculpturing, which is much more delicately wrought. The dentition presents a similar range of variation observed in the above and other species, while the persistency of the specific characteristics readily affords the means of identifying the isolated teeth from various parts of the jaws

*Position and locality*. Common in the lower fish bed of the Kinderhook; Burlington, Iowa.

### ORODUS MAJOR, St. J. and W.

Pl VII, Fig 10

Teeth of large size, strong, symmetrical proportions. Lateral diameter of base equal to that of the crown, in depth exceeding the general elevation of the crown, but narrower, massive, moderately oblique, posterior angles sharply rounded, posterior face gently arched in both directions, with a more or less marked depression parallel with and just beneath the coronal border, anterior face moderately and broadly excavated, the shoulder beneath the coronal margin apparently obscurely defined, inferior surface gently arched vertically, and moderately beveled to the obtuse posterior margin, anterior and posterior surfaces coarsely roughened or pitted. Crown gently and regularly arched between the extremities, which latter are more or less curved forward, rising into a strong, obtusely conical median cone, which is somewhat strongly produced before and behind, and broadly rounded, rapidly narrowed to the nearly linear lateral extensions, which are abruptly truncated or broadly rounded, strongly constricted basally, traversed by a low, undulated, obscurely defined median crest, which bears at irregular and infrequent intervals obtuse, or nearly obsolete, secondary prominences, from which descend obscure plicæ, which bifurcate below, forming numerous vertical ribs in the region of the basal margins; the median prominence, as well as the lateral crests, is smooth, only the middle and basal portions of the crown are distinctly costate, the relatively narrower anterior surface is even less strongly folded, and the entire coronal surface is regularly and minutely punctate Greatest diameter of medium sized tooth about two inches, greatest hight of tooth .95, antero posterior diameter at base of median cone 70, breadth of lateral wings .43, greatest hight of crown 50, elevation near the extremities .18; greatest thickness of root 40 inch Other examples attain above three inches in length.

The above species, of which we have examined but three or four representatives in the collections of Messrs. SPRINGER and WACHSMUTH, is one of the largest and finest of the genus, and the interest which attaches to these specimens is further enhanced by the fact that they are among the very few examples of ichthyic remains which the researches of the above gentlemen have brought to light in the Lower Burlington limestone. The specimens unfortunately are not perfect, although their state of preservation is such as to enable their form and superficial characteristics to be quite fully determined. The coronal region bears unmistakable signs of abrasion, by which the vertical rugæ have been obliterated in the region of the crest, and consequently obscured in the basal portions, but their general form and direction is still discernible, and aid in the determination of the characteristics by which the form is especially distinguished in the absence of the enamel layer and any delicate markings it may have preserved.

These teeth have only remotely intimate resemblances with any of the numerous species of *Orodus* now known, bearing, perhaps, as close resemblance to *O ramosus*, Agass, as to any of its congeners from American localities. It has little in common, save the uniformly punctate condition of the abraded coronal surface, with the form so numerously represented in the Upper Burlington fish bed, to which we have applied the name *O variocostatus*, the costæ being less widely and irregularly spaced, and the median prominence less prominently produced.

*Position and locality:* Rare in the Lower Burlington limestone, Burlington, Iowa

## ORODUS VARIOCOSTATUS, ST. J. and W.

Pl. VII, Fig. 1-9.

Teeth ranging from small to above medium in size, presenting considerable variation in form and coronal contour. Large teeth laterally elongated, extremities more or less curved anteriorly, generally inæquilateral, gently arched vertically. Base moderately thick, more or less oblique to the crown, moderately excavated in the outer face, superior shoulder narrow but well-defined, posterior surface slightly arched in both directions, both faces coarsely roughened, inferior surface smooth, beveled to the obtuse posterior border in nearly the same horizontal plane as the crown, postero-lateral angles sharply rounded. Crown produced into a median, or generally submedian, turgid, more or less quadrangular or pyramidal, and often obtusely truncated cone, which is protruded beyond the basal line in front and behind, and well defined from the lateral wings, which latter are also constricted basally, very gradually tapering toward the extremities, which are broadly rounded, and equal or slightly exceed the lateral extension of the base; the crown is traversed by an irregular, tortuose, usually obscurely defined, though sometimes sharply angular submedian crest, which is continued nearly to the apex of the principal prominence in some individuals, from which sharp or obtusely angular, very irregular and obliquely deflected costæ descend to the basal margins, where they often form buttress-like supports, flanked by faint secondary ridges or bifurcations, which sometimes produce the appearance of rude basal folds; the median prominence is surrounded by similar vertical plicæ, which, however, become obsolete before reaching the upper third of the cone, except the more or less prominent angular mesial ridge, which is generally discernible in either face, and often continued to the apical extremity in examples which have not been abraded; in some individuals the coronal carinæ present a vermiculose appearance, and are clustered at the base of the median cone in an elegantly, though irregularly plicated belt. Teeth possessing the above mentioned characters range in size from those above one inch in lateral diameter to small forms not exceeding one fourth inch in length. With these more regular teeth there is found a variety represented by smaller teeth, which are especially distinguishable by their abbreviated lateral extent, relatively greater antero-posterior diameter, and depressed summit. In some of the latter teeth the base is very strong and deep, and deeply excavated in the anterior face, the crown strongly produced in front, and gently arched along the posterior border, the median prominence very depressed, and occupying the greater portion of the coronal area, lateral extremities bearing one to three irregularly developed lobes, but in general appearance and surface markings intimately agreeing with the preceding variety, and varying in lateral diameter from 15 to 55 inch, (Pl VII, Fig. 2, 3, 4) Some of the latter may be individuals of the former variety, whose median prominences have been worn down by attrition; but it seems probable that the majority of them represent the dental armature of the posterior portions of the jaws, and that of the extreme anterior portion of the jaws may be represented by a peculiar form of small, proportionately slender, high-crested, strongly buttressed teeth, which bear some resemblance to the first mentioned variety, as shown in the illustrations, Pl VII, Fig 1 *a*, *b*.

This interesting form is one of the most numerously represented in the Upper Burlington fish bed It is not apparently allied with other species from the same horizon, but a form occurs in the Keokuk limestone, originally described under the name of *Helodus gibbosus*, N and W, (Ill Rep II, p. 79, Pl. V, Fig 3,) which bears most intimate relationship with the present teeth Fortunately the collection of Mr. VAN HORNE affords a fine large example from Hamilton, Illinois, which, though slightly worn, exhibits the specific identity as also the true generic relationship of the original specimen above referred to, showing the latter to be a very worn tooth Our collections from the same vicinity and from Keokuk and Bentonsport, Iowa, furnish several additional smaller specimens of the same form, so that now we have the means to institute a very satisfactory comparison between them and the form described above. The Keokuk form, while it exhibits about the same variability, is chiefly recognizable by its generally more robust proportions, thicker and more massive base, generally less attenuated lateral extremities, less sharp crested vertical ridges and coarser punctation of the coronal surfaces.

There are few species, the dental remains of which are so variable, that possess peculiarities which are so readily recognizable as those which facilitate the identification of the isolated teeth of the present form Some of its variations are at first sight scarcely recognizable, and especially is this true of the small posterior (?) teeth, the depressed contour and broad, subcircular outline of which widely contrast with the large laterally elongated teeth. But in all varieties the same style of coronal ornamentation and form of base prevails, and a careful scrutiny cannot fail to reveal the same pattern of form, though modified to a greater or less extent, according to the place the teeth held upon the jaw.

*Position and locality* · This form is apparently confined to the fish-bed stratum in the Upper Burlington limestone, and its geographical distribution is probably as extensive as that of any other species of the same horizon; at the numerous exposures of the horizon in Louisa and DesMoines counties, Iowa, Henderson county, Illinois.

## ORODUS FASTIGIATUS, St J and W.

Pl VI, Fig 1-3

Teeth small, robust, triangular in general outline Base very oblique to the crown, thick, laterally expanded below, (in worn examples the margins are quite parallel or rounded) and slightly concave along the lower edge, lateral diameter little greater than the vertical, posterior face gently convex, opposite side more or less deeply excavated, with a well defined shoulder parallel with the coronal margin, inferior surface forming a rather wide, angular area, obliquely beveled to the posterior edge Crown inbeveled below and sharply defined from the base, strongly arched vertically, rising into a high pyramidal prominence, flanked by the lateral wings, which are sharp crested and marked upon either side by two or three angular vertical ridges which terminate below in nodose prominences, sometimes bifurcated, meeting in the crest where they sometimes produce obscure denticulations; the median cone is flanked in the outer face by a very strong, angular buttress, abruptly descending and strongly produced towards the base, and ornamented with lateral ridges similar to those occurring in the lateral wings, besides being delicately marked with undulated rugæ, the posterior face of the crown is also occupied by an angular, though less prominent, mesial ridge, which rises from a turgid basal prominence, and marked above by delicate decussations similar to those observed in the sharp crest of the lateral wings, originally the crown was acutely pointed, but in the larger number of specimens it is truncated, and in some examples it is reduced to less than half the original elevation The coronal surfaces are uniformly enveloped in a dense, highly polished enamel like coating A specimen of ordinary size measures in greatest lateral diameter 25 inch, greatest antero posterior diameter of crown 16, hight of tooth ·31 inch

The form here indicated is represented by numerous individuals in the collections from the Upper Burlington fish bed horizon, and withal they present considerable individual variation, we have been unable to trace their specific identity with other forms known from the same localities The peculiar form of the teeth strongly impresses one with the belief that they occupied an anterior position upon the jaws But we know of no species whose median teeth can be satisfactorily identified with those under consideration, while they vary in size and in certain coronal features among themselves to such an extent as apparently to justify the conclusion that they are specifically distinct from their associates In the depth and excavation of the outer basal region there is strong resemblance to *O. tuberculatus*, N and W; but the coronal portion is so markedly different as to render their identity with that species hardly probable, and the peculiar pyramidally produced apex and strongly arched contour of the crown afford characters which may be relied upon in the determination of the identity of the individuals.

Associated with the above mentioned teeth, there are a few individuals of the same general form, but which have their crests reduced to the condition of a smooth arched plate—indeed such as might be produced by the wearing away of the crown to a line little above the basal margin The individual variations of the latter teeth are almost as striking as are the differences by which they are distinguished from the teeth above described, and with which they are probably specifically identical.

The Keokuk limestone fish bed horizon also affords teeth which somewhat closely resemble the present form, but which are in too imperfect condition for satisfactory determination.

*Position and locality:* Common in the fish-bed of the Upper Burlington limestone, Louisa and DesMoines counties, Iowa

## Orodus carinatus, St. J. and W.

Pl V, Fig 24

We have from the Keokuk limestone a couple specimens of a peculiar form of *Orodus*, which seems to be distinct from those with which it is associated at the same locality, and which are distinguishable by the following characteristics Teeth of small size, a medium sized specimen measuring in lateral diameter 13 inch, and in hight nearly .05. Base thick, obliquely produced behind, more or less arched vertically, anterior face moderately channeled, inferior surface relatively broad, both anterior and posterior faces marked by rather coarse vertical grooves or pits The crown forms a very compressed, gently and regularly arched sharp crested prominence, slightly overreaching the lateral borders of the base, and constricted before and behind, and occupied in either face by strong, buttress like, laterally deflected carinæ, which culminate in the crest and give rise to a series of delicate tuberculations in the lateral portions, the posterior basal portion of the crown is further delicately ornamented by the peculiarly interrupted plicæ, such as characterize certain species of the genus, but the character of the opposite basal border is not satisfactorily exhibited by the specimens before us The crown is remarkably thin, resembling in this respect *Chomatodus*, but its vertically ridged surfaces clearly indicate its generic identity with *Orodus*

From *O. minutus*, N. and W, with which it is most intimately allied of all its associates, it differs in the relatively thinner crown, also in the less numerous and stronger vertical ridges; but in the character of the basal plicæ it strongly resembles the above species In *O minutus* the vertical ridges of the crown show a tendency to decussate, recalling a similar style of coronal sculpturing observed in the form called *O ornatus*, N and W, but in the present teeth we fail to detect the slightest semblance of similar decussations, although it is barely possible they may have become obsolete from wear *Orodus parvulus* of the St Louis limestone, perhaps, bears the most striking resemblance to the present form, it is, however, distinguished by the slighter and more numerous vertical ridges, and deeper base

*Position and locality*: Rare in the upper fish-bed horizon of the Keokuk limestone; Bentonsport, Iowa

### Orodus neglectus, St J. and W

Pl VI, Fig 26

Teeth of medium size, robust. Crown more or less strongly arched vertically and moderately so backward, culminating in an obtuse, swollen median prominence, at the base of which, in front, occurs a slight callosity, lateral portions marked by obscure mammilloid undulations with an indistinctly defined, angular crest, sharply constricted along the basal borders, from which ascend with more or less regularity strong vertical ridges, in worn surfaces the crown presents a coarsely punctate structure Base oblique to the vertical plane of the crown, posterior surface slightly convex and forming a rather broad area projecting behind and parallel with the base of the crown, deeply excavated in front, with broad beveled interior surface; both sides coarsely roughened and pitted, inferior surface comparatively smooth Greatest diameter 50 to 75 inch

The present form is apparently closely allied to the teeth described under the name *O variocostatus* from the Upper Burlington, also *O. gibbosus* (N. and W. sp) of the Keokuk division; it is, however, distinguishable from those forms by the greater regularity of coronal coutour, and the more regular disposition of the vertical ridges

*Geological position and locality* It is a very rare form, only two specimens being known to us, one from an arenaceous bed in the St Louis division of Monroe county, Ill, and the other (represented in Pl. VI, Fig. 26) was obtained by Mr Van Horne, in the calcareous shales of the same formation at Pella, Iowa

ORODUS PARVULUS, St J and W.

Pl VI, Fig 6

The form for which we have proposed the above designation is represented in our collections by two minute teeth, the perfect preservation of which, however, readily enable the determination of their affinities and distinctive peculiarities. The form may be distinguished from the species so numerously represented in the same horizon, *O. plicatus*, N and W., by the marked dissimilarity in the outline and contour of the crown, which is thinner, more evenly crested, it is gently arched between the extremities, which latter are very slightly curved outward, slightly constricted basally, culminating in the middle in a well defined, though not prominent median cone, the lateral wings, which are abruptly terminated at their extremities, are occupied by numerous, closely set, vertical or laterally deflected, bifurcated ridges, which terminate in delicate tuberculations along the sharp crest The base is nearly or quite equal to the lateral diameter of the crown, thin, deep, exceeding in depth the elevation of the crown, obliquely produced behind and broadly arched in both directions, anterior face broadly channeled and defined above by the well marked superior shoulder, inferior surface narrow, beveled to the obtuse posterior border in nearly the same horizontal plane as the crown, postero lateral angles sharply rounded, anterior and posterior faces dense, or delicately roughened or pitted. Lateral diameter of tooth .27 inch, hight about 08

The above form also bears a close resemblance to *O minutus*, N and W., of the Keokuk limestone, but the vertical ridges are stronger and less elaborately wrought, besides there is no indication of the presence of a delicately sculptured basal belt, such as occurs in the latter form From *O carinatus*, also from the Keokuk, it differs in the relatively thicker crown, and more closely approximated, rounded vertical ridges As in *O elegantulus*, N and W , of the Upper Burlington limestone, the vertical plicæ terminate in the crest along its lateral extensions in minute tubercles, and the median prominence is also similarly marked by radiating ridges, but the latter are much stronger and fewer in number than those encircling the median cone in the latter species, while the crest is much more compressed antero posteriorly, and the base proportionately much deeper

*Position and locality* · Rare in the upper beds of the St. Louis limestone. Alton, Illinois.

### ORODUS TURGIDUS, St J. and W

Pl VI, Fig 4, 5

Teeth very small, robust, gently arched posteriorly Base of moderate depth, less than that of the crown, as also its transverse and lateral diameters, moderately oblique, posterior face vertically arched in nearly the same plane as the posterior coronal slope, anterior face deeply channeled, shoulder of slight prominence, both faces coarsely punctate or roughened, inferior surface broad, smooth, and gently beveled to the sub acute posterior margin, gently arched vertically, postero lateral angles sharply rounded Crown moderately and more or less regularly arched between the extremities, inflated below, unbeveled along the basal margins and sharply defined from the base, a strong turgid or obtusely conical, more or less eccentric median prominence occupying the middle region, the lateral wings regularly diminishing towards the extremities, traversed by an obtuse subcentral crest, interrupted by a few relatively strong tuberculations, from which descend one or two prominent vertical or diverging carinæ, the median cone being apparently similarly though less strongly and more numerously plicated. The coronal surfaces, when perfect, enameled and highly polished. Lateral diameter of tooth about 17 inch, hight about 04

The form described is known by only two minute and somewhat worn teeth, but which are readily recognizable by the stout build and turgid median cone. It bears some likeness to *O plicatus*, N and W, with which it is most intimately allied, but apparently lacks the delicately plicated belt characteristic of that form, besides it is relatively much stouter.

*Position and locality*· Rare, in the upper fish-bed of the Chester limestone; Chester. Illinois.

### ORODUS ALLENI, St J and W.

Pl VII, Fig 19

Teeth medium in size. laterally elongated, and strongly arched upward in the middle Crown moderately elevated, with an obtusely angular crest centrally traversing the lateral portions, the sides irregularly corrugated vertically, the median region occupied by an obtusely conical prominence, oval in outline, projecting forward and backward beyond the line of the lateral wings, bordered by numerous vertical folds similar to, though smaller than those in the lateral portions, and which reach upward from the base half way or more towards the summit of the cone; the surface is evenly and rather finely punctate, the punctæ being encircled by a slight rim or raised border—a not unusual feature in the surface structure of teeth of widely distinct families of Carboniferous *Selachians*. The base is thick, massive, nearly as extensive laterally as the coronal region, in depth somewhat exceeding the hight of the crown, from which it projects backward at a slight angle to the vertical plane, posterior face gently arched, postero lateral angles sharply rounded, anterior face moderately excavated, inferior surface smooth, beveled at a slight angle to the horizontal plane, posterior margin obtuse, anterior and posterior faces roughened by vertically disposed vermiculose markings. Viewed from above the crown presents a gently arched outline, the extremities directed forward, the transverse diameter equaling, if not exceeding the elevation of the same parts. Greatest length of tooth .87 inch, hight .38, antero posterior diameter across the median cone .30, greatest elevation of crown .17 inch.

The present form is described from a specimen obtained from the upper portion of the Lower Coal Measures of Iowa, by Mr. J. A. ALLEN, to whom we have dedicated the species as a slight token of esteem. Not absolutely entire, it preserves the median cone and one of the lateral wings and base in a nearly perfect condition, enabling its distinctive characters to be tolerably clearly defined, as also a satisfactory comparison with other forms. Of the Coal Measure *Orodi*, the above species bears closest resemblance to *O. (?) corrugatus* N. and W., it differs, however, from that form in the more prominent median cone, and fewer and proportionately stronger coronal corrugations. Its closest ally is found in a species from the Upper Burlington limestone, *O. variocostatus*, from which it is distinguishable by its more symmetrical form, relatively deeper and more massive base, and more regular corrugation of coronal surfaces. In consideration of its geological position, it deserves close comparison with the forms of *Agassizodus* from the same deposits, but its apparently equally strongly vertically plicated anterior and posterior coronal surfaces would seem to preclude its reference to that genus, while they suggest intimate relationship with typical *Orodus*.

*Position and locality.* Upper part of the Lower Coal Measures; Greene county, Iowa.

## GENUS AGASSIZODUS, St. J. and W.

*Lophodus*, NEWBERRY and WORTHEN 1870, Ill Rep., Vol IV, p. 360, not *Lophodus*, ROMANOWSKY, 1864.*

Late in the autumn of 1873, one of the writers was favored with a communication from Prof. B. F. MUDGE, Director of the Geological Survey of Kansas, in reference to the discovery of the remains of a

* Disc de quelques restes de Poissons Fossiles, trouvès dans le calcaire carbonifère du Gouvernement de Toula. Par Hennadius Romanowsky, Moscow, 1864.

remarkable fish, consisting of a part of the jaw preserving about three hundred teeth in their natural position, and which was obtained from Upper Coal Measure strata in Osage county, Kansas. Subsequently, or late in the following January (1864,) Mr SPRINGER, while passing through Topeka, chanced to come upon another specimen, which he kindly forwarded to Cambridge, the examination of which, together with the fact that the latter specimen was derived from the same locality as that reported by Prof MUDGE led us to suspect that the two specimens might prove to be fragments of one and the same individual—an inference which was most conclusively confirmed not long thereafter, on bringing the two specimens together The former proved to be about two thirds the posterior portion of what appears to be the left ramus of the mandible or lower jaw, the latter apparently completing the anterior prolongation of the ramus, besides showing along the inner margin, though much displaced by compression, a series of teeth belonging to five or six of the anterior rows of the opposite ramus. But the posterior portion of the right ramus has been broken away, and it is apparent only a few teeth belonging to consecutive rows from the symphysis backward remain of what constituted this side of the mandible.

Considering the left ramus, which apparently presents quite the entire dentition of this side of the jaw, the specimen exhibits the posterior two thirds, or the teeth from the first row in advance of the row of large median teeth, in the normal condition as refers to the natural relative position of the rows, but in the anterior portion of the ramus the rows towards the inner margin have been displaced or crowded forward so as to give to the vertical or symphysial line a reversed deflection approaching that of the postero outer dentary border The above features of the ramus are well shown in fig 1, Pl S, which besides showing the accidental displacement or spreading of the rows of teeth above alluded to, also shows the ramus much flattened, so as to obscure the convoluted inrollment, characteristic as well of the *Cestracionts*, giving to the jaw almost precisely the same appearance the spread out diagram of the dental armature of *Cestracion* would present, as obtained by stripping off the teeth and spreading them upon a flat surface. Hence, in attempting the restoration, (Pl S, fig. 22.) it is obvious that sufficient allowance may not have been made for the inrollment of the anterior portion of the jaw, thus producing an outline more obtusely angular in front than may have obtained in reality Yet, compared with the modern *Cestracion*, the jaws of the remarkable fish under consideration were doubtless less acutely produced forward, and in this particular holding a mean between its modern representative and some of the *Rays* (*e g Trygon*) in the relative obtuseness of the anterior extremity of the jaws. But the resemblance here ceases In all other respects, as the form of the individual teeth and their arrangement upon the jaws, we observe unmistakable *Hybodont* affinities

The articular extremities of the jaw are not preserved, though fragments of the substance of the cartilage are scattered through the rock-mass upon which the teeth are imbedded These cartilages were doubtless comparatively thin, the outer and inner folds giving away to the pressure which flattened the rami, as shown in their present condition.

The teeth are disposed in serial rows having a convoluted inrollment from the inner to the outer border, and gradually increasing in size from the posterior extremity to the row of large median teeth, anterior to which the rows as regularly diminish in size towards the symphysis Posterior of the median row the ramus presents six to nine rows, the extra three rows apparently not reaching the extreme outer borders, but spreading over the inner portion of the jaw, the extreme posterior row diminished to half the vertical extent of the fourth in the series, the mature teeth of which present no perceptible difference, except in their diminished size, to the teeth of the other rows These teeth are remarkably uniform in their shape They may be described as laterally elongated, very slightly arched along the obtuse angle of the crest, and slightly curved forward, the anterior end perceptibly slightly more thickened than the opposite extremity, but without defined median prominence The crown, therefore, is very uniform in proportions, and robust. The middle portion of the ramus is occupied by a row of proportionately very large teeth, which differ from the posterior teeth in having the outline of the crest quite strongly arched vertically between the extremities and produced into a strong, obtusely conical, eccentric prominence which culminates at a point more or less posterior of the middle of the tooth. It should be here stated that the teeth of the posterior contiguous row also show faint indication near their posterior extremities of an apical culmination, from which point the crown very slightly tapers anteriorly. The teeth of the anterior portion of the ramus are very similar to those situated posterior of the median row, and of which there are eight, possibly nine rows, gradually diminishing in size anteriorly, or in the reversed order to that mentioned above. The teeth of the row immediately in advance of the median row are distinguished from the teeth of the corresponding row next behind the median teeth, by their slightly greater length and more slender proportions, very slight forward curvature, and the more marked definition of the eccentric apical culmination, which is situated about a third, or less, the distance from the posterior extremity. The teeth of the other rows do not show the latter feature so distinctly, though it extends to the third or fourth row, and in the latter there is a tendency to irregularity in the more central position of the obscure apical point. The teeth of the several rows, as mentioned in connection with those of the posterior portion of the jaw, present but slight differences to one another, until reaching the extreme anterior rows, where they appear to assume irregularities which give rise to considerable diversity, especially in the presence in the extreme anterior row of minute, nearly circular teeth, which exhibit in the form of the crown and its sculpturing strong likeness to *Petrodus*, besides other scute like and irregular forms, the position of which is not so clear, more particularly noticed further on

The single ramus above described shows about four hundred and fifty individual teeth, and in its perfect state there were probably not less than five hundred, or one thousand teeth for the entire mandible.

Remarkable as this specimen is, showing as it does the nearly complete details of the dentition of the jaw, it unfortunately reveals no facts relative to that of the maxillaries or upper jaw, detached teeth of which, for all the aids afforded by the example before us, might be mistaken for representatives of distinct specific forms. But it is a matter of much importance to the student of these remains, the discovery by Prof TODD, in the shales of about the same stratigraphic horizon of the Upper Coal Measures of south-western Iowa, of a mass of detached teeth, occurring within so limited a compass and under conditions which leave little room to doubt but that they constituted the dental remains of a single fish Prof TODD obtained in all some two hundred specimens of individual teeth, the greater number of which are quite detached, though a few are still associated in rows and parts of series precisely as represented in the before mentioned specimen from Kansas. Unfortunately the existence of these interesting fossils was not made known sufficiently early to secure the entire set, as many, in fact the great majority of the teeth were lost by being concealed in the *debris* from the quarry, from which, indeed, many of the specimens here alluded to were rescued Yet this collection, assuming that it represents the dental armature of one and the same individual, supplies, in part at least, exactly the data not exhibited in the previously noticed specimen, inasmuch as the same sort of teeth are found amongst these Iowa specimens, besides other forms which it were difficult to account for on the ground of abnormal development, but which probably pertain to the opposite or maxillary portion of the jaws. While these materials afford additional data contributing to a more extended knowledge of the somewhat variable dentition of this group, we are still left in doubt as to the character and the extreme extent of the variableness of the teeth which occupied the anterior and posterior portions of the maxillaries, as the collection last referred to affords no individuals of a kind of extremely acuminate teeth, examples of which have been discovered in the Upper Coal Measures of Illinois.

Generically considered, the teeth present closest affinities to *Orodus*, Ag., a group prevalent in the Lower Carboniferous formations. But the present group of teeth is distinguished by the prevailing prominence of the buttressed condition of the anterior coronal borders, and the relative uniformity or evenness of the posterior face, besides the relatively fewer rows of acuminate teeth, as inferred from this feature being so prevalent in all collections of *Orodi*, while the linear forms are least commonly met with. The teeth of the extreme anterior rows present the most marked divergence from the normal features just alluded to, assuming a more or less circular outline as seen from above, sometimes with the anterior face produced into a single more or less prominent buttress. The latter feature may be readily explained by examining the tooth figured Pl. 8, fig. 15, in which the extremity of a small linear tooth shows a tendency to throw off a pair of minute independent teeth whose anterior angulation correspond to the buttresses in the other portion of the crown. The variety assumed by the teeth of the extreme rows of the jaw, as they occur in at least one specific form, is partially shown in the figures Pl. 8, fig. 15–20; of these, 15–17 probably belonged to the maxillaries, 18–20 to the mandibles. The basal portion of the teeth would seem to partake to greater or less extent in the variableness observed in the coronal region; the normal teeth presenting a quite persistent uniformity in general outline and proportions, being more or less compressed antero-posteriorly and obliquely produced downward and backward, vertically arched below with a more or less prominent transverse ridge beneath the coronal border, extremities angular, one or other (probably the anterior) more produced laterally; anterior face vertically concave, interrupted along the upper borders by the supports of the coronal buttresses which originate in the basal surface; inferior surface well defined, flattened nearly in the same plane as the crown, with which it agrees in proportionate outline, though relatively narrower antero-posteriorly, plane or faintly channeled, smooth or obliquely striated, the striæ or ridges being directed from the inner margin obliquely forward to the outer edge; either face of the base more or less deeply and irregularly pitted. The coronal region is enveloped in an enamel like layer, and which is almost universally of a light color, often a lustrous white, producing a marked contrast to the black basal portion of the tooth, only rare examples obtained from pyritose shales having a uniform black color. In the details of coronal ornamentation, as well as those persistent proportional features, the various specific forms are recognized.

Besides the teeth, there remain to be mentioned some peculiar little bodies which are intermingled in the mass of shale in which the teeth were imbedded, with fragments of the cartilages of the skeletal frame, and which do not appear to be referable to the dentary system. These bodies are exceedingly small, irregularly circular in outline, with a depressed convex coronal portion which rises into an eccentric acumination or transverse ridge along one side, and delicately sculptured with irregular carinæ radiating from the apex towards the marginal borders. The base is sometimes slightly produced opposite the abrupt face in a thin border, and more or less concave below. There is great diversity of form, no two specimens presenting precisely the same shape, though all partaking in a general resemblance, and especially in the dark, horny lustre of the enameled crown, by which they are readily distinguishable from the teeth with which they are associated. It seems not improbable that these minute bodies constituted part of the dermal or shagreen covering of the fish. One of the better preserved of the scales is shown in fig. 21, Pl. 8. Often the long slope of the crown exhibits greater or less indications of abrasion in the smooth surface it shows, and which may indicate the relative position of the anterior and posterior sides.

Neither of the remarkable suites of fossils noticed above furnish any clue to the nature of the dorsal fin defenses, if with such these fishes were provided. Remains of the firmer cartilages occur, which probably belonged to the supports upon which the teeth rested. These fragments are of variable thickness, portions from the dentary ridge of the jaw attaining a thickness of .40 inch, while fragments of what may have constituted the inner fold or other less exposed walls of the jaw, are of extreme thinness, sometimes not more .05 inch in thickness. These masses appear to be composed, in the one case of an aggregation of semi-ossified particles, and in the latter of similar points presenting an elongated polygonal outline, the sutures between the hard parts are often filled by mineral matter, giving to the mass a minute reticulated or honey-combed appearance when the substance of the partially ossified tissue has been dissolved away.

The present group of teeth was first brought to notice by the investigations of Messrs. NEWBERRY and WORTHEN, published in 1870, in the preceding fourth volume of this Report, where it is designated under the generic name *Lophodus*. This term having been previously employed by Col. ROMANOWSKY to designate a group of teeth from the Lower Carboniferous formations of Russia, and which are also common in the same deposits in Great Britain and America, it is obvious that the above name must give way.

In the above mentioned volume, two species were described under the names *L. variabilis*, from the Upper Coal Measures near La Salle, and *Orodus corrugatus*, from the Lower Coal Measures near Alton, in this State. The latter, as suggested by Messrs. NEWBERRY and WORTHEN, is unquestionably generically allied to the teeth described under the former name, the specimen figured (Vol IV, Pl III, fig 18,) preserving four teeth of the median row, probably of the right ramus of the mandible, or left maxillary, besides three successive rows of two and three teeth Specifically, however, the latter species exhibits strongly contrasted characters in comparison with the former, in the more tumid, spreading figure and the more elaborate tracery of the superficial coronal ornamentation. One of the specimens figured by Messrs NEWBERRY and WORTHEN, (Pl IV, fig 11,) which is referred to the former species, exhibits in its lofty median summit, flanked by comparatively slender, diverging lateral prolongations of the crest (which converge at an angle of about 90°) a most striking contrast to the form generally presented by the teeth of this species Neither of the magnificent series of teeth from Kansas and Iowa, have representatives of the form here referred to, and yet, from the symmetrical form of this tooth, it seems very improbable that it is abnormal. It is possible that the anterior portion of the upper jaw bore a single row of these cuspidate teeth, or it may be the representative of a distinct specific form The Iowa and Kansas specimens, above described, are apparently specifically identical with the teeth here referred to.

In a former volume of this Report, Messrs. NEWBERRY and WORTHEN described a tooth under the name *Helodus denticulatus* (Vol. II, p. 81, Pl. V, fig. 6,) which was reported from the Keokuk division of the Lower Carboniferous series This unique specimen certainly possesses marked affinities with the teeth of the genus under consideration, indeed it might readily be mistaken for an abraded tooth from the anterior portion of the median row of acuminate teeth, showing the buttress like projections in the anterior face, but possessing at the base of the posterior crown face, beneath the eccentric median cone, a protuberance or callosity, such as occurs in some forms of *Helodus (Lophodus*, Rom ,) as well as in *Orodus* Since the above description was published, we have had opportunity to examine large accessions illustrative of the ichthyic fauna of the Keokuk epoch, but without meeting a solitary companion to the tooth here referred to. This naturally suggests the possibility of some error in assigning the specimen in question to the Keokuk limestone.

With the single exception just alluded to, the present genus would appear, for anything to the contrary furnished by present data, to be confined to the Upper Carboniferous or Coal Measure period in our earth's history, in the lower and upper members of which examples are known to occur It is not at all improbable, as suggested by Messrs. NEWBERRY and WORTHEN, that this group constitutes the representative of *Orodus* in these horizons, since only a single form of the latter genus has been noticed from the Coal Measures, (*O Alleni*, St. J. and W.,) and this form may prove to belong to the present genus.

In the dedication of this remarkable genus of *Hybodonts* to the memory of Professor AGASSIZ, we but poorly, however appropriately, express our appreciation of the profound labors of the great naturalist in this field, and the impetus his researches gave to the cultivation of fossil ichthyology; and, in no less degree, the affection of a pupil for his lamented preceptor.

There remains to be noticed the following forms relating to the genus above described, of which it is thought there have already been determined four distinct species.

## AGASSIZODUS VARIABILIS, (N and W., sp.)

Pl VIII Fig 1-22

*Lophodus variabilis* NEWBERRY and WORTHEN, 1870, Ill Rep, Vol IV, p 361 Pl 4, Fig 4, 5 11

The typical species upon which the genus was based, is that here referred to, and which was described from fragments of two teeth, and the nearly perfect specimen, fig 11, Pl IV, of the fourth volume of this Report The two former specimens, figs 4 and 5, respectively represent unequivocal examples of teeth from the median and probably one of the anterior rows of the mandible of the same species as that to which the great jaw specimens previously noticed belong; fig 4 showing the median prominence of the crown of the new tooth, as indicated by the unabraded state of the triturating edge, and fig. 5 preserving a fragment of the anterior extremity of a tooth probably referable to one of the anterior rows of the right ramus, as indicated by the direction of the oblique striation of the inferior basal surface. The tooth figured in Pl. IV, fig. 11, however, apparently presents the anomalous condition of a perfectly symmetrical tooth, the center of which is suddenly produced into a very strong, lofty, laterally compressed cone, the apex rounded from front to back, the angles presenting a delicate cutting edge marked in the upper portions by the minute decussations or downward curved carinæ common to the other examples. Towards the base in the antero-lateral portions of the cone, the crown is continued in a pair of lateral crests of apparently the same symmetrical proportions, and which diverge forward and downward at an angle of about 90°. Only about one third of their extent is represented in the figure cited, and which partake of the characteristic conformation of the more regular formed teeth. The lateral arms equal, at least, in length the entire elevation of the median cone, differing from the normal appearance of the teeth of the lateral rows only in their comparatively more slender proportions, being much compressed antero posteriorly, and the apparent obliquity of the anterior butteresses to the sloping crest line, though they are nearly vertical to the general horizontal plane of the tooth. The base presents the same outline as the crown, the comparatively thin lateral portions gradually expanding in thickness and depth posteriorly, terminating in an obtusely rounded angle behind, the inferior median portion being deeply channeled, the vertical or transverse striæ becoming oblique when extended into either lateral prolongation In the direction and contour of the anterior and posterior faces of the base, as also the lateral portions of the interior surface, no essential differences are observed by which it might be distinguished from the prevailing individuals But in the symmetrical form of the tooth, as indicated not only in the coronal region, but also in the conformation of the inferior basal surface, there would seem to be strong evidence that there existed but a single row of these teeth and that this row was confined to the symphisis, the lateral wings resting respectively upon either ramus As no similar shaped teeth are present in the mandibular specimen described at length above, it would seem apparent that, in case the present form belongs to the above species, it probably pertained to the upper jaw.

On the position of the teeth upon the jaw, reference has already been made in the foregoing description. It remains to note in general the variability of the individual teeth, and to what extent it is dependent upon the relative position they occupied upon the jaw In the rami of the lower jaw there occurs as many as eighteen rows of teeth, or eight at least anterior and nine posterior to the large median row, which latter possessed above twenty five individual teeth, while the lateral rows ranged from forty to fifty and more, the posterior rows apparently possessing the larger number. The diminution in size consequently from the inner to the outer teeth of a row is very gradual, and the evidence afforded by the large, mature ramus from Kansas would seem to indicate the persistency of the teeth to an extent far in excess of that of the modern *Cestracion*, or even of the Liassic *Hybodonts*, the deciduous character of which, however, affords but a faint idea of the number of teeth shed from the jaws as compared with the comparatively small number permanently in use and in process of development at the same time upon the jaws. It is evident that both jaws of a mature fish probably possessed at least two thousand to two thousand five hundred teeth. It may be of some interest here to make some estimate of the probable size attained by this species. The common *Cestracion* of the Australian seas, one of the most nearly allied living representatives of these Carboniferous *Selacians*, presents the most accessible data upon which to base our calculation. Of the latter an individual thirty inches in length from snout to the caudal extremity, possesses jaws the mandibular portion of which are about four inches in length.

Assuming that the Carboniferous fish was of similar shape, which seems highly probable, that is remarkable for the breadth of the anterior or cephalic region, the mandibles of the ancient fish, which were near twenty-eight inches in length, would indicate a total length of from fifteen to twenty feet—truly formidable dimensions compared with the largest known individuals of the existing *Cestraceonts*

The teeth of the posterior rows are generally distinguishable by their more robust proportions and the rounded extremities Those of the anterior rows are appreciably more slender, their extremities more angularly terminated Only the teeth of the median row are prominently acuminate, though the first contiguous rows either side present a partially developed eccentric cone As seen from above, the teeth are slightly sigmoidally curved, those of the median row with the arch backward, while those of the lateral rows are slighly arched forward. In the relative number of buttresses in the anterior face there is marked irregularity, the buttresses increasing in number in the same row with age, at the same time subject to numerical modification by accidental causes, yet the extreme posterior rows appear to possess a relatively larger number of buttresses than the teeth of the corresponding rows in front, while there would also appear to be an irregular diminution in the number in the successive rows from the median row towards either extremity of the ramus The same irregularity obtains in the disposition of the buttresses of contiguous teeth in the same row, so that no two individuals present precisely the same details of superficial conformation, although in general proportions and outline the most marked persistency prevails, which may also be applied to the lesser details of ornamentation.

The examples given in illustration of the various forms of teeth from different portions of the ramus at the same time exhibit the details of modification presented by the various individuals. We have included therein certain specimens found with the group of teeth discovered by Prof TODD, which it is supposed probably belonged to the upper jaw These latter are represented by teeth which differ in certain particulars to such an extent as to present strong contrast to the teeth of the opposite jaw, as determined by comparison with the great mandibular specimen from Kansas The teeth here especially referred to are represented in Pl. 8, fig. 6 and 7 The former, on account of its very eccentric median cone, is not comparable to the teeth constituting the median row of the lower jaw, which, as shown by comparing the Iowa and Kansas specimens, possess marked persistency in form and proportions; it would therefore seem more probable that we have here a tooth which occupied a corresponding position upon the right ramus of the upper jaw. The latter specimen, fig 7, also presents characters which appear not to admit of its reference to the mandibular rows no similarly shaped teeth occur on the lower jaw, their marked sigmoidal curvature, and the central position of the slight apical prominence, constituting the chief distinguishing features. Their comparatively slender form would indicate that they belonged to the anterior rows, and it would seem very probable that they constituted the row contiguous to that of the median teeth of the right maxillary In figures 15, 16 and 17, Pl 8, we may possess representatives of teeth pertaining to the extreme posterior rows of the upper jaw, since the mandibular specimen from Kansas affords no similar teeth. On the other hand, the latter specimen exhibits teeth in the extreme anterior rows unmistakably like those represented in figures 18 and 19

The shagreen scales and other semi ossified fragments of the cartilaginous jaws which pertain to this species, have been mentioned in the foregoing notice of the genus.

*Position and localities* · So far as our data show anything to the contrary, the present species appears to be restricted to the Upper Coal Measure strata, in which position authentic specimens from the following localities have been obtained LaSalle and Springfield, Illinois, at both places above the horizon of coal No 9 of the Illinois section; Fremont county, Iowa, Osage county, Kansas.

## AGASSIZODUS VIRGINIANUS, St J and W.

Pl 8 Fig 23. a b, c, d

A unique specimen of a tooth discovered by Prof J J STEVENSON in the Upper Coal Measures of West Virginia, seems to possess distinctive features, as compared with the forms prevailing in the Coal Measure strata in the Mississippi valley, sufficient to establish its distinct specific character. The tooth in question is small in size, half an inch in length, and about 30 inch in greatest hight The crown is very stout in its build, slightly arched backward, the crest forming an acute angle, and regularly rising into the somewhat prominent, slightly eccentric median cone, rounded and inflexed at the extremities; the posterior face is considerably distended about midway between the basal line and the crest, and besides the sharp ridges descending from the faint secondary cones half way to the base, and the delicate intermediate carinæ marking alike both sides of the crest, the inferior half of the surface is ornamented by delicate, wavy vertical lines, the anterior face presents six buttresses, which are relatively strong, three in the long extremity, and two in the opposite extremity, with a wide space intervening between them andthe median buttress—the inferior half of the surface between the buttresses similarly ornamented as described in the opposite face. The base is relatively shallow, stout, in depth about two-thirds the hight of the crown, and proportionately thick antero-posteriorly.

The little tooth above described, which has apparently never been brought into use for triturating purposes, and therefore in perfect condition, probably belonged to one of the lateral rows, either anterior, or more likely posterior to the median row, and indicating a species in this respect quite strongly contrasting in its dentition to that previously noticed However, the specimen may have belonged to a median row, but in either case its distinctive peculiarities are too marked to suggest identity with the other forms of the genus It probably belonged to a young fish, else it represents a species which never attained the formidable size of the fish which bore the teeth of *A variabilis.*

*Position and locality* From strata about 100 feet above the Mahoning sandstone, or lower part of the Upper Coal Measure series of the Appalachian region; near Morgantown, West Virginia The above strata have afforded Prof. STEVENSON a few very interesting ichthyic remains, some of which are described in the present report

### AGASSIZODUS SCITULUS, St. J and W.

Pl 6, Fig 16 a, b, c, d, 17 a, 18 a, b, c

This form is represented by very small and minute teeth prevalent in strata of the Middle Coal Measures, or upper part of the Lower Coal Measures, of which only a few detached teeth are thus far known to us. These would indicate some variableness in shape, but no more than is consistent with their relative position upon the jaws, and of which it is believed we have examples pertaining to the median and lateral rows. The superficial characters presented by the various forms at present known are illustrated in the figures in Pl. 6, and need not be detailed in the text, further than to remark their distinguishing characters as compared with the previously noticed species The teeth of the supposed median rows of this form bear a somewhat close resemblance to the unique Virginia example noticed in the foregoing description, only the coronal faces are more strongly ornamented, and the posterior face more gibbose and abruptly unbeveled to the basal line below. The opposite face between the prominent vertical buttresses exhibits traces of what appear to have been transverse striæ, the latter feature is indistinctly shown in a group of three teeth from Iowa, although it is not represented in the figure given of the specimen, Pl. 6, fig 17 a The relative shallowness of the base (which is made to appear of greater depth than is really the case in the figure just cited, as also in fig. 18,) in all these examples, together with their small size, distinguish them from the teeth of *A variabilis*, of the Upper Coal Measures A tooth of one of the lateral rows, probably anterior of the median row, is illustrated Pl 6, fig 16 a, b. c, d, showing enlarged views of the various aspects of the tooth, which was also from Iowa, in a stratum a little above that whence the preceding specimen was obtained. While the figure 18 a, b, c, Pl 6, shows a tooth obtained by Mr FULLER from the shales overlying coal No. 5, near Springfield—a horizon probably nearly corresponding to the lower coal bed of the Middle Coal Measures of the Iowa survey.

We also possess an interesting specimen preserved in a nodule from Mazon creek, which apparently shows the remains of the entire cranial and jaw cartilages of a fish of the present species, but which is in so crushed and distorted a condition as to afford little additional information From the size of the teeth and the traces of the extent of the jaw, there would appear to have been comparatively fewer rows than obtained in the species *A variabilis;* but further than this the specimen scarcely affords more than conjectural evidence on those more important details of the arrangement and character of the teeth of the opposite jaws. The cartilages present the appearance of minutely reticulated sheets, the substance of the semiosseous matter having been quite dissolved, leaving in relief the mineralized interstices, the apertures having the same elongated outline described in connection with the cartilages of *A variabilis* under the preceding generic notice

*Position and locality* Specimens of the teeth of the above described form are known to occur in the lower strata of the Middle Coal Measures of southern central Iowa, also in nearly the same or subjacent horizons of the Lower Coal Measures of Illinois, near Springfield, Bloomington, and Mazon creek, in Grundy county.

### AGASSIZODUS CORRUGATUS (N. and W., sp.)

Pl 8, Fig 24

*Orodus corrugatus*, NEWBERRY and WORTHEN, 1870, Ill Rep, vol IV, p 358, Pl III, Fig 18, 18a

Our collections afford a few detached teeth from various localities and horizons, representative of the species formerly described by Messrs. NEWBERRY and WORTHEN under the name *Orodus corrugatus*, a brief notice of which is here offered The original specimen was obtained from a position referred to the lowest workable coal bed of the Lower Coal Measures, near Alton, Illinois Mr FULLER obtained from the shales of coal No 7, near Danville, a tooth of one of the median rows of the same species, while Mr. ALEX BUTTERS procured from the roof of coal No. 5, near Carlinville, teeth also probably referable to the same species But one of the most interesting discoveries in this connection is that by Prof MUDGE, of a tooth represented Pl 8, Fig. 24, from the Upper Coal Measures in the vicinity of Manhattan, Kansas. The latter specimen pertained to one of the median rows, and exhibits in the details of ornamentation and general conformation precisely similar features possessed by the original specimen, the only dissimilarity is in the comparatively great elevation of the median cone. But we would hardly venture to place great stress on this character alone—indeed, the tooth from Danville presents an intermediate condition in this respect Hence, it would seem highly probable that we already possess authentic evidence of the extensive stratigraphic range of this species

## GENUS PERIPLECTRODUS, St. J and W

Teeth symmetrical Base more or less expanded laterally, or sometimes very compressed, symmetrically inrolled from within outward, sometimes embracing, as in the whorls of *Nautilus*, again but gently arched vertically, the lateral edges beveled and grooved, inferior surface excavated. Crown consisting of a transverse series of strong median cusps, flanked by at least a pair of small lateral denticles, one on either side, and which regularly increase in size from the outer to the inner extremity or with age: coronal cusps enameled, smooth or vertically striated.

The marked resemblance in form of the teeth above indicated to the detached teeth of *Plectrodus*, Agassiz, of the British Upper Ludlow "bone bed," suggested the term by which they are here designated. But their mode of implantation and apparent succession is quite different from that of the Upper Ludlow teeth, the present teeth apparently, as in the *Cochliodonts*, constituting a complete row, in which only the coronal portion exhibits the individual elements and which are merged into a common basal support. Taking the coronal region, a single set of the transverse cusps, the large median cone flanked on either side by a small lateral denticle, and we have almost the counterpart of an individual tooth of *Cladodus* But here the intimate resemblance ceases; the basal region scarcely presents the least element in common with *Cladodus*, lacking the broad, posterior expansion—indeed the posterior face of the base more markedly suggesting the anterior aspect of the latter tooth

The symmetrical or exact vertical inrollment of the teeth would appear to indicate that they occupied an isolated position, either constituting the sole dental element of the fish by which they were possessed, or restricted to some part of the mouth other than the maxillary elements, or, if associated with other and probably quite differently shaped teeth, they may have occupied the symphysial position upon the jaws

Representatives of the genus have been found only in the Lower Carboniferous formations, which have afforded the forms noticed in the following descriptions

PERIPLECTRODUS WARRENI, St. J. and W.

(Pl 8, Fig 25, a, b, c

The form here indicated is distinguished by its robust proportions and relatively large size The basal portion is moderately expanded laterally, the beveled superior edge nearly equal to one-fourth the transverse diameter of the tooth, slightly channeled, and rounded into the thick inferior edge, the surfaces roughly striato punctate; the lateral borders regularly and somewhat rapidly converge from the moderately produced, obtusely rounded postero-lateral angles towards the outer extremity, the posterior face is relatively deep, nearly plane vertically, slightly arched inward laterally and below, and defined from the crown above by a faint shoulder, as shown in fig. 25c; the inferior surface presents a deeply excavated area, bordered laterally by the downward produced walls of the lateral borders, which is, however, concealed in a mature specimen by the inrolled anterior extremity, as seen in fig. 25c. A mature specimen exhibits at least seven transverse series of coronal cusps, of which the median one is very strong, rapidly tapering to the acute apex, slightly curved sigmoidally with the apex directed slightly forward, slightly compressed antero-posteriorly, giving an oval transverse section, with delicate cutting edges, and ornamented in both faces by numerous, delicate vertical costæ, much as in *Cladodus;* the lateral denticles, of which there is one on either side the great cone, from which latter they are quite detached, are relatively very small and similar in shape and ornamentation to the median cone; the several sets of coronal cusps rise from transversely elongated coronal bases, which completely isolate the contiguous sets, but which are firmly connected with the basal portion without any visible suture or other line of demarcation The specimen figured represents a large-sized specimen, which, but for the abrasion of the anterior portion of the crown by which the cusps are more or less worn down, is quite entire

The collections afford above a score of examples of the above form, including specimens in various stages of growth, and some abnormally developed individuals worthy of particular notice Amongst the latter, it is apparent that large and mature teeth sometimes produce extra cusps in the newer or posterior portion of the crown, or, perhaps, by accident one set of cusps has been displaced or crowded to one side, thus destroying the perfect symmetry observable in the normal condition, and sometimes two median cones are placed side by side or in alternating order In certain examples of medium sized teeth, which show only three or four sets of coronal cusps, the antero inferior margin presents a broad, inbeveled area, in shape nearly corresponding to the posterior face, and from its smooth condition appearing never to have been articulated or cemented to the teeth in advance, which must have preceded these more mature developments. The latter examples would seem to indicate that, by accident, perhaps, the dental plate sometimes presents two or more segments quite perfect in themselves, but parts of the complete series as represented by a perfect specimen Again, in very young examples, showing three or four sets of cusps, we find the same proportions as are maintained in the older examples. But there occur in the collections very small specimens, showing as many as eight set of coronal cusps, completely inrolled or embracing, but with the cusps and lateral basal borders so worn down as to leave little room to doubt but that these minute examples are but part of the dental plate which has become detached from the newer or posterior portion of the series This would indicate that a perfect, mature example may present all the way from eight to twelve, or even more, sets of cusps, but those of the anterior extremity being hidden from view by the inrollment of the older extremity of the plate.

The present form is dedicated to the memory of an esteemed young friend and companion, Master WARREN SPRINGER

*Position and locality* Upper Burlington limestone, Buffington creek, Burlington and Augusta, Iowa

PERIPLECTRODUS COMPRESSUS, St. J. and W.

Pl. 8, Fig 26 a, b, c

The present form is represented by a unique and perfect specimen, discovered by Mr VAN HORNE It is characterized by the extreme lateral compression of the base, the lateral walls of which are but slightly produced outward in their descent and relatively shallow, defining the lateral boundaries of the correspondingly narrow, deeply channeled inferior surface, and but moderately arched antero-posteriorly The crown partakes equally in the lateral compression of the basal region, the specimen showing four sets of cusps, of which the two anterior ones are much worn by attrition; the median cones are relatively very large, the long diameter of their elliptical transverse section extending in the direction of growth or antero posteriorly, instead of transversely as in the preceding form, they taper to the rounded apex, with a faintly defined lateral carina in either face, but without visible striation or other ornamentation, the anterior and posterior faces sharply rounded, at the base in either side, sometimes nearly median but generally slightly anterior to the median line, arise a pair of tumid, almost rudimentary lateral denticles, which are not nearly as distinctly defined from the median cusps as in the preceding and following forms herein described.

The tooth above described differs so markedly from the two other species of the genus at present known, as scarcely to need further comparison, while, in its general features, it presents unmistakable generic affinities with those more typical forms.

*Position and locality* Upper beds of the St Louis limestone, Alton, Illinois

PERIPLECTRODUS EXPANSUS, St J and W

Pl 8, Fig 27, a, b, c

The single example of the present form which has come to our notice, is distinguished by the great lateral expansion of the base, the gently beveled upper edges being grooved in a manner similar to that observed in *P. Warreni*, moderately arched antero posteriorly, the anterior extremity obtusely pointed, the posterior face of moderate depth, interrupted by a shallow median sinus defined on either side by tumid protuberances which converge into the acute postero lateral angles, the inferior surface is somewhat deeply excavated, the concavity being transverse, the lateral walls not so conspicuous as in *P Warreni* The coronal region preserves three set of cusps, the anterior ones nearly obsolete from wear, and which are characterized by the stout median cone, which is nearly circular in transverse section or but slightly compressed antero posteriorly, with extremely delicate lateral edges, and ornamented with numerous delicate, sharp, widely spaced vertical costæ, the lateral cones, which are separated from the base of the principal cusp by only slight intervening space, are exceedingly minute, rapidly tapering and recurved, and ornamented similarly to the median cone.

The unique example shows the two posterior set of coronal cusps in perfect state of preservation as to abrasion, but the median cones are broken off so that their entire length and shape is not shown. The form bears closest resemblance to *P. Warreni*, described from the Upper Burlington formation, from which, however, its extreme lateral expansion and relatively shallow base readily distinguishes it

*Position and locality* Lower fish bed of the Chester formation, Chester, Illinois

## GENUS STEMMATODUS, St. J. and W.

Amongst the collections from the Upper Burlington limestone, our attention was first drawn to a group of teeth, quite numerously represented, but of so anamolous and withal variable character as seemingly to indicate representatives of several distinct though closely allied generic groups Subsequently, however, we have had opportunity to examine a fine lot of these remains in the collection of Mr SPRINGER, from a single locality, but all as detached or isolated teeth, which has resulted in the conviction that they all probably belong to a single genus, and of which there would appear to be several kinds, varietal or specific As to the character of these latter forms, whether they merely represent the variableness of the dental elements according to the relative position of the teeth, or really indicate specific distinctions, may remain an open question so long as our material consists of these isolated elements of the dental armature.

These teeth may be arranged under at least two typical subgroups, which, taken by themselves separately, would appear to offer distinctive features sufficient to suggest their possible generic distinctness, but, as we shall attempt to show, these subgroups seem to be connected by a most varied and almost complete gradation, as shown by a large suite of specimens exhibiting the intermediate stages almost uninterruptedly The first of these subgroups above alluded to may be represented by teeth possessing the following general features. Teeth, as seen from above or below, triangular in outline, the anterior extremity forming the more or less acute, rounded angle, one or other of the lateral margins exceeding in length the opposite side, therefore conclusively showing that there were rights and lefts, whether associated in pairs or greater numbers. The basal portion is but slightly produced beyond the coronal region anteriorly and laterally, is generally rounded, possibly by abrasion, into the inferior surface, which latter presents a slightly arched outline between the front and posterior extremities, plane or slightly concave laterally. The crown consists of three or more longitudinal rows of stout, depressed denticles, which originate near the anterior extremity, gradually diverging and increasing in size posteriorly, the individual cusps of the various rows alternating, their apices directed backward, and in worn specimens, especially towards the front, scarcely individualized on account of the attrition to which they have been subjected while in use, the perfect cusp is more or less compressed antero-posteriorly, with more or less well defined lateral angles or cutting edges, and striated as in *Cladodus*, the posterior ones are much produced backward, projecting far beyond the posterior basal border, from which the crown is defined by the more or less distinct termination of the enamel layer. See Pl 8, fig 30

The second subgroup alluded to above, is represented by comparatively simple teeth, in which the basal region is much narrower, though probably presenting much the same contour as in the preceding teeth, but generally being worn to a rounded ridge below, gently arched between the extremities, and surmounted by a single row of coronal cusps, which in shape and succession are much like one of the single rows in the teeth above noticed See Pl 8, fig 37.

The intermediate forms, or those connecting the extremes above described, are represented by (1) teeth possessing basal features generally preserved in the condition last noticed above, but which when perfect show a more or less deeply excavated inferior surface, bounded by the walls of the lateral margin, and terminated anteriorly in a downward produced process, the crown occupied by two rows of teeth, the cusps depressed and irregularly alternating. See Pl. 8, fig. 32 (2) Teeth, represented in fig 33, Pl 8, in which the two rows of cusps are less individualized, seeming to originate in a single row towards the extreme front, though probably the two rows becoming merged in widely spaced irregular alternating order, such as is maintained throughout the crown in (3) the variety represented in fig. 35, Pl. 8 The latter teeth are also apparently in pairs, but those represented in figs 32, 33, appear to be symmetrical and therefore may have occupied a median position.

As to the nature of these little dental bodies, whether they pertained to the jaws or other part of the mouth, it may not be possible conclusively to decide They may have occupied the tongue or back part of the roof of the mouth, a supposition suggested at least by their resemblance to the dental plates of some of the Devonian ganoids, *e g.*, *Dipterus*; while, on the other hand, they are not so strikingly unlike the dental armature occurring on the jaws of *Ceratodus* But the latter suppositions, again, seem less probable on account of the occurrence amongst these remains of apparently symmetrical teeth, so that, were they referable to the maxillary elements, they must have occupied the extreme anterior portion of the jaws, and hence indicating a fish whose jaw extremities were not edentalous In the former position, they may have occurred in pairs or threes, as also in case they belonged to the anterior or symphysial region of the jaws

The several more or less distinct forms thus far observed are further noticed below, where the several varieties are designated by a provisional term, in the absence of data showing their true character and relationship

## STEMMATODUS CHEIRIFORMIS.

Pl 8, Fig 30 a b,c

Under this term is included the form represented in the above referred to illustrations, teeth which exhibit the extreme development of coronal cusps, of which there are from three to four rows—the outline, as previously stated, being triangular, with one or other of the lateral margins considerably more extended than the opposite side, thus producing an unsymmetrical figure suggestive of the lateral position of the tooth or its association with one or more companion teeth. The basal portion has already been described, it deserves mention, however, that this portion of the tooth, as shown in the several specimens, is more or less modified by accidental causes, so that none of the specimens may exhibit a perfect individual in this respect But in the coronal region, save what is due to attrition while the teeth were in use, there is quite persistent uniformity in the number and disposition of the cusps and rows. A specimen of medium size, as that figured, shows seven cusps in the longer marginal row, five in the shorter or opposite row, and six in the median row. In all these specimens the first three or four cusps of each respective row in the anterior portion of the crown, seemingly present a disproportionately small size as compared with those in the posterior portions of the tooth; but this may be attributable, in part at least, to abrasion by which the anterior cusps have been reduced in size, appearing as mere tuberculose prominences. In the larger and more perfect posterior cusps, the form is moderately compressed antero-posteriorly, rapidly tapering to the acutely rounded apex, the lateral angles sharp, and both faces marked with numerous, sharp vertical costæ, those in the posterior face being relatively finer. In the majority of specimens, perhaps, not a vestige of the coronal ornamentation remains, and in some examples the cusps are so worn down throughout as to give to the crown a striking resemblance to the teeth of *Ctenodus*, which they also recall in shape The specimen shown in fig 29, Pl. 8, is probably a very eccentrically developed tooth referable to the present form.

## STEMMATODUS BIFURCATUS.

Pl 8, Fig 31 a,b,c

The singular form here indicated is represented by a unique specimen. In shape it is like that above described, possessing three rows of coronal cusps in the anterior half, but the median row suddenly terminates with the fifth cusp, the two lateral rows being continued posteriorly in independent rami, bearing respectively eight and nine cusps, which latter, though forming but a single row, are somewhat irregular in their disposition or alternating from side to side, instead of forming a direct line. Taking into view the posterior rami of this tooth, there is no perceptible distinction between them and some of the irregularly single crested teeth noticed further on. The crown is worn, and although the shape of the cusps is well preserved, there remains no trace of the vertical costæ or other ornamentation.

### STEMMATODUS BICRISTATUS.

Pl. 8, Fig. 32, 33, 35.

Of the present form the collections contain several specimens, that illustrated in fig. 32 being a very small individual but in a more perfect state of preservation than its associates, which latter are much worn, the basal region rarely indicating its true contour. In the perfect condition, the teeth present a postero anterior elongated outline, the base slightly expanded laterally beyond the limits of the crown, and produced downward forming the rather strong lateral walls of the excavated inferior surface, the anterior extremity considerably produced downward in a laterally compressed wedge shaped process, between which and the tumid posterior extremity the outline is moderately arched upward and rounded into the posterior coronal face; a faint median ridge extends from the anterior process into the inferior basal area, which is also irregularly pitted. The coronal region is occupied by two slightly sinuose rows of cusps, of which latter there are respectively seven and eight in one or other row, depressed and quite regularly succeeding and increasing in size from front to rear, but without visible ornamentation, the rows are separated by a deep, angular median groove, and seem to originate in a single primary cusp at the anterior extremity, the cusps of the respective rows are arranged in an irregular alternating order.

A variety apparently of the same form is represented in fig. 33, Pl. 8, in which the principal dental plate, though much worn, exhibits quite the same characters, the only observable difference consisting in the less distinct individualization of the rows of cusps, which are more crowded, and towards the posterior extremity an extra denticle is developed in one side, which was probably succeeded by others—the extreme posterior portion of the tooth being broken off, so as not to show a third row of denticles if such existed. But the most remarkable feature of the specimen is the possession or association with a pair of very small, similarly shaped dental plates, one on either side of the extreme anterior extremity, between which accessory teeth the principal plate seems to have been wedged from below, but with which they are apparently firmly welded. The relative position of these accessory teeth is shown in the figures In shape they are not unlike worn examples of the large tooth to which they are attached, and though firmly cemented where they impinge upon the central tooth, their basal outline is perfectly preserved by the presence of the deep groove shown in the side view of the specimen, they are much worn, and the character of the coronal region is consequently indistinctly shown, there would appear to be but a single row of cusps, such as obtains in the variety illustrated in fig. 37, Pl 8, an extremely abraded individual of which these accessory teeth strongly resemble At all events, we evidently here possess an intimation of the relative position of three individual dental plates, since it is difficult to conceive accident could have any share in their so symmetrical disposition, and, further, it seems very probable that the intimate relation of two quite distinct varieties is hinted at at least

One of the most common varieties contained in the collections is that represented in fig. 35, Pl. 8, a form which it is not always easy to distinguish from the middle tooth of fig. 33. These teeth, however, always appear to be rights and lefts, as shown by the curvature in their outline viewed from above The basal region does not differ from that of the tooth alluded to, but the crown presents a double row of alternating cusps, but which are so intimately associated as scarcely to indicate their real character, and which in the anterior portion of the crown become still less distinct and finally merge into a single row towards the extreme front The unsymmetrical form of these teeth readily suggests their identity with the accessory teeth in the specimen above referred to The latter form is quite variable in the minor details of size and the number of cusps along the crown, but not to the same extent as occurs in the form representing the median tooth, fig 33, isolated examples of which, or those in which the accessory teeth have become detached, show the cusps originating anteriorly in a single row, diverging into two rows in the middle, and towards the posterior extremity presenting three such rows of cusps

### STEMMATODUS SIMPLEX

Pl 8. Fig 36 37

Teeth represented by four examples, showing similar outline to the varieties last noticed above, apparently symmetrical, and in which the cusps are arranged quite regularly in a single row The tooth fig. 36, which preserves the enamel, shows no trace of striæ, from which it is inferred the cusps were smooth The specimen just referred to exhibits the anomalous feature of the budding of an accessory arm bearing three cusps, from one of the lateral surfaces about midway between the extremities. This accessory branch is unmistakably firmly attached to the parent body, there being not the faintest trace of suture or other indication of its independent origin. The specimen is unique in this respect, though recalling the appearance of the tooth shown in fig 33, but no similar detached teeth have as yet been found—the oblique direction of the cusps of the accessory branch, which appear nearly at right angles to the direction of those in the principal plate, would at once attract the attention in case they are hereafter discovered

A specimen of the form under consideration, in which a portion of one of the lateral faces has been broken away, reveals something of the internal structure, or sufficient to show that in the dentine portion of the tooth the individuality of the cusps is maintained nearly to the inferior plane of the base, presenting a segmented condition, which is quite concealed by the external coating of enamel in the crown and the density acquired by the exposed portion of the base. Were these dental plates always found in the symmetrical condition of the specimen, Fig 37, the question might arise whether they are referable to the dental apparatus of the fish, but pertain to the dorsal defense and akin to the segmented defensive spine originally described by Dr. LEIDY under the generic name *Edestus*, which they also somewhat intimately resemble in general shape.

## STEMMATODUS SYMMETRICUS.

Pl 8, Fig 28

A form, of which we have seen very few examples, represented by very small teeth, having the lateral diameter equal to or exceeding that from front to rear, and nearly symmetrical in shape. The basal region is considerably produced laterally, beveled above to the lateral edges, which are sharply rounded and rapidly converge towards the anterior extremity from about the middle, whence posteriorly they are nearly parallel or but slightly diverge, in front the superior borders are marked by a pair of lateral and median folds, the inferior surface presenting an elliptical outline, moderately excavated and defined by the strong, obtuse anterior and posterior border, sometimes arched downward laterally, as shown in the specimen figured. The coronal region presents two rows of cusps, which gradually diverge posteriorly, the cusps in the respective rows irregularly alternating, and regularly or irregularly increasing in size posteriorly—the specimen figured shows five and six in each respective row, depressed, the posterior ones strongly produced beyond the basal line; the cusps are moderately compressed antero-posteriorly, sublenticular in transverse section with sharp lateral angles, which rapidly converge towards the sharply rounded apex, the anterior face occupied by relatively strong, sharp vertical costæ, which in the opposite face are much less strongly marked.

The very few specimens of the present form indicate considerable individual variableness, and which, it is interesting to note, is precisely of the nature observed in other forms of the group, as in that cited in connection with *S cheiriformis*, wherein in one or other, or both, of the rows the cusps present the appearance of arrested growth near the middle of the tooth, thence continued by disproportionately large cusps. So far as refers to the coronal elements there is much similarity to the form described above under the name *S bicristatus*, though the rows diverge more rapidly posteriorly, in which respect they recall a pair of the rows in the form *S cheiriformis*, as also in the shape of the cusps, the costation of which, however, is stronger.

*Position and localities* · All the above described forms occur in the fish bed of the Upper Burlington limestone, intermingled with the various other remains of fishes peculiar to this horizon; Buffington creek, Burlington and Augusta, Iowa, the former locality affording the majority of the specimens, and all those, with a single exception, employed in the illustrations.

The Keokuk limestone has afforded a few examples of the present group of teeth, but the specimens, unfortunately, are in so imperfect a state of preservation as scarcely to permit of satisfactory comparison with the Upper Burlington forms. There occur amongst these specimens apparently the same varieties as noticed in the preceding descriptions, though the teeth resembling *S. cheiriformis* are most common. But the Keokuk specimens of the latter type seem to have the cusps more erect and arranged in three or four rows, and the basal region would appear to be shallower. It is, therefore, very probable that a suit of well preserved specimens of these teeth would show distinctions of specific value. The *cheiriform* examples are labeled *S. Keokuk* All the Keokuk specimens are from the vicinity of Warsaw, Illinois, Keokuk and Bentonsport, Iowa

## STEMMATODUS COMPACTUS, St. J. and W.

Pl 8, Fig 38, a b, c.

Tooth very small, robust, long-elliptical in outline viewed from above. Base deep, lateral walls slightly converging in their descent, laterally compressed in front and produced downward into a process, posterior extremity rounded, interior surface moderately excavated and forming less than half the antero-posterior diameter of the entire tooth Coronal region moderately produced laterally, though the longer axis extends antero posteriorly, and occupied by a single median row of depressed cusps, which regularly increase in size posteriorly and as regular in the order of their succession, the posterior one produced nearly its entire length beyond the basal border, the crown is enveloped in a polished layer of enamel, the cusps are apparently destitute of ornamentation.

A solitary specimen is all we possess from which to recognize the above described form, but which is amply sufficient to show its distinguishing features in comparison with the previously noticed forms from the Upper Burlington formation. Of the latter, that described under term *S. simplex* most intimately approaches the form here indicated. But the present tooth is distinguished by its more compact, robust build, and especially by the more produced lateral borders of the crown, and proportionately deeper base

*Position and locality*. Lower fish bed of the Chester formation, Chester, Illinois

## Genus LEIODUS, St. J. and W.

Teeth of medium and small size, in general form like *Orodus*. Crown more or less arched laterally and vertically, basal margins constricted and sharply defined from the base, culminating in a more or less produced apex with obscurely defined lateral crests, convex in either face, the anterior face generally produced or buttressed beneath the median cone, and both faces occupied by comparatively faint, simple vertical sulci, which sometimes extend to the crest, producing obscure secondary prominences, surfaces generally smooth, polished, punctate, and sometimes, especially in immature teeth, verrucose or reticulately roughened in the basal margins Base, as in *Orodus*, relatively deep, gently convex behind, concave in front, with a more or less prominent shoulder above parallel with the inferior coronal margin. below obliquely beveled to the inferior edge.

The teeth here referred to are closely allied to *Orodus*, from which they are mainly distinguished by the comparative smoothness of the coronal surfaces, which are simply and generally obscurely lobed, or quite plain, instead of being corrugated. And the apparent diversity in the form of the teeth from different parts of the jaws, indicates a much more varied dentition than obtains in *Orodus*, in this particular approaching the modern *Cestracion*. The following are the sole species as yet indicated.

LEIODUS CALCARATUS, St J. and W.

Pl VII, Fig 11-13

Teeth variable in size and form, and separable into three or four varieties, which, however, are not persistent, blending into each other by almost imperceptible gradations, but which may be distinguished under three heads, (posterior, median and anterior teeth,) according to their supposed position upon the jaws Of these the median teeth are the largest, presenting a massive build and a somewhat strongly arched outline; base as long, and more or less oblique to, the crown, deep, thick, angular in outline, deeply channeled on one side, with a more or less angular convexity occupying the opposite side, both sides coarsely roughened and vermicularly pitted, inferior surface smooth, and obliquely beveled to an edge along the inner margin, crown generally strongly arched vertically, sharply constricted basally, rising into a more or less tumid, eccentric prominence, which is more or less produced inferiorly in the outer margin, surmounted by a slightly recurved acute apex; lateral wings gradually narrowed towards the extremities, which are obliquely truncated or rounded, and usually slightly curved forward, more or less undulated along the margins, with an obscurely defined median crest, surfaces nearly equally and regularly convex vertically, obscurely and irregularly lobed, with one to three or four narrow vertical sulci in one or other extremity, giving rise to an annulated appearance and faint secondary cones in the crest, basal margins marked by more or less numerous, faint rugæ—otherwise the coronal surfaces are smooth and finely punctate From individuals possessing the above characteristics there seems to be a gradation into smaller forms, some of which are of minute size, and which are readily recognizable by the extremely produced, slender, eccentric cone, which latter is also more or less deflected laterally, as well as recurved, more strongly produced basally in front, and seldom, if ever, lobed, though in in the larger individuals the lateral extremities are faintly undulated vertically, in the smaller ones laterally abbreviated, and the apex less eccentrically produced, in other respects presenting a community of characters which intimately connect them with the larger teeth A third form, which may have formed the posterior rows, is represented by individuals differing in no respect from the median teeth, except in the truncated or obtuse cone and depressed lateral wings. A fourth and sparsely represented variety is distinguished by the rather elevated, sharp-pointed, antero posteriorly compressed crown. Coronal surfaces enveloped in a thin, polished enamel-like layer, and very faintly verrucose; in worn surfaces the punctate structure is much more distinct, and in immature teeth the crown presents an elegant verrucose or roughened appearance. In transverse diameter the teeth range from less than .15 to 1.05 inch.

The varied dentition indicated by these teeth renders this one of the most interesting of the numerous *Orodont* species occurring in our Carboniferous rocks. In the mature or larger teeth, the coronal lobes approach more nearly the condition ascribed to *Orodus*, while in the small teeth, with the exception of the acutely produced median cone, the superficial characters even more resemble certain forms of *Helodus*, or the small teeth of certain *Psephodi*. In their diversity they recall the dentition of *Cestracion*—the small, acutely conical teeth corresponding to the prehensile teeth in the anterior part of the mouth, while the posterior teeth become less and less prominent and acutely apiculate, until reaching the low, obtusely conical or depressed teeth which composed the rows in the posterior portion of the jaws.

The collections from the Keokuk limestone also afford a few examples of teeth, which are indistinguishable from the Burlington specimens, except that they are apparently more coarsely punctate. Our series of these specimens is so small, however, as not to exhibit their distinguishing characteristics, if such they possess, by which they may be recognized from the form described above, though they may be indicated provisionally by the name *L. grossipunctatus*. The latter specimens occur in the Keokuk fish bed horizon at Keokuk, Iowa, and Warsaw, Illinois.

*Position and locality*: Not uncommon in the fish-bed of the Upper Burlington limestone; Louisa and DesMoines counties, Iowa; Henderson and Warren counties, Illinois.

## GENUS DESMIODUS, St. J. and W.

Teeth occurring in series or rows extending from the inner to the outer border of the jaws. Individually the teeth are of small size, robust. Crown laterally elongated, more or less strongly arched vertically, culminating in a strong, subconical, median prominence, which is strongly buttressed in the outer or concave face by an angular vertical ridge, laterally flanked by the obtusely angular crests, which are more or less strongly denticulated, inner face more or less regularly arched in both directions, anterior face gently concave or plane vertically, more or less strongly produced along the basal line in the median region, extremities rounded, basal borders unbeveled and occupied by a simple, wide coronal fold, which slightly overlaps the produced borders of the superior coronal region; surface polished, smooth or delicately marked along the crest by sharp thread like costæ, and in the edge of the coronal fold exceedingly delicate striæ. Base narrower and thinner than the crown, relatively deep, and produced posteriorly slightly oblique to the vertical plane of the crown, rectangular in outline, posterior face slightly convex, anterior face of less depth, moderately excavated, with a narrow shoulder parallel with and just beneath the coronal border, which is produced into a more or less conspicuous basal protuberance corresponding to the median angulation in base of the coronal region, inferior surface well defined, very obliquely beveled to the posterior edge; basal surfaces more or less coarsely roughened or pitted.

Many specimens present the teeth in serial order, in which condition they are sometimes soldered at the impingement of their bases into a common basal support, the inrollment of which strikingly recalls the form of the large triturating plates of *Psephodus;* again, in other series, each tooth is distinctly separated by suture from the contiguous teeth, and in isolated specimens the basal portion is entire, proving that all the teeth were not intimately associated by the co-ossification of their bases.

From the general figure of these series of teeth, it is difficult to avoid the use of the same descriptive phraseology employed in defining the outline and contour of the large inrolled crushing teeth of the *Cochliodonts*. Whether the small apical or terminal teeth are defaced by the effects of attrition while in use, or that they have suffered abrasion subsequent to their removal from the jaws, it is difficult to determine. In the latter case these terminal teeth might appear to be the immature inner teeth of the series, but we cannot overlook the fact that in most of the *Cochliodonts* the apical extremity of the inrolled teeth was buried in the integument of the jaw upon which they rested, and whether or no they were so buried, they always present the imperfectly preserved or abraded condition which is noticeable in connection with the lesser teeth of the series of the present forms. Further, in all individuals of *Cochliodonts* the coronal surface bordering the inner margin of the teeth is usually without blemish, except in such as bear evidence of having been beach worn prior to their having been imbedded, and it is a noteworthy fact that quite all the specimens of the species noticed under the present genus present the large teeth of the series in a remarkably perfect state of preservation. In view of these facts it is difficult to resist the conclusion that these teeth constituted part of the dental apparatus of a *Cochliodont* genus. On the development of the teeth some of our material exhibits interesting data. In rare instances, and in none better than in a specimen discovered by Mr VAN HORNE, series show the innermost or newest formed tooth to be markedly less in size than its immediate predecessor, thus it would appear that the formative matrices do not at the outset determine the full dimensions of the tooth, but the peripheral region and base is left to later processes for completion. It is often of importance in determining the identity of isolated teeth to be able to recognize the comparative degree of development of the individuals under examination. In the present examples the much-worn anterior teeth, with their strong and usually entire base, would scarcely be recognized as specifically identical with the immature coronal shell of the incomplete teeth, whose partially formed bases have entirely perished, but whose coronal markings are preserved with extremest sharpness.

In the group under consideration a combination of characters occurs which seem to indicate affinities with both the *Orodi* and *Chomatodi*, as represented by the genera *Mesodmodus* and *Venustodus*. Yet they may prove to be widely distinct from either of the above groups, and more closely allied to the *Cochliodonts*.

The representatives of the group belong to the Lower Carboniferous formations. The *Orodus minusculus* of Messrs. NEWBERRY and WORTHEN, of the Keokuk limestone, is a representative species, and closely allied to the typical form *D. tumidus*, of the St. Louis limestone.

### DESMIODUS TUMIDUS, St. J. and W.

Pl. Xa, Fig. 7-9.

Teeth minute, varying in outline from subtriangular to long elliptical, strongly built. Crown moderately arched laterally, obtusely rounded at the extremities, with an obtusely angular crest culminating in a strong, tumid, median prominence, which is nearly central in the laterally abbreviated varieties, but more or less eccentric in the elongated teeth, lateral portions of the crest bearing three to five, more or less, rather strong denticulations, which diminish in size towards the extremities and similar in shape to the median prominence, posterior face gently arched in both directions, sometimes sigmoidally so, anterior side more abrupt, faintly concave or nearly plane vertically, more or less produced in the median region where it is interrupted by the strong vertical angulation supporting the median cone, at the base of which, in the angle of the basal fold, occurs a small node-like protuberance; basal borders of the crown abruptly inbeveled and occupied by a simple wide coronal fold, the sharply defined upper edge of which slightly overlaps the produced borders of the superior coronal region, and which encircles the crown in a continuous band, gently arched upward in the median region and at the produced lateral extremities; coronal surfaces quite smooth and polished, the denticulations in the crest being defined by faint vertical sulci, and the anterior median buttress distinctly carinate. Base equal to the crown in depth, slightly less in lateral diameter, and but slightly produced posteriorly to the vertical plane of the crown, subrectangular in outline as seen from the posterior face, which latter is gently arched laterally, nearly plane vertically and faintly beveled below, anterior face rather deeply excavated, shoulder well-defined, produced into a delicate basal protuberance beneath the coronal angulation, inferior surface well defined and very obliquely beveled to the thin posterior edge, surfaces coarsely pitted. A specimen of medium size measures in lateral diameter .17 inch, antero posterior diameter .06; the abbreviated variety is proportionately shorter and wider in the same diameter, and the base relatively deeper.

The above species, examples of which were first discovered by Mr. VAN HORNE, is numerously represented in our collections, the majority of the specimens being in a very perfect state of preservation. It is usual to find three teeth arranged in a row, and some specimens present as many as seven teeth thus associated, and which are sometimes apparently firmly co ossified at the impingement of their bases. That the consolidation of the teeth upon a common basal support is not the normal condition, is shown not only by the examples, which are visibly separated by suture, but also by those detached individuals in which the basal portion presents no indication of such intimate union with the teeth of the same vertical series. Both the short and the elongated varieties occur in the above condition. In examples in which several teeth are associated, the same general proportion of parts is preserved in each individual of the series, except that in the small terminal teeth the crown is more or less abraded, other individuals exhibit eccentric enlargement of one or other extremity, and along the inner border of the series is sometimes present the coronal cap of an immature newly formed tooth; in the number of tuberculations of the coronal crests there is slight variation.

These teeth constitute a remarkably well-defined specific form, the variations of which are more dependent on individual proportions than on the modification of the characters which equally distinguish the abbreviated robust as well as the elongated teeth, as intimated in the foregoing description Intimately allied to *D minusculus* of the Keokuk limestone, it is distinguishable from that form by the strongly defined coronal fold, the elongated teeth by their broader and more regularly elliptical outline, while the short teeth differ from the corresponding variety of the above form in the proportionately greater elevation of the posterior crown face and the more strongly arched basal line

*Position and locality* · Although the teeth are found in greater or less abundance in certain layers, they range through a vertical thickness of strata of thirty feet, more or less, in the upper part of the St. Louis limestone; Alton, Illinois, St. Louis, Missouri.

### DESMIODUS COSTELLIFERUS, St J. and W.

Pl Xa, Fig 10, 11

Teeth minute, strong, more or less symmetrical Crown more or less strongly arched between the extremities, long elliptical in outline, obtusely rounded at the extremities, crest sharply defined, obtusely angular and gradually ascending from the extremities towards the middle, where it is more or less suddenly produced into a strong subconical, more or less eccentric median prominence, which is strongly produced in front forming a sharp vertical buttress, which is crossed by one or two delicate lateral carinæ, giving rise in the lower portion of the angulation to as many small node-like prominences of which the inferior one is largest, posterior face moderately arched laterally and vertically, sometimes with a broad convexity in the region of the median prominence, anterior face abrupt, gently concave in the lateral portions, but abruptly and sharply produced in the median buttress; basal borders strongly inbeveled, broadly arched upward in the middle and sharply so at the produced extremities, coronal fold wide, strongly defined along the obtuse angle of junction with the superior coronal region, the upper edge slightly overlapping and delicately striated vertically; the coronal surfaces are polished and smooth in the lower portion, along the crest sharp vertical costæ appear, which culminate in the delicate denticulations, of which latter there occur four to seven, more or less, in either one or other extremity, in the abrupt lateral declivity of the median prominence still fainter thread-like lines are observed, and in the more or less tumid convex face a few stronger costæ converge in the apex of the median prominence, sometimes only a single ridge occurs, forming a delicate vertical carina descending half way to the coronal fold. Base strong, nearly vertical to the crown, which it exceeds in depth, though considerably less in lateral and antero posterior diameter, posterior face rectangular in outline, slightly arched laterally and faintly depressed vertically in the middle, with a faint fold at the base of the inbeveled coronal border, and slightly beveled along the inferior margin, anterior face moderately excavated, superior shoulder prominent, with a relatively strong basal protuberance beneath the median angulation, inferior surface well defined, and very obliquely beveled to the posterior edge, basal surfaces coarsely roughened and pitted. The teeth seldom exceed .15 inch in lateral diameter

Of the present form perhaps two more or less well marked varieties are noticable, as represented by laterally elongated teeth, on the one hand, and on the other laterally abbreviated, stouter teeth, in which the median prominence is relatively stronger and the lateral portions of the crest with fewer denticulations We have also observed in the collection of Mr VAN HORNE a very minute tooth, apparently referable to the present form, in which the convex or posterior crown face is proportionately much deeper, regularly arched laterally, the lateral extremities of the basal fold more considerably curved upward in rounding the extremities, while the anterior face is exactly similar to that in the teeth noticed.

Notwithstanding their diminutive size, the specimens are usually absolutely perfect, even the most delicate carinæ and serrations in the crest and upper edge of the coronal fold are distinctly and sharply defined Compared with other forms, the peculiar ornamentation of the coronal region and the comparatively strong basal protuberance readily distinguishes the present teeth from *D. tumidus* of the same horizon, as also from *D. minusculus* of the Keokuk limestone.

*Position and locality* Not rare in the upper beds of the St. Louis limestone, Alton, Illinois, and St Louis, Missouri

## DESMIODUS? LIGONIFOMIS, St J. and W.

Pl XA, Fig 12-14

Teeth very small, subtriangular in general outline Crown strong and thick, gradually compressed towards the slightly obtuse crest, which is nearly horizontal or but faintly acuminate and minutely denticulate, each denticle being marked before and behind by a short carina, the apical point bearing a few faint radiating carinæ and which are rather more widely spaced than their lateral diameter, lateral extremities abruptly truncated; concave face nearly plane above the coronal belt, which latter occupies the broad inbeveled space, broadly arched downward along the lower margin and rapidly contracted laterally, upper margin less strongly arched and somewhat irregular in its direction, or slightly arched upward in the middle, apparently without imbrications but bearing a few obscure vertical plicæ in the region of its greatest vertical expansion; convex face about two thirds the hight of that just described, lateral portions above the coronal belt nearly plane, median region occupied by a strong angular vertical fold, which descends from the apex and rapidly increases in prominence towards the edge of the coronal fold, from which point it gradually decreases in elevation, terminating in a small basal protuberance, basal belt similar to that in the opposite face, though somewhat less in depth, simple, inbeveled, moderately arched upward in the middle and apparently considerably narrowed in crossing the median ridge and nearly parallel with the crest Coronal surfaces, in certain conditions, ornamented with short irregular vertical or slightly diverging thread like striæ, but usually, perhaps in the majority of specimens, nearly smooth Root short, thick, oblique, lateral margins slightly converging below, in breadth much narrower, and in depth less than the hight of the crown. Greatest lateral diameter of tooth of medium size 15 inch, or nearly equal to the entire elevation of tooth, hight of concave crown face about 10 inch

Of the several individual representatives of this interesting form, those furnished by Dr. WILLIAMS, of Boonville, are the most perfect. None of the specimens preserve the root entire, and most of them are otherwise mutilated, but the characters which distinguish them from other forms are sufficiently well displayed in all the examples In regard to the generic relations of these teeth, it seems not improbable that perfect examples might prove them to be distinct from *Desmiodus*, to which genus they are here provisionally referred, and with which they possess many features in common The rigid root, vertical crown and rather strong median fold in the convex face, together with the unbeveled coronal belt, present the same general characters which pertain to the above mentioned genus. They are readily recognized from *D minusculus* of the same deposits by the stronger and more compressed crown They may, however, hold the same relation to that form as does *D costilliferus* to *D tumidus* of the St Louis beds

*Position and locality* Upper fish bed horizon of the Keokuk limestone, Boonville, Missouri, and Bentonsport, Iowa.

## DESMIODUS? FLABELLUM, ST. J. and W.

Pl X A, Fig 15

Teeth small, moderately strong, flabellate in outline. Crown moderately thick, crest broadly arched, lateral margins low and slightly divergent from the ill defined extremities formed by the union of the coronal belt, and irregularly notched by more or less widely spaced, shallow serrations; concave face suboval, lateral diameter and hight nearly equal, gently arched vertically, very slightly arched or nearly plane laterally, with the lateral border slightly raised into a faint marginal rim, basal belt broad, well defined, rapidly contracted below, and occupying the unbeveled region, upper edge slightly arched upward in the middle and again curved upward in rounding the lateral angles, and marked by a few relatively strong vertical folds in the median region; convex crown face about one third less elevated than the opposite face, very gently arched laterally, in which direction it presents a broad, shallow channel in consequence of the slight vertical ridge, coronal fold very similar to that in the opposite face, though slightly narrower, simple, unbeveled, the upper edge approximating the curvature of the crest, both crown faces marked by short, irregular, diverging, thread-like lines, which increase by implantation and are much disconnected on approaching the crest, and much more strongly developed in the concave face where they reach half way to the upper edge of the coronal belt, enveloped in a polished enamel like layer Root apparently stout, thick, somewhat rapidly converging toward the inferior border, at its origin about half the lateral diameter of the crown. Lateral diameter of crown 16 inch, hight of concave face above the coronal belt .10 inch, including the coronal belt .14 inch, antero posterior diameter 05 inch.

The form under consideration is known to us by only a single specimen, an exceedingly handsome little tooth, which is nearly perfect with the exception of the root, which latter, unfortunately, has been broken away In its general aspect it recalls the form referred to under the name *Desmiodus ligoniformis*, from the same geological position, the resemblance being especially striking in the character of the coronal belt encircling the broad, inbeveled base of the crown, together with the superficial ornamentation It differs, however, markedly in the outer coronal aspect, as its less angular outline, the regular arching of the crest with its peculiar irregular serration, and the absence of the strong median ridge in the convex face, in each and all of which particulars it presents a striking contrast to the above mentioned form. The root was probably very short and stout, and set in nearly the same vertical plane as the crown. The variations of the individuals of *D. ligoniformis* present no approximation to the peculiarities apparent in the present form, while our material is insufficient to demonstrate, perhaps, their generic identity, much less their specific identity, by supposing these two forms to represent the dental armature of opposite jaws of the same species.

*Position and locality* Discovered by Dr. WILLIAMS in the upper fish bed of the Keokuk limestone, Boonville, Missouri.

## GENUS VENUSTODUS, St. J. and W.

Teeth laterally elongated, vertically arched. Crown abruptly constricted at the base and defined by imbricating folds, which form a proportionately broader belt along the concave side than in the opposite border, crest moderately elevated and usually well-defined, uniform or rising into a strong, obtusely conical, more or less eccentric median prominence, lateral portions more or less distinctly marked by obtuse denticulations, which gradually diminish in size towards the extremities, coronal surfaces enveloped in a polished enamel-like layer. Base forms a broad, shallow plate, more or less obliquely flattened inferiorly with well defined angles in front and behind, lateral and antero-posterior diameter less than that of the crown, with which it is nearly vertical.

The above group of teeth includes a form originally described by Dr LEIDY under the name *Chomatodus venustus*, which may be regarded as a typical example of the genus Besides the above, two or three additional forms from the superimposed and subjacent formations have come to our notice, which together form a remarkably well defined generic combination Each of these forms presents in kind and degree about the same individual variability, conclusively indicating their intimate relationship, while, at the same time, each retains its own well marked characteristics by which it is readily distinguishable from its congeners.

*Chomatodus (Helodus) denticulatus*, McCOY, (Brit Palæ Foss, p 618, Pl 3 k, fig 9 a, b,) of the Carboniferous limestone of Armagh, may possibly prove to be congeneric with the above. The genus is thus far known only from the Lower Carboniferous formations, from which the forms noticed in the following descriptions have been recognized

## VENUSTODUS ROBUSTUS, St. J and W.

Pl IX, Fig 15-13

Teeth having the same general form as the following described forms, and presenting two well marked varieties, especially distinguished by the angular extremities and vertically arched convex face of the crown. The first or larger variety is distinguished by the gently arched outline and the somewhat sudden culmination of the crest in a strong, obtusely pointed median cone, which is often truncated from wear; crest well defined, nearly central or nearest the convex border, lateral portions low or moderately elevated, and more or less distinctly denticulated; coronal folds forming a relatively narrow belt in the convex face, sometimes obsolete in the region of the swollen median prominence, the upper imbrications often broken into short, oblique plicæ terminating in the smooth area, lower folds forming a continuous belt with the broad, well marked band of the concave face, where it is composed of four to six folds, which are usually quite regular, or bifurcated at intervals. Base low, narrow, deepest beneath the convex border, inferior surface plain and defined in the angular inner and outer margins Of the second variety numerous representatives occur in the collection, distinguished by their smaller size, linear or gradually tapering outline, and low, uniform crest line which generally traverses the crown centrally, giving to the gently convex face a relatively greater depth than observed in the preceding variety; the concave face forms a narrow, shallow depression, limited below by the broad coronal belt, which is composed of as many as five folds, but which are generally less regular than in the large teeth, and which by frequent anastomosis present a net-work of raised lines. In many examples the upper fold is similarly interrupted by brief oblique plicæ as described above, the folds of the opposite face are less numerous, forming a narrow belt, often interrupted, or obsolete in the greater portion of the median region, the denticulated character of the crest also varies widely, the undulations generally obscure and irregularly developed, or obsolete. The base is proportionately massive, in form like the preceding variety

The varieties above noticed seem to be specifically identical, as determined by the community of their characters, while at the same time they diverge from those noticed in the following description in the same manner and degree. There appear to be no indications of gradation of characters sufficient to account for the peculiarities distinguishing these forms, yet it is possible they may prove to be only varietal expressions of one and the same species.

The small linear teeth bear, in some respects, striking resemblance to the group of teeth represented by *Helodus angularis*, N and W, especially in the uniform convexity of the one face and the relatively strong base. The imbricated belt encircling the crown, however, offers a contrast which readily distinguishes the present teeth from that above referred to, and associates them with the large acuminate teeth first noticed. In the marked convexity of the one side, the large teeth exhibit a somewhat intimate relationship with *V. Leidyi*, but the large size, central position of the crest, and more simple disposition of coronal folds, constitute features quite in contrast with those presented by the St. Louis species.

*Position and locality* Common in the Upper Burlington fish-bed, Louisa and DesMoines counties, Iowa

### VENUSTODUS VARIABILIS, St J. and W

Pl IX. Fig 7-14

The collections from the Upper Burlington, especially that of Mr. SPRINGER, contain fine and beautifully preserved series of a form which is so intimately related to *V. tenuicristatus* of the Keokuk, that, notwithstanding the somewhat striking contrast presented by extreme examples, it is extremely difficult to define them from the Keokuk form. Indeed, in many worn specimens, there is no distinguishable difference by which the teeth from different horizons might be recognized, and it seems hardly possible to foretell the results of an examination of a larger suite of the Keokuk specimens The Burlington teeth, however, may be recognized as a group, however variable the individuals, and this fact has led to their being noticed, provisionally, under a distinct head.

While the present form presents all the variability observed in the preceding and above mentioned forms, it is distinguished by the appreciably less robust proportions, though attaining the same size. The lateral extremities are more acutely rounded, and there is a very apparent increase in the number of coronal folds, especially along the concave crown face, although in this latter respect there is noticeable very considerable variation—many examples closely agreeing with the Keokuk teeth in possessing only three or four imbrications, while in some extreme example they attain double the ordinary number, and when strongly developed they increase by bifurcation, and more rarely by implantation, the folds along the convex face are also very like the above form, ranging in number from two to four, often interrupted at the median line by the more or less angular ridge of the principal cone, the median prominence is also quite variable in shape, always more or less eccentric, laterally deflected, the apex produced over the concave face, generally laterally compressed, though sometimes presenting a remarkably produced, symmetrical prominence vertical to the horizontal plane of the crown; the lateral portions of the crest exhibit the same variableness in the distinctness of the denticulations, which are always present in well preserved individuals, while the body of the crest is compressed, low, and striking the convex margin from which it is separated by the shallow intervening sulcation—rarely traversing the crown centrally. The base is the same as in the preceding and above named forms, outer and inner margins angular, shallowest beneath the concave face, inferior surface flattened and beveled as in the above. The coronal surfaces are smooth and polished, but in worn specimens coarse punctæ appear in the abraded spaces; in many teeth either one or other, sometimes both surfaces are ornamented with a delicate tracery of thread like lines which ascend more or less obliquely from the upper border of the coronal belt, becoming obsolete near the crest

Representatives of the second variety, as alluded to in connection with the Keokuk form, have escaped notice, and this seems not a little singular, taking into consideration the comparative abundance of the material in the present instance However, the collections contain teeth in which the median cone forms a relatively inconspicuous prominence, and the lateral elongation is an approach, at least, to the linear outline of the above referred to form

The third variety is also known from but few examples, which present the same general outline and contour, but which are distinguishable from the Keokuk form by the undulated or plicated and, perhaps, vertically more plane convex crown face, the angle in the convex face of the median cone being very obscurely developed, lateral portions of the crest obscurely and irregularly denticulate, the concave face is also sometimes more or less distinctly undulated in a manner similar to that observed in the large teeth, with which they otherwise bear features in common. Of the latter style of teeth the collections contain few examples, and this is true in relation to all the other forms of the genus, with the exception of *V. Leidyi*, of which the collection of Mr. VAN HORNE affords a fine series of both the large median teeth and the anterior teeth, and the variety represented by the teeth just described.

In regard to the geographical distribution of the present form, it is known to occur at nearly all the localities in the Upper Burlington where the fish-bed stratum is exposed. A noticeable feature of these collections is the persistency of the characters which distinguish, even though it appear slight, the Upper Burlington from the Keokuk teeth, and the present form from that previously described, with which it is associated at the locality which has received the most exhaustive exploration. But, however similar species may appear when comparisons are limited to a few examples of one or other form, experience oftener than otherwise proves, on the examination of large materials, a much greater divergence in the characters peculiar to each than it was possible to detect in a comparatively limited series of specimens.

*Position and locality:* Common in the Upper Burlington fish-bed, Louisa and DesMoines counties, Iowa, and Henderson, Warren and Adams counties, Illinois.

### VENUSTODUS TENUICRISTATUS, St. J. and W.

Pl. IX, Fig. 19-24.

Teeth attaining medium size, variable in outline and proportions, in which latter respect at least three varieties may be recognized.

The first of these attains the largest size and most robust proportions, ranging from .35 inch to 1 inch in lateral diameter, and .10 to .33 inch in antero posterior diameter, presenting from above an irregular long-elliptical outline, sometimes sigmoidally curved, and moderately arched between the extremities. Crown very gradually converging from the median region towards the lateral extremities, which are obtusely rounded, one narrower than the other, lateral portions of the crest low, compressed, forming a sharp, more or less distinctly and numerously denticulated crest, which is suddenly produced into a relatively strong eccentric prominence, which in mature individuals is laterally compressed, erect or laterally deflected, generally towards the short extremity, and usually flanked in the convex face by an angular vertical buttress and a more or less prominent gibbosity in the opposite face, the concave face is but slightly depressed vertically, averaging in width about one-third greater than the opposite face, which in the majority of specimens is also depressed vertically on either side of the principal cone—in rare examples the angle of the median cone is much distended, producing a broad convexity in the median region of the narrow face; coronal belt well marked, consisting of three or four imbrications in the concave face, and three in the opposite border, generally regularly disposed throughout the median region, but often interrupted by intercalated folds on reaching the extremities—in some instances the uppermost fold terminating in the acutely angular buttress of the median cone. Base forming a strong plate, considerably narrower than the crown, the narrow face beveled to the angularly defined, flattened inferior surface, and about half or two thirds the hight of the face beneath the convex crown face, which latter equals the greatest depth of the base. In worn teeth the crest is more or less reduced in elevation, the median cone is almost always truncated and frequently worn down to the level of the lateral portions of the crest; coronal surfaces smooth or faintly undulated, and polished, basal region more or less roughened.

We have recognized a variety differing from the above by their more slender proportions, and linear or slightly curved outline, relatively inconspicuous and eccentric median prominence, the crest being remarkably uniform throughout, the coronal belt containing an additional fold. Lateral diameter of crown .54 inch, antero posterior diameter .11, elevation about .05. A third variety is distinguished by its relatively short lateral diameter, and strongly arched vertical outline, and the predominance of the concave crown face over convex face in vertical hight, the lateral portions of the crest are faintly denticulated, the median cone sometimes flattened in the convex face, the coronal belt showing three folds in the concave and two in the opposite border, where they are sometimes interrupted, presenting a beaded appearance. Lateral diameter of crown .30 inch, lesser diameter about .12, or equal to the depth of the concave face, hight of median cone in the convex face about .07 inch.

The differences which distinguish the several varieties noticed above one from the other are not sufficiently characteristic to be deemed of specific importance, and probably indicate no greater difference than that dependent on the position the teeth occupied upon the jaws. The first variety probably held a median position, the third occupying the anterior portion, and the second variety may have filled the intermediate space, or, perhaps, more probably the posterior portions of the jaws.

However variable these teeth may appear on casual examination, a more intimate acquaintance derived from the comparison of a large suite of specimens reveals a remarkable identity of features common to all, such as readily distinguish them as a whole from the allied though specifically distinct forms noticed from other horizons Nor does this variability shade off into these other specific forms, each of which, while they present an equal degree of variation, are marked by certain persistent features peculiar to them.

From the St Louis and Chester species, the present teeth may be recognized by the proportionately greater size, narrower coronal belt, and the peculiar compressed, carina like crest, and the laterally compressed median cone As in those forms, the denticulated character of the crest is quite variable, often almost obsolete, though, perhaps, never entirely absent except when obliterated by attrition

*Position and locality* Common in the ichthyic horizon of the upper part of the Keokuk limestone, vicinity of Warsaw, Illinois, Keokuk and Bentonsport, Iowa, St Francisville and Boonville, Missouri, apparently rare at the latter locality, since few examples occur in the interesting collection of Dr. WILLIAMS, made at that locality

## VENUSTODUS LEIDYI, St J and W

Pl IX. Fig 1-4

*Chomatodus venustus*, LEIDY 1856 Trans Am Phil Soc Phila, vol xi Pl v, fig 19-21

The teeth which are arranged under the above specific designation present considerable individual variation in form, but which may be considered under two heads or varieties, as represented by individuals from different parts of the jaws

First, teeth of small size, rectilinear in outline viewed from above, gently arched between the extremities, a tooth of average size 50 inch in greatest length, and in breadth across the median portion of the tooth 15 inch The crown forms a rectilinear plate, very slightly disturbed in the middle, lateral extremities angularly rounded, rising into a subconical, more or less eccentric and usually truncated apex, which forms an obtuse angle in the arched outline from which the crest gradually declines to the extremities, the crest is more or less sharply angular, and occupied by a variable number (10 to 18) of delicate though well defined denticulations, which are generally more strongly developed and numerous in one than in the other wing of the crest; the concave face of the crown is gently depressed, about one third higher than the opposite face, which latter is slightly arched vertically, and more or less protuberant in the median region beneath the apex; the coronal folds form a continuous belt encircling the crown, broadest along the concave margin, diminished to a narrow belt in the convex border, and composed of a series of delicate interwoven thread like imbrications, of which only the uppermost forms an uninterrupted line spanning the crown, both coronal surfaces are covered by a thin, smooth, enamel-like layer, usually worn away for a short distance below the crest on the convex side, exposing to view a minute punctate structure The base forms a very low, relatively narrow plate, inferior surface slightly oblique to the horizontal plane of the crown, with more or less angular margins in front and behind, and in lateral extent nearly equal to that of the crown.

The second variety is represented by smaller teeth, which are principally distinguishable from those above described by their strong bow-shaped or vertically arched outline and acuminate apex, but which show a gradation from the acutely angular crest into the less strongly apiculate teeth In the more prominently arched examples, a sharp, angular ridge descends from the tip of the apex to the base of the crown in the convex side, which latter is almost imperceptibly arched vertically, the opposite face gently channeled in the long diameter; towards the extremities, which are more or less asymmetrical, the crest is delicately denticulated, the same as observed in the larger teeth In the character of the coronal folds, punctation of the convex margin of the crest, form and position of the base, they are in no particular essentially dissimilar to the large teeth The relative position occupied by these small teeth was probably anterior to those first noticed above—the extremely arched forms may have occupied the symphysis of the jaws corresponding to the prehensile teeth of the *Cestracionts* In size they also exhibit considerable variability, however, apparently never attaining the dimensions of the posterior or median teeth

We are indebted to Mr VAN HORNE for the use of a fine series illustrative of the varied phases presented by the interesting form under consideration The species was first made known by Dr LEIDY, who described it under the name *Chomatodus venustus* The original specimen, which was kindly loaned us for comparison, was derived from the upper portion of the St Louis limestone, probably from St. Louis, Mo., and from Warsaw, Ill., as we have most conclusively determined from the nature of the matrix as well as the fossil itself, in both which respects it agrees with the St Louis specimens, and presents the same strong contrast to the Keokuk species from the latter locality Having adopted the original specific application to designate the generic group, of which the present form is regarded a typical representative, it gives us pleasure to rededicate the species in honor of its discoverer.

The above form is closely allied to *V. angutus*, from which it is particularly distinguishable by the more rectilinear outline and the interwoven or reticulated character of the coronal folds, and which are discernible in almost every condition in which the individuals are met with With the Keokuk and Upper Burlington forms it scarcely needs comparison

*Position and locality*: In the middle and upper beds of the St. Louis limestone; Alton and Monroe county, Illinois; St. Louis, Missouri.

VENUSTODUS ARGUTUS, St. J. and W.

Pl. IX, Fig. 5, 6

Teeth of small size, gently arched along the convex border, more or less arched vertically, extremities rounded or angularly truncated, distance in a direct line between the extremities of a medium-sized specimen .32 inch, antero posterior breadth of crown .09 inch. Of this form two more or less well marked varieties may be recognized, the smaller of which is distinguished by its more strongly arched outline, and in some instances faint sigmoidal curvature, obtusely rounded at the extremities; besides, the crown is centrally traversed by a low or moderately elevated crest, which culminates in a strong, conical, laterally deflected median cone, which in worn specimens is tumid, and flanked in either extremity by a row of more or less prominent denticulations, which regularly decrease in size on nearing the extremities, and are more strongly developed upon that side overshadowed by the eccentric median cone, varying from eight to eleven in number; the convex surface is slightly arched vertically, often interrupted in the median region by a tumid distension of the basal portion of the principal cone, in hight little less or even exceeding that of the opposite face, which latter presents a shallow depressed area, terminated below by a comparatively wide coronal belt composed of as many as three more or less regular and strongly marked imbricating folds, which are reduced to one or two narrow folds in the convex face.

The second variety, which we have identified with the present species, is characterized by its rectangular outline as seen from above, is less strongly arched vertically, and traversed by a subcentral crest, which rises more abruptly from the convex border, culminating in a somewhat eccentric vertical cone, with from four to seven lateral denticulations in either extremity; convex face relatively low, lunate in outline, gently arched in both directions, and margined below by two or three narrow imbricating folds, which fold round the extremities coalescing with the much wider belt of the opposite face; the concave face is about one-third higher than the opposite side, of which fully one half is embraced in the numerously imbricated coronal belt, which forms a broad border projecting outward and downward in a less abrupt descent than the declivity of the superior surface, lateral extremities abruptly truncated or but slightly rounded; the thread-like imbricating plicæ of the coronal belt more or less frequently and irregularly anastomose, with intercalated folds in the stronger and more widely spaced upper portion of the belt, where they are upturned at their extremities, and becoming obsolete before reaching the lateral extremities of the crown, where the main belt is more or less suddenly deflected, sometimes at right angles, and curved round the extremities.

In all these varieties the base forms a thick, more or less angular plate, the inferior surface of which is slightly oblique to the horizontal plane of the crown, from which it is strongly defined on either side by a deep sulcation, and constituting less than half the vertical elevation of the tooth. The crown is highly polished, but in worn specimens the crest is more or less distinctly punctate, in which condition the lateral denticulations are often nearly obsolete.

The present form was first recognized in a few specimens in the collection of Prof. WORTHEN, all of which represented the small arched teeth. Subsequent discoveries brought to light larger and more symmetrical teeth, corresponding to the varieties in the St. Louis limestone which have been specifically associated under the name *V. Leidyi*. Some examples among these teeth are remarkable for the prehensile character of the strong apiculate median cone, and this feature is confined apparently to certain of the more strongly arched specimens, and has led to their reference to the anterior portion of the jaws, recalling the acuminate teeth occupying a similar position upon the jaws of *Cestracion*. Others, again, though strongly arched, have the median cone nearly vertical and angularly buttressed in the convex face, the lateral denticulations being less prominent, and the concave face more nearly approximating its condition in the last above described variety. Although, regarded separately, these varieties may appear to be characterized by persistent differences, yet, when we bring to our aid the evidence afforded by other forms of the type, one can hardly fail to recognize in these seeming differences the local and individual variations of the teeth of one and the same species. The evidence which may hereafter be obtained from a more complete series of specimens, will as likely prove the specific identity of these varieties as is the result in the numerously represented and equally and similarly variable dentition of the previously described forms.

The present form is readily recognized from the species occurring in the subjacent St. Louis formation, by the more regular disposition of the imbricating folds; indeed, it bears a more intimate resemblance to the forms described from the Keokuk and upper Burlington formations than to *V. Leidyi*.

*Position and locality*. Not uncommon in the upper fish bed of the Chester limestone; Chester, Illinois.

## GENUS HARPACODUS, Agassiz.

Teeth laterally elongated, vertically arched, and gently curved outward in the concave face, with nearly parallel margins. Crown compressed along the crest and deeply and regularly serrated, expanded below, convex face relatively low, nearly vertical, opposite face gently concave vertically, coronal borders more or less produced and sharply inbeveled to the base in either side, laterally produced and sharply rounded. Base strong, more or less obliquely produced to one or other side, less the lateral diameter of the crown, lateral angles well defined, the relative depth of the two faces the opposite of the coronal faces, that beneath the convex crown face being deepest, gently excavated or plane, the opposite side also laterally channeled, defined below by the obtuse angle of the inferior surface, which latter is obliquely beveled to the more acute posterior (?) margin The coronal surfaces present the usual dense, polished enamel like external layer.

Amongst some teeth from the Carboniferous limestone of Armagh, belonging to the collection of Lord ENNISKILLEN, Prof AGASSIZ recognized a peculiar type to which he gave the above generic appellation, and which, as originally understood, was supposed to be represented by two distinct forms. One of these was designated by the specific term *H dentatus* and so published in the catalogue of types belonging to the collection of Lord ENNISKILLEN, in 1869, the other form, which was represented by one or two imperfectly preserved specimens, had received no specific designation. In the course of our investigations, we have been so fortunate as to secure additional material, representing several species which are closely allied to the forms noticed by Prof AGASSIZ, and from which may be derived a somewhat more satisfactory idea of their character and relations than was afforded by the few European examples accessible to him.

From the study of these data, we have been led to transfer the form *H dentatus* to the genus *Ctenopetalus*, Agassiz, with which it apparently has the most intimate relationship; although strongly marked specifically by the extremely developed serrations amongst the American forms, however, we find those which, in the above respect, occupy an intermediate position, thus more closely connecting this extreme form with the more delicately serrated forms of the genus

Of the type represented by the unnamed form above referred to, our collection also afford a few quite entire individuals, representing two forms, which fully illustrate the distinctive and congeneric characteristics which they in common possess with the European form alluded to above, at the same time furnishing conclusive evidence as to their generic distinctness from the first noticed form, *H. dentatus* Thus limited and defined as above, *Harpacodus* constitutes a well characterized generic group, the affinities of which would appear to be near *Chomatodus*, as indicated not only by the low, compressed crown, but also the conformation of the basal region.

### HARPACODUS OCCIDENTALIS, St J and W.

Pl X A, Fig 2

Teeth small, laterally elongated, gently arched outward along the concave border and also along the crest. Crown compressed along the crest, expanded below in the concave face, deeply pectinated with from ten to twelve rounded denticulations, the intervening sulci extending downwards nearly to the basal border, very gradually diminishing in size towards the extremities, which are abruptly rounded, the convex face forms a long, narrow crescent shaped area, more or less strongly curved downward at the extremities, rising vertically from the basal margin; concave face about a third higher than the opposite side, gently depressed, and laterally and vertically gently arched, basal borders prominent, abruptly curved upward at the extremities, and continuous with the less prominent coronal border of the convex face, in both faces abruptly inflexed to the basal region. Coronal surfaces smooth, the crest sometimes delicately striated. Base moderately thick, laterally nearly as long as the crown, which it equals in depth, the deep side beneath the convex crown face gently excavated and nearly in the same vertical plane, a third deeper than the opposite side, which is somewhat more deeply channeled, inferior surface plane, obliquely beveled to the acutely angular posterior (?) border, lateral angles well defined Greatest diameter of a medium sized specimen .25 inch, vertical elevation of tooth .10, antero posterior diameter at base of crown .05, elevation of concave crown-face 07 inch.

The above form is based upon specimens discovered by Mr. VAN HORNE, in whose collection there is a nearly perfect example, while we have obtained other more or less perfect examples, which exhibit but slight individual variation, and so well marked is the form that even fragmentary specimens are readily determinable.

*Position and locality* Upper beds of the St. Louis limestone; Alton, Illinois, and St. Louis, Missouri.

### HARPACODUS COMPACTUS, St. J. and W.

Pl. X A, Fig 1

A specimen obtained by Mr. WORTHEN from the Chester formation, which exhibits the concave aspect of the tooth, constitutes a second and closely allied form of the above genus known from American horizons The present form is distinguished from that last described from the St Louis, *H occidentalis*, by its stouter proportions, strongly arched outline, the obliquity of the deep face of the base, and relatively shallower opposite face, and more obliquely beveled inferior surface. The coronal region is very similar to the above mentioned form, the pectinations, perhaps, are more tumid and the crest slightly acuminate

There remains to be noticed another form with which the present species is closely allied. This is represented by small teeth occurring in the Mountain limestone at Armagh, Ireland, specimens of which, with a rare suite of other forms, had been borrowed by Prof. AGASSIZ from the collection of Lord ENNISKILLEN, which we were so fortunate as to be permitted to examine at the museum in Cambridge before they were returned to Florence Court. These teeth are but little larger than the American form, from which they mainly differ in the less vertically arched and laterally curved outline, and, perhaps, fewer pectinations, the median one of which is perceptibly more strongly produced and elliptically pointed at the apex, than is the case in the present form.

*Position and locality* Upper fish bed of the Chester limestone, Chester, Illinois

## GENUS CHOMATODUS, Agassiz

### CHOMATODUS COMPTUS, St J. and W

Pl X, Fig 19-22

Teeth attain large size, strong variable in general proportions, and presenting at least two somewhat distinctly marked varieties One of these varieties is represented by teeth which are mainly distinguished by their abbreviated lateral extremities, which are sharply rounded, and traversed by an obtuse though well defined median crest, from which both sides alike rapidly slope to the abruptly constricted basal margins, the median portion of the crown is broadly produced in front and behind, and rises into a very strong, prominent, obtusely conical median cone whose apex overhangs the concave face, which is gently concave vertically, the opposite face presenting a gibbose prominence gradually expanding below and distinctly defined from the lateral wings, the basal margin is regularly curved along the concave side, very slightly arched upward in the middle and gently rounded to the extremities, in the opposite face it is suddenly interrupted in the median region by a more or less deeply notched border, in both faces occupied by a narrow, more or less obscurely imbricated coronal belt, from which arise irregular oblique lines which produce an exceedingly delicate and highly ornate sculpturing extending over the greater portion of the coronal surfaces, except in the convexity of the median prominence, which is smooth and towards the apex finely punctate. The root forms a relatively deep, strong, angular plate, nearly equal to the lateral diameter of the crown as also in depth, the deeper face nearly plane, the opposite side occupied by a broad depression terminating above in the strongly produced basal margin of the concave face, inferior surface well defined, gently arched upward and beveled at a slight angle to the horizontal plane of the crown from the concave to the inferior margin. Lateral diameter of crown about .80 inch, entire hight of tooth .68, greatest slope of crown in the convex face .50, greatest slope of crown in the concave face .31, antero posterior diameter of crown .38 inch.

A specimen of less robust proportions, in which the lateral extremities are greatly developed, presents a laterally elongated outline, the median portion of the crown—though smaller and slightly eccentric, and, perhaps, more regularly obtusely conical and less produced over the concave face—closely resembles that described above, the wings, however, are extremely produced laterally, and traversed by a high angular median ridge which is very gradually narrowed to the rounded extremities; the concave face but slightly depressed vertically or about equal in degree to the convexity of the opposite face which slightly exceeds it in elevation. The coronal ornamentation is the same as observed in the first mentioned variety, with the obliquely ascending plicæ perhaps a little more distinctly marked. The root forms a very deep plate nearly vertical to the crown, rhomboidal in outline, contour of outer and inner faces and basal surface similar to the base of the first described teeth. Lateral diameter of tooth 1 inch, hight .58, slope of convex side of median prominence .31, slope of concave side .25, antero posterior diameter .32.

Associated with these teeth Mr SPRINGER has found several specimens of smaller size, ranging from half an inch to a quarter of an inch in lateral diameter, the proportions and other characters of which seem to prove their specific identity with the larger teeth above described. These smaller examples, or at least some of them, have the median portion of the crown less produced, and in very small specimens the coronal surfaces are quite smooth and polished. The form is intimately related to *C. angulatus* (N. and W. sp.), and, perhaps, more so to *C. elegans*, N. and W., of the Keokuk limestone. It is distinguished, however, by the peculiar sculpturing of the coronal surfaces and the obscure definition of the coronal folds.

*Position and locality.* Fish bed of the Upper Burlington limestone; Louisa county, Iowa.

### CHOMATODUS PARALLELUS, St. J and W.

Pl X A, Fig 3, 4

The Warsaw beds have furnished a few examples of a form of the above genus which seem to be specifically distinct from the forms indicated from the St. Louis, as also those known to occur in the earlier Keokuk and Burlington deposits, and to which we have applied the above specific designation.

Teeth of medium or small size, laterally elongated, with the upper and lower margins parallel, moderately thick through the basal margins. Crown symmetrical, more or less compressed and sharp crested, rounded at the extremities, the convex face equals in elevation half the entire hight of the tooth, plane or slightly arched vertically, nearly straight laterally, with a narrow coronal belt consisting of two or three imbrications; the concave face is occupied by a rather deep lateral depression, and bordered by three or four well marked imbricating folds, which are gently curved upward at the extremities where they are confluent with the folds of the opposite face; the crest and basal margins are for the greater extent horizontal and parallel, and in the perfect condition the crown is enveloped in a coating of enamel, which is usually more or less distinctly striated vertically, in worn specimens a coarse punctation appears and the crest presents a more or less jagged outline The base is thick and strong, nearly perpendicular to the crown, inferior surface relatively wide and obliquely beveled from the concave side to the opposite margin, the convex face nearly plane and vertically furrowed, the shallower concave face deeply channeled beneath the produced coronal margin. None of the specimens before us are entire, but some of them plainly indicate a length of three-fourths of an inch, with a hight of .20, elevation of concave face .15, elevation of convex crown face 10.

The finest example of the above form which has come to our notice was kindly loaned us for description by Dr. G. A. WILLIAMS, who obtained it from the Warsaw beds near Boonville, Mo It is related most intimately with that described from the St Louis limestone under the name *C incrassatus*, but, at the same time, its less robust proportions, more symmetrical form, parallel margins, less angular basal extremities, and greater inequality in the elevation of the respective coronal faces, will readily serve to distinguish it from the latter form. Authentic specimens are known to occur only in the Warsaw beds, where it has been found on the Piasa, above Alton, while in the St. Louis limestone in the same region its presence has not been detected, although these deposits have been most thoroughly studied by Mr. VAN

HORNE with especial reference to the stratigraphic range of the ichthyic remains occurring therein.

*Position and locality:* Warsaw beds, Booneville, Missouri, and on the Piasa, above Alton, Illinois.

### CHOMATODUS INCRASSATUS, St. J. and W.

Pl. X, Fig. 18.

Teeth of small size, seldom exceeding half an inch in lateral diameter, in outline linear, or slightly arched in the convex side, tapering towards one or other extremity, both extremities obliquely truncated from the convex to the concave border. The base is nearly vertical to the crown, which it nearly equals in length and depth, very stout, compressed and sharply defined beneath the coronal margins, expanded or thickened below, the deep side slightly channeled laterally above, and broadly beveled below, opposite side relatively low, deeply channeled, interior surface well defined, very broad, plane, and strongly beveled to inferior acute angle, in outline long subrhomboidal as seen from the deeper face, which is more or less strongly furrowed vertically. Crown slightly exceeding the length and breadth of the base, the convex face rising abruptly from the basal margin, gently arched vertically and laterally, crest compressed, culminating in an eccentric prominence near one extremity, broadly arched towards the opposite end, the opposite face descending in a broad, shallow concavity, which is limited below by a strongly marked coronal band composed of from three to five imbrications, which form a continuous band with that of the convex face, where it is only about half as wide and composed of fewer imbrications, the basal border in the convex face is nearly direct, sharply curved round the lateral extremities and somewhat prominently defined from the basal region, in the concave face, the basal border is strongly produced, the median portion gently arched upward and inward, and sharply curved to the extremities in the obliquely truncated lateral portions. The coronal surfaces are polished and present a delicate vertical striation in the lower portions, on nearing the crest delicate vertical sulci often appear, which produce a minute denticulation, and which is especially discernible in the convex side.

Mr. VAN HORNE has brought together a beautiful series of teeth from the St Louis beds, which we have been led to regard as the representatives of a distinct form At Alton and St. Louis these teeth are associated with the *C insignis*, Leidy, and a more slender form closely allied to *C. cultellus*, N and W, of the Chester limestone The latter form also occurs at the Pella (Iowa) locality, associated with *C. inconstans*, with which latter form the present teeth may possibly prove to be identical. But, taking into consideration the distinctive features presented by the above described teeth, it would be mere assumption to recognize such specific identity in the present state of knowledge regarding their variableness, and the absence of material showing the gradations such as have been illustrated by the large series of specimens of *C inconstans*, whose association render their evidence almost conclusive, and which are equally strongly marked from the few examples of the present form occurring at the same locality. The teeth under consideration present some individual variation in size and form, though more to the extent noticed in the above mentioned form They approach *C insignis* in the outline of the convex aspect, but are distinguishable by their stronger proportions and more angular general figure.

*Position and locality* Upper beds of the St. Louis limestone; Alton, Illinois, St. Louis, Missouri, and Pella, Iowa.

## CHOMATODUS INCONSTANS, St J and W.

Pl X, Fig 5-14

The collections from a single locality and stratum, in the St Louis limestone of Iowa, afford a fine series of isolated teeth, which present considerable variation in form and size, constituting three or four quite well marked varieties, but which are intimately united by the gradation of characters common to all, and which seem to furnish conclusive evidence of their specific identity, however widely extreme examples may appear to differ from one another. 1 The teeth here designated possess in common the same coronal characters, which undergo the least modification of any part of the tooth in the mutations which are traceable in the various individuals which depart most widely from the normal condition of the species But in the basal region occur the principal variations, which give rise to the more or less strongly marked vertical forms herein noticed The crown forms a rather stout, regularly sloping ridge, the crest of which is subcentral or nearest the convex border, which latter is gently arched in both directions, while the opposite face is occupied by a wide and usually deeply excavated furrow extending the entire length of the concave face, and margined below by the thin, straight or slightly arched border, the upper surface of which often presents a delicately wrought basal band composed of several imbrications, the crest of the crown usually culminates near one or other extremity, whence on the one side the slope is abrupt to the rounded or somewhat obliquely truncated extremity, while on the other it gradually diminishes in elevation towards the obtusely pointed extremity of the tooth; the basal band, instead of forming a narrow belt, as in *C. incrassatus*, extends well up the convex face in a wide belt interrupted by obscure imbrications, it is, however, in comparatively few individuals that the coronal folds are well preserved, and probably in no instance were they as strongly developed as in the above mentioned form. In the teeth which represent the normal aspect of the present form, the root is apparently produced downward in a plane nearly vertical to that of the crown, moderately thick, nearly median, deeply channeled beneath the produced border of the concave face, less so in the opposite side, and slightly beveled along the lower margin, inferior surface well defined, very oblique, or nearly corresponding to the plane of the convex crown face, in depth equal to or exceeding the greatest elevation of the crown. 2. Among these teeth there are some which present a strong, irregular serration of the crest, as shown in fig 7, Pl X; the root is vertical as in the before mentioned variety, while in other respects they are very similar, the denticulate character gradually merging into those in which the crest is quite worn. 3 A third variety presents a more regular crest line, which, although it is not central, shows the side corresponding to the convex face to be slightly excavated, the root more obliquely produced in the plane of the convex crown-face, and constituting a connecting link between the above mentioned and the following extreme varieties. 4. Under this head is included a series of teeth which might at first seem to be quite dissimilar from their associates, as above described. They are distinguished by their uniform outline, the two longer sides being nearly parallel, the coronal crest nearly central and moderately arched, the concave face gently depressed, the opposite face but slightly arched vertically, sometimes quite plane or faintly depressed, the basal folds are obsolete in all the examples before us. The root, which in the previously mentioned varieties is more or less nearly vertical, in the present examples is remarkable for its extravagant obliquity, indeed so much so that in some extreme cases it forms an uninterrupted plane with the convex crown face, or even uniting at the basal limit at a slight angle, in some the basal border being slightly raised, in others, again, simply defined by the angulation and the perceptible difference in the superficial structure of the crown as compared with that of the basal portion, as shown in fig. 10. However, the gradation which these latter teeth exhibit, in connection with the gradation observed in the preceding varieties, seems to afford conclusive evidence of their specific identity. The surface ornamentation is much the same in all the varieties, consisting of a more or less distinct, minute striato punctation when not concealed by the dense, smooth, enamel like coating.

From a careful examination of the above noticed teeth, it would appear that they probably constituted the variable dentition of one and the same species. Among themselves the various forms are linked together by the unmistakable gradation of characters, while at the same time they are not easily confounded with others which are regarded as specifically distinct Of the latter, the Keokuk and Burlington formations have afforded many beautiful examples, and which exhibit precisely the same range of individual variation, though associated with other features of presumably distinctive importance. The latter forms were originally indicated under the name *Helodus angulatus* in the second volume of the present report

Indubitable examples of the form under consideration have been obtained only from the St. Louis limestone, at a single locality in the northern extension of the formation in Central Iowa. However, our collections contain a few examples of teeth from the Warsaw beds, which are difficult to distinguish from the present form, since they present precisely the same variations as have been observed in connection with the St. Louis specimens Most of these teeth are so worn that a satisfactory comparison is out of the question; but a single specimen obtained by Mr VAN HORNE in the Warsaw beds at Barrett's Station, Missouri, is deserving of particular notice The tooth is of average size, and is distinguished by its linear or very slightly curved convex border, nearly uniform and prominent crest, relative great depth of the convex face, the lower half of which is occupied by a broad coronal belt composed of five or six strong, regular imbricating folds, which are seldom branched or implanted, concave face rising abruptly from the narrow marginal border, which is apparently composed of two folds, and presenting a relatively narrow, deeply channeled outline quite in contrast to that observed in the numerous representatives from the St. Louis beds. The base formed a strong plate projecting downward in a plane closely corresponding to that of the convex crown face, from which it is defined by the produced and sharply unbeveled marginal border, the convex crown face is coarsely striato punctate in the triturating surface along the crest, the opposite face is smooth and polished. From the same horizon, in the exposures above the mouth of Piasa creek, Mr VAN HORNE has obtained other specimens, but which, in the abraded condition, afford at best unsatisfactory comparison with the allied if not identical form from the superimposed beds.

The Chester limestone, also, have afforded a few teeth, which present the same general features, but which, unfortunately, are not sufficiently well-preserved to trace more intimate relationship than in the case of the Warsaw form They are, however, apparently distinguished by the fewer, stronger, and more regular coronal folds, perhaps more rectangular outline, stronger base, and perceptibly finer punctation. But in view of the variableness of the surface structure under the varying conditions of the preservation of the crown, little dependence can be placed on the latter feature

Of the last mentioned forms, which we have provisionally indicated by the designations *C. Varsouviensis* and *C. Chesterensis*, we have introduced illustrations of a few of the better preserved specimens, hoping by this means to call attention more particularly to their consideration when the organization of more complete materials shall enable a satisfactory comparison with the form described above, and thereby settle their relationship with one another.

*Position and locality:* Common in the calcareous shales of the St. Louis formation; Pella, Iowa The locality of the Warsaw form is indicated above; the Chester form occurs at Chester, Illinois.

## GENUS LISGODUS, St. J. and W.

Teeth laterally abbreviated, strong. Crown thick, or moderately compressed, more or less acuminate, sharp crested, and sometimes obscurely serrated, basal margins well defined from the base, descending lowest, or most produced, in the concave face, which is more or less strongly arched laterally, the convex face lowest, forming a more or less vertical plane area, coronal belt encircling the crown, and composed of one or more imbricating folds. Base nearly vertical to the crown, rectangular in outline, thick, less than the lateral diameter of the crown, in depth equal to or exceeding the elevation of the crown, inferior surface well-defined from either face above, and generally slightly beveled from the concave to the opposite border. Coronal surfaces invested with a polished enamel like layer, the worn crest striato punctate

In regard to the affinities of the forms herein included to the species with which they are associated, we have sought in vain to discover features which would more than vaguely suggest their intimate relation to, much less their specific identity with, other generic forms No gradation into the elongated forms of *Chomatodus* is observed, such as would hardly fail to be represented, did they exist, in the splendid collections which have been so generously made available to us; while the mutual identity of characters of the several forms included in the present group would seem to be sufficient evidence of their generic distinctness. Yet one cannot fail to note the affinities or resemblances which these teeth bear to typical *Chomatodus*, as represented by *C. pusillus*, N and W, or the representative of that species in the Upper Burlington fish bed, and this gives rise to the suspicion that the acquisition of a series of the latter teeth in their relative natural position might prove these to belong to the dentition of one and the same form—an arrangement something like the triturating plates of the *Mylodonts.*

Thus we might expect to find the *L curtus* associated with *C pusillus*, and the *L sellaliformis* with *Chomatodus insignis*, Leidy. But as we have no facts leading to the positive demonstration of such relationship, and as they constitute amongst themselves a well defined type, we have preferred to recognize their apparent distinctness in preference to assuming a probable generic and specific indentity with the above mentioned forms.

## LISGODUS CURTUS, St J. and W.

Pl X A, Fig 20-22

Teeth very small, lateral diameter and hight about equal, robust, symmetrical in form The crown forms a prominent, regularly arched, or slightly acuminate, sharp ridge, presenting from above a semi oval or subelliptical outline, the convex face is sublenticular in outline, vertical, nearly plane or slightly arched laterally, inferior angle gently or broadly arched downward in the middle, sharply beveled to the basal region, and bearing two comparatively strong coronal folds; concave face about one third higher than the opposite face, elliptical in outline, crest and basal line nearly equally arched, gently concave vertically, and more or less arched or convex laterally, basal margin prominent, abruptly curved downward from the extremities and gently arched upward in the median region, and occupied by two or three well marked imbrications, both coronal faces are enveloped in a dense, polished enamel layer, except along the crest, which is usually more or less worn and beveled along the concave side, in some instances it is worn down to half its original elevation, presenting a long, narrow, triturating area, roughened by the exposed extremities of the tubular structure The base varies somewhat in depth, the smaller the tooth the greater is its proportionate depth, but in all cases it equals the hight of the convex crown-face, and in the small teeth it is as deep again, somewhat narrower and thinner than the crown, and apparently always nearly vertical to the crown, broadly channeled in either face, the one face being prominently defined from the projecting margin of the concave crown face, lower angles well defined in perfect specimens, inferior surface flat and slightly beveled to the convex edge. A specimen of large size measures in lateral diameter of crown 36 inch, entire hight of tooth 26, elevation of convex crown face 15, depth of base in the same side 11, hight of concave crown-face 18, lateral diameter of base nearly 30 inch. A specimen of much smaller size is .18 inch in lateral diameter of crown, which is equal to the entire hight of the tooth, showing a relatively much deeper root than in the large teeth

This elegant little form is not uncommon in the fish bed horizon of the Upper Burlington, and is quite numerously represented in all the collections from that horizon. A few imperfect specimens from the Keokuk limestone, which have come to our notice, are undistinguishable from the teeth in the above mentioned subjacent deposits, yet they may prove to be specifically distinct The individual variation in size observed in this form has lead us to believe that it does not constitute a part of the dentition of other forms known from the same horizon. They are essentially dissimilar in many of the superficial details from other *Chomatodi* with which they are associated, and taking into account the variation in size and the slight modifications of relative proportions, we can scarcely fail to recognize in these variations those features common to the more or less variable dentition of a *Petalodont* species

*Position and locality* Upper Burlington fish bed, at the several localities in DesMoines and Louisa counties, Iowa, Warren county, Illinois The Keokuk teeth mentioned above occur at Warsaw, Illinois, and Dr. WILLIAMS has obtained the same form in the Keokuk limestone at Boonville, Missouri.

## LISGODUS SERRATUS, ST. J. and W.

Pl X V, Fig 17-19

Teeth exceedingly small and variable in relative proportions. Crown stout, semi elliptical in outline viewed from above, more or less acuminate, sharp crested, and interrupted by vertical sulci, which produce an irregular serration, which, however, is scarcely perceptible in some of the more acuminate individuals, or limited to one or two faint indentations well down in the lateral edges of the crest; convex face nearly vertical, slightly arched laterally or nearly straight, basal margin well-defined from the root and marked by a proportionately wide coronal band, consisting of two imbrications, which span the tooth in a direct course, or sometimes gently arched upward in the middle, and again at the extremities, opposite face half as high again as convex face, but in the more strongly acuminate specimens the two faces are nearly equal in elevation, moderately concave vertically, gently and irregularly arched laterally, median region more or less swollen, basal line prominently produced beyond the root, arched upward in the middle, and again abruptly curved upward to the extremities, and occupied by three imbricating folds, which form a band but little wider and continuous with that of the opposite face The crown is covered with a polished enamel layer, the triturating surface being most strongly marked in the concave side, (though in none of the specimens is it as distinct as in *L. curtus*,) and giving rise to the vertical striation and striato punctate appearance commonly observed for a greater or less distance below the crest. The base is well developed, angular in outline, nearly vertical to the crown, a little narrower and not as thick, in depth usually less than, though in some instances nearly or quite equal to, the hight of the crown, both faces slightly channeled laterally, lower edges worn or less angular, inferior surface gently beveled to the concave side. A very acuminate specimen is .20 inch in greatest lateral diameter, hight of crown .14, a low, serrated tooth measures in lateral diameter .18, entire hight of tooth .17, elevation of crown .08. There are individuals with even a lower crown, but that last mentioned probably represents the normal proportions of these teeth.

This form is much like that described under the name *L. cultus*, presenting nearly the same general outline and proportions. It differs, however, in the serrated character of the crest, and the medially upward arching or horizontal basal line of the convex face, also in its smaller size. Otherwise it is most intimately allied to the above mentioned form, in the serrated condition of the crest does it depart most widely. Yet we find examples in which the latter character is nearly obsolete, and which, but for the slight lateral position of the apex, as well as those other distinctive features noted above, might be mistaken for the form with which it occurs. From *L. selluliformis* of the St. Louis limestone, it differs in its less symmetrical outline and proportions, and the vertical position of the base; in the character of the coronal serration it closely resembles that form.

We are largely indebted to Mr. SPRINGER for the means of comparing a large number of individuals of this and the previously described form, all of which were obtained from a single locality in the ichthyic stratum of the Upper Burlington limestone, the same association is also known at other localities, but the Louisa county (Iowa) locality has afforded by far the largest and most interesting suite of these teeth.

*Position and locality.* Fish-bed of the Upper Burlington limestone, Louisa and Des Moines counties, Iowa, Warren county, Illinois.

### LISGODUS SELLULIFORMIS, St. J. and W.

Pl. X A, Fig. 16.

Teeth very small, thick, greatest hight exceeding the lateral diameter. The crown is strongly arched, sharp, terminating in a thickened, more or less acutely rounded point, and low down upon the flanks one or two faint serrations give to the lateral edges an obscure denticulate character; the convex crown face presents a subtriangular, vertical area, sometimes moderately arched laterally, and margined below by a well-marked horizontal coronal fold; concave face obtusely curvilinear in outline, broadly rounded below, gently concave vertically, its greater area occupied by a strong median ridge descending from the apex and giving rise to the prominent lateral convexity in the coronal contour, and bordered by a rather wide coronal belt composed of at least two imbricating folds. The coronal surfaces are usually smooth, in worn surfaces coarsely striato punctate, and sometimes enlarged in a dense, vertically undulated or corrugated enamel layer. Base strong, thick, rectangular in shape, in depth nearly equal to the hight of the crown, somewhat less in lateral diameter, slightly compressed in the middle and expanded below, interior surface well defined and beveled from the convex to the concave border, slightly produced beyond the vertical plane of the convex crown face, and sharply defined above by the projecting basal angles of the crown. A specimen of ordinary dimensions measures in lateral diameter of crown .12 inch, hight of convex crown-face .06, hight of concave face .10, lateral diameter of base .08, entire elevation of tooth .14 inch.

Although we have seen but few examples of this exceedingly small and handsome form in the collection of Mr. VAN HORNE, their state of preservation, fortunately, is such as to render their distinctive features easily discernible. It is most intimately related to *L. serratus* of the Upper Burlington limestone; but, besides being scarcely half the size of that form, it is further distinguished by the relatively larger root, the vertical position of the convex crown face and its nearly horizontal basal line, while that of the opposite face is more strongly and regularly arched downward, also the unequal elevation of the coronal faces; the denticulations of the crest are more remote from the apex.

*Position and locality.* Upper beds of the St. Louis limestone; Alton, Illinois; St. Louis, Missouri.

## GENUS TANAODUS, St. J. and W.

In recognizing the generic distinctness of the group of teeth embraced under the above designation, we have not been led to such disposition by the assumption, if *Antliodus* differs generically from *Petalodus*, so *Chomatodus* in like manner differs from the present group; but it has rather been with the hope of eliminating from the heterogeneous assemblage of forms usually referred to *Chomatodus* such well-characterized groups which have an equal value as distinctive expressions with the various groups already recognized, which constitute the family of *Petalodonts*. In the present instance we have a peculiar expression of characteristics which pertain to certain individuals or forms which extend through a considerable time space in the Carboniferous period—indeed, appearing early in the period and continuing to the close of the Upper Coal Measure epoch. And these peculiarities, as compared with what may be regarded as typical of *Chomatodus* in the restrictive sense here recognized in the elongated, vertical teeth to which Prof. AGASSIZ gave the name *Chomatodus linearis*, (Poiss Foss. tom. III. Tab 12, fig. 9; not fig 5, 7, 12,) the group under consideration, will be found to present a marked contrast in the relative position of the base, which closely adheres to the margin beneath the basal border of the concave crown-face, the basal area beneath the opposite coronal face more nearly corresponding to that of *Anthodus* In the laterally extended linear outline of the crown there is strong resemblance to typical *Chomatodus;* but in the disproportionate depth of the coronal surfaces and the marginal position of the root, it presents affinities with *Anthodus* From the latter, however, it is distinguished by the linear or rectangular outline of the crown, and perhaps also the distinct definition of the inferior surface of the root, which in *Anthodus* appears to be rounded as in *Petalodus* and *Ctenopetalus*.

We have, however, observed in certain forms from the St Louis and Chester formations, an association of individuals the specific affinities of which we strongly suspect, and which exhibit a combination of outline and contour which might be regarded as evidence positive of their relationship with *Anthodus*. But if we restrict *Anthodus* to those forms which possess a crown essentially like *Petalodus*, with a shallow root, it may be admissible to recognize in the above mentioned form a type intermediate between the true *Chomatodus* and *Anthodus* Yet, if we adhere to the strict interpretation of the facts at present represented, it seems highly probable that the forms referred to under the above head may prove to represent the extremely varied dentition of one and the same genus

Of the present type of teeth the following representatives have already been described. *Chomatodus gracillimus*, N and W, *C. multiplicatus*, N and W., of the Upper Burlington, *C obscurus*, Leidy, of the Keokuk, *C angulatus*, N. and W., of the Coal Measures. In the study of the collection of Mr SPRINGER, we have been led to suspect the possible specific identity of such forms as represented by *C gracillimus* and a form closely resembling *Anthodus politus*, N and W, which it represents in the Upper Burlington deposits. Should these inferences prove correct, then all the forms hereinafter noticed will probably fall under the genus *Anthodus*, as amended and extended.

### TANAODUS SUBLUNATUS, St J and W.

Pl XI, Fig 27

We have provisionally recognized the specific distinctness of a form, represented by a single specimen in the collection of Mr. VAN HORNE from the St. Louis, which bears certain resemblances to the teeth referred to under the above genus with which it is here associated The tooth is very small and delicate, and so imbedded as to reveal only the basal and convex coronal aspect Viewed from below, the basal area presents an irregular trapezoidal outline, a little broader at one extremity than the other and rounded or obliquely truncated, gently arched outward along the concave border, beneath which is situated the low, comparatively short root The basal margin of the convex face is slightly arched inward, and defined by a simple coronal fold, which forms the well-marked angulation between the basal area and the convex crown-face, which latter is low, nearly plane, gently arched along the crest, which is produced beyond the basal line, and gradually declines in elevation from the broader extremity, and interrupted by delicate vertical sulci which produce a faint denticulate appearance Lateral diameter of crown about 23 inch, antero posterior diameter 10.

The sublunate outline shorter, relatively wide, and more strongly arched concave border, also the more central position of the root, constitute the more prominent features which distinguish the present form from its congenus. In its short lateral extent it bears resemblance to *Anthodus*, but the straight convex margin and vertical inequality in the crest line present characters more or less strongly in contrast with the symmetrical outlines of the typical examples of the latter group

*Position and locality* Upper beds of the St Louis limestone, Alton, Illinois

## Tanodus pumilus, St. J. and W

Pl XI, Fig 1, 2, 3, 4, 5

Teeth small, moderately strong though variable in proportions, crown moderately compressed or rapidly thickening towards the base, broadly arched along the crest, sometimes obscurely denticulated near the extremities, and usually projecting at a considerable angle beyond the basal margin of the convex crown-face; the concave face is irregularly elliptical in outline, in some examples the longer sides converge towards one or other extremity giving rise to a more or less subtriangular outline, very gently arched laterally and slightly depressed vertically, basal margin slightly undulating in its downward and outward course, and defined by a very wide basal band composed of five or six imbricated folds, from the upper margin of which the plain coronal surface ascends at a slight angle, lateral extremities unequally and more or less acutely and obliquely rounded or truncated, the convex face is about half the hight of the opposite side, irregularly lunate in outline, gently arched laterally, or sometimes strongly so in laterally abbreviated, acuminate examples, nearly plane vertically, basal margin generally very gently arched upward, sometimes curved downward or irregularly sinuose, and limited by a narrow, though well marked coronal belt consisting of as many as five imbrications, coronal surfaces smooth or faintly striated, striato-punctate along the worn crest. Basal area broad, gently depressed and more or less distinctly defined from the root, which latter varies considerably in depth in different individuals, antero posteriorly compressed or wedge shaped, sharply defined from the projecting margin of the concave crown-face, descending more or less obliquely backward or outward, laterally converging, inferior surface slightly oblique to the horizontal plane of the crown, but generally obscurely defined and often terminated in a sharp edge, both faces more or less coarsely roughened. A small symmetrical and unusually well preserved tooth measures in lateral diameter .32 inch, hight of concave crown face .15, hight of convex face .07, greatest diameter of root .23, depth of inner face about .05 inch.

This form presents considerable individual variability, which probably, in consequence of the larger number of specimens which exist in the collections, is even more striking than in the case of *T. bellicinctus*, with which it is intimately allied. Regarding the specific identity of these varied forms, the only evidence is their association in the same stratum and certain well defined peculiarities of coronal or basal conformation common to all, however variable and dissimilar in outline are the extreme examples. Compared with *T. bellicinctus*, besides its smaller size, it is distinguishable by the more strongly developed coronal bands encircling the basal margins of the crown, and the relatively deeper and more oblique root, all the specimens thus far known are less elongated laterally, and of less symmetrical proportions, upon which latter feature however, little stress should be placed in the present state of our knowledge of the Chester forms.

The particular horizons and localities which have afforded indubitable examples of the present form, also afford teeth having the same general outline, but which present unmistakable evidence of extreme abrasion in the roughened coronal portion and the sulcation of the basal area immediately beneath the convex coronal border. In these teeth the convex crown face is worn down to an obtuse ridge, the coronal folds being obsolete in either face, though along the inner margin a strong ridge defines the basal limits, while the intermediate space presents a more or less deep, broad excavation, which occupies the concave crown-face, in all these teeth the root is wedge shaped and terminated inferiorly in a sharp edge. Notwithstanding the absence of specimens showing a gradation into the more perfect teeth of the above description, as in the instance of *T. bellicinctus*, their relationship seems to be unmistakable, since they exhibit the same evidences of attrition, possibly of immaturity, which characterize the worn teeth of the former species indeed so intimate is the resemblance between the worn examples of these two species, that, were they known only from the imperfect teeth, they might be mistaken for one and the same species

Associated with the present form there is a group of teeth equally well represented, and which holds precisely the same relationships to that above described, as do the teeth noticed under the head of *T depressus* to *T bellicinctus*, and which, for the same reasons as assigned in that instance, are provisionally referred to a distinct group, which is noticed at length in the description under *T prænuntius*.

*Position and locality* Upper beds of the St Louis limestone; Alton, Illinois, Pella, Iowa

## Tanaodus Prænuntius, St. J and W

Pl XI, Fig 6 7 8 9, 10

Teeth small, laterally elongated, long elliptical or gently arcuate, outer and inner margins more or less nearly parallel, extremities rounded or obliquely truncated The concave crown-face is gently depressed vertically, very slightly so or nearly straight in the long diameter, and sometimes gently arched, basal margin slightly raised and forming a right angle with the abrupt face of the root, destitute of distinct imbricating folds, straight or slightly arched inward and upward, and more or less abruptly curved round the lateral extremities, gently arched in both directions along the crest, which forms a low, obtuse ridge, sometimes obscurely and irregularly denticulate, and closely bordering the convex side of the crown, which latter is correspondingly low, nearly plane or faintly channeled vertically, broadly arched laterally, very gently and sometimes irregularly curved downward along the lower margin, which is sharply defined from the inferior region, and sometimes, though rarely, marked by obscure, irregularly disposed, thread like lines, the coronal surfaces present a coarse, irregular vermiculose appearance, and along the crest a coarse punctate or striato punctate structure, the vertical tubes being often gathered into irregularly spaced bundles, which give rise to the obtuse denticulations frequently observed in the crest The root forms a strong, laterally narrowed, wedge shaped process, faintly channeled laterally and abruptly defined from the margin of the concave crown-face, upon the opposite side scarcely definable from the wide basal area, the contour of which is more or less irregularly convex, and defined above by a faint sulcation extending along and just beneath the basal angle of the convex crown-face; the basal area is faintly roughened or smooth, and faint vertical sulci sometimes appear in the root. Greatest diameter of a large size specimen about .53 inch, antero posterior diameter .20, or but a trifle more than the hight of the concave crown-face, elevation of convex face .05, depth of root beneath the concave face .14 inch.

The individuals of the present form are somewhat variable in outline, and in many of the teeth some of the characters noticed above are obsolete; very few examples show any trace of coronal folds along the basal margin of the convex crown face, though all present the same rugose coronal structure and absence of coronal folds in the concave face, the crest also varies from a vertical position in relation to the horizontal plane of the crown, being sometimes slightly inclined from within, which, however, is probably due to the wearing away of the convex surface, the crest rarely shows distinct denticulations, and in some teeth the interior region exhibits evidence of greater or less abrasion along its outer margin, as though by the impingement of the contiguous tooth, to which may be attributed certain irregularities in the basal contour But in all these teeth there prevails a marked uniformity in general appearance, requiring but slight experience to be able to recognize their identity

This form is closely allied to that described from the Chester division under the name *T. depressus;* yet, notwithstanding in both may be traced the same kind of individual variability, a critical comparison of a fine suite of teeth from the two horizons discloses certain slight but persistent differences, which together strongly impress one with the conviction of their specific distinctness In all the St. Louis teeth the crest is less elevated and less erect or produced outward over the basal line of the convex crown face, the superficial markings of the crown also differ, in the present form being coarser and rougher than in the Chester teeth But in these teeth one cannot fail to observe those appearances which seem to indicate the action of abrading influences to a more considerable extent than is presented in the latter form; and in this feature, too, the same uniformity prevails as observed in other respects

Regarding the affinities of these teeth with apparently allied forms from the same horizons, the same suggestions are presented and the same difficulties encountered in determining the nature of their resemblances, and the character of their relationship, as has been observed in connection with *T depressus.* However remote their resemblance may be to *T. sculptus*, it is of the same nature as that of *T. depressus* to *T. polymorphus* In the present instance the resemblance is most strikingly portrayed in the general contour of the basal region, the same as in the Chester forms, but the most thorough comparison of the materials in hand fails to prove their identity, while their relationship to *T pumilus* seems to be even more remote than in the case of *T depressus* and *T bellicinctus* The wedge shaped condition of root is more or less prevalent in all these forms—in *T. praenuntius* and *T depressus* as a permanent feature apparently, while in the other named forms it is evidently, in part at least, the result of accidental causes These peculiarities are strongly suggestive of generic importance, but in view of the uncertainty (which may indeed exist only in the mind) of their permanence, it is deemed more consistent with the nature of the facts possessed to retain them provisionally in the same generic association Indeed were it possible to study the complete dention of the forms enumerated, even a more intimate specific relationship might be proved than can be derived from the study of the isolated material now accessible

*Position and locality* Upper beds of the St. Louis limestone, Alton, Illinois; Pella, Iowa, St Louis, Missouri

## TANAODUS SCULPTUS, St. J and W

Pl XI, Fig 20, 21, 22, 23

Teeth small, presenting as viewed from above a somewhat variable oval or broad elliptical outline. Concave crown face broad elliptical or irregularly circular in outline, but subject to considerable variation in this respect—in some examples more or less hexagonal, in others triangular or curvilinear—lateral extremities acutely or obtusely rounded, in some of the more circular teeth less distinctly defined, nearly plane or more or less depressed in the middle, and rising into a low, regularly or eccentrically arched, obtuse crest, which slightly projects beyond the basal line of the opposite face, the lower margin is generally less regularly and more angularly arched downward, more or less produced and in some examples sharply inbeveled to the base, and bordered by five to six well defined, narrow imbricating folds, which pass round the lateral angles in a broad abruptly curved belt, which merges into the narrower though equally well-marked basal band of the convex face, the convex crown face presents a low, lenticular outline, nearly plane vertically and broadly arched laterally, the crest and inferior margin nearly the same in curvature, the basal margin being gently arched downward in the middle, sometimes angularly so, and again gently curved towards the extremities, forming an obtuse angle with the basal area from which it is well defined by the imbricated coronal band, except in examples which have suffered from attrition, in which the folds as well as the peculiar sculpturing in the entire surface are obsolete. The lower portion of the concave face is elegantly sculptured, presenting a delicate tracery of undulating and frequently interrupted lines, variously disposed, but most frequently slightly deflected to one or other side, or in some instances diverging from the median line in their upward course until lost in the papillose surface occupying the upper space, as also the greater portion of the convex face, and the striato punctate belt immediately along the crest; also, in well preserved specimens, the coronal folds are more or less distinctly and finely striated vertically. The basal area nearly corresponds in outline to the concave crown face, in contour moderately convex, rarely plane, defined from the basal line of the convex crown-face by a faint sulcation, gradually curved downward and merging into the short, wedge-shaped, laterally constricted and vertically sulcated root, the inner face of which forms an abrupt declivity projecting slightly outward, laterally channeled, and nearly parallel with the concave coronal margin from which it is more or less sharply defined by the produced border of the coronal folds; the inferior surface in the majority of the specimens is reduced to an exceedingly narrow area, giving to the root the appearance of terminating in a sharp edge, but in well preserved examples it forms a well marked though very shallow and relatively narrow appendage, the flattened inferior surface of which agrees with the horizontal plane of the crown, and at the same time it is more abruptly defined on the one side from the broad basal region. A tooth of large size measures .48 inch in greatest diameter of crown, hight of concave face nearly .30, elevation of convex face .08, greatest diameter of root .30, depth beneath the concave coronal border .10; a minute, oval shaped tooth is .20 inch in lateral and .11 in transverse diameter, hight of convex crown face .05, or about equal to the depth of the root.

Although hardly any two individuals of this elegant little form present precisely the same outline, in which respect it is very variable, yet all are easily recognizable by the peculiar coronal sculpturing as well as by the general contour features common to all. The form is apparently restricted to the St. Louis division, and the examples at present known, which were derived from localities more or less distant from one another, present a persistency of characters which afford the best evidence of their specific identity. Its most intimate ally is found in the upper (?) ichthyic horizon of the next succeeding or Chester formation, and so close is their relationship, that it is only by comparing a suite of each form that they may be satisfactorily distinguished one from the other. However slight these distinctive features may appear in the comparison of solitary examples from either horizon, collectively, each presents a combination of features which at once arrests the attention and leads to the conviction of their specific distinctness. These differences are noticed more at length in the description of *T. polymorphus*.

In regard to the generic relations of the present form, it would appear that, in the outline of the crown, it approximates *Anthodus*, but by following out its affinities with the preceding forms, it seems to present equally intimate relationship with the latter The features in common with *Tanaodus* consist in the wedge shaped outline of the root, the convexity of the basal area, and the peculiar coronal contour, characters which present a strong contrast to the typical forms of *Antliodus*

*Position and locality* Upper beds of the St. Louis limestone; Pella, Iowa, Alton, Illinois, St. Louis, Missouri

TANAODUS GROSSIPLICATUS, St. J. and W.

Pl XI, Fig 26

Teeth small or medium in size, viewed from above elongate trapezoidal in outline Crown culminating along the straight convex face in a low, even crested ridge slightly produced outward, the basal angle defined by a narrow coronal fold, nearly straight throughout the greater extent, but gently curved upward and downward at the extremities; concave face descending in a wide, gradual and gently depressed inclination to the basal margin, which is defined by a rather prominent coronal belt composed of two or three strong imbricating folds, in the median half straight and parallel with the opposite face, more or less suddenly and obliquely truncated in the lateral portions, the coronal belt continuous with that in the convex face, the coronal surfaces are invested with a delicately wrought enamel layer, and in the worn triturating surface along the crest a striato punctate structure appears The basal area presents in outline very nearly the figure of the concave crown-face, nearly plane or laterally traversed by a faint ridge; the root is placed close beneath the concave margin, produced downward and outward in nearly the same plane as the convex crown-face, which it nearly equals in depth, moderately strong, in transverse diameter considerably less than the crown, inferior surface more or less well defined and beveled in the horizontal plane of the crown

The single representative of the form above described, unfortunately, preserves only about half the entire lateral diameter of the tooth, which is otherwise in an unusually perfect state of preservation In general form it bears closest resemblance to the Coal measure form *T angulatus* (N. and W. sp,) from which it differs not only in its smaller size, but in the less numerous imbrications in the coronal belt of the concave face Its resemblance to some of the Keokuk and Upper Burlington congeneric forms is also quite striking, yet it is distinguishable by its straight concave border, even crest, and stronger proportions

*Position and locality* Probably from the lower fish-bed of the Chester formation; Chester, Illinois

### TONAODUS BELLICINCTUS, St J and W

Pl XI Fig 14-16, 25

Teeth of medium or small size, strong, in outline long elliptical and acutely rounded at the extremities Concave crown-face but slightly depressed, sometimes gently arched in the long direction of the tooth, culminating along the convex margin in a sharp more or less regularly arched crest, and bordered below by a wide, strongly marked basal band, which is composed of three to six narrow and more or less regular, vertically striated imbricating folds, gently arched upward in the middle and usually sharply curved round the extremities, inferiorly inbeveled and prominently defined from the root, concave face less than half the hight of the opposite face, in outline arcuate and broadly or gently arched laterally, generally very faintly channeled laterally, the crest projecting beyond the basal line, and limited below by a more or less well defined basal band, which presents along the greater extent of the median portion only one or two distinct imbricating folds, but which on nearing the extremities branch into several delicate secondary folds, which apparently terminate in the crest, or, in part, from a continuous belt with that of the concave face The coronal surfaces are ornamented with vermiculose markings, immediately above the basal band faint vertical plicæ, and in the triturating surface along the crest, where the exceedingly thin enamel like layer has been exfoliated, a fine striato punctation appears The basal region forms a long, narrow area, which, together with the face of the root, presents a broad, shallow depression extending in the long diameter of the tooth, the root proper is very short, antero posteriorly compressed and laterally constricted, in depth beneath the concave face nearly equal to or slightly exceeding the hight of the convex crown face, projecting outward and downward in nearly the same plane as the convex crown face, and inferiorly flattened Lateral diameter of tooth .81 inch, transverse diameter of concave crown face 24, hight of convex face 12, greatest length of root 63, depth of inner face .09 inch

In the collection from the Chester limestone several varieties of teeth occur, which are apparently intimately allied, though in some instances it is exceedingly difficult to decide the nature of the differences by which they are distinguished from one another It is not difficult to separate these teeth into three or four forms, all of which present a greater or less individual variability, but in the extremes of some of these forms may be observed such intimate resemblances with the teeth, referable to other forms, as to cause one to hesitate in the determination of their identity. Yet, however strongly we may suspect the validity of these groups, our resources are inadequate to a satisfactory conclusion, and the attempt to limit them within definite specific bounds has resulted in the conviction that it were more advisable, at this time, to notice not only the seemingly distinctive characters by which each form may be recognized, but also to carefully note those features of gradation which may seem to indicate a probable specific identity. The same observations are equally applicable to certain forms found in the subjacent division, or St Louis limestone, and which are consecutively noticed in the preceding pages

The above described form is represented by only a single perfect specimen, that upon which the description is mainly based This tooth is most intimately allied to the laterally elongated teeth of the type of *Tanaodus obscurus* of Leidy, differing in a marked degree from the typical examples of *Antliodus*, which latter may be defined as a *Petalodus* having a very horizontal basal area and short root It also bears intimate resemblance to the St. Louis form mentioned under the name *T pumilus*, from which it chiefly differs in its relatively narrower coronal folds and more shallow root. In specimens which have undergone much attrition, the basal bands are more or less obscurely preserved—that along the convex crown-face is often quite obsolete, while that which limits the opposite basal margin forms a more or less prominent ridge, the imbrications of which may be entirely obliterated. Also, individuals in the latter state of preservation have the concave coronal region deeply excavated, while the inferior region presents evidence of greater or less wear, and the root assumes a wedge-shaped condition, strongly contrasting with its angular outline in perfect teeth, indeed, but for the fortunate possession of specimens showing intermediate stages of abrasion, the relationship of the extremely worn examples of this form might be entirely overlooked. Moreover, the latter bear evidence of wear in the roughened appearance of the coronal surfaces, and the greater the extent of the abrasion, the more apparent are its effects noticeable in the region along the basal angle of the convex face, which is reduced in hight by the wearing away of the coronal folds, in which process a more or less distinct sulcation is produced in the basal area just beneath the coronal angle, and after extending the entire length of the tooth, and which may have been caused by the wearing action along the line of impingement of the contiguous tooth The latter character, together with the attenuation of the root, is sometimes observed in connection with teeth in which the concave coronal region remains nearly perfect, and which forcibly recall very similar features observed in the worn teeth of *T polymorphus*, but in the latter case this is most probably a resemblance the result of similar causes, since the differences (as the coronal ornamentation) which distinguish the perfect teeth of these forms one from the other are well-marked and apparently persistent. The root, in specimens which have been subjected to extreme abrading action, often shows a tendency to divide into radicles which, however, differ from those characteristic of *Polyrhizodus* in their extremely irregular disposition, plainly indicating their accidental origin—the result of the attenuation of the originally thick root and the deepening or exposing of the irregularly spaced vertical sulci which appear in nearly all *Petalodont* forms

*Geological position and locality*: From the lower fish bed in the Chester division; Chester, Illinois

## TANAODUS DEPRESSUS, St. J. and W.

Pl XI, Fig 11-13

Teeth small, of strong proportions, curvilinear-elliptical as seen from above, though variable in outline, the longer sides nearly parallel or sometimes gradually converging towards one or other extremity, which latter are oblique, rounded or obtusely pointed Crown depressed, concave face faintly excavated vertically and more or less considerably arched laterally, rarely plane, inferior margin direct, or usually gently arched inward along the greater median extent and obliquely truncated or rapidly rounded to the lateral angles, gently or broadly arched along the crest, which generally projects beyond the inferior line of the convex face, forming a more or less well defined obtuse angle along the middle portion, but gradually diminishing in elevation towards the extremities where it is sometimes reduced to a simple convexity but slightly raised above the general plane of the crown, often obscurely denticulated in the prominent part, convex face very low, laterally arched, slightly channeled, inferior margin irregularly and very gently curved upward in the median region, gently or acutely rounded at the extremities, in perfect teeth sharply defined from the basal region; in a few examples the convex coronal margin presents traces of exceedingly delicate imbricating folds, of which there are three or four, but in the opposite basal margin the coronal folds are almost always obsolete—the fine vermiculose markings occupying the entire surface, except a narrow space immediately along the crest which is coarsely striato punctate. The outline and contour of the basal area varies considerably and in the same manner as does that of the crown, irregularly convex or concave, forming a plane nearly at right angles to that of the convex crown-face, and nearly continuous or uniform with the root, which latter, however, makes an abrupt descent from the concave coronal margin, faintly channeled, laterally converging below, forming a strong wedge-shaped process terminating in an acutely rounded edge, in depth equal to or exceeding the hight of the convex crown-face, with which it is nearly vertical A specimen of ordinary size and proportions measures in lateral diameter .58 inch, antero posterior diameter .16, hight of convex crown face about .06, depth of abrupt face of root .09 inch.

Of the present form there are several representatives in the collections, and taken together they constitute a well marked group, the individual variations of which do not depart in an unusual degree from the normal condition Notwithstanding its marked peculiarities, unmistakable as they appear in the examples before us, we have hesitated in separating these teeth specifically from the last preceding form, *T. bellicinctus*, on the one hand, and *T polymorphus* on the other, from either of which forms the chief distinguishing difference in the present one is the absence of coronal folds Yet, it is impossible to overlook certain other characters apparently of a permanent nature, which in either of the above forms are probably due to accidental causes, as instanced by the wedge shaped condition of the root. Again, in individuals which bear evident signs of attrition, the same effects are produced in the wearing away of the interior basal angle of the convex crown-face, and sulcation of the basal area, as has been observed under similar circumstances in the teeth of the above mentioned forms. It would seem very improbable that these permanent distinctive features are attributable to the immaturity of the teeth, since it is well known that the tissues of the coronal portion of the teeth of sharks are the first to arrive at maturity, while in the present teeth, which seem to bear greatest resemblance to the forms with which they are above compared, the resemblance is largely due to the abrasion of the *mature* basal portions. Its resemblance to certain forms of *Polyrhizodus* is remotely indicated by the general similarity of coronal contour, also the obscure vertical sulci often observed in the edge of the root. But it is impossible, with the data at present in hands, to prove a specific identity with any of the above mentioned forms Possibly the acquisition of more extensive material may show these differences to be of varietal importance only, since we should expect to find considerable variableness in the teeth from different parts of the jaws, also those features originating in accidental causes, as for example the the exfoliation by attrition of the greater or entire portion of the superficial layer of the crown, thus exposing to unusual abrasion the less dense tissues of dentine which compose the bulk of the crown and the entire basal region, producing under like circumstances similar results, and giving rise to these peculiarities of individual teeth the specific identity of which may be exceedingly difficult, if not impossible, to ascertain In the study of the fossil teeth of this class, such difficulties are of constant recurrence, and in the present instances, the desire to comprehend the actual relationship, and not the recognition of a new form, has induced us to dwell more at length on the features which the individuals of the present form possess in common with those of other supposed congeneric forms

*Position and locality*: From the lower fish-bed of the Chester formation; Chester, Illinois.

## TANAODUS POLYMORPHUS, ST. J. and W.

Pl. XI, Fig. 17-19, 24

Teeth small, variable in outline from irregularly circular to broad-elliptical, the transverse sometimes exceeding the lateral diameter of the tooth. Crown but moderately elevated and arched along the crest, which is obtuse and faintly denticulated, one or other, sometimes both, of the lateral extremities broadly rounded or obtusely angular; convex face low, generally projecting beyond the basal line, though sometimes inclined from within, often slightly channeled, more or less strongly arched laterally according to the outline of the crown, basal margin nearly horizontal or gently arched downward in the middle, and again very slightly curved downward on nearing the lateral angles, and marked by a narrow band of two to four or five quite regular imbricating folds, the concave face is much more variable in outline and contour, subcircular or elliptical, very gently ascending to the crest, nearly plane or but gently depressed, in some instances presenting a slight convexity in the lower median region, basal margin closely agreeing with the curvature of the crest, though perhaps never as strongly arched, in the more oval individuals forming an obtuse angle in the median region, and bordered by a usually well marked coronal band composed of from three to five regular, vertically striated imbrications, which are continuous with those of the opposite face though relatively wider. In well preserved specimens the coronal surfaces present a delicate vermiculose ornamentation in the convex face, also in the median portion of the concave face, the lower portions of which are beautifully marked with more or less numerous, regular rugæ which arise in the upper margin of the coronal belt, deflected laterally or converging in their upward course, becoming obsolete in the middle region, and which are quite distinct from the vertically elongated punctæ which often appear in the worn surfaces along the crest. The root forms a narrow, sharp edged, wedge shaped process, in nearly the same vertical planes as the crown and which is reduced almost to a reversed conical condition in short, oval teeth, inbeveled and slightly channeled laterally along the abrupt face beneath the basal margin of the concave crown face, with which it forms an acute or right angle, while its opposite face forms a nearly uninterrupted plane with the basal area, which latter is slightly bulging in the middle, smooth, and meeting at an obtuse angle with the inferior border of the convex crown-face, the proportionate depth of the root varies considerably, nor does this variation seem to be dependent upon any particular form or size of tooth. A specimen of large size measures in lateral diameter .42 inch, antero posterior diameter .33, or nearly that of the concave crown face, hight of convex face .09, depth of abrupt face of root about .11, while an exceedingly minute oval tooth has the transverse and lateral diameters of the crown nearly equal, or about .08 inch, the abrupt face of the root slightly exceeding .08 inch in depth, showing a remarkably produced wedge-shaped process

The collection of Mr VAN HORNE contains a beautiful suite of the above designated form, many of the individuals of which are so perfectly preserved as to afford a very satisfactory comparison with other and allied forms It is very closely related to the teeth which we have described from the St Louis formation under the name *T sculptus*, presenting even a greater individual diversity than has been observed in the latter form In order to appreciate the differences, however slight, which distinguish the individuals of these forms, it is not necessary to select some particular example, nor does the possession of a large variety of teeth render one's judgment and conclusions confused and unsatisfactory, on the contrary, in connection with the data which has been carefully noted bearing on the association of the teeth in the two horizons, the distinctive peculiarities pertaining to each, though slight, appear to be persistent and readily recognizable Compared with *T. sculptus*, with which form alone it is likely to be confounded, in the present form the convex face is less uniformly depressed, the coronal folds generally less prominent, and the rugæ and vertical striæ coarser, also the root is stronger, generally deeper, and more nearly vertical or less obliquely deflected outwards. The style of coronal ornamentation is essentially the same in all varieties of the present form, and the gradation of the individuals is of a nature that furnishes the best evidence accessible of the specific identity

As to their affinities with the preceding forms, *T. depressus* and *T. bellicinctus*, of the same horizon, the present teeth hold precisely the same relationship as observed in the case of *T. sculptus* with *T prænuntius* and *T. pumilus* of the St Louis formation But in the present state of our knowledge of these forms, it would seem mere presumption to recognize their specific identity, though such may prove to be the actual fact

*Position and locality* Lower fish bed of the Chester formation; Chester, Illinois.

## Genus CTENOPTYCHIUS, Agassiz.

### Ctenoptychius pertenuis, St. J. and W.

Pl. X A, Fig. 27.

Teeth very small and fragile. Crown very compressed, crest rather strongly arched, slightly acuminate, the apex nearly central, subacute, minutely serrated, the denticulations more or less regularly increasing in size from the lateral extremities where they are nearly obsolete, tumid, subacute or rounded and separated by very short, faint sulci, which appear in both faces in the perfect condition of the crown; concave face oval in outline, gently depressed vertically, nearly straight laterally, basal margin broadly and more or less regularly arched downward, or slightly sinuous in curvature, and a little more rapidly converging towards one or other extremity, the opposite end less acute or more rounded; coronal belt moderately prominent, narrow, consisting of at least two imbrications; convex face subcrescentiform, very slightly arched in either direction, or nearly plane, basal angle slightly though irregularly arched upward in the middle, and limited by a single narrow coronal fold, which generally, perhaps always, terminates in the crest on one or other side before reaching the extreme lateral angle, giving to this aspect of the tooth the eccentric, unsymmetrical contour observed in all the representatives of the form; both faces apparently smooth, highly polished. Base proportionally thick and strong, low, oblique, lateral diameter slightly less than that of the crown, from which it is strongly defined in both sides, inferior surface nearly in the same horizontal plane as the crown, broad and well defined along both margins, gradually narrowed toward one extremity in the same direction as the crown, as also noticable in the moderately channeled region beneath the convex crown face, which occupies about one third of the entire vertical diameter of that side of the tooth; surfaces more or less roughened. Lateral diameter of a small perfect tooth .16 inch, hight .13, depth of convex face of base .03, or nearly equal to the hight of the opposite crown face, elevation of concave crown face .10, or slightly greater than the hight of the deep side of the base; breadth of inferior surface of base .05 inch. A large specimen measures in lateral diameter .24 inch, vertical diameter .20, showing a proportionately greater elevation than in the preceding example.

The form under consideration is represented in our collections by only three or four examples, fortunately in a good state of preservation, plainly exhibiting their distinctive characteristics. There seems to be the most intimate relationship between these teeth and *C. apicalis*,

Agassiz, exhibiting precisely similar basal characters, while the crown differs chiefly from the typical species, as well as from *C. Stevensoni*, in the less acuminate and minute serration of the crest, and fewer indications in the coronal belt; the base is relatively stronger than that of the latter species, while it nearly agrees in this particular with the typical European form. It is also much smaller, the largest examples attaining scarcely half the size of either of the above named forms

*Position and locality:* Chester limestone; Chester, Illinois, upper fish bed

### CTENOPTYCHIUS STEVENSONI, St. J. and W.

Pl XII, Fig 15

Teeth small, delicate, in outline polygonal. Convex crown face semi-elliptical, plane or slightly arched laterally, regularly and considerably arched along the crest, which slightly projects beyond the line of the nearly straight basal angle, which latter is bordered by a narrow coronal belt composed of two or three folds, which are gently deflected at the lateral angles, forming a band continuous with that of the opposite face, concave face irregularly and broadly oval, gently and somewhat angularly depressed in the middle, basal border strongly produced and sharply unbeveled below, composed of four or five wide imbricating folds, widening at one extremity, nearly straight in the median region and abruptly rounded into the lateral extremities, the crest line is strongly and somewhat irregularly arched, slightly acuminate, and acutely denticulated, the denticulations more or less regularly diminishing in size from the strong median one towards the extremities, of which there are six or seven in either side, faintly striated along the abraded edge; both coronal faces enveloped in a dense, polished enamel like layer. The base is proportionately slender, considerably less in lateral diameter than the crown, eccentric, as seen from below, the region beneath the convex crown face narrowing towards one extremity, gently depressed and defined above and below by an obtuse angle, the opposite face relatively low, deeply channeled beneath the produced coronal border, inferior surface relatively wide, irregularly rectangular in outline, beveled to an acute edge in nearly the same horizontal plane as the crown.

The description of this elegant form is based upon one of three specimens which were discovered by Prof. J J. STEVENSON in the Coal Measures of West Virginia It differs so widely from any species thus far made known from the American Carboniferous series, that it scarcely requires a detailed comparison to distinguish it When, however, comparison is made with the type of the genus *C apicalis*, Ag , (not *C apicalis* referred to by McCoy, Brit Pale. Foss , p 626,) one cannot fail to be impressed with their intimate relationship It differs from *C. apicalis* in its thinner crown, straight basal border, more slender and shorter base, and greater number of serrations in the crest, also the absence of pectinations in the coronal band

The original specimen described by Prof AGASSIZ, (Pois. Foss, tom III, pp 99, 173 tab. 19, f. 1, 1a,) belongs to the collection of Sir PHILIP EGERTON, which we were permitted to examine while it was in the possession of Prof. AGASSIZ, who at one time had in contemplation the revision of the fossil *Selachians*, in aid of which purpose both Lord ENNISKILLEN and Sir PHILIP had contributed the use of their valuable collections, which were for a time at the Museum of Comparative Zoology; thus it was that we have enjoyed the rare privilege of studying material which has been rendered doubly valuable both on account of its historical and scientific interest. The type specimen above referred to was derived from the carbonaceous shales of the Coal Measures, Staffordshire near Manchester, England It presents very peculiar and at the same time marked distinctive features which can scarcely be mistaken. A careful examination of this specimen, and comparison with that above described, leads to the recognition of affinities more nearly allied to *Chomatodus* or *Antliodus* than to *Ctenopetalus* and other thick, long based *Petalodonts* The character of the basal region offers striking contrast to *Ctenopetalus*, and even the coronal region may be distinguished by its plane concave face—in the latter respect exhibiting intimate relationship with the abbreviated forms of *Chomatodus*, and in the former resembling both *Chomatodus* and *Antliodus*

*Position and locality*: In a calcareous bed holding a stratigraphic position about one hundred feet above the Mahoning sandstone, Coal Measures, near Morgantown, West Virginia.

## GENUS POLYRHIZODUS, McCoy.

### POLYRHIZODUS WILLIAMSI, St J and W.

Pl X A, Fig 23, Pl XIII, Fig 11

The collection of Dr. WILLIAMS affords a single nearly perfect example of a form of *Polyrhizodus* apparently specifically distinct from the several forms at present known from our Carboniferous deposits. It is distinguished by its strong, robust crown, which presents a lenticular outline, lateral extremities acutely rounded, the lateral diameter about two and a half times greater than the hight of the concave face; the convex crown face is worn down, reducing the elevation at least one-third, the present crest line well defined, but forming an obtuse angle, the triturating surface occupying its entire area, to the broadly and gently arched basal margin, which forms an acute angle with the broad basal area, but without a trace of coronal folds, subcrescent shaped in outline, concave crown face originally presenting a broad, regular lenticular outline, but in the present condition the crest is very gently arched, while the basal border is more strongly arched downward and moderately produced beyond the basal region to which it is sharply inbeveled, the extremities somewhat more abruptly curved upward to the lateral angles, and bordered by a strong coronal belt composed of three or more well defined parallel imbrications, which gradually narrow on approaching the extremities, the superior region gently depressed or nearly plane, smooth and polished, or with vertical striæ above the basal band The base is relatively small, low, lateral extent considerably less than the crown, well-defined from the broad basal area beneath the convex crown-face, inferior surface more or less distinctly defined, or rounded, beveled in nearly the same horizontal plane as the crown, and irregularly divided into six, more or less, radicles, coarsely roughened. A tooth .70 inch in lateral diameter, measures in transverse diameter 26 inch, depth of base beneath the concave crown-face about 07, lateral diameter about 15 inch across the lateral angles.

Mr SPRINGER has obtained another representative of the present form, in the same horizon at Keokuk, Iowa, represented in Pl. XI, fig. 23, which shows a very worn tooth from the inferior side, the coronal region having been even more reduced from attrition than the former example, but exhibiting the same abbreviated or transversely widened outline These teeth are intimately allied to the Upper Burlington form described by Messrs NEWBERRY and WORTHEN under the name *P porosus*, from which they may be distinguished by their shorter and more lenticular outline, narrower and more strongly downward arched basal belt. In the latter respect they bear some resemblance to *P. amplus* of the St. Louis; the latter form, however, should it prove to be distinct from *P Littoni*, N. and W., is less symmetrical in outline, and the concavity of the concave crown-face is much greater than obtains in the teeth under consideration

The form is dedicated to Dr G. A. WILLIAMS, to whom we are indebted for the use of valuable material from the Keokuk and Warsaw beds at Boonville

*Position and locality* Upper fish bed horizon of the Keokuk limestone, Boonville, Missouri, and Keokuk, Iowa

## POLYRHIZODUS NANUS, St J. and W.

Pl XIII, Fig 15

Teeth minute, stout, subelliptical in outline. Concave crown-face broadly elliptical in outline, moderately excavated, basal margin moderately prominent, broadly rounded, crest sharp, gently and regularly arched, convex face about half the hight of the opposite face, irregularly lenticular in outline, basal margin forming an obtuse angle with the rather narrow basal area, somewhat irregularly arched downward and broadly curved to the acute lateral angles, and occupied by a narrow coronal fold, surface broadly arched laterally, gently convex vertically and nearly at right angles to the basal area. Base nearly equal to the lateral diameter of the crown, in depth beneath the concave face less than the elevation of the convex crown face, thick, nearly vertical, well defined from the basal area beneath the convex face, inferior surface rounded, irregularly lobed with five, more or less, strong radicles Lateral diameter of tooth .12 inch, greatest hight .07, elevation of convex crown-face 04 inch.

The above form is represented by a single example, which shows the convex crown face and basal aspect. The fact that this is the only representative of the species, in a horizon abounding in ichthyic remains, is not so surprising when we take into consideration its minute size, rendering its discovery at all mere chance. We have not met with any form with which the present is intimately allied. It is in every respect dissimilar from *P. Williamsi* of the same horizon, being proportionately more robust, and the base of greater lateral extent. In the comparative strength and vertical diameter of the crown it seems to present affinities with *Dactylodus*, but the short base is essentially characteristic of *Polyrhizodus*.

*Position and locality:* Fish bed horizon in the upper part of the Keokuk limestone, Bentonsport, Iowa.

## POLYRHIZODUS PIASAENSIS, St J. and W.

Pl XIII, Fig 12

Teeth of medium size, extremely elongated laterally Crown moderately strong, compressed and gently arched along the crest, which is somewhat abruptly rounded to the acute lateral angles, nearly parallel with the basal margin; the convex face is nearly vertical, presenting an irregular, flattened lenticular outline, slightly channeled, about half the elevation of the opposite face, bordered by a prominent coronal belt consisting of one or more narrow folds, forming an obtuse angle with the basal area, nearly straight or but slightly arched downward in the median region, and very gently curved towards the lateral extremities; concave face long elliptical, with sharply rounded lateral angles, moderately excavated, basal border moderately produced and gently arched, imbrications not shown, but apparently forming a comparatively narrow belt. Basal area narrow, nearly linear, and at right-angles to the convex crown-face, base proper very low, moderately thick, considerably less than the lateral extent of the crown, well defined from the basal area, as also from the concave coronal margin, inferior surface rounded, and deeply fissured, with nine or ten irregular radicles The coronal surfaces are enveloped in a polished enamel like layer, which is more or less abraded by attrition in the convex face, exposing a striato punctate structure usually met with in the triturating surface of these teeth Greatest diameter of crown about .85 inch, hight of tooth 16, elevation of convex crown face .12, or about half that of the concave face, depth of base beneath concave basal margin .07 inch.

A unique example of the present form was discovered by Mr. VAN HORNE in the Warsaw beds above the mouth of Piasa creek, which we believe is the only representative of the genus thus far known from that horizon Its relatively great lateral elongation readily distinguishes it from other described forms, although in shape it bears a close general resemblance to *P. Littoni*, N and W, of the St Louis limestone. From the latter form it may be distinguished by its more slender proportions, less massive base, and more numerous radicles, and the outward or downward arched basal margin of the concave crown-face, more acutely rounded lateral extremities, and probably narrower coronal folds of the same side

*Position and locality*. In the escarpment exposure of brown, friable limestone of the Warsaw beds; in the Mississippi bluffs one mile above the mouth of Piasa creek, Jersey county, Illinois.

## POLYRHIZODUS AMPLUS, St. J. and W.

Pl XIII, Fig 13

Teeth of medium or large size, strong, unsymmetrical in outline. Crown moderately thick below, compressed to a thin edge along the broadly and somewhat irregularly arched crest; convex face irregularly long elliptical in outline, produced and attenuated at one or other extremity, regularly converging and acutely rounded at the opposite extremity, gently arched laterally, triturating surface occupying nearly the entire area, and nearly plane vertically, basal margin obtusely rounded, forming a sub acute angle with the basal area below, more or less broadly and irregularly arched downward from one extremity, and more abruptly curved upward to the opposite angle, and bordered by a moderately wide and, in the present state of preservation, obscurely imbricated coronal belt, concave crown face somewhat deeply excavated laterally and vertically, broadly and irregularly elliptical in outline, basal margin irregularly broadly arched and produced beyond the basal surface, sharply inbeveled, basal band wide, consisting of as many as six imbricating folds, gently rounded at one extremity, more abruptly so at the other, invested with a delicate, polished enamel layer, through which is visible the minute punctate structure, the opposite crown face is denuded of its enamel coating, presenting a fine granular structure, and in the crest striato punctation Base following the strong curvature of the basal margin of the concave crown face, considerably less in lateral diameter, moderately thick, and obliquely produced in the plane of the concave face, well defined from the broad basal area, inferiorly rounded, and irregularly divided into six or eight radicles of unequal size and shape Lateral diameter of crown 1.37 inch, hight of tooth .77, elevation of convex crown face .42, lateral diameter of base 1.05 inch, depth beneath the basal border of concave crown face .26

The above form was originally described from specimens in the collection of Mr. VAN HORNE but subsequently it has been found at two or more other localities in the same horizon, and with the evidence adduced by this additional material, the variations presented by individuals of the form do not appear to be remarkable. In some respects it bears somewhat intimate resemblance to *P radicans*, McCoy, with specimens of which, from the Carboniferous limestone of Armagh, in the Museum of Comparative Zoology, we have had opportunity to make direct comparison. Especially noticeable is this resemblance in the broadly arched, produced basal margin of the concave crown-face; it differs, however, in the more compressed crown less robust and shorter radicles The basal area is quite wide and plane, forming an acute angle with the convex crown face, instead of an obtuse angle as in the European form From *P dentatus*, N and W, of the Chester formation, it is distinguished by its broad elliptical outline, more compressed and higher crown, in which character it presents even greater contrast with *P. Littoni*, N and W, with which it is associated. The latter form is remarkable for its long-elliptical outline, which, however, may be attributable, in greater or less degree, to the wearing down of the convex aspect of the tooth by trituration; yet the basal border of the concave crown face, which forms a nearly straight belt gently curved outward at the extremities and sharply rounded, contrasts so widely with the teeth above described that we can hardly believe these distinctions represent merely individual variation. We have introduced illustrations of a remarkably fine example of the latter form, belonging to the collection of Mr. VAN HORNE, for comparison with that above described

*Position and locality:* Not rare, upper beds of the St Louis limestone, Alton and Waterloo, Illinois; St. Louis, Missouri

### POLYRHIZODUS CARBONARIUS, St J and W

Pl X A, Fig 24, 25 Pl XIII, Fig 1

Among the many interesting announcements made during the prosecution of the present investigations, that of a form of the genus *Polyrhizodus* from the Coal Measures of Illinois may claim no inconsiderable share of interest, on account of the extensive stratigraphic range it gives to the genus in the Carboniferous formations of the Mississippi valley, as contrasted with its more restricted range in the Lower Carboniferous strata of Europe

The present form is represented by a very few and imperfectly preserved individuals, but sufficient to exhibit not only their generic identity, but also their specific characteristics. The teeth are moderately strong, symmetrical, and of medium and large size. Concave crown face regularly elliptical in outline, more or less deeply excavated, thick below and rapidly attenuated in the upper portion to the broadly arched crest, lateral angles more or less acutely rounded, basal margin broadly and regularly arched downward, moderately produced, and traversed by a prominent coronal belt of two or three, or more, wide, regular imbrications, gradually narrowing towards the lateral extremities, convex face about half the elevation of the opposite side, gently arched laterally and vertically, sublenticular in outline, basal margin sharply defined, gently arched downward in the median region and broadly curved to the acute lateral angles, basal folds obsolete from attrition, in which condition the entire surface and crest is more or less reduced, and granulo punctate; concave face with a polished enamel coating, where it has not been exfoliated by corroding agencies. Base moderately strong, as deep again as thick, scarcely more than half the lateral diameter of the crown, slightly obliquely produced, inferior surface well defined, rounded, deeply divided into seven, more or less, irregular radicles, well-defined from the broad, laterally arched basal area, which is nearly at right angles to the convex crown face Lateral diameter of a large tooth 1.35 inch, hight of concave crown face .50, lateral diameter of base about 90, depth beneath the concave coronal border 16

The apparent symmetrical proportions and regularity of outline of the present form readily distinguishes it from other described forms. It has some general likeness to *P radicans*, McCoy, though it is much less robust in build and the base shorter vertically. The relative pro portions of the convex face and outline of the crest are subject to considerable modification, according to the degree of attrition which has taken place while the teeth were in use. By this means, as is the case with all the species of the genus, the convex face rarely exhibits its perfect contour and outline, and in many examples the abrasion has been carried to such an extent as to reduce the vertical diameter of the concave face until it is even less than that of the triturating surface of the convex face.

*Position and locality:* The typical example of the above species was obtained by Prof WORTHEN from the limestone overlying coal No 5 ? at Belleville, Illinois A single specimen discovered in the limestone horizon above coal No 8, at Springfield, Illinois, may prove to be specifically identical with the above; it represents a smaller individual, and the convex face is less abraded, but the base is broken away, although in lateral diameter, as well as in the general outline of the coronal region, it presents most intimate resemblance to the tooth described.

## GENUS DACTYLODUS, N. and W.

### DACTYLODUS CONCAVUS, St. J. and W.

Pl. XIII, Fig 17, 18

We have, provisionally, recognized the specific distinctness of a form of teeth represented by a few individuals in the collection of Mr VAN HORNE, which were obtained from the same beds which have afforded a magnificent series of *Dactylodus princeps*, N. and W, with which the present teeth are intimately allied. Indeed the chief distinctions by which they are characterized consist in the deep, angular excavation of the concave face of the crown, the basal border of which is more strongly produced horizontally, the convex face forming a greater angle with the basal area than is observed in the large number of typical examples of *D princeps*, the teeth are narrower laterally, and relatively of greater vertical extent, the radicles of the base probably not exceeding four, and more strongly defined from the basal area. The basal band in the concave crown face is equally wide and prominent, consisting of three to four strong imbrications, strongly produced and inbevelled to the base The convex face is more or less abraded, and granulo-punctate, the punctæ becoming vertically elongated near the crest which is obtusely angular, culminating in an eccentric, rounded apex; concave face smooth, or roughened by the appearance of the minute tubular structure. The outline of the basal margin in the convex crown-face is not dissimilar to that of *D. princeps*, although it is principally more strongly arched downward in the middle, and forms a much less obtuse angle with the basal area In size the teeth are smaller than the majority of typical specimens of *D princeps*, measuring in greatest hight 1 inch, lateral diameter of crown 77, elevation of concave face .57, elevation of convex face 45, lateral diameter of base 50, depth beneath base of concave crown-face 10 inch. We strongly suspect the form here indicated will be found to represent a part of the somewhat varied dentition of the above referred to species.

*Position and locality* Upper beds of the St Louis limestone; Alton, Illinois.

## DACTYLODUS MINIMUS, St. J. and W.

Pl XIII, Fig 19

Teeth minute, of robust proportions Crown lozenge shape as seen from above, rather depressed or tumid, crest gently arched laterally, strongly so from the concave face, obtusely rounded, convex face elliptical in outline, lateral extremities sharply rounded, gently arched in both directions, basal margin gently arched downward in a less degree than the crest, slightly eccentric at one or other extremity, and bordered by a faintly defined, narrow coronal fold, concave face broadly oval in outline, strongly arched and obtusely acuminate along the crest line, but slightly depressed vertically and gently arched laterally, giving the surface a full though not tumid appearance, basal margin gently and quite regularly arched downward and outward, moderately prominent and produced beyond the basal region to which it is abruptly inbeveled, coronal folds very obscure or obsolete Base massive, thick, in width scarcely more than half the lateral diameter of the crown, obliquely produced in the direction of the concave face, in depth equalling if not exceeding the elevation of the crown, and divided into three or four radicles, well-defined from the narrow basal area, which forms an acute angle with the convex crown-face Greatest diameter of crown .08 inch, antero posterior diameter .06, elevation of convex face 04, greatest depth of base 10 inch.

The description is founded upon a unique and well preserved specimen belonging to the collection of Mr VAN HORNE In diminutiveness this little tooth almost rivals some of *Polyrhizodi* which we have described. The coronal portion bears a somewhat marked resemblance to some of the narrow, obtusely crested *Chomatodi*, but the very strong, lobed base seems to indicate generic identity with *Dactylodus*—its abbreviated lateral dimensions and depth of base offering well marked distinctions from *Polyrhizodus.* In the present state of our knowledge, it is impossible to detect other than congeneric affinities with the other forms of *Dactylodus* known from the same horizon.

*Position and locality* Upper beds of the St Louis limestone; Alton, Illinois.

### DACTYLODUS EXCAVATUS, St J. and W.

Pl XIII, Fig 16

Teeth of small size, moderately strong Crown thick below, culminating in a sharp, broadly arched crest, concave face oval in outline, the crest and base inequally arched, rather deeply excavated towards the base, which is defined by a rather strong basal band composed of three or four folds, strongly arched downward in the middle and regularly and gently curved at the extremities, strongly produced along the exterior margin and unbeveled, superior coronal surface nearly plane laterally smooth and polished ; convex crown face irregularly lenticular in outline, sharply rounded at the extremities, very gently arched laterally, nearly plane vertically, crest line moderately and regularly arched, basal border gently and irregularly arched downward, and broadly curved to one or other extremity, defined by a narrow basal fold continuous with that of the concave face, but obscure from wear, the entire surface showing evidences of attrition. The basal area forms a narrow, plane surface nearly at right angles to the convex crown face, merging into the thick, massive radicles below, of which there are indications of three, possibly four, which are produced in a direction corresponding to the plane of the concave crown face, probably equaling if not exceeding in depth the hight of the crown, and about half or two-thirds the lateral diameter of the crown. Lateral diameter of crown 23 inch, hight of concave crown-face 15, hight of convex face 09 inch.

We have seen but a single example of the present form, which presents the coronal region of the tooth nearly entire, but the fangs of the base are broken away. Its relation to *Dactylodus* is inferred from the general character of the crown and the apparently long, narrow base It seems to have closer relationship with the teeth described under the name *D. concavus* of the St Louis limestone, which is similarly excavated in the concave face, but sufficiently distinct to be readily recognized, the crown being relatively broader and not acuminate From *D inflexus*, N and W., of the same horizon, it may be distinguished by its narrow base and fewer radicles It may, however, prove to be a young or small tooth of the latter form. Our knowledge of the variableness of these forms is, as yet, insufficient to make it possible always to trace out the specific identity of variable individuals

*Position and locality* Upper fish-bed of the Chester formation, Chester, Illinois.

## GENUS ANTLIODUS, N. and W.

### ANTLIODUS PEROVALIS, St J. and W.

Pl XI, Fig 28

Teeth small, very compressed, nearly circular in outline viewed from the concave aspect, broadly and strongly arched along the crest Concave crown face moderately depressed, basal line probably well defined from the root, broadly arched downward, forming an obtuse angle at the lateral extremities; the convex face is much lower than the opposite face, nearly plane vertically and gently arched laterally, slightly produced outward forming an obtuse angle along the basal margin with the basal area below, and bordered by a rather wide coronal fold which spans the crown in a nearly direct course The surface is smooth, or striato-punctate along the crest especially in the convex face Lateral diameter of tooth 14 inch, hight of convex crown face 06, hight of concave face about 15

Of the present form only a single specimen is known to us, and this is imperfect in the basal region. The root was probably very small, and the concave crown face was bordered by a coronal belt, of which only a faint trace is visible in the specimen The tooth is somewhat like *A sarcululus* of the Upper Burlington limestone, but it is readily distinguished by its circular outline and laterally worn strongly arched convex crown-face

The original, which belonged to the collection of Prof. WORTHEN, was lost at the time of the fire in the building occupied by the State Geological Museum, in Springfield, February, 1871

*Position and locality* Warsaw beds; Warsaw, Illinois

### ANTLIODUS GRACILIS, St. J and W

Pl XI, Fig 29

Teeth small, oval in outline Crown moderately compressed, crest regularly arched and sharp, presenting a striato punctate structure in worn surfaces; convex face irregularly elliptical in outline, but slightly arched in either direction, basal line nearly horizontal in the median region, but towards the extremities suddenly and gracefully curved upwards forming obtuse angles about one fourth the distance from either extremity, coronal fold narrow and apparently simple, concave side broadly elliptical in outline, moderately depressed in the longest diameter, and curved backward at the lateral borders, basal line probably nearly corresponding to the outline of the crest, but in the specimen before us this portion of the crown is not preserved The root is probably short, and of considerable less extent laterally than the crown, with which it is nearly vertical Lateral diameter of crown 31 inch, elevation of concave face about 17, elevation of convex face 14, lateral diameter of base about 21 inch

The sole representative of this elegant little form, unfortunately, does not preserve the entire outline—the basal margin of the concave crown face and the root having been broken away, but enough remains for satisfactory description and comparison with other forms, and which exhibit its specific distinctness and also its probable generic identity with *Antliodus*. It is apparently allied to *A. sarcululus*, N. and W, of the Upper Burlington limestone, the basal outline of the convex crown-face being much as in that form, but its much more elevated crown and more abrupt declination of the concave face distinguish it from that as well as from other forms of the genus The above features, together with its symmetrical figure, will readily facilitate the identification of other individuals, although we have to regret the imperfect condition of the unique example before us, and the lack of a more complete series such as would afford a better knowledge of its specific relations

*Position and locality* The unique specimen was discovered by Mr. VAN HORNE, in the Warsaw beds; mouth of Piasa creek, Illinois

## GENUS PETALODUS, Owen.

### PETALODUS HYBRIDUS, St J and W

Pl XII, Fig 10

We have examined a form of *Petalodus* represented by two specimens in the collection of Mr VAN HORNE, one of which exhibits a nearly entire individual, and the other shows the concave face of the crown in a very satisfactory manner A cursory examination at first induced us to refer these teeth to *P linguifer*, a species originally described by Messrs. NEWBERRY and WORTHEN, from the Chester formation; but the acquisition of additional material illustrative of that form, and a detailed comparison with the teeth herein mentioned, seem to prove conclusively their specific distinctness Hence, in consequence of its apparent resemblance to *P curtus*, N and W, of the Warsaw beds, and the species above referred to, we have designated the present form by the above specific appellation

The teeth attain large size Crown long elliptical or narrow lozenge-shaped in outline, compressed along the crest and moderately acuminate, gradually thickening below, concave face moderately excavated, bordered by a prominent basal band composed of five to seven narrow, regular imbrications, strongly arched downward in the middle and making a slight sigmoidal curvature towards the extremities, sharply inbeveled to the base; the convex face is long-elliptical or sublenticular in outline, in hight less than that of the opposite face, gently arched laterally, basal line broadly and regularly curved downward in the middle, and marked in the deeply beveled inferior margin by a rather wide imbricated belt which is made up of irregularly interrupted, delicately wrought folds, and which is distinctly defined from the base proper by a faint raised line; both coronal surfaces are invested with a smooth, polished enamel like layer, which becomes delicately striated along the crest by the exposure of the vertically disposed medullary tubes in the trenchant triturating edge. The base is relatively thick, thickening below and more strongly beveled beneath the concave face, broadly rounded below, with obtusely defined lateral angles, and slightly diverging to the base of the crown, in width about two thirds that of the crown, and nearly equal to the hight of the crown, coarsely roughened vertically A large specimen measures in lateral diameter of crown 1.65 inch, hight of tooth 1.14 inch, greatest elevation of convex crown face .55, greatest elevation of concave face about .65 inch

This form bears a marked resemblance to *P linguifer*, and in some particulars it also recalls in a striking manner *P. curtus*. Indeed, so marked is this intermediate relationship both as to structure and occurrence in time, it might readily be assumed that they were derived by processes of evolution one from the other. In the acuminate outline of the crown, it resembles the Chester form first mentioned, but the basal margin of the concave face is suddenly arched downward, producing a median angulation not observed in that form; also the basal belt of the opposite face is composed of much finer and more numerous imbrications, the crown is proportionately less massive, the base is less deep, wider and more angular in the lateral margins—in this latter particular intimately resembling the base of *P curtus* of the Warsaw beds. The crown differs from the latter form in its long elliptical outline, acuminate crest, more nearly equal elevation of the coronal surfaces, as also in the character of the basal belts, and the crown is less deeply concave than is the case in either of the forms with which the present one is compared

*Position and locality:* In the upper beds of the St Louis limestone; Alton, Illinois

### PETALODUS PROXIMUS, St. J and W

Pl XII, Fig 11

Under the above name we have designated a peculiar form of teeth, of which we have seen no absolutely entire individuals, but of which the collection of Prof. WORTHEN contains several more or less fragmentary examples, besides the nearly perfect tooth figured These fragments exhibit a uniformity of characters which has led provisionally to their recognition as a distinct form From *Petalodus Alleghaniensis*, Leidy, with which they are associated, they are distinguished by the regularly arched crest, the comparatively horizontal direction of the basal border of the concave face, relatively low convex face, and apparently short, broadly rounded base, which is produced downward in nearly the same vertical plane as the convex crown face, comparatively slight antero posterior diameter, and about two thirds the lateral diameter of the crown The concave crown face presents an elliptical outline, broadly rounded at the extremities, and nearly as high again as the opposite face, which latter is irregularly lenticular in outline The basal belt in the concave face is composed of three or four wide, regular imbrications, occupying more than a third of the entire elevation, about half their breadth produced beyond the plane of the base, in the convex face the coronal belt is composed of four or five narrower folds, about half the width of that in the opposite face, and strongly inbeveled to the basal region, the crest is compressed, with the usual vertical striation produced by the abrasion of the enamel like layer and exposure of the tubular structure Lateral diameter of crown of a full-sized specimen 88 inch, hight of concave face 35, hight of convex face about 20 inch

It will be observed that the teeth described present striking features in contrast with the large teeth originally described by Dr LEIDY under the name *Petalodus Alleghaniensis*, the originals of which he kindly submitted to us for examination, and to which we are satisfied belong the teeth subsequently described in the second volume of the present report under the name *P destructor*, N and W. The teeth under consideration possibly hold the same relation to the above mentioned form as does *P Hastingsii*, Owen, to *P acuminatus*, Agass, of the British Carboniferous limestone Prof McCOY has suggested the probable specific identity of the latter forms; but we have never seen immature or small individuals of *P. Alleghaniensis* that might be confounded with the present teeth, although such may yet be discovered

*Position and locality* • In the limestone above coal No 8, Upper Coal Measures, near Springfield, Illinois

## GENUS CTENOPETALUS. Agassiz

### CTENOPETALUS VINOSUS. St. J. and W.

Pl XII Fig 13

Under the designation *Ctenopetalus*, Prof AGASSIZ recognized the generic distinctness of a *Petalodont* form of teeth, which had previously been transferred from *Petalodus* to *Ctenoptychius*, and finally became to be regarded as the type of the present group, under the name *Ctenopetalus serratus*, which was published in the widely distributed list of type specimens in the well known collection of Lord ENNISKILLEN.* The genus has certain strongly marked facies, as the serrated or denticulated crest, which serve to distinguish it from *Petalodus*, with which it otherwise bears a much more intimate resemblance than to *Ctenoptychius*, indeed holding the same relationship to *Petalodus* as the latter genus does to *Antliodus*.

The present form attains medium size. Convex face of crown sub-lenticular in outline, gently arched laterally, and quite plane vertically, moderately thick, strong, acutely rounded at the produced lateral extremities, which are slightly curved downward at one or other, or both extremities, crest very gently arched along its greater length, suddenly curved downward on nearing the extremities, somewhat obtusely and minutely denticulated, the denticulations becoming strong and sub angular toward the lateral margins, where they are quite strongly developed; lower margin defined by a strong imbricated basal band, consisting of at least three faintly crenulated folds, broadly and regularly arched downward in the middle, gently deflected laterally, and relieved at a sharp angle from the coronal surface above, more or less inbeveled below, the concave face apparently presents an elliptical outline, gently concave in both directions, basal margin not shown; both coronal surfaces are enveloped in a dense, polished enamel like layer, towards the crest faintly marked with numerous slightly diverging striæ, which mark the course of the medullary tubes which terminate above singly, or in pairs, or threes, forming the denticulations. Base unknown. Greatest lateral diameter of crown .95 inch, elevation of convex face .36.

This elegant form is represented by a unique specimen in the collection of Mr. SPRINGER, which was obtained from the ichthyic horizon in the upper part of the Keokuk limestone. The generic reference is based upon the coronal characters alone, since the base and basal border of the concave crown face unfortunately are not preserved. But judging from the superficial characters presented by the crown, we have little or no hesitation in regarding it generically identical with the forms recognized under the above generic title, whether or not this group is sufficiently distinct from *Petalodus* to be regarded as a well defined genus. Specifically, however, the present form is readily distinguished by its laterally elongated outline and slightly arched crest. In shape it is nearest the form from the St. Louis limestone, *P. (Ctenopetalus) bellulus*, which we have provisionally referred to this group; but its

* Alphabetical Catalogue of the Type Specimens of Fossil Fishes in the Collection of the Earl of Enniskillen, at Florence Court. Geol Mag., vol vi, Dec., 1869.

great size, more minutely denticulated crest, and regularly arched basal margin, are sufficient to establish its distinctness from that form

*Position and locality:* Keokuk limestone, Bentonsport, Iowa

CTENOPETALUS (PETALODUS) BELLULUS, St J and W

Pl XII, Fig 9

Teeth very small, oval or subelliptical in outline, rather strongly proportioned Crown moderately thick at base, sharp and regularly arched along the crest, with acute lateral extremities; concave face elliptical in outline, gently excavated, basal margin regularly arched downward in the middle, and bordered by three more or less imbricated folds, which expand in the median region to twice their breadth nearer the extremities, the upper fold spanning the crown in an irregular though nearly horizontal direction, and but slightly produced below beyond the plane of the basal region, convex face of irregular outline, long-elliptical or sublenticular, gently arched laterally, nearly plane vertically, basal margin irregularly curved downward, forming an obtuse angle, and limited by two narrow imbrications, which are sometimes slightly deflected at the extremities, but usually describe a slight sigmoidal curvature Base short, broadly rounded below, and obtuse, somewhat distended in the middle, well defined at the lateral angles, in breadth considerably less than that of the crown, with which it is nearly in the same vertical plane. Greatest lateral diameter of crown of large-sized tooth .25 inch, hight of entire tooth 15, elevation of concave crown face .10, elevation of convex face 06 inch

Only two specimens of this pretty little form have come to our notice, and these are respectively from widely separated localities, though evidently from nearly the same horizon. One of the specimens, that from Iowa, presents a group of teeth of which the larger and more perfect one is that upon which the above specific description is based The other teeth of the group are all of smaller size, though presenting a remarkable persistency in form, but they are not apparently in the relative order in which they occurred, being irregularly dispersed, having the appearance of two contiguous rows of teeth crowded together, as shown in the figure illustrating the convex aspect of the group; otherwise, if their occurrence in the above specimen does indicate their relative natural position, it indicates a degree of irregularity in the arrangement of the teeth such as has not been observed in other *Petalodont* genera, of which series of teeth have been found in their natural order The crest of some of these teeth is interrupted by slight vertical sulci, giving to the crown a delicate denticulate appearance, which strongly recalls the appearance presented by *Ctenopetalus serratus*,

Agass But as this serrated character is not apparently constant—even portions of the crown in the same individual exhibiting both the plain and serrated conditions of the crest, and in the larger tooth the entire crest is even—it may not be regarded as an important character Nor does it appear that in the case of *Ctenopetalus serratus* of the European Carboniferous deposits the serrated crest should be considered as its most important generic character, since a series of that species, which we have examined in the collection of the Museum of Comparative Zoology, is sure to lead by almost imperceptible gradations from individuals in which the crest is strongly serrated to forms in which the coronal serrations are scarcely more prominent than is the striation in *Petalodus laevissimus*, Agassiz, with which they are associated The collection of Mr VAN HORNE, from Alton, affords a single imperfect specimen apparently referable to the present form, in which the denticulated character of the crown is well displayed.

*Position and locality*. In the upper beds of the St. Louis limestone; Pella, Iowa, and Alton, Illinois

CTENOPETALUS LIMATULUS, St. J. and W

Pl XII, Fig 18

Teeth very small, strong and symmetrically proportioned Crown moderately thick below and gradually attenuated towards the crest, which is moderately arched, acuminate, and somewhat deeply serrated, with as many as seven strong, subtumid, subacute denticulations, of which the median one is strongest, the lateral ones regularly decreasing in size towards the extremities, and defined from one another by rather deeply impressed sulci extending nearly to the basal line in the convex face; convex face slightly arched laterally, nearly plane vertically, basal angle well defined, broadly arched downward in the middle and again gently curved downward at the extremities, and marked upon the inferior or beveled surface by a relatively broad coronal belt apparently without imbrications, concave face apparently more regularly oval in outline, but slightly depressed, basal margin broadly arched downward, coronal folds unknown, both surfaces smooth and polished. Base strong, constricted above, slightly expanded and thickened below and broadly rounded, in depth equal to the hight of the crown, but considerably less in lateral diameter, more or less roughened. Lateral diameter of crown 24 inch, elevation of convex face .10, entire hight of tooth 23, lateral diameter of base 17 inch

This elegant little form is intimately allied to *C dentatus* (Agassiz sp) of the British Mountain limestone, with authentic specimens of which, as also the type belonging to the collection of Lord ENNISKILLEN, we have had opportunities for making direct comparison at the Museum of Comparative Zoology The apparent distinctive characters by which the present form may be distinguished from the above mentioned species, consists in the less deep serration of the crest, shallower concave face, and relatively narrower base as compared with the lateral diameter of the crown

*Position and locality* Rare in the Chester limestone, Chester, Illinois

## CTENOPETALUS MEDIUS, St J and W

Pl X, Fig 26

The teeth herein referred to, and which we have, provisionally, recognized as a distinct form, present the same general form and size as the preceding species, *C limatulus*, but are recognized by the proportionately greater lateral diameter of the crown as compared with the entire hight of the tooth, which obtains in the majority of examples, the narrower and obtusely pointed inferior extremity of the base, the exceedingly minute and numerous serration of the somewhat acuminate crest, each serrature being flanked, especially in the convex face, by short, sharp crested carina, which regularly though slightly diverge, but which are scarcely discernible in the absolutely perfect condition, when the entire crown is invested with an exceedingly delicate, polished enamel like mantle In the latter condition, as also in shape, these teeth bear a marked resemblance to *Petalodus linguifer*, N and W, a species described from the same formation and locality, but a careful comparison reveals other and apparently permanent characteristics which seem to render its identity with that form extremely improbable. Thus, in the present teeth the basal belt along the convex crown face forms a simple, broad fold in the unbeveled portion, sometimes showing quite distinctly along the upper edge an extremely delicate imbrication, which only extends through the broadly arched median region, while, in *Petalodus linguifer*, the inferior or unbeveled area occupied by the coronal belt is distinctly imbricated, even in minute examples, with three or more folds The inner crown face is moderately excavated and defined below by a well-marked broadly downward arched, imbricated coronal belt

We are aware of the variableness of the serration in *C. serratus* Agassiz, but these variations are not apparently accompanied by other features, such as distinguish the present teeth from *Petalodus linguifer* On the other hand, the fine serration of the crest readily distinguish it from *C limatulus*

The intimate relations which exist between *Ctenopetalus* and *Petalodus* find an additional exemplification in the present form Indeed, it would appear that the non-serrate forms of the one pass by almost imperceptible gradation into the serrate condition of the other while in general form the species of both groups are most intimately related.

*Position and locality:* Uncommon in the Chester limestone, Chester, Illinois

CTENOPETALUS OCCIDENTALIS, St. J and W

Pl XII, Fig 14

Teeth small, symmetrical Crown moderately thick below, rapidly attenuated towards the crest, which is slightly acuminate and broadly arched, with ten to twelve obtusely rounded denticulations, which more or less regularly diminish in size towards the lateral extremities, the median one forming the apex being the most conspicuous, concave crown face long oval in outline, more or less sharply rounded at the extremities, rather deeply and uniformly depressed, and limited below by a relatively narrow, slightly produced basal band, which is apparently composed of not more than three or four imbrications, gently and regularly arched downward in the middle and slightly deflected laterally, the opposite face is more elliptical or sublenticular in outline, moderately convex in both directions, and acutely rounded at the extremities, in hight above the basal angle, about half that of the concave face; the basal band in the convex face is remarkable for its great width, the uppermost fold being usually narrow, but the lower fold, or folds, reaching far down and investing nearly half the vertical extent of the inferior basal area in a thin coating of enamel, in the downward curvature somewhat more sharply arched than the opposite border with which it nearly corresponds The base is of moderate dimensions in proportion to the crown, slightly eccentric, lateral angles and basal margin uniformly rounded, thickened, lateral margins diverging to the crown, gently beveled along the inferior convex border, more or less roughened The coronal surfaces present a firm smooth enamel like layer, which is usually more or less abraded along the crest and delicately marked with slightly diverging striæ Greatest lateral diameter of crown .66 inch, hight of tooth 52, elevation of concave crown face 35, hight of convex crown-face above basal angle .24 inch.

The above species is known from two examples, one of which exhibits a nearly entire specimen, which were discovered by Mr. W. R Morley in strata near the base of the Coal Measures The species falls under the genus *Ctenopetalus* of Agassiz, and is intimately allied to the typical

—54

form *C serratus*, Agassiz. It differs, however, from that form by readily distinguishable peculiarities, as the less robust proportions of the crown, more obtusely acuminate apex, and the stronger and fewer serrations of the crest, narrower basal band in the concave face, and the less strongly though more broadly arched basal margin of the convex face.

*Position and locality* · From a stratum of limestone overlying a thin bed of coal near the base of the lower Coal Measures, Fort Dodge, Iowa.

## GENUS PRISTODUS, Agassiz.

### PRISTODUS? ACUMINATUS, St J. and W.

Pl X A, Fig 6

We have provisionally referred to the genus *Pristodus*, of Agassiz, a minute form represented by a unique example in the collection of Mr. SPRINGER, which possess distinctive features which seem to indicate a more intimate relationship with that genus than with any other group of teeth known in the American Carboniferous deposits The tooth is distinguished by its lateral elongation and comparatively thin or compressed crown, which is slightly curved backward, sharply rounded at the extremities, basal border sharply inbeveled behind and defined along the line of the superior coronal region by an obtusely produced basal ridge, gently arched vertically, crest strongly denticulated and rising into a strong, laterally deflected, eccentric median prominence, the denticulations very similar throughout, though gradually and more or less regularly diminishing in size laterally, in shape lanceolate terminating in an acute apex, and defined by relatively well-marked vertical sulci, which descend nearly to the produced basal angle; posterior (?) face faintly convex vertically, though slightly expanded on nearing the basal border, the inbeveled portion being apparently occupied by a simple coronal fold, anterior face gently concave in both directions, slightly exceeding in hight the opposite face, sharply inbeveled along the base, both faces smooth and polished Lateral diameter of tooth 09 inch, greatest hight of crown 04 Base unknown

The exceedingly delicate little tooth above noticed, unfortunately, reveals only one side of the crown in full, only a portion of the concave face can be seen, and the base has either crumbled away, else it forms so inconspicuous an object as to appear obsolete. The specimen presents peculiarities in coronal conformation which more closely resemble the *Pristodus falcatus*, Agass., of the Yorkshire Carboniferous limestone, than any of the forms with which it is associated or those occurring in superimposed strata. Its basal region in the posterior face, however, recalls the simple coronal fold characteristic of *Desmiodus*, but there is no indication of the strong anterior buttress and basal protuberance, while the very compressed crown and its sharp denticulations still further contrast with the latter genus. The character of the basal borders, also, bear some resemblance to *Harpacodus*, Agass. In view of its minute size, could we detect a horny structure in the place of the apparently true dentine of the tooth, it might be suspected to belong to those curious little fossils known under the general term *Conodonts*.

*Position and locality:* In the lower fish-bed of the Kinderhook, Burlington, Iowa

## Genus CALOPODUS, St J. and W.

Teeth in general form like *Petalodus* Crown massive concavo-convex, concave face deepest, and especially distinguished by its laterally arched or swollen contour, obtuse crest terminating in a strong, subconical, more or less eccentric apex, convex face broadly rounded laterally, and more or less arched vertically, coronal margins more or less prominent, beveled to the base, and occupied by a broad basal band composed of more or less regular or interrupted imbrications, broadest in the concave face and continuous with that of the convex face Base very similar to that of *Petalodus*, strong, more or less compressed and constricted above, inferiorly rounded and beveled to an obtuse edge beneath the concave coronal region.

A single species of the above genus is known to us, which was derived from the Middle Coal Measures Allied to *Petalodus*, it may be distinguished by the turgid, subconical, unsymmetrical crown. The strata whence the following species was obtained, though carefully searched, afford no examples of *Petalodus*, the non-occurrence of which further renders it improbable that these teeth formed a part of the dental apparatus of that genus

### Calopodus apicalis, St. J. and W.

Pl XII, Fig 16, 17

Teeth very small, robust, unsymmetrical, variable in form. Crown forming a stout, subconical or unequally compressed prominence, crest obtuse, apical extremity eccentric, subacute, directed over the concave face and sometimes laterally deflected, concave face curvilinear or irregularly triangular in outline, lateral diameter nearly equal to the hight, slightly concave vertically, gently arched laterally, basal border moderately and more or less irregularly arched downward, with four or five imbricating folds, of which the uppermost ones are curved upward and lost in the smooth surface, basal border gently produced and gently beveled, sometimes abruptly, to the basal region, the convex face is usually slightly less elevated than the concave face, moderately convex in both directions, basal angle very obtuse, nearly horizontal, or viewed obliquely from below appearing gently arched upward in the middle, more or less sharply rounded at the lateral extremities, gently beveled to the base, the beveled area rather wide and occupied by at least three imbricating folds, continuous with the opposite coronal belt; coronal region invested with a dense, polish enamel like layer. Base proportionately strong, obliquely produced, usually as broad and deep as the crown, eccentric, compressed beneath the basal margins of the crown, expanded and thickened below, lateral angles sharply rounded, beveled in the deeper face to the broadly rounded, obtuse inferior margin, surfaces more or less roughened. A small and unusually symmetrical specimen measures in hight .18 inch, greatest lateral diameter at base of crown .13, hight of concave crown face .12, hight of convex face nearly .10 inch.

The only two representatives of this interesting species at present known to us, were obtained at the same locality—indeed so intimately associated that the one was discovered in developing the other from the shaly matrix—in a stratum which has afforded no other *Petalodont* forms or other ichthyic remains, except *Petrodus* and scales of *Palæoniscus*. The smaller and more symmetrical specimen is that upon which the preceding description was based, but the other tooth exhibits such marked individual variation from what may be regarded as the normal aspect of the species, that it is not merely a matter of interest but important carefully to note the variations so far as may be necessary for the satisfactory definition of the species. The individual teeth are subject to considerable variableness in the symmetry of outline and relative proportion of parts. The large specimen presents a more distorted outline than the small tooth, the base being strongly deflected, without, however, losing its general shape, the crown is conical, both surfaces very full or arched laterally, and nearly equal in hight, apex conical, laterally deflected, and slightly curved over the concave face, lateral edges of the the crest very obtuse, scarcely defined, basal margin slightly arched downward in the middle and beveled gently to the basal region, imbricated belt very wide and composed of three or four continuous, though irregularly disposed folds, with several secondary thread like folds reaching two thirds the distance to the apex. This tooth is unquestionably specifically identical with that first noticed, differing chiefly in the less distinct definition of the concave crown face and lateral obliquity of the base. The species differs so widely from other *Petalodont* forms as scarcely to require more minute comparisons than those detailed above to distinguish it.

*Position and locality* Black carbonaceous shales overlying the "Panora coal bed" of the Middle Coal Measures; Guthrie county, Iowa.

## Genus PETALORHYNCHUS, Agassiz

### PETALORHYNCHUS PSEUDOSAGITTATUS, St. J. and W.

Pl XII, Fig 1-4

Teeth small or of medium size Crown irregularly pentagonal in outline, moderately thick, sharp crested, acuminate or broadly rounded between the prominent lateral angles of the convex face; the concave face forms a spatulate area, gently depressed in the middle, lateral angles slightly produced, from which the basal border is profoundly arched downward, the lateral margins gradually converging in a slight curvature to the obtusely rounded inferior border, where the coronal belt is very wide and gently beveled to the base, and composed of several imbrications, of which the lower and narrower ones follow the curvature of the margin, the upper folds gradually increasing in width and more or less angularly arched upward in the middle, where they occupy from one fifth to one-third of the vertical diameter of the crown, but as they diverge towards the lateral angles of the crown they suddenly narrow, and are seldom present. rarely being even faintly discernible in the present condition of the teeth, the convex crown-face is relatively low, probably in the majority of individuals not more than half the vertical diameter of the opposite face, gently arched laterally, nearly plane vertically, the basal margin forming a more or less prominent angle and gently beveled below, produced in the median region into a nearly horizontal shoulder, from the angles of which the beveled imbricated belt arches upward and again strongly curved downward on nearing the acute lateral angles of the crown The coronal surfaces are invested with a thin enamel layer, which, however, is generally exfoliated to greater or less extent, especially in the convex face, giving rise, by the exposure of the minute tubular structure, to the diverging striation observable in the majority of specimens The base as seen from the convex side, slightly expands laterally below the coronal border into an obtuse lateral angle, below which the margins gradually converge to the rounded inferior border, the surface gently convex below and rising into a more or less angularly defined ridge above, corresponding to the angulation in the coronal margin, from which it is beveled to the lateral margins, the concave aspect presents a short lingulate pro cess, gently arched laterally and less than half the vertical extent of the opposite face, surfaces more or less roughened by irregular vertical striæ A medium sized specimen measures in vertical diameter .63 inch, lateral diameter of crown 37, or but little greater than the diameter across the angles of the base, elevation of concave crown-face 45, hight of convex face .30 inch

The fine series of the present form which we have had for examination exhibits considerable individual variability, which is in part attributable to attrition, probably also to the position the teeth respectively occupied upon the jaws. Probably the majority of the specimens were worn down while in use, since the crest and convex face bear every evidence of abrasion in the exfoliation of the enamel layer, and the consequent exposure of the minute tubular structure, to which is due the striated appearance of specimens in this state of preservation. In the outline of the crest there is also considerable variation—many specimens being prominently acuminate, while others are broadly rounded between the coronal angles indeed, the rounded outline would appear to be the actual condition of perfect individuals, as indicated by examples in which the enamel-like layer remains, although the same condition of surface obtains in acuminate specimens, and, *vice versa*, rounded examples present unmistakable evidence of attrition. A large specimen in the collection of Mr. VAN HORNE exhibits an anomalous feature, the base being deeply cleft producing a pair of radicles.

In the present form we have another example of the intimate specific relations existing between many of the American Carboniferous fishes and those of the same formations in Europe In the present instance we observe the closest resemblance with a form in the Carboniferous limestone of Armagh, the *P. sagittatus*, Agassiz The present form, however, is distinguished by its shorter base, less rapidly converging outline of the crest, and the more numerous imbrications of the coronal belt—characters which equally serve to distinguish it from *P striatus*, N and W., of the Upper Burlington limestone.

*Position and locality* Upper beds of the St Louis limestone; Alton, Illinois, Pella, Iowa, St. Louis, Missouri.

## PETALORHYNCHUS DISTORTUS, St J and W.

Pl XII, Fig 7 8

In the collections from the St Louis formations occur a form represented by very small teeth, which we have failed satisfactorily to identify with either of the two species known from the same horizon, although we have not overlooked analogous resemblances, but these are apparently irreconcilable with the characters which especially distinguish those forms, from which we have provisionally recognized its specific distinctness.

Teeth irregular or eccentric in outline. Crown moderately thick, irregularly arched along the crest, sharp, acuminate, apex submedian; the concave crown-face is but slightly depressed, lateral angles strongly produced, subacute, inferior border strongly and eccentrically arched downward and rounded below, deflected to the lateral extremities above, and margined by four or more imbricating folds, which are well defined below, attenuated in the lateral borders on nearing the extremities, where they are usually obsolete or broken away; convex face semielliptical in outline, in elevation much less (one third to two thirds) than that of the opposite face, rather strongly arched laterally, sharply rounded at the lateral angles, inferior border moderately prominent, gently beveled to the base, gently arched downward from one or other extremity and suddenly curved upward near the opposite extremity, and bordered by two or three narrow imbrications continuous with the basal belt of the concave face The coronal surfaces in the specimens before us are delicately ornamented with vermiculose striæ, and along the crest diverging striæ appear in the triturating surface. The base is too indifferently preserved to determine its entire form; it appears to have been thin, tapering to the broadly rounded extremity, which probably extended but little beyond the extreme basal margin in the concave face, forming a broad convexity in the opposite face Greatest lateral diameter of crown .22 inch, elevation of convex face .12, elevation of concave face about .18 inch.

The basal band of the concave face is not shown in its lateral extension, where it was probably very attenuated before reaching the lateral angles. The eccentric outline of the concave face is due to the irregularly arched basal borders, as also that of the opposite face. In this particular these teeth bear a remarkable resemblance to some of the distorted teeth found associated with and referable to *P. striatus*, N and W, in the Upper Burlington limestone But in the case of the present form, we have been unable to trace such intimate specific features with either of the two forms described from the St. Louis limestone, while the identity of the specimens from widely separated localities, would seem to furnish additional evidence of their specific distinctness In the direction of the basal folds, and the rather prominent convexity of the median region of the convex crown face, there is a less or more remote resemblance to *P. spatulatus*, but there exist no such intimate features in common with the latter form, such as enable the probable identification of the abnormal individuals of the Upper Burlington form from those above referred to, and which the teeth under consideration more closely resemble than they do either of the forms with which they are associated

*Position and locality.* Upper beds of the St. Louis limestone; Pella, Iowa, Alton, Illinois, and St. Louis, Missouri.

PETALORHYNCHUS SPATULATUS, St J. and W.

Pl XII, Fig 5,6

Associated with the preceding species occurs a form of teeth which present peculiarities strikingly in contrast with the distinguishing features of *P. pseudosagittatus*, and holding the same relation to that form in the St. Louis limestone, as does *P. psittacinus* with *P. sagittatus* in the Carboniferous limestone of Armagh. The chief distinguishing peculiarity consists in the swollen condition of the basal portion of the teeth, which is particularly noticeable from the convex side, the base presenting a massive, laterally expanded surface, elliptical in outline, very convex laterally and compressed in the gently rounded lateral margins, broadly rounded below, slightly converging above and compressed beneath the lateral portions of the coronal margin; opposite face less than half the vertical extent of that described, laterally flattened, perhaps faintly depressed, strongly rounded to the extremity, both faces more or less roughened, with irregularly disposed foramina. Crown proportionately strong, convex face broadly arched laterally, lateral margins sharp, more or less rapidly converging towards the strongly acuminate apex, which is sometimes truncated or rounded, basal margin slightly prominent, broadly arched downward in the median region and more or less strongly curved laterally, the rather wide, gently beveled inferior belt occupied by three or more regular imbricating folds, which gradually narrow towards the extremities, and apparently continuous with the coronal belt of the opposite face, concave crown face twice the hight of the convex face, subovate in outline, moderately excavated, basal margin well defined from the base, strongly arched downward in the middle and lightly produced at the lateral extremities, coronal belt wide and composed of several imbrications—in the specimen before us the folds are very obscure as though from abrasion. Vertical dimensions of a tooth of large size 90 inch, greatest lateral diameter of base 45, elevation of convex crown face 38 inch.

The collection of Mr. VAN HORNE contains three examples of the present form of large and medium size, none of which, however, show the concave aspect of the teeth. But a fragment of the basal portion of one of the specimens plainly reveals the outline of the concave crown-face, with the strongly downward arched basal belt, which is apparently made up of several imbricating folds, the upper folds being slightly arched upward in the middle, much in the same manner as observed in *P. pseudosagittatus*, though relatively narrower than in the latter form. We have a few imperfect teeth from the same formation, at Pella, which are probably referable to this species The latter specimens, however, are very small and somewhat peculiar in the truncation or broadly rounded condition of the apical extremity, although in other particulars they are not dissimilar from the Alton specimens

At the localities mentioned, an anomalous form occurs, which we have, provisionally, referred to a distinct species, under the name *P distortus*, the affinities of which are noted in detail under that head. As there stated, their relation to the present form was suggested by their resemblance to abnormally developed individuals of the form common in the Upper Burlington limestone, *P striatus* of Messrs NEWBERRY and WORTHEN, but it is exceedingly difficult to reconcile the variations presented by these teeth with the marked distinctive characteristics of the form described above, though to a much less degree when they are compared with *P pseudosagittatus*

The present form is most nearly allied to that originally recognized by Prof AGASSIZ under the name *P psittacinus*, from the Carboniferous limestone of Armagh, Ireland. It differs, however, from the European form in the less tumid condition of the basal region, and also the less horizontal direction of the basal band of the convex crown face However, in the collection of the Museum of Comparative Zoology, there is a single specimen of the European form, in which the basal band is gently curved upward and downward on approaching the lateral angles in the convex crown face, much in the same manner, though in a less degree than in the present form, instead of being perfectly horizontal as represented in the figures given by Prof McCOY in the British Paleozoic Fossils, Pl. 3 I., fig 11

*Position and locality* Upper beds of the St. Louis limestone; Alton, Illinois, and Pella, Iowa

## GENUS PELTODUS, N. and W.

This genus was founded upon a species from the Upper Coal Measures, which was described in Vol IV of this Report (pp 362, 363, Pl II, fig 7, 7 a,) under the specific designation *P. unguiformis*, N and W From the notes appended to the generic diagnosis above cited, it would appear that the genus was regarded as intimately allied to the *Cochliodonts*, or "intermediate in character between *Psammodus* and *Cochliodus*" The material now possessed, perhaps, more clearly illustrates the affinities of the genus, and which has suggested the following observations on the homologous features which it possesses in common with the *Petalodonts*, to which the genus belongs The general figure of the teeth is that characteristic of the *Petalodonts*, consisting of a flattened crown, whose concave face occupies the greater extent of the tooth, while the opposite face, instead of the strong definition in the typical genera of the family, forms a more or less regular convexity with the basal area (not the "crown surface"), from which, however, it is defined by a distinct though very narrow fold or thickening of the coronal border, as shown in the figures above cited, and lunate in general outline; the concave crown-face is gently depressed, broadly oval or sub quadrate in outline, the direction of the greater diameter varying in different species, but usually vertically elongated, crest broadly arched, subacute, lateral margins sometimes more or less parallel or slightly converging towards the base, as in the above typical species, basal margin gently arched downward and generally forming an angle at the lateral margins, abruptly truncated or beveled, and bordered by an imbricated belt, as in *Petalodus*, etc. The inferior or basal area is similar in outline, though less in superficial extent than the concave crown face, moderately convex; the root arises in the lower border, projecting slightly downward and suddenly outward, gradually tapering to a rounded point, vertically flattened, narrow, excavated in the inner side of the shoulder, and trowel-shaped Both crown faces are invested with an enamel like layer, sometimes more or less rugose, the basal area is quite smooth, and the root proper more or less roughened.

All the above mentioned characters are present in the original specimens of *P. unguiformis*, even the root is shown in the above cited figures, though its extremity is imperfect, having been broken away. By reference to the figures of the following described forms, it will at once be apparent that the genus is a true *Petalodont*, the teeth holding the same position upon the jaws as do those of *Petalorhynchus*, *Antliodus*, etc, etc, from which they chiefly differ in the less erect crest and the peculiar shape of the root.

According to our present knowledge, the genus has no representatives below the middle or St. Louis division of the Lower Carboniferous series, extending into the Upper Coal Measures.

## PELTODUS QUADRATUS, St. J. and W

Pl XIII, Fig 6, 7

Teeth of small size, quadrangular in outline. Convex crown face low, broadly arched laterally, basal border forming an obtuse angle with the basal area, somewhat strongly arched downward in the middle, broadly and regularly curved to the lateral borders, and defined by two or more delicate imbricating folds; general contour of the concave face moderately depressed, flattened or plane below, crest rather sharp and projecting outward beyond the basal margin of the convex face, broadly and usually regularly arched between the angles of the straight lateral margins, inferior border gently arched downward and abruptly defined or unbeveled, and marked by a relatively wide coronal band composed of three or more imbrications, which abruptly terminate at the inferior angles of the lateral margins. The coronal surfaces present a fine granulo punctate structure. The inferior or basal area is nearly equal in extent to the concave crown-face, gently convex laterally, smooth and well-defined from the convex crown face, the root forms a trowel shaped process projecting from the lower border of the basal area, the antero posterior diameter of which it nearly equals in its outward prolongation, slightly contracted at the shoulder and rather deeply excavated, rapidly tapering to an obtusely rounded point, and plane below. Length and lateral diameter of crown nearly equal, the largest tooth measuring .35 inch, smaller teeth .16 inch in length and breadth

This elegant little species is known to us by several individuals, the first having been discovered by Mr. VAN HORNE, at Alton, and others subsequently obtained at St Louis, all from the same horizon in the St. Louis limestone In general form it bears a somewhat close resemblance to *P. transversus* from the Coal Measures. Its quadrangular outline as seen from the concave side, and prominent coronal imbrications, however, will readily distinguish the present form from that mentioned above, which it is even more strongly marked in contrast with *Peltodus unguiformis* of the Upper Coal Measures.

*Position and locality* Upper beds of the St. Louis limestone; Alton, Illinois, and St Louis, Missouri.

### PELTODUS? PLICOMPHALUS, St J. and W.

Pl XIII, Fig 9

Teeth small, subovate in outline. Crown moderately thick, crest subacute, rather strongly arched, acuminate, or truncated from wear, concave crown-face broadly ovate, antero posterior diameter equal to, if not exceeding the lateral diameter, lateral margins gently rounded, median line occupied by a somewhat prominent vertical fold, which is flanked on either side by nearly parallel though obscurely defined plicæ, intermediate lateral portions slightly depressed vertically, basal margin unknown—probably broadly arched downward, and bordered by a narrow, irregularly imbricated coronal belt, convex face sublunate in outline, relatively low, gently arched laterally, slightly depressed in the middle towards the base, where it is defined by a well marked coronal fold, which is abruptly arched downward in the middle and strongly deflected or curved laterally, both coronal surfaces are enveloped in a delicate enamel like coating, through which are discernible minute punctæ, and along the worn, triturating surface of the crest comparatively coarse punctæ appear. Basal area smooth, subcordate in outline, in contour very like the concave crown face, the mesial line being raised into a slight vertical ridge, which is faintly depressed below, and forming a regular convexity with the convex crown-face above; root unknown. Lateral diameter of crown .26 inch, vertical diameter of concave crown-face about .28, elevation of convex face about .08, or when entire .10 inch.

The fragment of tooth upon which the above description is based, and which belongs to the collection of Mr VAN HORNE, presents some anomalous features which we have not observed in any of the numerous forms of teeth from our Carboniferous deposits, the real nature of which, as well as its generic relations, in consequence of the imperfect condition of the base, we have not been able satisfactorily to determine. It presents, however, a marked resemblance to the typical forms of *Peltodus*, with which genus it is here provisionally associated. The basal region suggests a comparison with *Chomatodus* (*Antliodus*) *truncatus*, Agassiz, from the Carboniferous limestone of Ireland, but its thickened crest and general uniform convexity of the convex crown-face and basal area widely distinguish it from that form. In the great depth and mesial fold of the basal region, and the produced apex, it presents features recalling *Petalorhynchus*, but all these resemblances are apparently subordinate to the characters which more strongly suggest *Peltodus*. Unfortunately, the basal portion, together with the root, is not shown in the solitary example here noticed; it is not improbable, however, the root formed a slight, narrow, tapering process, originating in the lower part of the depressed median ridge of the basal region, and produced outward in nearly the same plane, or presenting the general characters common to *Peltodus*.

*Position and locality.* In the lower fish-bed of the Chester formation, Chester, Illinois.

## PELTODUS TRANSVERSUS, St. J. and W.

Pl. XIII, Fig. 8.

Teeth very small, broadly ovate in outline, lateral diameter a little greater than the antero posterior length. The concave crown face forms a suboval area, apparently but slightly depressed, basal border strongly arched downward and rounded. The convex face and basal region forms a continuous convexity, the crown being defined from the basal area by an indistinct coronal fold which is slightly arched downward in the middle and greatly deflected to the lateral extremities, though in a much less degree than in *P. unguiformis* Behind the coronal border the basal area is gradually narrowed and produced into a proportionately strong root, which exhibits the vertically excavated inner shoulder and trowel-shaped interior outline common to the genus. The coronal surfaces are ornamented with vermiculose lines and punctæ, much in the same manner as in *P unguiformis*

This form is represented by only one specimen, from the middle division of the Coal Measures and exhibits only the convex aspect of the tooth It differs from that described from the Upper Coal Measures, *P. unguiformis*, N. and W, in its greater lateral extent as compared with the antero posterior diameter, also in the character of the coronal fold in the convex face, which is not continued down the lateral margins as far as in the last mentioned form From *P quadratus* of the St. Louis limestone, it is distinguished by its more oval outline and relatively stronger root; otherwise all the forms are intimately allied

*Position and locality:* In the limestone overlying coal No. 5; Belleville, Illinois

## Genus FISSODUS, St J. and W

Teeth small Crown forming a comparatively thin concavo convex plate together with the basal region, subcurvilinear or trapezoidal in general outline, as seen from the concave side, the basal margin of which is produced or strongly arched and rounded from the ear like lateral angles, and bordered by an imbricated coronal belt, convex face relatively low, more or less uniformly convex with the basal region, from which it is defined by a slight coronal fold, which describes a broad arch outwards from the lateral angles and more or less curved downwards in the middle, crest more or less compressed, and deeply cleft, or divided into two or more strong, acuminate, uniform, trenchant cusps; both coronal surfaces, in perfect state, enveloped in a dense, polished enamel like layer The root originates in the gently convex basal area just beneath the lower crown face, proportionately small, and produced in a thin, trowel shaped process, which is somewhat deeply channeled longitudinally in the region of its origin, narrowed and truncated below

The teeth embraced under the above generic description comprise a group closely allied to *Peltodus*, which it resembles in the form of the root and general contour, but from which it is distinguished by the cleft condition of the crest—differences akin to those which distinguish *Ctenopetalus* from *Petalodus*. It also presents, in the outline of the basal portion of the crown, resemblances with *Petalorhynchus*, although the relationship is more remote than in the case of *Peltodus*, but in both the root is totally different from that of *Petalorhynchus* The genus has two representative species in the Chester division of the Lower Carboniferous.

FISSODUS BIFIDUS, ST. J. and W.

Pl XIII, Fig 1, 2

Teeth small. Convex crown face very low, sublunate in general outline, gently arched laterally and more strongly so along the compressed crest, which is deeply cleft midway, forming two strong, acutely pointed lobes, basal fold indistinct, gently arched downward in the middle and strongly curved downward terminating in the auriculate lateral angles; concave face gently depressed, faintly swollen above in the coronal cusps and again in the basal region, which is deeply and somewhat angularly arched downward, abruptly defined from the root below, and occupied by a relatively wide coronal belt composed of three to four or five narrow imbrications, which become exceedingly attenuated ascending the diverging lateral margins towards the acutely produced lateral angles of the crown, where they are usually obsolete, coronal surfaces invested with a smooth polished enamel layer, which on being worn away along the crest exposes to view a vertical striato-punctate structure. Inferior or basal surface of tooth irregularly oval or subcircular in outline, moderately convex, and more or less uniform with the convexity of the convex crown-face, from which it is faintly defined by a slight sulcation extending along and just beneath the very narrow coronal fold, lower surface slightly flattened and suddenly produced into a long, narrow, tapering root, which is flattened in the same plane as the crown, somewhat deeply excavated in the inner face and flanked by rather prominent lateral bosses, which shade into slight lateral ridges along either margin of the root towards the lower extremity, which is slightly rounded or truncated; basal region and root faintly roughened or quite smooth. Lateral diameter of tooth .29 inch, vertical diameter .38. elevation of convex crown face .08 inch, or about half the hight of the concave face

The teeth comprised in the present species are remarkable for their elegant and symmetrical proportions, and the persistency of the distinctive characteristics, as shown by the slight individual variation observed in a fine suite of specimens. The deeply cleft, æqui-lobed crest readily distinguishes the form from others occurring in the same horizon.

*Position and locality*· Not uncommon in the upper and lower ichthyic horizons of the Chester formation; Chester, Illinois.

### Fissodus tricuspidatus, St J. and W.

Pl XIII, Fig 3

Teeth small, concave in outline, lateral diameter somewhat less than the antero posterior diameter, thick. Convex crown face low, gently arched laterally, the convexity uniform with that of the basal area, from which it is obscurely defined by a faint coronal fold, or in worn specimens by a shallow sulcus, gently arched downward in the middle and again regularly curved to the obtuse lateral angles, the opposite face presents a broad ovate outline, faintly convex laterally, with a submedian depression in some instances, worn surfaces rather coarsely punctate on approaching the crest, which is divided into three obtusely acuminate lobes, of which the central one is a little the largest, the lateral lobes being apparently of equal size. Basal area moderately convex, interior portion, as also the basal border of the concave crown-face, unknown. The root probably resembles that of *F bifidus*, and the concave coronal border was probably similarly bordered with imbricating folds.

We have examined only two specimens of the form above indicated, neither of which are entire, showing evidences of wear to which is probably attributable the obtuse condition of the coronal cusps and the absence of the imbricating folds, as also the obtuse, ill defined lateral angles of the crown Yet these teeth present characters which unquestionably distinguish them from the previously described form. They are remarkable for their robust proportions and tricuspidate crest, in which respects they differ markedly from *F. bifidus*, and equally so from the form of the allied genus, *Cholodus inæqualis*, from the Upper Coal Measures.

*Position and locality* · Lower (?) fish-bed of the Chester limestone, Chester, Illinois

## Genus CHOLODUS, St J. and W.

Teeth presenting the general outline and coronal contour of *Peltodus*, but specially characterized by the division of the crest into two or more eccentric, inequal cusps, of which the culminating cusp is lateral or eccentric in position; convex crown face more or less regularly arched with the basal area, broadly arched laterally, base defined by a faint coronal fold, which is more or less eccentrically or obliquely arched downward in the middle, and strongly deflected to the lateral margins, terminating near the infero lateral angles; concave face more or less depressed, and probably broadly rounded below, and defined by imbricating folds Root unknown Coronal surfaces smooth or punctate

The present genus is recognized in a single species from the upper division of the Coal Measures Unfortunately none of the specimens are entire along the basal margin, affording no clue to the form of the root and outline of the basal margin of the concave crown face The root is probably small, and from the general similarity in contour of the other parts to *Peltodus* and *Fissodus*, it seems not improbable that it may prove to be similar in shape to the root in those genera The superficial markings are also similar to those observed in the above named genera, the distinctive generic characters being chiefly presented in the eccentrically lobed crest and the extreme downward prolongation of the lateral extremities of the coronal fold in the convex face.

The association of the individuals of the sole representative species known at the present time with the teeth of *Petalodus unguiformis* might raise a suspicion of the generic, possibly specific, relations or identity of these forms But the facts possessed do not sustain such a conjecture, unless it proves to be a species of most extraordinary variableness, the mutations of which in some instances would be even more remarkable than the characters by which many of the *Petalodont* genera are distinguished from one another.

## CHOLODUS INÆQUALIS, St. J and W.

Pl XIII Fig 4, 5

Teeth of medium size, in general outline subovate or rhomboidal. Basal area forming a gentle convexity uniform with the convex crown-face, from which, in the worn specimens usually met with, it is defined by a low, distinct border, produced by the thickening of the upper rim of the basal area and thus raised slightly above the plane of the crown, but in well preserved teeth, in which the original external coating of the crown still exists, an exceedingly delicate raised line marks the basal limit of the crown, corresponding to the imbricated folds in allied genera, the basal line spans the tooth in an irregular direction, more or less oblique from one or other side, slightly arched downward in the middle or quite direct, but on nearing the lateral margins it is suddenly curved downward in the direction of the infero lateral angles of the tooth The concave face of the crown presents a gentle concavity, gradually rising into the irregularly cuspidate crest, and slightly rounded into the thickened or compressed lateral margins, which are nearly parallel though slightly and irregularly curved, and slightly diverging from the basal angles; the crest presents an irregular outline, being divided into two prominent, unequal lobes, which culminate in subacute, eccentric apices—in some individuals rudimentary lobes appear in either lateral margin below the principal cusps, but these are discernible only in exceptionally well preserved specimens, if indeed they are always developed Unfortunately none of the specimens before us preserve the basal portion of the teeth, hence we are lead to conjecture the broadly downward arched basal border of the concave crown face, and its probable imbricated belt, as also the probable relative diminutiveness of the produced root portion, which latter probably more or less intimately resembles the root in *Fissodus* and *Peltodus*, with which these teeth otherwise are intimately related Lateral diameter of tooth 45 inch, antero-posterior diameter above .60, thickest portion about 09, greatest hight of convex crown face .21 inch

The distinctly lobed character of the crest of the present form definitely distinguishes it from *Peltodus unguiformis*, N and W, which occurs in the same horizon, and with which it has one striking feature in common, viz the general uniformity in the convexity of the convex crown face and basal region, and the delicate demarkation defining the basal from the coronal region But the singular bifid character of the crest strongly contrasts with the regular outline of the crest of *Peltodus*, and almost equally so with the symmetrical cuspidations of *Fissodus*, differences which would seem to remove them from the same generic category, unless, indeed, the opposite jaws bore teeth so very dissimilar However we have no evidence of a nature that more than vaguely suggests such specific relationship, and the non occurrence of both forms in the Chester and St Louis formations, both of which horizons have yielded peculiar examples of one or other type, seems further to militate against such identity

The present form is, so far at least as our information extends, restricted to the upper division of the Coal Measures, examples of which have been found at distant localities in Iowa and Illinois Some of the Iowa specimens are not quite as strong, and the rudimentary or lateral lobes are more distinctly developed than in the ordinary examples, as shown in the illustrations introduced in Pl XIV, fig. 4

*Position and locality* Upper Coal Measures, above the horizon of coal No 8, near Springfield, Illinois, and in a similar horizon near Clarinda, Iowa

## GENUS PSEPHODUS, Agassiz.

### PSEPHODUS ? RETICULATUS, St. J. and W.

Pl VI Fig 19-21

Teeth attain large size, ranging from 20 to 1 15 inches in lateral diameter, more or less irregular in outline, massive, depressed or strongly acuminate. In large, mature teeth, the base presents a broad, thick, rhomboidal plate, with more or less parallel, curved sides and sharply marked angles, inferior surface in nearly the same horizontal plane as the crown, faintly concave, smooth or striated, abruptly beveled and coarsely roughened in the thickened face, the opposite face deeply channeled and strongly defined from the anteriorly produced basal border of the crown, in lateral diameter equal to and in breadth exceeded by that of the crown. The crown forms a massive, rather low, broad, moderately convex prominence, the greatest prominence of which extends in an antero posterior direction, and produced into a low, obtuse, subcentral ridge, culminating above the abruptly sloping outer face, declining in a broad gentle convexity to the opposite margin, which is gently arched posteriorly and approximately parallel to the anterior margin, both of which are more or less irregular or undulated in outline, constricted along the base, one extremity abruptly truncated, one of the angles obliquely so, the opposite end broadly rounded and slightly narrowed, the coronal surface is ornamented with numerous delicate, slightly undulating plicæ, which appear as flattened or sharp thread-like lines over the body of the crown, obsolete in the region of the obscurely defined crest, but towards the basal margins in either face becoming more strongly marked and intricately interlaced, producing the delicate reticulated ornamentation encircling the basal borders of the crown.

Small teeth presenting essentially the same form and coronal features noted above; but the base is more obliquely produced and gradually beveled to a sharp edge along the posterior margin, and the corresponding channel of the opposite face is relatively broader The crown is elliptical in outline, extremities broadly rounded, the median prominence less eccentric and comparatively more strongly developed, forming, as in the large teeth, an obtuse ridge traversing the crown at right angles to the obscurely defined, submedian crest; the coronal plicæ are well-marked, forming an elegantly wrought belt along the inferior borders, precisely as in the large teeth, in both of which the crown is enveloped in a polished enamel-like layer, except along the crest and median prominence, where it has usually been abraded to greater or less extent, exposing in the triturating surface a delicate punctate structure.

By a remarkably uniform gradation the latter teeth pass into smaller and more and more acuminate individuals, until we arrive at minute teeth in which the median prominence is excessively developed, forming a lofty, anteriorly flattened, posteriorly broadly arched, laterally deflected, obtusely pointed cone, around the basal borders of which are clustered a few relatively strong plicæ, the base presents essentially the same features previously observed, and the coronal ornamentation, traced through the intermediate gradations, presents no striking contrast to that of the larger teeth But regarded independently, the extreme examples bear strongest contrast to the teeth first noticed above, yet, in view of the evidence actually within reach, there seems to be no question as to their specific identity The latter teeth are about .20 inch in lateral diameter, and .30 in hight

A tooth of large size measures in lateral diameter 1 15 inch, antero-posterior diameter of crown .70, elevation of crown .40.

The description of this remarkable form is based upon a fine suite of specimens, mainly belonging to the collections of Mr. SPRINGER and Mr. WACHSMUTH, all of which were derived from the same locality Varying greatly in size and contour, we have seldom met with similar instances where specific identity is so unequivocally demonstrable as in the present case. The large teeth present features in outline and general contour, which suggest relationship with some of the peculiar *Psephodi* of the same horizon, but to what extent this resemblance should influence the determination of their generic relations, we have not been able to decide They, however, apparently hold the same relation to *Psephodus* as *Helodus planus* of the European Carboniferous limestone does But such interpretation of their affinities necessarily presumes a combination of *Cochliodont* and *Cestraciont* features of the most extraordinary latitude, such, indeed, as obtains in no other family, ancient or modern, of the class to which these remains belong

Messrs WACHSMUTH and SPRINGER have placed in our hands a large collection of the above form, and from the study of this material we have encountered many difficulties in the way of determining the limits of the individual specimens in their relation to other and perhaps generically allied forms. Worn examples, and which, unfortunately, is the prevalent condition of these teeth, are scarcely distinguishable from other forms allied to *Helodus biformis*, N and W, regarding the affinities of which latter with *Psephodus* of the same deposits, we have scarcely a doubt. In a communication with which we have been favored from Lord ENNISKILLEN, it appears that there is no longer reason to doubt the specific identity of the Irish Carboniferous teeth originally described under the names *Helodus planus* and *Psephodus magnus*, Agass We have ourselves observed similar combinations in some of the American representatives of *Psephodus*, as for example, that from the Chester limestone, to which Messrs NEWBERRY and WORTHEN gave the name *Aspidodus crenulatus* Considering the apparent affinities of the teeth under consideration, however marked the contrast of individuals, we have been led, provisionally, to refer them to the same genus

*Position and locality* Kinderhook formation; the same form, apparently, occurring in both fish-bed horizons, Burlington, Iowa.

## GENUS CTENACANTHUS, Agassiz.

### CTENACANTHUS SPECTABILIS, St. J. and W.

Pl XV, Fig 1a, b, c d, e

Fin spine robust, attaining a length of seven or eight inches, rapidly tapering, the line of insertion indicating a posterior inclination at an angle of about 45°, transverse section sublenticular, truncated behind. Lateral faces of the exposed portion broadly expanded at base, flattened or very slightly arched in the posterior half, more rapidly rounded in front to the obtusely angular and gently arched anterior margin, which bears a prominent, eccentric marginal ridge, from which frequent bifurcations are sent off on either side, and these again bifurcate descending, each offshoot being more attenuated and curved posteriorly on approaching the posterior margin, forming throughout closely approximated, rounded ridges, of which there are about fifty, counting along the inferior margin, and less than half that number two-thirds the distance to the apex, the longitudinal costæ are occupied by numerous obtuse, apparently smooth, brightly enameled tubercles, more or less regularly spaced by once or twice their own diameter, along the anterior margin they present the appearance of closely approximated decussations, apparently the result of abrasion, the entire crest of the ridges being reduced to a smooth polished surface, but towards the base where they are less worn, they present the usual condition of more or less transverse tubercles abruptly rising from the rounded costæ, similar to those occurring in the posterior rows, the intercostal furrows are very narrow, in diameter less than that of the ridges, and minutely punctate or striato-punctate. Posterior face slightly channeled either side of the low, obtusely angular median ridge; postero lateral margins forming right angles, and occupied by apparently small, closely arranged denticles. Pulp cavity ovate or sublenticular in section, situated in the posterior two thirds of the spine, less than one third the diameter of the spine a third the distance from the apex, but running out near the line of insertion, deeply channeling the postero-inferior margin Basal portion rapidly tapering to the proximal extremity, nearly straight in front and gradually rounded behind to the point, surface finely striato punctate.

The unique example of the elegant form above described was discovered by Dr E N. WHIPPLE, of Legrande, Iowa, to whom we are indebted for its possession It represents a nearly entire fin spine, perhaps an inch and a half of the distal extremity and one inch of the opposite end are broken off, but otherwise the specimen is in a remarkably perfect state of preservation. Its great breadth along the oblique line of insertion and the abrupt posterior deflection in the curvature of the costæ, producing a frayed appearance in that portion of the posterior margin, bear close resemblance to the form which we have indicated under the name *C. speciosus*, from the same formation, the peculiar tuberculation of the costæ and more robust proportions, however, serve to distinguish it from the last named form, while these and the above mentioned characters offer marked contrast to other forms from the American Carboniferous deposits. In general outline it closely resembles *C. brevis*, Ag., a form originally described by Professor AGASSIZ, from the British Carboniferous limestone. Its differences, however, are obvious at a glance—the costæ in *C. brevis* being far less numerous and not bifurcated, while the tubercles are distinctly marked with radiating carinæ.

*Position and locality:* In the uppermost beds of the Kinderhook formation, vicinity of Legrande, Marshall county, Iowa.

### CTENACANTHUS SCULPTUS, St. J. and W.

Pl. XIV, Fig. 1.

Fin ray of medium size, anterior and posterior margins converging towards the apical extremity at the rate of one-fourth inch in three inches, slightly curved, line of insertion somewhat irregular and forming an angle of 35° to 40° with the posterior inclination of the spine. Lateral surfaces flattened and gradually converging to the rounded anterior margin, occupied by numerous, irregularly disposed, rarely bifurcated costæ, which more or less regularly diminish in size posteriorly, intercostal spaces equally irregular, varying from half to the full diameter of the ridges, and longitudinally traversed by one to three delicate thread like carinæ. The costæ are elegantly ornamented with stellate sculptured tubercles of variable shape and size in different parts, generally spaced by once or twice their diameter, but sometimes closely approximated, in the anterior portion of the spine, especially above, they generally occur as oblique or transverse protuberances, abruptly truncated above and sloping inferiorly, and along the anterior margin a slightly eccentric row of relatively large transverse tubercles occur, the bifurcations of which carry longitudinally elongated tubercles, similar to those occurring throughout the lower portion and in the posterior costæ. Posterior face rather deeply channeled either side of the prominent median ridge, lateral angles prominent, subacute, with indications of a row of small tubercles along the crest in the upper portion of the spine. Base apparently of moderate length, rounded at the extremity, and beautifully striated externally, the thread like lines terminating above in the costæ, the intermediate ones continuous with those occupying the intercostal furrows; posterior face deeply excavated by the pulp cavity, which latter occupies above half the transverse diameter of the spine a third the distance from the apex, sublenticular in section

The above description is based upon a beautiful specimen discovered by Mr. WACHSMUTH, which presents a nearly entire and well preserved spine, above six inches in length. In general outline, and number of costæ, it strikingly resembles *C. formosus*, Newb, a form occurring in a similar horizon, the Waverly formation of Ohio. But the costæ in the present form bear distinctly sculptured tubercles, which do not appear as simple decussations, being quite isolated or separated by spaces destitute of enamel, and extremely diverse in shape, also, the posterior face instead of being "flattened and slightly concave," is distinctly carinated longitudinally. As represented in the unique specimen described, it constitutes a remarkably well defined and readily distinguishable form

*Position and locality:* In the lower fish-bed (No 1) of the Upper Kinderhook beds; Burlington, Iowa.

## CTENACANTHUS VARIANS, St. J and W.

Pl XIV, Fig 2

Fin spine of robust proportions, rapidly tapering from the broadly expanded basal line, elliptical in transverse section Anterior margin rounded, nearly straight below, but gently arched above, lateral faces flattened posteriorly and gently rounded in front, and occupied by numerous longitudinal ridges, which more or less regularly diminish in size towards the posterior borders, where they are less than one fourth the bulk of the anterior costæ, that along the anterior margin being perceptibly stronger and frequently bifurcated descending towards the basal line; intercostal spaces forming narrow and usually angular channels traversed by a line of minute punctæ, in front very crowded, but more irregular in width behind, where they sometimes equal the diameter of the costæ The costæ are ornamented by beautifully sculptured tubercles of diverse shape and variously disposed in different parts of the spine, in the front ridges they frequently form double, rarely triple, rows, which are separated by a faint depression, but still very irregular, the pairs of nearly circular tubercles often coalesce forming a single transverse tubercle, which latter is the prevailing, if not persistent, form in the posterior costæ, in appearance they generally present a broad, gently convex, sometimes concave, inferior slope, sculptured by delicate ridges converging toward the apex, with a more or less well defined transverse crest and abrupt descent above, spaced by once or twice their diameter; in the front ridges they are apparently smooth, possibly the result of wear, and in other parts both the transverse and round forms are associated on the same rib It is exceedingly difficult to portray the minutiæ of details of the tuberculose ornamentation here observed, except through the medium of illustrations, of which we have made such use as seems to meet the requirements of their identification. The base appears massive in front, of moderate depth, rapidly converging to the inferior extremity, deeply channeled posteriorly by the pulp cavity which occupies more than half the diameter of the middle portion of the spine, where it presents an elliptical transverse section. The posterior face is occupied by a strong median ridge slightly channeled on either side, and which becomes exceedingly prominent on reaching the middle of the spine, the postero lateral angles are sharply defined for a short distance below the apex, where they are armed with a row of prominent, obtusely hooked denticles, slightly compressed laterally and closely approximated, or separated by spaces less than their greatest diameter; lower, the posterior angles appear rounded and destitute of denticles

The solitary example which we have examined of the present form, represents a spine probably seven inches in length, and, though broken and parts missing, sufficient remains, together with the perfect condition of the superficial characters, to show its distinctive characters as contrasted with other forms One feature not alluded to in the above description and which may be merely individual in its appearance, is the regular bifurcation of the costæ along lines of growth corresponding to the line of insertion, and which is partially shown in the illustration, Pl XIV, fig 2 A This feature is apparent in both faces, and in regard to the relative obliquity of these lines of growth and the present line of insertion, the observations on the growth of spines made in connection with *C speciosus*, are equally applicable to the present form In the specimen before us the anterior margin for two thirds or more of its extent from the apex is quite smooth, apparently from wear, and for a short distance from the apex the lateral costæ are equally smoothed from the same cause, the surface of the ridges, denuded of their tubercles, being delicately striated longitudinally

Compared with *C speciosus*, with which it has in common the same general outline and similar style of tuberculose ornamentation, its distinguishing peculiarities consist in its more robust proportions and greater lateral thickness, the double row of tubercles along the anterior ridges and the more prominent denticles arming the postero-lateral angles.

*Position and locality*. The specimen described was discovered by Mr GILLS in the upper fish bed of the Kinderhook formation; Flint river, near Burlington, Iowa.

## CTENACANTHUS SPECIOSUS, St J and W

Pl XIV, Fig 3 4

The present form, as indicated by a large and nearly perfect fin ray discovered by Mr. WACHSMUTH, bears, in its rapidly tapering outline as seen from the side, much resemblance to *C. spectabilis*, perhaps even a stronger likeness to *C varians*, in the above and other respects. The anterior margin is gently arched and rounded, from which the lateral faces very gradually diverge in a slight curvature to the posterior margin in the upper portion, but apparently very slightly converging in the lower part, as shown in the transverse section, which above is wedge-shaped and below long elliptical, truncated behind. Posterior face nearly plane near the apex, the median ridge gradually increasing in strength and quite prominent below, gently channeled either side and limited by the well defined postero lateral angles, which bear a row of low, broad, obtusely pointed denticles, spaced by once or twice their own diameter, and which are probably confined to the upper third of the spine. Line of insertion presenting a slight sigmoidal curvature, very oblique, the posterior limb being almost parallel with, or diverging at an angle of 5° to 10° from the anterior margin. Successive lines of growth, so to speak, of less and less obliquity the further removed from the present dorsal line, seem to show that in the development of the spine accessions to its substance were more abundantly supplied to the dense anterior portion, hence the line of insertion, as exhibited in individuals of different stages of growth, would indicate various degrees of inclination, a young spine occupying a relatively more erect position than is the case in the mature condition—a fact which is probably equally applicable to all ichthyodorulites of this class. The basal portion extends half way to the apex in the posterior margin, broadly rounded to the inferior extremity, exterior surface delicately punctate or striato-punctate, deeply excavated behind by the pulp cavity, which latter occupies the posterior two thirds of the diameter of the spine above. The exposed portion of the spine is ornamented by the most exquisite and varied sculpturing, the anterior edge is occupied by a more or less eccentric ridge, slightly more bulky than the others, which rarely bifurcates until nearing the basal line, and this is true of all longitudinal ridges occupying the body of the spine, which send off most frequent branches toward their bases in the expanded portion of the spine, where, in a mature individual, they number above eighty, very irregular in size and arrangement, closely crowded, separated by interspaces rarely half their diameter, the ridges present the appearance of minute decussated costæ, the narrow, transverse, vertically ridged tubercles resting in various directions and degrees of obliquity, generally abruptly descending and sometimes unbeveled above, more gently sloping in the lower side, usually sculptured with a few delicate vertical ridges, or often quite smooth, scalloped along the crest or deeply cleft, sometimes widely spaced, again separated by vertical spaces of scarcely more than their own diameter Under an ordinary lens they present the most beautiful appearance, the varied details appearing in all parts and always associated with the transverse style of tuberculation.

The collections contain several fragmentary specimens of the form described, indicating spines of various dimensions, of which the fine example, figured Pl XIV, fig 3a, was probably above eight inches in length. As above remarked, in general outline these spines resemble *C. spectabilis* and *C. varians*, from the former, however, it distinctly differs in ornamentation, and its laterally compressed and less robust figure equally distinguishes it from both the above named forms In the details of ornamentation, as the form and sculpturing of the individual tubercles, it more closely resembles the latter form; but the double arrangement of tubercles, as well as the frequent tendency to become longitudinally elongated in the latter, afford ample distinctive features by which the form under consideration may be recognized.

*Position and locality* All authentic examples of the form at present known pertain to the lower icthyic bed of the Kinderhook formation; Burlington, Iowa

## CTENACANTHUS GRADOCOSTUS, St J and W

Pl XV Fig 2, 3

Fin-ray moderately strong, long, gradually tapering towards the apex, gently curved, lenticular or long-elliptical in transverse section Lateral faces flattened for half or two thirds their posterior diameter, thence somewhat rapidly converging to the anterior margin, along which extends a narrow, compressed, or sometimes rounded ridge, usually smooth along the crest, but in some specimens possessing well-marked lateral prominences, and which are really connected forming singular transverse tubercles, the lateral wings of which are more or less crescent shaped, with the convexity directed upward; the costæ are prominent, more or less decreasing in size posteriorly, and beautifully wrought in apparently plain transverse tubercles throughout, though they are less distinct in the posterior than in the middle and anterior ridges, and separated by a space half to twice their diameter; the tubercles vary in shape from more or less obtuse prominences to narrow bands clasping the ridge in variable degrees and directions of obliquity, and in all the specimens examined presenting evidences of wear; intercostal spaces generlly less than the diameter of the costæ, forming deep, narrow grooves Posterior face forming an obtuse angle along the median ridge, either side of which is faintly channeled and coarsely striated longitudinally, postero lateral angles angularly rounded but well-defined, and apparently destitute of denticles throughout the greater length of the spine Pulp cavity relatively large Base unknown

A fragment of a spine from Quincy, indicating a specimen at least ten inches in length, Pl. XV, fig. 2, and a few very imperfect individuals from Louisa county, constitute the meagre material from which the above description is derived The Quincy specimen, however, shows about two inches of the middle or lower portion of a finely preserved spine, which plainly exhibits the specific peculiarities of the form as compared with others from the same and other horizons In the style of its tuberculose ornamentation it recalls *C Mayi*, N. and W, from the same position, its long and gradually tapering outline and prominent posterior keel, as also the narrower costæ, present characters which readily distinguish it from that species In form and general proportions it also intimately resembles *C Burlingtonensis,* but the prominently keeled posterior face and the general tuberculation of the costæ, offer marked contrast with that form.

*Position and locality* · In the fish bed of the Upper Burlington limestone . Quincy, Ill , Louisa Co , Ia.

### CTENACANTHUS BURLINGTONENSIS, St J. and W.

Pl XV, Fig 6 7

Fin spines long, slender, slightly curved and very gradually tapering, laterally compressed, lenticular in transverse section, truncated posteriorly, where the thickness is about one-fifth the greatest diameter. Lateral faces gently convex and converging to the acute anterior edge, which is occupied by a single well-defined ridge bearing in places laterally compressed closely arranged stellate tubercles, but which in other parts have the appearance of lateral decussations, possibly due to the wearing down of the crest of the tuberculose ridge; lateral faces of a medium sized specimen occupied by about fifteen prominent, rounded or flattened, rarely bifurcated costæ, which very gradually diminish in size posteriorly until nearing the beveled border, in which the posterior ridges become obsolete descending and equal the anterior ones in size; the anterior costæ also bear oblique, closely approximated tubercles, sculptured by radiating ridges, occurring on the third or fourth costæ from the margin, the posterior ridges being destitute of ornamentation, except occasional traces of minute tubercles and the delicate longitudinal striation; intercostal spaces varying from half to nearly the full diameter of the costæ and striated similarly Posterior faces gently depressed and rather coarsely striato punctate, median carina forming a low, obtusely angular ridge, and laterally defined by the somewhat prominent, compressed postero lateral angles, which are armed by moderately prominent, slightly hooked, laterally compressed denticles, which are regularly spaced in the same individual, but varying in the different specimens in the ratio of one to three, apparently more crowded below than near the extremity. Internal cavity of moderate size, transverse section as represented in the illustrations Base unknown

The form here referred to occurs quite common, but unfortunately, the specimens are generally in an unsatisfactory state of preservation; they indicate spines of six to eight inches or more in length, but it is seldom a specimen is found which exhibits the tuberculose ornamentation, though the costæ are well shown in nearly all. Compared with *C. Keokuk*, its nearest ally and representative species in the next succeeding formation, it is distinguishable by the perceptibly less curvature, more numerous or closely approximated denticles, and more compressed postero lateral angles, the tubercles of the anterior ridge more compressed laterally, often thereby giving rise to a sharp serrated crest, and the relatively larger size of the tubercles of the first two or three costæ on either side, the direction of their obliquity being apparently the opposite or from left to right. The specimens figured (Pl XV, fig 6, 7,) belong to the fine collection of Mr SPRINGER

*Position and locality* A common fine-spine in the fish-bed of the Upper Burlington limestone, at the various localities of its exposure in Louisa, Des Moines and Lee counties, Iowa; Quincy, and Henderson county, Illinois

## CTENACANTHUS KEOKUK, St. J and W.

Pl XV, Fig 8a, b, c, d, e

Fin spines eight to ten inches, more or less, in length, gently arched and very gradually tapering, lateral faces flattened behind and beveled to the postero-lateral borders, very gradually converging towards the front and somewhat rapidly rounded on approaching the anterior edge, in transverse section long elliptical, truncated posteriorly. Anterior rib moderately prominent and marked by somewhat tumid, radiate-sculptured tubercles, spaced by about their own diameter; lateral costæ twelve to sixteen in either face, equally prominent, rarely bifurcating descending and still more seldom implanted, very gradually and more or less irregularly diminishing in size posteriorly, in some examples the middle ridges most prominent, the posterior ridges terminating descending in the narrow, slightly beveled space along the posterior borders; intercostal spaces usually equaling or slightly exceeding the diameter of the costæ, faintly striato punctate. The first pair of costæ on either side the anterior ridge bear delicate, obliquely transverse tubercles, spaced by about twice their diameter, but sometimes connected by the thread like lines descending from the long inferior slope of the tubercles; the succeeding ridges are smooth or faintly striated longitudinally, with the exception of the first and second which are sparcely occupied by minute, irregularly spaced tubercles Posterior face slightly channeled, median keel inconspicuous, postero lateral margins forming prominent rounded angles above, less obtuse below, and bearing relatively strong, slightly hooked, sculptured denticles, separated by about twice their diameter, perhaps more widely spaced above Pulp cavity nearly half the diameter of the spine in the middle, long elliptical in section Base unknown.

The spines here referred to bear striking resemblance to the Upper Burlington form which we have described under the name *C Burlingtonensis*, so strong is the likeness, indeed, that the majority of the imperfect specimens of the two forms are scarcely distinguishable one from the other. The collection of Dr. WILLIAMS contains several more or less perfect specimens of the present form, and the careful examination of this material seems to justify the disposition we have here made, in accordance with the apparent peculiarities enumerated in the observations under *C Burlingtonensis* It is not improbable more complete material would show even more intimate relations between these spines, or differences such as the better to serve their characterization.

*Position and locality* · Not uncommon, but generally in fragmentary condition, in the Keokuk fish beds, vicinity of Warsaw, Illinois, Keokuk and Bentonsport Iowa Boonville and Le Grande, Missouri

### CTENACANTHUS EXCAVATUS, ST J and W

Pl XV, Fig 4-5

Fin spine of moderate length, very strong, rapidly tapering, moderately curved, transverse section ovate, truncated posteriorly Lateral faces gently arched behind and slightly converging to the posterior borders, rapidly rounded in front to the anterior margin, which is occupied by a strong broadly rounded ridge, apparently smooth along the crest with indications of transverse decussations or tubercles in the lateral margins The lateral surfaces are covered by a few very prominent, decussated costæ, spaced about their own diameter by deep intercostal grooves Posterior face broad, more or less concave or deeply channeled, keel apparently inconspicuous, postero lateral angles relatively prominent with indications of strong, closely arranged denticles near the upper extremity Pulp cavity, above, occupying about one third the diameter of the spine, broadly ovate in section. Base unknown.

We have had opportunity to examine only two imperfect specimens of the present species, but these exhibit such strongly marked peculiarities as to preclude any hesitation in recognizing their specific distinctness The specimens show respectively one and two inches of the upper extremity, in the one instance of a fairly preserved individual, the other or larger fragment being considerably abraded along the anterior ridge, which presents the appearance of a broadly rounded, perfectly smooth surface—the costæ in the lateral faces also bear evidence of wear, which has nearly obliterated their decussated or tuberculose ornamentation. The smaller spine exhibits the superficial characters in a very satisfactory manner, though here some allowance must be made on account of wear, but to a much less extent than in the former case The costæ are very prominent, slightly imbeveled laterally and broadly rounded along the polished crest, which is crossed by delicate thread-like ridges or decussations which terminate laterally in more prominent projections, and which cross the costæ in varying degrees of obliquity or arched upward, three or four occurring in the space of one tenth inch

In outline and general proportions, it resembles *C Mayi* of the Upper Burlington limestone; it is, however, proportionately thicker, the costæ narrower and more widely spaced.

*Position and locality* In the upper fish-beds of the Keokuk limestone; Bentonsport, Iowa, La Grange, Missouri

### CTENACANTHUS GEMMATUS, St J and W.

Pl XV, Fig 9, 10

Fin ray long, gradually tapering, gently curved, lenticular in transverse section, abruptly truncated posteriorly, the posterior face nearly plane either side of the narrow median keel, meeting at the postero-lateral borders in a right angle. The lateral faces gradually converge in a slight convexity to the anterior margin, which presents a narrow, prominent, sharply rounded ridge, regularly crossed by beautifully sculptured tubercles, which meet in an obtuse angle along the crest, the swollen lateral extremities being gently directed downwards. Lateral costæ sixteen, more or less, in either face, prominent, more or less regularly spaced by about their own diameter, very gradually, though somewhat irregularly, diminishing in size posteriorly, and ornamented with elegantly wrought stellate tubercles, which form in the anterior costæ transverse or slightly oblique prominences, but less prominent and more circumscribed in the posterior ridges, where they are more widely spaced Pulp cavity elliptical in section, about one third the lateral diameter of the body of the spine, and apparently extending to the line of insertion before appearing in the posterior face Base of moderate length, strong, moderately excavated posteriorly. line of insertion forming an angle of about 45° with the posterior inclination of the spine.

The present form is recognized from a couple of fragments of spines in the collection of Mr. VAN HORNE, one of which shows about three inches of the inferior extremity of a mutilated specimen, the smaller fragments exhibiting a section from the middle region of the spine in a beautifully perfect state of preservation Neither of these fragmentary examples preserves any trace of denticles along the postero-lateral angles, though such probably existed, possibly confined to the upper extremity of the spine.

In outline it bears intimate resemblance to *C gracillimus*, N and W., of the same horizon, its peculiar and generally distributed tuberculation constituting its chief distinguishing features The latter, however, show a striking likeness to the Upper Burlington spines which we have noticed under the name *C gradocostus*, from which the present form differs in the relatively greater size and more elaborately sculptured tubercles of the anterior costæ, and the flattened, faintly keeled posterior face

*Position and locality* In the upper beds of the St Louis limestone; Alton, Illinois

### CTENACANTHUS PUGIUNCULUS, St. J and W

Pl XXI Fig 9

Fin-spine long, nearly straight or but gently curved posteriorly, gradually tapering to the acute apex, suboval in transverse section Lateral faces regularly and broadly rounded into the anterior margin, the longitudinal costæ, of which there are nine or ten in either side, of uniform size and spaced by about their own diameter in front, but diminishing in size posteriorly and more closely approximated, decussated, or those in front bearing more prominent, oblique tubercles, separated by vertical spaces equal to two or three times their diameter, the posterior ones less widely separated or more numerous, forming sharp, oblique ridges abruptly terminated above, the tubercles are apparently smooth and polished, and there appears to be much regularity in the direction of their obliquity, or ascending from the anterior to the posterior side, though probably subject to variation in the latter respects. Posterior face equal to the greatest lateral diameter, or nearly so, of the spine, with a prominent sharp-crested median keel, moderately channeled either side, with obscure secondary longitudinal ridges, and faintly striated, bearing along the inner side of the postero-lateral angles, which latter are sharply defined, a row of irregularly developed, straggling, obtuse tubercles, whose apices culminate in a rounded rim which is in some instances obliquely directed downward and inward, perhaps more frequently in the opposite direction, and extending from the apex to a point at least below the middle. Base unknown Pulp cavity, in the middle of the spine, less than half the greater diameter of the spine, in transverse section subcircular, or lateral diameter exceeding the antero posterior diameter, posterior walls about half the thickness of that in front Length of spine at least three inches, lateral diameter between the postero-lateral angles near the middle of the spine 13 inch, or but slightly less than the antero-posterior diameter

The present form is described from a unique example of a nearly entire and well-preserved spine, but which is so imbedded in its matrix as to exhibit only the posterior face and the posterior portion of the lateral surfaces, except a section from the middle of the spine which shows the entire lateral surface and anterior margin. Towards the apex, the costæ are more or less smoothly worn, and the tubercles in the posterior face are relatively larger than in the middle region below. The great lateral breadth of the spine, as compared with its antero-posterior diameter, the absence of a distinct angulation in the broadly rounded anterior margin, and the irregular development of posterior denticles, constitute the chief distinguishing features by which the present spine may be recognized from other forms of the genus to which it is here referred.

*Position and locality* · Upper beds of the St Louis limestone; St. Louis, Missouri

CTENACANTAUS SIMILIS, St J and W.

Pl XV, Fig 11 a b c, d

We here refer to a form apparently not uncommon in the Chester formation, but which is represented by imperfect specimens in the material accessible to us In general outline it is exceedingly like *C. angulatus*, N. and W, a fin spine described from the same horizon, being rigid or very slightly curved in outline. It is, however, apparently distinguishable from the above, with the original of which we have compared the present examples, by the more uniform and relatively stronger costæ, of which there are also fewer, and the peculiar decussation of the same, which latter recalls *C gradocostus*, or perhaps even more strikingly *C. excavatus* of the Keokuk formation. It is possible these spines may prove to be specifically identical with *C angulatus*, representing certain conditions of preservation not apparent in the solitary example examined by Messrs. NEWBERRY and WORTHEN.

*Position and locality* In the lower fish bed of the Chester limestone, Chester, Illinois

## GENUS ACONDYLACANTHUS, St. J and W.

Fin rays long, gradually tapering, laterally compressed, and moderately curved posteriorly. Lateral faces longitudinally fluted, the costæ being smooth and enameled, increasing by occasional bifurcation, perhaps more rarely by implantation. Posterior face uniformly excavated longitudinally, apparently without median keel, postero lateral angles bearing a row of downward hooked denticles, which extend in the majority of species well towards the base Pulp cavity occupying the posterior half or more of the spine Base unknown.

Regarding the generic identity of the Carboniferous ichthyodorulites heretofore referred to *Leptacanthus*, Agassiz, expressions of doubt have from time to time been made by investigators who have had to deal with these remains The genus *Leptacanthus* was based upon spines occurring in the *Jurassic* formations of Europe, the oldest representative, as originally determined by Professr AGASSIZ, belonging to the *Lias*. Subsequently Professor AGASSIZ identified certain Carboniferous fin spines with the genus, and other authors, at a later date, have extended the list of species of the same period, however, in every case pointing out the difficulties in the way of determining the real affinities of these earlier forms, and the necessity of their provisional reference to the *Mesozoic* genus There is one exception, that of Col ROMANOWSKY, who, in an interesting paper on the fossil fishes of the Lower Carboniferous deposits of Russia, describes a fin-spine which is apparently generically identical with the Carboniferous so called *Leptacanthi*, and which he has named *Cladodus tenuistriatus*, inferring their generic identity with *Cladodus* from the circumstance that the spines are associated with the remains of the dentition of that genus The ichthyodorulites for which Professor AGASSIZ proposed the generic term *Cladacanthus* in the lists of new forms appended to the Poissons Fossiles, III, are cited from the British mountain limestone, but of which we have failed to gain any definite knowledge. I am aware, however, that Professor AGASSIZ was strongly inclined to regard the spines to which he gave the name *Ctenacanthus* as probably belonging to the fishes which bore the teeth called *Cladodus* The latter inference was probably based upon as extensive data as was the case in that of the Russian fossils, and of the same kind; it is apparent, therefore, in the present state of our knowledge of the facts, that it is matter of individual opinion merely, and that we must seek a fuller acquaintance with facts to be derived only in the field where we may carefully note the occurrence and association of these fragmentary remains, before we can hope to satisfy ourselves in regard to their generic and specific identity. Although in several instances our American collections have been made with the utmost care, in the hope of securing every fact that might throw the least light on the affinities of the remains associated in the same beds, our data do not furnish unequivocal evidence by which the generic identity of fin-spines and teeth may be determined. Many suggestions may be derived from the study of this splendid material, but where suggestions are so conflicting their reliability is questionable.

In relation to the identity of the Carboniferous spines under consideration with the *Mesozoic Leptacanthi*, judging from the descriptions of Professor AGASSIZ and the illustrations accompanying the Poissons Fossiles, there is apparent in the distinctive features of the more ancient spines the uniform deep groove of the posterior face, the *Liassic Leptacanthus* being nearly plane across the posterior face; the costation is apparently very similar in the spines from the widely removed geological positions, and the denticulation of the posterior borders is equally similar.

The genus embraces the following described species, all of which pertain to the Carboniferous period: *Leptacanthus junceus*, McCoy, *L. Jenkinsoni*, McCoy, *Cladodus tenuistriatus*, Romanowsky, *Leptacanthus occidentalis*, N. and W.

### ACONDYLACANTHUS GRACILIS, St. J. and W.

Pl. XVI, Fig. 8-11

Fin spines of small or medium size, probably attaining the length of four or five inches, laterally compressed or sublenticular in transverse section, gradually tapering in the lower and middle portions, but rapidly converging near the apex, which forms an acute point. Lateral faces gently arched, flattened posterior to the middle, and regularly converging in front to the more or less sharply rounded anterior margin, and occupied by a few, about ten, relatively strong, irregular costæ, which increase by infrequent bifurcation descending, the anterior ridge sending off more frequent branches near the apical extremity, and quite regularly spaced by narrow, shallow intercostal furrows; the costæ are low and flattened or gently rounded along the crest, and generally more delicate along the posterior border, though their development varies considerably in different parts of the spine. Posterior face apparently uniformly though moderately channeled, irregularly striated or punctate, and bordered by relatively strong, prominent, obtusely rounded postero-lateral angles, which bear prominent, acutely pointed, hooked denticles, separated by about their own diameter in the upper portion of the spine, but becoming smaller and more widely spaced below, and probably extending well towards the base. Pulp cavity ovate in transverse section, about one third the lateral diameter of the body of the spine. Base unknown.

The collections of Messrs. SPRINGER, WACHSMUTH and GILES contain several imperfect specimens of the form above described, all of which show the upper extremity, and one large specimen, belonging to the collection of Mr. SPRINGER, indicating a spine probably four or five inches in length when entire, exhibits the smooth, enameled costæ in a perfect state of preservation. It is apparently referable to the same generic group as the spines which we have described from the Keokuk formation under the name *A. æquicostatus*. It differs from the Keokuk form in the more irregularly developed costæ, proportionately stronger, and more numerous denticles along the postero-lateral angles, less deeply excavated posterior face, and more strongly curved outline.

*Position and locality.* Not uncommon in the lower fish-bed, and apparently the same form occurs in the upper fish bed, of the Kinderhook formation, Burlington, Iowa.

### ACONDYLACANTHUS ÆQUICOSTATUS, St. J. and W.

Pl. XVI, Fig. 12, 13.

Fin-spine long, gradually tapering to the apex, and gently curved, transverse section lenticular, truncated behind. Lateral faces flattened or faintly convex in the posterior half, more rapidly converging to the anterior margin, which is occupied by a prominent, sharply rounded ridge, similar to the costæ covering the body of the spine, of which latter there are ten to sixteen, more or less, in either face, quite uniform in size, rarely bifurcating descending, and closely arranged, the intercostal spaces narrow, or generally less than half the diameter of the ridges, except sometimes along the anterior border the occurrence of a broader groove above the bifurcation of the anterior ridge. Posterior face deeply excavated, postero-lateral angles prominent and sharply rounded, bearing along their inner edges a row of depressed, hooked denticles, spaced by about or little more than their own diameter, and apparently extending at least half the distance from the apex towards the base. Internal cavity subelliptical in section, about half the lateral diameter of the body of the spine. Spines attain the length of eight to ten inches. Base unknown

Intimately related to *A occidentalis*, (N. and W. sp ) of the St Louis limestone, the present form is distinguished from that species by its laterally more compressed figure, the perceptibly narrower and more numerous costæ, less erect and more widely spaced denticles along the postero lateral angles Comparatively few specimens have been identified from collections made by Prof. WORTHEN, and these are imperfect from accident, though sufficient to show their distinctive features. Much worn examples of *Ctenacanthus Keokuk*, from the same horizon, bear some resemblance to this form, but they are readily recognizable by the wider intercostal spaces, and the median keel of the posterior face.

*Position and locality*: Not common in the Keokuk limestone; Warsaw, Illinois.

## GENUS ASTEROPTYCHIUS, Agassiz

### ASTEROPTYCHIUS VETUSTUS, St J and W.

Pl XVI, Fig 1

A fragment of a small spine, showing less than an inch of the upper extremity, appears to be the earliest representative of the genus *Asteroptychius* found in our Carboniferous formations Though imperfect from wear, it differs so unmistakably from its associates in the same horizon, that, taking into consideration its general features, we have little doubt as to its identity with the above genus

The spine is long, narrow, or very gradually tapering and moderately curved, thick, and probably subtriangular in transverse section Lateral faces gently arched and rapidly converging to the obtusely rounded anterior margin, occupied by at least three narrow, prominent, widely spaced costæ, the posterior one abruptly beveled to the postero lateral angles, the costæ apparently more crowded posteriorly than in front; intercostal spaces varying from the same to twice the diameter of the ridges, and longitudinally marked by one or two thread like striæ, but without any trace of intercostal tubercles. Posterior face faintly depressed, the channeled area relatively narrower, median keel apparently obsolete, postero lateral angles moderately prominent, obtusely rounded, armed with relatively large, laterally compressed denticles, spaced by little more than their greatest diameter Pulp cavity comparatively large, equaling half the lateral diameter of the spine, posterior wall very thin. Base unknown

We have thus far examined only the unique example described, so that we have no means of determining the character and extent of individual variation, but it presents distinctive characteristics by which it may be easily distinguished from other forms of the genus occurring in our Carboniferous deposits It is perhaps most intimately allied to the form which we have described under the name *A Keokuk*, with which it corresponds in the number of costæ and the more or less nearly obsolete condition of the posterior keel, but the lateral angles are more prominent, the posterior face more deeply channeled, and the general outline less rapidly tapering.

*Position and locality*. In the lower fish bed of the Kinderhook formation; Burlington, Iowa.

### ASTEROPTYCHIUS KEOKUK, St. J. and W.

Pl XVI, Fig 2

A fragment of fin spine, showing the upper extremity of a worn specimen apparently referable to *Asteroptychius*, presents the following characters Spine strong, slightly curved in outline and gradually tapering, subtriangular in transverse section, lateral faces moderately arched and rapidly converging to the more or less sharply rounded anterior edge, and occupied by relatively narrow, widely spaced costæ, of which there are three or four in the specimen before us, the lateral surfaces beveled to the inconspicuous postero lateral angles, posterior face faintly channeled on either side of the low, or nearly obsolete, median keel In the imperfect condition of the spine the intercostal spaces preserve no trace of tubercles, appearing roughened and coarsely striated longitudinally, and from the same cause the character of the denticles of the postero-lateral angles cannot be determined The pulp cavity is large, occupying half the lateral diameter of the spine The specimen was probably at least three inches in length, and perhaps .15 inch in breadth one inch from the apex.

The specimen described above, however imperfect its state of preservation, is unmistakably distinct from the associated forms in the same deposit, while it differs from *A St. Ludovici* in the rarer costation of the lateral faces, and from the Chester form, *A tenuis*, by its apparent shorter, more robust and rapidly tapering outline The intercostal spaces are relatively broader and deeper than in *A triangularis*, N. and W, of the Upper Burlington limestone, with which it is closely allied in form.

*Position and locality* Rare in the Keokuk fish-bed; Warsaw, Illinois.

## Asteroptychius St. Ludovici, St. J. and W.

Pl XVI Fig 3, 4

Spines of medium size, moderately strong, slightly curved backward, very gradually tapering to the distal extremity, near which the opposite margins more rapidly converge, transverse section sublenticular, forming an acute angle in front, lateral faces gently arched and slightly converging to the abruptly truncated posterior margin The anterior marginal carina rounded, prominent, and similar to the longitudinal carinæ which occupy the body of the spine, from which it is separated for the greater length of the spine by a plane space of variable width, but towards the extremity the costæ are more crowded and uniformly spaced by about their own diameter; in the middle and lower part the intercostal spaces are of variable width, generally narrower and more uniform in the posterior half, and often equal to more than twice the diameter of the costæ in the anterior half, and delicately striated longitudinally, the broad space on either side of the anterior margin is generally occupied by irregularly disposed minute tubercles, which also occur sparsely in the second and third furrows from the margin, but these do not appear invariably, being absent in some specimens. The lateral costæ rarely bifurcate descending, generally near the apex, enlarging below. Posterior margin traversed by a well defined median ridge throughout its greater length, but less prominent above, gently depressed on either side and finely striated longitudinally. Postero lateral angles marked by more or less closely arranged and hooked, laterally compressed denticles, those near the distal extremity being perceptibly stronger, more closely approximated and more strongly hooked downward, while the central and lower denticles are more erect with their apices directed upward; the transition in the reversed direction of the apices of the denticles appears quite suddenly, the intermediate denticle of the upper series being more obtusely pointed, the same as is the case with that of the lower series, where they are perhaps generally less uniform in shape Pulp cavity oval in transverse section, occupying half or more the diameter of the spine in the central portion, but relatively greatly reduced in the upper part, restricted to the posterior half Base unknown.

The collections afford several examples of this elegant ichthyodorulite, but they are generally quite fragmentary, the individuals figured being the most perfect we have met with From the examination of this material, it would appear that these spines present considerable individual variability, such as the variable spacing of the longitudinal costæ as also the denticles along the postero lateral angles, and the absence of the tubercles in the anterior channels, which latter may be due to accident. But, on the whole, it is a well marked form, any fragment showing a complete transverse section and the superficial ornamentation being sufficient for its identification.

Compared with *A triangularis*, N and W., of the Upper Burlington limestone, its more slender proportions are sufficient to distinguish it from that form. It bears a somewhat intimate general likeness to *A ornatus*, Ag., and *A semiornatus*, McCoy, of the Irish Carboniferous limestone, but may be recognized by its more slender proportions and the downward direction of the denticles in the upper portion of the spine.

The plainer examples of the present form present also marked resemblance to the form from the Chester limestone which we have designated under the name *Asteroptychius ? tenuis*, the more closely approximated costæ and the reversed direction of the posterior denticles are sufficient to enable its recognition.

It seems not improbable that the reversion in the direction of the two series of denticles in the postero lateral angles, as shown in the present species, may constitute a generic feature; but as the majority of specimens only show the upper portion of the spine, it is very rare that this peculiarity is observable.

*Position and locality*: Upper beds of the St Louis limestone; Alton, Illinois, and St. Louis, Missouri.

## ASTEROPTYCHIUS ? TENUIS, St. J. and W.

Pl XVI, Fig 5, 6

Spine of medium size, nearly straight or very slightly curved backward, and very gradually tapering from base to apex, transverse section subovate. Anterior angle formed by a simple rounded ridge, postero-lateral angles less acute, with traces of numerous minute denticles separated by a space above twice their vertical diameter in the middle portion of the spine, lateral faces slightly arched and beautifully fluted, with seven, more or less, smooth low rounded, parallel, enameled costæ, separated by a shallow depression of somewhat irregular breadth, about twice the diameter of the ridges in the middle, but more crowded towards either margin, the interspaces delicately striated or striato-punctate vertically. Posterior face abruptly truncated, transverse diameter about two thirds that of the lateral faces, median keel somewhat prominent, forming a subacute angle, bordered by wide, gently excavated spaces, which are striated in the same manner as the interspaces between the lateral costæ. Pulp cavity ovate in transverse section, occupying about half the antero posterior diameter of the spine midway between the extremities, but proportionately much smaller towards the apex, lateral and posterior walls about the same thickness. Base or inserted portion unknown.

The form indicated above is known by a somewhat imperfect specimen, both extremities being broken away and distorted along the one side of the posterior face, but which clearly exhibits the superficial characters and thereby its distinguishing features as compared with other forms. From previously described ichthyodorulites from American formations, which have been referred to this group, it obviously differs widely Apparently intimately allied to the Coal Measure form, *A. bellulus*, the crowded condition of the costæ along the anterior margin on either side at once affords a distinguishing feature in contrast with that form. The apparent absence of intercostal tubercles renders its identity with the present group open to a doubt, but the arrangement of the costæ and the intervening spaces indicate its intimate relationship with the forms referred to this genus

*Position and locality:* In the upper division of the Chester limestone, Carroll s place, Pope county, Illinois

## ASTEROPTYCHIUS BELLULUS, St J and W.

Pl XVI, Fig 7

A fragment of a small spine from the horizon of coal No 5, referable to the above genus, is characterized by its somewhat stout proportions, gradually tapering from base to apex, and very slightly curved outline viewed from the side, transverse section subtriangular with curvilinear lateral faces Anterior margin forming an acute angle traversed by a relatively strong, rounded enameled keel, similar to the longitudinal ridges which occupy the body of the spine, from which it is separated by a broad, shallow space about equal to that occupied by two of the lateral ridges, of the latter there are seven or eight in either face, gradually becoming smaller towards the posterior angles, in diameter about equal to the intervening grooves, and rarely interrupted by faint nodes; intercostal spaces delicately striato punctate, which extends into the base as also in the posterior face, with rarely occurring, minute tubercles. The posterior face is mutilated by pressure, but it is apparently gently concave or laterally grooved, with obtusely angular postero lateral edges, forming a thin posterior wall to the pulp cavity, which occupies about half the bulk of the spine at the middle, and subovate in transverse section. The line of insertion, as shown in this imperfect specimen, was apparently very oblique, indicating the posterior inclination of the spine at an angle of about 30°. The specimen was probably at least one and three fourths inches in length, near .20 inch in greatest diameter, and about .14 at the thickest part near the base.

This pretty little ichthyodorulite bears a striking likeness to *Asteroptychius? tenuis*, of the Chester limestone, but is distinguished by its apparent shorter and stouter proportions and more closely approximated costæ, and the broad plane space either side the anterior margin. The intercostal tubercles occur very sparsely; in the fragment described there are traces of only two or three nodes in the first and second spaces from the anterior border.

*Position and locality*: Discovered by ALEX BUTTERS, in the roof shales of coal No 5, Coal Measures; Carlinville, Illinois Also in the Lower Coal Measures near Fort Dodge, Iowa

## GENUS GEISACANTHUS, St J. and W.

Ichthyodorulite more or less curved posteriorly, anterior angle occupied by a simple raised border or keel; lateral faces ornamented with tubercles arranged in parallel longitudinal rows, anterior keel and tubercles enveloped in a polished enamel like layer. Posterior face longitudinally keeled

The spines under consideration bear striking resemblance to peculiar ichthyodorulites found in the *Triassic* of Europe, to which Professor AGASSIZ applied the name *Nemacanthus*, indicating two species from the "bone bed" vicinity of Bristol, England But the American forms may be distinguished by the apparent absence of hooked denticles along the postero lateral angles. Besides, when we recall the faunal association of the *Triassic Nemacanthi*, as compared with that of the present form, it seems hardly probable they appertain to one and the same genus, since the ichthyic assemblage in the two respective geological formations bears in no instance generic identity among the class to which these spines belong Our data is too meagre to warrant even a conjecture as to the probable specific identity of these spines with other imperishable remains of the class described from the same geological position. The typical examples belong to the Chester and St. Louis formations, or upper members of the Lower Carboniferous

### GEISACANTHUS STELLATUS, St. J. and W.

Pl XXI, Fig 10

Fin-spine of small size, very slightly curved, gradually tapering to the apex Anterior ridge relatively small, sharply rounded along the edge, laterally compressed, and marked by delicate, impressed, oblique striæ,

Lateral faces moderately convex, gently compressed posteriorly, more rapidly converging in front, and ornamented with rather coarsely sculptured stellate tubercles, which are arranged in closely approximated longitudinal rows and irregular oblique order ascending from the anterior to the posterior border, with faint intervening sulci, and vertically spaced by two to four times their diameter, the tubercles present considerable variation in sculpturing, their apices are obtusely acuminate and directed toward the base, perceptibly diminishing in size posteriorly, though not regularly, small tubercles being interspersed with the larger ones in the anterior portion of the spine. Intercostal spaces marked with delicate impressed striæ Posterior face about two thirds the breadth of the spine in its thickest part, prominently keeled, faintly depressed laterally and distinctly defined in the obtuse postero-lateral angles. Internal cavity about half the diameter of the body, similar in section, posterior walls very thin, and probably opening below the dorsal line, deeply excavating the posterior face of the base. Base strong, deeply inserted, tapering to the obtusely pointed inferior extremity, dorsal line indicating a posterior inclination of about 15°.

The only specimen of the above species which we have examined, represents a nearly entire spine about two and a half inches in length. The thin walls of the posterior face have been crushed in along the lower portion of the spine, showing the extent of the internal cavity, otherwise the state of preservation of the specimen clearly exhibits its generic identity and specific peculiarities In general outline and size it is very like *G bullatus* of the Chester formation, but the anterior keel is less broadly rounded in front, and the tubercles are far less crowded vertically, while their coarse radiating ridges offer marked contrast to the smooth or faintly sculptured tubercles of the Chester form.

*Position and locality* Upper beds of the St. Louis limestone, St. Louis, Missouri.

## GEISACANTHUS BULLATUS, St. J. and W.

Pl XVII, Fig 3, 4

An imperfect specimen, indicating a spine probably at least two inches in length, but broken away at either extremity and otherwise mutilated, so that only a small part of the specimen preserves the superficial characters by which its generic peculiarities have been recognized, affords the following specific features Spine strong, somewhat rapidly tapering towards the apex, transverse section subtriangular or conical, thickness about half the antero posterior diameter Anterior edge gently arched and traversed by a prominent, rounded and laterally unbeveled keel; lateral surfaces moderately arched transversely, occupied by five or more longitudinal rows of rather strong, closely approximated tubercles, which are arranged in such order as to form diagonal rows in either direction, those along the postero lateral angles being slightly smaller and apparently more conical. Posterior face abruptly truncated and longitudinally channeled by a rather deep, angular depression. Pulp cavity confined to the posterior half of the spine in the middle, compressed, oval in transverse section. Base deeply imbedded, pointed, dorsal line indicating posterior inclination of spine equal to 20°

The characters above noticed are clearly shown, notwithstanding the imperfect condition of the unique example. The surface ornamentation has been obliterated with the exception of a small area, in which the bases of the tubercles are distinctly shown, besides a few apparently worn tubercles, which present faint traces of vertical or radiating sulci. The tubercles forming the row adjacent to the postero lateral angles are slightly compressed laterally, but not hooked A section obtained by breaking the specimen across the middle indicates a rather deep, angular depression in the posterior face, with slightly convex sides rounding into postero lateral angles Whether the channeled condition of the posterior face is due to the imperfect or mutilated state of the specimen, we have not been able to determine; but the strongly keeled condition of the St. Louis species, *G. stellatus*, would seem to indicate that such is probably the case, and that the thin posterior walls have been forced in upon the pulp cavity by pressure

*Position and locality:* Lower division of the Chester limestone; Fountain Bluff, Jackson county, Illinois.

## GENUS ANACLITACANTHUS, St. J. and W.

A fragment of a large dorsal spine, obtained by Mr. WACHSMUTH from the Upper Burlington fish bed, presents anomalous characters which seem to indicate generic relationship with none of the several ichthyodorulites with which it is associated Unfortunately the specimen is imperfect, bearing evidence of distortion from pressure by which parts of the spine are so thrown out of place as to render the determination of the section and entire outline exceedingly difficult, if not wholly unsatisfactory. Apparently, so far as it is possible to ascertain, both sides present quite the same appearance, from which fact it is inferred that the fragment before us may be relied upon for such characteristic features as have not been destroyed by mechanical attrition and pressure. Towards the lower extremity the spine has been fractured across, and the anterior edge so folded under and broken as to appear displaced, as shown in the figure, Pl XVI, fig 14 a, the upper half, however, apparently shows nearly a perfect transverse section, as determined by breaking the specimen in several places, by which means we have been enabled to make out the following general characteristics.

Fin-spine recumbent if not imbedded along its entire inferior extent, laterally compressed, subovate in transverse section; basal or imbedded portion of greater or less depth, anteriorly produced beyond the limit of the antero inferior shoulder of the exposed body, thick, and coarsely osseous in structure, exposed body of the spine constricted along the line of union with the base, lateral faces converging to the more or less obtusely rounded anterior margin, and longitudinally costate. Internal cavity?

## ANACLITACANTHUS SEMICOSTATUS, St J and W.

Pl XVI, Fig 14

The base of the spine nearly equals the greatest transverse diameter of the exposed portion, nearly as thick as it is deep and broadly rounded along the lower edge, the striated appearance of the surface being produced by the coarse, fibrous structure, the striæ diverging inferiorly from the basal or insertion line; the crown or exposed body gradually rises from the antero inferior point into a long, elevated, obtusely rounded ridge from which the sides gradually diverge, probably gently convex, to the sharply constricted or inbeveled margin along the line of insertion, presenting in connection with the base a subelliptic or long ovate transverse section; the lateral faces are covered with numerous bifurcating costæ, which are larger and more or less irregularly disposed in the middle and anterior portion, gradually diminishing in size posteriorly and apparently more regular and parallel with the basal line, generally smooth, but with occasional traces of minute pectination, intercostal spaces moderately deep, of variable width, probably averaging half the diameter of the costæ.

The specimen described exhibits about two thirds of the entire length, indicating a spine of at least six inches in length The peculiar and anomalous feature is the great extent of the inserted base, which probably extended nearly if not quite to the tip, and the semi costation. The costæ are very irregular in the middle and front portion of the spine, often extremely roughened, but in the imperfect state of preservation it is difficult to assign the cause of this appearance, though it is apparently indicative of tuberculation; indeed the obscure traces of pectination would seem to corroborate this last inference There is no trace of an internal cavity, nor of segmentation, but the basal portion is exceedingly coarsely fibrous in structure.

*Position and locality* In the fish-bed of the Upper Burlington limestone, Burlington, Iowa.

## GENUS BYTHIACANTHUS, St. J. and W.

Fin spines deeply imbedded, laterally more or less compressed, exposed portion relatively limited and but moderately produced vertically, but extending along the back in a recumbent position; line of insertion very oblique and more or less coextensive with the anterior margin, which latter is arched posteriorly, terminating in an obtuse, beak-like apex; lateral surfaces marked by more or less prominent, conical, vertically striated tubercles, arranged in more or less regular rows which obliquely descend from the anterior margin to the inferior border, increasing below by implanation. Posterior face relatively low and vertically keeled. Pulp cavity forming a deep channel in the posterior side of the base and extending to the angle formed by the junction of the posterior face with the shaft or base, possibly penetrating the body of the spine towards the apex

The recumbent position of the exposed part of the ichthyodorulite forms a striking feature of the forms for which we have proposed the above generic designation, and which in connection with the associate characters as described above present an ensemble of characteristics which readily serve to distinguish it from allied genera The species thus far determined pertain to the Lower Carboniferous, probably both belonging to the St Louis limestone, that described in the present work under the name *By Van Hornei*, and a similar form mentioned by Dr LEIDY from the Lower Carboniferous of Tennessee under the term *Astracanthus siderius*.

The affinities of these ichthyodorulites with the *Mesozoic Astracanthi* are made to appear more remote by the examination of the fine example representing the species first referred to above than was the case with the imperfect specimen possessed by Dr. LEIDY, from which the real form of the spine could not be determined. There are points of resemblance between these spines and the form described by Prof. AGASSIZ under the name *Ctenacanthus brevis*, from the Carboniferous limestone of England, a very recumbent form with vertically striated tubercles; but the latter are apparently disposed in rows parallel with the anterior margin instead of descending obliquely to the inferior border as in the present examples

## BYTHIACANTHUS VAN HORNEI, St J. and W

Pl XVII Fig 1

Fin-spines large, exposed portion massive, subelliptical in section, basal line nearly corresponding to the anterior margin, presenting as seen from the side a long elliptical figure, obliquely truncated behind by the low, prominently keeled posterior face, which scarcely equals in hight the greatest transverse diameter of the exposed portion of the spine. Lateral faces very slightly convex and gradually converging to the rounded anterior margin, which is smooth from wear above, and terminated in an obtuse beak, tubercles arranged in more or less regular rows obliquely descending from the anterior edge in a slight forward curvature to the basal line, probably multiplying by implantation, the interspaces narrow, faintly depressed and irregularly striato punctate, in a mature specimen there being about fifteen such rows diverging from the anterior border and twenty to twenty five along the inferior border, the tubercles are large, conical, slightly compressed laterally, or eccentric, with more or less distinct trenchant edges, rising from a broad base, and beautifully sculptured by fine radiating ridges which abruptly terminate below in a faint constriction below which the broad base expands to the body of the spine The posterior face, as previously remarked, is very low and strongly keeled, the lateral surfaces gently concave and coarsely striato punctate in the same manner as the interspaces in the lateral faces, along the crest of the median keel near the apex occur obscure traces of what appear to have been denticles, but this denticulate appearance may be the result of accident Base constituting more than two thirds the bulk of the spine, line of insertion distinctly marked by the termination of the tuberculose surface, below which it is gently compressed, long elliptical in transverse section, anterior margin rounded and broadly curved inferiorly to the obtusely rounded extremity, posterior face deeply excavated by the pulp cavity, which latter apparently terminates at the junction of the posterior face with the line of insertion, exterior surface of the base coarsely and irregularly striato punctate

The remarkable form above noticed is represented by a unique and quite perfect example,* which was discovered by Mr VAN HORNE, to whom we have dedicated the species We are aware of but a single other allied species, that described by Dr LEIDY under the name *Asteracanthus siderius*, (Dr Joseph Leidy, 1873, Ext. Vert. Fauna, p 313, Pl XXXII, f 59,) purporting to have been derived from the Lower Carboniferous deposits near Glasgow, Tennessee, and possibly belonging to the St. Louis division of the group. There seems to be no question as to the generic identity of these two individuals, and their specific relationship is doubtless most intimate However, the form under consideration appears to be especially distinguished, as compared with that cited above, by its relatively broader base, the striation of which is posteriorly deflected instead of being nearly parallel with the anterior edge as represented in the Tennessee specimen, the tubercles are relatively smaller and more numerous, with distinct cutting edges, and more finely striated vertically, their apices being directed upward, though truncated from wear, as mentioned in the description of *B sidereus*.

*Position and locality:* In the upper beds of the St Louis formation; Alton, Illinois.

## Genus GLYMMATACANTHUS, St. J and W.

Fin ray apparently vertically elongated and posteriorly arched, laterally compressed, the lateral faces converging to the more or less sharply rounded anterior margin, and occupied by stellate or vertically striated tubercles, arranged in longitudinal rows more or less nearly parallel with the anterior edge, but increasing by implantation below, and often disposed in irregular transverse or oblique rows. Posterior face and base unknown. Pulp cavity posterior occupying half, more or less, of the transverse diameter of the spine.

The solitary fragment of ichthyodorulite affording the above diagnosis, would doubtless be regarded as probably referable to the *Mesozoic* genus recognized by Prof AGASSIZ under the name *Asteracanthus*, but we believe we are justified in recognizing the distinction between them as based upon even so indifferently preserved specimen as the example before us. The tubercles are much more closely arranged laterally, the interspaces between the longitudinal rows being exceedingly narrow and scarcely at all depressed, the tubercles are also much more delicately sculptured and their stellate character far less conspicuous than is the case with the *Asteracanthi*

In the disposition and form of the tubercles there exists marked resemblance to the *Drepanacanthi*, but the fragment here noticed presents in the apparent, however slight, posterior deflection in the descent of the rows of tubercles evidence of the posterior curvature of the spine, which fact precludes its reference to the latter genus.

The tendency of the tubercles to assume more or less irregular transverse or oblique disposition, also recalls a similar arrangement of the tuberculation in the *Oracanthi*; the massive structure and symmetrical proportions, however, together with the probable truncation of the posterior border, serve to define it from the typical examples of that genus.

## GLYMMATACANTHUS IRISHII, St J. and W.

Pl XVII, Fig 2

Fin spine attaining large size, moderately curved, transverse section lenticular, (truncated posteriorly?) Lateral faces very gradually converging in a regular though slight convexity from the posterior to the anterior margin, which latter is sharply rounded, sides covered with numerous (above twenty) closely approximated rows of strong, subconical, enameled and vertically striated tubercles, the impingement of which gives rise to irregular transverse or oblique arrangement, which, but for its irregularity, is more conspicuous, though not so uniform as the longitudinal disposition, the tubercles being spaced by once to twice their diameter, the interspaces delicately striato punctate vertically, but with scarcely a trace or very faint intercostal sulcation, the vertical rows increasing by implantation below; individually the tubercles present much uniformity in shape and size, being more or less circular or vertically oval, rarely transversely elongated though often two or more tubercles coalesce by lateral impingement, constricted at the base, and rising into a low, obtusely conical prominence, whose more or less eccentric apex is generally above the middle, and delicately sculptured by sharp radiating ridges. Posterior face and base unknown Pulp cavity large, probably limited to the posterior half of the spine and similar in transverse section.

The above described form, upon which the preceding generic description is based, is represented by a fragment of a large spine which was probably at least ten inches in length when entire, but of which the part before us exhibits a section of about two inches along the anterior border; the posterior borders, unfortunately, are broken away, so that it is impossible to determine the character of the posterior face As noticed under the preceding generic description, the affinities of the spine in question are somewhat doubtfully compared, on the one hand with the *Asteracanthi*, and on the other with *Drepanacanthus* But in the absence of more complete material, its nature and relationship can not be satisfactorily determined.

The species is dedicated to Mr CHARLES IRISH, the discoverer of the unique specimen described

*Position and locality* In the upper beds of the Kinderhook formation; near Le Grande, Iowa.

## GENUS PHYSONEMUS, Agassiz.

The first authentic notice of the genus *Physonemus*, though first recognized by Prof AGASSIZ, (Poiss Foss, III, appended list of new and undescribed forms,) we owe to the investigations of Prof MCCOY, who introduced a diagnosis of its generic characteristics in his work on the British Palæozoic Fossils, p 638, wherein he notices the supposed original form referred to by Prof. AGASSIZ, *Ph. subteres*, together with the description of a species new to science. *Ph. arcuatus*, p. 638, Pl. 3 I, fig 29

From the description above referred to, the spines were apparently regarded as having a posterior curvature, reversing the relative position of parts, by which the convex posterior border was supposed to constitute the anterior margin Later, Messrs NEWBERRY and WORTHEN, in a notice of a remarkable species belonging to the Upper Burlington limestone, which they described in a preceding report of the Illinois Geological Survey, (Vol IV, p 373, Pl II, f 1,) under the name *Ph gigas*, correctly interpret the position or forward curvature of the apex of the spine; and though comparison is made with *Ph arcuatus*, McCoy, of the Irish Carboniferous limestone, no reference is made to the generic diagnosis preceding the description of the latter form.

The material accessible to us, through the labors of Messrs SPRINGER, WACHSMUTH, VAN HORNE and ourselves, though not extensive, embraces more or less satisfactory representation of the several forms afforded by the various formations of our Lower Carboniferous group, first appearing in the Kinderhook or lowest member, and extending up into the Chester or upper division, from which latter a single small specimen has come to our notice With this material we have been enabled to arrive at a pretty thorough understanding of the generic peculiarities as represented in the several species now determined, and from which the following amended description is presented

Dorsal spine generally strong, laterally compressed, deeply imbedded, curved with the apex directed towards the front. Exposed portion of the spine more or less flattened laterally, truncated posteriorly, rounded in front along the concave anterior margin which arises from a more or less prominent or laterally expanded shoulder; lateral faces occupied by parallel longitudinal costæ which bear sculptured tubercles whose apices are directed downward, and form a pair of perhaps less prominent costæ, on either side of the anterior edge arise a row of similar but much larger, alternately disposed tubercles, which extend at least to the antero-inferior shoulder. Posterior face depressed (?) or convex and traversed by a more or less prominent median keel. Pulp cavity relatively large, extending well towards the tip, and opening out into a more or less profound excavation along the postero-inferior borders of the spine Basal portion compressed beneath the antero-inferior shoulder, often deeply notched in front, and more or less produced anteriorly, terminating in an acute or rounded extremity, line of insertion marked by the termination of the costation of the exposed lateral faces. Attain large size

A striking feature observed in a large collection of these ichthyodorulites, is the denuded condition of the external surface by which the tuberculation has been removed, and in most instances every vestige of the costation has also disappeared, leaving a perfectly smooth surface, in which latter condition they would be most puzzling objects but for the fortunate possession of specimens exhibiting various conditions of preservation. As often occurs in spines whose surfaces are studded with prominent, isolated tubercles, the superficial characteristics are seldom preserved in other than mutilated condition; but it is notable amongst these *Physonemi* that very few examples show all the distinctive features of the genus, or more than the general outline, and under these circumstances a perfectly trustworthy definition of their specific characteristics cannot, in many cases, be given, or at least carried beyond the particulars of form and proportion

There are also other characters which pertain to the development of the individual, as indicated in apparently old and young specimens of the same species, by which the outline of extreme examples offers considerable contrast, as noticed in connection with the description of the Kinderhook form, *Ph proclivus.* But probably the origin of most of these eccentricities in shape is directly traceable to the effects of abrasion, by which the comparatively thin posterior walls of the spine have been destroyed, opening to view the entire extent of the internal cavity, which in the majority of specimens before us forms a more or less deep channel in the posterior face, gradually becoming obsolete on approaching either attenuated extremity So great are the modifications in outline produced by the accidental removal of a greater or less extent of the posterior portion, that it is often difficult to appreciate the specific identity of individuals exhibiting different degrees of abrasion, as instanced in the examples of *Ph Altonensis* of the St. Louis formation

From the figures of *Ph arcuatus*, McCoy, it is apparent Prof McCoy possessed a nearly perfect specimen The original of *Ph gigas*, N. and W, of the Upper Burlington limestone, though quite perfect as to the completeness of the body, the exposed surface does not exhibit the tuberculose ornamentation of the longitudinal costæ which formed a beautiful feature of its ornamentation, and which is shown in specimens subsequently obtained by Mr SPRINGER and one of the writers The entire surface was beautifully tuberculated, the tubercles being closely arranged along the costæ or separated by a space equal to or exceeding their own diameter, very gradually diminishing in size posteriorly, but presenting a marked contrast in size to the large, widely spaced tubercles along the anterior margin, which, however, they intimately resemble in form and radiate-sculpturing, the intercostal spaces about equal the diameter of the ribs except along the anterior edge where they form a rather wide, gently depressed area on either side The lateral faces slightly converge posteriorly, giving to the transverse section a long-ovate figure, the narrow extremity of which is truncated by the posterior face, which latter is but gently raised along the median keel and faintly channeled either side, the postero-lateral edges forming an obtuse angle without any sign of denticles, though such may have existed. The basal portion, as usual, is deeply excavated by the pulp cavity, which latter has a clavate section in the upper part of the spine, antero-inferior shoulder prominent, rounded above and moderately expanded laterally, beneath which in front the base is deeply notched and laterally compressed, and continued anteriorly into an obtuse point. Most of the examples of this form, of which we have had for examination those of less than an inch in length to the fine original of the species which probably attained the length of ten inches, are in a perfectly nude condition and much modified in outline by attrition As compared with *Ph arcuatus*, McCoy, these spines are proportionately longer and narrower, and probably less strongly arched forward, and, as remarked by Messrs NEWBERRY and WORTHEN, the tubercles are less symmetrical or more eccentrically apiculate, more finely sculptured, and the large anterior ones apparently isolated by wide vertical spaces.

The chief distinction of the genus as here defined, compared with *Xystracanthus*, Leidy, of the Coal Measures, and *Drepanacanthus*, N. and W., consists in the relatively greater prominence of the antero-inferior shoulder, and the prevalence of a plain space of greater or less breadth either side of the anterior margin which is occupied by the comparatively extravagantly developed tubercles, distinctions which are probably of generic value. The first authentic examples of the latter genus appear in the Keokuk formation, and which are very closely related to, if indeed not identical with *Xystracanthus*, Leidy.

Professor AGASSIZ described in the *Poissons Fossiles* (III, Pl 1, fig. 7 and 8,) a species of dorsal spine from the Carboniferous limestone of Bristol, England, under the name *Onchus hamatus*, which presents a striking resemblance to denuded specimens of the present genus. Subsequently Professor AGASSIZ recognized the above species as the type of a distinct genus, to which he gave the name *Cladacanthus*, *Pois. Foss*, III, appended list of new forms In a list of the species of Carboniferous fishes contained in his collection, kindly communicated by Lord

ENNISKILLEN, it appears that *Cladacanthus paradoxus*, Ag., is identical with, and, as I understand it, founded upon the *Onchus hamatus*. Since it appears very uncertain what relation *Physonemus subteres*, Ag., holds to the spines represented by *Ph. arcuatus*, McCoy, it may result in the transfer of all the species heretofore described under *Physonemus*, except *Ph. subteres*, the original form recognized by Professor AGASSIZ, to *Cladacanthus*, Ag.

## PHYSONEMI OF THE KINDERHOOK.

### PH. PROCLIVUS, PH. DEPRESSUS, PH. CARINATUS.

Pl. XVIII, Fig. 1, 2, 3, 4, 5

The following forms are determined from worn specimens, none of which retain a complete transverse section of the exposed portion of the spine, the posterior walls, which were doubtless very thin, having been destroyed, thus exposing to view the internal cavity which forms in the present condition of the spines a more or less deep channel in the posterior face in front of which the solid anterior body extends to the anterior edge. In shape and size the specimens exhibit much individual variation, and which may possibly be attributable to the greater or less abrasion to which the individual specimens have been exposed, and by which their outline has been more or less modified. Under these circumstances it is exceedingly difficult to determine the relative importance of certain characters, as the extreme erect and depressed position of the exposed body, the relative prominence of the antero-inferior shoulder, and the anteriorly produced basal portion, though they may prove to be dependent upon age, or indicative of developmental origin.

Taking into consideration the apparent characters, in the absence of those which would afford a knowledge of the superficial ornamentation, but of which latter none of our specimens reveal the faintest trace, two, perhaps three, more or less distinctly marked forms occur, to which we have applied the distinctive terms *Ph. proclivus*, *Ph. depressus* and *Ph. carinatus*, in allusion to the predominant feature by which they are respectively distinguished in the imperfect state of preservation of the spines before us.

### PHYSONEMUS PROCLIVUS

Pl. XVIII, Fig. 1, 2

Authentic examples of the present form have thus far been obtained only from the lower fish bed of the Kinderhook, and of which there are several in the collections of Messrs SPRINGER and WACHSMUTH. It is especially distinguished by the erect or strong forward curvature of the external body, the sharp anterior margin terminating below in the broadly expanded and slightly convex though laterally sharply defined antero inferior shoulder, which, instead of being notched in front, gradually narrows and slopes into the superior basal edge, terminating in a blunt point, the lateral surfaces are traversed longitudinally and nearly centrally by a distinct groove, transverse section near the middle sub-lenticular, the posterior face moderately channeled by the exposed pulp cavity The largest specimen was probably above an inch in length.

### PHYSONEMUS DEPRESSUS

Pl XVIII, Fig 3

Is represented by a few imperfect specimens, also from the lower fish-bed, which are particularly recognizable by their larger size, depressed position or comparatively gentle curvature, the antero-inferior shoulder broadly rounded from side to side, notched in front and produced anteriorly into a long, slender point; transverse section similar to the preceding form, perhaps less sharply rounded in front, and moderately excavated by the open pulp cavity behind. Length of the largest example above two inches

### PHYSONEMUS CARINATUS

Pl XVIII Fig 4,5

Two fragments of spines from the upper fish bed of the Kinderhook, preserving the inferior portion, are the sole representatives of the present form in the collections The spines were probably near the last above mentioned in form and position, and especially characterized by the more or less laterally compressed and keeled antero inferior shoulder, more or less deeply notched in front and produced anteriorly, and in transverse section laterally more compressed than is the case in either of the above named forms In size the specimens here referred to probably attained the length of two inches

With the material in hands, however apparently well defined the forms mentioned above, we are not prepared to express an estimate of the value of the characters upon which they are founded, nor can this be ascertained without the aid of larger collections and specimens showing the external ornamentation. But the study of the collections under consideration seems to anticipate at least two distinct species—the two first mentioned may prove to be identical, their differences attributable to difference in age

Compared with forms from other horizons, the first named, *Ph proclivus*, bears perhaps closest resemblance to the Keokuk form which we have indicated under the name *Ph. parvulus*, but is apparently less robust and relatively shorter That above referred to under the name *Ph depressus* equally resembles the medium size individuals in the Upper Burlington fish bed, which we believe to be identical with *Ph gigas*, N and W, the only appreciable difference consisting in the relatively less strong and laterally more compressed figure of the present spines The sharply carinated antero inferior shoulder of the last described form, *Ph. carinatus*, distinguishes it from any form with which we have had the means of instituting a comparison

## PHYSONEMUS PARVULUS, St. J. and W.

Pl XVIII, Fig 11, 12

This little spine is distinguished by the strong curvature and proportionately stout build, the transverse section showing gently convex lateral faces which rapidly converge towards the anterior edge, the posterior face relatively broad, antero posterior shoulder moderately prominent, gently convex above, and reaching probably half way across the base posteriorly, below which the inserted portion is compressed, slightly notched in front, and terminated in an obtuse point The largest specimen is a little less than one inch in length, about 35 inch in breadth at the basal line, and about .15 inch across the posterior face in the lower part of the exposed portion

We have seen only a couple of specimens of this form, both of which are denuded of every trace of external ornamentation, and the posterior walls are worn away, the posterior aspect being deeply channeled by the pulp cavity. One of these specimens, belonging to the collection of Dr WILLIAMS, of Boonville, exhibits nearly the entire outline and the basal region, the other, obtained by Mr. WORTHEN, though less perfect, shows the transverse section of an individual of about the same size Its stout proportions, strong curvature, and thick transverse section, distinguish it from *Ph proclivus*, the young of *Ph gigas*, N and W, as also *Ph. Chesterensis*.

*Position and locality* Rare in the fish-bed horizon of the Keokuk limestone, Boonville, Missouri, and near Warsaw, Illinois

## PHYSONEMUS ALTONENSIS, St. J and W.

Pl XIX, Fig 1-3

Fin spine attains large size External portion erect, sublenticular in transverse section, rapidly tapering to the apex which is posterior to a vertical median line, hight less than the horizontal dimension of the base, anterior margin regularly curved and forming one fourth of a circle, merging below into the laterally expanded, gently convex, elliptic antero-inferior shoulder, beneath which the base forms a sharp constriction; lateral surfaces flattened above, very slightly convex below, gradually converging to the obtusely angular or rounded anterior margin, more or less compressed inferiorly along the posterior borders, broadly expanded along the basal line, the denuded surface finely striato punctate. Posterior face very gently and somewhat irregularly arched, occupied by a prominent median keel and gently channeled either side, postero lateral angles well defined above, inferiorly obsolete or merging into the body of the spine Base sharply compressed beneath the antero inferior shoulder and deeply notched in front, produced anteriorly into a long, slender point, posteriorly merging into the exposed body of the spine, and similarly striato punctate, the channel of the internal cavity reaching to the extremity Internal cavity large, extending nearly to the apex, lenticular or long ovate in transverse section, the obtuse extremity anterior and encroaching on the anterior wall towards the apex which is even slighter than the dense body along the posterior borders, and deeply excavating the postero-inferior margin A large specimen about seven inches in length, measures two inches in greatest diameter, 60 inch in thickness, basal line about 4 25 inch, elevation of the external portion over the horizontal line continued from the shoulder above three inches

All the specimens of this species examined by us are imperfect in the nonpreservation of the external ornamentation, of the special character of which we have no intimation. The collection of Mr. VAN HORNE affords a fine, large individual exhibiting the entire outline of the spine, and perfect with the exception of the tuberculose ornamentation; and from the same locality (Alton), Mr VAN HORNE has obtained a smaller specimen, which latter is in the condition of the majority of the specimens of the genus, that is, the denuded external surfaces and the broken posterior face. Together, these specimens contribute important data to our knowledge of the actual outline of the ichthyodorulite and the modifications produced by abrasion, and which is very similar in all forms Thus the imperfect spine above referred to scarcely affords a suggestion of the entire outline as it is exhibited in the large specimen, and yet in every other respect their resemblance is so intimate as to leave no doubt as to their specific identity The breaking away and erosion of the posterior borders results in reducing the entire posterior aspect to a curved line corresponding more or less nearly with the anterior limit of the internal cavity, the lateral walls becoming the boundaries of the more or less deep channel which it forms in the posterior side In the spines under consideration, by this means the diameter of the body is reduced to less than one third its entire breadth, besides greatly reducing its vertical elevation, so as to give the basal portion disproportionately large dimensions, though the anteriorly produced portion suffers equally from abrasion, being diminished horizontally and vertically to the extent of the thin lateral walls protecting the inferior prolongation of the pulp cavity; hence, it will be observed, the process of abrasion is chiefly confined to the posterior and inferior borders, and in the successive stages of its progress, the region in the vicinity of the antero inferior shoulder assumes successively a relatively more and more exaggerated predominance.

Amongst some small spines obtained from the same formation at Pella, Iowa, there are several fragments of *Physonemus* of which the only appreciable distinction, aside from their relatively diminutive size, consists in the truncation and broadly rounded extremity of the antero-inferior shoulder and the consequent reduction of the notch in front, the sharp superior edge of the base terminating at the edge of the shoulder. The condition of these latter spines recalls that of the Kinderhook form to which we have referred under the name *Ph proclivus*, and which holds about the same relation in this particular to *Ph depressus* of the same deposits, as do the present examples to the large specimens described above, the origin of which may be partly due to abrasion and partly to the development of the spine

*Position and locality*. In the upper beds of the St Louis limestone; Alton, Illinois, and Pella, Iowa.

### PHYSONEMUS CHESTERENSIS, St. J. and W.

Pl XIX, Fig 4

Dorsal spine represented by a small and imperfect specimen, in which the external ornamentation is entirely obliterated and the posterior portion worn away so as to expose the external cavity, which forms a moderate depression in the present aspect of the posterior face. The basal portion is also broken away, and the antero inferior shoulder worn down so as to appear as a moderately laterally expanded, depressed prominence. Outline strongly curved, transverse section long elliptical, truncated posteriorly, lateral faces flattened and nearly parallel in the posterior half, sharply rounded in front to the anterior margin, and marked in the worn condition by a comparatively deep longitudinal sulcus, slightly anterior to the anterior wall of the internal cavity. Length along the strongly arched outline 40 inch, lateral breadth near the basal line about .16, greatest thickness in same region 05 inch

The specimen above described may be recognized by its general symmetrical outline and proportions, probably approaching the young spines which we have referred to *Ph gigas*, more closely than other determined forms; but the more strongly arched outline and flattened transverse section offer distinguishing features. It is also less lenticular in transverse section, and probably more gradually tapering than *Ph proclivus* of the Kinderhook, with which, in the condition of the sole representation here noticed, it bears intimate resemblance

*Position and locality* · Rare in the Chester formation; Chester, Ill

In dealing with most of the forms of this genus of ichthyodorulites, we have been compelled, in most instances, to rely upon forms and proportions for discriminating features, and these have been given as they appear in the specimens examined, and which it is believed will require little modification, though the discovery of specimens which shall display those other superficial features most essential in the definition of intimately allied forms will largely add to our knowledge of the affinities of the foregoing forms

## DREPANACANTHUS REVERSUS, St. J and W.

Pl XIX, Fig 5 6

A fragment of a dorsal spine, discovered by Mr. VANHORNE, showing little more than an inch of the inferior portion above the line of insertion, appears to be referable to the genus *Drepanacanthus.* The spine is moderately curved and rather rapidly tapering, in which respect it approaches the Coal Measure form *Xystracanthus acinaciformis* more closely than *D gemmatus*, N and W., of the Keokuk limestone. Transverse section sublenticular, truncated posteriorly, lateral surfaces flattened or very slightly convex, gradually converging and rounded along the anterior margin, and occupied by numerous, probably not less than twenty, tuberculose costæ, spaced by less than their own diameter. The tubercles are quite variable in shape and degree of radiate sculpturing, varying from vertically to transversly elongated, culminating in a transverse apical crest over the inferior border, and more or less regularly diminishing in size posteriorly, those of the posterior costæ plain or relatively meagerly sculptured and more widely spaced vertically; but a marked peculiarity presented by the specimen is the apparent reversed position of the apical crest in the large transverse tubercles along the anterior margin, the inferior declivity gently descending and the superior slope abrupt, as shown in fig. 5 b, enlargment showing the slightly eccentric middle row and the two large lateral rows immediately occupying the anterior margin The line of insertion is very oblique, indicating a correspondingly depressed or moderate inclination of the spine

A specimen from the same horizon at St Louis, representing an apparently young spine, fig 6 a, may prove to be specifically identical with the above, having the same general outline and showing the basal characteristics of the genus, or the inconspicuous antero inferior shoulder and general slender, elongated outline, but in a nude condition without trace of tuberculose ornamentation.

*Position and locality*: Rare, upper beds of the St. Louis limestone, Alton, Illinois, and St Louis, Missouri

## GENUS XYSTRACANTHUS, Leidy.

*Xystracanthus arcuatus* LEIDY, Proc Acad Nat Sci Phila 1859 3 Extinct Vert Fauna Dr Hayden's U S Geol Survey of the Territories, 1873, p 312 Pl XVII, fig 25

The above referred to genus and species was recognized by Dr LEIDY from a unique and nearly entire spine, discovered by Messrs HAYDEN and MEEK in the Upper Coal Measures at Leavenworth, Kansas. From the solitary example, which does not preserve the inserted extremity, it would be difficult to clearly define the characteristics of the spine, but which are quite apparent in the light of other and generically identical specimens which have since been discovered in the Coal Measure strata of Illinois On application, Dr. LEIDY kindly loaned us the original specimen noticed by him, a comparison of which with the Illinois spines conclusively establishes the generic identity of the latter with the Kansas specimen.

Allied to *Physonemus*, Agassiz, from which it is mainly distinguished by the more slender, straighter outline, and the less preponderance of the antero inferior shoulder, it remains to be ascertained in what essential feature the spines of this genus differ from *Drepanacanthus*, N and W, occuring in the Lower Carboniferous formations. Presenting nearly the same proportionate characters, perhaps slightly more rapidly tapering, it would appear that we must look for distinguishing features, if such exist, in the style and arrangement of the external ornamentation But as far as our observations extend, there would appear to be quite as great variableness in this respect amongst the Coal Measure forms as there is between them and the Lower Carboniferous forms In view of this marked similarity, it would seem highly improbable that the spines from the two periods are of more remote relationship than subgeneric, if, indeed, they prove not to be congeneric.

The spine described by Messrs NEWBERRY and WORTHEN under the name *Drepanacanthus anceps* (Ill Rep., Vol. II, p 122, Pl 12, fig 8), from the Upper Coal Measures near Springfield, Illinois, is generically identical with the form above alluded to, making with the two additional forms noticed below, in all four species at present known from the Coal Measures

## XYSTRACANTHUS MIRABILIS, St. J and W.

Pl 20, Fig 1

Spine large, moderately curved, anterior and posterior margins rather rapidly converging towards the apex, compressed laterally, sides flat, obtusely rounded in front, abruptly defined along the obtuse postero-lateral angles of the gently arched posterior face, which is rather strongly keeled with slightly channeled spaces on either side, which slope at an angle of about 35°; pulp cavity posterior to the median line, probably oblong or obtusely elliptical in transverse section, lateral diameter less than half the greater diameter, lateral and posterior walls comparatively thin Base unknown. Superficial tubercles variable in form and size in different parts of the spine, arranged in close longitudinal rows, which increase by implantation towards the base, where they are relatively much smaller than nearer the apex, in general appearance they are slightly constricted at base, abruptly rising along the inferior border into an obtusely angular and acuminate transverse crest, above which the surface gradually descends in a broad, smooth convexity to the low rounded, unbeveled superior border, and ornamented by more or less distinct, irregularly disposed sharp carinæ; in front towards the base, the median line is occupied by a row of medium sized, narrow tubercles which extend probably two inches above the dorsal line of insertion, flanked on either side in the lower half by one, two or three rows of similar denticles, the exterior row continuing above in larger eccentric transverse prominences which gradually change into vertically elongated, high crested tubercles towards the apex, forming a prominent row on either margin of the median line throughout nearly the entire length of the exposed spine; behind the latter one or two rows of similar but much smaller tubercles occur on either side, followed by numerous rows which successively diminish in size to the postero lateral angles, the last row being composed of slightly larger denticles than the preceding; near the base there are forty five to fifty of these rows, which diminish to half that number two thirds the distance to the apex, in which region the tubercles are also relatively larger The transverse crest of the larger tubercles, especially those in front, often presents an exceedingly sharp carina, and though generally smooth, sometimes the basal portion is marked by short carinæ; throughout the tubercles present a polished enameled surface, and are delicately ornamented with sharp ridges arranged in irregular radiating manner, sometimes reaching the summit, but generally confined to the borders, the upper slope being quite smooth. Where the tubercles have been broken off, leaving only the cicatrices of their bases, the surface presents a longitudinally fluted appearance, the shallow channels or interspaces being fine striato punctate similar to the smooth posterior face

The remarkable ichthyodorulite herein described was discovered by Mr JOHN WOLF, to whom we are indebted for the use of the specimen. It represents a spine the exposed part of which was probably ten to eleven inches in hight, two or three inches of the upper extremity having been lost, while the entire base, or that portion which was imbedded in the body of the fish, is broken away, only a faint trace of the smooth area which marked the junction of the dorsal line being visible in the middle angle of the broken spine The body of the spine in the region of the pulp cavity is crushed so as to bring the opposite walls of the cavity in close contact, causing the distortion shown in the illustration, and which is the condition of nearly all the *Xystracanthi* The anterior half retains its form, enabling the accurate restoration of the posterior portion It is evident also that the opening of the cavity was situated very low, if at all above the dorsal line.

From the forms described from the Lower Carboniferous formations, under the term *Drepanacanthus*, the present species differ so markedly as scarcely to require detailed comparison, while its relation to other forms is noticed in the following description under *X acinaciformis*.

*Position and locality:* In the carbonaceous shales overlaying coal No 4 or 5, Coal Measures; near Canton, Fulton county, Illinois.

XYSTRACANTHUS ACINACIFORMIS, St J. and W.

Pl 20, Fig 2

Spine gently arched forward, gradually tapering to the extremity, laterally compressed to a nearly uniform thickness which is about one-fifth the greatest width, obtusely rounded in front, posterior face carinate with a slight channel on either side of the keel, postero lateral angles sharply defined and forming a thin edge below the opening of the medullary cavity. Base more compressed, terminating in a sharp angle in the anterior shoulder, extremity thin and rounded, gently and regularly arched with the posterior margin of the body, line of insertion distinctly marked by slight compression, and indicating a posterior inclination of the spine equal to 45° to 50°. Pulp cavity oblong in transverse section, thickness about half the width, occupying the posterior half of the body, and concealed for two thirds or more its length from the apex, below the opening of which it forms a deep groove gradually becoming shallower as it approaches the extremity of the broadly rounded base The surface ornamentation above the basal portion consists of nearly round or oblong, obtuse and apparently smooth tubercles, slightly constricted at base, arranged in longitudinal rows, also with obscure or irregular oblique rows ascending from the anterior to the posterior margin, the rounded anterior margin is occupied by a single row of large transverse tubercles, flanked on either side by rows of gradually diminishing tubercles, of which rows there are about fifteen in the middle of the spine on either side, flanked by a row along the postero-lateral angles, which latter have their apices slightly turned downward though not hooked, the vertical spaces between the tubercles are relatively greater in the posterior rows than in the anterior ones, while the rows themselves are closely crowded, the anterior tubercles are five times more bulky than those of the posterior rows. The basal portion is faintly and irregularly striated vertically. Length of spine about four inches, breadth half an inch, thickness about 16 inch

The above description is based upon a nearly entire ichthyodorulite, which presents characters by which we are led to infer its specific distinctness from allied forms described in the present and preceding Reports Towards the base the tuberculose ornamentation has been worn off, as also patches in the body of the spine, but their bases are still quite distinctly shown, exhibiting their arrangement in close longitudinal rows It is closely allied to *N anceps* (N and W. sp) from the horizon of coal No 8, from which it differs in being proportionately thicker, less compressed along the anterior edge, and the nonstellate or smooth tubercles, of which the larger ones forming the anterior row are more transverse than is the case in the above form From *N. mirabilis*, with which it agrees in general proportions, it may be distinguished by the character of the tubercles, which neither possess the transverse carina or crest nor the stellate ornamentation characteristic of the latter form, besides the absence of the double row of large tubercles which occupy the anterior border in that form; it is also apparently less erect, the dorsal line indicating a greater backward inclination of the spine. In the present form the tubercles are apparently destitute of any sculpturing, low and rounded, with the highest point or obscure apex eccentric or slightly below the middle, which feature is perhaps more apparent in the tubercles along the posterior angles than in those occupying the body of the spine It is possible these differences are merely characteristic of age, but as yet our materials are insufficient for the successful investigation of the development of these defensive spines. The relatively narrower and more strongly curved outline, and laterally elongated, sharp crested tubercles distinguish *X arcuatus*, Leidy, from the present form.

*Geological position and locality* Discovered by Mr ALEX BUTTERS, in the carbonaceous root-shales of coal No 5, associated with *Edestus Heinrichsii*, N. and W, *Petrodus occidentalis*, N. and W., etc, Carlinville, Illinois.

## GENUS ERISMACANTHUS, McCoy.

### ERISMACANTHUS MCCOYANUS, St J and W.

Pl XXII, Fig 1-5

Fin spine of medium size Basal shaft nearly vertical or at right angles to the anterior and posterior arms, with a slight forward direction, very compressed, apparently in part at least due to pressure, the walls of the inserted portion being very thin and readily yielding to external compression, bluntly rounded inferiorly, gently concave posteriorly, and correspondingly convex along the thickened anterior edge, which was exposed far down its extent, and terminated in a projecting shoulder, beneath which the true base is slightly notched and obliquely truncated something after the fashion of *Physonemus*; line of insertion gently and regularly arched from the antero inferior shoulder to the angle of the posterior basal margin and posterior arm. Anterior spine long, very gradually diminishing towards the apparently obtuse extremity, more or less circular or oval in transverse section in the anterior and middle region, compressed near its origin, and marked by numerous relatively large, depressed or subconical tubercles, disposed in somewhat obscure oblique, crowded rows, overspreading the lateral surfaces of the inferior portion or shaft, where they are relatively small and even less regularly arranged, and extending along perhaps a third of the posterior margin of the posterior spine, those along the anterior (inferior) side of the anterior spine being somewhat produced tubercles, whose eccentric apices are directed forward, and which constitute a row extending to the antero inferior shoulder, but along the inferior edge they are much less prominent The posterior arm consists of a relatively short spine, about one-third the length of the anterior arm, rapidly tapering, moderately curved, laterally compressed, low inclined, anterior margin thickest, and forming an obtuse angle at the point of union with the opposite spine, posterior margin regularly curved with the posterior basal margin, lateral surfaces ridged with three or four low, rounded, enameled longitudinal costæ, rarely bifurcated, and spaced by about their own diameter, except in front, where a broad intercostal space intervenes between the first lateral ridge and the broad, rounded ridge of the anterior margin. The posterior face is very indistinctly shown in our specimens, but appears to be of moderate breadth and rounded or keeled, in one specimen from St Louis, the tubercles, described above as ascending the lower third of the posterior face, appear as high up as the middle, or even higher, where they form a single row of rather widely spaced, laterally compressed, hooked denticles, apparently confined to the keel or median line, as shown in figure 1 a The pulp cavity is relatively small, slightly posterior to the centre, but it apparently expands inferiorly, occupying the greater diameter of the basal portion in the condition of a deep channel opening along the posterior borders of the inserted shaft. A specimen of small size affords the following comparative measurements: greatest diameter of base .20 inch, hight to the angle of the anterior and posterior arms .35, greatest diameter of anterior arm .12, diameter near extremity about .05, length in a direct line .95, greatest diameter of posterior spine .12 inch, length .31, the largest specimens attained at least twice the dimensions of that given above.

The above species is represented by several fragmentary and more or less perfectly preserved specimens in the collection of Mr VAN HORNE and those of the authors, which afford sufficient details for the definition of their distinctive characteristics, but which unfortunately do not exhibit certain features necessary for a perfect understanding of the generic characters, so far as they depend upon external features, and which are not apparent in the original described by McCOY These consist in the imperfect condition of the extremity of the singular anterior appendage, which recalls in shape and position the bony appendage which arises from the cranial region of the existing *Chimæra*, and the apparent distortion of the basal shaft and posterior spine, which render it difficult to arrive at a correct understanding of the outline and transverse sections, the pulp cavity and the contour of the posterior face. As mentioned above the posterior face of the posterior spine appears to be rounded or moderately keeled, the postero-lateral angles very obtuse, and in worn specimens scarcely observable, but in others apparently occupied by an enameled ridge. A single small specimen in the collection of Mr VAN HORNE, however, exhibits the superficial features of the posterior spine in nearly perfect state, showing the delicately ridged postero-lateral angles, and the median keel bearing upon its crest a row of relatively long, compressed, trenchant and slightly hooked, closely approximate denticles, which might at first glance be mistaken for a continuous sharp enameled ridge, but which under the lens are seen to be isolated though very closely arranged denticles, their abrupt inferior acclivity rising into a delicate transverse carina, the long superior slope culminating in a sharp ridge, as shown in figure 3 c, d. Whether the approximate arrangement of the denticles observed in the above specimen is indicative of specific distinctness from its associates we have not the means of determining; it is, however, probable that these closely arranged denticles gradually merge into the widely spaced and finally obtuse tubercles occuring near the base of the spine, as shown in fig. 1 a, and fig 4 a

In nearly all specimens the strong anterior ridge of the posterior spine is distinctly shown, though the lateral costæ may be completely destroyed, and often so compressed basally as to appear like a flat scale without the least indication of internal cavity, presenting in transverse section a wedge shaped outline, the broad extremity formed by the anterior ridge. But an otherwise much worn individual obtained by one of the writers at Alton, and the first example of the genus found in our rocks, fortunately shows the entire section of both arms, though the base as usual is flatly compressed. In the latter specimen the posterior spine in the upper third has an ovate transverse section, the pulp cavity occupying about one-third the diameter, and subcentral or situated within the posterior two thirds of the diameter, it doubtless rapidly expands inferiorly, where the comparatively thin walls offer slight resistance to pressure exerted from without, as is the case with the basal region. The anteriorly produced appendage is traversed throughout by the internal cavity, which is continuous with that of the posterior spine and basal region, inclosed interiorly by very thin walls, but diminishing towards the extremity, where the pulp cavity is about half the diameter of the body of the spine, and closely crowding the superior (posterior) wall, while along the inferior (anterior) side the inclosing walls are relatively massive From these facts alone, even in the absence of any knowledge of the direction of the inserted base in relation to the external processes, the relative position of these appendages would be readily inferred from the posterior position of their internal cavities

Intimately allied to *E Jonesii*, McCoy, of the Carboniferous limestone of Armagh, Ireland, it is chiefly distinguished by the more restricted posterior extension of the tuberculose surface, which in that form extends up the posterior spine a third of the distance from its base, and the less numerous costæ which reach to an oblique line descending from the angle of divarication Whether or not the apparent dissimilarity in the transverse sections of these spines is real, or that the flattened condition of the specimen figured by McCoy, Brit. Pal. Foss. p 628, Pl 3 k, fig 26, 27, is attributable to compression, we have no means of determining.

The present species is dedicated to Professor McCoy, who first recognized the generic peculiarities of this remarkable genus of ichthyodorulites, as a slight testimonial of appreciation of his labors in this field of paleontology.

*Position and locality* Not uncommon in the upper beds of the St. Louis limestone, Alton, Illinois, and St Louis, Missouri

## Genus AMACANTHUS, St. J. and W.

Dorsal spine firmly implanted, curved forward, more or less laterally compressed, posterior face truncated and longitudinally keeled or denticulate along the median line, rounded in front along the concave anterior margin, which is occupied by a row of more or less strongly developed tubercles, which extend from apex to base, lateral surface longitudinally traversed by irregularly spaced, bifurcated, tuberculose costæ, that bordering the postero-lateral angles bearing laterally compressed denticles more or less similar to the posterior keel, the tubercles in the front rows radiately sculptured Spines of small or medium size.

In the above genus is recognized the form originally described by Messrs NEWBERRY and WORTHEN under the name *Homacanthus gibbosus.* As inferred from the above generic diagnosis, the spines here referred to are entirely distinct from *Homacanthus*, Agassiz, their affinities being with *Xystracanthus*, from which latter they are distinguished by the peculiar truncated or serrated condition of the posterior keel, as also the character of the costation and the tuberculose anterior region.

### AMACANTHUS GIBBOSUS.

Pl XXII, Fig 6

*Homacanthus gibbosus*, NEWBERRY and WORTHEN, 1866 Geological Survey of Illinois, Vol II, p 113, Pl XII, Fig 1

The species is characterized by the gentle, regular curvature of the spine, which gradually tapers from the somewhat expanded base to the obtusely pointed apex, laterally compressed, subelliptical in transverse section, anterior margin angularly rounded, supporting numerous, relatively strong, acute, generally slightly recurved, vertically sculptured tubercles, which rise from a broad base, closely and regularly spaced in the upper half or two-thirds, gradually increasing in size towards the base, where they are apparently less regularly and more widely spaced. The lateral faces present five to seven, or more, relatively strong costæ, which are widely spaced above, but approaching the base frequently bifurcate, becoming more crowded and scarcely distinguishable from the intercostal ridges, which latter also bifurcates, and of which there are two to four in the upper intercostal spaces and separated by delicate punctate sulci, the costæ swell at regular, though rather widely spaced intervals of four or five times their diameter, into obliquely elongated tuberculose prominences, the interior bifurcations being more frequently interrupted, and the anterior ridge marked by distinct conical, closely arranged tubercles, similar to those in the anterior margin, but smaller, the intervening anterior intercostal space is relatively wide, the bifurcated ridge below terminating in isolated, minute tubercles. The posterior face is abruptly truncated, the median line occupied by a row of prominent, laterally compressed, vertically elongated, confluent, smooth denticles, whose apices are directed slightly downward, and forming an interrupted and deeply notched keel, the postero lateral angles occupied by a strong ridge bearing tuberculose denticulations, similar to those of the posterior keel Base strong, rapidly converging interiorly, deeply inserted forward at an angle of about 50° with the dorsal line Pulp cavity small, subovate or circular in section, and situated posterior of the middle The largest specimen known attains two and a half inches in length, greatest diameter in the middle .12, thickness about .05, pulp cavity about .03 in greatest diameter at the same point

A rare form, we have had for examination only a few fragments of spines, besides the beautiful and well preserved original specimen described by Messrs NEWBERRY and WORTHEN But so strongly marked are the generic and specific characters in these spines that the merest fragments, showing the superficial ornamentation and section, are sufficient for their identification

*Position and locality*. Upper beds of the St Louis limestone, St Louis, Missouri.

## GENUS MARRACANTHUS, St. J. and W.

Dorsal spine nearly straight or with a forward curvature, obtusely terminated, rounded in front, truncated behind or rounded into the posterior face, which is longitudinally ridged in apparent continuity with the lateral costæ Lateral face and anterior margin longitudinally ridged, the costæ being tuberculated, those in front more or less strongly developed, with their apices directed upwards, and especially in the upper part where they gradually increase in size, forming strong, more or less deflected hooks, transversely carinated, intercostal spaces minutely ridged and striato punctate. Base moderately inserted, forming a comparatively thin plate, more or less laterally expanded posteriorly from the angular ridge in front, with more or less prominent marginal angles behind. Pulp cavity moderately large, similar in section to the body, and occupying the posterior two thirds of the diameter of the spine. The spines thus far determined are of small size.

The present genus is founded upon *Homacanthus rectus*, N. and W., which constitutes the sole representative species at this time known. It is perhaps more intimately allied to *Amacanthus* than it is with *Nystracanthus*. In costation it is strikingly like the former genus, while the transversely carinated tubercles bear some resemblance to the latter, though their convexity is reversed, besides they are less individualized, their connection with the costæ being more intimate than is the case with the tubercles in either *Nystracanthus* or *Batacanthus*. The uniform distribution of costæ in the anterior region as well as in the posterior portion, and the peculiarly expanded base, constitute its most marked contrast with the former genus. Were the posterior face uniformly ridged with the lateral surfaces, which it certainly appears to be, its affinities should be transferred to *Batacanthus*, probably holding an intermediate relationship with that genus and *Amacanthus*.

In the antero-posterior compression, especially as observed in the flattened base of insertion, it is interesting to note the analogy to the sting with which the caudal appendage of some of the *Rays* (*Trygon*, etc.) is armed.

## MARRACANTHUS RECTUS.

Pl. XXII, Fig. 7-9.

*Homacanthus? rectus*, NEWBERRY and WORTHEN, 1866. Geol. Sur. Ill., Vol. II, p. 115, Pl. XII, fig. 6.

Dorsal spines of small size, deeply imbedded, inclined backwards at an angle of about 50° with the dorsal line, very gently curved forward, gradually and uniformly tapering towards the extremity, transverse section subtriangular. Lateral faces gently arched, rapidly converging to the rounded anterior margin, beveled along the posterior margins, with five to eight moderately prominent angular costæ, closely arranged and rarely bifurcated in the posterior portion and the three or four ridges occupying the anterior border, but interrupted in the anterior half by a row of large tubercles, which often extends half way or even more towards the base in mature individuals, flanking the margin on either side, and extravagantly developed near the apex, which they terminate in two strong beak-like hooks; these singular tubercles are more or less laterally compressed, the thin concave inferior slope rising into the more or less acutely rounded apex, the superior slope abruptly descending in a broad convexity, merging laterally in the keeled crest, enameled and apparently smooth The costæ bear similar but comparatively minute tubercles, occurring quite regularly at intervals equal to four or five times their diameter, diminishing in size posteriorly, where they are also less transverse. Intercostal spaces form narrow, punctate sulci in the posterior region, with one or two slightly wider ones in the middle, which are traversed by a thread like line. Posterior face flattened, rounding into the postero lateral angles, and apparently longitudinally ridged with about five delicate, faintly tuberculated costæ, very like and in continuation of the lateral costæ. Base comparatively thin, sharply carinate in front, laterally expanded, the posterior margins somewhat rapidly diverging from above, forming an obtuse angle, from which the inferior borders are broadly rounded to the extremity, presenting from the front concave surfaces gently descending and laterally expanding from the anterior angle. in outline spatulate Pulp cavity relatively large, transverse section more obtuse in front and equal to about half the diameter of the body, posterior walls about half the thickness of those in front, and opening at or just below the dorsal line in the posterior side, forming a rounded, broad excavation in the inner face of the base A mature specimen measures little more than two inches in length, of which the base constitutes about one-fourth.

The form described is abundantly represented in our collections by more or less perfect specimens, exhibiting various stages of growth, the study of which has furnished a very clear idea of the persistent characters, as well as those attributable to age. In young specimens the tuberculation is generally more conspicuous, and the outline quite erect. Considerable variation in the relative extent of the series of large tubercles flanking the anterior margin on either side is noticed in individuals of different sizes, and therefore is apparently of merely individual importance But in the majority of specimens these large tubercles do not descend below the middle of the spine, while in a few individuals they extend even to the base It is rare to find a specimen which exhibits the posterior face, and our knowledge of the character of its surface has been derived from carefully developing perfect specimens by cutting away the matrix By this means the costate condition of the entire external surface of the spines has been conclusively demonstrated, and which offers a marked distinguishing peculiarity as compared with the serrated keel of *Amacanthus gibbosus*, with which the present species was originally generically associated.

*Position and locality* Upper beds of the St Louis limestone, Alton, Illinois, and St. Louis, Missouri.

## Genus BATACANTHUS, St. J. and W.

Spines long, more or less gradually tapering and curved forward, terminating in an obtuse or turgid apex, in transverse section subcircular or oval, without distinctly defined anterior angle and posterior face, the lateral surfaces rounding regularly into either margin, and occupied by more or less distinctly stellate tubercles arranged in longitudinal rows, with faint intercostal sulci, and less regular diagonal series, the tubercles are often much produced along the concave anterior side, especially on approaching the summit, where they form in some instances strong, hollow hooks, bristling the swollen extremity, and sometimes forming a few rows of obtusely conical tubercles in the posterior side for a greater or less distance below the apex. Base moderately inserted, tapered inferiorly. Pulp cavity subcentral or nearest the posterior border, similar in section to that of the body of the spine, and apparently concealed throughout the extent of the external body.

Perhaps the most marked peculiarity of the spines above designated consists in their symmetrically rounded transverse section and absence of a defined posterior face. In curvature they resemble *Xystracanthus* and *Marracanthus*, with which latter their affinities would appear to be most intimate, as indicated by the denticulate character of the tubercles towards the extremity.

As here understood the genus embraces *Drepanacanthus? stellatus*, of Newberry and Worthen, who have remarked its anomalous character, (Ill. Rep. II, p. 125), and possibly the large spine described by Prof. AGASSIZ from the Carboniferous limestone of Bristol, England, under the name *Oracanthus pustulosus*, (Pois. Foss., III, p. 15, Tab. 2, fig. 3, 4,) which presents apparently the same arrangement of the tuberculose ornamentation and similarly rounded anterior and posterior borders, while the thickened wall inclosing the pulp cavity along the concave side would seem to indicate the reversed or anterior curvature of the spine, the base not being preserved in the original noticed by Professor AGASSIZ.

A small ichthyodorulite from the Carboniferous limestone of Russia, described by Col. ROMANOWSKY under the name *Myriacanthus semigranulatus*,* may also prove to be referable to the genus here recognized. The latter form is distinguished by its straight, very gradually tapering outline, nearly circular transverse section, with a large central cavity, and bearing externally along one side two rows of obtuse, closely arranged tubercles, the base is not shown in the specimen, which is

---

* Desc. quelques restes de Poissons Fossiles trouvés dans le calcaire carbonifère de Gouvernement de Toula. Par Heunadius Romanowsky. Moscow, Imp. l'Un. Imperiale, 1864.

about 1 inch in diameter, and probably above one inch and a half in length.

The species thus far determined belong to the Lower Carboniferous formations, and that described under the specific term *B. baculiformis* is regarded as the typical representative of the genus.

### BATACANTHUS BACULIFORMIS, St. J and W.

Pl XXI, Fig 4, 5, 6, 7, 8

Spines of medium size, gently curved and very gradually tapering from the base toward the turgid, bluntly terminated summit, transverse section oval, slightly compressed posteriorly, and uniformly rounded along both margins External surface occupied by ten to thirteen, more or less, faint longitudinal costæ in either side, separated by a narrow sulcus, and bearing numerous radiately sculptured tubercles, arranged in more or less regular oblique series gently descending from the anterior to the posterior border, though subject to considerable variation in the latter respect, especially in the posterior region, where the transverse arrangement is very irregular The tubercles in the anterior portion of the spine, where their apices have been more or less abraded, are obliquely transverse or crescentiform, the concave side toward the apex, and vertically spaced by three times their own diameter, posteriorly they become slightly elongated vertically, and more acuminate, smaller and more crowded, their eccentric apices, as in the anterior rows, generally directed above Towards the summit the tubercles suddenly develop into strong, conical processes, which are apparently smooth, and which form a singular bristling armature of the turgid extremity, occupying the greater part of the lateral surfaces and the anterior margin Base, as shown in a fragment of a small spine, inserted at an angle of about 40° with the dorsal line, strong and tapering to an obtuse point, excavated posteriorly. Pulp cavity nearly half the diameter of the spine, lateral walls nearly the same thickness as the posterior, and about half the strength of the wall along the concave anterior border, extending quite to the summit, and probably opening posteriorly below the line of insertion. A specimen half an inch in greatest diameter near the base probably attained seven or eight inches in length, about the dimensions of the largest examples at present known.

The fragments of spines of the present species are readily recognizable by the transverse and generally obliquely arranged tubercles of the anterior region, their posterior half being generally distorted by the yielding of the thin walls inclosing the pulp cavity to external pressure. A beautiful example which we owe to Mr. WACHSMUTH, showing nearly an entire spine, wanting only an inch or two of the inferior extremity, exhibits the connection of the singular swollen apex, with its claw-shaped tuberculose processes, to the body of the spine, a relationship which would hardly be suspected were the two parts found detached, as they generally are. The large spinose hooks of the extremity in this specimen seem to be traversed by a cavity connecting with the internal or pulp cavity, and filled with a soft chalky substance. Other specimens, however, exhibit, on removing the smooth external shell, an inner dense core, but with an exceedingly delicate perforation, which is apparently in direct communication with the coarse medullary canals which traverse the body walls.

*Position and locality:* Not common, fish bed horizon in the upper part of the Keokuk limestone, Lagrange and St Francisville, Missouri; Keokuk, Iowa; and possibly in the fish bed of the lower or division beds at Nauvoo, Illinois.

## BATACANTHUS STELLATUS.

Pl XXI, Fig 1 2 3

*Drepanacanthus? stellatus*, NEWBERRY and WORTHEN, 1866, Geol Sur Ill, Vol II, p 125, Pl XII, fig 7

Spines of medium size, gradually tapering to an obtuse point, moderately curved, transverse section subovate, lateral surfaces compressed and regularly rounded into either border. Lateral face marked by twelve to sixteen, more or less, obscure, closely approximated, longitudinal costæ, ornamented in the middle region by delicate, subconical, strongly sculptured tubercles, separated vertically by twice or three times their diameter, and arranged in irregular diagonal order, the series generally extending obliquely upwards from the anterior border. Towards the upper part in the convex posterior side the tubercles become suddenly enlarged to several times their dimension in the lateral faces, widely spaced vertically, laterally compressed or vertically elongated, strongly ridged, with their obtuse, eccentric apices below the middle, and forming about five rows embracing the rounded margin; in the lower portion of the spine the tubercles of the posterior border present scarcely appreciable difference in size and form from those in the lateral faces. Along the anterior border, and perhaps extending nearly to the base and probably reaching to the apex, several more or less regular rows, at least four in some examples, of strong, more or less laterally compressed, trenchant, recurved denticles occur, those on either side of the median line being largest, and apparently irregularly interspersed with small tubercles similar to those in the lateral surfaces; the large denticles are sometimes scattered at irregular intervals in the body of the spine, especially in the upper portion, and in most instances they are strongly ridged vertically, though the two largest anterior rows are generally quite smooth, probably in consequence of wear Base unknown. Pulp-cavity of moderate size, in section similar to that of the body, rapidly diminishing in diameter above, the posterior wall exceeding the thickness of the lateral walls and about half that of the anterior wall. The largest examples attain seven inches or more in length

The species originally described by Messrs NEWBERRY and WORTHEN was based upon an imperfect, worn specimen, obtained from the geode beds immediately overlaying the Keokuk limestone. Subsequently additional and in some respects more perfect material has been obtained, the study of which has afforded a clearer knowledge of the generic as well as specific peculiarities by which these spines are distinguished

Our specimens do not show the actual extent of the denticles in the anterior border, indeed they would seem not to reach beyond the middle descending towards the base, though this appearance may be deceptive. In a much worn fragment of a large spine, which we have doubtfully referred to this form (fig 3, Pl XXII,) the lateral tubercles become somewhat transverse in the lower anterior portion of the spine, recalling the shape of the tubercles in the preceding form, but the specimen is generally so abraded, except along the anterior margin where the strong denticles are still preserved, as to render the determination of its identity with the present form unsatisfactory

The form here described strikingly resembles *B baculiformis*, with which it is associated, but may be recognized by its perhaps more tapering and curved outline, less tumid apical extremity, more compressed lateral surfaces, and the opposite direction of the oblique disposition of the tubercles; also the occurrence of strong tuberculose denticles along the anterior border, as also in the upper portion of the posterior side, offer marked contrast to the form cited above

*Position and locality* Not common, in the fish bed horizon of the Upper Keokuk limestone, at Hamilton, and in the immediately superimposed geode bed at Warsaw, Illinois

## GENUS GAMPSACANTHUS, St. J. and W.

Spines long, laterally compressed, tapering, curved backward (?) Lateral faces obscurely costate longitudinally, ornamented with more or less regularly disposed, radiatingly sculptured or nearly smooth tubercles, whose apices are directed upward, often interspersed with larger tubercles of the same style, especially in the convex border, posterior or concave margin occupied by large, laterally compressed, subtrenchant denticles, slightly curved downward, widely spaced, of nearly uniform size, or diminishing inferiorly, sometimes with minute downward hooked tubercles in the interspaces, apex armed with one or more strong denticles similar to those occurring in the concave border. Base transversely expanded and more or less laterally dilated, apparently not inserted or but slightly buried in the integuments. Pulp cavity large, nearly central, walls thin below, more dense near the apex, and apparently thickest in the convex margin. Spines of small size

The above general description applies to two or three forms occurring in the St Louis and Keokuk limestone, and which have close affinities with the spines indicated under the designation *Lecracanthus*? Their main distinctive features are the uniform denticulation of the concave margin and the apparent greater regularity in the longitudinal arrangement of the tubercles in the lateral faces The character of the base is not well shown in the specimens before us, but it apparently intimately resembles that of the spines just referred to, and was probably lightly imbedded In the latter particular, and the posterior curvature, these spines differ widely from *Batacanthus*, with which they have certain resemblance of general outline The form of the larger tubercles, such as occur in the convex border of some of the species, bears a striking resemblance to the large anterior tubercles in *Dipriacanthus*, McCoy, and the resemblance is further carried out in the peculiarly expanded base But Prof. McCoy does not mention whether the form described by him was a hollow spine, though he compares it with *Oracanthus*, but particular stress is laid on its resemblance to the comparatively solid, articulated spines of some of the *Siluroids*; while those under consideration undoubtedly belong to *Selachians*, the character of the basal attachment strongly suggesting relationship with the *Rays* or *Mylodonts*.

### Gampsacanthus typus, St J and W.

Pl XXII Fig 12

Spines of small size, considerably curved, and gradually tapering, the basal portion very thin and more or less expanded before and behind, the apex apparently bluntly terminated and possibly armed with three or four flattened processes, that behind (?) largest and in all respects like the posterior denticles, that in front smallest, with an intermediate one, possibly two rising from either lateral face immediately beneath the crest The body of the spines is almost invariably crushed flat, but a fragment of apparently the same form shows an oval transverse section, a very large and nearly central pulp cavity extending to the tip and thin lateral walls, thickened in the margins, that of the convex margin apparently strongest; this would seem to indicate the posterior curvature of the spine The lateral faces are marked with delicate scutiform tubercles, arranged in quite regular longitudinal rows, closely approximated laterally, and vertically spaced by once to twice their diameter, though irregular and often crowded towards the base, and interspersed with large, similarly shaped tubercles, which form perhaps three, more or less, rows in either face, widely and irregularly spaced vertically, except in the convex margin, where they are more numerous and more uniform in size and disposition; the tubercles, large and small, are oval in outline, with delicate arched transverse crest, the acutely rounded apex directed above and generally projecting beyond the base of the abrupt concave superior face, the inferior side gently sloping and faintly sculptured with radiating ridges, the smaller tubercles are generally more nearly circular or transversely oval, their summits adpressed, while the larger ones are longer and often produced into a sharp-pointed apex The intercostal spaces are more or less clearly defined by a sharp impressed line, and the interspaces, or costæ, between the tubercles are delicately striato punctate The concave margin is set with a row of strong, laterally compressed, subtrenchant tubercles or denticles small or faintly striated vertically at their expanded bases, slightly curved or hooked downward, widely spaced, the distance regularly decreasing towards the apex, a medium size specimen bearing perhaps six to eight denticles A specimen one and a half inches in length has a transverse diameter near the middle of about .12 inch, probably as great again as the lateral diameter

The few specimens of the above described form which we have examined, though more or less imperfect in one or other respect, are singularly persistent in their distinctive characteristics. Only one example preserves the extreme apex, which presents the appearance described above, while its body ornamentation is precisely like that observed in other individuals One large fine specimen obtained by Professor WORTHEN, at St. Louis, shows the very thin, transversely expanded base, so very like that of *Lecracanthus unguiculus.*

*Position and locality*. Upper beds of the St. Louis limestone; Alton, Illinois, St Louis, Missouri

## GAMPSACANTHUS SQUAMOSUS, St. J. and W

Pl XXII, Fig 13

Spines proportionately short, rapidly tapering, very slightly curved backward, apex obtusely pointed or terminated in a strong, slightly curved spur, basal borders expanded, transverse section elliptical, though usually flattened by pressure Lateral surfaces thickly studded with relatively large tubercles, arranged in more or less regular longitudinal rows and diagonal series in both directions, vertically spaced by about their own diameter, closely approximated laterally, largest and most crowded in front and occupying the convex margin, apparently scattered posteriorly, abruptly truncated above with an arched transverse crest, sloping below and more or less distinctly radiatingly striated, though generally quite smooth The costæ do not appear to be distinctly defined, the vertical interspaces beneath the tubercles are finely striated, or striato punctate. The posterior or concave edge set with rather strong, laterally compressed, slightly downward curved denticles, spaced by little more than their diameter, and rapidly diminishing in size inferiorly A specimen, probably imperfect, half an inch in length, measures about 20 inch across the expanded base.

The form described is known from only two specimens, one of which is quite perfect so far as relates to its external features, though the basal portion is doubtless broken away It is most intimately allied to *G latus* of the Keokuk limestone, both in shape and general ornamentation, the only marked distinguishing feature being the less strongly sculptured tubercles and their more crowded arrangement

In case the specimens noticed represent nearly the entire length attained by the spines, of both these forms, one can scarcely fail to recognize affinities which almost equally ally them with *Pnigeacanthus*—their chief distinction, assuming their basis of support to be the same, consisting in the occurrence of a row of strong denticles in the concave margin.

*Position and locality* Upper beds of the St. Louis limestone, St. Louis, Missouri

GAMPSACANTHUS ? LATUS, St J and W.

Pl XXII, Fig 14

A fragment of a spine, discovered by Dr. G. A. WILLIAMS, showing about half an inch of the upper extremity of a medium-sized specimen, seems to be allied generically with the form noticed under the name *Gampsacanthus typus* The specimen is characterized by its somewhat rapidly converging anterior and posterior margins, terminated in an obtuse point, laterally compressed, broadly rounded in the gently arched convex margin, lateral faces apparently slightly converging to the more sharply rounded concave margin, which is occupied by a row of very strong, slightly compressed and recurved denticles, which are smooth or perhaps faintly ridged vertically, widely spaced and apparently diminishing in size below, where they may assume much the appearance of the tubercles The flattened or very gently arched lateral faces and convex border present numerous scute like, coarsely stellate tubercles, whose apices are directed towards the summit, and more or less regularly arranged in closely approximated longitudinal rows and oblique series in both directions, vertically spaced by once to twice their diameter, and of nearly uniform size, or diminishing in size above The interspaces are occupied by rather coarse, interrupted striæ, with more distinct but irregular intercostal sulci Pulp cavity very large

The solitary fragment under consideration exhibits so small a section of the spine as to render a perfectly satisfactory comparison with other forms impossible. The character of its tuberculation bears a marked resemblance to *Pnigeacanthus deltoides*, as also the rapidly tapering outline; but the presence of strong denticles in the concave margin, also the more definite longitudinal disposition of the tubercles in the lateral surfaces, distinguish it from that form, and at the same time present close affinities with *Gampsacanthus*, to which it is here referred.

*Position and locality:* In the upper fish bed horizon of the Keokuk limestone; Boonville, Missouri.

## GENUS LECRACANTHUS, St J. and W.

Spines elongated, laterally compressed, rounded in front and behind, tapering posteriorly (?), curved, base expanded before and behind, very thin, apparently resting upon or but slightly imbedded in the integuments, apex more or less transversely expanded and armed with strong denticles Lateral surfaces rounded into either margin, and occupied by irregularly disposed stellate tubercles, those in the upper portion have their apices above the middle, while in the lower portion of the body they are more symmetrical, or subconical Pulp cavity very large, central, the inclosing walls correspondingly thin, apparently thickest in the convex margin Spines of small size.

The spines here indicated are closely allied to *Pnigeacanthus*, apparently possessing the same basal expansion and very similar tuberculation of the lateral surfaces and borders The tubercles appear to be uniformly distributed in the sides and anterior and posterior borders, though they are sometimes enlarged in one or other margin, large and small intermingled without distinct arrangement. But the most marked distinguishing feature is the singularly distended, spinose tip, which presents a striking contrast to the simple tuberculated apex of the above mentioned spines In general outline, and perhaps tuberculation, these spines seem to be intimately related to *Dipriacanthus*, McCoy; but their relationship is no more intimate than is that of *Gampsacanthus*, while the description of *Dipriacanthus* (Brit Palæ Foss., p. 627, Pl. 3 k, fig 18,) does not permit the satisfactory determination of its affinities with either of the genera here indicated.

### LECRACANTHUS UNGUICULUS, St. J and W.

Pl XXII Fig 10, 11

Our collections contain numerous fragmentary remains of a peculiar form, the exact affinities of which it is difficult positively to determine, but which seems to be closely allied to *Pnigeacanthus* (*Oracanthus pnigeus*, N and W) The specimens in no instance, save one, show the entire length of the shaft, they are about equally abundant, portions of the inferior body and short sections of the curiously spinose tip. But one specimen, found at St Louis, shows the connection of the almost universally dissevered parts, though it is not improbable some of the short specimens may prove to be immature spines It is quite conjectural whether the direction of curvature was forward or backward If, as is inferred, *Pnigeacanthus* was curved in the latter direction, assuming from the character of the thin, transversely expanded inferior portion, which presents no appreciable differences distinguishing it from the above genus, then these spines are probably similarly arched posteriorly The body walls are exceedingly thin and of nearly uniform thickness, perhaps slightly strengthened in the margins, in consequence of their frail build they are almost always crushed, the inner surfaces of the walls more or less closely approximating. But in the collection of Mr. VAN HORNE, a fragment of a rather large individual exhibits the sub-lenticular transverse section quite satisfactorily, showing the large internal cavity and compressed or gently arched lateral surfaces, which are rounded into the broad concave (posterior ?) margin, and from which they gradually converge to the narrower and more sharply rounded convex side The curvature, viewed from the side, is considerable, the basal portion rather suddenly expanding both in front and behind, but none of the specimens retain any indication of an inserted extremity, on the contrary, the inferior borders become exceedingly thin, and, as mentioned by Messrs NEWBERRY and WORTHEN in connection with *Pnigeacanthus* (*O pnigeus*), the structure is that of semi osseous cartilage, the osseous particles of which, in the process of growth, becomes firmly impacted in the body of the spine The middle portion of the shaft to near the extremity is of nearly uniform dimensions, or very gradually tapering to the suddenly and irregularly expanded apical extremity, which appears to be thrown slightly forward and terminated with several strong, talon like, smooth processes or denticles, which spring from the anterior (?) margin and lateral surfaces, more or less compressed laterally, rounded and thickest along the convex side, and curved forward In many examples occurs a sudden tuberculose expansion in the posterior (?) margin of the spine just beneath the tip, and which is probably a persistent feature of the form The surfaces of the spine are studded with relatively large, coarsely stellate tubercles, interspersed with smaller ones, and more or less irregularly disposed, and which are coarsely sculptured in radiating ridges, though generally worn smooth, abruptly terminated above, the apices directed toward the summit of the spine, which latter features are, perhaps, most apparent in the upper portion, where the larger tubercles themselves present the appearance of eccentrically apiculate scutes. The interspaces are irregularly and finely striated or striato-punctate. A specimen below the medium size has a length of at least 1 inch, transverse diameter near the middle .07, greatest expansion near the tip about .10, transverse basal expansion about .20 inch: lateral diameter reduced to the minimum by the compression of the opposite sides.

The general aspect of the spines described above bear a striking resemblance to *Pnigeacanthus;* but their greater length and peculiar armature of the apex widely distinguish them Whether the absence of the apical processes in the above form should be regarded as evidence of its generic distinctness from the spines under consideration, we may not presume to have conclusively demonstrated, but that the facts bear such interpretation seems, to us, unquestionable

*Position and locality*. Upper beds of the St Louis limestone, St Louis, Missouri, Alton, Illinois

## Genus ORACANTHUS, Agassiz

### Oracanthus? obliquus, St J and W.

Pl XXII. Fig 16

A fragment of a spine, too imperfect for satisfactory description, but presenting anomalous features distinguishing it from forms previously noticed in our Carboniferous collections, we have provisionally referred to *Oracanthus*, with which in some respects it seems to be closely allied The spine appears to have been of moderate length and rapidly tapered to the obtuse apex, but the posterior borders are broken away and the remaining lateral surfaces bear evidence of compression, thus suggesting the presence of a large central cavity. The anterior margin, which is gently curved posteriorly, presents an obtuse angle bearing prominent eccentric, obliquely transverse decussations, which gradually diminish and are finally replaced by simple tubercles on approaching the apex similar to those occurring in the lateral faces, the transverse tubercles are widely spaced, narrow along the crest, abruptly descending above, sometimes interrupted giving rise to a series of small tubercles, and in their worn crests coarsely punctate. The lateral faces are studded with small subconical tubercles, very variable and irregularly disposed as to size, but with indistinct traces of longitudinal ridges, which, however, are subject to frequent interruption by the interpolation of large tubercles, which is especially the case towards the summit, and with obscure, irregular oblique disposition, the lateral tubercles also present a coarse punctation in their worn crowns, with indications of vertical or radiating ridges in their sides

The decussated anterior ridge, or transverse tubercles, resemble the decussated ridges of *Ctenacanthus;* but this appearance cannot be associated with any of the *Ctenacanthi* occurring in the same horizon, while the character of the very irregular tuberculose lateral surfaces exhibit still more remote affinities with these forms. The unique example, however, is scarcely sufficient for the determination of its generic relationship

*Position and locality* Fish-bed horizon upper part of the Keokuk limestone, Warsaw, Illinois.

### ORACANTHUS CONSIMILIS, St J and W.

Pl XXII, Fig 15

The form here indicated is represented by a few fragmentary specimens, which generally show only the surface tuberculation, with the exception of a single individual discovered by Mr VAN HORNE, which exhibits the entire transverse outline of a section apparently from near the middle of a medium sized spine. The latter specimen, which is much distorted by the compression of the lateral walls of the large pulp-cavity, indicates a moderately or somewhat rapidly tapering outline, long elliptic transverse section, laterally very gently arched, and the anterior border, as indicated by the apparent greater thickness of the wall in that portion of the spine, is broadly rounded and apparently very slightly curved backward or nearly straight, the opposite or posterior side faintly concave vertically, relatively broader and more angularly rounded, or flattened along the median region and somewhat abruptly rounding into the lateral faces along the postero lateral angles. The superficial ornamentation consists of relatively large, transverse or oval, vertically sculptured tubercles, arranged upon obscure longitudinal ridges separated by faint sulci and striato punctate, closely approximated laterally, vertically spaced by about twice their diameter, disposed in irregular transverse order, or generally descending in a slight oblique course from the anterior to the posterior border, and uniformly dispersed throughout the spine, occurring equally in the posterior and anterior margins. The tubercles culminate in a subacute apex directed towards the summit of the spine, the inferior slope gently convex, that above more abrupt and concave but presenting considerable variation in form and size in various parts of the body, two or more coalescing at the point of bifurcation of the costæ, forming laterally elongated prominences traversed by an interrupted transverse crest, and one or more eccentric rows in either margin consisting of strong oblique, irregular tubercles, in size nearly as large again as those occupying the lateral faces Base unknown Internal cavity large, nearly central, the lateral walls less than half the strength of those in front and behind Transverse or greatest diameter near the middle of the spine 1 inch, lateral diameter across the postero lateral angles .32, lateral diameter in front across the anterior limit of the cavity .25, antero posterior diameter of the internal cavity 70 inch.

Notwithstanding the imperfect condition of the specimens referred to above, a careful reference to the description and comparison with the illustrations given by Professor AGASSIZ of *Oracanthus Milleri* (Pois. Foss 3, p 13, Tab 3, fig 1–4,) of the Carboniferous limestone of England, leaves scarcely a doubt as to the generic identity of these fossils with *Oracanthus* as the genus is defined by the typical representative *O. Milleri*, Ag. Specifically the present form is distinguished from that just named by its relatively more numerous and less obliquely disposed tubercles, which in shape are very like in both forms, though they appear to be more isolated laterally and, perhaps, vertically than is the case in *O Milleri*

Dr. LIEDY has described a spine reported from the "Missouri Territory," and probably belonging to the Lower Carboniferous, under the name *Oracanthus vetustus* (Jour. Acad Nat Sci, Phila, Vol II, [second series,] p. 161, Pl. 16, fig. 1, 2, 3,) which undoubtedly is closely allied to the above described form It is chiefly distinguishable by the less robust and more numerous tuberculation, features with regard to the variation of which we are not sufficiently familiar to decide their import

In regard to their relationship with *Pnigeacanthus deltoides*, we have little hesitation in recognizing their generic distinctness, the latter having the appearance of, and probably more intimately homologous with dermal scutes than with true fin or defensive spines—affinities no less distinct than those which distinguish the teeth from the spines, and though they are differences of degree, nevertheless they are always strongly marked and unmistakable, by which the thin solid elements of the integument are distinguishable one from the other.

*Position and locality* Upper beds of the St. Louis limestone; Alton, Ill, St Louis, Mo, Pella, Ia.

## Genus PNIGEACANTHUS, St. J. and W.

Spines comparatively short, conical, laterally compressed, base broadly expanded before and behind, without insertion, rapidly tapering to the obtuse apex, which is directed posteriorly, transverse section elliptical, rounded into the slightly sigmoidally curved anterior border and concave posterior margin. Pulp cavity very large, extending nearly to the tip, lateral walls very thin, slightly thickened in the margins. External surface occupied by irregularly disposed, radiatingly sculptured tubercles, sometimes arranged in obscure or interrupted longitudinal and diagonal order.

The affinities of the spines embraced under the above generic term would appear to be more intimate with *Oracanthus* than with the spines which we have described under *Lecracanthus*, differing from the former in the irregular disposition of the tubercles and less solid build, and from the latter by their shorter proportions and absence of spinose tubercles in the apical extremity.

The *Oracanthus pnigeus*, N. and W., of the Keokuk limestone is regarded as the typical example. In connection with the original description of the latter form, Dr. NEWBERRY refers to a Devonian species, which he has recognized under the name *O. abbreviatus*, and which he regards as closely allied to the above species.

### PNIGEACANTHUS DELTOIDES, St. J. and W.

*Oracanthus pnigeus*, NEWBERRY and WORTHEN, 1866 Ill Rep., Vol II, p 117, Pl XII, fig 3

The present form has a triangular outline, the anterior border nearly straight or with a slight sigmoidal curvature, the opposite side gently concave, and both rapidly converging to the bluntly pointed apex. In the present condition of the original and thus far only authentic example, the opposite lateral walls are pressed close together, the breaking away of a portion of one side revealing the great extent of the internal cavity and the comparatively thin crust of the inclosing walls. The tuberculation consists of relatively strong, eccentrically conical, coarsely sculptured, stellate tubercles, those in the lower portion of the spine being more symmetrical than those towards the apex, which latter are projected upward forming scute-like bosses, with a gentle inferior slope and abrupt concave superior face; the tubercles are arranged in obscure interrupted longitudinal series, large and small intermingled, but the largest occurring in the front half of the spine; the interspaces are occupied by coarse, interrupted longitudinal striæ. The specimen exhibits no trace of spinose processes in the tip, the uniform tuberculation prevailing throughout, though more or less worn near the extremity, but in the concave margin near the extremity occur large tubercles similar to those in the anterior portion of the spine, and which are apparently irregularly disposed

Towards the mutilated inferior border, the inner surface of the walls present much the appearance of semi ossified cartilage, the individual tubercles seeming to have had independent origin in the extreme borders, but later to have become more and more intimately connected by the impingement of their edges, and finally became incorporated in the solid bony basis of the spine, their inner surface no longer showing suture or other signs of isolated origin. Indeed the structure of the base of these spines, as it appears under the ordinary lens, seems to be almost exactly like that of the semi-osseous cartilage of the jaws, remains of which we have discovered in our Lower Carboniferous deposits. Yet, it is not improbable that these bodies present all the phases of developmental origin discernible in ordinary spines, *i e*, distinct formative organs by which the basis or inserted portion was formed and subsequently the enameled or external coating was produced, though here we have what at first thought seems to be the anomalous feature of the intimate peripheral association of the organs, but which, in fact, seems to be identical with their occurrence in the development of dormal scutes

*Position and locality* Upper fish bed horizon of the Keokuk limestone; Keokuk, Iowa

# SYSTEMATIC AND CHRONOLOGICAL TABLE

## OF FOSSIL FISHES DESCRIBED IN THE PRESENT VOLUME.

---

## SELACHIANS.

### HYBODONTS.

## PETALODONTS

## COCHLIODONTS.



## ICHTHYODORULITES.

# PALÆONTOLOGY OF ILLINOIS.

## SECTION II.

## DESCRIPTIONS OF INVERTEBRATES.

By A. H WORTHEN and F B MEEK.

# LOWER SILURIAN SPECIES.

---

## SPONGIÆ.

### Genus CNEMIDIUM? Goldf.

Cnemidium? Trentonensis, Worthen.

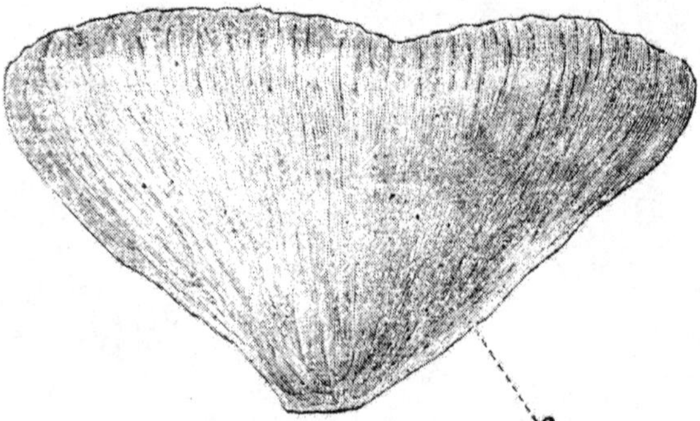

6

*Cnemidium Trentonensis.* Side view, natural size.

General form discoidal, hight about half as great as the breadth at the summit; summit deeply and broadly concave, the base of the con cavity being a little to one side of the center. Furrows both on the side and in the concavity numerous at the summit but decreasing rapidly by coalescing below. Hight of a medium-sized specimen 1.50 inch; greatest breadth at the summit 3 inches in one direction and 3.25 inches in the opposite one; depth of concavity 0.70 inch.

This fine sponge seems to be more nearly related to the genus *Cnemidium*, established by Goldfuss for certain *Jurassic* forms, than to *Astylospongia* of Roemer founded on the Upper Silurian sponges of Tennessee.

*Locality and position:* Three miles north-east of Dixon, Lee county, Illinois, in the lower division of the Trenton limestone.

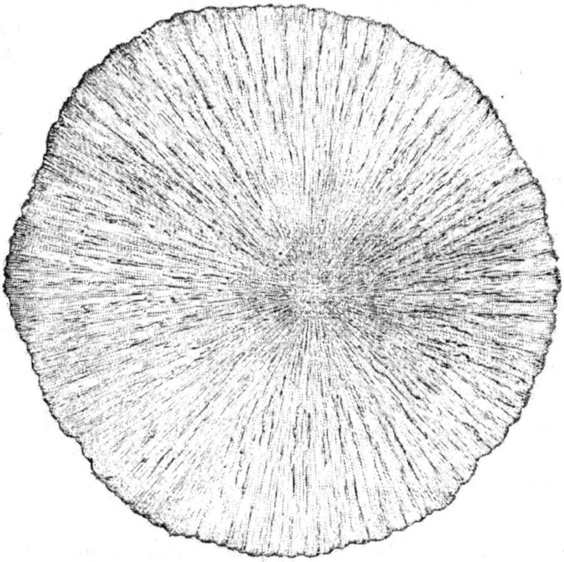

a

View of calice.

I am indebted to Dr. OLIVER EVERETT, of Dixon, for the very fine specimen from which the above figures and description were drawn. For the opportunity of comparing this with a typical form of *Cnemidium*, from the Upper Jurassic formation of Wurtemberg, in Bavaria, I am indebted to Dr. C. ROMINGER, State Geologist of Michigan.

# ECHINODERMATA.

## GENUS HOMOCRINUS, Hall.

### HOMOCRINUS ANGUSTATUS, M. and W.

Pl. 23, Fig. 8.

*Homocrinus angustatus*, MEEK and WORTHEN, 1870; Proceed. Acad. Nat. Sci., Philad., p. 30.

Body below the first radial pieces more or less obconic, or somewhat constricted below the middle. Base forming a narrow cup, sometimes nearly as high as wide, with vertical sides; composed of convex pieces, once and a half to nearly twice as wide as high. Subradial pieces as long as the basals, or sometimes a little longer, and always wider; more or less convex, all hexagonal excepting one on the anal side, which is heptagonal. First radial pieces nearly one third wider than high, being as wide as the subradials, but shorter, and not so tumid, all pentagonal, with the upper side truncated their entire breadth. Succeeding radials, of which there are three in each of the rays seen,* as wide as the first, but much shorter, or only one third to one fourth as long as wide, thus forming free arms so wide as to be nearly in contact all around except on the anal side; last or fourth radial supporting upon its superior slightly sloping sides the first divisions of the arms, which, at least in one of the posterior, and one of the lateral rays, bifurcate on the third piece, while some of the divisions appear to divide again on the fourth piece, which is as far as they can be traced in the specimens examined. Column large, or nearly two thirds as wide as the base at its connection with the latter, but suddenly tapering downwards, and, at least in one of the examples, ending with the sixth piece in a rounded point, evidently showing this individual to have been free at maturity.

Connecting or upper joint of the column in the only two examples seen, very thick, and in one quite tumid.

Hight to summit of first radial pieces, 0.48 inch; breadth at top of first radial pieces, 0.50 inch; hight of base, 0.20 inch; breadth of rays below the first division, 0.17 inch.

This species seems to be most nearly related to *H. polydactylus* of Shumard, from which it differs in the remarkable narrowness of its base, and the proportional greater thickness of its column. It also differs in having only three to four primary radials to each ray, instead of five or six.

*Locality and position:* Mount Carroll, Illinois, in the Cincinnati Group of the Lower Silurian.

## HETEROCRINUS CRASSUS, M. and W.

Pl. 23, Fig. 1.

*Heterocrinus crassus*, MEEK and WORTHEN, 1865. Proceed. Acad. Nat. Sci., Philad., p. 117. Geol. Survey of Ill., Vol. III., p. 324. Pl. 4, fig. 1a, b, c.

For the use of the very fine specimen figured in this volume, I am indebted to Mr. STEWART, of Plano, Kendall county, Illinois.

---

* The right posterior ray seems to be an exception to this statement, as it *appears* to have only three radials including the first, with the second one nearly as large as the first. Its parts, however, are not well preserved.

# MOLLUSCA.

## LAMELLIBRANCHIATA.

### MODIOLOPSIS SUBNASUTA, M. and W.

Pl 23, Fig 9 a, b

*Modiolopsis subnasuta*. MEEK and WORTHEN, 1870 Proceed Philad Acad Sci, p 41

Shell rather small, elongate, narrow and slightly arcuate, rather distinctly convex, the most gibbous part being along the posterior umbonal slopes above the middle of the valves, dorsal and ventral margins slightly diverging posteriorly, so as to make the widest (highest) part of the valves nearest the posterior end, while the most sinuous part of the ventral margin is a little in advance of the middle; anterior end narrow, a little produced, with an oblique forward slope of its upper margin, to its narrowly rounded edge, posterior margin somewhat cuneate, with an oblique truncation more or less convex in outline, to the posterior basal extremity, which is narrowly rounded; cardinal margin long, and a little arched, beaks much depressed, and placed rather nearer the anterior edge than the middle, posterior umbonal slopes prominent, and forming an obtuse ridge extending obliquely backward to the posterior basal edge of each valve, anterior muscular scar comparatively large, round, shallow, and placed near the edge of the valves; small pedal muscular scars distinct above those of the anterior adductors: surface of internal cast, showing moderately distinct, irregular, concentric undulations, which are most strongly defined below, and in front of the posterior umbonal slopes, on the flattened or concave flanks.

Length, 1.31 inch; hight, 0.50 inch; convexity, 0.40 inch

This is a neat symmetrical shell, resembling *M nasuta*, Conrad, (sp.) but differs in having the narrowed anterior less produced, the beaks being placed farther forward; while its posterior end is broader, and obliquely truncated, instead of being rounded Its general outline is more like that of *Orthonota contracta*, Hall, (Palæont. N. Y., Vol. I, Pl. 32, fig 8,) though its lower margin is less distinctly sinuous, its beaks more depressed, and its posterior margin oblique, while it wants the oblique dorsal wrinkles seen on casts of that shell, being a true *Modiolopsis*

On comparison with foreign species, our shell will be found to be very closely allied to the Upper Silurian species, *M. platyphyllus*, of Salter.

It differs, however, in having its anterior end narrower and more produced, with more prominent posterior umbonal slopes

*Locality and position:* Galena limestone of the Lower Silurian, in Carroll county, Illinois.

AMBONICHIA ILLINOIENSIS, Worthen.

Pl 23, Fig 4 a b

Shell above the medium size, subovate in outline, not compressed, convexity of valves nearly equal, beaks pointed, terminal, slightly oblique and rising above the cardinal margin Hinge line straight and fully one half as long as the longer axis of the valves, with which it ranges at an angle of about 35° to 40° A low ridge commences just below the beak on the cardinal margin, and gradually widening extends to the base of the shell, and is separated from the umbonal slope by a very shallow depression Surface of the cast shows twenty or more simple rounded costæ separated by narrower interspaces Other surface characters unknown Greatest length of the valves in the best example seen 3 inches, breadth at the lower extremity of the hinge line 1.88 inch; convexity of the two valves 1.50 inch.

*Position and locality* Magnesian beds of the Cincinnati Group, Savannah, Carroll county, Illinois

# GASTEROPODA.

## GENUS SUBULITES, Conrad.

### SUBULITES INFLATUS, M. and W.

Pl 23, Fig 5

*Subulites inflatus*, MEEK and WORTHEN, 1869 Proceed Philad Acad Nat Sci

Shell very ventricose, subfusiform; volutions about five and a half to six, those of the spire moderately convex in (external?) casts, last one very large, ventricose, and forming much the larger part of the whole, produced and contracted below so as apparently to terminate in a short canal; aperture narrow, rhombic in outline, and pointed or angular above and below; suture well defined in cast; surface unknown. Hight of a specimen with apparently about two whorls at the apex, and a portion of the lower extremity of the produced body whorl broken away, 1.55 inch, breadth of body volution, about 1.15 inch.

It is barely possible that this may be a ventricose, fusiform *Murchisonia*, as we only know it from rough casts, apparently of the exterior. As it shows no traces, however, of any revolving band, or lines, and has much the general physiognomy of *Subulites*, we have concluded to refer it provisionally to that group Its most marked characters are the large size, and the ventricose form of its body volution, in which it reminds one of some of the Carboniferous species of *Macrocheilus* It differs from these, however, in the produced and subcanaliculate peculiarity of the lower part of its body whorl

*Position and locality*. Galena beds of the Lower Silurian; Carroll county, Illinois.

# CEPHALOPODA.

## GENUS CYRTOCERAS, Goldf

### CYRTOCERAS CARROLLENSIS, Worthen.

Pl XXIII, Fig 3

Shell of medium size, moderately curved and laterally compressed. Section ovate, the greatest diameter being near the middle of the chamber of habitation, which is strongly constricted above the middle, and about an inch in depth Septa about eight to an inch on the dorsal side. Dorso-ventral diameter of the last chamber 7 lines, lateral diameter of same 5 lines Siphuncle of moderate size, dorsal and nearly in contact with the shell Surface markings unknown.

This shell seems to be nearly related to *C macrostomum*, of Hall, Palæont of N Y., Vol. I, page 194, Pl. 42, fig 1, and also to *C. Isodorus*, of Billings, Paleozoic Fossils of Canada, Vol. I, page 175, but may be distinguished from both by the characters given above.

*Position and locality:* Galena division of the Lower Silurian; Carroll county, Illinois.

# ARTICULATA.

## GENUS ASAPHUS, Brongniart.

### ASAPHUS (ISOTELUS) VIGILANS, M and W.

Pl 23, Fig 6

*Asaphus (Isotelus) vigilans* MEEK and WORTHEN, 1870 Proceed Acad Nat Sci, Philad, p 53

Body small, elliptic in general form, and moderately convex Head rather more than half as long as wide, approaching a sub-crescentic outline, with the posterior lateral angles abruptly rounded or subangular; anterior margin apparently somewhat narrowly rounded, posterior outline broadly and distinctly concave, but rather straight along the middle, without any traces of marginal or occipital furrows. Glabella not rising above the general convexity of the head, and entirely undefined by any traces of dorsal furrows Eyes situated about their own antero posterior diameter in advance of the posterior margin, and apparently about half way between the latter and the front, rather widely separated from each other, and very prominent, nearly round, and truncato sub conic in form, visual surface elevated almost entirely above the general convexity, and curved around so as to form about three-fourths of a circle, presenting a smooth surface; palpebral lobes as elevated as the eyes, and much contracted, or merely connected with the glabella on the inner side by a narrow neck Facial sutures extending obliquely outward and backward from the eyes behind so as to intersect the posterior margin about half way between a line drawn longitudinally through the middle of each eye, and posterior lateral margins of the cheeks; and in front, at first curving slightly outward a little in advance of each eye, beyond which point they converge forward so as apparently to intersect the front margin in such a manner as to leave a rather narrow anterior edge to the glabella *

Thorax longer than the head or pygidium, as measured over the curve of a rolled up specimen, showing scarcely any traces of trilobation, and composed of eight segments. Mesial lobe, as indicated by very faint impressions on each side of the body segment, very wide and depressed, with segments nearly flat Lateral lobes very narrow, sloping off regularly from the mesial one on each side, pleuræ without furrows, and

* As the specimen is imperfect here it is possible these sutures may not reach the anterior margin in front

—64

with the exposed surfaces seen in a rolled up specimen, narrowing off laterally very rapidly with a strong backward curve, all more or less angular at the extremity, the posterior ones being rather pointed, lapping surfaces apparently wide.

Pygidium subtrigonal, and of near the same size as the head, entirely without any indications of trilobation or segments.

Whole surface smooth, excepting a minute pitting, most distinct on the movable cheeks.

Length (measuring over the curve of a rolled up specimen) 2.75 inches, breadth 1.30 inch, length of head at the middle about 0 75 inch, breadth between the eyes 0 47 inch, hight of eyes on the outer side 0 20 inch Breadth of axial lobe of thorax 0 85 inch, antero posterior diameter of each of the first four or five segments of same near the middle 0 15 inch

This species seems not to be nearly related to any of the described species with which we are acquainted Its most marked characters are the prominence of its eyes, and the almost entire absence of any traces of trilobation in its thorax and pygidium, as well as the great breadth of the mesial lobe of the same, as indicated by a very obscure depression, and a minute projection on the anterior margin of each thoracic segment, on a line nearly behind the outer edge of each eye. These little projections do not extend upward, but forward, and fit into corresponding notches in the posterior margin of each succeeding segment in front As the margin of its head and the posterior edge of its pygidium are in the specimens more or less imperfect, we cannot determine exactly their outlines.

In some respects this species resembles the young individuals of *Isotelus megistos.* of Lock, though it differs in not having its cheeks produced into pointed terminations behind, while its eyes are more prominent and situated farther forward, and the mesial lobes of its thorax much less defined and distinctly wider Its pleuræ also differ in being angular, or a little pointed, instead of rounded at the ends.

*Position and locality* Carroll county, near Mount Carroll, and near Oswego, in Kendall county, in this State, in the Cincinnati shales of the Lower Silurian

# UPPER SILURIAN SPECIES.

## SPONGIÆ.

### ASTYLOSPONGIA PRAEMORSA, Goldf? (sp)

Pl 25, Fig 2 and 2a

*Astylospongia praemorsa* Goldf, 1826 Petref Germ, vol 1, tab 6, fig 9, Heisinger (1837), Leth Suec 94, tab 26, fig 7, Eichwald Silur Schicht, in Esthland 209, Maximilian (1843), Herzog von Leucht Beschr einiger neuen Thierreste der Urwelt aus den Silurisch Kalksch von Zarskoje Selo., 24, F Roemer (1852-1854), Leonh u Bronn's Jahrb, 684, and in Lethae geog ed. 3d Th 154, tab 27, fig 21

*Siphonia excavata*, Goldf, 1826 Petref Germ, I tab 6, fig 8, Bronn (1851-1852), Leth geog ed, 3d Th, V 75

*Siphonia stipitata* Heisinger Leth Suec 94, tab XXVI fig 8

*Jerea excavata* d Orbigny, 1850 Prod de Pal strat 11, 286

*Astylospongia praemorsa*, F Roemer, 1860 Sil Fauna des Westl Tennessee, p 8

Depressed subglobose, the breadth being to the hight as 90 to about 65; concavity of summit shallow, furrows of sides about 24, somewhat flexuous, and more or less interrupted (Under side unknown.) Hight 1.80 inch, breadth 1.30 inch

The only specimen of this fossil we have seen is entirely silicified, and compact in structure (in its present condition), while its surface is considerably worn. Consequently we are by no means clearly satisfied that it belongs to the same species as that figured by GOLDFUSS, ROEMER and others, but merely refer it provisionally to that species, until better specimens can be obtained for comparison. On comparing it with specimens of the Tennessee form figured by ROEMER, it is seen to present a smoother, less porous appearance, but this we believe is due to its worn and more densely silicified condition. It also appears to want the canal openings in the depression of the summit generally seen in the Tennessee specimens, but this may be due to the accidental filling of these openings with silicious matter.

*Position and locality:* Found loose in Carroll county, Illinois, but believed to be from the Niagara division of the Upper Silurian.

# FORAMINIFERA?

## GENUS RECEPTACULITES, Defrance.

### RECEPTACULITES FORMOSUS, M. and W.

Pl 24, Fig 1

*Receptaculites formosus*, MEEK and WORTHEN, 1870 Proceedings Acad Nat Sci, Philad, p 23

Body obovate, the breadth being about three fourths the hight, and the widest point a little above the middle; upper end rounded and without any umbilicoid concavity or opening, unless it may be a very small one, sides gradually tapering with a slight convexity from a little above the middle to an apparently moderate sized base of attachment. Cell openings or depressions shallow, quadrangular, or transversely rhombic (those on the upper part wider than high), arranged in spirally ascending rows, which make nearly one turn in passing from the base to the center of the top; each with a transverse linear central furrow, from which a similar furrow passes to the lower angle; central perforations of the cell depressions minute, and generally closed in the typical specimen

Hight 1.75 inch; breadth 1.22 inch.

This species differs from all others known to us, especially from any Upper Silurian horizon, in its elongated, obovate form, its outline being almost exactly obovate, excepting the truncation of the lower (smaller) end In general appearance it perhaps most nearly agrees with a form found in the Galena limestone, and referred by us doubtfully to *R. globularis*, Hall, in the third Vol Ill. Geol. Reports, Pl 2, fig. 2 a, b. It differs, however, from that species in having the upper end more round, or less depressed, and without any umbilicoid impression Its cell impressions are also very different, not being near so crowded, and instead of becoming more crowded and narrower on the lower half, they are less so there than above, while the central perforation of each is smaller

*Position and locality* Bridgeport, Cook county, Illinois Niagara Group Upper Silurian.

# ECHINODERMATA.

## GENUS EUCALYPTOCRINUS, Goldf.

### EUCALYPTOCRINUS MAGNUS, Worthen.

Pl 25, Fig 3

Body above the medium size, broadly discoidal below the arm bases, forming a shallow cup Base rather deeply impressed, basal plates small and concealed in the depression for the reception of the first columnar facet. First radial plates large, hexagonal, wider than high, with the upper lateral angles truncated for the reception of the first interradials, and the lower angle depressed into the basal cavity, second radials quadrangular, wider than high, but varying in their proportions, third radials hexagonal, a little wider than high, and supporting a rather high and narrow fourth radial or supra-radial, the upper portion of which turns abruptly upward for the support of an arm plate. First interradial quite large, longer than wide, with ten distinct angles, and supporting on its upper angles two long hexagonal pieces that extend upward nearly as high as the fourth radials, and like them curve upward at their upper extremities On each side of these pieces there are four other plates, the lowest and largest being pentagonal and resting against one of the lateral angles of the first interradial, and giving support to a smaller hexagonal plate above, that in its turn supports two small triangular pieces on its upper angles. Arms and column unknown.

This large and fine species is so unlike any of the forms usually met with from this horizon that a comparison seems hardly necessary Possibly it may be included in Dr. TROOST'S catalogue of the crinoids of Tennessee, published in 1850, in the Proceed Amer. Asso, Cambridge meeting, p 60; but as no descriptions of the species there catalogued have ever been published so far as is known, this point can only be decided by a comparison of specimens.

*Position and locality:* Wayne county, Tennessee, in the red limestone at the base of the Upper Silurian

# BRACHIOPODA.

## Genus STRICKLANDINIA, Billings.

### Stricklandinia deformis, M. and W

Pl 24, Fig 5 a, b

*Stricklandinia deformis*, Meek and Worthen, 1870 Proceed Philad Acad Nat Sci, p 37

Shell (internal cast) longitudinally subovate, oblong or sometimes in young examples nearly or quite as wide as long, valves very nearly equal and sometimes showing very faint traces of an obscure mesial prominence on the dorsal valve, and of a corresponding depression near the front of the ventral valve; hinge line straight, and less than the breadth of the valves surface apparently smooth or only with concentric lines on the young shell, while casts of the adult show some traces of a few obscure irregular radiating ridges Beaks, area and finer surface markings unknown.

Length of a young internal cast 1 inch, breadth .97 inch, convexity .46 inch. Length of a larger specimen 1.93 inch, breadth 1.58 inch, convexity 1 inch.

This shell varied so greatly in form at different stages of growth that it is very difficult to give a description that will convey a correct idea of it Young examples from .70 to 1 inch in length approach a broad ovate form, being truncated on the hinge line, and somewhat narrowly rounded at the middle of the front, while their posterior lateral margins are more or less straightened and inflected as we often see in *Rensselaeria* After attaining this size and form, the shell, judging from some adult examples we have seen, seems to have suddenly commenced a more vigorous growth, mainly forward and antero laterally, so as to attain a much larger size, leaving the valves of the young shell as it were, open and spread upon the beaks, thus completely destroying the symmetry of the entire shell At this stage of growth the shell has a curious constricted appearance at the connection of the young and adult shell; while the whole breadth posteriorly is only that of the young shell, and the widest part is then some distance in advance of this, and the posterior margins are strongly flattened by their sudden inflection towards each other there

The casts show that the chamber in the beak of the ventral valve is of moderate size, and supported on a rather short mesial septum. The socket processes are seen, by their impressions in the cast, to be small not united, and scarcely assuming the character of plates; while the crural processes extended from their inner lower sides forward nearly parallel, so as to leave two slender, deep perforations in the cast. The surface of the young shell appears to have been smooth, or only marked with concentric striæ, but internal casts of large individuals sometimes show very faint traces of a few broad, irregular, radiating flattened ridges

It is probable that this species is most nearly allied to *Stricklandinia Davidsoni*, of Billings (Geol Mag, Vol V, Pl. IV, fig 1, 1 a), which in some stages of its growth it resembled rather nearly in form. In all the large examples, however, it differs extremely from that shell in its remarkable narrowness across the umbones, and its truncated or flattened posterior lateral margins Its front is also less produced and less narrowly rounded in the middle in these larger specimens.

*Position and locality*. All the specimens of this species we have seen were found loose in Carroll county, Illinois, near rocks of the age of the Niagara Group They are all in the condition of white quartz casts of the interior

# CEPHALOPODA.

## Genus ORTHOCERAS, Auct.

### Orthoceras crebristriatum, M. and W.

Pl 26, Fig 2

*Orthoceras crebristriatum* Meek and Worthen 1865 Proceed Philad Acad Nat Sci, p 255

Shell attaining a medium size, rather rapidly tapering, compressed, (in part probably due to accidental pressure), section elliptical, septa transverse, rather deeply concave, distant less than one third the greater diameter of the shell at the point of measurement, siphon apparently subcentral Surface ornamented with numerous closely and very regularly arranged, equal, thread like annular striæ, of the same breadth as the depressions between, and differing but slightly in size throughout the entire length of the shell

Length of the typical specimen (which is partly septate and imperfect at both extremities) 12 50 inches, greater diameter at larger end 4 20 inches, smaller diameter of same 2 56 inches. Greater diameter of the smaller end about 2 13 inches smaller diameter of same 1.08 inch.

Angle of divergence, measuring along the narrower sides, 11°. Annular striæ 8 in 20 inch at the larger end, and 9 or 10 in the same space at the smaller end. The specimen figured shows only the septate portion of the shell.

The most marked character of this species is its very regularly arranged, equal striæ, which seem to pass almost, if not quite, directly around the shell. They appear to be simple, uninterrupted and everywhere arranged their own breadth apart. It differs from *O. Laphami*, from the same rock, in its much more rapid expansion from the smaller to the larger extremity, and in its compressed instead of cylindrical form, as well as in having its striæ passing directly around, instead of obliquely.

*Position and locality* Joliet, Illinois; Niagara Group, Upper Silurian.

## ORTHOCERAS MEDULLARE, Hall?

Pl 26, Fig 1

*Orthoceras medullare*, HALL, 1860 Rep Prog Geol Survey Wisconsin, p 4 20 Regents' Rept N Y State Cab, p 412, Pl 20, fig 1 and 2

*O strialineatum*, MCCHESNEY, 1861 New Paleozoic Fossils, p 94

*Position and locality*. Niagara limestone, Joliet, Illinois.

## ORTHOCERAS ANGULATUM, Wahl

Pl 24, Fig 8

*Orthoceras angulatum*, WAHLENBERG, 1827 Nova Acta Sci Upsal p 90

*O angulatum*, HALL, 20 Regents' Report, p 413 Pl XIX figs 10 and 11, and Pl XXIV, fig 1

*Position and locality* Niagara limestone Joliet, Illinois

## ORTHOCERAS RECTUM, Worthen

Pl 26, Fig 3

Shell of medium size, very gradually tapering, septa moderately concave, two of the intervals being a little less in width than the diameter of the shell. Length of specimen with twelve septa preserved, 8 87 inches, length of outer chamber about 3 inches Surface markings and siphuncle unknown

This shell seems to be nearly related to *O crebescens* of Hall, but differs from that species in its much less tapering form, and in the proportional width of the septa

*Locality and position* Joliet, Illinois, in the Niagara limestone, Upper Silurian.

### ORTHOCERAS UNIONENSIS, Worthen.

Pl 26, Fig 4

Shell below the medium size, rather rapidly tapering, especially along the upper half of its septate portion, and more gradually below, slightly arcuate, (though this may be due to accident,) septa transverse, rather deeply concave, distant on the upper half of the shell a little less than one half the greatest diameter at the point of measurement, surface markings and siphuncle unknown.

This species differs from the last in its more slender and more rapidly tapering form, and the comparative distance of its septa. Length of the septate portion of the shell in the specimen under examination, 9 inches, diameter at the base of the chamber of habitation 1 50 inch, diameter at the lower extremity, 0 15 inch

*Locality and position:* Union county, Illinois, from the red layers at the base of the Niagara, Upper Silurian.

### ORTHOCERAS JOLIETENSIS, M and W

Pl 26, Fig 5

*Orthoceras Jolietensis*, MEEK and WORTHEN, 1865, Proceed Acad Nat Sci Philad, p 256

Shell much elongated, very gradually tapering, section oval or narrow elliptic; septa very concave, unusually distant or separated by spaces three fourths the greater diameter of the shell at the point of measurement. Siphuncle and surface unknown

Length of a septate specimen, imperfect at both extremities, 14.50 inches, greater diameter of septate specimen at larger end, 2 75 inches, smaller diameter of same, 1 77 inch; greater diameter at smaller end, 2.16 inches, smaller diameter of same, 1.30 inch. Number of septa in the entire 14½ inches, 8.

This species is remarkable for its very gradually tapering form, and unusually distant septa. The latter character will alone distinguish it from any Upper Silurian species known to us, excepting *O pauciseptum*, Hall, from the shaly limestone of the Lower Helderberg Group From this New York species it will be distinguished by its compressed instead of cylindrical form It is true this compression may be in some degree due to accidental pressure, but it seems to be too regular along the entire length of the shell not to be mainly the natural form.

*Locality and position* · Joliet, Illinois. Niagara division of the Upper Silurian series

## GENUS PHRAGMOCERAS, Broderip.

### PHRAGMOCERAS BYRONENSIS, Worthen.

Pl 24, Fig 6

Shell rather above the medium size and moderately arcuate, the septate portion of the shell as preserved in a cast in magnesian limestone being about once and a half the depth of the chamber of habitation This outer chamber is ovate in outline, measuring 2 62 inches in its dorso ventral diameter, by 1 60 inch in a lateral direction, about 2 inches in depth and constricted at its junction with the septate portion of the shell. The greater and lesser diameter of the septa are as 10 to 5. Siphuncle rather large and close to the inner border of the shell

This species differs from *P nestor* of Hall, (20th Regents' Report on the N Y State Cabinet, p. 405,) in the comparative size of its septa, and more moderate curvature, as well as the form of its outer chamber and position of its siphuncle.

*Locality and position* The specimen from which the foregoing description was drawn was found at Rock Island, in a block of Niagara limestone evidently transported from the vicinity of Port Byron, Ill.

## GENUS CYRTOCERAS, Goldfuss

### CYRTOCERAS DARDANUS, Hall ?

Pl 25, Fig 6

*Cyrtoceras dardanus* HALL, 1861 Report of Progress, Geological Survey of Wisconsin p 43, and 20th Regents' Report on the New York State Cabinet of Natural Hist, p 406, Pl XVII, fig 3, 4, 5

"Shell robust, strongly curved, moderately expanding from the apex, and slightly contracting near the aperture, transverse section broadly elliptical, the greater diameter in a dorso ventral direction. Dorsal and ventral sides equally rounded, septa distant, measuring only four in a distance equal to their transverse diameter, deeply concave and strongly arched forward on the dorsum The siphuncle of moderate size, dorsal"

The above is the original description of this species, and our shell appears to differ in the following characters General form more robust, not quite so strongly curved, septa not so strongly arched forward on the dorsum, and apparently not so deeply concave and measuring five in a distance equal to their transverse diameter. Not knowing to what extent this form may vary, we place it provisionally under this species Should further comparison prove it distinct, it might take the name *Cyrtoceras Fultonensis*

*Locality and position.* Fulton City, Illinois, in a buff limestone at the base of the Niagara, Upper Silurian

## Genus LITUITES, Breyn.

### Lituites Graftonensis, M and W

Pl 25 Fig 1

*Lituites Graftonensis*, Meek and Worthen, 1869 Proceed Acad Nat Sci, Philad

Shell rather small, with the involuted portion discoid, planorbicular, and slightly concave on both sides; volutions four or more, slightly embracing, increasing very gradually in size, with transverse section nearly or quite circular, excepting the shallow concavity along the inner side. Surface ornamented by numerous, distinct, very regularly arranged costæ, which cross the sides of the volutions very obliquely backward from the inner side, curving strongly backward as they approach the periphery, and after crossing the middle of the same, again deflected abruptly forward as on the opposite side; this indicating a profound sinus in the outer side of the lip, the sinus being very narrow, but not quite angular at its termination, and widening rapidly forward; fine, somewhat imbricating striæ of growth also run parallel to the costæ Septa apparently rather distant and running nearly straight across the sides of the volutions. Siphuncle and free portion of the outer volution unknown.

Greatest diameter of the coiled part, 2 10 inches, transverse diameter, 0 54 inch; dorso ventral diameter of outer volution, 0 52 inch.

As we have seen neither the siphuncle nor the free part of the body chamber of this species, we cannot be positively sure it has exactly the characters of the genus *Lituites* Yet as it does not show the slighest appearance of the obliquity of the volutions seen in *Trochoceras*, we have scarcely any doubt in regard to its being a true *Lituite* Compared with *Lituites Marshii*, of Hall, (20th Ann Rep. Regents' University N Y. on State Cab Nat Hist, Pl. 16, fig. 6, 7,) from the same horizon at Kankakee in this State, our species will be found to differ in having its volutions more compactly coiled together, much less rapidly increasing in size, and ornamented with smaller and much more closely arranged costæ Its costæ also make a stronger, or deeper backward curve, in crossing the periphery, which is rounded instead of being flattened, as in the *Marshii*. This flattening along the outer side of the whorls of *L. Marshii*, seems to indicate that it belongs to the subgenus *Ophidioceras* of Barrande, while our species agrees, in the rounded character of its periphery, with the typical *Lituites*.

In general appearance our shell is more like *L* (*Trocholites*) *ammonius*, of Conrad, from the Lower Silurian, though its costæ are much more oblique, and differ in being separated by rounded furrows quite as wide as the costæ themselves, while its surface shows no traces of the finer sculpturing seen on that shell

*Position and locality* Grafton, Illinois, from a light drab magnesian limestone of the age of the New York Niagara Group Upper Silurian

# CRUSTACEA.

## GENUS LICHAS, Dalman.

### LICHAS BOLTONI, Bigsby (sp)

Pl 25, Fig 5

*Paradoxides Boltoni* BIGSBY 1825 Jour Acad Nat Sci, Philad, Vol IV p 362 GREEN, (1832,) Monogr, p 6, Pl 1 fig 5 Also (1832) Monthly Am Jour Geol, p 360 HARLAN (1834,) Trans Geol Soc Pa Vol 1 p 103 and Med and Phys Researches, p 401

*Platynotus Boltoni* CONRAD 1838 Ann Rep Palæont N Y, p 118, HALL Geol Rep, Fourth Dist N Y

*Actinurus Boltoni* CASTELNAU 1843 Ess Sur Sil Syst de l Amer Sept, p 21 t 3 fig 3

*Lichas Boltoni* HALL 1852 Palæont N Y, Vol 2d p 311, Pl 69 70 fig 1 a b, etc, (not 1e)

The only specimen of this species yet known to us from any Illinois locality, consists of the pygidium, in a tolerable good state of preservation. It agrees with the New York species too nearly, we think, to be regarded as a distinct species, though we can see some slight differences in its details. For instance, the anterior end of its mesial lobe is more convex than that of any New York specimens we have seen, but as the latter are all in soft shale, it is probable this difference may have been produced by pressure. The angular projections of its posterior margin are also rather more pointed than is usual in New York examples In these characters, and its rather distinctly and coarsely granular surface, it seems to agree well with a form described by Prof HALL under the name *L Boltoni* var *Occidentalis*, from Waldron, Indiana, but as we have seen no figure, and but a brief description of that type, we cannot be sure of the identity of our specimen with it

*Position and locality* Niagara Group, of the Upper Silurian. Grafton, Illinois.

## GENUS ILLÆNUS, Dalman.

### ILLÆNUS (BUMASTUS) GRAFTONENSIS, M. and W.

Pl 25, Fig 4

*Illænus (Bumastus) Graftonensis*, MEEK and WORTHEN, 1869 Proceed Acad Nat Sci., Philad

Attaining a rather large size Head (determined from internal cast) transversely subelliptic as seen from above, when placed with the under side on a horizontal plane, its breadth being to its length very nearly as fifty to thirty; moderately convex, the hight being rather distinctly less than half the breadth, and the most prominent part a little behind the middle, while the curve over the middle, from its posterior to its anterior margin, forms about a quarter of a circle. Anterior margin, as seen from above, presenting a nearly transversely semielliptic curve, and a subquadrangular outline, as seen in a side view; lateral margins rather narrowly, and regularly rounded in outline, into the posterior side. Axial furrows distinct, converging forward to a point nearly opposite the middle of each eye, where they terminate in little flattened oval depressions Eyes large, forming nearly semicircular curves, with their posterior ends as near the posterior as to the lateral margins of the head; each with a broad, very deep furrow around beneath its outer side, so as to form a kind of obtuse shoulder below, from which the cheeks drop off nearly vertically, with a slight convexity of outline, to the inferior margins, palpebral lobes less elevated than the middle of the glabella, and sloping a little outward, with an even convexity over their whole surface, visual surface forming a rather narrow convex band, and showing (in internal casts) under a magnifier, numerous very minute reticulations Facial suture cutting the anterior margin distinctly within a line drawn antero-posteriorly through the inner ends of each eye, and intersecting the posterior margin nearly on a line with the middle of each eye Rostral shield flat, with a subfusiform outline, and obtuse lateral extremities; just three times as wide as its antero-posterior diameter Surface of the internal cast of the whole upper part of the head, without lines, furrows or other markings, but rather distinct transverse furrows are seen on the rostral shield. Body and other parts unknown

Length of head, about 1 20 inch, breadth of head, 2 17 inches; hight or convexity, 1 05 inch Length of eyes, 0 55 inch, hight of visual surface, 0 10 inch; distance between the eyes at posterior and anterior ends, 1 65 inch

This species is perhaps most nearly related to the common and widely distributed *I Barriensis* of Murchison It may be readily distinguished, however, by several important differences in the head, which is the only part yet known to us In the first place, its head is much wider in proportion to its length, and has its lateral margins, as seen from above, much more narrowly and regularly rounded, so that the cheeks do not project any farther out from the eyes posteriorly, than laterally, the outline of the lateral margins having almost exactly the same curve as the eyes themselves Its rostral shield also has a very different form from that of Murchison's species, being narrow in its antero posterior diameter, and distinctly obtuse, instead of pointed at the lateral extremi ties. Our species likewise shows no traces of the furrows on the cast of the upper side of the head, so strongly marked on *I. Barriensis*.

It is still more widely removed from *I. insignis* of Hall; and we know of no other described species, having the head so nearly elliptical in outline, as seen from above, excepting possibly *I. Salteri* of Barrande, which, however, differs widely in other characters, belonging, as it does, to the small eyed section of the group.

*Position and locality:* Grafton, Illinois; from the Niagara division of the Upper Silurian.

## GENUS SPHÆREXOCHUS, Beyrich.

### SPHÆREXOCHUS ROMINGERI, Hall.

Pl. 24, Fig. 4.

*Sphærexochus Romingeri*, HALL, 1862. Geol. Rep. of Wis., p. 434, and 20th Regents' Report, p. 425. Pl. 21, figs. 4-7.

*Position and locality:* Joliet, Illinois; Niagara Group.

---

# DEVONIAN SPECIES.

## GENUS CALCEOCRINUS, Hall.

### CALCEOCRINUS BARRISI, Worthen.

Body above the medium size and composed of thick massive plates. Lower dorsal plate triangular and about three times as wide as high.

*Calceocrinus Barrisi.* View of the body.

Upper dorsal plate less than half the size of the lower, and triangular in outline. Dorso-lateral pieces presenting an irregular pentagonal outline, with abruptly rounding lateral sides, and projecting upper angles. Arms and column unknown.

This species may be readily distinguished from any other known to us by its thick massive plates and robust appearance. We are indebted to the Rev. Mr. BARRIS, of Davenport, Iowa, for the only specimen we have seen, to whom we dedicate the species.

*Position and locality:* Davenport, Iowa; in beds of Devonian age.

# MOLLUSCA.

## LAMELLIBRANCHIATA.

### GENUS AVICULOPECTEN, McCoy.

AVICULOPECTEN UNIONENSIS, Worthen.

Pl 23, Fig 3

Shell of medium size, broadly subovate in outline exclusive of the ears, left valve moderately convex and oblique, anterior and postero-basal margins rounded, the latter rounding up to meet the obliquely sloping edge of the posterior margin Anterior ear rather small, triangular, flat; posterior ear about three times as large as the anterior, and more acutely angular, beak depressed, scarcely reaching beyond the cardinal margin and placed considerably in advance of the middle of the hinge; surface ornamented with numerous simple linear costæ, of which about twelve may be counted on the lower margin in the space of half an inch, alternating somewhat in size, the smaller ones dying out towards the umbo. Crossing these linear costæ are distinct lines of growth Right valve unknown. Length of hinge line 1 20 inch, greatest length from the umbo to the basal margin 2.25 inches, greatest transverse breadth 2 10 inches.

*Position and locality* Union county, Illinois, in a dark fœtid limestone, probably representing the Corniferous beds of the Devonian.

## CEPHALOPODA.

### GENUS PHRAGMOCERAS.

PHRAGMOCERAS WALSHII, M and W.

Pl 28, Fig 2 a, b

*Phragmoceras Walshii*, MEEK and WORTHEN, 1866 Proceed Acad Nat Sci, Philad, p 257

Shell attaining a large size, clavato sublunate, being moderately arched, increasing rather rapidly in size (particularly in the dorso ventral diameter), from the smaller end to near the middle, and thence apparently somewhat tapering towards the aperture, which is not preserved in the only specimen seen More or less compressed laterally. Body chamber apparently rather short. Septa oblique (in part from accidental pressure in the specimen examined), comparatively closely arranged, the chambers between scarcely equalling one sixth the greater diameter of the shell at the widest part, and one eighth towards the smaller end. (Siphuncle, surface markings and aperture unknown.)

Length of specimen (imperfect at both extremities), measuring along the middle of the side parallel to the curve, about 15 inches Greatest breadth near the middle, 5 inches, greater diameter at the smaller end, 2 10 inches. Of the whole length of the specimen, 22 of the chambers form 10 inches, and the remaining portion of the body chamber the other 5 inches

The only specimen of this large shell we have seen is very imperfect, and much distorted, so that it is quite probable some of the characters given may have to be modified more or less, when perfect examples are found Its large size, general form, and rather closely arranged septa, however, will probably render its identification not very difficult

The specific name was given in honor of B. D. WALSH, Esq, the well known Entomologist, of Rock Island, Illinois

*Position and locality* Rock Island, Illinois; Hamilton division of the Devonian.

## GENUS ORTHOCERAS.

### ORTHOCERAS WINCHELLI, M. and W.

Pl 28, Fig 1

*Orthoceras Winchelli*, MEEK and WORTHEN, 1866 Proceed Acad Nat Sci Philad., p 257

Shell rather rapidly tapering, section nearly circular, its greater and smaller diameter being as 106 to 100, septa moderately concave, not oblique, distant one fifth the greater diameter of the shell at the point of measurement, and showing a gentle backward curve in crossing the dorsal and ventral sides; siphuncle very small, at the points where it passes through the septa (but probably swollen between), placed on the shorter axis of the septa only about its own breadth from the margin. Surface nearly smooth, or with more obscure lines of growth, which, like the margins of the septa, make a slight backward curve in crossing the dorsal and ventral sides

Length of a specimen imperfect, 3 25 inches

This species seems to be somewhat similar to *O occidentale* of Prof. WINCHELL, from the Michigan Marshall group (Am Jour Sci., XXXIII, 356, 1862), but differs in being more rapidly tapering, and in having its siphuncle nearly marginal, instead of placed midway between the centre and the margin of the septa It much swollen between the septa, its siphuncle must be really marginal at these points

The specific name was given in honor of Prof. A. WINCHELL, State Geologist of Michigan.

*Position and locality*: White Sulphur Springs, Delaware county, Ohio, Devonian.

---

# LOWER CARBONIFEROUS SPECIES.

# ECHINODERMATA.

## GENUS DORYCRINUS, Rœmer.

### DORYCRINUS KELLOGGI, Worthen

Pl 23, Fig 8

Body below the medium size, obconical below the arms, tapering rapidly to the truncated base, and depressed convex above, base truncated, excavated for the reception of the columnar facet, and slightly depressed at the sutures, first radials a little wider than high, three hexagonal and two heptagonal; second radials nearly twice as wide as high, two pentagonal and three hexagonal, third radials twice as wide as high, pentagonal and hexagonal, each supporting on its superior sloping sides a pentagonal secondary radial, which is succeeded by another heptagonal secondary radial, the latter supporting on each of its superior sloping sides two brachial pieces, giving four arm openings to each ray First anal piece heptagonal and about the same size as the first radials, supporting three others above, one of which is pentagonal, one hexagonal and one heptagonal; these are succeeded by a dozen or more minute and irregular shaped pieces extending up to the spiniferous or mammillary plate at the apex of the summit. Around this central plate on the summit there are six other mammillary plates of smaller size forming three quarters of a circle, the opening being on the anal side, and beside these there are from one to three other protuberant plates on the summit of each ray making in all from eighteen to twenty protuberant plates on the vault. First interradial a little larger than the second radials, hexagonal, and supporting two smaller pieces above, that extend up nearly to the base of the arms. Anal opening minute, slightly protuberant, and located immediately at the base of the mammillary plate that forms the apex of the summit Surface of all the plates finely rugose

Dedicated to Dr GEO W KELLOGG, of Keokuk, Iowa, from whom I received the typical specimen.

*Position and locality* Keokuk, Iowa; Keokuk limestone, Lower Carboniferous

## GENUS SYNBATHOCRINUS Phillips.

### SYNBATHOCRINUS ROBUSTUS, Shumard.

Pl 29, Fig 4

*Synbathocrinus robustus*, SHUMARD, 1866 Trans St Louis Acad of Science, Vol 2, p 397

"Body below the second radials depressed conical, enlarging rapidly from the base, width not quite double the hight, plates thick, surface finely granulose. Base pentagonal above, short, widely truncated and excavated below by the upper joint of the column, margin of excavation finely but distinctly crenulate. First radials wider than high, quadrangular, gently convex, double the hight of the base, facets for second radials broad." The foregoing is Dr SHUMARD'S original description, to which the example figured enables me to add the following: Second radials quadrangular, wider than high and tapering very gently upward Arms stout and composed of slightly rounded plates from one half to one-third as high as wide, forming when closed a cylindrical prolongation which in the example figured is about 2.60 inches in length Column round, and composed of rather short plates, of which about every fourth one is a little longer and wider than the others, forming rim-like projections.

*Position and locality* Greene county, Illinois, and Buttonmould Knob, Ky, Keokuk Group, Lower Carboniferous

## Genus DICHOCRINUS, Munster.

### Dichocrinus ficus, C and L.

Pl 29, Fig 7

*Dichocrinus ficus* Casseday and Lyon, 1860 Proceed Am Acad Arts and Sci, Vol 5, p 24

Body subovoid, inflated near the middle of the first radials, from which it gradually contracts both above and below. Basal pieces similar in form and size, and when united presenting five slightly curved depressions and one angular notch for the reception of the radial and anal pieces First radials five, similar in form and size, longer than wide, sub quadrangular; the upper margin slightly indented for the reception of the second radials; second radials, six very small, semicircular, third radials, six small, cuneiform, axillary, supporting on their upper sloping sides two arms Anal piece similar in form but narrower than the first radials, and like them it supports a second and third radial and a pair of arms Arms twelve, composed at their bases of rather stout pieces nearly as long as wide, but growing shorter above, and giving off numerous *pinnulæ* to their extremities

*Position and locality* Crawfordsville, Indiana; from the shaly beds of the Keokuk Group, Lower Carboniferous.

## Genus BARYCRINUS, Wachsmuth

### Barycrinus striatus, Worthen.

Pl 29, Fig 5

Body rather large, broadly obconic and composed of massive plates. Basal series very small and almost entirely concealed in the columnar depression Subradials large, pentagonal ? nearly triangular in outline, the upper angle being a little longer than the laterals First radials nearly quadrangular, a little wider at the top than the length to the middle of the facet for the reception of the next range of radials. This facet is moderately concave, and sloping outward occupies about one-half the width of the first radial pieces. Anal piece large, a little longer than its greatest width, and rather more than half as large as the first radials. Surface ornamented with four or five prominent striæ that begin at the base and run parallel with the lateral borders of the subradials to their upper angles, and thence diverge to the centre of the facet on the upper margin of the first radials. A granulose structure is also observable on the remaining portion of the body plates These surface markings will serve to distinguish it from any other species of the genus at present known in the Lower Carboniferous limestone. Arms and column unknown.

*Position and locality:* Otter creek, Jersey county, Illinois; Keokuk limestone, Lower Carboniferous.

## Genus POTERIOCRINUS.

### Poteriocrinus Hoveyi, Worthen.

Pl 29, Fig 6

Body below the second radials obconical and tapering very gradually from the top of the first radials to the column. Base nearly twice as wide at the top as long, truncated below the breadth of the column; basal plates longer than wide, pentagonal in form, with salient angles above; subradials comparatively large, length and breadth about equal, and, so far as can be seen in the specimen under examination, hexagonal; first radial plates smaller than the subradials, pentagonal and truncated squarely across their upper margins for the reception of the next radial pieces; second radials a little longer than wide, rounded and slightly constricted in the middle, pentagonal, and supporting the arms on their superior sloping sides.

Arms very long, two to each ray in two of the rays seen, and one only in the other or anterior ray (as in *P. Coryi*), and composed of rather short, rounded, wedge-shaped pieces, and giving off long slender *pinnulæ* to their extremities Ventral tube very long, cylindrical, composed of rather large plates with short, stout spines at the summit. Column round and composed of rather thin plates at the base

*Position and locality:* Crawfordsville, Indiana, in shales of the Keokuk group, Lower Carboniferous.

I take pleasure in dedicating this fine species to Prof E O Hovey, of Wabash College, Crawfordsville, Indiana.

### Poteriocrinus Coreyi, Worthen.

Pl 29, Fig 2, 3

Body below the base of the arms rather deeply cup-shaped or truncato-obconic, basal plates small pentagonal, and projecting about half their length above the truncated base. Subradials moderately large, higher than wide and hexagonal First radials pentagonal and about once and a half as wide as high, rather smaller than the subradials, and four of them truncated their whole width for the reception of a second radial piece Second radials less than half as high as the first and rounded on the outside; third radials about as high as the first, four in number and giving support on their upper sloping angles to two arms that continue single to their extremities The middle ray on the anterior side gives off a single arm from the summit of the first radial piece, which, like the others, continues simple to its extremity First anal plate hexagonal, about as large as the subradials, upon the upper angles of which it rests, and supporting two smaller plates above, which are succeeded by others still smaller that extend up to the base of the ventral tube. Ventral tube composed of very small plates, and strongly inflated at the summit, with a well marked anal opening on its anterior side about half an inch above its lower extremity. The plates surrounding this opening form a prominent projecting rim, such as may be seen around this opening in the crinoids where it is located on the side of the body as in *Agaricocrinus Americanus*, and many others This character may also be seen more distinctly expressed in the example of *Scaphiocrinus unicus*, figure 1 of the same plate.

This species is nearly related to *P. Indianensis*, M and W., Vol. III, Geological Survey of Illinois, p 515, Pl. 20, fig 4, but differs from that in the form and proportion of its body plates, and in the number and arrangement of its arms.

*Position and locality* Crawfordsville, Indiana, in shales belonging to the Keokuk group, Lower Carboniferous.

This species is dedicated to Mr L W Corey, of Crawfordsville, Indiana, from whom the typical specimen was received For the specimen showing the ventral tube, I am indebted to Prof E O Hovey, of Wabash College

## Poteriocrinus Van Hornei, Worthen

Pl 31, Fig 2, 3

Body obconical below the arms, surface smooth, basal plates pentagonal as seen beyond the facet for the reception of the column, a little wider than long and uniting to form a shallow cup, subradials, three pentagonal and two hexagonal, length and breadth about equal; first radials nearly once and a half as wide as long, pentagonal and a little concave on their upper margins so as to leave a suture between that and the second radial plate; second radials on the anal side nearly twice as long as wide, strongly rounded and constricted in the middle and supporting the arms on their superior sloping angles Arms, two to each ray, as far as can be seen on our specimens, composed of smooth wedge formed pieces, and apparently continuing single to their extremities Anal plates, seven or eight visible, the two lowest less than half the size of the subradials, pentagonal, and resting on the upper mar gin of one of the irregular shaped subradials, those above are smaller and decrease in size upward Ventral tube long and apparently cylindrical (the apex is broken off in our specimen) and composed of small pentagonal plates, crenulated or indented on their margins, giving them a stellate appearance Column distinctly pentagonal at its junction with the base and for an inch below, which is as far as it can be seen in our specimens. This feature alone will serve to distinguish it from any other species known to us from this horizon.

*Position and locality:* Alton, Illinois, from the upper division of the St Louis group, Lower Carboniferous

Dedicated to my friend W. C VAN HORNE, Esq, to whom I am indebted for the use of one of the examples figured

### POTERIOCRINUS PROBOSCIDIALIS, Worthen.

Pl 31 Fig 1

Body below the base of the arms depressed obconical, base small, scarcely projecting beyond the circumference of the first columnar joints; basal pieces rather small, nearly twice as wide as high and forming a shallow cup Subradials, so far as they can be seen on the anal side, a little wider than long and hexagonal, first radial plates about once and a half as wide as high and pentagonal, second radials a little shorter than the first, quadrangular; third radials as long as the second, pentagonal, and supporting two arms on their superior sloping sides Anal plates, eight to ten visible, extending up and overlapping or merging into the ventral tube The two lowest ones are the largest and hexagonal, the succeeding ones growing smaller as far as they can be traced, and all pentagonal or hexagonal. Arms, two to each ray on the anal side, and they appear to bifurcate on the sixth or tenth plate, which is produced laterally into a short, stout spine Ventral tube nearly two inches long, and apparently a little inflated at its upper extremity, where it is surmounted by three or more short pointed spines. The surface of this organ is ornamented with longitudinal ridges, which seem to be dotted along their upper extremities with minute dimples or oval depressions, and are connected by oblique striæ, that give a beautiful cancellated appearance to its surface under a magnifier. Column round, and composed of alternating thin and moderately thick joints, the latter projecting a little beyond the others

*Position and locality:* Carondelet, Mo., in the upper division of the St Louis limestone, Lower Carboniferous.

## SUBGENUS SCAPHIOCRINUS, Hall.

### SCAPHIOCRINUS UNICUS.

Pl 29, Fig 1

*Scaphiocrinus unicus* HALL 1861 Prelim Descr New Crinoidea, p 8 *S unicus*, MEEK and WORTHEN, 1873, Geol Survey of Ill, Vol V, p 493, Pl 15, fig 5

"Body broadly cup shaped, with a deeply depressed base, somewhat abruptly spreading at the summit of the first radials Basal plates and lower ends of the subradials forming the bottom and sides of the cavity. Arms dividing on the second radial plate, each division bifurcating twice and rarely three times The anterior ray has a single arm, which is undivided throughout. This single arm is a strongly distinctive character."

The above is the original description of this species as published in 1861, and the figure of an unique specimen is introduced here, showing the full form of the ventral tube, with a well marked anal opening on its anterior side, situated about midway between the apex and base of this organ. The ventral tube is strongly inflated at the upper extremity, and is surmounted by three or more strongly pointed spines. So far as I am aware this and the *Poteriocrinus Coreyi* are the only examples of crinoidea yet discovered showing the position of the anal opening in the *Poteriocrinidæ*.

*Position and locality*: Crawfordsville, Ind, Keokuk group, Lower Carboniferous I am indebted to Prof E O HOVEY, of Wabash College, for this unique specimen.

### SCAPHIOCRINUS ABNORMIS, Worthen

Pl 31 Fig 6

Body truncato-obconic, basal plates small, and concealed in the columnar depression, subradials not well shown in our specimen, in which the body plates are somewhat distorted by pressure; two of the radial pieces longer than wide and hexagonal, the others about as wide as long and pentagonal, each giving support above to a second radial piece Second radials about as wide as long, constricted about the middle, and two of them supporting two arms on their upper sloping sides, which continue single as far as they can be seen On two of the other rays, and probably on all three of them, a single arm proceeds from their upper oblique margins, and not dividing, make but seven or eight arms altogether Arms composed of a single series of stout, wedge shaped pieces, giving off numerous *pinnulæ* from their inner margins, composed of rather stout, round pieces, two or three times as long as wide. The number and arrangement of the arms of this species, which suggested the specific name, will distinguish it from any other form at present known from this horizon

*Position and locality*. Monroe county, Illinois, in the upper division of the St. Louis group. Lower Carboniferous

## GENUS ONYCHOCRINUS, L. and C.

### ONYCHOCRINUS MAGNUS, Worthen

Pl 31, Fig 5

Body large, and composed of massive and apparently smooth plates Basal pieces small, and entirely concealed in the columnar depression. Subradials of unequal size, the two on the anal side much smaller than the others, and the three on the anterior side showing a pentagonal form beyond the columnar facet First radial pieces twice as wide as long, hexagonal and heptagonal, counting the slight angular depression on their upper margins, second, third and fourth radials nearly as wide and rather shorter than the first; fifth radials as long as the first, measuring to the top of their upper angles, and supporting on their upper sloping margins the first of a double series of secondary radials or brachial pieces, of which about 27 or 28 can be counted in each series on two of the rays, but gradually diminishing in size to their extremities, where they are no larger than their pinnulæ Each of the ten arms gives off on alternate sides from the third, fourth or fifth plate clusters of stout pinnulæ composed of plates similar to those of the arms, but gradually decreasing in size to their extremities. All the arm plates, as well as those of the pinnulæ, are angular below, the angle fitting into a depression in the subordinate plate. A single anal plate only is visible in our specimen, and by an oversight this is not represented in the drawing. It is small, about twice as long as wide, and apparently pentagonal Column round, comparatively large at its junction with the base, composed of very thin equal segments connecting by crenulated sutures, and decreasing in diameter nearly one half in the space of an inch below the base.

*Position and locality* · Monroe county, Illinois, in the upper division of the St Louis group. Lower Carboniferous.

## GENUS PENTREMITES, Say.

### PENTREMITES (TRICŒLOCRINUS) VARSOUVIENSIS, Worthen

Pl 31, Fig 8 and 9

Base strongly triangular, becoming pentagonal above, and a little more than half as long as the radial pieces. Radials rather narrow, elongate, borders nearly parallel, angulated below and flattened on the sides, and truncated for the reception of the interradial pieces. Interradials rather small, lanceolate, and reaching nearly or quite to the summit Pseudo ambulacral fields narrow, linear, and extending downwards less than half the length of the radial pieces, and each containing about sixty pore pieces arranged in a double row.

This species is closely allied to *P. lineatus*, Shum., from the Burlington limestone, but differs in its more triangular base, in the proportions of its principal pieces, and in the number of pore pieces in its pseudo-ambulacral fields.

*Position and locality* Warsaw, and Monroe county near Columbus, Illinois, in the Warsaw division of the St. Louis group Lower Carboniferous.

### PENTREMITES (TRICŒLOCRINUS) OBLIQUATUS, Rœmer, sp

Pl 31, Fig 4

*Pentatrematites obliquatus*, RŒMER, 1852, Monog Blast., p 47, Pl 3, fig 11

This species also occurs in the Warsaw division of the St. Louis group in Monroe county, Illinois, and not in the *Archimedes* beds of Randolph county, as cited by Rœmer

## GENUS SPIRIFER, Sowerby.

### SPIRIFER FASTIGATUS, M and W

Pl 30, Fig 3

*Spirifer fastigatus*, MEEK and WORTHEN 1870 Proceed Acad Nat Sci., Philad, p 36

Shell attaining a rather large size, moderately convex, very transverse, or distinctly more than twice as wide as long; greatest breadth on the hinge line, lateral extremities very attenuate and acutely pointed in young specimens, but becoming more obtuse in larger individuals. front and anterior lateral margins broadly and rather regularly rounded Dorsal valve nearly as convex as the ventral, beak depressed, somewhat incurved, and scarcely projecting beyond the hinge line; area of rather more than usual breadth for that of a dorsal valve, and arched with the beak; mesial fold commencing at the beak scarcely larger than one of the ribs on each side of it, but increasing gradually in breadth and prominence to the front, where it is occupied by about six to eight costæ, which, however, coalesce into one or two at the beak. Ventral valve regularly convex over the central region, and somewhat compressed toward the lateral extremities; mesial sinus commencing narrow and very small near the beak, and widening and deepening gradually to the front, where it is occupied by about eight depressed, rounded costæ, which, like those on the fold of the other valve, coalesce with those on each side and with each other, so as to leave but one that extends quite to the beak; beak rather depressed and not projecting much beyond the hinge line, arched or moderately incurved; area rather narrow, and extending, with almost perfectly parallel margins, quite out to the lateral extremities of the hinge, marked by the usual transverse and vertical striæ; foramen wider than high, rather large, and extending close up under the rather flattened apex of the beak.

Surface ornamented by depressed, rounded, bifurcating or trifid, more or less fasciculated costæ, about five or which, on each side of the mesial and sinus fold, are larger than the others, and divide before reaching the front so as to form as many fasciculi of two or three ribs each, the furrows between which are less strongly defined than those between the bundles. Toward the lateral extremities some eight or ten smaller, simple, obscure costæ, that do not reach the beaks, may also be counted on each side of each valve, gradually becoming obsolete near the ends. Crossing the whole, fine obscure, undulating striæ, and a few stronger marks of growth may be observed on well preserved specimens, the striæ, however, excepting near the front and lateral margins, not being readily seen without the aid of a magnifier.

Length about 1.15 inch, breadth 2.20 inches, convexity about 1.50 inch, hight of area at the beak .26 inch.

We have had specimens of this fine *Spirifer* under consideration for a long time, and after numerous careful comparisons we have been unable to identify it with any of the described species. It seems to be most nearly allied to our common Coal Measure species *S. cameratus*, of Morton, with which it agrees in the fasciculated character of its costæ, and in general appearance. It differs, however, in several characters by which it can be readily distinguished on comparison. In the first place, its larger fasciculated costæ are distinctly broader, and rather more depressed on the anterior slope of its valves, and proportionally less numerous. The incurved apex of the beak of its ventral valves is always less abruptly curved, and much more flattened. The most marked character, however, is to be observed in its cardinal area, which has its margins almost perfectly parallel, instead of being always sloping from the beak to the lateral extremities. The same characters and its narrow mesial fold and sinus distinguish it from the variety of *S. striatus* with somewhat fasciculated costæ. It belongs to the subgenus *Trigonotreta*.

*Position and locality*. Crawfordsville, Indiana, in the shales of the Keokuk group Lower Carboniferous.

### Spirifer neglectus, Hall.

Pl 30, Fig 2 a, and 1 c

*Spirifer neglectus*, Hall, 1858 Geol of Iowa, Vol I, Part 2, p 642, Pl 20, fig 5

"Shell transversely oval, gibbous, hinge line less than the greatest width, rounded at the extremities. Dorsal valve convex; mesial fold small at the beak, increasing rapidly towards the front, where it is very prominent, not plicated, beak a little elevated above the hinge, incurved Ventral valve a little more convex, elevated in the umbonal region, mesial sinus broad and deep, with one broad, faint plication in the middle, and indications of another on each side; umbo very gibbous, beak strongly arched, area high arcuate, its lateral margins rounding gradually on each side, foramen large, triangular, a little higher than wide

Surface marked by about six broad, depressed and rounded, simple plications on each side of the mesial fold and sinus, concentrically crossed by fine undulating striæ and a few stronger wrinkles of growth."

*Position and locality* Warsaw, Hamilton and Nauvoo, Illinois, and Keokuk, Iowa Keokuk limestone, Lower Carboniferous.

### Spirifer suborbicularis, Hall

Pl 30, Fig 1

*Spirifer suborbicularis*, Hall, 1858 Geol of Iowa, Vol I, Part 2, p 644

"Shell suborbicular, length and width nearly equal or somewhat wider than long, hinge line much shorter than the width of the shell; cardinal extremities regularly curved. Dorsal valve convex, gibbous above the middle, with the mesial fold becoming defined below the beak, and somewhat prominent at the base. Ventral valve convex, gibbous above the middle, with elevated umbo and beak abruptly incurved over a narrow area, which in length is about equal to half the width of the shell, foramen with the dental lamellæ projecting, and partially closed by pseudo deltidium

Surface marked by broad, flattened, scarcely defined plications, of which there are seven or eight on each side of the mesial fold and sinus, with two or three more faintly defined on these parts of the shell, and some appearance of a small plication in the center of the sinus."

*Position and locality*: Warsaw, Hamilton, Nauvoo, Niota, and various other places in Illinois, and Keokuk, Iowa. Keokuk limestone, Lower Carboniferous.

## GENUS MYALINA, deKoninck.

### MYALINA KEOKUK, Worthen.

Pl 30, Fig 5

Shell of medium size, subquadrate, about once and a half as high as wide, rather oblique, hinge nearly straight and as long as the greatest breadth of the valves below; anterior side a little sinuate, posterior side compressed towards the margin, sinuate or deflected inwards immediately below the hinge and rounding into the base below, beak of the left valve pointed, projecting beyond the hinge and curving forward and inward. Surface marked by distinct, rather irregular laminæ, of which five or six may be counted in the space of half an inch

Length of an average sized specimen, 2.2 inches; breadth, 1 25 inch, convexity of left valve, about 0 37 inch

*Position and locality* Keokuk, Iowa, and Warsaw, Nauvoo and Hamilton, Illinois, Keokuk limestone, Lower Carboniferous

## GENUS PINNA, Linn.

### PINNA SUBSPATULATA, Worthen

Pl 30 Fig 4

This shell is only known from casts of single valves which do not admit of a minute description. It is above the medium size, the specimens seen usually ranging from 8 to 10 inches in length, by 1½ in breadth at the posterior end Valves very gradually tapering, sides apparently flattened towards the posterior end, which seems to have been obliquely rounded, judging from the lines of growth to be seen on the surface of the cast Cardinal margin slightly thickened with a rather well defined cardinal ridge at the edge. Surface markings unknown

In general form it resembles *P spatula* of McCoy, from the Carboniferous limestones of Derbyshire, but ours is a larger shell than the European species, and rather wider in proportion to its length.

*Position and locality* Quite rare in the Keokuk limestone, at Keokuk, Iowa, and Warsaw, Illinois A single example of apparently the same species, has been found in the Warsaw division of the St. Louis Group, at Warsaw, Illinois.

# COAL MEASURE SPECIES

## Genus AXOPHYLLUM, Edwards and Haime

### Axophyllum rudis, White and St John.

Pl 32, Fig 6, a, b, c

"Coral irregularly turbinate, contorted, often attached along a great portion of its length, usually expanding rapidly, surface marked by irregular concentric undulations of growth, and often also by numerous rootlets, some of which clasp the objects to which they may be attached. Outer portion of the calyx shallow, central portion rather deep, columella small, flattened, the greater diameter being from the concave to the convex side"

The above is the original description of this species by the authors cited above, as published in the Trans of the Chicago Acad of Sciences, Vol. I, p 117, and agrees very well with the Illinois specimens illustrated on Pl. 32, fig. 6.

*Position and locality* Near Collinsville, St. Clair county, Illinois, from a calcareous shale 117 feet above the Belleville coal

### Axophyllum infundibulum, Worthen

Pl 32, Fig 7

Coral turbinate, sometimes showing indications of attachment at the lower extremity, epitheca thin, and showing on its surface numerous undulations of growth, the young individuals originating at the bottom of the calyx, and the old examples presenting the appearance of a series of deep cups placed one within the other Septa about 40 Columella nearly obsolete in some examples, and much less strongly defined than in *A rudis*

*Position and locality*. Clark county, Illinois, about the horizon of coal No 12

## GENUS CYATHOXONIA, Michelin

### CYATHOXONIA DISTORTA, Worthen.

Pl 32, Fig 4

Coral small, cylindrical, more or less distorted and gradually tapering at the lower extremity, where, in some examples, it shows the bases of several small spines or rootlets; surface showing numerous distinct longitudinal striæ, crossed by rather indistinct wrinkles of growth. Calice circular, rather deep, with a small columella visible in one of our specimens. Septa 22 to 24 or more

*Position and locality* Cumberland county, Illinois Rare in the limestone over coal No. 16, associated with *Fusulina cylindrica*, etc.

## GENUS CHÆTETES, Fischer.

### CHÆTETES ? CARBONARIA, Worthen.

Pl 32, Fig 5

Coral cylindrical or ramose, calices rather unequally developed. *corallites* small and radiating from the center with closely arranged *tabulæ*.

We refer this form to the genus *Chætetes* with hesitation in view of its rather undefined characters, but as the species illustrated is a well marked form in the Coal Measures, it seems desirable that it should have some designation

*Position and locality:* St. Clair county, Illinois, in the calcareous shales over the Belleville coal.

### POTERIOCRINUS LASALLENSIS, Worthen.

Pl 32, Fig 3

Body below the base of the arms obconic, very gradually tapering to the middle of the subradials and more rapidly below; base small, truncated for the reception of the columnar facet, and about twice as wide as high; subradials of moderate size, length and breadth nearly equal, three hexagonal and two heptagonal, first radials about once and a half as wide as high, pentagonal, first anal plate smaller than the sub radials between the upper angles of which it rests, pentagonal, second anal plate longer than wide, hexagonal, and resting on the upper truncated margin of a subradial; third anal plate rather wider than long, hexagonal or heptagonal, and resting on the upper truncated margin of the first anal piece All the body plates are depressed at the angles, giving it a pentalobate character somewhat like *Barycrinus pentagonus* of the Keokuk limestone

*Position and locality* LaSalle, Illinois; Upper Coal Measures

## Genus EUPACHYCRINUS, Meek and Worthen.

### Eupachycrinus Craigii, Worthen.

Pl 32 Fig 1

Body subhemispherical below the summit of the first radial pieces, composed of rather thick smooth plates, with a moderately deep concavity on the under side Basal plates small and concealed in the basal depression, subradials rather large, the form of some of them not shown in our specimen from its slightly distorted condition, but four of them are probably hexagonal and one heptagonal, with their superior angles projecting upwards about two thirds the length of the first radial pieces, and strongly incurved below. First radials twice as wide as high, pentagonal, and beveled on their upper margins so as to leave a well defined suture between them and the second radial pieces Second radials as wide as the first below, but gradually narrowing upwards, and produced laterally into short stout spines, and supporting on their upper truncated margins two stout brachial pieces that give origin to two arms to each ray Arms commencing with a single series, but changing on the second or third piece to a double series of rather short stout interlocking pieces, that are at first more than twice as wide as high, but gradually diminishing in width towards their upper extremities One very small anal piece only is partly visible. Column unknown.

The basal portion of this species might be mistaken for Shumard's *Scaph ? hemisphericus* but it differs from that in its more massive body plates, and the more triangular form of the upper portion of its subradials From *Eupach Fayettensis* it may be distinguished by its larger size, more robust form and less convex body plates

*Position and locality* Vandalia coal shaft, from a bed of black argillaceous shaly limestone at the depth of about 230 feet, and probably near the horizon of No 10 coal

Dedicated to Mr. R. M. Craig, of Vandalia, to whom I am indebted for the use of the unique specimen figured.

### EUPACHYCRINUS BASSETTI, Worthen

Pl 32, Fig 2.

Body large, sub-hemispherical, width about once and a half as much as the hight. Base small, depressed, with the basal plates hidden by the columnar facet. Subradials large, hexagonal so far as can be seen from the examples under examination, length and breadth nearly equal, and curving into the basal concavity below First radials about once and a half as wide as high, pentagonal, second radials as wide as the first, less than half as high, except one on the anal side, which is about three fourths the hight of the first radial on which it rests, and more decidedly pentagonal than the others, and all supporting on their margins two nearly quadrangular brachial pieces that support the arms. One anal plate only is visible, about twice as high as wide, apparently hexagonal, resting partly on two of the subradials, and extending upward nearly or quite as high as the upper lateral angles of the second radials, and curved inwardly at its upper extremity. Arms, four on the two posterior rays, and apparently but two on the others, though the anterior side is but partially seen in our specimens, composed of rather short stout plates, the first ones single, but soon merging into a double series of short interlocking pieces, that decrease very gradually in width towards the upper extremities of the arms The entire surface of the body and arms ornamented with numerous irregularly disposed wart-like prominences, giving to it a very strongly marked verrucose appearance.

Column slender, and composed of round alternating thin and thicker joints, the latter a little projecting, with numerous lateral appendages, or side arms, composed of small, rather thick round joints, connected by strongly crenulated sutures

This species is nearly related to the one described by Messrs WHITE and ST JOHN, in the Trans. Chicago Acad. Sci. Vol. I, page 117, under the name *Hydreinocrinus? verrucosus*, but differs from that in its more robust form, in not having the margins of its body plates beveled, in the form of its anal plate, and in its somewhat different style of ornamentation.

*Position and locality* Same as the last. Dedicated to Dr. G. W. BASSETT, of Vandalia, to whom I am indebted for the use of one of the examples figured, as well as for liberal contributions of interesting fossils from Fayette county, and for many acts of personal kindness and attention

## GENUS CONOCARDIUM, Bronn

### CONOCARDIUM OBLIQUUM, M and W.

Pl 33, Fig 4

*Conocardium obliquum* MEEK and WORTHEN, 1865 Proceed Acad Nat Sci, Philad, page 249

Shell rather small, obliquely subtrigonal, gibbous, anterior side (posterior of Woodward) very obliquely and abruptly truncated with a forward slope, and flattened so as to present a regular cordate outline in a front view, anterior auricle narrow, but of unknown length, base very short, posterior margin sloping up from the base so as to intersect the hinge at an angle of about 15°, rather widely gaping, and crenate its entire length. Beaks moderately prominent, small, strongly incurved; umbonal slopes very prominent, angular, and directed obliquely forward to the angular anterior basal extremity. Surface ornamented with rather sharply elevated, thread-like, subcrenate radiating ribs, narrower than the depressions between, each of these depressions on the posterior and flattened anterior sides of the valves occupied by a smaller intermediate rib; entire surface also marked by fine very regular radiating and concentric striæ, so as to produce a neat, minutely cancellated sculpturing, as seen under a magnifier.

Length from the posterior extremity to the produced antero basal angle, 0 70 inch, hight from the latter to the beaks, 0 50 inch; length from the beaks to the posterior extremity, 0 37 inch; convexity, 0 44 inch, breadth of posterior hiatus, 0.17 inch.

We know of no other species liable to be confounded with this Its most marked features are the great backward obliquity of its umbonal axis, by which its beaks are placed even a little behind the middle of the body part of the shell, and the beautiful regular cancellated style of ornament seen between the ribs, under a magnifier.

*Position and locality*. Coal Measures; Wabash cut off, Posey county, Indiana.

## GENUS PLEUROPHORUS? King.

### PLEUROPHORUS? ANGULATUS, M. and W

Pl 33, Fig 5

*Pleurophorus? angulatus*, MEEK and WORTHEN, 1865 Proceed Acad Nat. Sci, Philad, page 247

Shell oblong, about twice and a half as long as high, rather convex; cardinal and ventral margins straight and parallel, or the latter very faintly sinuous along the middle; posterior side (which is a little imperfect in our specimen,) apparently obliquely truncated above, and very narrowly rounded below, anterior side very short, sloping abruptly from the beaks above, and abruptly rounded beneath; hinge line very straight, rather long, but shorter than the base Beaks depressed upon a line with the dorsal outline, and located very near the anterior margin, umbonal ridge prominent and distinctly angular from the beaks to the posterior basal extremity Surface of internal cast, showing faint traces of two or three distant, very obscure, concentric ridges, or undulations

Length 0.52 inch, hight 0 20 inch, convexity 0 16 inch.

The most marked peculiarities of this species are its oblong form, straight and parallel cardinal and ventral margins, and distinctly angular umbonal ridge Its anterior muscular impression seems not to be as distinct as usual in the genus *Pleurophorus*, but this may be due to a defect in our specimen, which is an internal cast. All we know of the hinge is an impression of a long, linear posterior lateral tooth, parallel to the cardinal margin, and most distinct behind. This tooth appears to have been double in the left valve, for the reception of a similar elongated tooth in the right.

*Position and locality* Wabash cut off, near New Harmony, Indiana; Upper Coal Measures

## GENUS CARBONARCA, Meek and Worthen.

Genus *Carbonarca*, MEEK and WORTHEN, 1870 Proc Acad Nat Sci, Philad, page 39

Shell (as determined from internal casts) equivalve, inequilateral, very convex, transversely oblong or oval; umbones gibbous, prominent, and strongly incurved with subangular or prominent posterior slopes; valves closed all around, with smooth margins, ligament external, cardinal margin a little arched, with, at the anterior extremity in each valve, two rather oblique comparatively stout teeth, and extending along its entire length from immediately behind these, a row of minute, interlocking teeth or crenulations, as in *Arca*

This genus seems to belong to the *Arcidæ*, near *Isoarca*. It differs, however, very decidedly from that genus, in having, in addition to the small interlocking crenulations along the whole length of the hinge, two well developed and independent larger teeth at the anterior end of the hinge. The specimens seen are all internal casts, but an impression of the hinge of a right valve, in the matrix, shows its characters very clearly There is no gradation from the series of minute teeth into the two large ones at the anterior end of the hinge, the first of the smaller series immediately behind the two larger ones being as minute as any of those farther back, so that the contrast between the two sets of teeth is well marked and abrupt The hinge margin was doubtless provided with a cardinal area, but as we only have internal casts, it has not yet been seen.

### CARBONARCA GIBBOSA, M. and W.

Pl 33, Fig 6

*Carbonarca gibbosa*, MEEK and WORTHEN, 1876 Proceed Acad Nat Sci, Phila, p 10

Shell transverse, short-oblong, very convex, posterior side wider than the other, and vertically subtruncated; anterior margin rather narrowly rounded; ventral margin nearly straight along the middle, but sloping and rounded up anteriorly, and more abruptly behind, cardinal edge equaling two thirds of the whole length; larger anterior teeth inclined forward and upward, and those of the small series ranging nearly vertically, or slightly inclined forward anteriorly, and a little backward behind; umbones gibbous, but with their outer and upper surfaces a little flattened, so as to impart a slightly subangular or prominent character to the post umbonal slopes; immediate *apices* of the strongly inclined beaks placed about one fourth the entire length of the shell behind the anterior extremity Surface markings unknown

Length 0 82 inch, hight to top of cardinal margin (of cast) behind the beaks 0 56 inch, hight to top of the umbones 0 65; convexity of the two valves 0 57 inch.

*Position and locality:* Springfield and LaSalle, Illinois, Upper Coal Measures. The specimens from the latter locality are, in some examples, more depressed and oblique than the typical form from near Springfield, and these may possibly belong to a distinct species, if the differences noted are not due to accidental distortion If really distinct, this form might be called *C. depressa*.

## GENUS NAUTILUS, Linnæus.

### NAUTILUS (DISCITES) HIGHLANDENSIS, Worthen

Pl 33, Fig 2

Shell of medium size, discoid, compressed; whorls about three, contiguous, nearly flat on the sides, the greatest convexity being near the inner margin, which is gently rounded. Septa rather closely arranged, crossing the sides with a graceful backward curve, and also curving backward on the narrow truncated periphery. Last or body chamber long and proportionally broad, forming about half the outer volution. Surface markings and siphuncle unknown

This shell in general form resembles *Nautilus (Discites) disciformis*, M. and W., from the Keokuk limestone, but differs from that in its much smaller size, (none of the specimens seen attaining a diameter of more than 3 50 inches,) and by its proportionally broader outer chamber.

*Position and locality:* LaSalle, Illinois, and near Highland, in Madison county, where it is found in the Shoal creek limestone above coal No. 9 I am indebted to Mr AD F. BANDELIER, of Highland, for the use of the example figured.

## NAUTILUS (CRYPTOCERAS) CAPAX, M. and W.

Pl 33 Fig 1

*Nautilus Cryptoceras) capax*, MEEK and WORTHEN, 1865 Proceed Acad Nat Sci, Phila., p 262.

Shell attaining a moderately large size, subglobose in form Umbilicus deep, with abruptly sloping walls—one third as wide as the dorso-ventral diameter of the outer whorl, and showing each of the inner turns Whorls about two and half, increasing rapidly in size, particularly in transverse breadth; last one so expanded laterally as to be apparently one-third to one-half wider than its dorso-ventral diameter; inner ones proportionally narrower All broadly rounded on the outer side, and more narrowly rounded with a flattened or slightly concave revolving space between a ridge bounding the umbilicus and the middle of each side; each provided with a narrow, shallow impression along the ventral side for the reception of the inner volutions Septa separated by spaces which measure on the outer side less than one-fourth the dorso ventral diameter of the volution at the point of measurement a little arched backwards on the slightly concave inner side of the whorls, and less distinctly so on the narrow revolving flattened space just outside of the umbilicus, after which they cross over the broadly rounded outer side, with a very low scarcely perceptible backward curve Aperture transversely oval, or subelliptic, and apparently angular, and effuse at each inner lateral margin Outer chamber very capacious, composing less than half a volution.

Greatest diameter across the disc about 7 inches; breadth (transverse diameter of the aperture) 6 inches; dorso ventral diameter 3 25 inches, breadth of umbilicus 1 inch.

The only specimen of this species we have seen is a cast, which shows along the outer side of the whorls the appearance of a tube 0 20 inch in diameter, extending backwards from each septum. It is possible this may be a small lobe of the septa, but we have scarcely a doubt in regard to its being the siphon, and hence that the species belongs to the group *Cryptoceras*.

Compared with *N dorsalis*, Phillips, (Geol Yorks II, Pl 13, fig. 1 and 2,) the type of the group *Cryptoceras*, our shell will be found to differ in its much more broadly rounded dorsum, and much wider mouth, as well as in the peculiar revolving flattened space near the umbilical side of the whorls, which imparts a slight angularity to the margin of the umbilicus, as well as an undefined longitudinal ridge or prominence near the middle of the whorls on each side

*Position and locality* Charboniere, Missouri Coal Measures

# INDEX.

# ERRATA.

---

Page 30—18th line from bottom, for "pawpaw" read "papaw"
Page 32—15th line from top for "limstone" read "limestone"
Page 63—12th line from bottom for "coats" read "coals"
Page 92—10th line from top for "*occidentalus*" read "*occidentalis*"
Page 151—2d line from bottom and 16th from top, for "*Machrocheilus*" read "*Macrocheilus*"
Page 203—13th line from top for "*carbonaris*" read "*carbonarius*"
Page 247—6th line from bottom for "horizon" read "horizons"
Page 249—12th line from top, for "in faunal facies" read "in their faunal facies"
Page 251—11th line from bottom for "burled" read "beveled"
Page 252—9th line from bottom, for "bevelled" read "beveled"
Page 254—21st line from bottom, for "sharp curved" read "sharp crested"
Page 255—21st line from top, for "our own" read "our"
Page 255—7th line from bottom for "inverted" read "inbeveled"
Page 256—20th line from top for "denticular" read "denticulate"
Page 261—6th line from top for "expressed" read "preserved"
Page 262—9th line from bottom for "wth" read "with"
Page 267—12th line from bottom for "teeth" read "tooth"
Page 268—15th line from bottom for "fragmentory" read "fragmentary"
Page 270—2d line from bottom for "represetation" read "representative"
Page 271—2d line from bottom, for "form" read "four"
Page 281—17th line from top for "forms" read "form"
Page 282—15th line from top for "beeled" read "keeled"
Page 284—15th line from bottom, for "clearly" read "closely"
Page 283—8th line from top, for "*Lambdodus hamulus*" read "*L. hamatus*," and same on page 424 6th line from top
Page 283—14th line from bottom, for "were" read "was"
Page 289—8th line from bottom, for "crust" read "crest"
Page 290—17th line from bottom, for "one" read "an"
Page 291—20th line from bottom, add "Pl VI, Fig 9"
Page 292—16th line from top, for "found" read "formed"
Page 299—7th line from top, for "*Actobatis*" read "*Aetobatis*"
Page 326—16th line from top, for "set" read "sets"
Page 329—7th line from bottom, "edeutalous" read "edentulous"
Page 347—21st line from bottom, for "striking" read "skirting"
Page 350—16th line from bottom, for "disturbed" read "distended"
Page 351—13th line from bottom for "and from Warsaw" read "and not from Warsaw"
Page 354—4th line from bottom, for "collection" read "collections"
Page 360—10th line from top for "more" read "never"
Page 360—12th line from bottom for "vertical" read "varietal"
Page 362—7th line from bottom, for "have" read "has"
Page 363—7th line from top for "organization" read "acquisition"
Page 369—18th line from top, for "congenus" read "congeners"
Page 376—15th line from top, for "from" read "form"
Page 377—10th line from bottom for "after" read "often"
Page 379—6th line from bottom, for "these" read "those"
Page 383—3d line from top for "indications" read "imbrications"
Page 385—12th line from bottom, for "Pl XI" read "Pl X A"
Page 389—6th line from top, for "Pl XIII, fig 1," read "Pl XIII, fig 10"
Page 393—12th line from bottom, for "worn" read "more"

# ERRATA.

Page 398—10th line from top, for "three more or less imbricated" read "three more or less, imbricated "

Page 401—19th line from bottom, omit comma between "angle" and 'about "

Page 404—10th line from top, for 'polish" read "polished '

Page 408—13th line from bottom, for "lightly" read "slightly "

Page 411—18th line from bottom for ' which ' read while '

Page 413—1st line from top, for "greatly' read ' gently '

Page 415—3d line from top, for concave ' read ' clavate

Page 416—15th line from top for *Petalodus* read ' *Peltodus* '

Page 417—9th line from bottom, for Pl XIV ' read ' Pl XIII "

Page 426—16th line from top, semi colon after ' position '

Page 426—6th line from bottom, for ' border ' read borders '

Page 427—2d line from top for ' faces read face '

Page 428—13th line from bottom for LeGrande' read 'Lagrange

Page 430—11th line from top for "fragments" read ' fragment '

Page 432—1st line from top, for ' *angularis*" read ' *angulatus* '

Page 435—8th line from bottom for narrower read narrow '

Page 441—12th and 11th lines from bottom for '*Astracanthus*' read '*Asteracanthus*" and ' *Asteracantha*

Page 448—6th line from bottom for ' form ' read from

Page 455—5th line from bottom, for ' external ' read internal

Page 456—17th line from top for forms" read 'form '

Page 459—13th line from bottom for 'differ' read differs "

Page 462—13th line from top for ' 1 a" read ' 4 a '

Page 464—17th line from bottom, for ' truncated read interrupted

Page 465—3d line from top for bifurcates ' read bifurcate

Page 465—6th line from bottom for 'face ' read faces

Page 468—2d line from bottom for trouvis read ' trouves

Page 471—18th line from top for 'Pl XXII" read "Pl XXI

Page 473—18th line from top for ' small" read smooth

Page 474—7th line from top, for beneath ' read between

Page 479—4th line from top for 'transvere read ' transverse

Page 479—4th line from bottom for ' thin read "three

Page 484—9th line from top for "*plicatilus* read "*plicatilis*

Page 495—12th line from top for "tho" read the

# PLATE I.

| | | | PAGE |
|---|---|---|---|
| Fig | 1-6 | CLADODUS EXILIS St. J. and W. | 258 |
| | 1 *a* | Outline of minute tooth. 1 *b*, view of outer face enlarged, showing two lateral denticles on one extremity and three in the opposite. 1 *c*, base from below, 1 *d*, profile section. Lower fish bed, Kinderhook. | |
| | 2 *a* | Outline of slightly larger tooth, with three lateral denticles on either side. 2 *b*, outer surface enlarged. 2 *c*, base from below. 2 *d*, profile section. Same horizon. | |
| | 3 *a* | Outline of medium sized, robust tooth. 3 *b*, view of outer face enlarged, 3 *c*, posterior face. 3 *d*, inferior basal surface. 3 *e*, profile section. Upper fish bed, Kinderhook. | |
| | 4 *a* | Outline of small worn tooth with two lateral cones on either side, 4 *b*, outer face enlarged. 4 *c*, posterior face. 4 *d e*, base from below, and profile section and transverse section of median cusp. Same horizon. | |
| | 5 *a* | Front view of small perfect tooth, enlarged. 5 *b c*, inferior basal surface and profile section. Same horizon. | |
| | 6 *a* | Outline of imperfect tooth of large size. 6 *b c*, outer and posterior faces enlarged, 6 *d e*, base from below and profile section. Same horizon. | |
| Fig | 7 | [illegible] St. J. and W. | 255 |
| | 7 *a* | Outline nat. size. 7 *b*, view of outer face enlarged. 7 *c*, inferior basal surface. 7 *d*, profile section and transverse section of median cone. Lower fish bed, Kinderhook. | |
| Fig | 8-11 | [illegible] St. J. and W. | 256 |
| | 8 *a* | Outer face of large tooth enlarged three diameters. 8 *b*, inferior basal surface, showing worn protuberances in front and median foramen in posterior margin. Upper fish bed, Kinderhook. | |
| | 9 *a* | Front view of smaller specimen enlarged two diameters. 9 *b*, posterior face showing broad convexity of upper basal surface. 9 *c*, inferior basal surface, showing pad like prominences in front less worn than in the preceding example, 9 *d*, profile section. Lower fish bed, Kinderhook. | |
| | 10 *a* | Outline of small tooth showing antero-inferior basal prominences. 10 *b*, front view enlarged. Same horizon. | |
| | 11 *a* | Anterior view of minute tooth enlarged. 11 *b*, posterior face. 11 *c*, base from below, showing [illegible] protuberances. Same horizon. | |
| Fig | 12-13 | [illegible] St. J. and W. | 252 |
| | 12 *a* | View of outer face of large tooth, enlarged. 12 *b*, posterior aspect. 12 *c*, profile and transverse sections of median cusp. Middle Devonian, Waterloo, Iowa. | |
| | 13 *a* | Front view of [illegible] nearly perfect tooth, enlarged. 13 *b*, posterior face, 13 *c*, inferior basal surface [illegible] profile section. Same horizon and locality. | |
| Fig | 14 | [illegible] St. J. and W. | 251 |
| | 14 *a* | View of anterior face of large tooth enlarged. 14 *b*, posterior face, showing well defined median prominence of superior basal surface, 14 *c*, inferior basal surface, 14 *d*, profile section. Middle Devonian, Waterloo, Iowa. | |

# GEOLOGICAL SURVEY OF ILLINOIS

FOSSIL-FISHES. (Devonian & Carb.) CLADODONTS.

A. H. Worthen, direxit. J. Mayer & Co., lith., Boston.

# PLATE II

| | | PAGE |
|---|---|---|
| Fig 1-13 | CLADODUS SPRINGERI St J and W | 259 |

1 *a* Outline of small tooth nat size 1 *b* outer face, enlarged two diameters, 1 *c*, base from below 1 *d* profile section Lower fish bed Kinderhook

2 *a* Outline of little larger tooth 2 *b c d* view of outer face inferior basal surface, and profile section enlarged two diameters Same horizon

3 *a* Outline of still larger specimen 3 *b, c* views of outer face and inferior basal surface, enlarged two diameters Same horizon

4 *a* View of outer face of large tooth, 4 *b* posterior face enlarged, 4 *c*, profile view, enlarged 4 *d* inferior basal surface Same horizon

5 *a* View of outer face of medium sized tooth enlarged 5 *b, c*, inferior basal surface and profile section nat size Same horizon

6 *a* Anterior face of medium sized, worn tooth, the two large lateral denticles alone remain, 6 *b* posterior face, 6 *c*, showing the worn inferior basal surface 6 *d*, profile section Same horizon

7 *a* View of outer face of slightly smaller tooth exhibiting other features due to attrition 7 *b*, base from below Same horizon

8 *a* Outer face of minute tooth much worn enlarged four diameters 8 *b, c*, inferior basal surface, profile section and transverse section of median cone Same horizon

9 *a* Outer face of very small, worn tooth, enlarged four diameters, 9 *b*, base from below Same horizon

10 *a* Outer face of minute tooth in which only one lateral denticle remains on one extremity and two on the opposite enlarged four diameters, 10 *b*, base from below Same horizon

11 *a* Outer face of an abnormally developed tooth enlarged one half 11 *b*, posterior face showing the contracted prominence of upper basal surface, 11 *c*, view of base from below Same horizon

12 *a* Outer face of minute perfect tooth enlarged four diameters 12 *b c d* posterior face inferior basal surface and profile section Same horizon

13 *a* View of outer face of small perfect tooth, showing excessive development of accessory denticles at base of crown enlarged three diameters 13 *b, c*, base from below and profile section Same horizon

| | | |
|---|---|---|
| Fig 14-18 | CLADODUS ALTERNATUS St J and W | 265 |

14 *a* Outline nat size 14 *b*, outer surface enlarged three diameters 14 *c d* inferior basal surface, and profile section nat size Lower fish bed Kinderhook

15 *a* Outline of little more robust tooth 15 *b c d e* views of outer posterior, and inferior basal aspects and profile section, enlarged three diameters Same horizon

16 *a* Outline of smaller tooth 16 *b* outer face, enlarged three diameters, 16 *c*, base from below 16 *d* profile section Upper fish bed Kinderhook

17 *a* Outline of very small tooth 17 *b c, d* views of outer face inferior basal surface, and profile section enlarged three diameters Lower fish bed Kinderhook

18 *a* View of outer face of medium sized tooth enlarged four diameters, partial restoration outline from tooth from upper fish bed coronal ornamentation from specimen from lower fish bed of the Kinderhook

# GEOLOGICAL SURVEY OF ILLINOIS

FOSSIL FISHES.

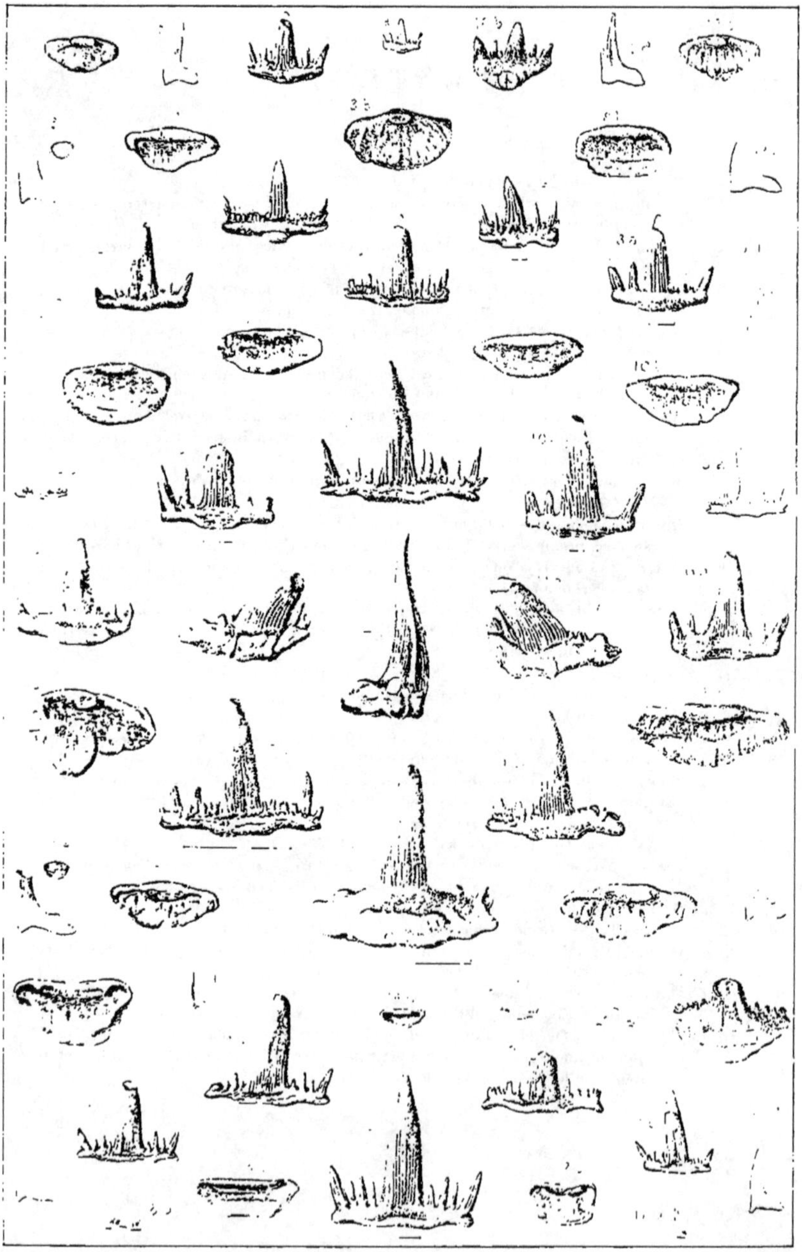

# PLATE III.

PAGE

Fig 1-7. CLADODUS WACHSMUTHI, St J and W. .. . 263

1 *a* View of outer face of tooth, 1 *b*, base from below, showing scarcely defined bosses in front, 1 *c* profile section. Upper fish bed Kinderhook

2 *a* Outer face of slightly smaller tooth, 2 *b* posterior face, showing superior basal region, 2 *c* inferior basal surface showing bilobed character of outer basal ridge, 2 *d*, profile and transverse sections of median cone. Same horizon

3 *a* Outer face of medium sized, perfect tooth, 3 *b* base from below, 3 *c* profile and transverse sections of median cusp. Same horizon

4 *a* View of outer face of large tooth. Same horizon

5 *a* Posterior aspect of medium sized tooth. Same horizon

6 *a* Outline of outer face of small tooth, 6 *b*, posterior face, 6 *c*, inferior basal surface. Same horizon

7 *a* Outline of outer face of very small tooth. Same horizon

Fig 8-12. CLADODUS SUCCINCTUS, St J and W. 265

8 *a* Outer face of medium sized, normal specimen, enlarged, 8 *b*, inferior basal surface, nat size, 8 *c*, profile section. Upper fish bed Kinderhook

9 *a* Outer face of slightly smaller tooth, showing absence of accessory processes at base of median cone, enlarged, 9 *b*, posterior face, 9 *c*, inferior basal surface, 9 *d*, profile and transverse section of median cone. Same horizon

10 *a* Outline of outer face, 10 *b* outer face enlarged, 10 *c* base from below, 10 *d* profile section. Same horizon

11 *a* Median cone of small tooth enlarged two diameters, showing ornamentation of posterior face, 11 *b* showing the outer face, 11 *c* profile view. Same horizon

12 *a* Outer face of large tooth, enamel layer partially exfoliated, 12 *b* posterior face, 12 *c*, base from below, showing constriction in outer basal ridge giving rise to pad like prominences at either extremity, 12 *d* profile section. Same horizon

Fig 13-15. CLADODUS EXIGUUS, St J and W. . 261

13 *a* Outline of outer face of medium sized tooth, 13 *b*, the same, enlarged two diameters, 13 *c*, inferior basal surface, 13 *d* profile section. Lower fish bed Kinderhook

14 *a* Outer face of smaller tooth, enlarged two diameters, 14 *b*, inferior basal surface showing faint bilobed condition of outer basal ridge, 14 *c*, profile section. Same horizon

15 *a* View of outer face of an abnormally developed tooth, enlarged two diameters, 15 *b*, base from below, 15 *c*, profile section. Same horizon

# GEOLOGICAL SURVEY OF ILLINOIS

FOSSIL FISHES. CLADODI.

# PLATE IV

| | | PAGE |
|---|---|---|
| 1-3 | CLADODUS LECYTHIFERUS, St. J. and W. . . . | 274 |
| 1 *a* | View of anterior face of minute tooth enlarged; 1 *b*, base from below. St. Louis limestone; Alton, Illinois. | |
| 2 *a* | Outer face of medium sized tooth, enlarged; 2 *b*, view of base from below. Same horizon; St. Louis, Missouri. | |
| 3 *a* | Outer face of large tooth enlarged two diameters; 3 *b*, view of posterior face; 3 *c*, base from below; 3 *d*, profile section. St. Louis beds; Pella, Iowa. | |
| 4 | CLADODUS ECCENTRICUS, St. J. and W. | 272 |
| 4 *a* | View of outer face of medium sized tooth enlarged two diameters; 4 *b*, inferior basal surface; 4 *c*, profile section. St. Louis limestone; St. Louis, Missouri. | |
| 5 | CLADODUS VAN HORNEI, St. J. and W. | 273 |
| 5 *a* | Outer face of medium sized perfect tooth; 5 *b*, posterior face; 5 *c*, inferior basal surface; 5 *d*, profile section. St. Louis limestone; Alton, Illinois. | |
| 6, 7. | CLADODUS CARINATUS, St. J. and W. . | 279 |
| 6 *a* | View of outer face of minute tooth enlarged; 6 *b*, base from below; 6 *c*, profile section. Middle Coal Measures; Guthrie county, Iowa. | |
| 7 *a* | Outer face of large symmetrical tooth enlarged; 7 *b*, outline of base from below. Coal Measures; Girard, Illinois. | |
| 8 | CLADODUS [illegible], St. J. and W. | 278 |
| 8 *a* | View of outer face enlarged four diameters; 8 *b*, postero superior basal aspect; 8 *c*, inferior basal surface; 8 *d*, profile section. Coal Measures; Carlinville, Illinois. | |
| 9 | CLADODUS FULLERI, St. J. and W. | 276 |
| 9 *a* | Outer face of minute tooth probably referable to this species enlarged four diameters; 9 *b*, posterior face; 9 *c*, base from below; 9 *d*, profile section. Middle Coal Measures; Iowa. | |
| 10 | CLADODUS [illegible], St. J. and W. | 270 |
| 10 *a* | View of outer face of large tooth; 10 *b*, posterior face; 10 *c*, profile view; 10 *d*, base from below. Upper Burlington limestone; Louisa county, Iowa. | |
| 11 | CLADODUS INTERCOSTATUS, St. J. and W. | 267 |
| 11 *a* | Outer face of tooth enlarged two diameters; 11 *b*, posterior face; 11 *c*, base from below; 11 *d*, profile section. Upper Burlington; Louisa county, Iowa. | |
| 12-16 | CLADODUS [illegible], St. J. and W. | 269 |
| 12 *a* | Outer face of small tooth; 12 *b*, posterior face; 12 *c*, base from below; 12 *d*, profile section. Upper Burlington; Louisa county, Iowa. | |
| 13 *a* | Outer face of minute tooth, enlarged; 13 *b*, base from below. Same horizon and locality. | |
| 14 *a* | Outer face of medium sized imperfect tooth. Same horizon and locality. | |
| 15 *a* | Outer face of tooth showing two denticles on either side of median cone; 15 *b*, posterior face; 15 *c*, profile section. Same horizon and locality. | |
| 16 *a* | Outer face of large less symmetrical tooth; 16 *c*, profile section. Same horizon and locality. | |
| 17 | CLADODUS [illegible], St. J. and W. | 270 |
| 17 *a* | View of outer face of nearly perfect tooth; 17 *b*, posterior face; 17 *c*, view of inferior basal surface. Upper Burlington; Louisa county, Iowa. | |
| 18 | CLADODUS [illegible], St. J. and W. | 271 |
| 18 *a* | View of outer face of tooth; 18 *b*, profile section. Keokuk limestone. | |

# GEOLOGICAL SURVEY OF ILLINOIS

FOSSIL-FISHES. (Lower & Upper Carboniferous) CLADODI.

C. S. P. & C. K. W. del. A. H. Worthen, direxit J. Mayer & Co., lith., Boston.

# PLATE V.

PAGE

Fig 1-2 — THRINACODUS NANUS St J and W . . 229

1 a — Front view of tooth 1 b same enlarged, 1 c, base from below Kinderhook beds, Burlington, Iowa

2 a — Side view of another specimen showing the base 2 b the same enlarged Same horizon and locality

Fig 3 — LAMBDODUS COSTATUS, St J and W . . . . . 230

3 a — Front view of tooth 3 b, side view, 3 c, outline from above Upper Burlington limestone, Louisa county Iowa.

Fig 4 — LAMBDODUS TRANSVERSUS St J and W . . 232

4 a — Front view of tooth enlarged two diameters, 4 b, side view St Louis limestone, Alton, Ill

Fig 5 — LAMBDODUS CALCEOLUS, St J and W . . . . 231

5 a — Front view, 5 b, view from above, 5 c, side view Upper Burlington, Louisa county, Iowa

Fig 6 — LAMBDODUS ROBUSTUS, St J and W . 233

6 a, b, c — Views from the front, above and side Keokuk limestone

Fig 7 — HYBOCLADODUS NITIDUS, St J and W . .... . ... 288

7 a — Front view of tooth, enlarged four diameters, 7 b, posterior face, 7 c, front view, showing inferior basal region, 7 d, base from below, 7 e, profile section Chester limestone Chester Ill

Fig 8 — HYBOCLADODUS COMPRESSUS (N and W sp) . . . 287

8 a b c — Views of outer and posterior faces and profile section Upper Burlington, Louisa county, Iowa

Fig 9 — HYBOCLADODUS PLICATILIS St J and W 286

9 a, b, c — Views of outer and posterior faces, and profile section Upper Burlington, Louisa county Iowa

Fig 10 — HYBOCLADODUS TENUICOSTATUS St J and W 286

10 a, b, c. — Outer and inner faces and profile section Keokuk limestone, Illinois

Fig 11 — HYBOCLADODUS var INTERMEDIUS St J and W 287

11 a b — View of outer face and profile section Keokuk limestone

Fig 12-14 — MESODMODUS ORNATUS, St J and W 294

12 a — View of outer face of tooth enlarged two diameters, 12 b, the same further enlarged, 12 c posterior face, 12 d base from below, 12 e, profile section, enlarged same as 12 b Upper Burlington, Louisa county, Iowa

13 a b c d. — Similar views of a less robust specimen Same horizon and locality

14 a, b, c, d — Similar views of a strong worn tooth Same horizon and locality

Fig 15-17 — MESODMODUS EXPLANATUS, St J and W . 293

15 a — View of posterior face of symmetrical tooth 15 b, outer face, enlarged two diameters 15 c base from below 15 d, profile section Kinderhook beds, Burlington, Iowa

16 a — Outer face of eccentric tooth enlarged two diameters, 16 b, view of base from below, 16 c, profile section Same horizon and locality

17 a b — Posterior face, and profile section of an abnormal or eccentrically developed tooth enlarged one half Same horizon and locality

# Plate V.—*Continued*

| | | Page |
|---|---|---|
| Fig. 13–22. | Mesodmodus exsculptus St. J. and W. | 291 |
| 13 *a*. | View of posterior face of a large, perfect tooth, enlarged one half. Kinderhook beds, Burlington, Iowa. | |
| 19 *a*, *b*, *c*. | Views of posterior and outer faces and profile section of smaller median tooth from opposite side of the jaw, enlarged one half. Same horizon and locality. | |
| 20 *a*, *b*, *c*, *d*. | Views of posterior and outer faces, outline from above, and profile section of a linear posterior tooth, enlarged two diameters. Same horizon and locality. | |
| 21 *a*, *b*, *c*, *d*. | Views of outer and inner faces, outline from above, and profile section of a large anterior tooth, enlarged two diameters. Same horizon and locality. | |
| 22 *a*, *b*, *c*, *d*. | Similar views of smaller anterior tooth from opposite side of the jaw, enlarged two diameters. Same horizon and locality. | |
| Fig. 23. | Orodus? parallelus St. J. and W. | 295 |
| 23 *a*. | Front view of two teeth, enlarged three diameters; 23 *b*, view from the inner side; 23 *c*, base from below; 23 *d*, outline from above; 23 *e*, profile section. Kinderhook beds, Richmond, Iowa. | |
| Fig. 24. | Orodus calinatus, St. J. and W. | 307 |
| 24 *a*. | View of posterior face, enlarged two diameters; 24 *b*, outer face; 24 *c*, outline from above; 24 *d*, profile section. Keokuk limestone. Bentonsport, Iowa. | |
| Fig. 25. | Lambdodus reflexus St. J. and W. | 284 |
| 25 *a*. | Front view of tooth; 25 *b*, side view, outline. Chester limestone. Chester, Illinois. | |
| Fig. 26. | Lambdodus hamatus St. J. and W. | 283 |
| 26 *a*. | Front view; 26 *b*, side view; 26 *c*, view from above, cone truncated, and section across base. Chester limestone, Chester, Illinois. | |

# PLATE VI

# GEOLOGICAL SURVEY OF ILLINOIS

FOSSIL-FISHES. (L. and U. Carb.) ORODI etc.

A. H. Worthen, direxit. J. Mayer & Co., lith., Boston.

# PLATE VII

PAGE

Fig 1-9 OBODUS VARIOCOSTATUS, St J and W . . . . . 304

1 *a* View of outer face of small, anterior (?) tooth, base broken away, 1 *b*, crown from above Upper Burlington limestone, Louisa county, Iowa

2 *a* Posterior face of a minute posterior (?) tooth, 2 *b* crown from above, 2 *c*, profile section Same horizon and locality

3 *a* View of inner face of similar but larger tooth 3 *b* crown from above, showing eccentric median prominence Same horizon and locality

4 *a* A larger subcircular tooth seen from above Same horizon and locality

5 *a* View of inner face of larger and more laterally elongated tooth, 5 *b*, crown from above Same horizon and locality

6 *a* Similar tooth posterior face, crown worn, 6 *b*, view from above, 6 *c* profile section Same horizon and locality

7 *a* Outer aspect of medium sized tooth, showing excavated interior basal region, superior shoulder parallel with the coronal margin, and beveled inferior surface of the base, and the outer crown face 7 *b* crown from above 7 *c* profile section Same horizon and locality

8 *a* View of inner face of similar tooth, the median cone truncated from wear, 8 *b* crown seen from above Same horizon and locality

9 *a* Posterior face of a large tooth, also more or less worn 9 *b*, crown seen from above Same horizon and locality

Fig 10 [illegible] [illegible], St J and W . . . . . 302

10 *a* View of inner face of medium sized tooth, 10 *b*, crown as seen from above 10 *c*, profile section Lower Burlington limestone, Burlington, Iowa

Fig 11-18 [illegible] CALCARATUS, St J and W . . . . . 336

11 *a* Posterior face of large tooth, 11 *b*, view of outer face, 11 *c*, profile section Upper Burlington Louisa county, Iowa

12 *a* Medium sized tooth inner face 12 *b* outline of crown from above Same horizon and locality

13 *a* Small acuminate tooth outer face, 13 *b*, outline from above Same horizon and locality

14 *a* Outer face of small, robust tooth, 14 *b* outline from above Same horizon and locality

15 *a* Outer face of a very small acuminate anterior (?) tooth, 15 *b* posterior face, 15 *c*, outline of crown from above Same horizon and locality

16 *a* Outer face of an eccentric acuminate tooth, anterior (?) 16 *b*, outline of crown from above Same horizon and locality

17 *a* View of outer face of posterior (?) tooth, 17 *b*, posterior face 17 *c*, outline of crown from above Same horizon and locality

18 *a* Outer face of a similar tooth 18 *b* view of crown from above 18 *c* profile section Same horizon Burlington Iowa

Fig 19 ORODUS ALLENI St J and W . . . . . 310

19 *a* View of inner face 19 *b* view of crown from above 19 *c* profile section Lower Coal Measures Iowa

GEOLOGICAL SURVEY OF ILLINOIS

FOSSIL-FISHES. (Lower & Upper Carboniferous) ORODI

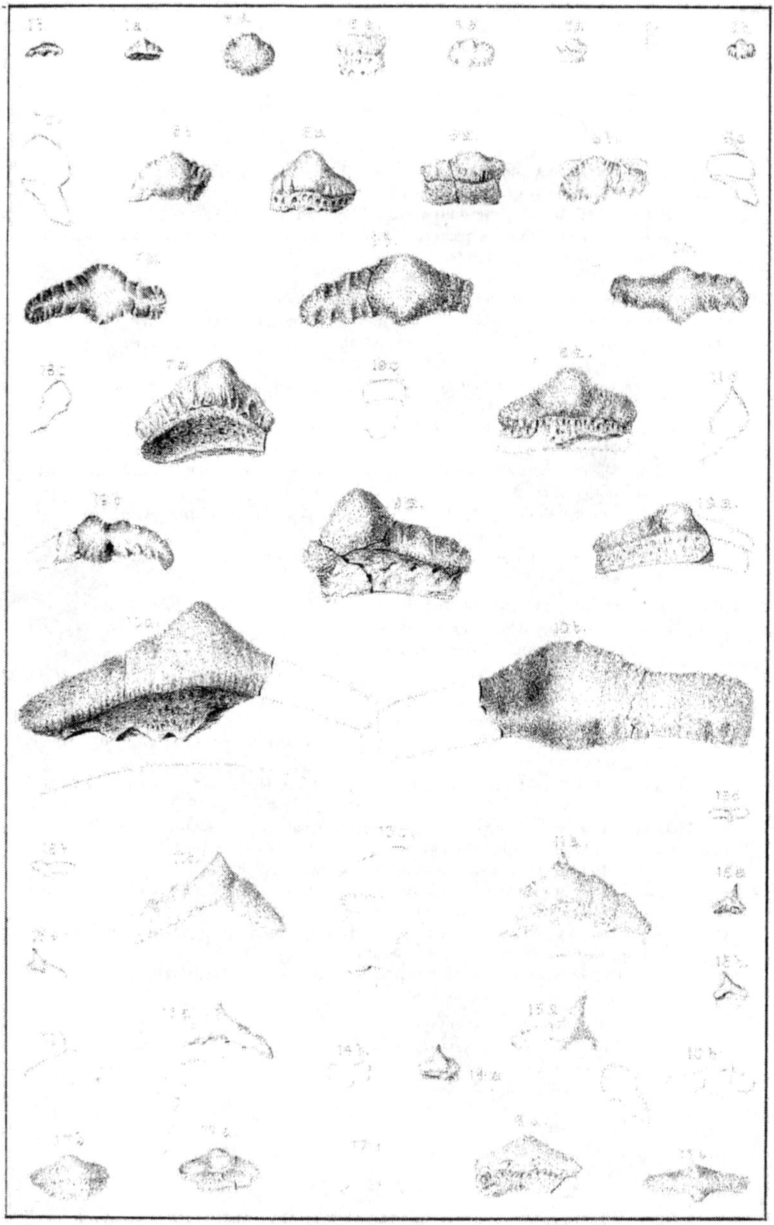

Geo. H. Worthen, del. A. H. Worthen, direxit. J. Mayer & Co., lith., Boston.

# PLATE VIII

| | | PAGE. |
|---|---|---|
| Fig 1 | Agassizodus variabilis | 318 |

View of specimen exhibiting the nearly complete dentition of one ramus, probably the left side of the mandible or lower jaw, reduced to two thirds the natural size Towards the anterior extremity of the specimen at *a* a series of teeth are shown which, from their reversed position, would appear to have formed part of the dental armature of the opposite ramus Upper Coal Measures Osage Kansas

2 *a, b* Views showing the posterior and anterior faces of a large perfect tooth belonging to the median row of ten minute teeth of the right ramus Upper Coal Meas, Mills county Iowa

3 *a, b c* Posterior and anterior faces and outline from above, of a small worn tooth from near the outer extremity of the same row Same position and locality as the preceding and from which were obtained the specimens of the following figures up to Fig 21 so associated as to leave no room to doubt that they formed part of the dental remains of one and the same fish

4 *a b, c* Views of a medium sized tooth belonging to the median row of the left ramus, showing the posterior and anterior faces and outline from above The abraded condition of the crown indicates its position in the outer half of the row

5 *a b c d* Similar views and profile section of a small outer tooth of the same row

6 *a b c* Posterior and anterior faces and outline from above of a specimen remarkable for the eccentric position of the median prominence and which may have belonged to the median row of the right ramus of the upper jaw

7 *a b c d* Similar views and profile section of a large perfect tooth probably belonging to the first row anterior to the median row the immature condition of the root as well as the unabraded state of the crown plainly indicating its inner position Possibly pertaining to the upper jaw

8 *a b, c d* Similar view of a mature tooth of the first row anterior to the median row of the left ramus of the mandible

9 *a, b c* Views showing the posterior and anterior faces and outline from above of a mature perfect tooth of the same ramus as the preceding and probably belonging to one of the anterior rows

10 *a, b, c* The same views of a small tooth probably referable to one of the posterior rows of the same ramus

11 *a b, c* Similar views of a still smaller mature tooth which probably belonged to one of the extreme posterior rows of the same ramus

12 *a b c* Similar views of mature tooth probably belonging to one of the anterior rows of the right ramus of the mandible

13 *a b c* The same views of small tooth of one of the posterior rows of right ramus

14 *a, b, c* Similar views of a very small tooth apparently belonging to one of the extreme anterior rows of the right ramus

15 *a, b, c* Similar views of a tooth probably belonging to one of the extreme posterior rows of the maxillaries showing the crown at one extremity divided into two minute secondary cones, which latter recall some of the entire teeth composing the extreme outer rows in front

16 *a b, c* Posterior anterior and profile views of a very small irregularly shaped depressed tooth possibly pertaining to the maxillary, or upper jaw

17 *a b c d* Outline from above natural size and enlargements showing the posterior (?) and lateral faces of a minute cylindrical tooth the continuation into the root restored in outline

18 *a, b, c* Views of a minute laterally compressed tooth, presenting the normal vertical proportions peculiar to the form, showing the crown from above, lateral and anterior aspects of lower jaw

19 *a b c* Views natural size and enlarged from above, and lateral aspect of an exceedingly minute tooth in which the root is relatively very shallow and proportionately broad antero posteriorly

20 *a, b* Views from above and posterior (?) face of a similar tooth to the last preceding but laterally more elongated with two distinct coronal prominences rising from the common basal support Enlarged two diameters

21 *a, b c* Enlarged views exhibiting the external surface from above, *a*, the abrupt face and foreshortened view of the shallow excavated interior surface *b* and profile *c* of a minute body supposed to pertain to the dermal covering of the same fish to which the previously figured teeth belonged These dermal or shagreen scales are quite common and very varied in shape

22 Restoration showing the probable angle of divergence of the rami from the symphysis in front posteriorly and the convoluted or involled arrangement of the rows of teeth, as indicated in the large specimen, Fig 1

| | | |
|---|---|---|
| Fig 23 | Agassizodus virginianus, St J and W | 321 |

23 *a* View of the posterior face of nearly entire tooth the lateral angles of the base restored in outline *b* anterior face showing relatively shallow root *c* view of crown from above, *d* profile section Position about 100 feet above the Mahoning sandstone, near Morgantown West Virginia. Coal Meas

## Plate VIII — *Continued*

PAGE

Fig. 24. AGASSIZODUS CORRUGATUS, N. and W. . . . 323

24 *a*. View of the posterior face of a medium sized tooth of one of the median rows showing the greater portion of the crown, the outline of the base restored; *b*, anterior face; *c*, crown as seen from above, the apex broken away and extremities restored in outline; *d*, profile section. Upper Coal Meas., near Manhattan, Kansas.

Fig. 25. PERIPLECTRODUS WARRENI, St. J. and W. 325

25 *a*. View of a nearly perfect tooth from above, showing the coronal cusps and the beveled lateral edges; *b*, profile view, showing the strong inrollment of the anterior extremity of the mature teeth; *c*, view of the posterior face, showing the deep, massive basal portion, beneath which appears the inrolled anterior portion of the crown. Burlington creek, Iowa. Upper Burlington.

Fig. 26. PERIPLECTRODUS COMPRESSUS, St. J. and W. 326

26 *a*. View from above, enlarged two diameters, showing the lateral compression of the tooth; 26 *b*, profile view, showing the slight inrollment; 26 *c*, posterior face. Alton, Illinois. St. Louis limestone.

Fig. 27. PERIPLECTRODUS EXPANSUS, St. J. and W. . 327

27 *a*. View from above of a small specimen exhibiting a pair of coronal cusps, enlarged one diameter; 27 *b*, profile view; 27 *c*, posterior face, showing the lateral expansion of the basal portion. Chester, Illinois. Chester limestone.

Fig. 28. STEMMATODUS SYMMETRICUS, St. J. and W. . .. 333

28 *a*. View from above, showing the coronal cusps and callosities at the anterior extremity of the tooth, enlarged; 28 *b*, profile view; 28 *c*, posterior view, showing the inferior surface of base, fore-shortened. Burlington creek, Iowa. U. Burlington.

Fig. 29. STEMMATODUS CHEIRIFORMIS, St. J. and W. . 330

29 *a*. View from above, showing the flattened anterior border, and irregular disposition of the cusps; 29 *b*, profile view; 29 *c*, inferior surface, enlarged. Burlington creek, Iowa. U. Burlington.

30 *a*. View from above of a nearly perfect tooth, showing the striation of the posterior cusps and the minute divided cusps in the angle of the anterior extremity, enlarged six diameters; 30 *b*, view from below, showing inferior basal surface and relative position of the posterior cusps, one of the large exterior ones broken away and restored in outline. Burlington creek, Iowa.

Fig. 31. STEMMATODUS BIFURCATUS, St. J. and W. 330

31 *a*. View from above, enlarged one diameter, showing the postero-lateral prolongations and the relatively brief or arrested median row of cusps; 31 *b*, profile view; 31 *c*, view showing the inferior basal region, evidently more or less abraded. Burlington creek, Iowa. U. Burlington.

Fig. 32. STEMMATODUS BICRISTATUS, St. J. and W. 331

32 *a*. Tooth as seen from above, a minute and apparently perfect specimen, enlarged; 32 *b*, profile view, showing the downward produced anterior or terminal extremity; 32 *c*, view from below, showing the excavated basal surface. Burlington creek, Iowa. U. Burlington.

33 *a*. Superior surface of a large specimen having firmly attached to the narrow anterior extremity a pair of apparently similar but much worn dental crests, between which the larger body is wedged; 33 *b*, profile view, the outline of base restored in outline; 33 *c*, view from below, the base much worn and showing the anterior inferior borders of the pair of anterior teeth. Burlington creek, Iowa.

Fig. 34. STEMMATODUS SIMPLEX, St. J. and W. 332

34 *a*. Profile view of a large single crested tooth, a portion of the external layer broken away in the posterior half, revealing the sutures defining the individual cusps in the body or dental portion of the tooth. Burlington, Iowa. U. Burlington.

Fig. 35. STEMMATODUS BICRISTATUS, St. J. and W. . 331

35 *a*, *b*, *c*. Superior, profile and inferior views of a medium size specimen, showing towards the anterior extremity only a single row of small appressed cusps, while towards the opposite extremity a double row of alternating cusps are seen. Burlington creek, Iowa. U. Burlington.

Fig. 36. STEMMATODUS SIMPLEX, St. J. and W. 332

36 *a*. View from above of a large single crested tooth, which exhibits the anomalous features of a kind of bifurcation abruptly arising from one of the lateral surfaces nearly midway between the extremities, and which consists of three strong cusps apparently firmly soldered to the main body of the tooth. Burlington creek, Iowa. U. Burlington.

37 *a*, *b*. Views from above and in profile of a symmetrical single crested tooth, the base, which is worn, restored in outline. Burlington creek, Iowa.

Fig. 38. STEMMATODUS COMPACTUS, St. J. and W. 334

38 *a*. View of upper surface of small tooth, bearing a median row of large cusps, with faint indications of rudimentary lateral cusps; 38 *b*, profile view, base partially restored in outline. Chester, Illinois. Chester limestone.

GEOLOGICAL SURVEY OF ILLINOIS

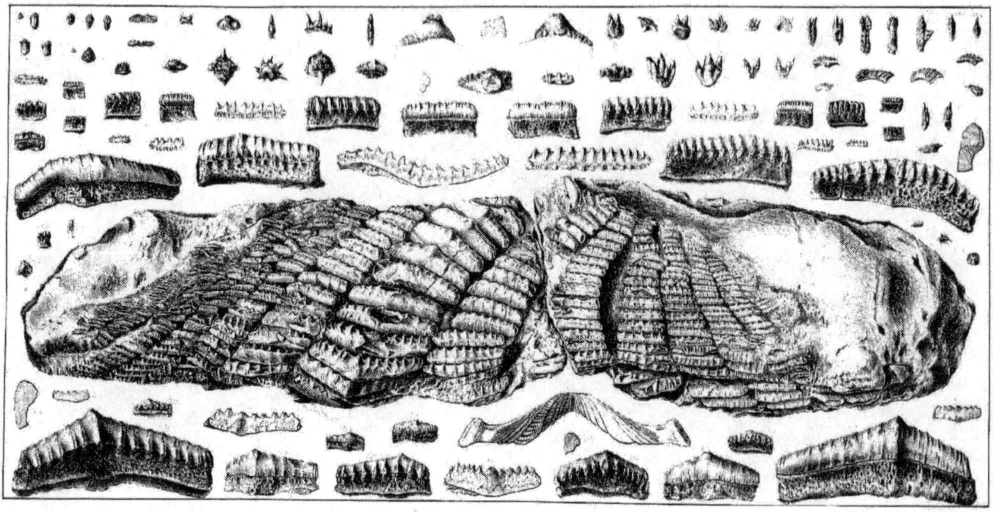

O. St. John, del. A. H. Worthen, direx. J. Mayer & Co., lith. Boston.

# PLATE IX

PAGE

Fig 1-4 VENUSTODUS LEIDYI St J and W 350

1 a View of concave face of tooth 1 b convex face 1 c view from above enlarged two diameters 1 d, enlargement showing the disposition of the coronal folds in concave face 1 e enlargement showing folds in convex face 1 f outline view in profile, enlarged 1 g profile section enlarged St Louis limestone Alton, Illinois

2 a Outline nat size, and enlargement showing the concave face of a minute tooth intermediate in form Same horizon and locality

3 a Concave face of small arched tooth enlarged two diameters 3 b showing the convex face 3 c outline view in profile Same horizon and locality

4 a View of concave face of still smaller tooth enlarged two diameters, 4 b, convex face 4 c outline of crown from above 4 d outline view in profile 4 e, profile section Same horizon and locality

Fig 5, 6 VENUSTODUS ARGUTUS St J and W 352

5 a Concave face of medium sized tooth 5 b convex face, 5 c view of convex face, enlarged two diameters, 5 d, outline from above showing arrangement of basal folds, enlarged 5 e enlargement showing portion concave coronal belt, 5 f, similar enlargement of convex face 5 g outline view in profile, enlarged 5 h, profile section Chester limestone, upper fish bed Chester, Illinois

6 a Concave face of smaller arched tooth, 6 b, view from above, 6 c, similar view, enlarged two diameters, 6 d, similar view of one extremity still further enlarged, showing disposition of coronal folds 6 e profile section enlarged Same horizon and locality

Fig 7-14 VENUSTODUS VARIABILIS, St J and W 346

7 a Tooth of normal size and form, seen from above, 7 b, profile section Upper Burlington limestone Louisa county Iowa

8 a Concave crown face of similar medium sized tooth 8 b, convex face base restored in outline 8 c profile section Same horizon and locality

9 a, b Similar views of a less denticulate variety Same horizon and locality

10 a View of convex face of large tooth with laterally compressed median cone, 10 b, profile view Same horizon and locality

11 a A small linear low crested tooth seen from above, enlarged two diameters, 11 b profile section Same horizon and locality

12 a View from above of a very flat variety in which the crest is but slightly raised above basal imbrications Same horizon and locality

13 a Concave face of small triangular, acuminate tooth 13 b convex face 13 c profile section Same horizon and locality

14 a Concave face of more robust tooth of same variety 14 b, convex face showing relatively deep base and interrupted coronal folds 14 c profile section Same horizon and locality

Fig 15-18 VENUSTODUS TENUICRISTATUS St J and W 345

15 a Medium size tooth seen from above 15 b profile section Upper Burlington Louisa county Iowa

16 a Convex face of large sharp crested form 16 b profile view Same horizon and locality

17 a Small linear variety view from above showing apex but slightly elevated above crest, 17 b profile section Same horizon and locality

18 a A very small linear form seen from above crest forms a low even ridge, coronal folds frequently interrupted enlarged two diameters 18 b, profile section Same horizon and locality

# PLATE IX—*Continued.*

PAGE

Figs. 19-24. VENUSTODUS TENUICRISTATUS, St. J. and W. . 348

19 *a*. Concave face of small tooth of normal shape, showing borders of convex side; 19 *b*, convex face; 19 *c*, profile section. Keokuk limestone, vicinity of Warsaw, Ill.

20 *a*. A more slender tooth in which the apex is less prominent, seen from above. Same horizon and locality.

21 *a*. View from above of large, robust tooth, showing compressed crest, and laterally compressed median cone; 21 *b*, convex face, basal band imperfect from wear; 21 *c*, profile section. Same horizon and locality.

22 *a*. A large elongated tooth, seen from above; 22 *b*, convex face, the worn crest restored in outline; 22 *c*, *d*, profile sections at middle and extremity of tooth. Same horizon and locality.

23 *a*. View from above of small, linear, even crested tooth; 23 *b*, profile section. Same horizon and locality.

24 *a*. Concave face of small triangular acuminate tooth; 24 *b*, convex face, base restored in outline; 24 *c*, outline view in profile. Same horizon and vicinity.

# GEOLOGICAL SURVEY OF ILLINOIS

FOSSIL-FISHES. (Lower Jaws). VERTEBRATA.

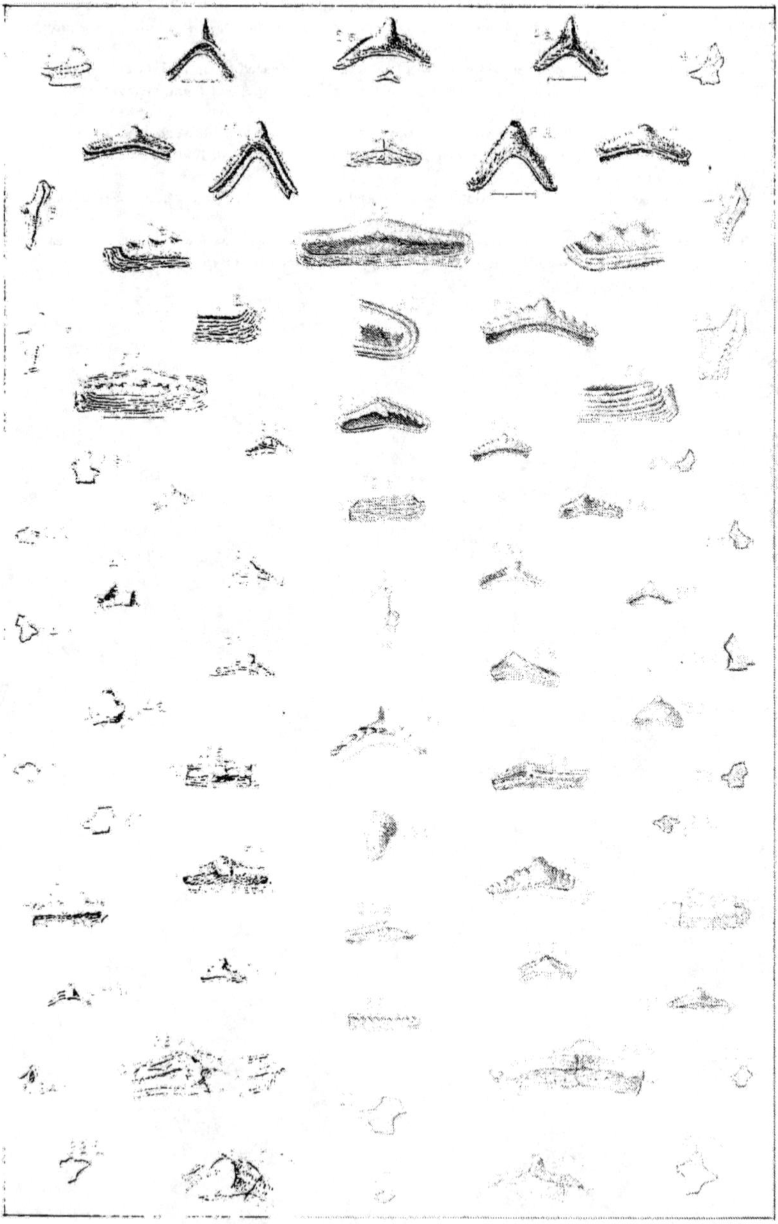

A.H. Worthen direxit. J. Mayer & Co. lith. Boston.

# PLATE X

PAGE

Fig 1-4 CHOMATODUS VARSOUVIENSIS St J and W 363

1 *a* View from above, 1 *b*. convex face, 1 *c*, profile section Warsaw beds above Alton Illinois

2 *a*, *b* *c* Similar views of a larger, worn specimen Same horizon and locality

3 *a*, *b*, *c* Similar views of large tooth showing extravagantly developed convex crown face Same horizon, Barretts Missouri

4 *a* Fragment of oblique tooth seen from above, 4 *b* profile section Same horizon above Alton Illinois

Fig 5-14 CHOMATODUS INCONSTANS St J and W . 360

5 *a* Concave face of tooth of ordinary appearance 5 *b* opposite face base restored in outline 5 *c* profile section showing nearly vertical root St Louis limestone, Pella Iowa

6 *a* A long slender tooth seen from above 6 *b*, convex aspect, 6 *c*, profile section Same horizon and locality

7 *a* Concave face of small tooth, irregularly serrated along crest, 7 *b* convex face, 7 *c*, profile section Same horizon and locality

8 *a*, *b*, *c* Similar views of small tooth with oblique root Same horizon and locality

9 *a* *b*, *c* Similar views of tooth with extremely oblique root Same horizon and locality

10 *a* *b*, *c* The same views of a more regular tooth, with oblique base Same horizon and locality

11 *a*, *b*, *c* Similar views of a more eccentric tooth Same horizon and locality

12 *a*, *b*, *c* Similar views showing both faces of base and the beveled inferior surface Same horizon and locality

13 *a* View from above of large tooth, with nearly median crest 13 *b*, convex face, showing relatively shallow root, 13 *c* profile section Same horizon and locality

14 *a* Profile section of large specimen with vertical root, both faces of crown vertically concave Same horizon and locality

Fig 15-17 CHOMATODUS CHESTERENSIS St J and W . 363

15 *a* Medium sized tooth, seen from above 15 *b* convex face, showing deep base, 15 *c* profile section Chester limestone Chester Illinois

16 *a* Concave face of fragment of small tooth, with oblique base, 16 *b*, convex face 16 *c* profile section Same horizon and locality

17 *a* *b*, *c* Similar views of large, nearly perfect tooth, 17 *d*, view of crown from above, showing nearly median crest Same horizon and locality

Fig 18 CHOMATODUS INCRASSATUS St J and W . . . 359

18 *a* View of concave face of medium sized tooth enlarged two diameters 18 *b* convex face and base 18 *c*. profile section St. Louis limestone Alton, Illinois

Fig 19-22 CHOMATODUS COMPTUS St J and W .. . . . .. . 356

19 *a* Concave aspect of large, symmetrical tooth, showing base and beveled inferior surface 19 *b* view of convex face 19 *c*, outline of crown from above, 19 *d*, *e*, profile sections Upper Burlington Louisa county, Iowa

20 *a* *b*, *c* Similar views of short robust tooth Same horizon and locality

21 *a*, *b*, *c* Same views of a similar shaped smaller tooth Same horizon and locality

22 *a*, *b*, *c* Similar views of small tooth Same horizon and locality

Fig 23 CHOMATODUS ARCUATUS St J . .. ... . .. 000

23 *a* View of concave crown face, showing part of base, 23 *b* convex crown face, base partially restored 23 *c* view of crown from above, 23 *d*, profile section Upper Coal Measures Adams county Iowa

GEOLOGICAL SURVEY OF ILLINOIS

FOSSIL-FISHES. (Lower & Upper Carboniferous) CHOMATODI.

Chas. K. Worthen, del. A. H. Worthen, direxit. J. Mayer & Co., lith., Boston.

# PLATE X A.

| | | | PAGE |
|---|---|---|---|
| Fig. 1 | | HARPACODUS COMPACTUS St. J. and W. | 355 |
| | 1 *a* | View of concave face of tooth enlarged two diameters, 1 *b*, profile section. Chester limestone. Chester, Illinois. | |
| Fig. 2 | | HARPACODUS OCCIDENTALIS, St. J. and W. | 355 |
| | 2 *a* | Concave crown face enlarged two diameters, 2 *b*, convex face. 2 *c*, outline from above, 2 *d*, profile section. St. Louis limestone, Alton, Illinois. | |
| Fig. 3, 4 | | CHOMATODUS PARALLELUS St. J. and W. | 358 |
| | 3 *a* | Concave crown face of nearly perfect tooth, 3 *b*, convex face, 3 *c*, profile section. Warsaw beds. | |
| | 4 *a* | Convex face of less robust tooth. Warsaw beds, above Alton, Illinois. | |
| Fig. 5 | | CHOMATODUS INSIGNIS (Leidy sp.) | 359 |
| | 5 *a* | Concave face of nearly entire specimen. 5 *b*, convex aspect. 5 *c*, profile section. St. Louis limestone, St. Louis, Missouri. | |
| Fig. 6 | | PRISTODUS ? ACUMINATUS St. J. and W. | 402 |
| | 6 *a* | Convex crown face enlarged, 6 *b*, concave face, 6 *c*, outline from above, 6 *d*, profile section. Kinderhook beds, Burlington, Iowa. | |
| Fig. 7-9 | | DESMIODUS TUMIDUS, St. J. and W. | 339 |
| | 7 *a* | Concave aspect of tooth enlarged four diameters, 7 *b*, convex face, 7 *c*, outline from above. 7 *d*, profile section. St. Louis limestone, Alton, Illinois. | |
| | 8 *a* | View of series of four teeth from above enlarged two diameters. 8 *b*, profile outline of anterior border, 8 *c*, outline from above, still further enlarged. Same horizon and locality. | |
| | 9 *a* | A series of seven teeth, seen from above, enlarged. Same horizon. St. Louis, Mo. | |
| Fig. 10, 11 | | DESMIODUS COSTELLIFERUS St. J. and W. | 341 |
| | 10 *a* | View of convex aspect of tooth enlarged four diameters, 10 *b*, concave face. 10 *c*, outline of crown from above. 10 *d*, profile section. St. Louis limestone, St. Louis, Missouri. | |
| | 11 *a*, *b*, *c* | Similar views of an elongated tooth, enlarged four diameters. Same horizon. Alton, Illinois. | |
| Fig. 12-14 | | DESMIODUS ? LIGONIFORMIS St. J. and W. | 342 |
| | 12 *a*, *b*, *c* | Views of concave and convex faces and profile section, enlarged two diameters. Keokuk limestone. Boonville, Missouri. | |
| | 13 *a*, *b* | Convex face and profile section of similar tooth enlarged two diameters. Same horizon, Bentonsport, Iowa. | |
| | 14 *a*, *b* | Concave and convex faces of larger, robust worn tooth enlarged two diameters. Same horizon. Boonville, Missouri. | |
| Fig. 15 | | DESMIODUS ? FLABELLUM, St. J. and W. | 343 |
| | 15 *a* | Concave face enlarged two diameters. 15 *b*, convex face. 15 *c*, profile section. Keokuk limestone, Boonville, Missouri. | |
| Fig. 16 | | LISGODUS SCUTULIFORMIS St. J. and W. | 366 |
| | 16 *a*, *b*, *c*, *d* | Views of concave and convex faces, outline from above, and profile section, enlarged two diameters. St. Louis limestone, Alton, Illinois. | |
| Fig. 17-19 | | LISGODUS SERRATUS St. J. and W. | 365 |
| | 17 *a*, *b*, *c* | Views of concave and convex faces, and outline of crown from above, enlarged two diameters. Upper Burlington limestone, Louisa county, Iowa. | |
| | 18 *a*, *b*, *c* | Concave and convex faces, and profile section of slightly stronger tooth enlarged two diameters. Same horizon and locality. | |
| | 19 *a*, *b*, *c* | Similar views of a large robust tooth enlarged two diameters. Same horizon and locality. | |

## Plate X a.—*Continued*

# GEOLOGICAL SURVEY OF ILLINOIS

FOSSIL FISHES. PETALODONTS

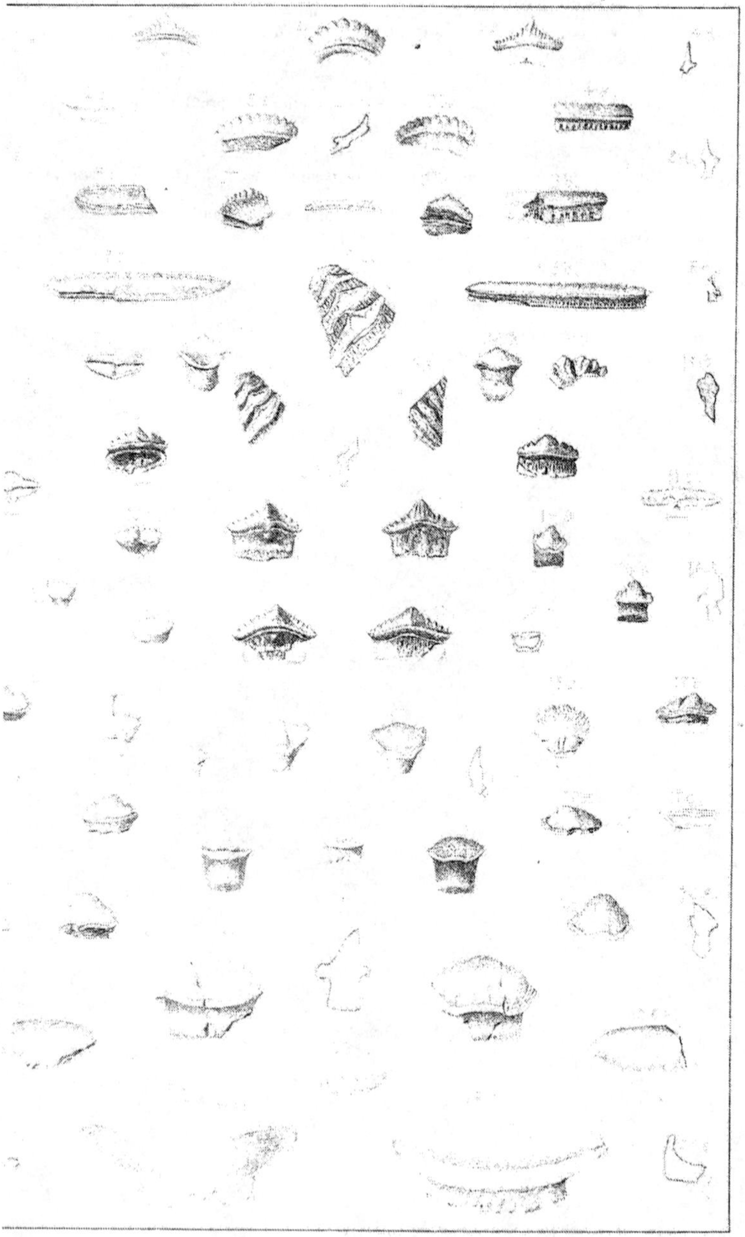

# PLATE XI.

## PLATE XI—*Continued.*

PAGE

Fig 20-23 TANAODUS SCULPTUS, St J and W . . 373

20 *a* Concave face of large symmetrical tooth. 20 *b*, convex face, coronal folds obsolete 20 *c* profile section St Louis limestone Alton, Illinois

21 *a* Outline of concave face of small eccentric tooth. 21 *b*, the same enlarged two diameters 21 *c* convex face, 21 *d* profile section St Louis beds Pella, Iowa

22 *a*, *b* *c* Similar views of small symmetrical tooth same horizon and locality

23 *a* Outline of concave face 23 *b* view of concave face enlarged two diameters, 23 *c*, convex face showing coronal folds 23 *d* profile section showing outline of perfect root, and unusual concavity of the concave face St Louis Alton, Illinois

Fig 26 TANAODUS GROSSIPLICATUS, St J and W . . . .. 375

26 *a* Concave face of tooth partially restored in outline, 26 *b*. convex face 26 *c*, profile section Chester limestone Chester Illinois

Fig 27 TANAODUS SUBLUNATUS, St J and W .. . . . ... 368

27 *a* Outline of convex aspect, partially restored enlarged two diameters, 27 *b*, profile section St Louis limestone, Alton, Illinois

Fig 28 ANTLIODUS PEROVALIS St J and W . .. 393

28 *a* Concave face basal border imperfect. 28 *b* convex face, 28 *c* profile section Warsaw beds

Fig 29 ANTLIODUS GRACILIS, St J and W .. . 393

29 *a* View of concave crown face, basal border broken away, 29 *b* convex face, 29 *c*, profile section Warsaw beds

# GEOLOGICAL SURVEY OF ILLINOIS

FOSSIL-FISHES. (Lower Carb) CHOMATODI, etc.

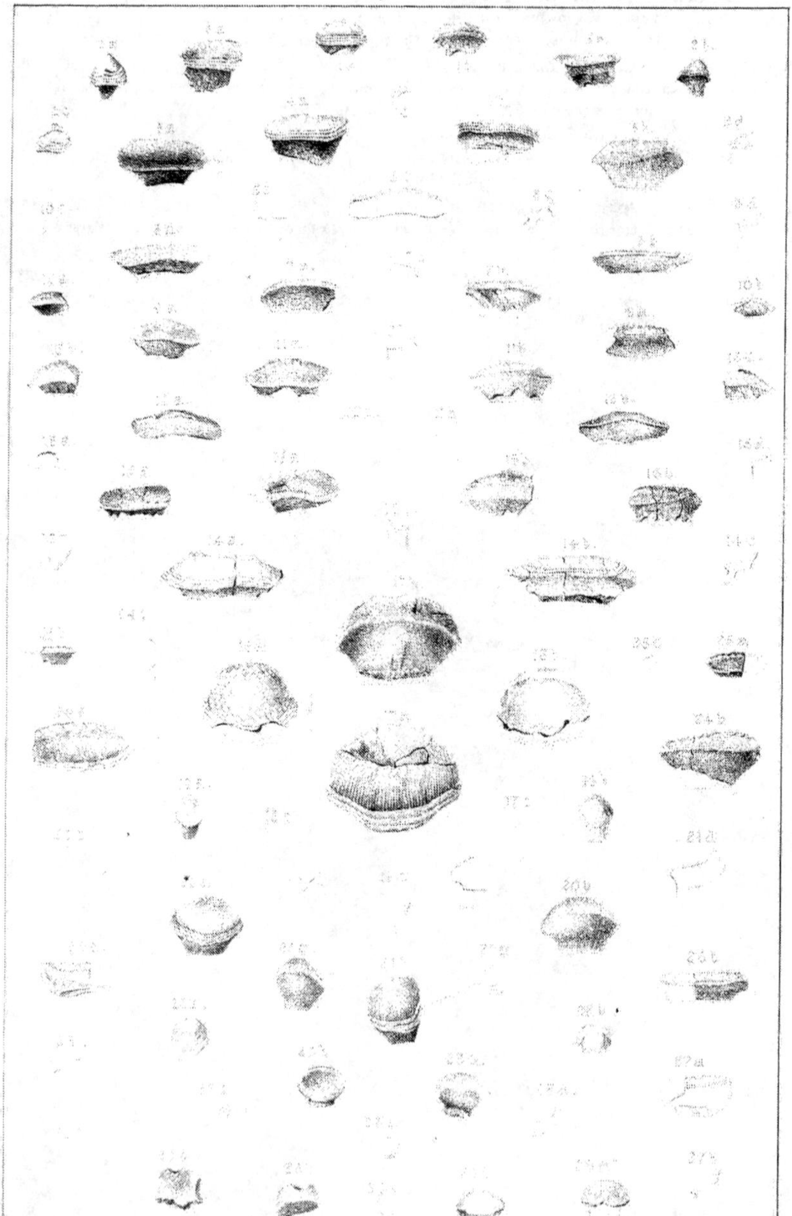

Chas. K. Worthen, del. A. H. Worthen, direxit. J. Mayer & Co., lith., Boston.

# PLATE XII.

| | | | PAGE |
|---|---|---|---|
| Fig | 1-4 | PETALORHYNCHUS PSEUDOSAGITTATUS St J and W . . | 405 |
| | 1 *a* | Convex face of small tooth, 1 *b*, concave face, 1 *c*, profile section St Louis beds, Pella, Iowa | |
| | 2 *a* | Concave face of large tooth, 2 *b*, convex aspect, 2 *c*, profile section St Louis, Alton, Illinois | |
| | 3 *a* | Outline of convex face of very large acuminate tooth, with forked root Same horizon and locality | |
| | 4 *a* | Similar outline of medium sized symmetrical tooth St Louis, Pella, Iowa | |
| Fig | 5, 6 | PETALORHYNCHUS SPATULATUS St J and W . | . 403 |
| | 5 *a* | Convex aspect of large tooth with rounded apex, 5 *b*, side view St Louis limestone, Alton Illinois | |
| | 6 *a* | Convex face of small tooth 6 *b* concave face 6 *c* profile section St Louis, Pella, Iowa | |
| Fig | 7, 8 | PETALORHYNCHUS DISTORTUS St J and W | . 406 |
| | 7 *a* | Convex face of medium sized tooth 7 *b*, concave face showing deeply arched basal margin, 7 *c* profile section St Louis beds Pella, Iowa | |
| | 8 *a,b,c* | Similar views of smaller specimen St Louis Alton Illinois | |
| Fig | 9 | CTENOPETALUS BELLULUS St J and W . .. | 393 |
| | 9 *a* | View of group of teeth from the convex side, enlarged two diameters, 9 *b*, view of opposite face showing entire outline of the largest specimen, 9 *c*, profile section of large tooth St Louis beds Pella Iowa | |
| Fig | 10 | PETALODUS HYBRIDUS, St J and W | 394 |
| | 10 *a* | Convex face of large tooth, 10 *b* concave face 10 *c*, profile section St Louis, Alton, Illinois | |
| Fig | 11 | PETALODUS PROXIMUS St J and W . . | 395 |
| | 11 *a* | Convex face of nearly perfect tooth 11 *b* view of concave face, 11 *c* profile section Upper Coal Measures, Springfield Illinois | |
| Fig | 12 | PETALODUS CURTUS? N and W | . 394 |
| | 12 *a* | View of convex face of medium sized tooth, crest worn nearly plane with convex basal margin 12 *b* concave face showing corrugated ornamentation, 12 *c*, profile section Keokuk limestone Bentonsport Iowa | |
| Fig | 13 | CTENOPETALUS SINUOSUS, St J and W | .. 396 |
| | 13 *a* | Convex crown face 13 *b*, profile section Keokuk limestone, Bentonsport, Iowa | |
| Fig | 14 | CTENOPETALUS OCCIDENTALIS St J and W . .... | . 401 |
| | 14 *a*. | View of convex face 14 *b* concave face 14 *c*, profile section Lower Coal Measures, Fort Dodge, Iowa | |
| Fig | 15 | CTENOPTYCHIUS STEVENSONI St J and W . | . 393 |
| | 15 *a* | View of convex face 15 *b* concave face 15 *c* profile section Coal Measures, West Virginia | |
| Fig | 16, 17 | CALOPODUS APICALIS, St J and W | 403 |
| | 16 *a* | Convex face of tooth enlarged two diameters 16 *b* concave aspect 16 *c*, profile outline Middle Coal Measures Iowa | |
| | 17 *a* | Convex face of smaller tooth, enlarged two diameters 17 *b*, concave face showing hooked apex 17 *c* profile outline Same horizon and locality | |
| Fig | 18 | CTENOPETALUS LIMATULUS, St J and W . .. | 399 |
| | 18 *a* | View of convex face, 18 *b*, profile section Chester limestone Chester Illinois | |

# GEOLOGICAL SURVEY OF ILLINOIS

FOSSIL-FISHES. (Lower & Upper) Carboniferous PETALODONTS

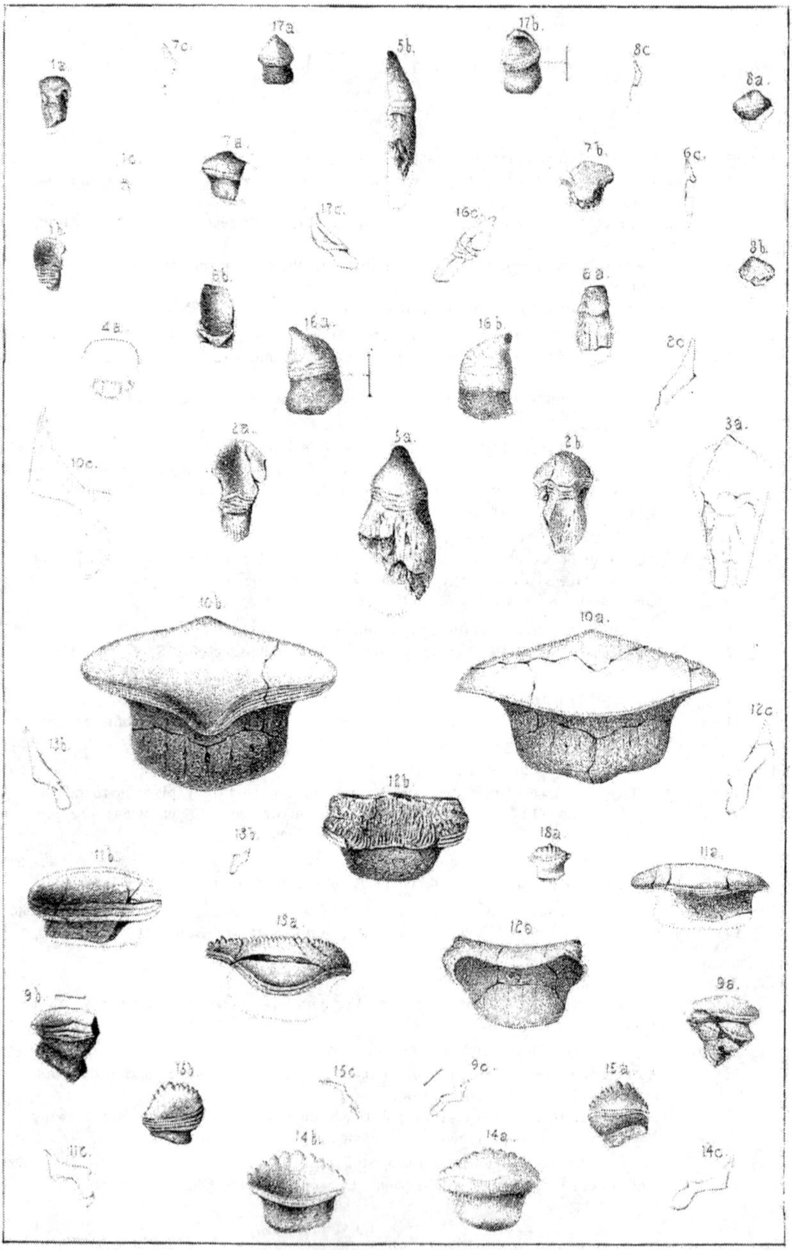

# PLATE XIII.

| | | | PAGE |
|---|---|---|---|
| Fig. 1, 2 | | FISSODUS BIFIDUS, St. J. and W. | 414 |
| | 1 *a* | Concave face of perfect tooth; 1 *b* convex face; 1 *c* profile section. Chester limestone. Chester, Illinois. | |
| | 2 *a* | Concave face of smaller, less perfect specimen; 2 *b* profile section. Same horizon and locality. | |
| Fig. 3 | | FISSODUS TRICUSPIDATUS, St. J. and W. | 415 |
| | 3 *a* | Concave face of an imperfect tooth, basal borders restored; 3 *b* opposite face; 3 *c* profile section. Chester, Illinois. | |
| Fig. 4, 5 | | CHOLODUS INEQUALIS, St. J. and W. | 416 |
| | 4 *a* | Concave face of an imperfect tooth, basal border broken away; 4 *b* view of convex face; 4 *c* profile section. Upper Coal Measures. Iowa. | |
| | 5 *a* | View of concave face of more robust tooth, basal border and root destroyed; 5 *b*, convex face; 5 *c* profile section. Upper Coal Measures. Springfield, Illinois. | |
| Fig. 6, 7 | | PELTODUS QUADRATUS, St. J. and W. | 410 |
| | 6 *a* | Convex face of perfect tooth, enlarged two diameters; 6 *b*, profile section. St. Louis limestone. Alton, Illinois. | |
| | 7 *a* | Concave face of an imperfect tooth; 7 *b* convex face; 7 *c* profile section. Same horizon and locality. | |
| Fig. 8 | | PELTODUS TRANSVERSUS, St. J. and W. | 412 |
| | 8 *a* | Convex face of nearly entire tooth, enlarged two diameters; 8 *b* profile section. Coal Measures. Carlinville, Illinois. | |
| Fig. 9 | | PELTODUS? [illegible], St. J. and W. | 411 |
| | 9 *a* | Concave face, basal margin imperfect; 9 *b* convex face, root restored in outline; 9 *c* profile section. Chester limestone. Chester, Illinois. | |
| Fig. 10 | | POLYRHIZODUS CARBONARIUS, St. J. and W. | 389 |
| | 10 *a* | Appearance of original example, convex face, partially restored in outline; 10 *b*, profile section. Upper Coal Measures. LaSalle, Illinois. | |
| Fig. 11 | | POLYRHIZODUS WILLIAMSI, St. J. and W. | 384 |
| | 11 *a* | View of concave face, showing dentate root; 11 *b* view of crown from above, showing triturating surface in the convex face; 11 *c* profile section. Keokuk limestone. Boonville, Missouri. | |
| Fig. 12 | | POLYRHIZODUS PIASAENSIS, St. J. and W. | 386 |
| | 12 *a* | Concave face of nearly perfect tooth; 12 *b*, convex face; 12 *c*, profile section. Warsaw beds above Alton, Illinois. | |
| Fig. 13 | | POLYRHIZODUS AMPLUS, St. J. and W. | 387 |
| | 13 *a* | Concave face of perfect tooth; 13 *b* convex face; 13 *c* profile section. St. Louis limestone. Alton, Illinois. | |
| Fig. 14 | | POLYRHIZODUS LITTONI, N. and W. | 385 |
| | 14 *a, b, c* | Concave and convex faces and profile section of nearly perfect tooth, introduced for comparison with preceding form. St. Louis. Alton, Illinois. | |
| Fig. 15 | | POLYRHIZODUS NANUS, St. J. and W. | 386 |
| | 15 *a, b* | Convex face and profile section; 15 *c, d*, the same views, enlarged two diameters. Keokuk limestone. Bentonsport, Iowa. | |
| Fig. 16 | | DACTYLODUS EXCAVATUS, St. J. and W. | 392 |
| | 16 *a* | Concave face, root broken away, enlarged two diameters; 16 *b* convex face; 16 *c*, profile section. Chester limestone. Chester, Illinois. | |
| Fig. 17, 18 | | DACTYLODUS CONCAVUS, St. J. and W. | 390 |
| | 17 *a* | Concave face of medium size tooth; 17 *b*, convex face; 17 *c* profile section. St. Louis limestone. Alton, Illinois. | |
| | 18 *a* | Concave face of large specimen, extremities of fangs broken away; 18 *b*, convex face; 18 *c* profile section. Same horizon and locality. | |
| Fig. 19 | | DACTYLODUS MINIMUS, St. J. and W. | 391 |
| | 19 *a* | Concave face of tooth, enlarged two diameters; 19 *b* opposite face; 19 *c*, profile section. St. Louis Limestone. Alton, Illinois. | |

# GEOLOGICAL SURVEY OF ILLINOIS

FOSSIL-FISHES. (L. and U. Carb) PETALODONTS

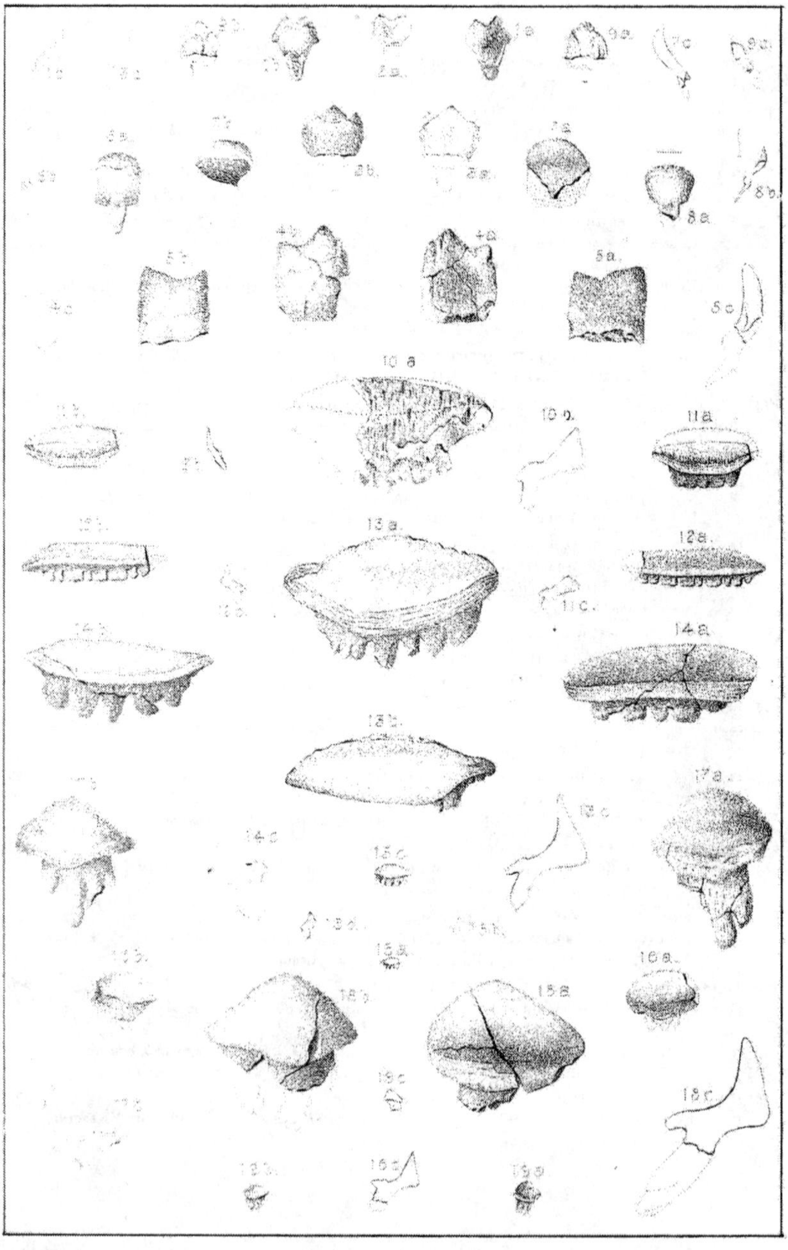

# PLATE XIV.

PAGE

Fig 1 CTENACANTHUS SCULPTUS, St J and W . . . 421

1 a Side view of a nearly perfect specimen, 1 b transverse section of spine near upper extremity, showing pulp cavity and contour of posterior face, 1 c, enlargement showing disposition and form of tubercles, the eccentric anterior ridge near the base with profile outline 1 d, enlargement of tubercle of third costa from front, near base, and profile outline, 1 e f enlargement of tubercles from middle costæ, 1 g enlargement of costæ and tubercles in middle and posterior portions above Lower fish bed Kinderhook, Burlington, Iowa

Fig 2 CTENACANTHUS VARIANS, St J and W . . . .. 422

2 a Side view of broken spine partially restored in outline the inner dotted lines showing the outline of the pulp cavity, 2 b view of upper half of posterior face showing the strong, rounded median keel and denticles along the postero lateral angles, 2 c transverse section about one fourth the distance from the apex, 2 d, transverse section near line of insertion showing the deeply excavated posterior border, 2 e, enlargement of costæ near base in front 2 f, enlargement of middle costæ of right side near base 2 g enlargement of tenth costa from front in lower third of spine of same side 2 h enlargement of posterior costa near base, 2 i profile enlargement of posterior denticles Upper fish bed Kinderhook Burlington, Iowa

Fig 3 4 CTENACANTHUS SPECIOSUS, St J and W 424

3 a Side view of large imperfect spine partially restored in outline 3 b transverse section below the opening of internal cavity 3 c transverse section near the upper extremity, posterior outline restored 3 d enlargement of costæ from various parts of the spine 3 e, enlargement of fragment of another individual, showing the posterior denticles, etc Lower fish bed Kinderhook Burlington Iowa

4 a Side view of a worn specimen probably referable to this form, in which the decussations of the costæ are obsolete, 4 b view of the posterior face, 4 c, d, transverse sections near base and upper part Same horizon and locality

GEOLOGICAL SURVEY OF ILLINOIS

FOSSIL FISHES. [illegible] ICHTHYODORULITES.

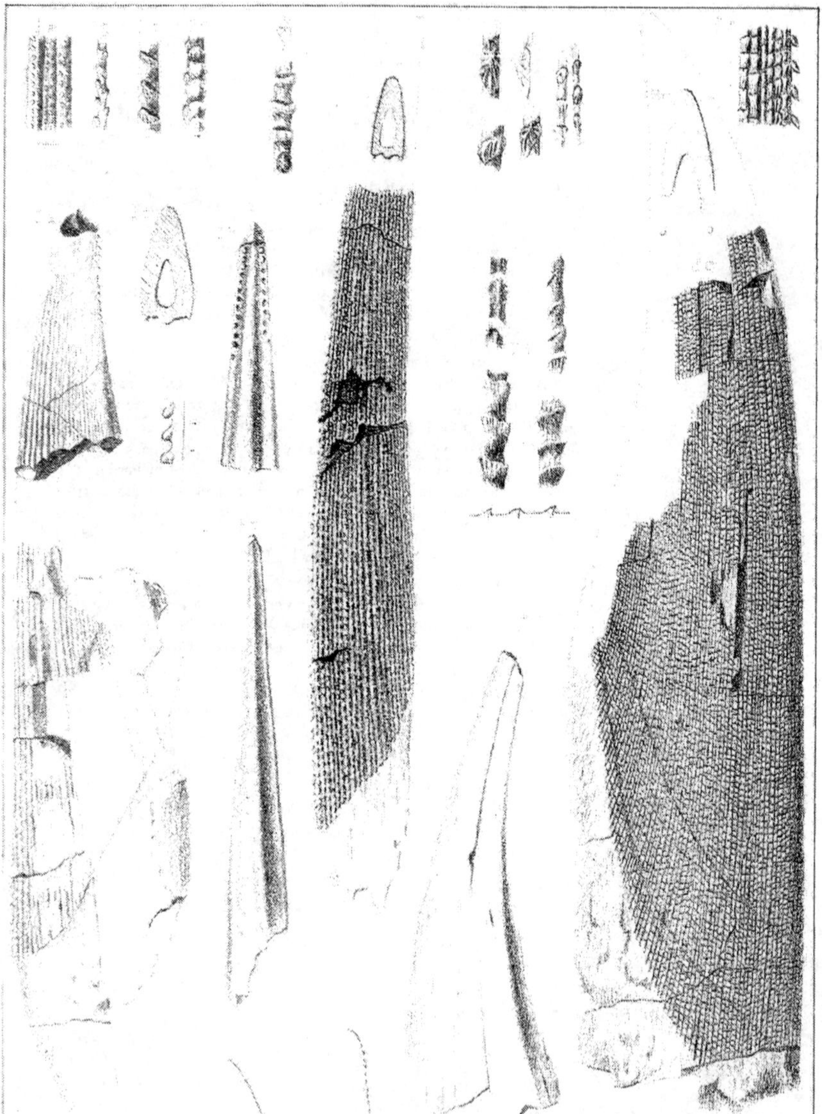

# PLATE XV.

PAGE

Fig. 1 CTENACANTHUS SPECTABILIS, St. J. and W. 420

1 *a*. Side view, tip and postero-inferior border partially restored in outline; 1 *b*, *c*, transverse sections at broken extremity and near basal line; 1 *d*, enlargement of costæ in the middle near base; 1 *e*, enlargement of costæ of anterior margin above, showing their appearance when worn. Kinderhook beds, LeGrande, Iowa.

Fig. 2, 3. CTENACANTHUS GRADOCOSTATUS, St. J. and W. 425

2 *a*. Side view of fragment of spine; 2 *b*, enlargement of a section from the upper extremity, showing details of ornamentation; 2 *c*, view of section of posterior face; 2 *d*, *e*, transverse section and enlargement showing contour of posterior face; 2 *f*, enlargements in outline showing elevation of costæ from the side and end. Upper Burlington, Quincy, Illinois.

3 *a*. Fragment from near the apex of a specimen referred to the above form, enlarged; 3 *b*, enlargement of posterior edge, and section showing outline of the anterior ridge. Same horizon, Louisa county, Iowa.

Fig. 4, 5. CTENACANTHUS EXCAVATUS, St. J. and W. 425

4 *a*. Side view of a broken spine, enlarged about two diameters; 4 *b*, further enlargement of anterior ridge; 4 *c*, view of posterior face near extremity, showing position of denticles and median concavity, enlarged about two diameters; 4 *d*, transverse section enlarged. Keokuk limestone, Bentonsport, Iowa.

5 *a*. Side view of a fragment showing the tip of a larger spine, and transverse section of the same. Same horizon, LaGrange, Missouri.

Fig. 6, 7. CTENACANTHUS BURLINGTONENSIS, St. J. and W. 426

6 *a*. Side view of upper portion of spine; 6 *b*, enlargement of posterior border; 6 *c*, transverse section. Upper Burlington, Louisa county, Iowa.

7 *a*. Side view of lower portion of spine, base restored in outline; 7 *b*, enlargement of posterior margin, showing relatively smaller and obtusely conical denticles than occur in the upper portion; 7 *c*, enlargement along the anterior border, showing ornamentation of three or four tuberculose costæ; 7 *d*, enlargement showing the anterior ridge and laterally compressed tubercles; 7 *e*, section of posterior face; 7 *f*, *g*, transverse sections, natural size and enlarged. Same horizon and locality.

Fig. 8. CTENACANTHUS KEOKUK, St. J. and W. 427

8 *a*. Side view of large well preserved specimen, the broken inferior extremity showing mould of pulp cavity, the ornamented costæ in front partially restored; 8 *b*, transverse section enlarged; 8 *c*, enlargement of posterior border, showing sculptured denticles, bifurcated and irradiated costæ, etc.; 8 *d*, enlargement of the anterior margin, showing tuberculose costæ, etc.; 8 *e*, enlargement of the anterior ridge, showing depressed tubercles. Keokuk limestone, Boonville, Mo.

Fig. 9, 10. CTENACANTHUS GEMMATUS, St. J. and W. 429

9 *a*. Side view of imperfect spine, with ornamentation partially restored; 9 *b*, transverse section. St. Louis limestone, Alton, Illinois.

10 *a*. Enlargements from a small fragment of a spine, showing anterior ridge and several costæ from the front, middle and posterior portions of the spine; 10 *b*, anterior ridge enlarged. Same horizon and locality.

Fig. 11. CTENACANTHUS [illegible], St. J. and W. 431

11 *a*. Side view of upper extremity of spine; 11 *b*, enlargement of the anterior and two of the lateral costæ, showing the obliquely striated lateral margins of the anterior ridge, etc.; 11 *c*, enlargement of anterior ridge; 11 *d*, transverse section. Chester limestone, Chester, Illinois.

GEOLOGICAL SURVEY OF ILLINOIS

FOSSIL-FISHES. (Lower Carb.) ICHTHYODORULITES.

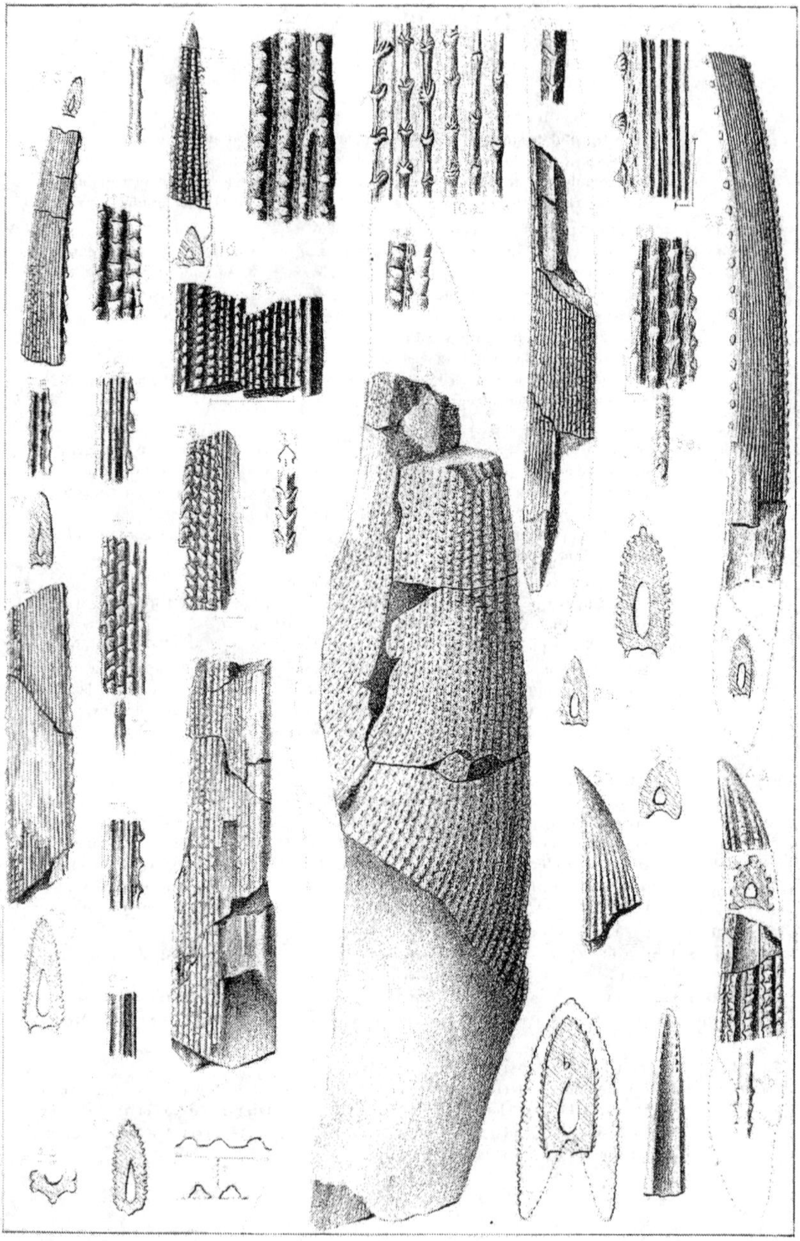

A. H. Worthen, direct. J. Mayer & Co., lith. Boston.

# PLATE XVI

PAGE

Fig 1 ASTEROPTYCHIUS VETUSTUS, St J and W . . 435

1 *a* Side view enlarged two diameters 1 *b* section of one side further enlarged, showing details of intercostal striation and appearance of the more or less worn posterior denticles 1 *c* enlargement of portion of posterior face showing position of denticles along the postero lateral angles also the faint median ridge 1 *d*, transverse section enlarged Lower fish bed Kinderhook Burlington, Iowa

Fig 2 ASTEROPTYCHIUS KEOKUK, St J and W . . 436

2 *a* Side view of an imperfect spine enlarged two diameters, and restored in outline 2 *b*, sketch of the posterior face enlarged two diameters 2 *c*, transverse section Keokuk limestone Warsaw Illinois

Fig 3 4 ASTEROPTYCHIUS ST LUDOVICI St J and W 437

3 *a* Lateral view of a perfect preserved specimen showing intercostal tubercles and posterior denticles—the latter are represented slightly too large—enlarged two diameters 3 *b* section of posterior face enlarged two diameters 3 *c d* side views of denticles belonging to the upper and lower series enlarged, 3 *e*, transverse section St Louis limestone Alton Illinois

4 *a* Side view of a nearly entire small spine 4 *b* section of the posterior face near the lower extremity enlarged one half showing median keel and position of denticles 4 *c*, section along the anterior margin enlarged showing two costae and striato punctate intercostal spaces 4 *d* enlargement of section from the posterior border near the lower extremity showing the irregular striae in the intercostal spaces and the posterior denticles 4 *e* enlargement of posterior face near upper extremity, showing the downward hooked denticles etc 4 *f g* transverse sections near the lower and upper extremities enlarged one half showing relative prominence of median keel in different parts of the spine Same horizon St Louis, Missouri

Fig 5 6 [illegible] St J and W . 438

5 *a* Side view of a large nearly entire spine 5 *b*, enlargement of a portion of the surface, 5 *c*, transverse section near the lower extremity Chester limestone Chester, Ill

6 *a* Lateral view of a fragment showing the top of a spine enlarged two diameters 6 *b*, enlargement showing portion of the posterior face which is faintly channeled instead of keeled as in the lower portion of the spine 6 *c* enlargement of the posterior border showing intercostal striation and denticles 6 *d*, transverse section, enlarged two diameters Same horizon and locality

Fig 7 [illegible], St J and W 439

7 *a* Side view of a small spine showing the base 7 *b* view of anterior edge 7 *c* transverse section 7 *d* enlargement of portion of lateral surface Coal Measures, Carlinville, Illinois

Fig 8 11 ACONDYLACANTHUS GRACILIS, St J and W 433

8 *a* Side view of spine of larger one half 8 *b* transverse section Upper fish bed, Kinderhook, Burlington Iowa

9 *a* Side view of a fragment near the upper extremity enlarged two diameters, 9 *b*, posterior face enlarged two diameters 9 *c* transverse section, enlarged Same horizon and locality

10 *a* Side view of the tip of a very small spine referred to the above form, enlarged two diameters 10 *b* transverse section 10 *c* enlargement of one of the denticles seen from the outer side Lower fish bed Kinderhook Burlington, Iowa

11 *a* Lateral view of a fragment of a large spine probably referable to this species, showing the surface in perfect state of preservation 11 *b* enlargement of a portion of the surface and profile section of the costa 11 *c*, transverse section Upper fish bed Kinderhook Burlington Iowa

Fig 12 13 ACONDYLACANTHUS [illegible], St J and W . . 434

12 *a* Lateral view of a large spine 12 *b* enlargement of a portion along the anterior margin, 12 *c* enlargement showing section of the posterior face, showing form of denticles, etc 12 *d* side view of denticle enlarged 12 *e* transverse section 12 *f*, enlarged section of anterior portion of spine Keokuk limestone, Warsaw, Illinois

13 *a* Side view of a smaller specimen 13 *b* enlargement showing the broad intercostal spaces along the anterior margin 13 *c* enlargement of portion along the posterior border 13 *d* enlargement of the posterior face 13 *e* transverse section enlarged. Same horizon, Keokuk, Iowa

Fig 14 ANACLITACANTHUS SEMICOSTATUS St J and W 443

14 *a* Side view of spine 14 *b* transverse section near the broken distal end 14 *c* transverse section near the inferior extremity Upper Burlington limestone, Burlington Iowa

# GEOLOGICAL SURVEY OF ILLINOIS

FOSSIL FISHES. ICHTHYODORULITES.

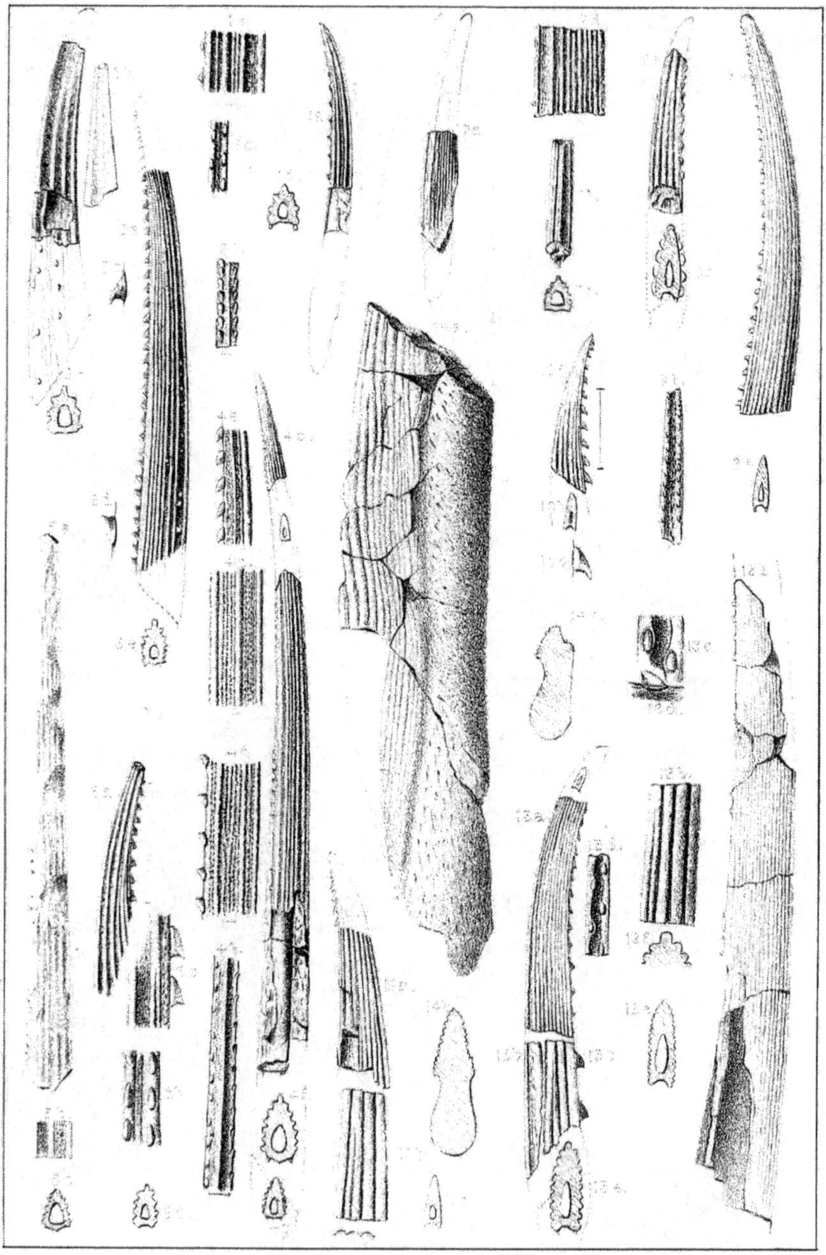

A. H. Worthen, direxit. J. Mayer & Co., lith., Boston

# PLATE XVII.

| | | | PAGE. |
|---|---|---|---|
| Fig 1 | | BYTHIACANTHUS VANHORNEI, St J and W | 445 |
| | 1 a | Side view of the spine 1 b, anterior aspect, reduced to one fourth natural size, 1 c, view showing posterior face 1 d, e, f, views of tubercles showing inferior side lateral view and seen from above 1 g, outline of an elongated tubercle seen from above 1 h, transverse section near the middle of exposed portion of spine, 1 i, similar section across the base midway between the anterior shoulder and the inferior extremity St Louis limestone Alton Illinois | |
| Fig 2 | | GLYMMATACANTHUS IRISHII, St J and W | 447 |
| | 2 a | Side view of fragment of spine base partially restored in outline, 2 b, transverse section partially restored in outline along the posterior side, 2 c, enlargement of tubercles as seen from above showing also the interspaces 2 d, side view of a single tubercle, enlarged Kinderhook beds Marshall county Iowa | |
| Fig 3, 4 | | GEISACANTHUS BULLATUS, St J and W . . . . . | 441 |
| | 3 a | Side view of a spine showing the base and part of the exposed portion, enlarged two diameters the upper portion of the figure representing the surface denuded of tubercles as seen in fig 4 a 3 b, enlargement showing one of the tubercles seen from above and lateral view in outline Chester limestone, Chester, Ill | |
| | 4 a | Side view of an imperfect spine showing patch of surface near tip denuded of tubercles and below the pulp cavity is exposed by the breaking away of the lateral wall Same horizon and locality | |

# GEOLOGICAL SURVEY OF ILLINOIS

FOSSIL-FISHES.    Lower Carb.    ICHTHYODORULITES

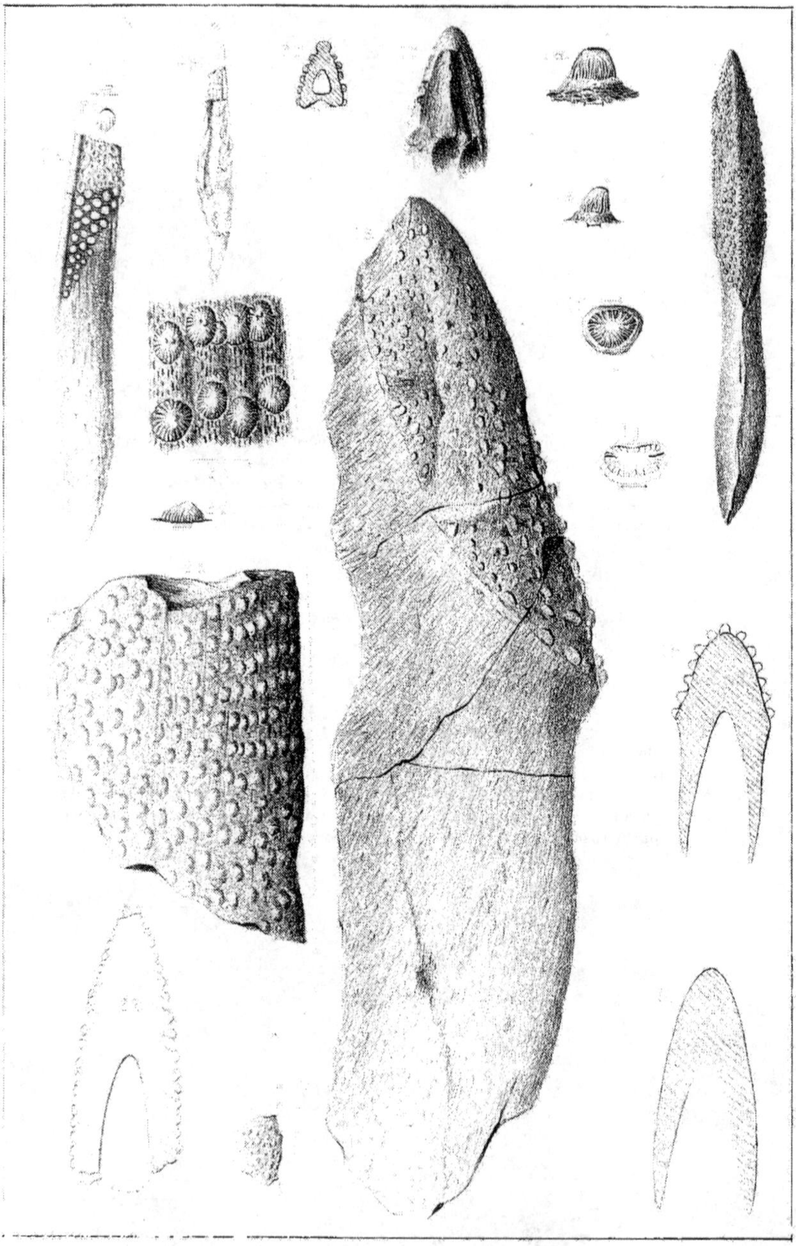

A. H. Worthen, direxr    J. Mayer & Co. lith. Boston.

# PLATE XVIII

PAGE

Fig 1 2 — PHYSONEMUS PROCLIVUS, St J and W .... 451

1 *a* Side view of small spine 1 *b* view of anterior face 1 *c* transverse section near the broken tip posterior face restored 1 *d* transverse section across the shoulder 1 *e* transverse section just above shoulder Lower fish bed of the Kinderhook, Burlington Iowa

2 *a* Side view of a smaller specimen enlarged two diameters posterior outline restored 2 *b* front view enlarged two diameters 2 *c d e* transverse sections at points indicated by corresponding letters fig 2 *b* the posterior face restored in outline Same horizon and locality

Fig 3 — PHYSONEMUS DEPRESSUS St J and W . 432

3 *a* Lateral view of spine posterior borders restored in outline, 3 *b*, anterior face 3 *c d e f* transverse sections Lower fish bed Kinderhook Burlington, Iowa

Fig 4 5 — PHYSONEMUS CARINATUS, St J and W 452

4 *a* Side view of fragment showing inferior extremity of spine restored in outline, 4 *b* front view 4 *c d* transverse sections Upper fish bed Kinderhook, Burlington, Iowa

5 *a* Side view of a more compressed specimen restored in outline 5 *b c* transverse sections Same horizon and locality

Fig 6-10 — PHYSONEMUS GIGAS N and W .

6 *a* Side view of fragment of large spine showing tuberculose ornamentation, 6 *b*, one of the anterior tubercles enlarged 6 *c* enlargement of two tubercles of one of the anterior ridges and profile outline, 6 *d*, similar enlargements of posterior costæ Upper Burlington limestone, Louisa county, Iowa

7 *a* Side view of imperfect smaller spine probably referable to above species Same horizon and locality

8 *a* Lateral view of smaller specimen, restored in outline, 8 *b*, view of anterior face, 8 *c d, e f*, transverse sections Same horizon and locality

9 *a b* Side view and transverse section of a very small specimen Same horizon and locality

10 *a*, *b* Transverse sections near the broken tip and base of the original specimen described by Messrs Newberry and Worthen, Vol IV Pl II fig 1 Same horizon, Quincy Illinois

Fig 11, 12 — PHYSONEMUS PARVULUS St J and W . . .. 433

11 *a* Lateral view restored in outline along the posterior face Keokuk limestone Boonville, Missouri

12 *a* Side view and transverse section of a fragment of spine, restored in outline Same horizon Warsaw, Illinois

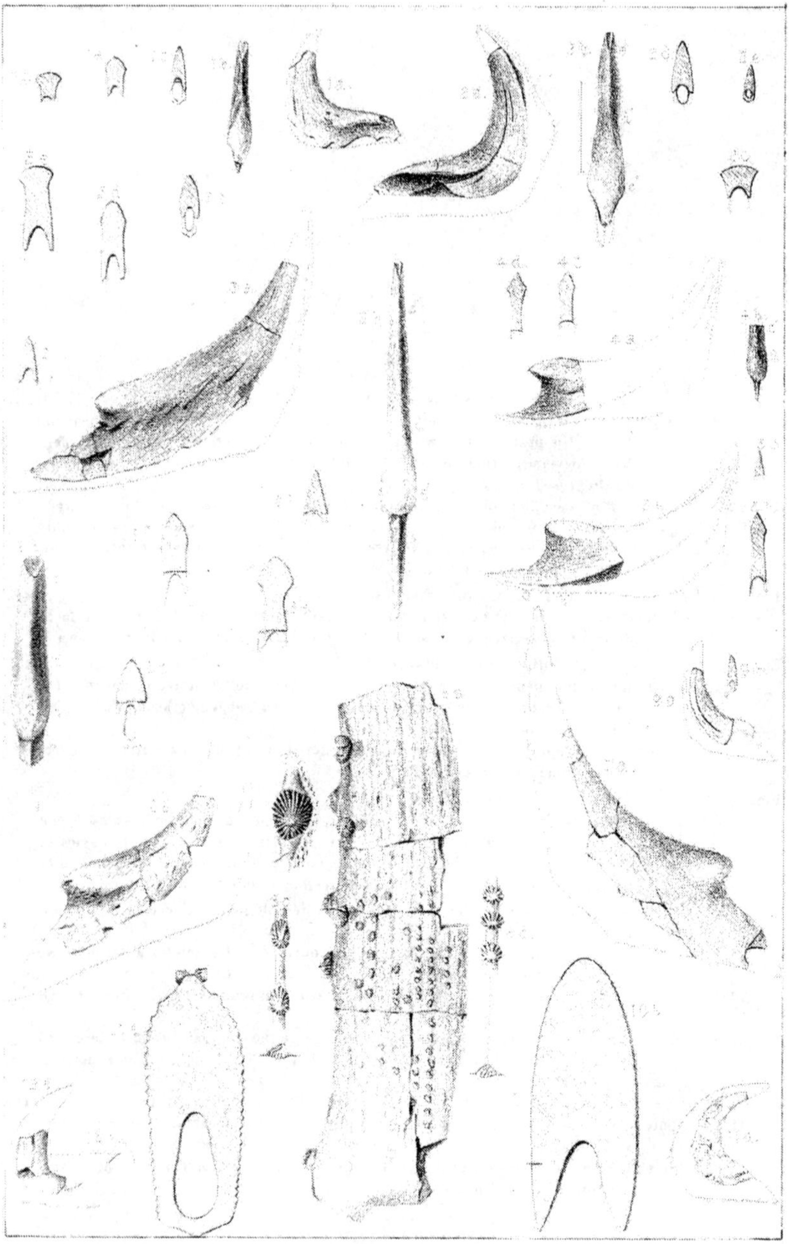

A. H. Worthen, direxit. Mayer & Co. lith., Boston.

# PLATE XIX

PAGE

Fig. 1–3 PHYSONEMUS ALTONENSIS St J and W 454

1 a Side view of large specimen 1 b front view 1 c view of the posterior face 1 d e, f, g, transverse sections at points indicated by corresponding letters fig 1 a St. Louis limestone, Alton, Illinois

2 a Side view of a smaller spine, the posterior face broken away, restored in outline 2 b c d e f transverse sections Same horizon and locality

3 a Side view of very small spine probably referable to the above species, but having the antero inferior shoulder truncated, 3 b, front view 3 c, d, e transverse sections St Louis beds, Pella, Iowa

Fig. 4 PHYSONEMUS CHESTERENSIS St J and W 455

4 a Side view enlarged two diameters and outline natural size. 4 b, front view, enlarged two diameters 4 c d e transverse sections enlarged two diameters Chester limestone Chester, Illinois

Fig. 5, 6 DREPANACANTHUS REVERSUS St J and W 456

5 a Side view of fragment of spine base restored in outline, anterior limit of internal cavity indicated by the dotted line 5 b, enlargement, showing tuberculation of the anterior border 5 c enlargement of tubercles of middle ridge, 5 d, enlargement of tubercles posterior ridge 5 e, transverse section, posterior face restored in outline St Louis limestone Alton Illinois

6 a Lateral view of small worn spine possibly referable to the above species and transverse section of the same Same horizon St Louis Missouri

# GEOLOGICAL SURVEY OF ILLINOIS

FOSSIL FISHES. (Lower Carb) ICHTHYODORULITES.

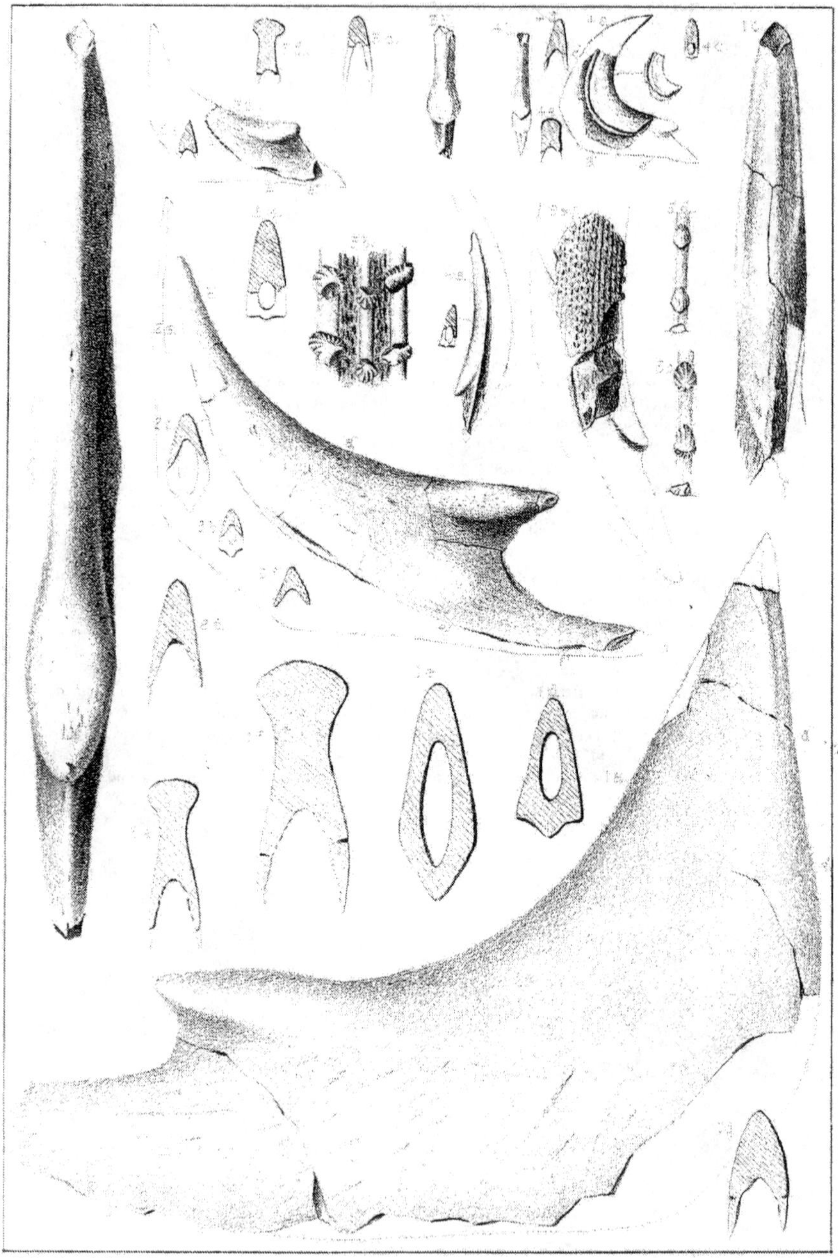

A.H. Worthen, direxit. J. Mayer & Co., lith., Boston

# PLATE XX

| | | PAGE |
|---|---|---|
| Fig. 1 | XYSTRACANTHUS MIRABILIS, St. J. and W. | 458 |
| 1 a | Side view, natural size; 1 b, view from front showing disposition of tubercles along the anterior margin reduced to one fourth natural size; 1 c, portion of posterior face reduced to one fourth natural size; 1 d, transverse section in upper part of the spine, partially restored; 1 e, similar section near base showing the walls of the pulp cavity distorted by pressure; 1 f–l various views of tubercles enlarged, 1 f tubercle from one of the middle rows near top of spine; 1 g from the third row near top; 1 h large tubercle from one of the anterior rows in middle of the spine; 1 i, large transverse tubercle near base; 1 k, l, small tubercles of middle rows near base. Coal No. 4 or 5, Fulton county, Illinois. | |
| Fig. 2 | XYSTRACANTHUS ACINACIFORMIS, St. J. and W. | 459 |
| 2 a | Side view of spine, natural size, with enlargements of tubercles; 2 b, view of posterior face; 2 c, transverse section near middle of spine; 2 d, portion of anterior margin showing arrangement of tubercles. Coal No. 5, Carlinville, Illinois. | |
| 3 | Fragment of an undetermined spine enlarged. Middle Coal Measures, Dallas county, Iowa. | |

GEOLOGICAL SURVEY OF ILLINOIS

FOSSIL FISHES. Upper Carb. ICHTHYODORULITES.

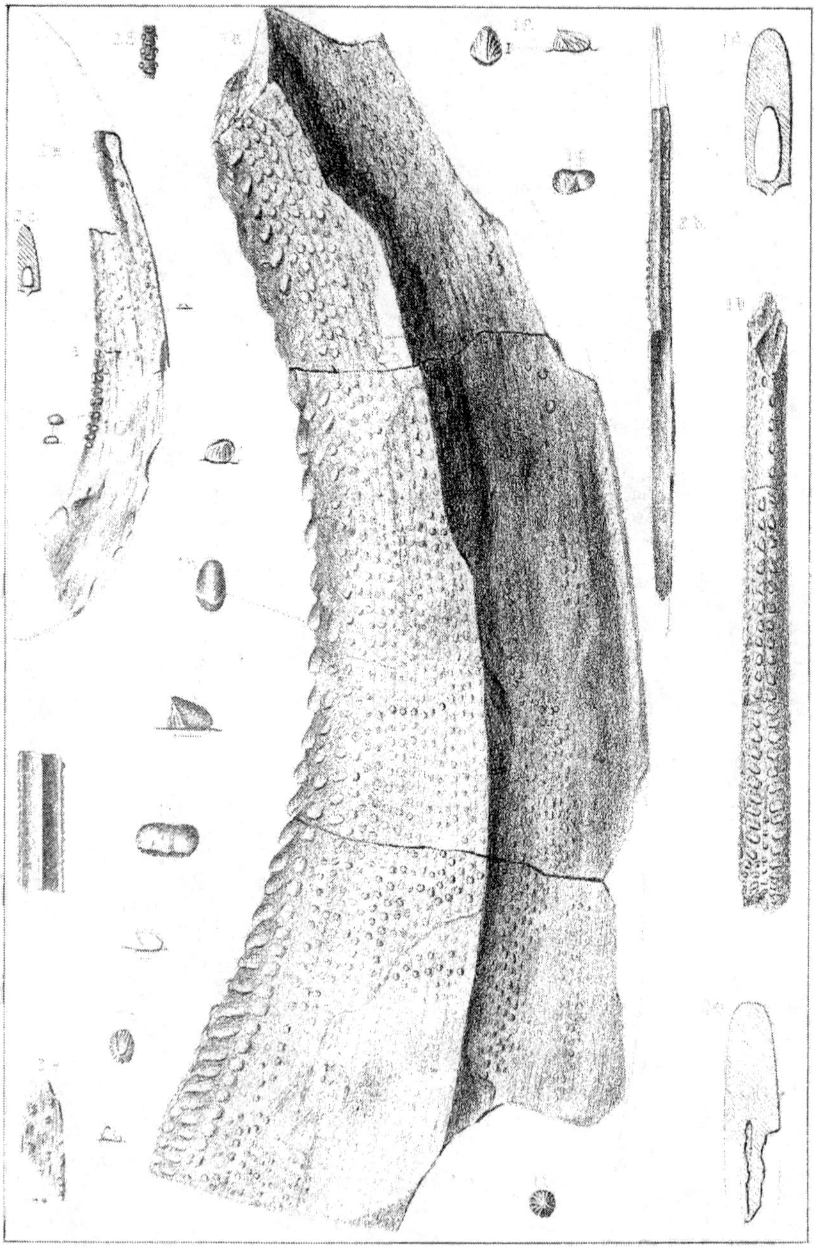

A. H. Worthen, direxit. J. Mayer & Co., lith., Boston.

# PLATE XXI

PAGE

Fig. 1-3 BATACANTHUS STELLATUS (N. and W. sp.) 470

1 a. Side view of an imperfect and worn spine, showing large tubercles in the upper portion of the posterior border, the spinose tubercles of the middle and lower anterior side, and outline of pulp cavity. 1 b, sketch of upper portion of the posterior side showing arrangement of tubercles. 1 c, transverse section. 1 d, enlargement of one of the large posterior tubercles, seen from above and profile outline. 1 e, enlarged sketch of tubercles of the lateral faces. The original specimen figured in Vol. II, Pl. 12, fig. 7. Geode bed of the Keokuk. Warsaw, Illinois.

2 a. Side view of fragment of the middle portion of a similar spine, the tuberculation of the lateral surfaces nearly obsolete from abrasion, but showing the bases of the anterior tubercles. 2 b, sketch of anterior face, showing disposition of tubercles. 2 c, transverse section. Upper fish bed Keokuk limestone. Hamilton, Illinois.

3 a. Side view of a larger specimen, preserving the anterior tubercles entire. 3 b, c, d, enlargements of tubercles from middle region near base, from the upper portion near the posterior side, and one of the large anterior tubercles and section. Same horizon and locality.

Fig. 4-8 BATACANTHUS BACULIFORMIS St. J. and W. 469

4 a. Side view of a nearly entire spine, showing the swollen extremity armed with strong tuberculose processes. 4 b, enlargement of one of the large spinose tubercles of the upper extremity. 4 c, d, enlargement of tubercles from upper and middle portion of the spine. 4 e, tubercles from the posterior portion. 4 f, transverse section. Keokuk limestone. Keokuk, Iowa.

5 a. View of the anterior face of a fragment of a similar but worn specimen. Same horizon and locality.

6 a. Side view of fragment of a large specimen. 6 b, c, d, enlargements of tubercles from the anterior, middle and posterior portions of the spine, and profile outlines of the same. 6 e, transverse section. La Grange, Missouri, in the same horizon.

7 a. Side view of fragment of a small spine, showing the base and outline of internal cavity. Same horizon. St. Francisville, Missouri.

8 a. Fragment of the upper extremity of a large spine, probably referable to the above form. Same horizon. Nauvoo, Illinois.

Fig. 9 CTENACANTHUS PUGIUNCULUS St. J. and W. 430

9 a. View of posterior face of spine, twisted towards the extremity so as to bring into view portion of one of the lateral faces; base imperfect. 9 b, transverse section. 9 c, enlargement of a section from near the middle of the spine, showing the character of the ornamentation on the lateral face. St. Louis limestone, St. Louis, Missouri.

Fig. 10 GEISACANTHUS STELLATUS St. J. and W. 440

10 a. Side view of a nearly perfect spine. 10 b, enlargement of anterior border near insertion. 10 c, section of the posterior face near the middle, slightly enlarged. 10 d, enlargement of portion of lateral face, showing the disposition of tubercles and faint costæ, with profile outlines of tubercles. 10 e, transverse section near middle of spine, natural size and enlarged. St. Louis limestone, St. Louis, Missouri.

Fig. 11 Fragment of an undetermined ichthyodorulite (?). Upper Burlington limestone. Louisa county, Iowa.

# GEOLOGICAL SURVEY OF ILLINOIS

FOSSIL-FISHES. (Lower Carb.) ICHTHYODORULITES.

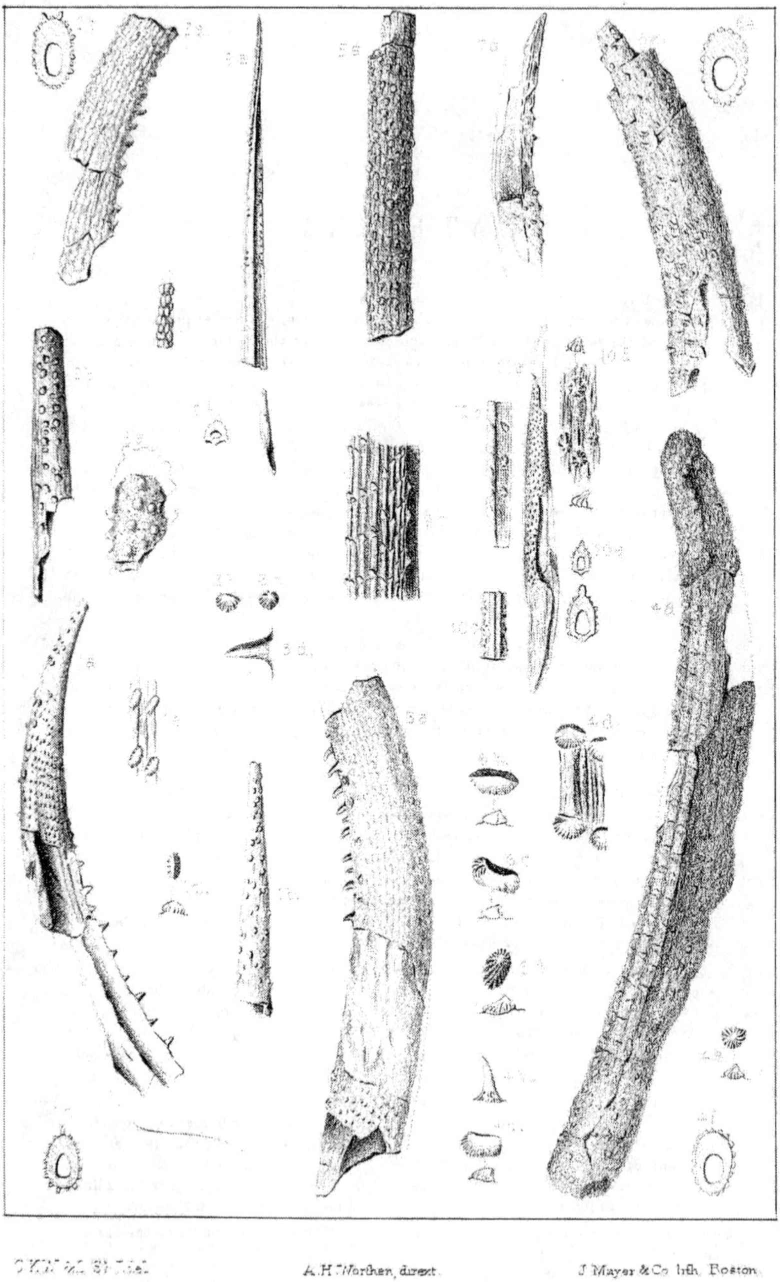

A. H. Worthen, direxit. J. Mayer & Co. lith. Boston.

# PLATE XXII.

PAGE

Fig 1-5 ERISMACANTHUS MCCOYANUS St J and W . 461

1 *a* Side view of nearly entire spine enlarged two diameters, 1 *b c d* enlargement of tubercles from various parts of the anterior prong St Louis limestone, St Louis Missouri

2 *a* Side view of an imperfect worn specimen exhibiting perfect transverse sections of either prong as shown in fig 2 *b c d*. Same horizon Alton Illinois

3 *a* Left side of posterior prong enlarged two diameters showing costation and dentition of the posterior border, 3 *b* anterior border folded longitudinally as though by pressure 3 *c* enlargement of posterior border showing form and arrangement of denticles etc 3 *d* enlargement of two denticles seen from above Same horizon and locality

4 *a* Side view of posterior spine enlarged one half showing more widely spaced denticles of posterior border and tuberculation of anterior intercostal space 4 *b*, transverse section compressed and 4 *c* restored outline 4 *d* side and view from above of one of the posterior denticles Same horizon St Louis, Missouri

5 *a* Section from a large anterior spine enlarged two diameters showing crowded arrangement of tubercles in some specimens Same horizon and locality

Fig 6 AMACANTHUS GIBBOSUS (N and W sp ) . . 464

6 *a* Side view of a nearly perfect spine enlarged one half 6 *b* enlargement of section near the middle of the spine showing bifurcated and interpolated costæ, denticulation of anterior and posterior borders 6 *c* transverse section enlarged The original specimen of *Homacanthus gibbosus* Vol II Pl XII, f 1 St Louis limestone St Louis Missouri

Fig 7-9 MARRACANTHUS STRICTUS (N and W sp ) 466

7 *a* Side view of perfect spine enlarged two diameters 7 *b* enlargement of portion of extremity 7 *c* similar enlargement of section from lower part of spine showing lateral face 7 *d* similar enlargement of a section showing the posterior face, 7 *e f g h* enlargements showing different views of the large anterior denticles near the summit of the spine 7 *k* transverse section, enlarged St Louis limestone St Louis Missouri

8 *a* Sketch of a small spine showing the anterior aspect and laterally expanded flattened base 8 *b* lateral view outline, 8 *c*, transverse section across the inserted base Same horizon and locality

9 *a* View of a fragment of a large spine, showing portion of the posterior face, the central cavity and posterior face of the expanded base 9 *b c d* transverse sections at points indicated by corresponding letters in preceding figure Same horizon and locality

Fig 10, 11 LECRACANTHUS UNGUICULUS St J and W 476

10 *a* Side view of a medium sized nearly perfect spine enlarged two diameters, 10 *b* enlargement of tubercles from near the middle of the spine 10 *c* transverse sections near middle and across the transversely expanded base the upper side being the posterior or concave border enlarged two diameters St Louis limestone, St Louis Missouri

11 *a* Lateral view of a fragment showing the upper extremity of a large specimen enlarged two diameters 11 *b* transverse section of one of the large apical denticles, 11 *c* enlargement of tubercles, 11 *d* transverse section across the posterior prominence, the [illegible] edge corresponding to the posterior margin Same horizon and locality

## Plate XXII—*Continued.*

| | | | Page |
|---|---|---|---|
| Fig. 12 | | Gampsacanthus typus, St. J. and W. | 472 |
| | 12 *a* | Side view of a nearly entire spine of medium size, enlarged two diameters, showing spinose processes at the apex, base partially restored from specimens in the collection of Mr. Van Horne and Prof. Worthen; 12 *b*, enlargement of a section near the middle of the spine, showing lateral surface and either border; 12 *c*, transverse section near base, enlarged two diameters; and 12 *d*, probable outline of the same when perfect. St. Louis limestone, St. Louis, Missouri. | |
| Fig. 13 | | Gampsacanthus squamosus, St. J. and W. | 473 |
| | 13 *a* | Side view of fragment showing upper portion of spine, enlarged one half; 13 *b*, enlargement showing form and disposition of tubercles; 13 *c*, transverse sections near tip and across the broken base, enlarged one half. St. Louis limestone, St. Louis, Missouri. | |
| Fig. 14 | | Gampsacanthus latus, St. J. and W. | 474 |
| | 14 *a* | Side view of tip of spine, enlarged one half; 14 *b*, enlargement of portion of lateral surface; 14 *c*, transverse section. Keokuk limestone, Boonville, Missouri. | |
| Fig. 15 | | Oracanthus consimilis, St. J. and W. | 476 |
| | 15 *a* | Side view of a fragment apparently from near the middle of the spine; 15 *b*, sketch of the concave margin showing form and arrangement of tubercles; 15 *c*, sketch showing convex border; 15 *d*, transverse section, distorted by pressure. St. Louis limestone, Alton, Illinois. | |
| Fig. 16 | | Oracanthus? obliquus, St. J. and W. | 477 |
| | 16 *a* | View of the anterior (?) margin of a fragment of the upper portion of a spine; 16 *b*, *c*, transverse section. Keokuk limestone, Warsaw, Illinois. | |

# GEOLOGICAL SURVEY OF ILLINOIS

FOSSIL FISHES. Lower Carb. ICHTHYODORULITES.

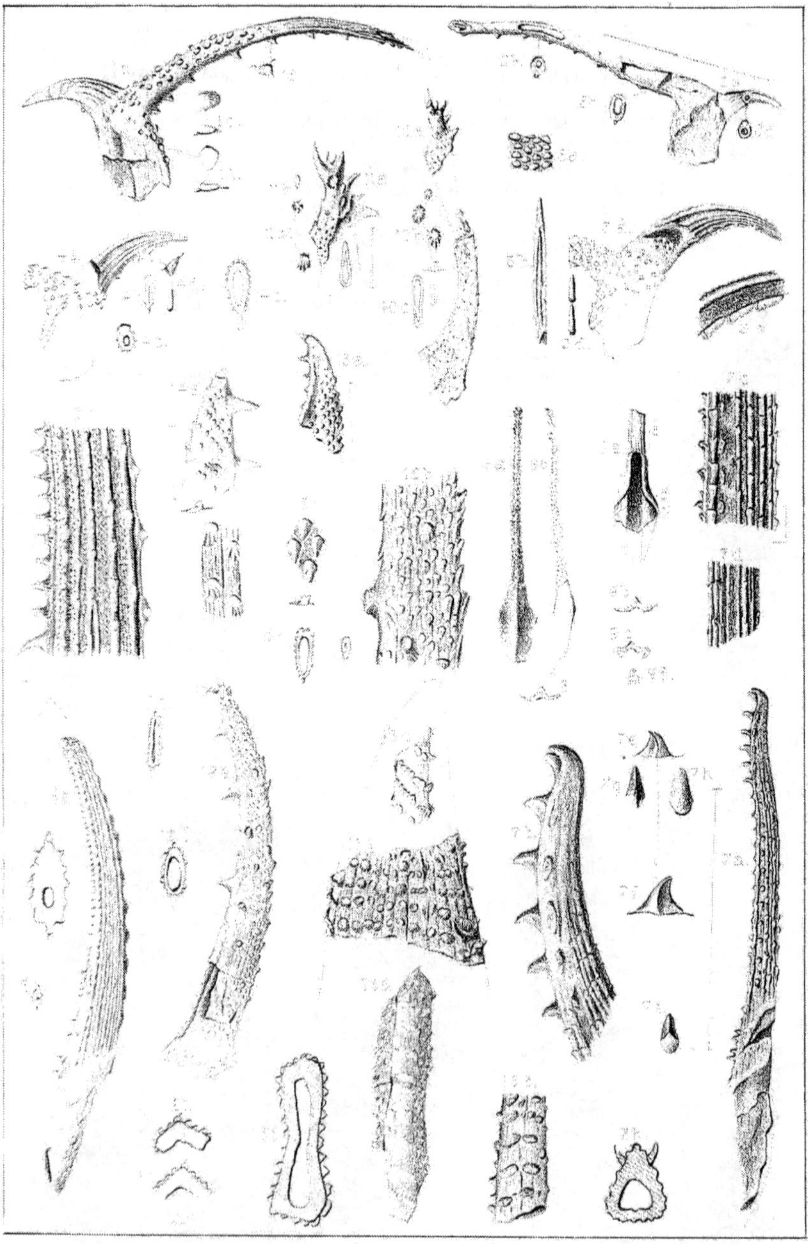

# PLATE XXIII.

| | | | PAGE |
|---|---|---|---|
| Fig. 1 | | HETEROCRINUS CRASSUS . | 493 |
| | | View of a nearly perfect example of this fine species, showing the arms to their extremities | |
| Fig. 2. | | MODIOLOPSIS, cast—undet. . . . . . . . . | |
| Fig. 3. | | CYRTOCERAS CARROLLENSIS . . . . . . . . . . | 496 |
| Fig. 4 | | AMBONYCHIA ILLINOIENSIS ... . ... . ... . .. .. . ... | 495 |
| | 4 a | Profile view showing the beak | |
| | 4 b | Side view of a nearly complete valve | |
| Fig. 5 | | SUBULITES INFLATUS . . ... . . .. . . . .. .. . | 495 |
| Fig. 6 | | ASAPHUS VIGILANS . ... . ... . . . . . . . .. .. ..... | 497 |
| | | View of a rolled specimen showing glabella | |
| Fig. 7 | | GONIOPHORA ? . . . .. .... . . | |
| | | Cast in magnesian limestone from the Trenton beds of Carroll county | |
| Fig. 8 | | HOMOCRINUS ANGUSTATUS . . .. . . .. . . . .... . . . | 493 |
| Fig. 9 | | MODIOLOPSIS SUBNASUTA . . .. . . . . . | 494 |
| | 9 a | Side view of a natural cast | |
| | 9 b | Dorsal view of the same | |

GEOLOGICAL SURVEY OF ILLINOIS

L. SILURIAN. (Cincinnati Group) MISCELLANEOUS.

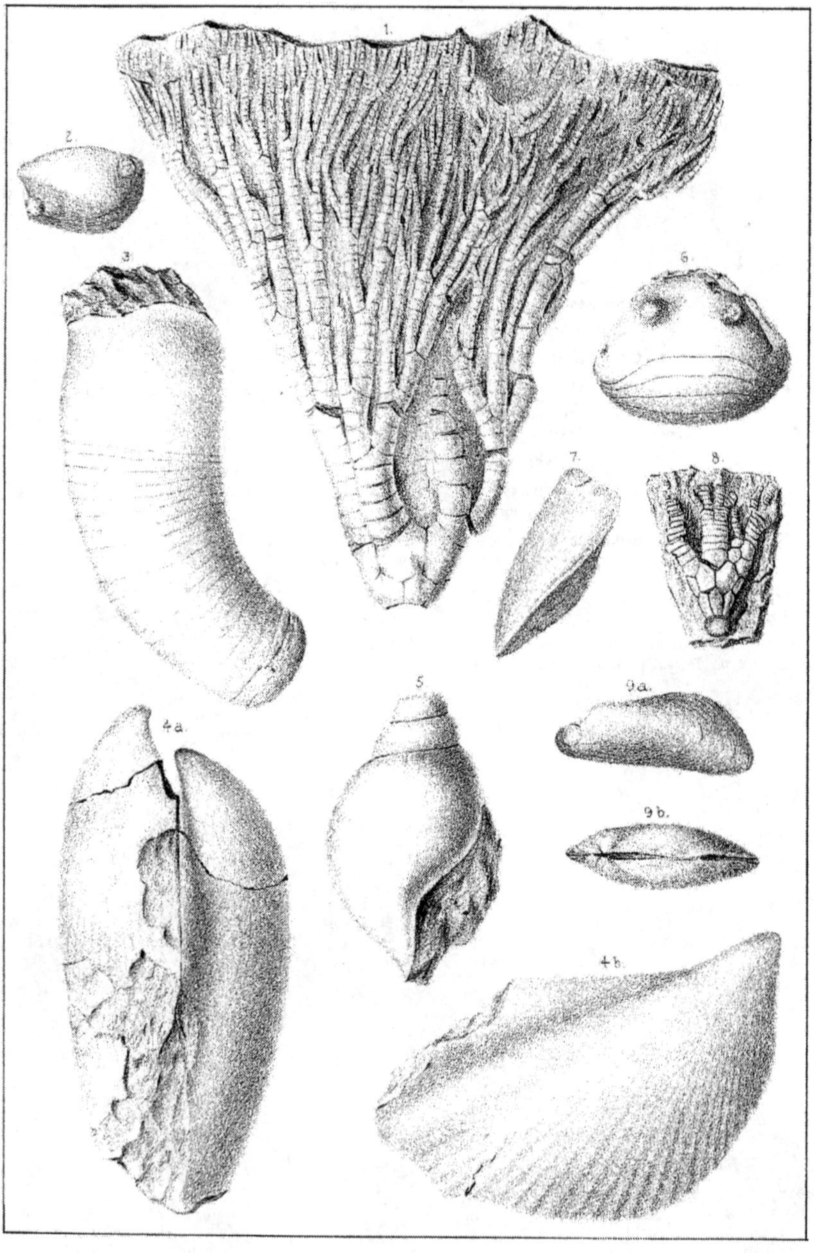


Chas K. Worthen, del. A. H. Worthen, direxit J. Mayer & Co., lith., Boston.

# PLATE XXIV

| | | | PAGE |
|---|---|---|---|
| Fig | 1 | RECEPTACULITES FORMOSUS . . | 500 |
| | | Side view of specimen, natural size | |
| Fig | 2 | EUCALYPTOCRINUS (*sp undet*) | |
| | 2 | View of the summit from a natural cast in magnesian limestone | |
| | 2 *a* | Side view of the same specimen | |
| Fig | 3 | ILLAENUS (BUMASTUS), *sp undet* . . . | |
| Fig | 4 | SPHAEREXOCHUS ROMINGERI . . | 510 |
| | 4 | Glabella seen from above 4 *a* side view of the same | |
| Fig | 5 | STRICKLANDINIA DEFORMIS . . | 502 |
| | 5 | View of ventral valve 5 *a* view of dorsal valve | |
| | 5 *b* | Profile view of the same | |
| Fig | 6 | PHRAGMOCERAS BYRONENSIS . . | 506 |
| | | Side view of a nearly entire internal cast | |
| Fig | 8 | ORTHOCERAS ANGULATUM . | 504 |
| | 8 | View of specimen showing the surface markings | |
| | 8 *a* | Section showing the position of the siphuncle | |

GEOLOGICAL SURVEY OF ILLINOIS

UPPER SILURIAN. MISCELLANEOUS.

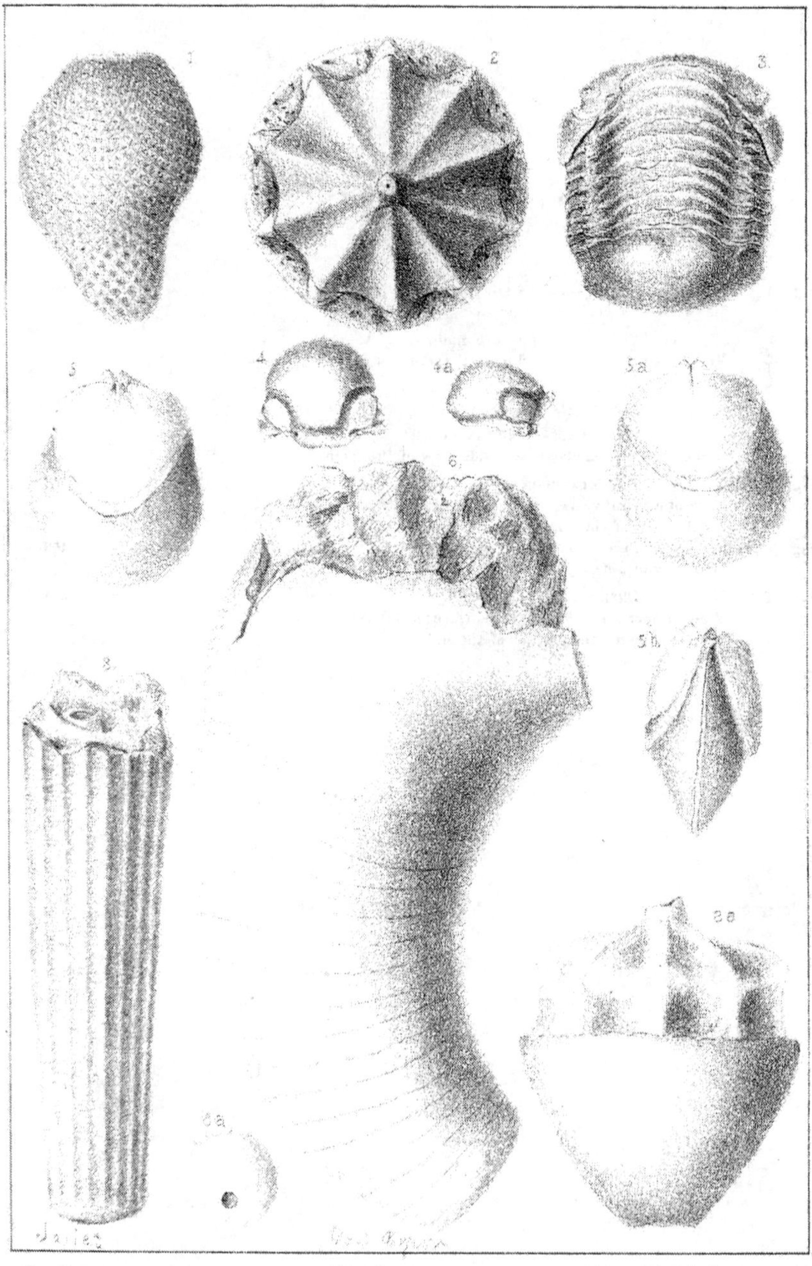


Chas K. Worthen, del. A. H. Worthen, direx. J. Mayer & Co. lith. Boston.

# PLATE XXV.

GEOLOGICAL SURVEY OF ILLINOIS

UPPER SILURIAN. (Niagara Group) MISCELLANEOUS.

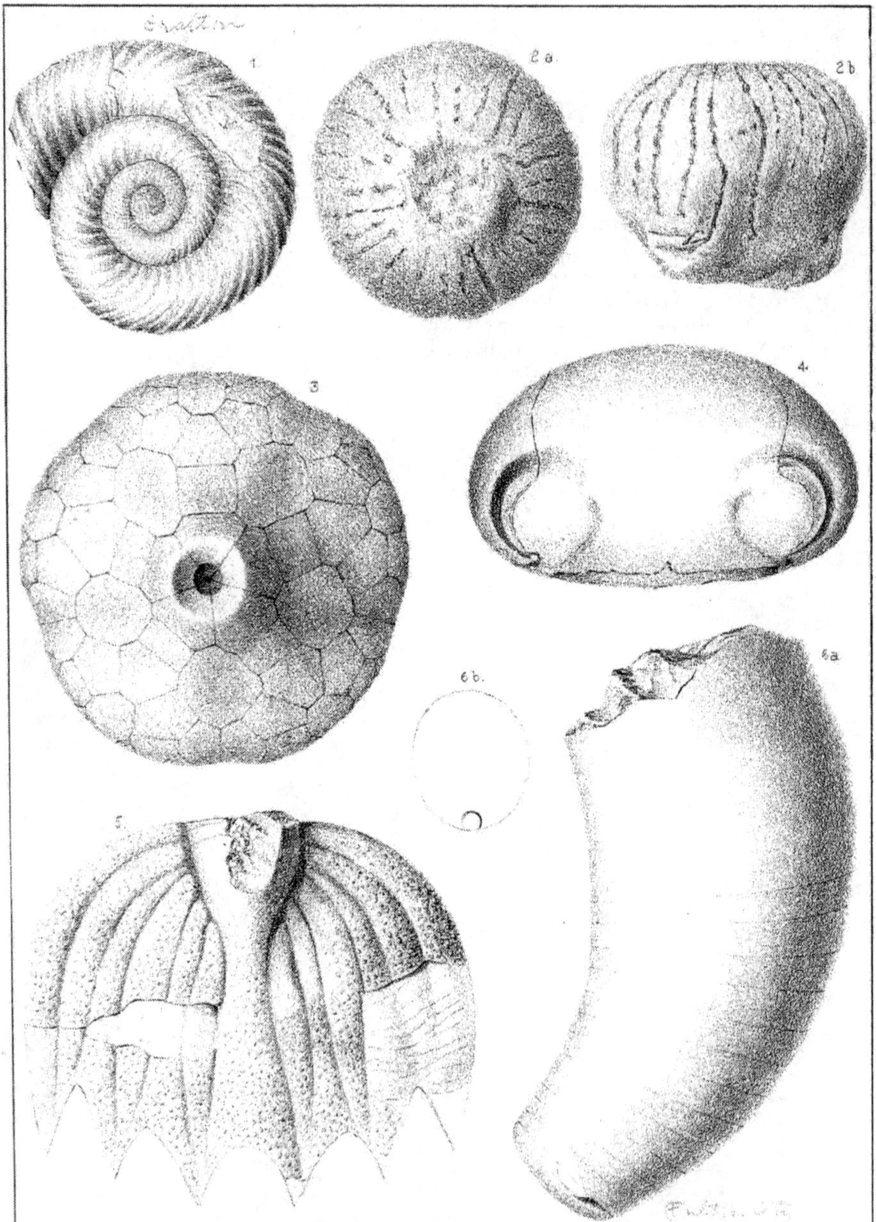


Geo. K. Worthen, del. A. H. Worthen, direxit. J. Mayer & Co., lith., Boston.

# PLATE XXVI.

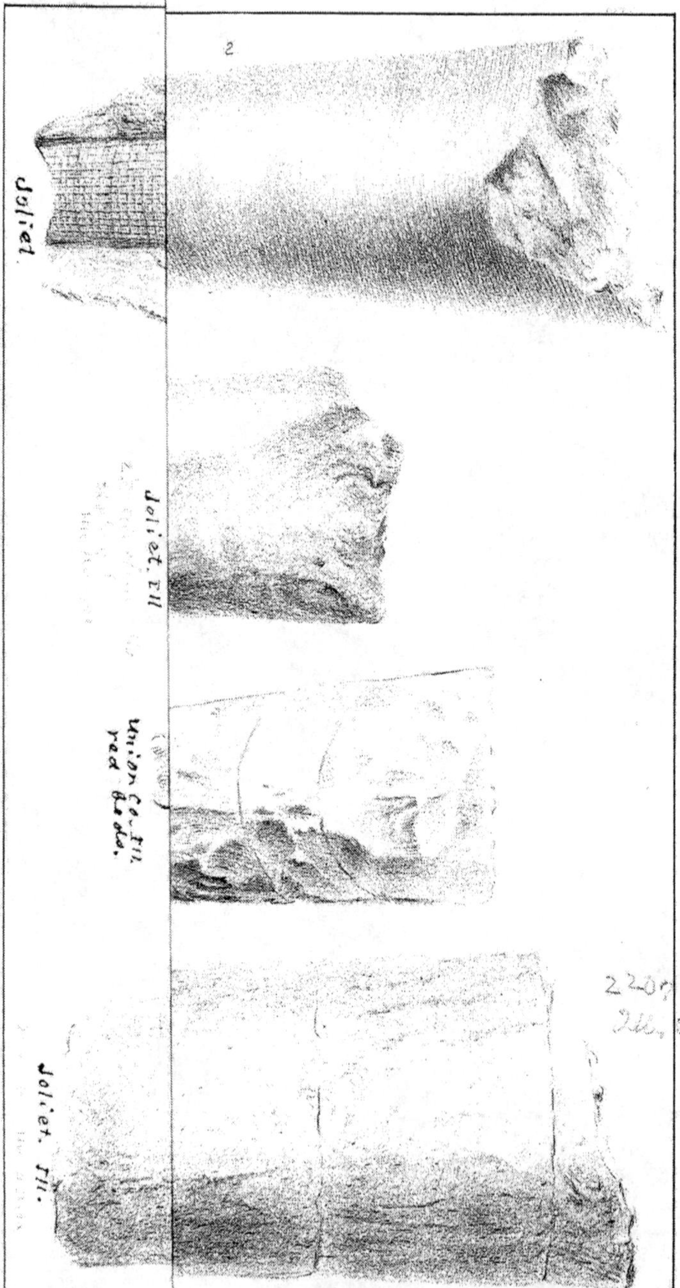


220?
Ill. St. Mus.

J. Mayer & Co. lith. Boston

# GEOLOGICAL SURVEY OF ILLINOIS

UPPER SILURIAN. CEPHALOPODA

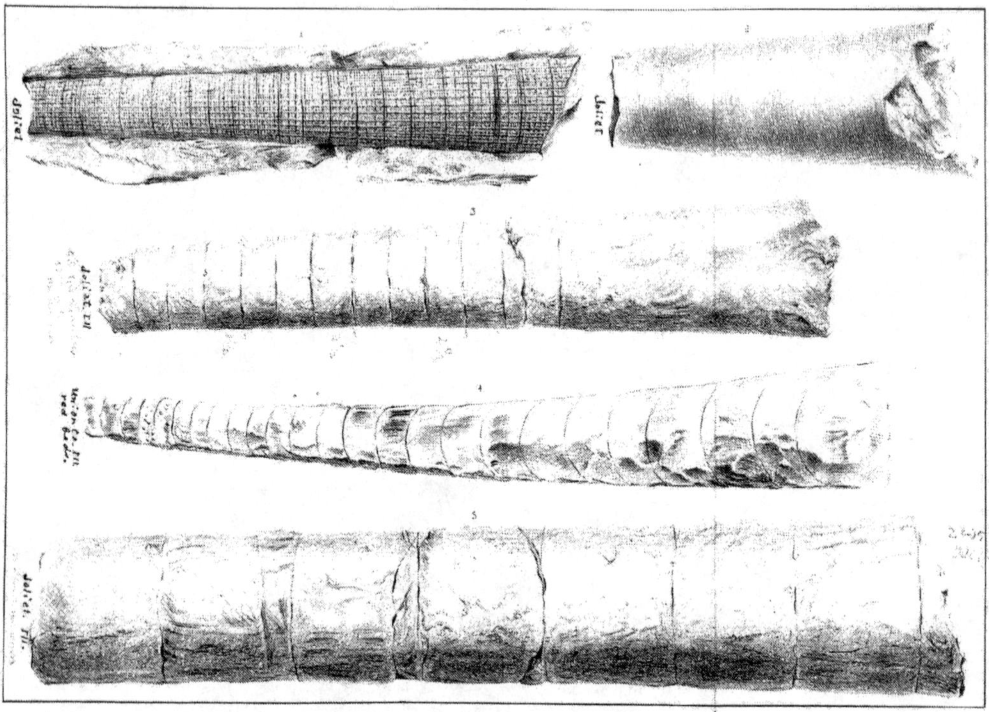


Chas K Worthen del. A. H. Worthen direxit J. Mayer & Co. Lith. Boston

# PLATE XXVII.

PAGE

Fig. 1 a. NAUTILUS (DISCITES) ORNATUS ? VAR. AMPLUS . . . .

1 a. View of the ventral or outer side of the curve of an imperfect internal cast, (one half nat. diameter), showing the curves of the septa in crossing the periphery.

1 b. A side view of same. *Nautilus (Discites) ornatus ? var. amplus*, Meek and Worthen, 1865. Proc. Philad. Acad. Nat. Sci., p. 265.

Fig. 2. GYROCERAS CONSTRICTUM .

A side view of imperfect internal cast. Two views of this same fossil were given on plate 12 of volume III., but the side view was not given there for want of room, and is added here to complete the illustration of the species as far as can be done at this time.

GEOLOGICAL SURVEY OF ILLINOIS

DEVONIAN. (Hamilton Group) CEPHALOPODA

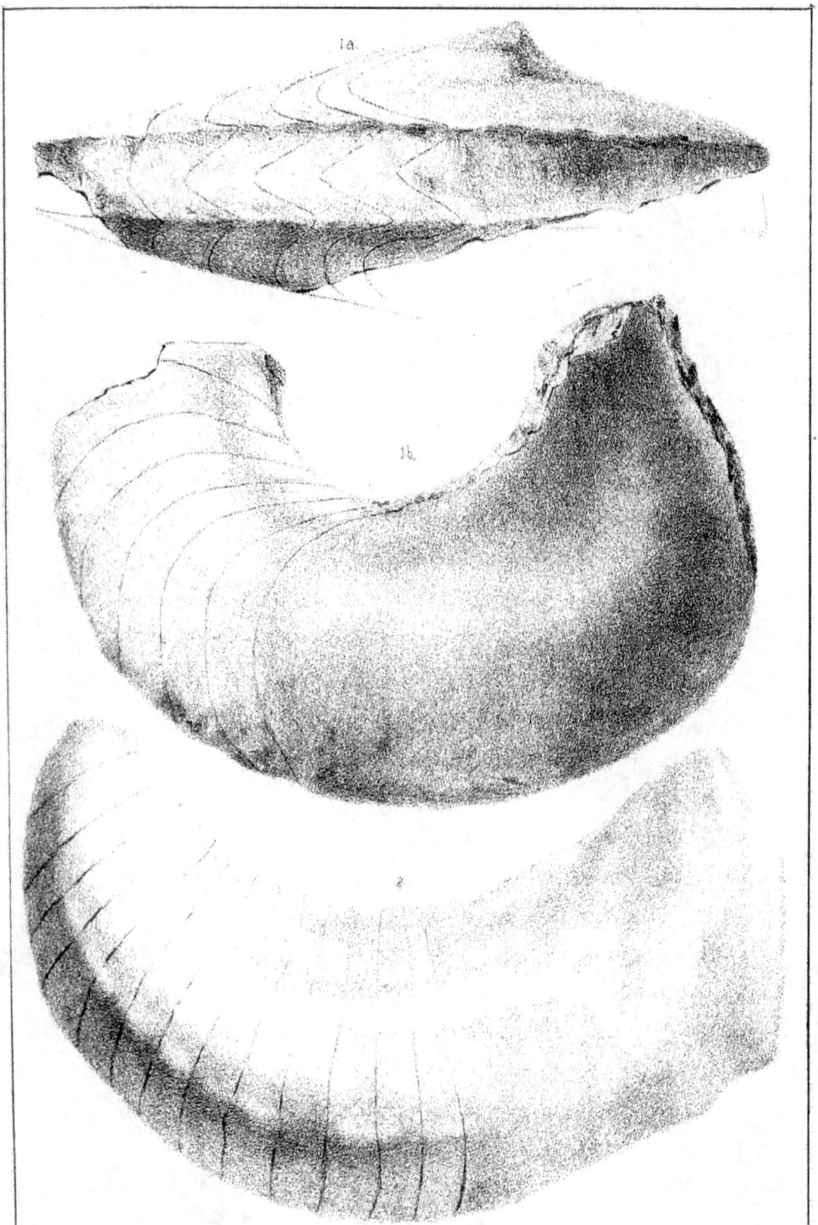


Chas. K. Worthen, del. A. H. Worthen, direxr. J. Mayer & Co. lith., Boston.

# PLATE XXVIII.

PAGE.

Fig 1 ORTHOCERAS WINCHELLII . . 512

Fig 2 PHRAGMOCERAS WALCHII . . . . . . . . 511

2 *a* Side view of an imperfect internal cast, distorted by accidental pressure, reduced to half the natural diameter

2 *b* Another view of same

Fig 3 AVICULOPECTEN UNIONENSIS . . 511

View of a left valve, natural size

# GEOLOGICAL SURVEY OF ILLINOIS

DEVONIAN. (Hamilton Group) MOLLUSCA.

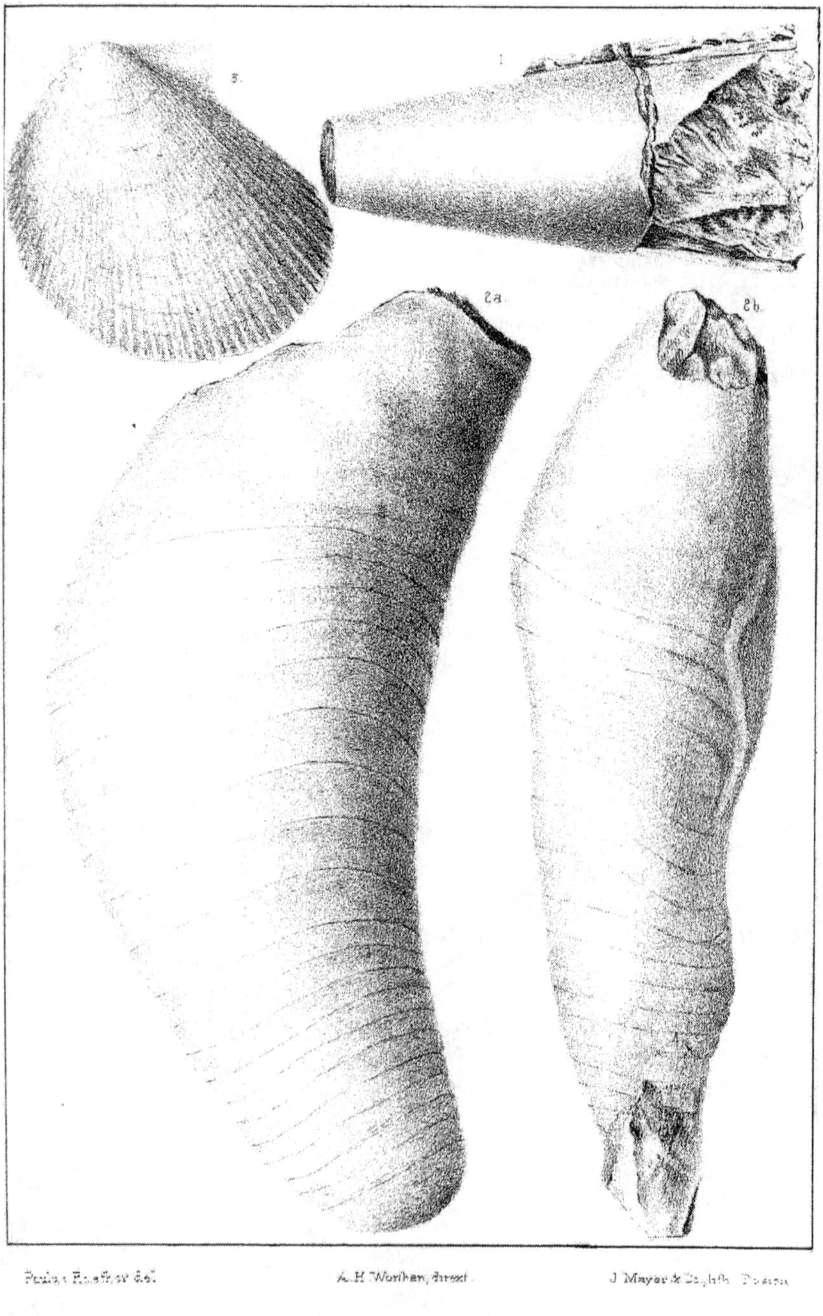


[illegible] del. A. H. Worthen, direct. J. Mayer & Co. lith. Boston.

# PLATE XXIX.

| | | | PAGE |
|---|---|---|---|
| Fig. 1 | | SCAPHIOCRINUS UNICUS . | 519 |
| | | Specimen showing the ventral tube with its anal opening. | |
| Fig. 2, 3. | | POTERIOCRINUS COREYI . . . | 516 |
| | 2. | Specimen showing ventral tube and anal opening. | |
| | 3, 3 a. | Opposite sides of a nearly perfect example showing the arms nearly entire. | |
| Fig. 4. | | SYNBATHOCRINUS ROBUSTUS . . . . . | 514 |
| | | View of a nearly perfect example. | |
| Fig. 5. | | BARYCRINUS STELLATUS . . . . . | 515 |
| | 5 a. | View of anterior side; 5 b, basal view; 5 c, view of the anal side. | |
| Fig. 6. | | POTERIOCRINUS HOVEYI . . . | 516 |
| | | View of a nearly perfect example showing the arms and ventral tube. | |
| Fig. 7. | | DICHOCRINUS FICUS . | 515 |
| | | Specimen with the arms attached. | |
| Fig. 8. | | DORYCRINUS KELLOGGI . . . . | 513 |
| | 8 a. | View of the anal side. | |
| | 8 b. | View of the anterior side. | |
| | c. | View of the crown. | |

# GEOLOGICAL SURVEY OF ILLINOIS

CARBONIFEROUS (Keokuk Group) CRINOIDEA.

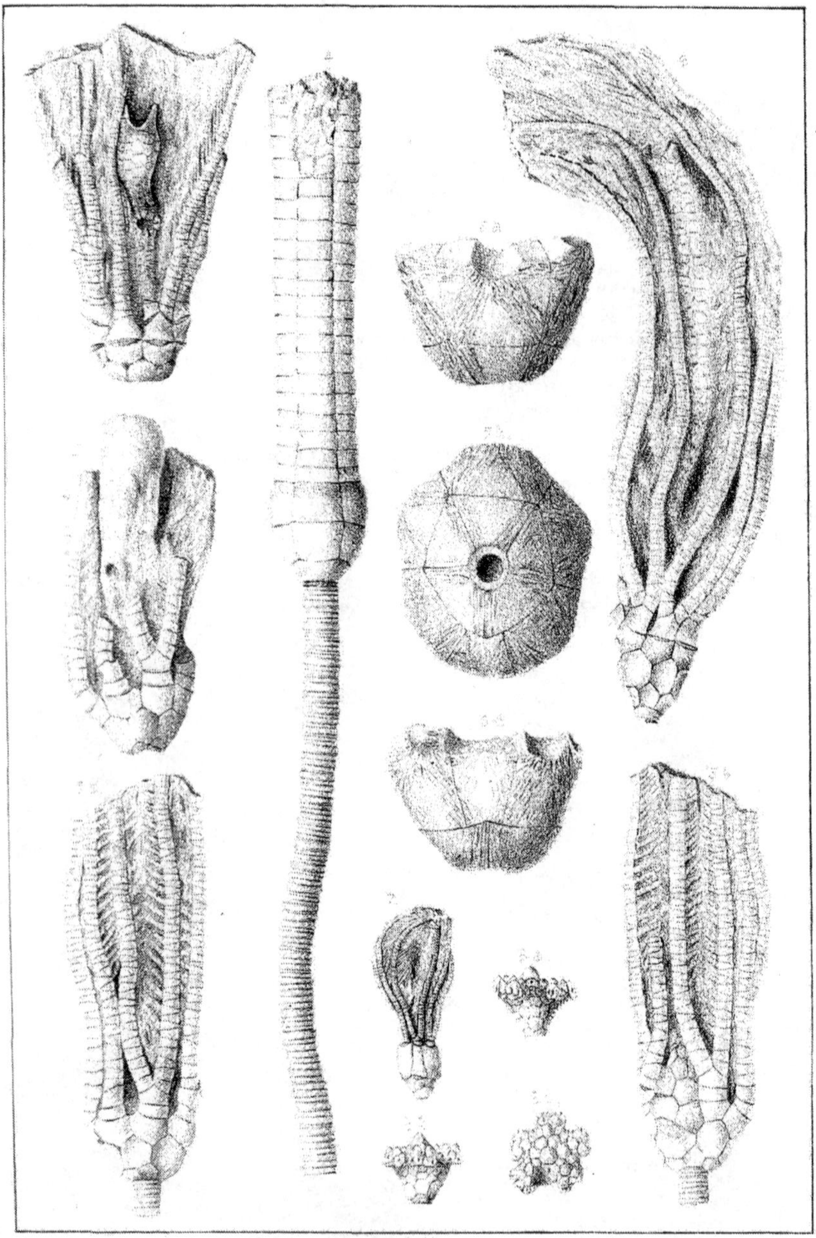

Chas. K. Worthen, del. A. H. Worthen, direx. J. Mayer & Co. lith., Boston

# PLATE XXX

| | | | PAGE |
|---|---|---|---|
| Fig 1 | | SPIRIFER SUBORBICULARIS | 523 |
| | 1 *a* | Dorsal view, 1 *b* view of ventral valve | |
| | 1 *d* | Profile view showing the beaks | |
| Fig 2 | | SPIRIFER SCULPTILIS | 523 |
| | 2 *a* | Profile view 1 *c* front view | |
| Fig 3 | | SPIRIFER FASTIGATUS | 521 |
| | 3 *a* | Dorsal view showing cardinal area | |
| | 3 *b* | View of the ventral valve | |
| Fig 4 | | PINNA SUBSPATULATA | 524 |
| Fig 5 | | MYALINA KEOKUK | 524 |
| | | View of a left valve | |

GEOLOGICAL SURVEY OF ILLINOIS

CARBONIFEROUS (Keokuk Group) MOLLUSCA

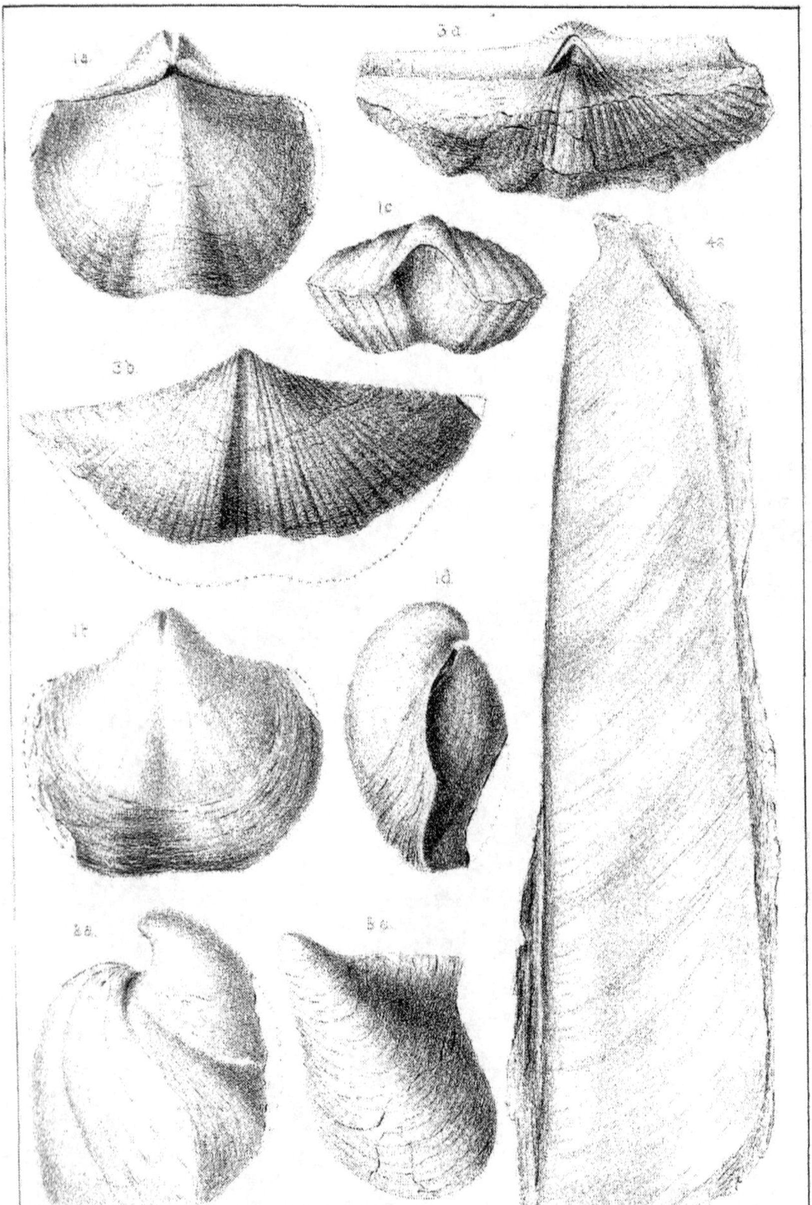

Chas K. Worthen del. A. H. Worthen, direxit. J. Mayer & Co., lith., Boston.

# PALTE XXXI.

GEOLOGICAL SURVEY OF ILLINOIS

CARBONIFEROUS (St. Louis Group) CRINOIDEA.

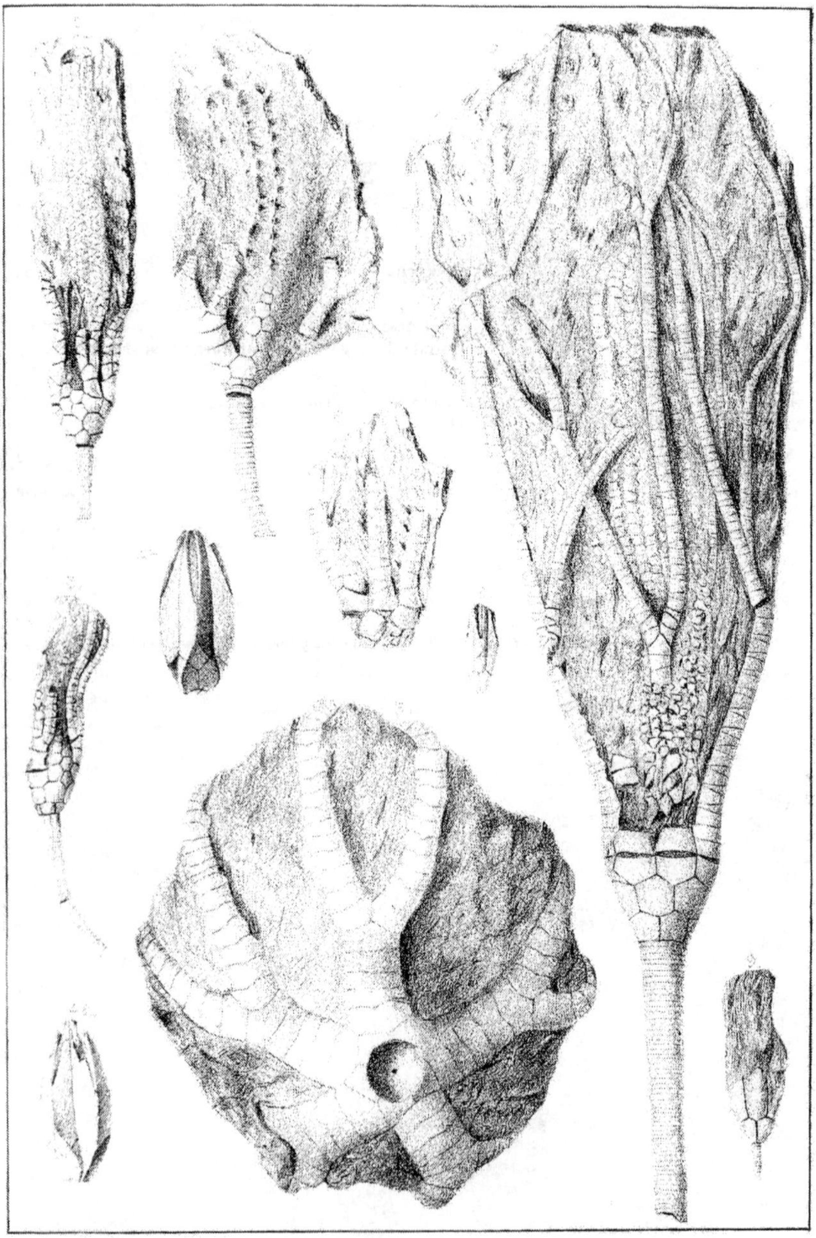

[illegible] A. H. Worthen, direxit. J. Mayer & Co., lith., Boston.

# PLATE XXXII.

(Coal measures) RADIATA.

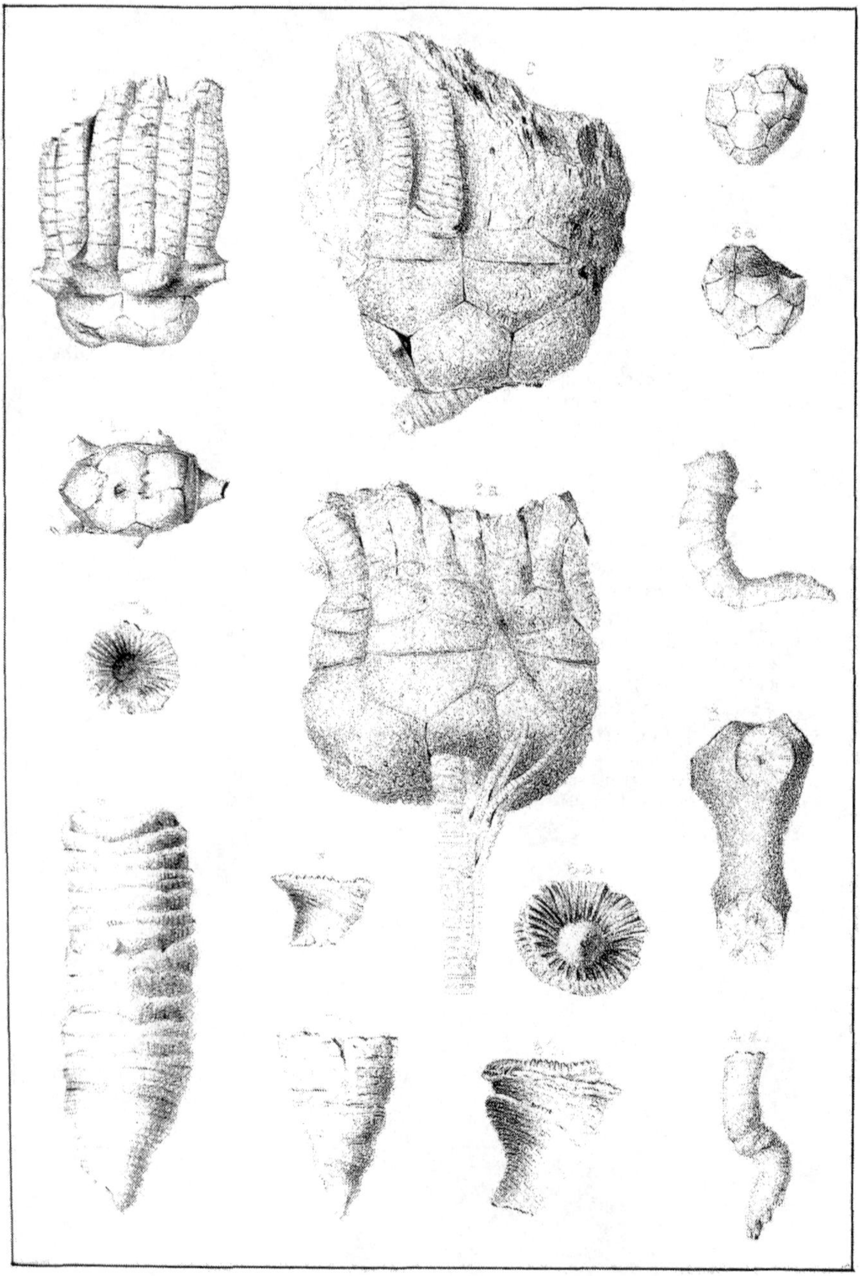

Chas K. Worthen del. A. H. Worthen, direct. J. Mayer & Co., lith., Boston.

# PLATE XXXIII.

Fig 1 NAUTILUS (CRYPTOCERAS) CAPAX . 532
1 Dorsal view 1 *a*, side view

Fig 2 NAUTILUS (DISCITES) HIGHLANDENSIS .. . 531

Fig 3 AVICULOPECTEN (*spec undet*) . . . . .. .
View of the interior of a right valve

Fig 4 CONOCARDIUM OBLIQUUM . . . . 529
4 *a* Dorsal view, 4 side view

Fig 5 PLEUROPHORUS? ANGULATUS. . . . 529

Fig 6 CARBONARCA GIBBOSA ... . 531
6 View of the crenulated hinge line
6 *a* Anterior view showing the beaks
6 *b* Lateral view.

# GEOLOGICAL SURVEY OF ILLINOIS

MOLLUSCA

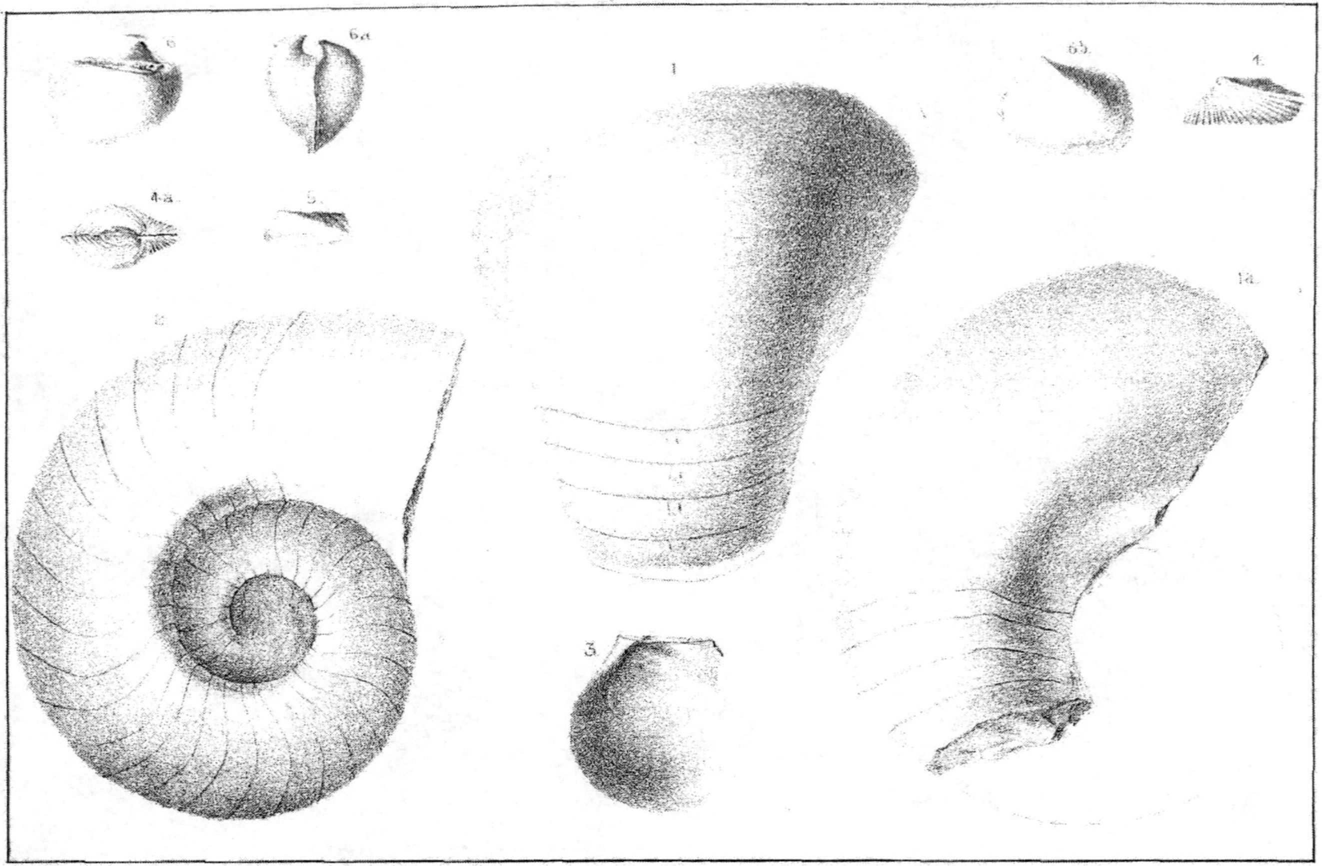


Chas K. Worthen, del. A. H. Worthen, direxit. J. Mayer & Co. lith. Boston

CPSIA information can be obtained
at www.ICGtesting.com
Printed in the USA
LVHW021527040921
696974LV00010B/739

9 781362 623410